MALICE THROUGH THE LOOKING GLASS

Reflections and Refractions of Envy, Greed & Jealousy

by

Joseph H. Berke

Jacket Photomontage by Pauline Duffy

While the cases described in this book are based on interviews with real persons, names, professions, locations and other biographical details have been changed to preserve their privacy and anonymity.

TEVA PUBLICATIONS

5 Shepherd's Close London N6 5AG
www.tevapublications.com
tevapublications@aol.com

Published by TEVA

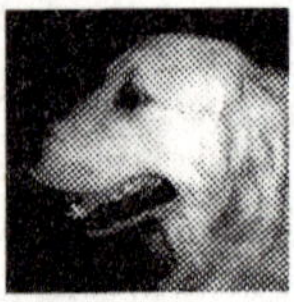

Looking into the Nature of Things

Library of Congress Cataloging in Publication Data

Malice Through the Looking Glass:
Reflections and Refractions of Envy, Greed & Jealousy

Joseph H. Berke.

Bibliography: p493
Includes indexes.
ISBN-10: 0-9552767-0-5
ISBN-13: 978-0-9552767-0-5
1. Envy. 2. Avarice 3. Jealousy. 4. Aggressiveness (Psychology) S. Envy–Social aspects. 6. Avarice–Social aspects. 7. Jealousy–Social aspects. 8. Aggressiveness (Psychology)–Social aspects. 9. Terrorism

Drawing on p. 243 by Lorenz; © 1986 The New Yorker Magazine, Inc.
Cartoon on p. 29 reprinted with permission of Punch.
Cartoons on pp. 296 and 299 by Pete Mastin, Black Flag, 1985.

ISBN 0-9552767-0-5
ISBN-13: 978-0-9552767-0-5

Previous Works

Counter Culture: The Creation of An Alternative Society

(Editor and Contributor)

Mary Barnes: Two Accounts of a Journey Through Madness

(with Mary Barnes)

The Cannabis Experience

(with Calvin Hernton)

Butterfly Man: Madness, Degradation and Redemption

I Haven't Had to Go Mad Here

The Tyranny of Malice: Exploring the Dark Side of Character and Culture

Sanctuary: The Arbours Experience of Alternative Community Care

(Co-Editor and Contributor)

Even Paranoids Have Enemies: New Perspectives on Paranoia and Persecution

(Co-Editor and Contributor)

Beyond Madness: PsychoSocial Interventions in Psychosis

(Co-Editor and Contributor)

For

Dr. Norman Cohen

"Beware the Jabberwock, my son.!
The jaws that bite, the claws that catch!
Beware the Jubjub bird, and shun
The Frumious Bandersnatch"

Jabberwocky (1)

"the bestial urges"

Table of Contents

Introduction

The 'looking-glass' is a very special mirror which can reflect and refract the deepest recesses of the mind, the utmost corners of the self. It is an instrument which can dazzle and dismay, something to stand apart from as well as step into. This 'glass' provides an opportunity to 'look' and discover basic truths about our inner nature and outer constructions. At propitious moments the resultant images pass beyond a wonderland of fear or self-satisfaction. They reveal the truth about the way we are as well as the way of the world.

This book is a looking-glass which allows the reader to explore the darkest components of character and culture, 'the shadow side of the self.' These elements tend to remain within the shadows of perception because they are chaotic, violent, dangerous and highly disturbing. Yet, a knowledge of their presence and of their intricate relations with the acceptable faces of reality, remains an absolute necessity for overcoming the damage that individuals and institutions do to each other. It is the sine qua non for liberating the world from the grip of what collectively may be termed, 'malice.'

Malice has three components: *perception:* an awareness of something provoking an intolerable feeling; *feeling:* intense displeasure and vexation; and *action:* forceful, attacking, annihilating behavior.

An aggressive response may be essential to survival when it is self-protective and an obvious reaction to provocation. All too often this is not the case. The person who goes around with a 'chip on his shoulder' is an unlikely example of constructive self-assertion, or even reactive revenge. I am concerned with another kind of malice, a passion which may not have an obvious cause, yet which is very intense, deep-rooted and is associated with hate, rage, chaos and evil. Such passions accompany consciousness and are uniquely human.

They are complex creatures, painfully private and publicly dangerous, fed by an 'inner world' of fact and fantasy brought about by the interplay of perception, memory and imagination.

Malicious hatred is all pervasive, yet it is curiously unfashionable. It is a subject relegated to fiction, while generally ignored by the social sciences. The many manifestations of this kind of hate tend to be ascribed to problems of environment or heredity. The 'yob' who stabs the old lady down the block, or the man who kills his child, 'must' have bad genes. Or maybe their biochemistry has gone haywire. Similarly, acts of outrageous criminality tend to be justified when done in the name of economic inequality, political oppression, or bad weather.

Man himself is the source of the malice against which he is constantly struggling. And it is only possible for him to transcend this basic malignity by knowing how, what, why and when it arises. The alternative is to continue the blind butchery of our environment and fellow creatures which otherwise permeates our lives. R. D. Laing has succinctly described the dilemma in an essay on "Violence and Love" written in 1965. He points out that in the previous fifty years we human beings have slaughtered over one hundred million of our own species (a figure that continues to climb). We all live under threat of total annihilation, yet seem to seek death and destruction as much as life and happiness. He suggests that we can only stop destroying others when we stop destroying ourselves, and that we have to begin by:

> "*.......admitting and even accepting our violence, rather than blindly destroying ourselves with it, and therewith we have to realise that we are as deeply afraid to live and to love as we are to die.* (2)

It is possible to know, albeit harder to accept the shadow side of ourselves, the essential darkness which breeds ill-will. Envy, greed and jealousy are the fundamental components of this malice. Their counterparts are gratitude, generosity and compassion. Each does not exist in isolation from the other. The interplay of these forces of love and hate create the structure of our lives, which on a personal level is called, character, and on the social level is called, culture.

Envy and gratitude, greed and generosity, jealousy and compassion, these sins and graces are the fundamental forces of human emotional life. Just as the arrangement of protons and electrons, the positive and negative forces of the physical world, define the atom, so do the relative strength of love and hate in a person, define character. Just as different combinations of atoms define the molecule, the smallest unit of matter which retains individual identity, so do different characters come together and create families, and families of families, the basic units of our society.

No-one can 'see' a proton or electron. Yet we postulate their existence and from this predict their effects. Similarly, with love and hate, one person can never know for sure what another feels inside himself or herself, yet, from what people say, when they can say, and from what the do, we postulate the existence of certain feelings, and can predict their effects. In fact, this process is easier with people. You don't need an atom smasher to look into a stranger's eye and detect abject loathing or good will.

'Malice' is a study of the negative or angry constituents of character and culture. But I shall not ignore love. On the contrary I shall demonstrate that when the negative components of our emotional life are denied or ignored (because of guilt or fear), then the positive ones suffer too. As always, love and hate are inexorably intertwined.

The overall purpose of my work is to develop a detailed understanding of our capacity for destruction, as well as for making good. This is not an easy task, either for me, the writer, or you, the reader. The relative absence of comparable studies is an indication of the anxiety that envy, greed, and jealousy arouse.

The sensational press provides some of the best source material on envy, usually to condemn it. Remarkably few scientific books or papers document the emotional havoc and implacable conflicts caused by sheer hate. Some major British and American journals of anthropology and sociology have not carried a single reference to envy, jealousy or resentment over periods of nine to fifty-two years. [3] And in the indices of two major studies of human aggression and destructiveness, one didn't mention envy at all (nor greed, nor jealousy), and the other mentioned it only once (greed once, jealousy not at all) [4]. Yet when you talk to people they are always aware of envy, usually in others. I think that envy is to modern times what sex was to the Victorians, an obsession best forgotten, denied or avoided.

In the *Parson's Tale*, Geoffrey Chaucer wrote:

> *"It is certain that envy is the worst sin that is; for all other sins against one virtue, whereas envy is against all virtue and against all goodness."* [5]

For this reason I have begun the book with a study of envy, the most malevolent of all the constituents of malice.

Historically, *envy* has been equated with 'the evil eye', which is synonymous with the envious 'I' or self. Indeed, the thirteenth century theologian, Thomas Aquinas, observed: *"The evil eye is affected by the strong imagination of the soul and then corrupts and poisons the atmosphere so that tender bodies coming within its range may be injuriously affected."* [6] This pernicious orientation to life seems to begin at birth, and if not tempered during the course of development, may lead to a hatred of all life giving experiences, essentially towards any 'source of supply'.

On the other hand, *greed* is an insatiable desire to take for oneself what another possesses. It is damaging because of its ruthless acquisitiveness. A greedy person can admit that what he wants is good and valuable. In contrast, an envious person is not concerned with possessing, just with preventing others from possessing. For the envious or evil eye goodness must not be preserved, only attacked, spoiled or destroyed.

Developmentally, *jealousy* is a later emotion concerned with relationships. Jealousy has to do with rivalry with one person for the love of another. Jealousy is always triangular, envy is dyadic. Jealousy consists both of a bitter hatred and a possessive love. Envy is pure malice.

Much of this work will be concerned with the interpersonal implications of these impulses, directed emotions felt by one person, the agent, the subject towards another person, the target, the object. Therefore they have to be considered from the point of view of both individuals. However, the subject or object, the 'envier ' or 'envied', for example, need not be an individual. Envious malice can be expressed by or can be directed to a larger group of people up to and including a whole culture.

When society is the envier we can speak about *institutionalised envy*, malevolence and spite embodied in and expressed by the representatives of major social, economic and political institutions towards individual citizens, the envied. Alternatively, in the case of vandalism, the envier is an individual, and it is society, or some aspect of society which is envied. The politics of envy culminates in the effective disguise of individual enmity and its expression through the relationships between institutions, cultures or nation-states. It is common knowledge, for example, that poor, less powerful states envy richer, more powerful ones. Thus North Korea, *"a political and economic failure, hates and envies successful South Korea,"* [7] and that Arab and Muslim societies applauded the destruction of the World Trade Towers on eleven September 2001 (9/11), for knocking the 'Great Satan' (The United States) down a peg or two, [8]. With complementary attacks on the London underground in July 2005, (7/7) in mind, [9] [10] I have also included a new, expanded section on the psychology of Muslim terrorism.

Opposed to this, I will query the resolution of envy, greed and jealousy, including the wide variety of false solutions to these feelings. Many psuedo-solutions strike at the hated object in the hope that if the envied person, culture or source of supply is eliminated, then malice and spite will be vanquished as well. Similarly they strike at the desired object in the hope of deleting greed. Egalitarianism and social leveling are the contemporary expressions of this wish to eliminate envy and greed. Clearly this is an impossibility without eliminating perception and apperception, freewill and imagination.

The best answer to the 'looking glass of malice' is by enhancing the life-sustaining elements in our lives. Most profoundly, gratitude counteracts the damage done by envy. If envy is destructive, gratitude is constructive. If the envious eye, 'I', spews forth bad looks and bad thoughts, then the grateful heart mitigates the malice. As many people attest, there are glances that heal as well as hurt.

But beforehand, I have divided the book into five parts, in order to review the reflections and refractions of malice. The first part looks at the nature of malice, what it is, why it exists and how it operates throughout history.

Part two considers the primary targets of malice. These are the breast, the womb and the penis. The breast represents the source of life, the womb embodies female potency and the penis stands for male potency in all their real and symbolic forms.

Part Three explores the influence of malice on citizens and society. This begins with the relationship between parents and children or brothers and sisters, both as agents and victims of envy, greed and jealousy. Eventually these interactions set the stage for more extensive and more damaging tyrannies, that of a culture or whole nation as an emissary of evil, or its chosen target. In these chapters I will discuss the damage done by the state or its institutions against the individual and conversely, I will trace the effects of malicious persons against the state. All this leads to the greatest predicaments, malice removed from individual intent but expressed by one nation or culture or religion against another. This discussion includes two sections, the first on national pride, and the second, particularly relevant at the start of the third millennium, is on the psychology of Muslim terrorism (written together with Stanley Schneider).

Part four is the concluding chapter on the resolution of malice and completes the basic body of the book.

The fifth part comprises the endnotes. It documents the material I have used in the text and elaborates on issues raised in the individual chapters. Although the text is an authoritative 'looking-glass' on its own accord, the reader should be able to gain an even richer understanding of the nature and impact of malice by following the references and commentaries as he goes along.

Acknowledgements

I would like to express my great appreciation to my friends and relatives, colleagues and patients, who have contributed to this book in many different ways. I am indebted for their incisive comments, criticisms, and suggestions, as well as for many detailed references and examples that they both directly provided and helped me to discover. Not least I am grateful for their encouragement over the many years it took to research and write this book. Many thanks to Mr. David Annesley, Mr. Sam Auspitz, Mr. Adrian Bailey, Lord Beaumont of Whitley, Dr. Eric Brenman, Ms. Jilly Cooper, Mr. Simon Callow, Mr. Simon Duberry, Mr. David Edgar, Mr. Robert Elzey, Ms. Susan Ford, Mr. William Frankel, Mr. Alex Gildzen, Rabbi Hugo Gryn, Mr. Roger Hacker, Mr. Colin Haycroft, Dr. T. T. S. Hayley, Mr. David Herrera, Mr. John Hill, Prof. Robert Hinshelwood, Dr. Alex Holder, Mr. Tony Jackson, Ms. Hazel Jacobs, Ms. Vickie Jaffee, Dr. Colin James, Mr. Martin Jenkins, Ms. Betty Joseph, Mr. Michael Kelly, Ms. Ilany Kogan, Ms. Sandi Lacey, Rabbi Shmuel Lew, Dr. Tali Loewenthal, Prof. Kate Loewenthal, Ms. Fiona Macpherson, Mr. Olivier Marc, Mr. Peter Marsh, Dr. Donald Meltzer, Ms. Suzy Menkes, Dr. Jonathan Miller, Dr. Loren Mosher, Dr. Donald Nathanson, Mr. John Newman, Dr. Dinora Pines, Dr. Malcolm Pines, Professor J. M. Roberts, Dr. Herbert Rosenfeld, Mr. Tom Ryan, Mr. Andrea Sabbadini, Dr. Morton Schatzman, Prof. Stanley Schneider, Ms. Julia Segal, Ms. Helen Silman, Mr. David Spanier, Dr. Joan Speck, Dr. Ross Speck, Dr. Harold Stern, Dr. Alex Tarnopolsky, Mr. Alan Taylor, Dr. Thorkil Vanggaard, Prof. Gabi von Bruck, Mr. Peter von Schreber, Prof. Peter Walcot, Dr. Paul Williams, Mr. Peregrine Worsthorne and Prof. Robert Young.

I am especially grateful to Prof. Helmut Schoeck for his active support and encouragement for the project, and for carefully reading and commenting on the chapters. Special thanks are also due to Drs. Nina Coltart and Peter Lomas for their active support and encouragement.

I wish to thank the staff of the Library of the Royal Society of Medicine, the London Library, and the Regent Bookshop for helping me research the book and gather the material I needed to review.

In particular, I wish to acknowledge the tremendous practical and editorial support given to me by my wife, Shree Pickar Berke, as well as the major contributions of my son, Prof. Joshua Berke, my daughter, Mrs. Deborah Armstrong, and Mrs. Roberta Elzey Berke.

Finally, many thanks to Abdul Azzam and Heather Macpherson of Bookchase for their patience and expertise in designing and producing this book.

Excerpts of some chapters have been previously published in various journals:

"Envy Loveth Not: A Study of the Origin, Influence and Confluence of Envy and Narcissism" *British Journal Psychotherapy,* Vol. 1, No.3, 1985.

"Penis Greed" *British Journal Psychotherapy,* Vol. 5, No. 3, 1989.

"Womb Envy" *Journal of Melanie Klein and Object Relations,* Vol.15, No. 3, 1997.

"The Good and the Bad Therapist" *Medical Psychotherapy,* Vol. 10, Issues 2-3, 1994.

"When Little Men Become Big" *History Today,* Vol. 45, No. 4, 1995.

"The Wellsprings of Fascism: Individual Malice, Group Hatreds and the Emergence of National Narcissism" *Free Associations,* Vol. 6, No. 39, 1996.

PART 1:
THE NATURE OF MALICE
Malicious Intent

Chapter 1

Malice throughout History: The Evil Eye

The *evil eye* is the power to harm or bewitch by a malevolent look or glance. It is a gaze imbued with hostility and wickedness. According to many peoples, it is an expression infected by the Devil.[(1)]

The belief in the *evil eye* is both primeval and universal, and has been often associated with magic, witchcraft and superstition. As to the threat it can pose, Rabbi Judah Low, the alleged creator of the Golem, commented, *"Know and understand that the evil eye concentrates within itself the element of fire,"* and so flashes forth destruction. [(2)]

In our times people are more aware that the harm engendered by a spiteful stare has more to do with the personal malicious wishes, than demonic possession. Yet, a penetrating gaze, a withering glance or a dirty look can strike terror in the most sophisticated of men, comparable to the feelings aroused in the ancients by the Furies of a Greek Chorus. [(3)] We need not be surprised. The *evil eye* is no less than the active expression of the *envious 'I'.*

The chill eye/ 'I' of envy has been acutely captured by the French painter, Jean Louis Gericault, in *A Mad Woman with the Mania of Envy.* [(4)] This painting portrays a thin, tense, nervous woman in her mid-fifties. Sharp, unbalanced eyes radiate agitation and suffering as they focus like daggers on whatever has excited her interest. A slight grimace exaggerates the comparisons she seems to register unceasingly. The woman, a servant according to her dress, is clearly obsessed by the thought of all that she doesn't have.

It is uncomfortable to look at her straight in her face, even in a picture, even in a copy of a picture. One soon wants to avert the eye and shrink away.

To fully comprehend this experience we have to consider two points of view, the mind of the maid and reaction of the onlooker, that is, of the envier and the envied, of the subject and the object. *Envy is not just an emotion. It is a profound emotional force which imposes a comprehensive alteration on the whole way that the envious person sees, feels and acts, and on the way that the envied other, the victim, responds.*

Envy begins in the eye of the beholder, an eye which exaggerates, misrepresents and selectively chooses things to hate. This eye is especially attracted to prosperity, fertility, vitality, fame, success, pride, power, and any other quality or characteristic or accomplishment which conveys, or appears to convey, superiority or special advantage. But these things do not always stimulate envy. Much depends on the life history of the envier, his inner state; and the context, whether he is comparing himself to relatives, to neighbors, to friends, or not.

In Gericault's picture the ominous expression of a servant's eyes hints at a background seething with frustration and deprivation. The left one is wide open as if to emphasize a sinister, if not supernatural transformation of whatever has caught her attention. This is an extravagant look which can turn a cloth coat into a mink and a house into a palace. As various folk sayings attest, this initial tendency towards the idealization of the object can turn toadstools into palm trees and midges into elephants. [5] Such a perception arises from a deep, gnawing sense of inferiority coupled with an instantaneous, and usually unconscious comparison with the envied object. It conveys the essential idea, *"Whatever I am, or have, you are much bigger and better"*. But, this evaluation cannot last long because it arouses intolerable anguish in the envier. Therefore the reverse inevitably happens. Denigration, equally extreme and unrealistic, follows idealization, in order to mitigate the effects of the original perception. Thus the elephant becomes a midge, the palm trees – toadstools and the cloth coat – a rag.

In the meanwhile, the woman's other eye is narrow and squinting, as if to zero in on its target, and hold it in its gaze. This eye sees selectively, focussing on enviable qualities, that is, on good ones, but ignoring the bad ones. There are many examples in Russian literature of this process:

> *"Envy may see the bearskin, but not the moths."*
> *"Envy can see the sea, but not the leak."* (6)

In other words, envious perception confirms, and adds to, envy. Again, such a perception cannot continue because of the pain it evokes. Soon the reverse will occur and the envier will refuse to register goodness, only what's bad in people, and in the world. The culmination of this process is emotional, moral, even actual blindness. It is likely that certain cases of 'hysterical' blindness are the result of an envy so intense, that the person refuses to see anything at all, rather than risk seeing any goodness in anyone, or any thing.

* * * * *

The power of the evil eye, and the fear it evoked, have long been acknowledged by the special names given to the eye, to an envious look, or to a person who looks in an evil or envious way. The Greeks used the word, *baskainein,* which meant, to look or bewitch with the evil eye. *Baskania* meant the evil eye, or, envy. The Roman counterpart was *fascinare.* (7) In contemporary usage *fascination* means strong, overwhelming interest in something, or someone. The word has lost its malevolent undertones. But for almost two millennia, *fascinate* and *fascination* connoted spells, witchcraft, and horror. [8] To get some idea of what the ancients felt when they fell under the influence of a *fascinator,* one only has to think of oneself held in the gaze of a rattlesnake posed to strike, or of the glowing eyes of a cat in the dark. The evil eye has been commonly attributed to any animal, real or mythological, with large, protuberant or brightly coloured eyes. These have included wolves, tigers, hawks, crocodiles, snakes and snake like creatures like the 'basilisk' which allegedly could kill at a glance. [9]

The eye with a magical power to cause harm has been called by many names. The Romans used *oculus fascinus,* the Syrians, *aina-basa,* and the Jews, *ayn-hara.* In modern Italy the evil eye is the *mal occhio* and one possessed of it is called a *jettatura.* [10] People are often considered to be a *jettatura* when bad luck or damage or evil seem to follow in their wake. [11] Pope Pius IX (1792-1878) was extremely popular in Italy during much of his pontificate. Nevertheless, a series of disasters that occurred during his reign led to his being attributed with the evil eye. The same held true for his successor, Pope Leo XIII (1810-1903) who was held responsible for the deaths of a large number of cardinals. [12]

In English speaking countries people tend to be aware of the evil eye, but not to refer to it by name, except among ethnic minorities. This was not always the case. In Shakespeare's time the term *overlook* was widely employed to denote the act of looking at someone with the evil eye. Therefore an *over-looker* was an evil person who was widely feared for *ill-wishing.* [13] Later on the owner of an evil eye was called a *blinker* whose victims were said to be *blinked, fore-looked,* or *eye-bitten.* [14]

The English philosopher, Francis Bacon, observed that an envious person looks at others obliquely, and it has been said that people who squint are exceptionally envious. Perhaps this is why the English country gentleman has long feared squinting neighbors and strangers. [15]

Nowadays people are not directly preoccupied with the evil eye. But they don't like 'dirty looks', or red, inflamed, enlarged, deformed eyes.

In fact, in China envy is called *"the red-eyed disease."* [16] Similarly, in the cinema, the most disreputable villains, and most horrific monsters, often have huge, blood-shot, shifty, squinting eyes. These caricatures of primitive fears also tend to be very sensitive about how others look at them: *"Don't look at me that way, or I'll plug ya full of holes!"* [17] And if this happens, or people die in any other circumstances, someone will quickly come and pull down their eyelids, not just for cosmetic reasons. It is part of a custom that can be traced back to Roman times, and further.

The Romans placed a coin on the eyes of the dead. This was to pay Charon, the boatman who ferried souls across the river Styx to Hades. But the coins also served as weights, to make sure that the dead could not stare at the living. Similarly, Aryan peoples closed the eyes of the dead and placed weights upon the lid. They wished to prevent the spirit of the dead person from casting a spell on those who survived. [18]

Closing the eyes of the dead remains a widespread custom. In our times it is the closest that many people come to acknowledging the power of the evil eye. This is especially strong at the moment of death, for envy is most intense, most vicious and dangerous, when it is directed by the dead, or those who feel dead, towards the living.

The German writer, Elias Canetti, has commented of the amazing power of the "the dead" to dominate the lives of the living:

> *"The first thing that strikes one is the universal fear of the dead. They are discontented and full of envy for those they have left behind. They try to take revenge on them, sometimes for injuries done them during their life-time, but often simply because they themselves are no longer alive."* [19]

* * * * *

What feelings fuel the envious perceptions and wishes that constitute the evil eye? When confronted by evidence of limitations and mortality, the envier feels assailed by an implacable, all-consuming anguish and despair, as exemplified by Ivan Babichev, Iago and Salieri. Then he or she responds with vindictive, burning hatred and rage towards the object of this envy. The immediate impulse is to eliminate the pain and torment by annihilating anything and everything that may have caused it. As the anguish and anger occur almost simultaneously, the two feelings tend to fuse and cause even greater suffering, evident as hostile desperation in the eyes of the envier.

An envious person will go to any length to reduce this intolerable inner state. He may refuse to recognize what he sees and refuse to acknowledge what he feels. Or, he may dissociate himself from his feelings and attribute them to whomever or whatever he envies, whether a prosperous friend, a comfortable home, or a bowl of soup. This happened with Kavalerov, Ivan Babichev's envy-ridden lay-about companion who discovered that *"things"* stopped liking him:

> *"Furniture tries to trip me up. Once the sharp corner of some polished thing literally bit me...Soup given to me, never cools. If some bit of junk – a coin or a collar button – falls off the table, it usually rolls under some almost unmovable piece of furniture. And when, crawling around on the floor after it, I raise my head, I catch the sideboard laughing at me."* [20]

The denial of reality, by evacuating bad feelings into the external world, may afford some temporary relief, but it is no solution to the anguish and despair aroused by envy. Therefore the envier seeks to alter, and to destroy reality, not just deny it. [21]

'Reality' is everything the envier hates. His first stratagem is psychological. He acts with words and gestures to rubbish whomever and whatever he envies. His intentions are to diminish, denigrate and debase that person or thing so completely, that it will appear and be totally worthless in his eyes, and in the eyes of everyone else. If the object of his envy is a person, he literally wants to fill that person with agitation and anger in order to effectively transfer his desperation to another. In this way the envier hopes that he will be released from his suffering. If not, at least he will have had a measure of revenge on his imagined tormentor.

Examples of psychic attacks are commonplace. Who hasn't heard children respond to the accomplishments of their sibs or parents with: *"That's shit!"*, *"That's nothing"* or *"You're all wrong!"?* The businessman or scientist who attacks a colleague's reputation on spurious grounds, or the housewife who spreads malicious rumors about a relative or neighbor are familiar figures. 'Put downs' allow the envier, whether child or adult, to feel superior. Boasting and bragging serve the same end. They enhance the speaker at the expense of his audience.

Kierkegaard, understood this process very well, for he attributed envy to anyone who aroused envy in others whether by self-promotion and self-flattery, or otherwise. (22) Interestingly, the latin word for envy, *invidia,* has given rise to the English word, *invidious,* which is often taken to mean offensive or envious. Yet, the principle definition of *invidious* is envy arousing. In effect, if not in intention, a braggart or show-off is an *invidious* person.

Excessive or undeserved compliments can lead the complimented person to feel anxious and embarrassed and easily make him a target for others' envy. The American anthropologist, George Foster, has described many instances where excessive praise, or compliments, serve or are seen as thinly disguised, envious attacks. In Mali people avoid direct compliments for fear of the harm they cause. And in the Arab world well meaning praise may be shunned because of the contrary feelings it may contain. Foster sums up by quoting from the Spanish novel, *Abel Sanchez: The History of a Passion*, where a truculent character always exclaims, whenever he hears anyone praised, *"Against whom is that eulogy directed?"* (23)

The Greeks were particularly aware of the dangers of excessive praise which they believed attracted the *Envy of the Gods – Phthonos Theon.* In the writings of Homer, *Envy of the Gods* seemed to represent an unnamed, indeterminate, but malevolent divine force that lay behind things when they went wrong. [24] This changed around 500 B.C. at a time when Greek society became much less rigidly hierarchical and more open – socially, politically and economically. [25] *Phthonos theon* came to mean the specific hatred and retribution of the Gods towards mortals who challenged their authority, prerogatives or power. This concept was defined and redefined by Pindar, Aeschylus and Herodotus in their poems, plays and histories. [26]

In the *Agamemnon,* the chorus, 'that frequent exponent of popular morality' exclaims, prior to the hero's murder:

> *"Grievous is the burden of excessive praise, for from the eyes of Zeus is cast the thunder-bolt."* [27]

Agamemnon prayed that *'envy's eye'* would not strike him from afar. [28] His prayers were misdirected, and unanswered. He was slaughtered by Clytemnestra, his wife.

Later writers, like Euripides and Plutarch were more precise when they declared that the *'evil stings'* and *'poisoned arrows'* of envy originated in the eyes of envious mortals. [29] Even Aeschylus, in his mature judgement, stated that it is impiety, the actions of men, not the envy of immortal deities, that unleashes disaster on mankind. [30]

The Greeks realized that the envious man was charged with hostility. Moreover, they appreciated that the consequences of this hostility were not just psychological – the besmearing a reputation, or arousing bad feelings, but that they were tangible, physical and deadly. For them *'thunderbolts', 'evil stings'* and *'poisoned arrows'* were part of a wide weaponry of envious anger and rage that posed a constant threat to man, to society, to life itself.

The English Classicist, Peter Walcot, points out that as far back as 500 B.C. the philosopher, Democritus taught that the envious released particles charged with envy ('angry atoms', 'evil atoms'), particles which *"established themselves securely in those bewitched and so damaged their bodies and minds."* [31]

This idea was embellished by the 3rd century novelist, Heliodorus, who seemed to equate envy's 'poisoned arrows' and 'evil particles' with the very air that emanates from an envious person. He explained that the air which surrounds us, goes deep into our body, and emerges charged with emotion. Therefore the air expelled by an envious person is charged with malice. It fills the atmosphere with a '*malignant quality*'. What we call the *evil eye* is this breath of bitterness which, when taken in by another, penetrates deep to the marrow and can cause sickness and death. [32]

Plutarch concluded that this evil air and similar noxious '*scents*', '*voices*' or '*any other defluxions and streams*' spew forth from the eye rather than any other conduit of the body because "... *sight, being a sense very swift, active, and nimble, doth send forth and disperse from it a wonderful fiery puissance, together with the spirit that carrieth and directed it.*" [33]

Fifteen hundred years later these views were echoed by Francis Bacon who called envy, '*an ejaculation, or irradiation of the eye*'. [34] He averred that the envious gaze "*emitteth some malign and poisonous spirit, which taketh hold of the spirit of another; and is likewise of the greatest force when the cast of the eye is oblique.*" [35] However, the active, destructive component of envy remained a mystery even for Bacon, a keen observer of human relationships. He postulated poison rays rather than accept that the damage caused by envy was the result of specific, concrete, malicious actions.

By this time few people believed in the *Envy of the Gods*, as such. The Greeks, themselves, didn't refer to it very much after Aeschylus. Yet, people still retained a need to distance themselves from the evil they waged on earth. So it became, indeed, it had long been the function of astrology to attribute 'bad fate', 'ill luck', 'divine retribution', or 'evil influence' to the position of the planets and the stars. Bacon commented on the preoccupations of astrologers. He connected what '*the Scripture calleth the evil eye*' with '*the evil aspects of the stars*' to what he termed envious irradiation. To this very day astrology remains the repository for popular beliefs in the *evil eye*, set far away, amid the heavenly bodies. [36]

* * * * *

Bacon, as others before him, clearly linked the *evil eye* with an envious anger. It is an important distinction. There are many kinds of anger, as there are many reasons for aggression. Envy is not the prime cause of all anger. Nor is all anger, evil.

There are angers motivated by greed and jealousy, or by frustration, indignation, rivalry and revenge, to name but a few. There is an assertive, self-protective anger or aggression and an instrumental aggression that is part of being a member of a group, whether a young gang, or the police. Their consequences may be negative, violent and wicked, or positive and constructive. All have been seen in, and attributed to the eye. Some eyes have been said to be 'devouring', 'possessive', and 'bigger than your stomach', while others have been considered 'dangerous', 'provocative' and 'penetrating.

A young patient of mine spent most of one session declaiming his insatiable hunger for women. I pointed out that it seemed that he wanted me to provide girls for him just as his nanny had provided sweets, and that he gave me dirty looks if I didn't. He grimaced, *"Ah yes, sweets, red and round,"* and proceeded to move both of his hands in a circular motion in front of him, as if he were depicting two breasts. "*You know,* he added, *"I sometimes feel my eyes are as big as soup plates."* (37)

As for jealousy, it has long been said that *"jealousy has a thousand eyes, yet none sees properly."* (38)

Love, desire and curiosity are frequent inhabitants of the eye. In the third century B.C.E. Pindar noted that there can be beneficent glances as well as destructive ones. In one ode the poet prays for *"the unenvious regard of the gods"* and asks Apollo *"to let your eyes rain melody on every step I take."* (39) And Bacon himself wrote that:

> *"There be none of the affections which have been noted to fascinate or bewitch but love and envy: they both have vehement*

wishes, they frame themselves readily into imaginations and suggestions; and they come easily into the eye, especially upon the presence of objects ... " [40]

Characteristically, the *evil eye* is an eye without love, a savage eye holding an anger without obvious merit or cause or restraint. This eye, full of ill-will, can be cunning and calculating. It can act by doing nothing such as when an envious person deliberately fails to warn someone in danger or distress, but whom he envies. The philosopher, Immanuel Kant, noted that in this way, by refusing to do his duty, the envier is able to give (bad) fate a helping hand. [41]

Usually the envier is too impatient to let fate take an evil course. He prefers *'to consort with the hangman'* as was the case with Iago and Salieri, who employed slander and swords, duplicity and poison. [42] That is what is so horrific, the sadistic quality of the envious attack, which specifically mimics the burning, consuming, spoiling, vitriolic turmoil within the envier.

* * * * *

On 19 July 1949, John Haigh was convicted of one of the more heinous crimes to have come before Lewes Assizes. [43] He had become friends with, robbed and disposed of nine men and women by immersing them in a vat of concentrated sulfuric acid (oil of vitriol). At his trial he showed no remorse for the victims, but he did object to the use of the word '*murder*'. He preferred *'killings'* and argued that they were necessary in order for him *'to fulfill his destiny'*.

Haigh came from a background that was very conducive to the envy of vitality and happiness – his destiny! He had been brought up in a fanatically religious atmosphere, one where newspapers and radio were forbidden and friends and neighbors were excluded from the house. The wrath and punishment of God was held over his head as a punishment for every trifling misdemeanor.

This man attacked nine members of three different families. His crime was one of 'grenvy'. He managed to steal property worth £30,000 (at 1949 prices). But his corroding, mutilating, annihilating violence was typical of envy. Also typical are crimes where the victims are gratuitously debased, denigrated or mutilated. (44)

It is somewhat more difficult to appreciate that whatever the envier does to someone or something outside himself, he also does to an image (psychic representation) of the envied person or thing inside himself. Since these internal images contribute to the contents and structure of his own mind, a very envious person can be devastatingly self-destructive. (45)

The state of affairs, whereby the *evil eye* turns inward, has been recognized by the folk sayings of many countries and cultures.

"Envy cuts its own throat."

"Envy devours its own master."

"Envy is its own scourge."

"Envy envies itself." (46)

Various writers have decreed that envy is a diseased state of mind, because the envious man is 'his own worse enemy'. (47) Certainly it causes a lot of mental 'dis-ease' which the envier seeks to minimize to himself by maximizing in another. The distorted perceptions and diabolical actions I have described all serve this purpose, to defend against envy (the anguish, despair, hostility of the subject) by arousing it (in the object).

In summary, envy affects the envier in three basic ways – *perception, emotion* and *action.* His *perceptions* are exaggerated and selective. This arises from, and gives rise to, *feelings* of great agony and anger, which, in turn, impel *actions* of extreme aggressiveness. They are a combination of psychic and direct physical attacks on whatever and whomever is envied, both externally, in actuality, and internally against oneself.

The envied person also responds according to the same three categories of perception, emotion and action. The specific effects have to do with the state of being envied, and may be similar to, or quite different from what occurs in the envier, for the envied person is the victim, not the victimizer. Nevertheless, these effects are in a dynamic relationship with the envy which precedes them. Therefore the impact of envy on awareness, feeling and volition (in the envied person) should be considered to be a component of envy, that is, part of the structure of the phenomenon.

Envy, like greed or jealousy, is a directed emotion. It needs an object. Without an object to focus upon, and to influence, envy remains a possibility, but not a practical reality. Envy is not a mood. Gloom or irritation may fill the mind without reference to anyone or anything. This cannot happen with envy, which may contribute to such a mood, but only if the envier has already fastened onto to something to be upset about.

It is particularly important to consider the experience and viewpoint of the envied person, because of the drastic changes that the envier can induce in him. I am not just referring to the impact of 'angry atoms' or specific destructive actions. Most commonly the envier enters into and affects the inner world of the envied person by the powerful psychological mechanism known as *projective identification*, which I will detail in the next chapter. Because of projective identification we can say that within the psyche of a person who feels threatened by envy, there exists an envier from whom he is trying to escape. This internalized envier may be a psychic representation of an envious friend or relative, or of envy as embodied in a social institution or state. [48]

In Egypt where the evil eye is known as "Hassad", people commonly talk about parts of the body as having been invaded by "Hassad", that is, an internalized envier in the form of their own or others' malicious intentions. Thus one resident of a fashionable Cairo suburb believed that her husband had "Hassad" in his broken leg. Although ostensibly 'Westernized', she asked priests to visit her home to sprinkle special oils and intone prayers against the scourge. Still she observed, "*......one thing after another keeps on happening. Now it's in his foot. Perhaps we are giving Hassad to ourselves.*" [49]

The wish to escape from the envier, whether real or imagined, external or internal, leads the envied person to have an extreme sensitivity to the malevolent intentions of others. All his senses may be constantly attuned to detecting shafts of hatred and misfortune emanating from inanimate as well as human sources. [50]

The American playwright, Tennessee Williams, suffered an unbearable sensitivity to malice after the "*catastrophic success*'" of *The Glass Menagerie* snatched him from virtual oblivion and thrust him into a sudden prominence. In his new expensive Manhattan suite things began to break "*accidentally.*" Cigarettes would fall onto and damage the furniture. Windows would be left open in a downpour and his room would be flooded – events that had never happened to him before. He became very depressed. [51]

> *"Sincerity and kindliness seemed to have gone from my friends' voices. I suspected them of hypocrisy, I stopped calling them, stopped seeing them."* [52]

Williams held the literal belief that if he stopped seeing them, they would stop seeing him, therefore he would gain protection from their enmity (the evil eye). He acted upon this belief by going to the hospital for an optional eye operation. For several weeks his eyes were covered with a gauze mask and he couldn't see. Only then did he allow his friends to visit him.

Upon leaving the hospital, with his sight restored, Williams escaped to Mexico. There he knew no one. It was a place "*where you can quickly forget the false dignities and conceits imposed by success*". The anonymity allowed him to write again. [53]

The hyper-awareness of envy figures in many cultures as a heightened susceptibility to and inexorable obsession with the *evil eye.* [54] But the opposite reaction may also occur. The envied person may shut down his perceptual facilities in order to avoid awareness of envy, or the evil eye. Thus, up until the last moment, Mozart showed an astonishing insensitivity to the machinations of Salieri, as did Othello to Iago.

The inability to realistically perceive and respond to the dangers posed by envy occurs within an emotional framework of fear, guilt, shame and embarrassment. Tennessee Williams was as terrified of the praise of his friends, as others were of the gaze of the Gods. They all anticipated that calamities would follow and could site 'hard facts' to justify their fears, although the 'facts' (a flooded room, a sudden death) were not necessarily caused by what they feared. The feelings which interfere with an appropriate response to malice also reflect people's preoccupations with themselves. In other words, a greedy or envious person may refuse to see in others what he refuses to see in himself. This was certainly the case with Mozart who was often described as a vain, pompous man who delighted in cutting down colleagues with his superior talents and attendant airs. [55]

The powerful, all encompassing fears engendered by the real or imagined envy of others can be destructive, in themselves, to the life of the envied person. Dr. Frank Gifford, a Philadelphia ophthalmologist and student of the folklore of vision, noticed that many of the physical symptoms of the patients who attended his south Philadelphia clinic, occurred after they believed that had been 'overlooked' by the evil eye. Their fear resulted in headache, weakness, fatigue, stomach ache and general discomfort. Many experienced an unpleasant sensation of warmth at the moment they had been overlooked, with subsequent mental and physical deterioration [56]

Newspapers like the London *Guardian* often print cartoon commentaries about the effects of envious looks. In a take-off on middle class problems, "Black Looks" describes a well-off man who became pale and wan after being seen by his daughter's jobless friends unloading a case of Rioja from his Volvo. He declaims, "Oh, its a terrible look, Wendy...black huddle of clothes...Look of ENVY....blunt ENVY... and DERISION! Oh heck! Utter DERISION!" [57]

Most readers would not immediately associate these symptoms with being overlooked or fear of the *evil eye*. However, they become quite familiar if thought of in terms of a fear of success. Marriage, the birth of a child, the purchase of a house, the publication of a book, public or professional recognition, and other forms of success are often followed by an incongruous period of retreat, turmoil and breakdown. Some people never recover. Others restrict their achievements, in the first place. [58]

The fear of success originates in the fear of the envy that success may attract. The psychologist, Matina Horner, and her colleagues have done systematic studies of the threats posed by success. In one test she asked 178 male and female college undergraduates to write about a girl called Anne, *"who finds herself at the top of her medical school class."* Three major themes emerged, They were: a fear that Anne would lose her friends because *"everyone hates and envies her";* a very negative internal state because *"Anne feels guilty, unhappy, unfeminine and abnormal";* and bizarre or exaggerated hostility due to an anticipated rejection by others. Many students did not wish to be Anne. For them the fear of envy was a predominant concern. [59]

Similar constrictions affect the Navaho Indians of the American Southwest. In recent years their lifestyle has elicited considerable sympathy and admiration, for they have little concept of material success or personal achievement. However, the individual Navaho is under constant social pressure not to possess what he might like, or to give away what he has become to possess. If he fails, *"the voice of envy will speak out in whispers of witchcraft"*, and he will be the object of constant attack. [60]

This reluctance to outdo others is rooted both in the fear of envy, and in guilt about greed. The fear and the guilt, arising from envy and greed, are inexorably linked. Each arouses and is aroused by the other, and each may have identical, inhibiting, self-damaging consequences.

'Envious' guilt occurs when a person holds himself responsible for a malevolent, spoiling attack on another person or thing. It is often confused with guilt about greed. [61] Envious guilt also occurs when a person displays or uses his possessions, skills or good fortune in a haughty, self-inflating, invidious (envy arousing) manner. A lot depends on the intentions of the guilty party. If he deliberately set out to make a relative or friend feel bad, then the guilt may be quite appropriate. Even when this is not the case, the person may still become the focus of ill-will. He need not blame himself, but often does.

A state of 'false responsibility' develops whereby the envied person feels guilty for being envied. This is very uncomfortable, but common, situation. It leads the individual to be terrified by, and apologetic for, others' envy. (62) This experience coincides with, and tends to be made worse by the belief that no one can prosper, or be rich (in anything, not just money), without depriving someone else of what he has, or might have. Then, life is like a zero sum game where ownership equals theft and one has to be on constant guard not to possess more than the next person. (63)

* * * * *

Over several millennia an intricate array of activities has evolved in order to enable people avert the malicious interest of relatives, friends or neighbors. Stratagems for avoiding envy range from economic camouflage to hermit-like isolation. They can be roughly divided into five categories: *Concealment, Denial, Magical Self-Defense, Aggressive Counter Attack,* and *Appeasement.*

The first principle of envy avoidance is to hide whatever may attract it. This is a universal phenomenon, well illustrated by illustrious singers like the former Beatle, Paul McCartney, certain German Mercedes owners, or poor and primitive Indians, like the Siriono of Bolivia.

Although said to be *"as rich as Croesus"*, McCartney has a marked reluctance to talk about or to display his wealth. When asked about money in an interview in the London *Evening Standard,* he commented:

"I try not to talk about it. It's a bit like discovering a gold mine at the bottom of your garden. It's embarrassing to talk

about, and there's always the fear that if you do, everyone else will want to take it off you." [64]

In Germany the very rich and powerful have taken to removing the chrome numbers from the left corner of the rear of their Mercedes which indicate that they are the top-of-the-line, the most powerful and expensive models. The car has become a symbol within the country of *"overdoing it"* and its owners and occupants a target for antagonism and terrorism. Driving the more economical diesel and four-cylinder models is a form of self-protection and fits in with the old Prussian dictum,

"Mehr sein als schein" – "Be more, seem less." [65]

The Siriono, a tribe organized in sub-units of fifteen to twenty-five people, leads a meager existence. Individual members generally eat alone and at night, because they do not wish to share food with others, even close relatives. The Indians hoard food, while constantly accusing each other of stealing it. Not only do the men hide anything edible, but the women tend to conceal bits of meat in their vagina, rather than allow others to have access to it. [66] These actions are not so dissimilar from those of McCartney, wealthy Mercedes owners, and others who fear the *evil eye*. If a Siriono does eat during the day, he tends to collect a small crowd which stares at him enviously. Celebrities like the Beatles also collect crowds which stare, both in wonder and anger. [67]

Conformity is a further way of avoiding recognition, and hostility, for having or doing anything outstanding. It is a capitulation to the fear of being successful, which may be fed by strong social as well as internal pressures. Sociologists have long noted, and sometimes ridiculed, the yearning for adjustment, acceptance and popularity in America. But conformism is hardly lacking in other countries or cultures. [68]

In order to appreciate why people conform, it is useful to consider what happens when they don't. In ancient Greece the penalty for unacceptable wealth or excellence was ostracism or death. [69] The philosopher, Socrates, was the most notable victim of the *"slander and envy of the many"* (Plato). [70] He was forced to drink poison.

Nowadays someone who works too hard or goes against the norm may be 'sent to Coventry'. [71] Yet, not long ago, Mr. Lester Summerfield, a dentist in practice in Coventry, had to leave the city, because he had been working too hard and making too much money. He was reprimanded and fined by the Coventry Family Practitioner Committee and the Dental Estimates Board after the Board noted that his practice had grossed over one million pounds in a ten year period.

Mr. Summerfield decided to dissolve the practice and return to his native New Zealand because he could not stand *"all the hassle"*. While this was happening, the secretary of the local dental committee admitted that other dentists were envious of Summerfield's capacity for work, although his patients were very happy.

> *"He ran foul of the system on the clinical side, although there is no case where any of his patients complained, and neither was he struck off the register.*
>
> *The local branch of the committee did not like the way the dental estimates board allowed the situation to develop. The board wanted to know why he was doing so much work."* [72]

Bureaucratic hassle was his punishment for hard work and success, a contemporary version of divine retribution (*Phthonos Theon*). To avoid this Summerfield decided to inhibit what he could do and diminish what he could earn. This is another method of secreting wealth and talent from the *evil eye*. [73]

The inhibition and diminution of whatever may attract envy is consistent with injunctions against ostentation one finds in the sacred writings of many peoples. The *Talmud*, for example, limits the number of guests at a wedding, the number of courses and the quality of garments worn in public. Not all Jews are so modest, but these rules are a reminder of the dangers of arousing envy, especially among gentiles. [74]

Modesty is an excellent character trait because it not only serves to defuse envy but also evokes praise in and of itself. By being modest the person (who may or may not be aware of being envied) seemingly adheres to egalitarian ideals and puts others at ease. In common parlance, *"Oh, it was nothing at all"*, or *"It wasn't anything, really"* are typical and expected responses to praise, awards and achievements. The words reduce hostility. [75]

To be most effective modesty must appear spontaneous and unaffected. We ascribe false modesty to vain or pompous men who linger too long on their alleged humble origins. The Washington Post has coined the term, *"Humble-Origins Chic"* to describe the posturing which characterizes American politicians who *"spend the first 40 years fighting their way out of borderline poverty and hardship and into country club posh, and the second 40 years bragging about how poor they used to be."* [76]

More than modesty, many people actively deny what they have, or could do. Such denial ominously expands the art of secreting resources, for the envied object, whether an individual or nation, does not only conceal things from others, but also from himself. One can see this process at work with people who never mention good news, or if they do, always couple it with worse news. Thus, any hint of prosperity, a new house, a new job, will be accompanied by a litany of imminent disasters, an ulcer, a heart attack, and so on. In a similar vein world figures, like the Secretary General of the United Nations, and other representatives of international agencies have an ominous tendency to diminish or deny good news (for example, the effectiveness of international aid programs) and exaggerate the bad. [77]

The consequences of such distortions of reality include a rise in international tensions and a collective helplessness and hopelessness. Thus, this very defense against envy can aggravate the envy it seeks to avoid. The same cycle happens with individuals who, in order not to be envied, convince themselves that they are worse off than they are.

They continue to be hated, because others still see them as they are. At the same time, these people may themselves be consumed with hatred (envy the enviers) because they imagine that those who envy them are really much better off.

Denial as a defense against envy proceeds from a simple self-diminishing to a deeper self-effacement and delusional sense of inferiority. [78] The English anthropologist Edmund Leach, sees all these processes at work in *"the contemporary British peculiarity of pretending to be poor, ill and already in trouble."* Leach observes that over and over business and government circles have moaned about the state of the economy, blaming one disaster after another on the *"Gnomes of Zurich or the Bankers of Wall Street"*, only to repeatedly discover that the country has been much more prosperous than it appeared:

> *The implication .... the English economic sickness is largely a response to fear of the envy of others: we have developed a sense of guilt about our power and affluence, and are taking it out on ourselves."* [79]

A similar attitude has been long established in Chinese thought. According to the *Tao Te Ching*, *"If you are rich and of high degree you become proud and so expose yourself to inevitable ruin. If all goes well with you, it is expedient to keep yourself in the background."*

But if self-deprecation isn't enough to divert the envious eye, then the threatened person or nation may escalate its self-hatred by idealizing the envier. This commonly occurs when members of a victimized class or caste excessively and indiscriminately praise their persecutors. Indeed, whole countries may act in such a manner towards their regional or economic antagonists. In the end the envied 'victims' may try to justify the malice of their tormentors, and become like them, to others, and to themselves, as when European countries ape the deprecations of Third World states at the U.N.

The idealization of the envier coincides with a reversal of values whereby poverty, sickness, failure and death are exalted, and the pleasures and benefits of earthly existence are spurned. The envied person may literally isolate himself from friends and relatives and withdraw from all material pursuits. Deliberate impoverishment and asceticism complete the renunciation from anything which could give offense to others. Long ago Francis Bacon observed that such detailed attention to avoiding envy was not without its practical advantages, such as arousing pity. He averred:

"Pity ever healeth envy." [80]

Pity, however, is not a satisfactory solution to envy, because in order to gain it, one has to maintain a facade of inferiority, or live in an impoverished manner. Moreover, pity itself, can be used for aggressive purposes, as I learned to my great discomfort while working with a man dying from cancer. [81]

Traditionally people have resorted to an array of extra ordinary words, gestures, amulets and talismans to protect themselves. These things interpose a magical, tangible barrier between the envied person and the envier. They operate by invoking a higher, greater, stronger or better power which can divert, deflect, absorb and thereby neutralize malicious looks and wishes. [82]

The Babylonians carved the names of Gods on incantation tablets. [83] The Egyptians carried representations of the eyes of their Gods. They even incised them on bodies for embalming. The eye of Horus (avenger of evil) was considered especially propitious, and in a complete or abbreviated form (the capital letter 'R'), it was painted on buildings, ships, documents – anything important. [84] The popularity of this symbol persisted into modern times when it was made part of the great seal of the United States. It appears on the back of every dollar note. [85]

The Greeks carried replicas of the head of Medusa, basing their protection on the principle, like cures like. This was also used by the

Romans, but their most popular amulet (charm worn on the body) or talisman (similar to an amulet but displayed about the house) was a sculpture of a phallus, called a *fascinum.* [86] Roman infants received a coral phallus to use as a teething ring. As they grew older boys carried a small *fascinum* in a box around their necks. At puberty this was placed over the hearth. Large *fascina* also decorated houses and were carried in the street during festivals. [87]

These phallic figures served as lightning rods to divert the attention of the envier and deflect it away from the bearer, or his home and family. Presumably, the bigger, and more elaborate or expensive the amulet, the greater their allure. The figurines also conveyed the message, *"I'm not afraid of you. I have greater strength and power than you. I defy you."* [88]

With the onset of Christianity, the phallus was gradually replaced by the horns of animals, or their look-alikes such as crescents, teeth and horse shoes. [89] These amulets were supplemented by special words and gestures. In Italy the mere pronunciation of the word for horn, *corno*, has magical protective power. [90] Italians have also persevered with two gestures which are said to be highly effective against the evil eye. The first was called *manus obscenus* by the Romans and *mano fico* by their descendants. It consists of clenching the fist with the thumb thrust between the first and second fingers. The other is known as the *mano cornuta* and is achieved by enclosing the second and third fingers with the thumb, and extending the first and fourth fingers of the hand. This gesture is known as, "making the Devil's Horns". When directed against the envier the *mano fica* and the *mano cornuta* are not just defensive, but highly aggressive counter attacks. [91]

Aggressive counter measures may be expressed magically, or non-magically. They are part of a strategy of striking first and immobilizing the envier, before he can hurt you. The ancients, for example, did not merely rely on the head of Medusa to avert the evil eye, but to paralyze it with fear and turn it to stone. Spitting three times in the presence of a stranger is another ritual that continues to be practiced. [92] It is a defensive maneuver with offensive intentions. Many sayings are purely offensive:

"Stomach ache for a long night." *(Morocco)*

"The curse be upon thine eye." *(Ireland)*

"Ill on your eye, bird shit on the back of that." *(Scottish Highlands)* [93]

These words aim to incapacitate the envier. I wonder whether the common toast, *"Here's mud in your eye"*, serves the same purpose.

George Foster has pointed out the dangers implicit in apparently innocuous bantering and compliments. Depending on the context, compliments may double as 'put-downs' or as a hostile over inflation of pride in order to deny a feared rival a reason for envy (blind him to what you have) and to provoke his downfall. [94] Alternatively, the envied person may flaunt his wealth and adopt a lofty superiority – *"a superiority complex"* – in the hope of becoming so far above everyone else that no-one would dare to envy him.

However, if an individual cannot destroy or immobilize his enviers, at least he can put them off their guard and mollify them. Aside from direct counter attacks, most of the measures I have described serve this purpose, to placate or appease those who overlook with anger. Self-diminution, self-deprecation and self-denial are all covert means of appeasement. They seek to change the relative balance of power, pride and possessions so that the envier can have a false sense of being bigger, stronger and more important than he is.

Overt appeasement is equally pervasive, often taking the form of carefully controlled, culturally sanctioned expressions of hostility (by the envier) and self-abasement (by the envied). Among the Hottentot people of South West Africa a successful hunter literally allows his fellow tribesmen to 'piss on him'. If he has killed a lion, an elephant or a rhinoceros, the heroic deed will be celebrated in the most dramatic fashion. The hunter has to stay in his hut until an elder invites him to come to the center of the village. In the meanwhile all the men will have gathered around in order to do him honor:

"The hero now crouches down on a mat and all the men squat down around him in a circle. The old man goes up to him and urinates all over him from head to toe. If he is a good friend of the hero he will deluge him with urine." [95]

Lest we titter with laughter, it is worth considering modern parents who tolerate and encourage the rebellious and delinquent acts of their children (which spoil the family honor) or international forums where small countries are permitted to hurl abuse (a verbal deluge) at bigger or more sophisticated ones. The Hottentots might find these events equally outrageous.

Sop behavior avoids the necessity of allowing the envier to vent steam. The sop is a small present, or token of good-will, or word of praise given in the hope of soaking up envious resentment. It can be thought of as the loser's compensation, a symbolic sharing of good fortune. Really it is a bribe, a device to buy off envy by appealing to greed (for self-esteem or goods). [96]

The giving of sops is such a pervasive practice that one rarely thinks of it as a bribe, just something that is done. The favors provided at the end of a child's birthday party are typical examples. Although the gifts may be a further expression of generosity on the part of the host, are they really necessary? [97] After all the children have been fed and entertained, usually at great expense and effort. But, they have not been the centre of attention, nor have they received the vast array of gifts as the birthday child. They share a position akin to Ivan Babichev when confronted by the *"queen of the ball"*. Anyone who has seen the wretchedness and barely concealed rage in the brother or sister of the birthday child, or the distress of a young guest who did not receive a going home present, would immediately understand this. The children 'need' a sop to make them feel better. [98]

Perhaps the most ubiquitous sops center around death and burial beliefs designed to diminish the envy of the bereaved and of the dead, themselves. Although the food given to a bereaved family by friends and relatives is an expression of sympathy and kindness, it is also a means of assuring good will, and warding off misfortune. Similarly, the annual visits to the grave and other propitiatory rites serve to assure the dead that their descendents still think of them and wish them well (so that they won't come back and haunt them!). [99] Foster believes that even these practices do not suffice. He speculates that the Judaeo-Christian and Moslem concept of heaven is *"basically a device invented to allay fear of the envy of the departed."* Therefore 'heaven' is sop behavior at its most imaginative. After all, what better means to ease the envy of the dead than to provide a celestial abode far more splendid than whatever has been left behind? Moreover, in societies riddled with great disparities in wealth among different social classes, Foster muses that the expectation of a glorious afterlife has been the best way to reduce envy between classes and to make life bearable for the poor and wretched:

> *And it so turns the tables that the living envy the dead, placing the latter on the defensive. Life, with its sorrows and suffering, is but a brief prelude to the true substance of existence, where all are equal before God, so that death can be anticipated with equanimity, if not with outright joy."* [100]

Sops do not have to be, nor are they always deceptive concepts or token presents. They often signify a tangible sharing of wealth, a form of generosity or charity motivated by compassion and the wish to put things right. Yet such charity is never entirely beneficent. And when things are given compulsively, anxiously and with contempt towards the recipient, then it is safe to surmise that a fear of envy is a significant factor. [101]

True sops are a temporary expedient. They reduce and delay hostility, but do not eliminate it. No matter how much the envied person gives up, no matter how much good he does, the envier will still believe that the gifts won't be missed and that the very act of giving is a sign of the other's superior character. No act of self-denial, nor self-abasement can make an envier happy. He will always insist that whatever people do, they are increasing their happiness, while he is left with bitterness and bile. For such a person, who denies or overlooks goodness in himself, the kindness and compassion of others are cruelties aimed to torment and humiliate him, stimulants for hatred and malice, and calls to the *evil eye.*

This attitude, and the dynamic relationship between the envier and the envied, has been eloquently portrayed by the cartoonist, Handelsman in his cartoon fable, *"The Story of the Envious Man and of him who was envied."* [102] The story begins with a picture of two neighbors, a happy dervish who always does good, and an envious one, steaming with resentment. As far as the latter is concerned, the good man can do nothing right. If he says, *"Good morning,"* his malevolent counterpart inevitably replies, *"Don't 'good morning' me, you sanctimonious swine! How come my roof leaks and yours doesn't?"*

Eventually the good man moves away, having had his fill of neighborly hostility. Naturally everything he does works out well. News of this reaches the envious man, who feels tortured by it, and decides to follow his former neighbor and throw him down a well. This happens, but he is saved by a benevolent spirit who also teaches him how to cure the misanthropic daughter of the sultan. Everyone is delighted and he gets to marry the girl. The fable concludes:

MORAL: One must be kind in order to be cruel.

Chapter 2

So Will I Turn Her Virtue Into Pitch

Envy is a state of exquisite tension, torment and ill-will provoked by an overwhelming sense of inferiority, impotence and worthlessness. It begins in the eye of the beholder, and is so painful to the mind, that the envious person will go to almost any length to diminish, if not destroy, whatever or whomever may have aroused it.

The Russian writer, Yuri Olesha, has provided a superb description of the spiteful, spoiling essence of envy in his short novel, *Envy*, written not long after the Russian revolution. (1) One of the central characters is Ivan Babichev, a self-hating lay-about and elder brother of an ambitious 'People's Commissar'. Ivan loathes the revolution, fears the new technology and longs for the old regime. For him life revolves around bitter obsessions, especially about his childhood when a girl upstaged him and love and attention seemed to pass him by. Consumed with self-pity, Ivan recalls a party at which he defamed and defiled '***a little beauty***' all dressed in pink and satin, who had the temerity to outsing, outdance, leap higher and play better than anyone else.

"She was the queen of the ball. She had it all her way. Everyone admired her, everything radiated from her and was drawn in around her.

I was thirteen, a high school student. I didn't have a chance, despite the fact that I was also used to admiration, to an enthusiastic following.

I caught the girl in the corridor and gave her a going over: tore her ribbons, mussed her curls, scratched her charming features. At that moment I loved that girl more than life itself, worshipped her, and hated her with all my strength. Mussing up her pretty curls, I thought I would dishonor her, dispel her pinkness, her glow; I thought I would show everyone they were wrong.

That is how I came to know envy. The terrible heartburn of envy. It is burdensome to envy! Envy catches you by the throat, squeezes your eyes from their sockets" (2)

Ivan loved that girl, not for herself, but because he wanted to be her. This couldn't be, so he ruined her ribbons and curls (beauty), disfigured her charming features (goodness) and dispelled her pinkness and glow (life). Here is an unusual man, not in the extent of his envy, but in the outspoken awareness of his ill-will. Ivan shares this quality with another outstanding personification of envy, Iago, the villain in Shakespeare's tragedy *Othello.* (3)

Othello is a successful General in the service of the Venetian state. Moreover his conquests embrace love as well as war, for he has just eloped with Desdemona, the beautiful daughter of a Venetian Senator. Iago is his ensign, recently passed over for promotion by another soldier who has become Othello's lieutenant. This is the ostensible reason for Iago's anger, but it is only a rationalization. Iago's villainy is part of his nature and, as the play develops, we see that his ruthless destructiveness is directed not only to Othello, but to Desdemona, and others as well.

Iago is a master of cunning and deceit. To Othello, to Desdemona, to his rivals he appears honest and helpful. But to himself and the audience his intentions are clear. After Othello has declared his joy and contentment, Iago asides that although the general may be *'well-tuned now'* , he will not find a right note, once his own plans take shape. [4] Later he adds: *"Knavery's plain face is never seen till used".* [5]

The ensuing knavery is far worse than physical abuse, or even murder. Iago attacks his victims from within. He is a psychic sadist who wreaks vengeance on Othello by destroying his peace of mind. Iago demonstrates a central feature of envious ill-will: the determination to undermine happiness and replace contentment and calm with agitation and anger, doubt and despair.

Othello confirms this mental torture. Previously he had been certain in his love for Desdemona, and trusted Iago. Now confusion reigns. One moment he thinks his wife is just and honest, the other not. One moment he sees a woman who is pure and white, the other one who is *"begrimed and black."* Poor Othello. He doesn't know where to turn or what to think. A once tranquil mind falls prey to an agony almost beyond endurance. [6]

But Othello's pain does not satisfy Iago, whose envy also touches Desdemona. Slowly, insidiously, he ruins her reputation, as he puts it, by purveying pestilence and poisoning Othello's love.

"I'll pour this pestilence into his ear–
That she repeals him for her body's lust
And by how much she strives to do him good,
She shall undo her credit with the Moor.
So will I turn her virtue into pitch,
And out of her goodness make the net
That shall ensnare them all." [7]

Envy corrupts and corrodes 'charming features' and love. It turns good into bad and makes life the rationale for death. To accomplish this Iago employs a lethal mixture of slander and duplicity, a process of bad-mouthing and back-stabbing made all the more effective because he is able to convince Othello to look to him for advice and support, while turning him into a fool, *"an ass"*, who must kiss the ass of the very person who attacks his peace of mind and drives him mad. [8]

According to a compelling, but incomplete legend, the eighteenth century Viennese court composer, Antonio Salieri, used similar tactics to humiliate, impoverish and ultimately murder Wolfgang Amadeus Mozart, who lived and worked in Vienna at the same time. This relationship has been dramatized by Peter Shaffer in his play *Amadeus.* [9]

Shaffer's Salieri is a cultured and immensely ambitious man who achieves considerable renown during his lifetime. [10] But in comparison to Mozart he is a musical mediocrity. And Salieri knows this. Overtly he tries to help Mozart and appears concerned about his career. But secretly, Salieri plots to grind Mozart into the ground–to deter his students, to prevent his advancement and to hinder the performance of his compositions. [11]

Fate intervenes to help Salieri in his machinations. [12] Mozart embarks on a new opera, *The Marriage of Figaro*. It is based on 'real people' and 'real places', instead of myths and folktales, as is the custom. The nobility becomes alarmed and raises a storm of objections, just as the court musicians who vehemently oppose Mozart's use of the vernacular. [13] At Salieri's suggestion Count Rosenberg, the Director of the Imperial Opera, takes exception to a dance sequence and tries to have it deleted. Himself alarmed, Mozart begs Salieri to use his influence to invite the Emperor to a rehearsal so he can present his case. Salieri agrees, while intending to do no such thing. But entirely against the usual practice, the Emperor does attend and takes Mozart's side. The dance remains. Believing that Salieri is responsible for his 'good luck', Mozart is grateful and decides Salieri is truely a friend. This allows Salieri to continue his dirty work and remain unsuspected. [14]

Although ill and overwhelmed by debt, Mozart continues to compose. In the meanwhile, Salieri prospers and is regarded by the public as infinitely the superior composer, a success spoiled by his continuing obsession with Mozart's genius.

"I confess that I poisoned Mozart's reputation with the Emperor by constant slander."

"I confess that I pushed him deeper into poverty by the simplest means." (15)

Not satisfied, Salieri turns to arsenic, to destroy Mozart in body as well as in mind. Again and again he comes to Mozart in disguise, and in secret, leaving bottles of poisoned wine. Finally, he appears, a dark messenger of death, and demands that Mozart rush a new commission, a Requiem Mass. But his victim protests. He can't do it. He is sick, has just shit himself, is covered in muck. And a bitter taste in his mouth makes him think he's been poisoned. So he demands a reprieve.

Suddenly Salieri casts off his mask and reveals himself. Mozart is incredulous. How could it be? Was it a joke? Was Salieri really behind everything that happened to him? *"Why.....Why?"* Yet to understood, Mozart would have had to know about a pact that Salieri had made with God at an early age, when he proposed to honor God with music in exchange for fame and fortune, and more important, inspiration.

The pact seemed to bear fruit. To all Vienna, indeed to all of Europe, Salieri was a prolific and respected composer, a musical giant. But, as befits the envious man, he did not measure his worth by intrinsic accomplishments. He only considered his work in comparison to another, to Mozart. By that token he and his music were nothing. (16)

Salieri sought a terrible revenge, like Ivan Babichev and like Iago. When aroused by envy, Ivan directed his ire against a pretty girl whose presence set his teeth on edge and made his lips tremble. In response he ripped her satins and bloodied her skin. He hated her beauty.

"I don't remember saying anything when I was beating her up, but I must have whispered: This is my revenge! Don't try to outdo me! Don't try to take what's mine by right." (17)

Iago directed his fury against a Venetian soldier. He hated his power. Iago's vengeance was more subtle, if not more cruel. He drove Othello to a jealous frenzy whereby he blew fond love, and his beloved, to hell.

"Arise, black vengeance, from the hollow hell!
Yield up, O love, thy crown and hearted throne
To tyrannous hate!
O, Blood, Blood, blood!" (18)

Salieri directed his rage against God, and that embodiment of the divine spark, the creativity of Mozart. He could not accept *'a giggling child'* whose casual notes were finer than his finest efforts. He refused the privilege of perceiving the incomparable, while remaining aware of relative mediocrity. Therefore, he denied his goodness, all goodness, and became an agent of evil, God's rival, the Devil. He hated himself! (19)

" I'll not accept it from You - Do you hear? .... They say God is not mocked! .... Dio Ingiusto! - You are the Enemy! - Nemico Eterno!
What use, after all, is Man, if not to teach God His lessons?" (20)

Envious revenge is fueled by arrogance and pride. It is based on imaginary hurts rather than actual injury. Although Mozart could be uncouth and derogatory, his bearing did not touch Salieri so much as his being. This was the grave offense. Similarly, Iago and Ivan Babichev did not seek revenge for what had been done to them in fact. The girl was probably not even aware of Ivan's presence until he attacked her. And Othello treated Iago well, like a friend and confidant. Yet, Ivan and Iago begrudged them their vitality and prowess, if not their very existence.

Begrudging is characteristic of envious people who take pleasure in depriving others of what they have or could have, without deriving any sort of advantage from this. Such people go to great lengths to inflict harm or unhappiness. In the summer of 1981 the London *Times* reported the sad story of two Greek, spinster sisters, one aged 80, and the other aged 85, who locked their sister, aged 75, in a stable for eight years as a punishment for marrying late in life and *"making us look ridiculous".* [21] These ladies were no more ridiculous than Salieri, who, after all, composed music that was widely enjoyed. But in their own minds, they felt humiliated, no doubt, when they thought of their own wasted lives. They gained nothing from locking up their sister, except, perhaps some temporary relief from their own anguish.

Similarly, Iago well understood the begrudging nature of envy when he commented to Othello:

"Who steals my purse steals trash.....
But he that filches from me my good name
Robs me of that which not enriches him
And makes me poor indeed." [22]

This characteristic helps to distinguish envy from greed. Greed does not begrudge. The greedy person wants as much as he can get, and more, in order to overcome a frightening inner emptiness. He is not concerned with preventing others from having what they have, but with getting whatever is good and life-giving for himself. Security consists of a freedom from emptiness.

The envious person feels inferior, rather than empty. He can't stand to see others full of life and goodness, because he is preoccupied with his own limitations and defects. So he aims to debunk and debase what others have. Security consists of an equality of emptiness.

Envy is a graspingness for self. Greed is a graspingness for life. Both are never satisfied because the envious person can always imagine someone else has more, or is worth more than he, while the greedy person can never imagine that he can get, or will have, enough.

As a writer who had been turned down for a lucrative MacArthur Fellowship realised, *"The envy in my soul now had to make room for its first cousin, greed."* [23]

Such greed recognizes life. The greedy person admits that there is goodness in the world. I mean that he can acknowledge and value care, tenderness, nourishment, beauty and love. That is why greed is not as shameful as envy, which denies all these things. For the envious person, love is delusion, life is death, and God is the Devil.

Greed hoards, envy abhors. The greedy person wants to get more and more, and keep more and more, and will go to any lengths to do this. Greedy destructiveness is unintended, but inevitable because of the ruthless, intemperate, gnashing, voracious manner of taking things in, and keeping them. Since damaged goods do not relieve hunger, the greedy person may feel compelled to seek out and acquire more of what he has damaged – a vicious, circular, self-defeating process.

Envious destructiveness is deliberate. The envious person denies good-will or love towards the object of his ire. What he wants is to remove the bilious anger and bitter vindictiveness from within himself, to get rid of it and put it elsewhere. Since he blames what he envies for how he feels, he sets out to make it feel bad or appear bad. Any relief is temporary because the source of his torment is not in what he envies, but in himself.

This wish to force gratuitous hurt into others is an important part of an envious, begrudging attack, typified by the case of a disgruntled Nigerian security guard who killed a visiting American banker out for a stroll in London. When caught, the man told police that he had long felt lonely and degraded, an outcast from society. One night while was walking in a well-to-do area he came across a large man who looked *'rich and comfortable'* , someone who went to plenty of *'posh places'*. All of a sudden he felt terribly cheated:

> *"I had to let off steam. I had to cut someone......I stabbed him in the stomach with all the force and hatred that had been building up inside me."* [24]

Crimes of theft and arson also illustrate the differences between greed and envy. The street thief and housebreaker want to empty you of what you have and get away as quickly as possible. They don't set out to do damage, which, nevertheless may happen, by accident, or out of frustration when they don't get what they expect. On the other hand, the arsonist who burns down a house does not wish to possess it, or its contents. He wants to evacuate his own burning displeasure by discomforting the owner, or by destroying the unique qualities of the house itself. (25) Thus, a man who had set fire to eight cars in Bridgeport, Connecticut, explained:

> *"I couldn't afford to own an automobile .... and I didn't want anyone else to have one."* (26)

On the larger social scene envy and greed seem to be predominant considerations affecting the style, if not policies, of many political figures. The envy-oriented politician tends to play on people's prejudices against the rich and privileged. He argues for a lower, but more equal national per capita income, and is against great disparities of wealth for whatever the reason. (27)

The greed-oriented politician stresses rapid and unrestricted economic growth and development, no matter who or what gets hurt or ruined in the process. He favors high profit policies, often associated with free-enterprise and capitalism. Not all capitalists are greedy, but 'capitalist' has become synonymous with greed. Terms like 'capitalist pig' or 'imperialist running dog' convey the contempt and derision of the envious, just like 'radical left' or 'trotskyite' are damnations which express the fear of people who want to hang on to their possessions. (28)

* * * * *

Envy and agreed rarely operate separately. My colleague, Dr. Nina Coltart, has suggested the term 'grenvy' to denote the fusion of these two emotional forces and the simultaneous expression of them. In 1730 Dr. Patrick Delany, a friend of the satirist, Jonathan Swift, wrote a telling verse which essentially describes the way Harpyes and slugs embody grenvy:

"At highest worth dull malice reaches
As slugs pollute the fairest peaches:
Envy defames, as Harpyes vile
Devour the fruit they first defile."

Devouring and defiling characterize grenvy, and distinguish the grenvious act from solely a greedy or envious one. The grenvious impulse is more common than pure greed or envy. At least it acknowledges goodness before trying to ruin it. Envy, itself, admits no desire, except to destroy.

The grenvious student, for example, combines stealing and spoiling. He yearns for the information and ideas his teachers possess, so much that he will go to almost any length to get them. Yet as soon as this happens he forgets what he has learned and debunks what he hasn't. Similarly, in therapy the grenvious patient is very demanding, for time, for interpretations, for help, while simultaneously mocking and distorting the therapist's thoughts. [29]

Newspaper reports of the antics of housebreakers who don't just steal, but leave places a wreck also refer to grenvy. A friend of mine owned a house in London which he was planning to sell. He had left if unoccupied, but locked up, after moving to another house. One Saturday he received a frantic call from a former neighbor who said that there was water pouring from the house onto the street. Hurrying to see what was the matter, my friend discovered that thieves had broken in and systematically ripped out the central heating pipes as well as taken anything else of value. But the intruders had not bothered to turn off the mains water so that it was cascading throughout the house. Worse than that they had left piles of their excrement all over the house, and had smeared it over walls and ceilings. During the course of their investigation the police told the owner that the damage was probably the work of a gang of teenage vandals. Professional thieves rarely disturb anything they don't take. But it is quite common for amateurs to break into a house and defile it. [30]

This crime demonstrates two forms of spoiling. Greedy spoiling occurs when the person or place robbed is emptied, injured or wrecked during the process of stealing. This spoiling is secondary to greed's ruthless, rapacious acquisitiveness. The plumbing damage indicated greedy spoiling, but the deliberate smearing of shit exemplified envious spoiling. By such extraneous damage, and by allowing water to flow all over the house, a pissing as well as shitting on things, the thieves expressed their contempt and hatred for the owner, and for the house too. It is this mixture of envy with greed which makes the grenvious impulse so damaging and difficult to alleviate. [31]

* * * * *

Envy can hide behind greed, as well as fuse with it. Many people accumulate things in order to numb an overweening sense of inferiority or worthlessness. In a materialistic society these 'things' might be clothes or cars. In another culture these 'things' might be titles, privileges or work-points. However, if the flow of 'things' slows or stops, then the same unhappy people tend to feel humiliated, unworthy and full of hate towards a world, which in their experience, has robbed and cheated them of their rights and privileges. [32] These grievances can quickly become an obsession, and their envious malice, previously held in check by the illusory fullness, may burst out against relatives, friends, neighbors, colleagues, "the system ' with annihilating accusations of selfishness, cruelty and greed! Giving more may be a palliative, or not, because once envy is aroused, people tend to rubbish whatever they get, while wanting more. Even good experiences tend to be trampled under the weight of ingratitude and discontent. Such envy surfaces in the child who 'bites the had that feeds him' and repays parental love with scorn, while demanding more.

* * * * *

Love scorned is a central theme of jealousy. The jealous person wants to love and be loved, but he or she fears the loss of a beloved to another. If this happens, or, even if there is a threat of it happening, jealous passions soon erupt. They aim to eliminate the unwelcome third party, the rival, so that the original relationship can continue. Alternatively, the jealous person may be the outsider, an excluded third party full of desire who comes between two others so that a new loving relationship can begin.

Here love is the primary issue, not hate. However, jealous anger and hatred can be quite as cruel, malicious and spiteful at that of envy. What differs is the focus - love lost; the direction of the anger - towards the rival; and the possibility of resolution - love regained and retained.

Jealousy is popularly associated with sexual jealousy, the subject of countless plays, films and books. Jilly Cooper, who writes on racy topics for the London *Sunday Times* has described her reaction when she thinks her husband is off with another woman:

> *"About once a year something triggers off a really bad attack of jealousy, and I turn from an insane irrational being into a raving maniac, all perspective blotted out. 'He's late home from work," I reason, He must be with another woman." Or he's early, "He must be feeling guilty about having a boozy lunch with her." And so on and on, lashing myself with misery. Once the octopus jealousy gets me in its stranglehold, it is almost impossible to wriggle free.* (33)

Ms Cooper highlights irrationality, infidelity, passion and possessiveness. These issues arise from relationships, any relationship where two people are having fun with each other, whether sex or a 'boozy lunch', to the exclusion of someone else. Jealousy is always group oriented. It involves a threesome.

In contrast, envy and greed are more primitive emotional states not concerned with relationships at all. They focus on things and qualities, aspects or attributes of a person without any reference to how this person things, feels, or what he needs in his own right. That is why envy and greed are bilaterally oriented, person to thing, person to quality in comparison to the triangular orientation of jealousy. (34)

The irrational component of jealousy stems from the tendency of the jealous person to exaggerate loss, when it has occurred, or to imagine loss, when it hasn't, as with Ms Cooper's husband. However, in the latter circumstance, there is usually some kernel of truth, a missed meeting, a delayed dinner which jealous fears can play on. Envy needs no basis in fact. Therefore, while conflict over love gives rise to jealousy, envy, itself, gives rise to conflicts which destroy love, including jealous conflict!

Jealous possessiveness signals the wish to hold on to one's partner and never let him go. It is a further response to the threat of loss and can also serve as a warning or punishment. There is a very aggressive, as well as adoring, quality to it, as with wives who won't let their husbands out of their sight. Such aggressiveness may explain why some people are ashamed of their possessive wishes, then deny them and attribute them to their loved one.

The wife who doesn't want her husband to spend a minute away from her may become a woman who constantly complains that her husband won't let her out of the flat, or won't let her do anything on her own. Ms Cooper is not like that, but she does attribute possessiveness to her own jealously. She then experiences the jealousy as an octopus threatening to strangle her with its emotional ramifications, as opposed to her own wish to tie her husband so he can't have an affair. This possessiveness is quite different from greedy possessiveness which treats people as if they were possessions. Ms Cooper did not say that she had a collection of husbands or lovers. Some woman do. This greedy accumulation of partners can also be a defense against anticipated infidelities.

Infidelity is the major issue for the jealous person who suspects that his loved one is having a close relationship with another. Suspicions of unfaithfulness indicate great insecurity, not only about relationships, but about the individual's own attractiveness, or lovability, as well as capacity for loving. [35] This can lead to obsessive feelings of unworthiness and inferiority, and murderous attacks on anyone who arouses them – the alleged third party for interfering, and the loved person, too. The direct attack on one's partner is an expression of the vindictive rage stimulated by jealousy – revenge for lost love and hurt pride. Jealous revenge is the operational link between jealousy and envy because the jilted man or woman is hitting back for disloyalty and for being cast in an excluded and inferior position. The malicious aggression that is a feature of such retribution is a form of envious spoiling of the former partner's happiness and superior charms.

The case of a man who disfigured his former girlfriend for life provides a typical example of jealous revenge, where love lost turns to hate. The man, a divorcee, had lived with the teenager for six months. Then she left him and returned to her family. After making defamatory calls to her family and employer, and trying to poison her dogs, the man threw a container of sulfuric acid at her face. In so doing, he essentially transferred his own burning jealous feelings to his former mistress and tried to ruin her chances for love with anyone else. [36]

Such retribution does not necessarily mean that jealousy and envy are identical. On the contrary, jealousy has a separate and distinct meaning and emotional flavoring. Unlike envy, or greed, jealousy is not present at birth, but only emerges after the infant is able to recognize his parents in their own right.

The distinction between the two terms can be traced back over two millennia. The ancient Greeks, who were keenly aware of envy, employed two terms, *phthonos* for envy, and *zelos* for jealousy. [37] Demosthenes, the greatest of the Athenian orators, claimed that *phthonos,* envy, was the sign of a wicked nature in every way and that the man who experienced envy was beyond pardon. [38] *Zelos,* jealousy, was considered much less bad, and even connoted admiration. [39] These moral associations might be expected as jealousy commands both love and hate, but envy is only concerned with hate.

In many countries the difference between envy and jealousy has been recognized in law. Crimes committed 'with malice aforethought' are punished in full, but 'crimes of passion' are treated more leniently. Obviously loss of love and infidelity are extenuating circumstances! [40] Still there remains considerable confusion about the two words. For example, Webster's New World Dictionary, erroneously defines 'jealous' as "resentfully envious". [41]

Jilly Cooper adds that people are invariably jealous of close friends or acquaintances. She herself would not mind if one of them won a Nobel Prize for chemistry, or a gold medal for discuss throwing. But should a chum marry a millionaire or win the pools she would be very irritated. The worst is when people threaten her own interests:

> *"...if one of them dyed her hair blonde and started pushing sex in a posh Sunday, I should be tempted to pop the odd bullet through her ... alas when one is in the grip of a grand passion all moral considerations go by the board. Beware my dears of jealousy. It is the green-eyed monster comes roaring out of the bedroom with a shotgun before you have time to leap out of bed and into the wardrobe."* [42]

Although Ms. Cooper has correctly used jealousy to describe a furious response to her husband's alleged affairs, she incorrectly uses the word to convey outrage at her friends' good fortune, knowledge or sexy characteristics. This outrage is envy. Qualities, characteristics, possessions (like a large bust, big lips, blonde hair) attract envy. Jealousy would imply a state of active conflict and competition with a friend who was deploying her sexiness to entice Cooper's husband. Maybe this happened. She did not say so in the article. [43]

Whatever the usage, Jilly Cooper gives a firm warning about jealousy. It is a 'green-eyed monster' liable to shoot first and ask questions after. Her allusion is to the warning that Iago gave to Othello about his dangerous state of mind:

"O, beware, my lord of jealousy!
It is the green-eyed monster, which doth mock
The meat it feeds on." [44]

The warning is double edged. It refers to Othello's jealousy, and to Iago's envy which makes a mockery of Othello, by driving him berserk with doubt, despair and rage. For Iago, jealousy, in as much as there is any case for it, simply serves to camouflage overweening envy. This is not an uncommon function of jealousy, to act as a defense against envy. It is especially evident in people who suffer from pathological jealousy. Sigmund Freud called this 'projected jealousy' and 'delusional jealousy'. It is also known as 'morbid jealousy'. [45]

Morbid jealousy manifests itself in men and women who develop a firm belief that their partners, and various named or unnamed third parties, want to rob them of everything: want to taunt, tantalize, outrage, strip them of self-respect and self-confidence, spoil their love and leave them feeling full of doubt and despair. Upon closer examination these thoughts are held by people with limited self-esteem and deeply ingrained feelings of inferiority. The accusations tend to be projections of what they want to do to others. [46]

Did Othello suffer from morbid jealousy? Did he succumb to Iago's intrigues because he secretly harbored great enmity towards the woman he married? Shakespeare provides considerable evidence towards this view. Othello is a Moor, a soldier of fortune, a hustler, while Desdemona is the daughter of a Venetian Senator, an aristocrat. And she is white, while he is black! I don't think these details are an accident. Shakespeare depicted the class and race conflicts of his time in order to mirror his society. Among the many reasons that we continue to be fascinated by his plays is because this mirror also depicts the endless, envious, guilt-laden preoccupations of the future. Iago is no more, but no less, than another side of the modern 'man' who cannot endure evil. Therefore 'he' blackens others and makes them suffer instead. [47]

* * * * *

Nowadays envy is just a prevalent as it was in Shakespeare's time, but people are less straightforward about it. The emotional meaning and motivation of the term tends to be clouded, if not actually reversed, by idiomatic usages and theoretical justifications. 'Chic' phrases deploy 'envy' in order to declare admiration interest, desire, strong feeling, frustration, resentment, indignation and identification (or the opposite) and have become part of common parlance:

"I envy you."

"You'll be envied for sitting in this seat."

"I so envy your new car."

"What an enviable position."

"I don't envy anyone with money these days."

"I don't envy him trying to write." (48)

Admen advise that envy is not to be feared. On the contrary, it's a useful stimulant for *'the folks back home'* (49) And sociologists imply that envy, influenced by *'uninhibited reference group choice'* may have a salutary effect on social reform. (50)

In September 1977 the Vickers Company placed a large cartoon advertisement in *The Sunday Times*. On one side of the page the reader sees a modern, open plan office block filled with new furniture, new equipment and smiling, cheerful people. On the other side there is an older, brick building from which a multitude of clerks, secretaries, typists and bosses peer out of rows of small, narrow windows exclaiming, *Envy! Envy! Envy!* Some of these faces are overcome with despair, resentment or rage, while others evince interest, admiration and desire. The caption comments that the cartoonist wanted to convey the whole range of Vickers' products as well as the envy of those who have to make do without them. (51)

This cartoon captures the multiple meanings ascribed to envy and demonstrates how envy can be used to sell products, if not a way of life, by preying on people's latent inferiority. The central image is two adjacent buildings and two adjacent groups of office workers. Their 'social proximity' provides the context for the 'invidious comparisons' that follow. [52] The advert assumes that the workers are unhappy about their conditions of employment. It seeks to awaken them to the relative impoverishment of their labors and implies that they should feel deprived in relation to the get ahead employees next door (even though they may previously have been content). [53] The cartoonist seems to be aware of the theories of the sociologist, W.G. Runciman, for whom envy signifies 'relative deprivation'. Runciman believes that: "*...the poorest appear to be entitled to a greater magnitude of relative deprivation than the evidence shows them to feel.*" [54]

Feeling appropriately deprived, one man is green, sick to the stomach at the thought of what he is missing. Another is crying and a third is in such a state of near total despair. Nearby, however, his colleague can be seen gnashing his teeth in rage and resentment, while another glowers with indignation. Down a floor someone else is so frustrated at the sight of the new equipment, he can't bear to look. [55]

Resentment, indignation and frustration are often used synonymously with envy. But they are not identical phenomena, rather reactions to actual injustice or deprivation, in other words, to an actual conflict of interest. Envy is rooted in imaginary conflict, although actual events can conceal or incite it. Vickers' products may also dispel resentment or indignation, but the grievances of a truly envious person do not disappear even when the alleged source of frustration is removed. [56]

The ad does try to foster positive feelings. Vickers obviously hopes and expects that all their potential customers in old brick-fronted buildings will be charmed and delighted by what they see and anticipate using. It wants everyone to emulate the new working practices of the glass-walled, fully automated 'get ahead' company next door. Why call this envy? Admiration is an 'antidote' for envy, not the expression of it. The use of 'admiration' is another example of the contemporary fashion to change envy into its opposite, in order to to conceal as well as defuse the malevolence inherent in envy. [57]

As Søren Kierkegaard has pointed out, envy embraces unhappy self-assertion, while admiration equals happy self-surrender. [58]

Similarly, emulation is quite different from an envious competitiveness which is spiteful, self-seeking and begrudging. The wish to be like someone is based on admiration, not ill-will. I presume the Vickers Company wants its new customers to equal or surpass its old ones, not disparage, damage or grind them to the ground [59] Yet this cartoon does incite envy, not by the overt use of the word, but by the covert message: 'You are not good or, at least not as good as everyone else, unless you use our products' [60]

Why don't people who are aroused by this message, and by the barrage of equivalent messages on TV, radio, newspapers, magazines and billboards immediately go on a rampage? Well, sometimes they do, collectively as in a ghetto riot, or individually, in a seemingly unprovoked attack on a relative or friend. Years ago the government of Indonesia ended commercial television solely because the sight of unattainable goods unsettled the inhabitants of their outer islands. [61]

Usually however, envy lurks behind a facade of probable hurts or is fused with greed and jealousy, as we have seen. Most importantly, envy is continually opposed by gratitude, generosity and compassion – all fundamental virtues which convey our love of life. Even Salieri was not totally motivated by malice. He admired Mozart and wanted to compose music like him so he could repay "God" for making him a famous man. Envy only got the upper hand when, in his view, this ambition was thwarted. Then he abandoned social duties and charitable pursuits and devoted himself to ruining Mozart's life.

Salieri, Iago, Ivan Babichev, they all demonstrate the essential criteria of unrestrained envy. It is an intense, implacable, irrational, irreconcilable, spiteful passion solely concerned with spoiling, corrupting, defaming and begrudging. No wonder it seems to operate in secret. It has always been considered one of the most deadly sins amply conveyed by the iconography of a Satanic serpent and more recently, by a bumper sticker seen on a car in Mexico: *"Down with everyone going up!"* [62]

Chapter 3

Envy Loveth Not: The Influence and Confluence of Envy and Narcissism

Envy is an inborn, destructive motivating force, opposed to love and antagonistic to life. Writing in *The Metaphysics of Morals* in 1797 Immanuel Kant had no qualms about describing envy as *"the vice of human hate,"* a moral incongruity that delights in misfortune (Schadenfreude and ingratitude. He called envy a *"hate that is the complete opposite of human love"* and concluded:

> *"The impulse for envy is thus inherent in the nature of man, and only its manifestation makes of it an abominable vice, a passion not only distressing and tormenting to the subject, but intent on the destruction of the happiness of others, and one that is opposed to man's duty towards himself as towards other people."* (1)

Over a hundred years later Sigmund Freud also commented on a hatred which opposes love. This is a hatred which strikes out against *"any source of unpleasurable feeling"* including: the absence of something needed; the presence of noxious sensations; and over-excitement - an intolerable inner tension associated with the very things a person wants. Mere relief from this distress does not necessarily diminish the displeasure. On the contrary, it can remain as a passionate hostility towards any stimulation, even rooted in desire, which has become too painful to bear. Freud said this was a hatred *"older than love."* [2] His description fits a rudimentary envy which averts love and transforms intense interest and excited desire (fascination) into malevolence.

Many physical and psychic activities arouse desire and displeasure from birth. Newborn babies ingest, inhale, take in all that they need and want. Similarly they evacuate, expel, put out whatever they don't need and dislike. The psychic equivalent of taking in is introjection, and of putting out is projection. Both the physical and psychic processes are means by which they interact with the 'world' - everything going on in and around themselves. [3]

Infants tend to use these mechanisms in a straightforward way to enhance pleasure and diminish pain. But they may not. Instead they have an inherent tendency to get angry at the very existence of pain in themselves and thrust it outside themselves with a vengeance in order to spoil and devastate a 'world' which (from their point of view) caused them to feel so bad in the first place. Vengeful evacuation and malicious projection provide an operational definition of envy.

* * * * *

At first Freud believed that angry attacks on the world were secondary to what he called *Eros,* or the *Life Instinct.* Later he concluded that destructive forces were equal in importance and power to life-enhancing ones, and that the *Life Instinct, Eros,* was opposed by a *Death Instinct, Thanatos.*[4] This view was strongly supported by his colleague, Melanie Klein. She wrote at length about the nature of envy and argued that envy is the earliest direct manifestation or 'externalization' of the 'death instinct'. [5]

The concept of a 'death instinct' is not easy to accept, not the least on ethical grounds. To many, 'death instinct' seems ominously close to 'original sin'. I think the duality, life – death, can best be understood as a struggle between forces aiming at growth, order, integration and structure – an upward energy flow, and forces leading to contraction, disorder, fragmentation and chaos – a downward spiral. [6] Conception is a psycho-biological impetus to structure which draws upon all the possibilities of the genetic code and the energies which flow from the mother's body to combat a return to randomness – physical and psychic entropy. *Life instinct* implies the former, *Death instinct* the latter. In fact 'impulse' is a much better term than 'instinct' for it denotes an impelling force rather than an unalterable one. [7]

What Freud termed 'pleasure' has to do with integration and structure. The attendant feeling is love. 'Displeasure' has to do with fragmentation and chaos. The attendant feeling is hatred. The primitive human being (fetus, neonate, infant) radiates displeasure in order to get rid of whatever opposes structure, that is, the creation of himself. This happens as a matter of course, such as when the infant evacuates urine, feces or wind. It can also happen wilfully when, during the course of development, the new being feels displeasure - gets upset and angry; and attacks - actively extends disorder at whatever has or seems to have hurt or threatened him. This rage is as likely to be directed at his own dissociated chaos and confusion – remnants of himself, in himself, as his environment – the womb, mother, father or others. [8] The passive projection of chaos and confusion is not envy, but the active, wilful, vengeful evacuation of 'displeasure' certainly is.

* * * * *

There exists considerable controversy among psychoanalysts about whether envy is a primary aggressive impulse, or not. Some believe that envy is a later derivative of character traits, interests and attitudes *"which only achieved their final, quasi-permanent, status towards the end of psycho-sexual development"*. [9] Others see it as a *"secondary motivating force which may have positive and adaptive consequences in on-going development, or may lead to malignant pathology".* [10] Both viewpoints treat envy purely as a reactive event. They also give it a libidinal component which envy intrinsically does not have, but which it often appears to have, because it occurs simultaneously with love, or fused with it, as in grenvy. Yet, as early as 1915, Freud commented:

> *"So we see that love and hate, which present themselves to us as complete opposites in their content, do not after all stand in any simple relation to each other. They did not arise from the cleavage of any originally common entity, but sprang from different sources, and had each its own development before the influence of the pleasure - unpleasure relation made them into opposites."* [11]

Regardless of this statement and Freud's later writings on the 'death instinct', the early analysts were very reluctant to grant a central place to aggression, or envy, in analytic theory. One reason was that libidinal energies were assumed to originate in somatic sources (the erotogenic zones: mouth, anus and genitals), while destructive ones did not. [12] In other words, *Eros* seemed to have a physiological and psychological basis, while *Thanatos* only had a psychological one. However, this distinction does not hold, if, instead of focussing on body parts, one thinks of body processes. Then libido has to do with taking in and building up (eating, drinking & introjection). Aggression has to do with putting out and breaking down (urinating, defecating & projection). Clearly libidinal and aggressive impulses are rooted in the soma and psyche. [13] Using projective processes for chaotic purposes, envy is a partial expression of the delicate interplay between life-sustaining and life-ruining tendencies. The latter is obvious physically when the envier, not necessarily a child, spews forth piss and shit, spit and farts, to soil and spoil the envied object. The psychological equivalent can be found in separate, or concomitant, penetrating, 'poisoned rays, 'venomous looks', 'angry atoms', 'malign spirits', 'malicious defluxions and streams', 'irradiations and ejaculations' – *the evil eye.*

Still, many theorists believe that envy is too sophisticated a state of mind and pattern of behaviour to exist at birth, and that the cognitive skills and sensitivity to relationships that I have described (such as in malicious comparison) only develop in the second or third year of life. From this point of view envy would have to be a 'later derivative' because the infant does not have sufficient 'ego strength' to be envious. However, studies of neonates demonstrates that this is not the case. They are enormously sensitive not just to physical stimuli, but to human relationships, and can respond according to what they see and feel. Obviously these capabilities expand as the infant grows older, but sufficient evidence does exist to confirm a potentiality for envious attack from birth. (14)

* * * * *

While malicious aggression is the active component of envy, not all aggression is malicious. Forceful, attacking behaviour may be constructively self-assertive and self-protective or destructively hostile to oneself or others. Whether aggression is constructive or destructive depends on context, motivation and feeling. It also depends on the creature who is being aggressive. All animals act in ways which are clearly self-assertive or defensive. They want food, sex and security.

Some zoologists and ethologists have considered territoriality or rank fighting (farmyard pecking order) to be examples of quasi-envious behaviour. (15) There is not a lot of evidence that these activities fit the essential criteria of envy: despair at others' advantages; spiteful rage; and destructive attacks without procuring any advantage or material gain. Jealousy, however, is no stranger to the animal kingdom. When two male hippopotami fight over a female, the battle is not a ritual. Each is trying to destroy the other as viciously as possible, a phenomenon readily seen with other species. And jealousy aside, field workers have noted that animals as different as orangutangs and elephant seals commonly engage in gratuitous violence, often committing gang rapes and killing the females without reason. [16]

Still, envious anger is different from that aroused by frustration, revenge, rivalry or indignation. The latter presuppose actual hurt, deprivation or injury and are assuaged when the cause of the hostility is overcome or removed. Envy lingers on even after a frustration has been overcome, a specific hurt repaid, a rival removed or an injustice made right. Envy may be associated with real events, but it is more than a reaction to them. Envy is both the tension and the hostile reaction to this tension in the envier, a tension which is not dependent on, or necessarily related to anything actually happening. Quite the contrary, the preverbal state of unpleasure is highly sensitive to mental activity, especially perception, and the power of the imagination. Aeschylus conveyed the envious state of mind through the voice of Agamemnon after he returned from Troy:

"*......For not many men, the proverb saith,*
Can love a friend who fortune prospereth
Unenvying; and about the envious brain
Cold poison clings and doubles all the pain
Life brings him. His own woundings he must nurse,
And feels another's gladness like a curse." [17]

Envious tension is aroused by the awareness of vitality and prosperity, indeed, by life itself. Although there is no specific word in English to denote such tension, the Czech word *litost* comes close. According to the writer Milan Kundera, *litost* denotes a gnawing sense of inner torment when faced by another's greater skills or accomplishments followed by the desire for revenge. [18] Kundera describes a young man out for a swim with his girlfriend. He is a beginner, she is an expert. Realizing his potential discomfort, she tries to keep to his pace, but at the end gives her sporting instincts free rein and sprints ahead. He tries to keep up but can't. Quick as a flash:

"He felt humiliated, exposed for the weakling he was; he felt resentment, the special sorrow which can only be called litost." [19]

Like envy, *litost* is too painful to bear and too shameful to reveal. In this instance the swimmer slapped his girl friend, but couldn't admit his true motivation. Passionate hypocrisy (he claimed he was worried that she might drown) protected a sudden insight into his own miserable self and the accompanying murderous response. As Kundera remarks, "Since revenge can never reveal its true motivation, it must plead false ones." [20]

In most situations the envier aims to eliminate the torment in himself by forceful, attacking, annihilative behaviour. This discharge, directed against the alleged source of the envy constitutes a means of self-protection as well as other-destruction. Therefore envy can be seen as a mechanism of defense at the service of the death impulse. It is opposed, mitigated, but never entirely vanquished by the opposite impulse associated with love. This view is consistent with Freud's theories of the life and death impulses, and the pleasure principle. [21] Life energies, or libido, promote pleasure when a person achieves growth, integration and structure. Pain is the result of the inability to achieve life needs (that is, reduce libidinal pressures). It also results from breakdown, chaos and disorder. [22]

The energies of the death impulse, akin to envious tension, continually resist libidinal (life) fulfilment. This is the action of entropy on the organism whereby pleasure consists of a return to randomness. Conversely pain lies in structure, order and growth, as the philosopher, Bertrand Russell noted, "... the envious person ... Instead of deriving pleasure from what he has, derives pain from what others have." [23] These two sets of tensions and tendencies are inborn. They can never be resolved, but both contribute to the richness, variety and complexity of existence.

* * * * *

Although I have said that envy is an inborn force, and have been critical of those who view it as a purely reactive phenomenon, it is more accurate to conclude that envy is both inherent and reactive. The tendency towards damaging, destructive wishes and behaviour is rooted in the very physical and mental make-up of a person. But what eventually transpires is a reaction to the internal tension aroused by actual or imagined events. How strong the tension will be, and how severe the response, depends on the particular envier. It also depends on the relative gradient of vitality, structure and plain good fortune between what the envier receives and how he perceives or experiences things in himself. Envy is not just a curse, but a consequence of consciousness.

If this is so, then on would expect envy to be a universal phenomenon. As far as one can tell, it is. Helmut Schoeck has pointed out that almost all cultures have a word for envy, or the equivalent state of mind, although they may lack such basic concepts as hope, love and justice:

> *"...virtually all people, including the most primitive, have found it necessary to define the state of mind of a person who cannot bear someone else's being something, having a skill, possessing something or enjoying a reputation which he himself lacks, and who will therefore rejoice should the other lose his asset, although that loss will not mean his own gain."* [24]

On the other hand, not all societies are like ancient Greece or Renaissance Italy where envy was accepted as a fact of life. People usually play down the contribution that envy makes to their state of mind, or social relations. They learn to keep the active expression of envy disguised and discrete, a collective practice that helps to avoid shameful guilt and retaliation. Indeed, "envy, by its very nature, is obstinate in its opposition to investigation". [25]

George Foster believes that it is almost impossible for the inhabitants of competitive, contemporary Western societies like the United States to concede the fundamental importance of envy because of the comparative elements involved which, when acknowledged, constantly threaten the envier with a massive loss of self-esteem:

> *"But in recognizing envy in himself, a person is acknowledging inferiority with respect to another; he measures himself against someone else, and finds himself wanting. It is, I think, this implied admission of inferiority, rather than the admission of envy, that is so difficult for us to accept."* [26]

* * * * *

Perhaps the most dangerous aspect of envy is not envy itself, but the denial of it. Then the envious impulse cannot be modified by loving, reparative wishes. More likely, the envier will use powerful projective processes, that is, the very mechanism of envy, to dissociate himself from a major part of himself, his own destructiveness. In these circumstances an individual may not just project a malign spirit, badness, to attack an envied object, but in order to get rid of an anguished and shameful side of himself, the side which had initiated the attack in the first place.

The consequence of such denial is a loss of self experienced as an increasing inner impoverishment. This loss stimulates murderous rage because the more impoverished the envier feels, the more angry he gets with others (with whom he compares himself) and the more angry he gets with himself (for hating, and for feeling so empty). The whole world (inner or outer reality) becomes full of dissociated destructiveness and appears to be a bad and threatening place. Hence envy gives a paranoid flavour to existence. Instead of desiring life, the envier comes to fear it.

Furthermore, the excessive projection of envious rage leads to a disturbance in introjection. This too may become excessive, as the envier, desperately trying to compensate for his inner emptiness, savagely sucks, bites and swallows whatever catches his eye. This explains why greed, destructive introjection, is often the companion of envy, destructive projection. (27)

Conversely, denied or unmodified envy (whether exceptionally strong from birth or aroused by hostile nurturing) can incite a harmful blockage of introjective processes. The envious child (or adult) may literally stop taking things in - food, words, ideas, stimuli. This frequently happens because the affected person believes that whatever he takes in will injure him.

An envy induced negativity especially interferes with the capacity to receive and return love. This can have a disastrous effect on learning. Having stifled and denigrated goodness, that is, the awareness of lovable qualities in oneself or others, the individual may conclude that everything is 'shit'. In other words, ideas or knowledge (equal to envied food and feelings) as well as the relationships which provided them, are poisonous. (28) Many learning difficulties, whether in children or adults, follow when ridicule, rage and fear, represented by a blank, impenetrable negativity, replace admiration and emulation. Then the envier may spitefully relinquish skills already learned, a response which feeds on itself and enrages him even further. (29)

Psychotherapy can be such a unlearning relationship. The negative therapeutic reaction, or the inability of the patient to profit from his treatment, is invariably connected with powerful envious impulses. (30) In fact, these sticky bits of hostility have probably contributed to the emotional disorder in the first place. Melanie Klein emphasized that '*excessive envy*,' a hatred so strong that life-loving or egoic forces have not been able to counter it, is usually accompanied by equally excessive anxiety and guilt. (31) So not only learning may suffer. These feelings often prove the prelude to catatonic negativism, extreme withdrawal and psychotic breakdown. (32)

* * * * *

A paranoid orientation, a loss of self, learning difficulties, excessive greed – they all follow in the footsteps of a defensive manoeuvre, projection, designed to evacuate envious anguish and anger elsewhere. The target may be the outer world, animate or inanimate, or it may be various aspects of one's self. Here the affected person or thing serves as a dustbin for painful, unwanted thoughts, feelings or sensations. But the envier (the subject) allows the target (the envied object) to preserve its separate identity. Thus a son may bad mouth his father in every way possible, but still admit that 'that shitty old man' is still his father. And 'the old man' may still feel and behave like a father.

However human or non-human 'trash cans' rarely satisfy the spiteful man, who wants to do more than simply evacuate the contents of a hate filled mind. Simultaneously and vengefully the envier may seek to totally alter and rubbish the object, to destroy any goodness in it and to control it so it can't fight back. In the example I have just cited, the boy can confer such an apparent power on his own words and actions, that when he looks at his father, he will literally see a piece of shit. And the father may forget who he is and be 'a shit'.

Traditionally, the scapegoat, an animal or human figure invested with the badness of the community, involves similar intentions. In the last chapter I showed how Dr. Lester Summerfield became the scapegoat for the greed and envy of his fellow dentists. For them he was not only a greedy man, but the embodiment of greed itself. Interestingly, when the ancient Israelites did the same, they poured their sins into two goats, one to be killed and the other to be sent away, or ostracized. In this way they tacitly recognized and preserved the shadier aspects of their lives. [33] Likewise the Coventry Family Practitioner Committee destroyed Summerfield's reputation, but allowed him to leave. Their envy and greed remained intact, but far away, on the other side of the world.

Enviers use the psychological mechanism of projective identification to equate the scapegoat or 'trash can' with its hated contents and to deny the original integrity and identity of the object. This is an offensive manoeuvre by which a person manipulates words, thoughts, actions or moods to put himself, or a part of himself, into another (person, thing, mental representation) and to combine with it. Hence, projective identification is both a perceptual transformation and interpersonal transaction.

From the standpoint of the subject (the envier), the envied person or thing no longer exists in its own right. The envier 'sees' and believes that the person or thing is identical with what he has put into it, or attributed to it (shit, urine, vomit, 'angry particles', badness). From the standpoint of the object, the envied person may have an inexplicable sense of being or feeling different. Or, he may not notice any change in himself, but realize that the envier is seeing him and treating him in a peculiarly inappropriate manner. If the behaviour strikes a certain chord, then slowly, involuntarily, the envied 'victim' will begin to feel, think and act as the envier sees him.

Projective identification is a form of communication which involves getting inside another and making him feel what you feel. When done maliciously, the quarry feels invaded and taken over by thoughts and wishes which he would normally reject. The experience is like being under attack from powerful, hostile forces which intend to drive you mad and destroy your mind, a view not far from the truth.

An unconscious appreciation of projective identification contributes to a fundamental fear of the *jettatura* and others possessed of the evil eye. The telltale glance of such an eye penetrates and fills you with malice. That is the result of projection and is bad enough. However, what strikes a note of absolute terror, is the anticipation of being changed into something evil. As Bacon put it:

> *".....the ejaculation or, irradiation (of the evil eye) emitteth some malign and poisonous spirit, which takes hold of the spirit of another."* (34)

This process of taking hold of the spirit of another perfectly describes the action of projective identification, and explains why, to the person so affected, envy is a disease, a terrible infection that can grab and subvert the soul with envious projectiles. [35] John Aubrey, a collector of gossip and folklore who was born in the same year that Bacon died (1626) recorded a similar opinion in his *Miscellanies:*

> *"The glances of envy and malice do shoot subtilly: the eye of the malicious person does really infect and make sick the spirit of the other".* [36]

Aubrey described the destructive side of projective phenomena, but I want to emphasize that projection and projective identification are normal and necessary intrapsychic and interpersonal mechanisms. Everyone employs them, for many reason, including, for example, to form symbols and think symbolically, and to establish and maintain close personal ties. [37] Envy is what gives these processes a pathological, if not deadly significance, all the more so because they operate internally. [38] They directly affect the contents and structure of the mind and personality, or as Bacon observed, the spirit and the soul.

* * * * *

Up until now, I have mostly emphasized external, tangible foci of hatred – fathers, therapists, successful professionals, and so forth. I have also pointed out that envious attacks do not just take place to rubbish these objects, but to evacuate and make them contain the tensions and hatreds that seem to be destroying the envier from within himself. However, all the transactions that take place between two separate people or objects, can also occur within the envier himself, that is, within the boundaries of his own psychic world.

Projection and projective identification are activities which influence different parts of the self. These, of course, include phantasized or internal representations of actual relationships. Thus a person can indeed feel under attack because he is attacking the mental images of his own father or teacher or therapist in himself.

However, a rather more ominous reaction occurs when, beset by envy, the envier tries to preserve himself, from himself, by splitting up and projectively identifying his spite and malice with and into parts of his own mind. Consequently the envier contains a multitude of envious others all threatening to attack him from within. These exist as split off and extremely hostile representations of his own envious self, or of envious parents and parental substitutes.

Hanna Segal has pointed out that envious internal figures contribute to the construction of and are comparable to what Freud called, the *"over-severe superego"*. On analysis it turns out that this superego is really an *"envious superego"*, perhaps one of many envious bits created by internal projective processes. The ensuing (inner) attacks then center on:

> *".......not only the individual's (own) aggression (inner enviers) but also, and even predominantly, against the individual's progressive and creative capacities."* [39]

In order to avoid such a psychic catastrophe, whereby a host of inner enviers assault each other, the afflicted person may utilize projective processes to deflect these enmities outwards. The net effect is like picking out a pack of piranhas and throwing them into the air. Because of the action of projective identification, when these vicious little enviers land on something, and they always do, the envious person (fleeing from his own envious selves) inevitably converts elements of external reality (benign people, places or things) into malevolent entities ('witches', 'evil influences', 'bad omens'). But instead of solving the problem, this manoeuvre compounds it, for the individual then feels threatened by malignity emanating from within himself and from without. Thus the envier becomes the envied, and the hunter becomes the haunted.

I have just been describing the creation of internal and external enviers (by splitting and by the subsequent projection of the split up bits). Consequently, one envier is usually many enviers, a bizarre configuration of malice that originates in one place but subsequently extends throughout one's internal and external perceptual worlds.

In yet another desperate attempt at self-protection, the envier, now a very envied figure as well, may try to deny and dissociate himself from whatever seems enviable, and make others the envied object. This is a ruthless form of envy avoidance literally employed by people who shower undue praise on friends or bystanders in the secret hope that these others will be hated and they will be spared. No wonder that excessive or undeserved compliments are generally unwelcome. They often denote insidious efforts to transform an ordinary person or thing into a focus of hatred.

Finally, the envious/ envied person may idealize one part of himself in order to protect another. Just like his phantasy world can become full of wicked little enviers, it can also become full of hated images, ideas or qualities. These are the equivalent of a host of envied objects. It takes a lot of work to hide these things, which, as Hanna Segal pointed out, may be aspects one's own creative capacities, from one's own ill-will. This is especially true when the malice appears in the form of an *"over-severe superego"* or other angry, alien figures. The ensuing game of cat and mouse with oneself can only lead to further fragmentation, confusion and chaos. Hence the counterpart of multiple internal and external attackers (envious subjects) are multiple internal and external foci of attack (envied objects). They survive as inner nightmares, or, because of projective identification, outer terrors.

* * * * *

The Canadian psychoanalyst, W. Clifford Scott, has described several patients whose lives were crippled by envious conflict with and within themselves. One was a doctor who suffered debilitating self-criticism and somatic symptoms just when his career was beginning to flourish. It transpired that one part of himself felt weak and inadequate and was identified with a small resentful child. Inwardly, this child hated and was determined to sabotage the efforts of his capable side identified with an strong adult. In fact, the attacks on himself, by himself and in himself, were a replay of the envy he had felt, but rarely acknowledged, towards his father. [40]

Another person was a businessman who had been thinking about embarking on a new, ambitious venture. However, after a brief period of deliberation, he decided that the project was too big and dropped it. In his therapy sessions the man mentioned that his work had taken on a dream-like quality, and that he was envious of people who could carry off big projects. During this time Scott noticed that his patient had found it very hard to dream. Those he did have were short, unproductive and quickly forgotten. Scott interpreted that the proposed new venture was "*the stuff that dreams are made of.*" It had become the focus of the same passionate hostilities that were otherwise directed towards his dream world. This was a man whose waking self tended to paralyze and spoil both his dreams and explicit hopes and aspirations. [41]

It is also possible to be very envious and jealous within a dream. A singer whom I saw in therapy turned up one morning very despondent and full of self-hate. She had just woken up from a dream in which a young man, a pianist, had been talking to her about himself at a party. He came from a wealthy family, had been living in London for several years and was in therapy. This treatment had been and continued to be very helpful. My patient immediately related the person to a pianist she had met the night before. He, like her, was just starting his career, and already had had some success. He too went to a therapist and taught at a school not far from my consulting rooms. In telling me about him, she became aware of intense jealousy and envy, jealousy because she assumed that he was a patient of mine, and envy because he was doing well and was more able to afford psychotherapy. [42]

I related this experience to her dream, and pointed out that the self-hatred she had suffered upon awakening was equivalent to the rage she harboured towards the pianist in her waking and dream life. She feared he would replace her in my affection. But this women also identified with the dream figure who embodied her achievements and ambition. Like Scott's patient, her self-hatred represented malign anger by one part of herself, that felt small, weak and helpless towards another, that was strong, capable and becoming increasingly successful.

Although it is tempting to describe the singer, the businessman and the doctor as victims of their own passions, to do so would be a gross distortion and oversimplification of their relationship with themselves and others. All three were the subject and object of envy.

The doctor's dilemma clearly illustrates this situation. In phantasy he was the aggressor who attacked his own capabilities, and the aggressed, the victim of entrenched images of critical parents who could never be pleased. In actuality he was vaguely aware of a deep seated enmity towards his father and feared, with some reason, reciprocal resentments towards his own growing accomplishments. So from his point of view, and ours, he was both envier and envied, the subject and object, of relationships which crossed the boundaries between conscious and unconscious life.

The businessman and the singer demonstrated similar patterns, although with them it was less clear that they were actually envied. No doubt further associations would have revealed that the businessman faced real rivals and I know that my patient is extremely sensitive to others' hostility towards her voice.

Multiple divisions between envier and envied exist in and between all people. They occur because of the pervasive use of projective and introjective mechanisms of defense and attack in intrapsychic and interpersonal relations. These splits are normal and natural and mean that we are all the subject and object of our own malice, aside from anyone else's. Although they extend across personal and social boundaries, at any given moment one pattern may predominate.

Significantly, whichever predominates, the outcome may be similar. There exist many points of confluence between the experience of the envier and the envied, each of which links the two sides and demonstrates that the perception, feelings and action of the envied person are part of the structure of envy as a state of mind, as a feeling, as an impelling force.

Both the envious person and the envied feel aggrieved and resentful. Aggressively, if not obsessively, they wish to strike back, denigrate and destroy the real or alleged cause of their distress, but for different reasons.

The envier is extremely sensitive to gnawing, tormenting displeasure, envious tension in himself. He tries to prevent it from happening by annihilating whatever arouses it. The impetus is a feared inferiority associated with a sense of unjust deprivation. The envied person is equally sensitive to and tormented by envious displeasure, but he experiences it as coming from outside himself. He aims to protect himself from this displeasure, and anticipated anger, by attacking the attackers (evil eyes, witches, over-severe superegos) before they can get him. Aggressive counter measures are common alternatives to defensive withdrawal, appeasement or self-effacement. The impetus is a feared superiority associated with a sense of unjust criticism.

Certainly, the envious person looks upon his envied counterpart with loathing and dread, as does the envied victim to his envier, both within the psychic domain, and without. Paradoxically these *dreaded objects* can also exert an almost irresistible fascination for each other, a phenomenon which demonstrates the narcissistic character of the relationship between the envier and envied. They are often aspects of the same person.

* * * * *

Narcissism is a state of self-preoccupation. Originally applied to a consuming self-love, the concept has expanded and includes any exclusive interest in and with oneself, especially as experienced in and through others. A narcissistic relationship is based on the prevailing use of primitive projective mechanisms as, for example, in envy. Hence the envious person, in defending himself against envious tension, can easily lock himself into a narrow, self-centered existence. Many enviers prefer to focus on their own image of the envied object, no matter how painful, or distorted, then take the chance of discovering someone or something in its own right. After all, the object might be better than imagined, or worse, and leave them feeling foolish.

Envy and narcissism are variations of the same problem–excessive mental pain, consciously perceived as overweening inferiority and inadequacy. To begin the envious and the narcissistic person attack this problem differently, the envier by deflating others, the narcissist by inflating himself, but their thinking, feelings and actions run along convergent tracks. (43)

In considering narcissism, I refer to a perverted or pathological self-absorption and pride that interferes with or precludes relations with others, not a normal or healthy self-esteem which is the prelude to mutual respect and reciprocal exchange. (44) The narcissist has little or no self-esteem. On the contrary he maintains a grandiose over-estimation of his capacities and virtues which he has built as a barrier against the underlying belief that he is unworthy and unimportant.

Like the envier the narcissist looks upon others with an eye which puffs them up and squashes them flat as soon as he perceives qualities or features better than his own. But the extremes of idealization and denigration do not only serve malicious comparison. This person actively searches for an ideal version of himself in others in order to enhance his self-importance. As in envy his perceptions fuel projections, little bits of charm designed to capture attention, evoke adoration and promote identification of another man or woman with himself. (45) The 'poisoned arrows' are reserved for those who don't suit this purpose, or resist it. Then narcissistic interest turns into envious hatred.

For such an individual, even a hint that he, or his partner, is not totally admirable and desirable is a blow which wounds his pride and inflicts severe psychic pain. (46) Such blows may call forth even greater degrees of self-inflation, often in the form of arrogance and inordinate vanity.

Hanna Segal recounts a scientist who was threatened by a single critical comment. (47) One day he dreamed that he was walking in London with a dinosaur. The beast was very hungry. The man had to keep on feeding it, otherwise disaster would strike. It transpired that the dinosaur represented his vanity, and the disaster a suicidal depression. The vanity maintained a fragile egotism and protected him from gnawing self-doubts. It allowed him to feel intellectually superior by making everyone else appear (and sometimes feel) like useless mental midgets. This state was both a defense against and expression of the envious hatred that this man directed towards his colleagues. But there was a price to pay. The vanity had a huge appetite. If he didn't feed it, he soon saw that his colleagues were actually creative and that his own research was less than first rank. Yet, when he did feed it, the ensuing insolence aroused the hostility of the very people he valued and spoiled his work. [(48)]

An aggressive narcissism is identical to envious self-assertion. [(49)] As we can see from the dilemma posed by the scientist's vanity, it can be life-threatening for the subject as well as his object. This view is found time and time again in classical mythology: vanity and hubris, indeed, any unjustified assertion of self which breaks the natural order of things calls forth retribution. The tragedy of Agamemnon illustrates this dimension of divine revenge. *Phthonos Theon* did not just mean, *Envy of the Gods*, but the inevitable downfall which follows the arrogant overstepping of bounds, as happened to a King who believed that wounded pride (the abduction of his sister-in-law, Helen) allowed him to abandon his family, sacrifice his daughter (Iphigenia) and destroy a mighty civilization (Troy).

Throughout this century the sudden and unexpected death and humiliation of public figures who have flaunted their fame, wealth, beauty or power has carried the same impact as a Greek legend. [(50)] In America Lee Harvey Oswald, Sirhan Sirhan and Mark Chapman were drawn, like the Furies, to John Kennedy, Robert Kennedy and John Lennon, famous men who epitomized many of the fatal contradictions of their age. [(51)] They preached tolerance and strength, but remained aloof, haughty and in many respects, weak. They advocated humility, but lived ostentatiously and had a genius for publicity and self-aggrandizement. And as politicians and super stars they championed the masses and evoked wild enthusiasms. Yet, in comparison to them, and by the standards of the mass media, these men could hardly fail to leave deep wounds in the many citizens who consider themselves to be non-entities, and try to make up for their failings by insisting that popular figures are extensions of themselves. [52]

This sketch illustrates an important aspect of the complicated relationship between famous people and their public, that of narcissistic arousal, infatuation and betrayal. [53] On a macro-social scale such transactions reflect and are reflections of countless small family dramas in which superficially competent, but chronically cold, indifferent or spitefully assertive parents keep their offspring in constantly devalued positions vis a vis themselves. From the child's point of view, their parents, or parental equivalents (authority figures), are people who substitute style for substance, who demand love and respect, but remain unwilling or unable to cope with real needs or feelings. The recipients of such treatment regularly reciprocate in kind, but still remain frustrated and vengeful.

* * * * *

Narcissism begets envy. For this reason world destroying rage can follow deprivation or gratification. A deprived child, for example, not only suffers from a lack of food, love, or warmth, but also from attendant fantasies that the depriving person has deliberately withheld these things and kept them for himself. Otherwise, he ponders, why aren't they (the tension reducers) right there when he wants them? Good care alleviates the doubts and subsequent pain and anger. However, the bad feelings may be made much worse by narcissistic parents who 'see' their appetites in their children and treat them in ways that are excitingly frustrating. Inevitably the tantalized infant (or child, or adult) becomes suffused with desires that cannot be contained and which have to be denied in order to prevent a state of utter confusion and fragmentation.

The denial of desire, or libidinal needs and feelings, creates conditions akin to an upsurge of envious displeasure. In order to avoid this, the persistent, but hidden hungers tend to be evacuated into the parents, an act which reinforces perceptions of them as greedy, selfish and self-satisfying. These images combine appropriate fears and projected impulses. They lead to even more hatred because the afflicted person feels completely powerless to get what he needs, or to prevent others from robbing him of the little he has. [54]

On the other hand, gratification does not necessarily lead to satisfaction. Whatever his parents give him, the infant may conclude that he will never be as good as them, or have as much as them. It's always, *"You're ripe, I'm rotten."* Again, this point of view can be modified by satisfying experiences. But it can also be made more poignant and bitter by relationships with people who do not give generously and altruistically. On the contrary, if they give at all, it is to prove their superiority and omnipotence. This leaves the child feeling small, helpless, unworthy, insignificant and important, while his parents or (parental) institution bask in malign, ill-deserved pride.

Attacks on the self lead to very painful inner states which have been variously described as narcissistic 'wounds', 'injuries', or 'losses'. The quality of hurt is equivalent to envious tension and seeks discharge by omnipotent self-inflation and other-denigration. This situation predominates in families where the parents or children are severely self-preoccupied and encourages a continuing 'narcissistic vulnerability' whereby the developing child, and later adult, remains exquisitely sensitive to actual or imagined infringements of his self-esteem.

Cold, aloof, spiteful parents do not cause envy. The tendency to death and disorder precedes them. What they do is stimulate destructive impulses that might otherwise be neutralized by kindness and compassion. Therefore a relationship which should be a model for nascent psychic integration, actually interferes with it, and perpetuates a state of war between the forces of life and death. An aggressively narcissistic child with adequate parenting often reaches a similar impasse. [55] In either case the child may retreat into a cocoon of grandiosity and omnipotence. [56]

The omnipotence represents a false solution to a fundamental problem – how to preserve life and love from the forces of destruction, one's own, and others. In a child, or adult, who is consumed with narcissistic pain, omnipotence becomes identical with goodness. Any omnipotence will do, whether creative or destructive, libidinal or anti-libidinal. The person postulates that he is the source of all life and goodness. Everything beautiful and valuable is either part of him or controlled by him. Or, he is Satan, the source of all evil and death, the centre of the universe.

In these circumstances anything which challenges this preeminent view of reality, whether the discovery of 'otherness', or the theories of a Galileo, comes as an intolerable deflation. It confronts the affected party (individual or institution) with an awareness of its own limitations and conjures forth a murderous rage which competes in intensity and intention with malicious anger. (57) Although often called 'narcissistic rage', these destructive wishes are not an expression of narcissism. Rather, they are an expression of the failure of narcissism, the failure of a particular strategy to protect against inadequate self-esteem or excessive hate. Hence 'narcissistic rage' represents a reversion to a primitive envious state of mind following a *'flaw in narcissistically perceived reality'.* (58)

For Salieri, this flaw, essentially an affront to his omnipotence, was the realization that the 'divine spark' resided in Mozart, and that the opera world comprised more than his own talent, or conceit. With Ivan Babichev the shock came at as party when he took a back seat to a pretty twelve year old, 'Queen of the Ball'. Babichev became enraged when he saw that the girl existed in her own right, not as an extension of himself.

Othello suffered a similar fate because false pride perverted his judgment and allowed Iago to play on his perceptions. He loved Desdemona so long as she appeared pure, loyal, white and beautiful, which is how he needed to see himself. When Iago turned her 'virtue into pitch', she became as black to Othello as he was to himself. Self-hatred prevailed and he replied with self-righteous abandon towards a version of himself he couldn't condone.

* * * * *

Many folktales, plays and novels celebrate the moment when 'narcissistic reality' becomes untenable. None are more striking than the story of *Snow White.* [59] It is about a princess raised in the household of a vain, self-centered step-mother. This woman, the Queen, cannot bear anyone to be more beautiful. She owns a magic mirror and frequently asks it,

"Mirror, mirror on the wall,
Who is the fairest of us all?"

The mirror always asserts:

"My lady queen is the fairest of all." [60]

Meanwhile Snow White has been growing up and has become *'as lovely as the bright day and more beautiful even than the queen'.* One day the mirror gives a new answer to the oft repeated question:

" My lady queen is fair to see,
But Snow White is fairer far than she." [61]

The reply shatters a fragile preeminence. The Queen is horrified. We can only presume that all her fears about being an undesirable, second rate wife, mother and sovereign come to the fore.

"At this the queen took fright and turned yellow and green with envy. From now on, whenever she saw Snow White, her heart turned over inside her, she hated the girl so. And envy and pride took root like weeds in her heart and grew higher and higher, giving her no peace by day or night. So she sent for a huntsman and said: 'Take that child out into the forest, I'm sick of the sight of her. You are to kill her and bring me her lungs and liver as proof.'" [62]

The Brothers Grimm vividly narrated the relationship between narcissistic failure and envy. In this instance the awareness of another's beauty provokes a storm of malice. The Queen is no longer concerned with inflating herself. She aims to wreak revenge on a figure who has dared disturb, however unwittingly, her lofty reveries. She launches her attack on the actual person, any reflection of that person, and her perception of the reflection. In the Grimm's tale the Queen spares the magic mirror, representing reality. In other versions of the story she smashes the mirror as well.

* * * * *

Rage, fuelled by an envious narcissism, does not stop at destroying the object. It aims to eradicate any vestige of attachment in the subject, any remnant of love, need or longing, such as between a mother and child, or husband and wife. Any loss of pride or self-esteem may herald the onset of a major internal battle (aside from an external one) whereby the forces of disorder, fragmentation and chaos overwhelm those of order, integration and structure. Initially there may be a period of psychic contraction, a withdrawal from relationships and dedifferentiation of self (regression), but the conflict often leads to a near total cessation of feeling, thought and perception, and can culminate in suicide. The wish is to return to an inanimate, intrauterine existence so that all tension and excitation vanish.

Freud described this phenomenon under the rubric of *The Nirvana Principle.* [63] It signals the point at which envy and narcissism converge, when an adult or child, who has been stripped of his illusions, and is unable to hide from an intolerable reality, yields to the forces of destruction. Then an angry state of mind reverts to an envious state of being and pleasure in death (auto-annihilation) supersedes pleasure in life. In gestures which are both defiant and defensive, the distraught person demonstrates the links between ostensibly different, but complimentary strategies for warding off mental pain. Simultaneously he inflates himself by assuming a posture of omnipotent destructiveness (*"Envy destroys what God creates."*) and deflates others. (*"They must be no good, otherwise why did I turn out so bad !"*)

Ultimately the envier seeks to triumph over life (experienced as painful feelings of inadequacy, inferiority and impotency) and to proclaim the primacy of death. For all too many people this convergence of envy and narcissism may be their finest achievement and serve as the final stage in a long history of unhappy self-assertion.

PART 2:

THE PRIMARY TARGETS OF MALICE

Malicious Foci

Chapter 4

On Attacking the Breast

The breast is anything and everything that sustains the body, warms the heart and calms the mind. Far more than an anatomical entity, it is a veritable cornucopia of love, security, pleasure and relief of pain. For these very reasons *the breast* lies at the center of human desire and hatred, and is the most appropriate starting point for considering the myriad real and symbolic objects which attract envy, greed and jealousy.

The earliest awareness of the breast consists of a comforting contentment and sensations such as warmth, fullness and softness that occur in a infant after a feed. Collectively these feelings and sensations mean goodness. Therefore, one's first relationship to the breast, really an abundant breast, is a relationship to a group of 'good' experiences. (1) During the course of development, this rudimentary conception gradually acquires a more objective, independent reality. However, human nature assures that this transformation is never complete. All people long for and try to recreate the moments of sheer pleasure which suffused the early part of their lives. (2)

The positive, delightful experiences that begin at birth have three principle components. There are pleasurable, satisfying feelings which include *"all that is promising, flourishing and nourishing".* [3] Then there are calm, blissful states of the mind and body that occur after painful tensions like hunger, colic and anger have been alleviated. Finally there is a proper level of arousal. This is something that is constantly changing, but can't be too little, too late or too much. The infant needs both sleep and stimulation. If he is over tired, then what might otherwise catch his interest simply becomes irritating. And without an adequate flow of human contact and activity, apathy replaces repose.

The gratification of physical needs, the prompt relief of pain and appropriate stimulation comprise the *milk of human kindness* to which infants, and adults, respond passionately and lovingly. [4] But this life-giving milk, as well as the giver, are constantly opposed by an equally strong mixture of noxious sensations, painful absences and over-excitement. Collectively they mean *badness* and conjure forth a hatred which equals a rudimentary envy.

The noxious experiences vie for space with the pleasant ones. A late feed brings emptiness and screams. A tense mother brings rough handling and a cold touch. Basic bodily or psychic processes which the infant cannot assess or appreciate quickly become tormenting. From the infant's point of view there exists, side by side with the *good breast*, a bad one which takes away goodness and revels in pain.

The *bad breast* is a reality permeated with chaos and discontent. It can result from unrequited desire as well as direct deprivation. The tingling in the lips, the smells and sounds of mother are intensely exciting, and demand immediate gratification. Delay is unbearable and can easily transform a potential pleasure into an agonizing persecution. A fragile self cannot cope with the outpouring of stimulation and tends to repudiate what it would otherwise welcome. As Freud pointed out in, "Instincts and their Vicissitudes":

"The ego hates, abhors and pursues with intent to destroy all objects which are a source of unpleasurable feeling for it,

without taking into account whether they mean frustration of sexual satisfaction or of the satisfaction of self-preservative needs." [5]

For an infant or child, the term 'object' can signify an overwhelming experience, just as for an adult, it can be a provocative thought. Both may protect themselves in similar ways, by denying and denigrating life-wishes in order to diminish excitement. This reaction is equivalent to an envious attack and underscores the connection between envious tension and undischarged excitement. If the envy appears to have life-affirmative elements, it is because the envious attack is part of a wider drama. This begins with an eager anticipation for food, sex or other pleasures - *greedy fascination.* It ends in angry, spiteful rejection once the feelings aroused have become unbearable - *envious fascination.* Wild swings from love to hate, from a life-loving to a life-hating posture are especially common with children born to self-absorbed, 'narcissistic' parents. They generally offer a breast which is excitingly frustrating, available one moment and gone the next. Or, some mothers try to turn the tables and make the baby care for them. For example, a young actress who suffered from sleeplessness after the birth of her daughter, developed a remedy for her nocturnal distress. Whenever she went to bed, she would pick up the baby and give her a feed. Then she would fall asleep while the baby woke up and fussed.[6]

In this instance the baby became the breast to her mother. The result was a residue of resentment and confusion which lasted late into adult life. Other women allow their babies to enjoy the breast and be nourished by it. By breast I refer to the actual bosom, a part of the body, or the baby bottle, a material object, as well as all the care and consolation, all the good feelings, which the mother can muster. [7] Therefore, within a short time, the developing child will begin to perceive that there is a source of vitality, a source of goodness separate from himself, despite the fact that he remains dominated by his own desires and sensations. Even when the feeding experience has been essentially positive, the sense of separateness may come as a painful shock, but it also sets the stage for the child to establish its own love and allow tender passions to easily flow back into mother.

* * * * *

The awareness of feeding, whether good or bad, focuses at or around the mouth, because the mouth of the infant is the specific part which seeks out and latches onto the nipple or teat. The mouth makes the first tangible links with the breast as an external object. Other organs, the eyes, ears, nose and musculature cement the growing bonds by taking in and responding to mother's sounds, scents and touch. However, for months, probably years, the ***mouth-bosom/nipple*** or *mouth-bottle/teat* couplet remains at the centre of the total nurturing experience. [8]

The mouth embodies all the infant's cravings while the *breast/nipple* embodies all he or she is craving for – provisions and containment. The provisions are both obvious and elusive. They include the usual ingredients of the stuff of life, the milk, food, love and care that come from mother or a mothering person (father, nurse) plus an abundance of sensual delights that spring forth from the child. Each enhances the other and makes a very rich brew that imbues the breast with mythological expectations. It becomes like the horn that suckled Zeus, a cornucopia that provides whatever its owner wants, a well spring magically renewed by its own impulses. But this creates a conundrum. The impulses vary from good to bad and the child has a limited capacity to hold in and hold on to the experiences he treasures. Constantly assailed by anxieties about emptiness, he immediately tries to disgorge the bad feelings into the breast (the bosom representing his entire physical and psychic worlds) by screaming, flailing about, vomiting, urinating, and other means. So the breast has to do more than pour back indiscriminate feelings and wishes. It has to hold on and contain the pains and hatreds, rather like a mother actually holds and comforts a crying baby. Then it has to give back something different. These *super-provisions* are love in place of pain, calm instead of chaos and, in general, a strength that transcends hunger and exhaustion. They reflect an essential function of the breast, containment, and are also a product of this function. [9]

Interestingly, the popular nursery rhyme, "Rockaby Baby" can illustrate containment or non-containment. The lyrics themselves would indicate a tired mother, like a bending tree, with arms like branches which can easily break and let the baby drop. On the other hand, when song softly and tenderly, the words matter less than the caressing sounds which indicate that trees may break but mother will always be around to carry her baby's burdens.

All persons lust for the life-giving and life-restoring foods that the breast provides. Adults have a slight advantage in that they can remember a good meal easier than an infant, and, hopefully have had more good meals to remember. In other words an adult mind has more clear-out, developed impressions or mental representations of mothering, images which help to sustain him when hungry. [10] Despite such imagos or 'internal objects,' greedy desires continue to buffet both infants and adults which even the best mother-child relationship or the fondest memories cannot eliminate.

The greedy mouth sucks, tears, scoops out and drains dry everything of value located in or attributed to the breast, including the breast itself. The ensuing damage is not necessarily intentional, rather a consequence of the ferocity of the attack. Any deprivation, but especially emotional deprivation, may provoke a ravenous onslaught. The provoker is frequently a non-containing mother who is so preoccupied with herself that she cannot cope with the needs of her offspring. Inevitably her child tries to make up for what he or she experiences as a 'rock-hard mommy' by draining the last drop of milk, energy, feelings or interest from her parent and everyone or everything else about. This certainly happened with the daughter of the actress I just mentioned. During her childhood she was an insatiable eater, all in a hopeless attempt to get back some of the things her mother had taken, and continued to take out of her. [11]

Greedy voraciousness tends to be fuelled by an unconscious image or comparable idea of an ever flowing, ever present source of supply. I am describing the wish for a state of continuous, total satisfaction, *the idealized internal breast.* In ancient times large or multi-breasted women like *Diana of Ephesus* represented this wish. (12) Or, in middle eastern cultures, it can be seen in the shape of a building such as the *Mosque of El Jazzar*, with a courtyard surrounded by dozens of breast-like domes. (13) For modern men the same longings come packaged within the pages of magazines like *Playboy or Forum.* The latter commonly carries ads which announce:

> *HUGE BREASTS!*
>
> *Are you a lover of Colossal Boobs?*
>
> *We offer you the very best in Mags & Videos. Great Value. Excellent Service. Try Us!!* (14)

All these pictures correspond with deep desires to possess the breast. And as we can see from those who commissioned the original sculptures or buildings or *Playboy* centerfolds, no effort is too great, for failure is almost too painful to bear. Those who don't fulfil this wish may deny it, but they never give it up. Inevitably the yearning for the ideal breast will be relocated in other people or places or things: for example in children, thumbs or toys; or adults, an ideal mate or a fabulous holiday on a deserted beach. Yet, the sequence - wish, denial and projection is a recipe for frustration and dissatisfaction, since the outside object rarely equals the internal expectations. This leaves the hungry person feeling even more greedy and vengeful.

Problems which primarily arise from within oneself, rather than from without, also arouse and exaggerate the same response as inadequate or destructive mothering. Greed thrives on fear. The greedy person is terrified of a lack or loss of sustenance such as, in an infant, milk, or in an adult, money. These provisions signify love, security, happiness and, in general, the perpetuation of life. They oppose and are opposed by forces which threaten dissolution and death, especially envy. The greedy response is an attempt to redress the balance between life and death, goodness and badness. Many things affect this balance including developmental traumas and deficiencies. They are not necessarily connected with an environmental failure, but they can restrict the ability of a person to take in, hold in and utilize nourishment.

Congenital feeding handicaps include poor reflexes, breathing difficulties, metabolic disease, and a damaged sensory apparatus, while mental impediments may emerge as poor memory, wild mood swings and an insufficient zest for life. However, even without these liabilities, everyone has to face the ebb and flow of noxious stimuli, an apparent bad internal breast which spoils calm and interferes with the wish to feed. The noxious events include wind, colic and teething, excessive excitement and emotional torment, in particular, guilt and fear. These feelings follow angry, savage attacks on mother for not immediately dispelling pain and, in general, for not living up to impossible expectations.

* * * * *

People's worse fear is that the bitten breast will bite back. In this vein, we know that young children frequently dream of being bitten or chased and devoured. These anxieties tend to be wishes projected onto the breast and nipple and acted out. Thus one little girl was referred for treatment because she would never spontaneously eat. However in the games she played during her analysis, and at home, she never stopped biting. Among many things she pretended to be a crocodile, a lion, a pair of scissors and a mincing machine. No wonder she wouldn't eat. She feared the terrible consequences, both to her mother, and to herself. [15]

In his book, *The Fear of Being a Woman: A Theory of Maternal Destructiveness*, Joseph Rheingold refers to a study of the dreams of forty-three children who had intense fears of being bitten, chased and eaten. Rheingold notes that older children frequently identify the threatening person as their mother. He concludes that children reveal their well justified fears and hatred of mother through their dreams and phobias. [16]

Woody Allen, demonstrated the dilemma in *Everything You Always Wanted to Know About Sex but Were Afraid to Ask.* [17] In one vignette he was chased through a field by a gigantic breast. One false step meant he would be engulfed and eaten. A late 90's lawsuit illustrates a related dilemma. The plaintiff alleged that he had suffered whiplash injuries after being buffeted about the head by a performer's 60-inch breasts at a topless club. He said the woman *"forced her huge breasts into his face and then jumped up and slammed (them) on my head and knocked me out. It was like two cement blocks hit me. I've never been right since."* [18]

Whether bitten or biting, squeezed or squeezing, the breasts focus further pain, guilt and an anguished self-reproach. This happens when either a child or adult hurts, or wants to hurt the very thing he loves and treasures. Such hurts also feed fear, since the greedy/guilty person is frightened of losing everything he has attacked (aside from being attacked by whatever he has lost.) So, in order to deny his impulses and overcome guilt, he may transform the breast into a beast, a monstrous mental construct, an ferocious animal like an alligator or shark.

The shark embraces greed, envy and guild-ridden retaliation. A primeval creature, it possesses an all-powerful mouth which can gnash steel chains as well as human flesh. Such an image is the perfect repository for passions which lurk in the depths of the mind just waiting to strike. It is a killer replete with appetites which know no bounds and recognize no ties. All mothers harbour shark-child-cannibals whose interests extend from their mothers' insides - mouth, brain and belly, to their outsides - skin, hair and clothes.

The primacy of oral sadistic impulses were initially delineated by Melanie Klein. According to Klein, "*.....(the child) gets possession of the contents of his mother's breast by sucking and scooping it out. This* *desire to suck and scoop out, first directed to her breast, soon extends to the inside of her body".* [19] Thus, the attackable breast is not just a part of the body, but the whole body, an Aladdin's cave, waiting to be discovered, explored robbed and defiled.

Primitive notions like these are not restricted to 'primitives', although sophisticated peoples prefer to think they are. The British anthropologist, Ioan Lewis, relates that during his travels in the West African bush, he noticed that the natives would hide when he, or other whitemen, walked down the roads. He wondered why and managed to stop a villager before he disappeared. The man was very wary, but eventually said that he was frightened of white people because they were all cannibals. Surprised, Professor Lewis asked for an explanation. The villager asserted that everyone know that whites ate black babies. For proof he obtained a tin of cooked meat. There were two pictures of healthy, smiling black babies on the label, ostensibly to demonstrate nutritious goodness. But the natives saw it as a confirmation of their worse fears, that white people liked to eat black baby meat! They refused to believe otherwise. [20]

Cannibalism, rather cannibalistic desires, is a universal phenomenon. As the German psychoanalyst, Karl Abraham observed, it is an example of oral sadistic savagery totally devoid of concern:

> *"Complete and unrestricted cannibalism is only possible on the basis of unrestricted narcissism. On such a level all that the individual considers is his own desire for pleasure. He pays no attention whatever to the interests of his object, and destroys that object without the least hesitation."* [21]

The narcissism Abraham described does not simply mean selfishness. It encompasses all the hurt and rage which I discussed in the last chapter to do with the realization that goodness is contained in another, and that it doesn't totally belong to the infant, or adult, and never can. The wish to devour, indeed to eviscerate the breast and body, tends to incorporate the wish to spoil and destroy the contents so that no one else, including mother, can enjoy them. Hence, envy accompanies greed, because the impetus is usually hunger plus a narcissistic wound.

Greed, however, can serve in its own right to diminish envy. The idea that everyone owns or possesses more valuable things consumes and torments the envier. Endless acquisition is a way of relieving this tension. The grenvious person believes that if he owned or possessed everything (all possible pleasures, all manner of love, all people and things), then the envy would evaporate. Unfortunately, the emotional protection that greed provides flounders when the rate of accumulation diminishes. Then an intractable malice reappears in full fury and the *evil eye* yields to the *malicious mouth.*

The dread aroused by creatures like sharks or insects, snakes and old hags has to do with envious intent located, directed and activated from and by the mouth. The Assamese people of Northeast India literally believe in the malicious mouth. Their word for envy means "*mouth putting*" and consists of two terrible creatures, Khoba and Khobee, who spring forth out of the mouth to burn and obliterate anything admirable. [22] Khoba and Khobee are themselves associated with biting insects and vermin which attack and ruin life-giving crops. In the Western world comparable anxieties extend to flies, mosquitoes and gnats, little devils which swarm at picnics and not only pollute the food, but ruin the pleasure of the participants. Our Khoba-Khobees also include any reptiles which inject poison, like the viper, or carnivores which appear to mutilate gratuitously. Carping, gossiping, back-biting men and women are no less abhorrent.

In *The Canterbury Tales,* Geoffrey Chaucer, provided many examples of the mouth destructive criticism which characterizes the envious person, [23] Writing a couple of centuries later, the poet, Edmund Spenser, similarly depicted the viperous tongue in, *The Faerie Queene:*

"He hated all good werkes and vertuous deeds

....

And eke the verse of famous Poets witt

He does backebite, and spightful poison spues

From leprous mouth and all that ever writt." [24]

Shakespeare did likewise in his characterization of Iago, a herald of evil eyes and malicious mouths. Contemporary Iagos, the gossip columnist, the political intriguer and the scurrilous critic deploy slander no less effectively and achieve similar results. Savage, often mutual loathings, among the famous and well-to-do exert an irresistible fascination for the public. The writer, John Walsh, has provided a more up-to-date review of biting, bitchy remarks on the contemporary English artistic and literary scene. After ranging from Boswell about Gibbon (*"Gibbon is an ugly, affected, disgusting fellow, and poisons our literary club for me. I class him among infidel wasps and venomous insects."*) and Tchaikovsky about Brahms (*"What a giftless bastard!"*), he zeros in on trenchant tongue lashings. (i.e. poets Horowitz vs Raine – a man who condemns us "...to video-skipping rhymes for evermore.")[25]

* * * * *

Ultimately the ferocious mouth represents the guilty conscience biting and tearing away at the peace of mind of the grenvious person who has damaged his loved ones. In this respect children are particularly at risk because their reparative capacities fluctuate. It is no wonder they are prone to nightmares in which savage beasts attack them. Guilt, and defenses against guilt, are important elements in these bad dreams. The torment would not arise, however, unless there was concern for the breast. Melanie Klein observed that a rudimentary regard for the caring person occurs very early in the life of the infant, a fact confirmed by subsequent research in child development. [26] An unrestrained onslaught may indicate the intensity of the impulse as well as an absolute need to deny concern in order to mitigate unbearable anguish.

Denial is an elementary response to guilt. At first it centers around the damaged person or thing, but the denial soon involves the destructive impulses too, in order to shun responsibility for them. Essentially the individual says to himself: "I don't want to know!" Therefore, he tries to ensure that none of the anger, guilt, awareness of damage, in other words, any aspect of the situation, remains in himself by getting rid of, or projecting it on to others. They become the scapegoat for what he hates about himself.

When these projections focus on outer figures, the troubled adult or child may behave with self-righteous savagery towards 'the evil in others' – the basis of religious and political fanaticism. However, when the projections flow the other way, they may sliver the self, that is, one's inner world. A hypochondriacal state will ensue, if these dissociated fragments of envy, greed, and guilt become associated with parts of the body. [27] More frequently they coalesce into a prohibitive, punitive figure – the basis of an 'over severe superego'. This can take the form of a shark or parents with shark - like faces which slash and mutilate thoughts and actions.

For the guilty person, 'the enemy' is anything that engenders guilt. This includes his own desires or any object of these desires. A breast, a bottle, a toy, a caress, a feed, a good feeling, they can all become pretexts for annihilating attacks when they get blamed for arousing anguish. Unless a positive, reparative exchange takes place, a vicious spiral of greed + envy -> guilt -> denial + projection -> vengeful rage will unfold which greatly exaggerates the original damage. The entire sequence mimics envious malice. It can culminate in the extermination of love and goodness either as felt in any by the subject, or as perceived in and towards the object. This rigid, absolute defense against alleged crimes and dreaded punishments involves multiple denials and reversals of the initial desires.

Thus, *I want everything,* an expression of greed, easily becomes, *I want nothing,* the denial of greed and avoidance of guilt.

Then, *I want nothing* reverses to *I want you to have nothing* or *I will destroy what you have,* a preemptive strike expressing envy.

Finally, *you have nothing* converts to *you are nothing* or *I will destroy you,* a verbal attack that encompasses anything that might rekindle remorse and reactivate guilt-ridden retaliation.

* * * * *

A patient of mine demonstrated all aspects of the greed-envy-guilt cycle, which reoccurred again and again in our work together. She was an intelligent woman who came to therapy desperate for insight. During the initial sessions she liked to ply me with dreams and images, while an ironic smile seemed to imbibe my interpretations. All this allowed her to leave relatively relaxed, although I would feel drained. Yet, in spite of the good beginnings, her mood turned ominous, for she inevitably declaimed that I had nothing to give and rued the fact that she had decided to see me.

Subsequently the resentment and defiance spiralled. She used to shriek to my face that I was a useless human being and a lost cause, a complete shit. (On several occasions she sent me shit in the post or left it outside the consulting room door). At the same time she carried on about knives and guns, threatening to cut me up or blow me to pieces.

Nothing helped, she hated my every word. I only began to make contact when I told her how bad I felt and conveyed my sense of desperation. Then she would calm and grudgingly reveal she was angry (for not getting more from me), worried (that she might hurt me) and frightened (that I would get back at her).

Essentially this person hungered for my ideas and feelings. Yet she hated my knowledge and peace of mind. She wasn't unaware of the things she did, but she took pleasure in my discomfort. No doubt she anticipated I would scream at her just like her parents had done when she was a child.

In a past that intruded far into the future, she felt all cut up inside. Therefore she was determined to excise that pain and get revenge. I think she was really terrified that I would reject her (give her the chop), or worse, make her feel guilty (drive her mad) and put her away (rubbish her).

The interplay of greed, envy and guilt I have just described took years to work out. As with all people these forces may oppose each other, or act in tandem, or fuse as in grenvy. There is rarely an occasion where one acts without the other. Yet, the simultaneous interplay of denial, reversal, projection and rage make this hard to realize. With my patient there often appeared to be no immediate reason for the stasis in her life, or the anxiety and confusion she contrived in mine. We had to unravel many layers of bile and bitterness in order to appreciate the tortuous strands of her destructiveness. These, in turn, were related to the different ways I represented *the breast.*

For her, indeed for all people, *the breast* means *good experiences* (peace of mind, calm, contentment, pleasure and security); *a part of the body* (the bosom, an exciting physical interior); *a material object* (any container, a glass, a plate, a bottle, a jewel, a safe, the sun, the light and warmth in her life); *a product* (milk, food, skills, knowledge, 'good's', possessions and 'super-possessions', love, calm and strength) and *qualities, capacities, characteristics and accomplishments* (patience, prosperity, vitality, creativity, fame and, in general, 'good werkes and vertuous deeds'). [28]

This woman wanted them these things. She wanted to have them or to prevent me from having them. And the more her greed and envy were frustrated, the more enraged she became. However, many people take a different tack. If they can't have the breast, they prefer to become the breast.

* * * * *

"I am a breast. A phenomenon that has been variously described to me as "as a massive hormonal influx," "an endocrinopathic catastrophe," and/or "a hermaphroditic explosion of chromosomes" took place within my body between midnight

and four A.M. on February 18, 1971, and converted me into a mammary gland disconnected from any human form.

They tell me that I am now an organism with the general shape of a football, or a dirigible; I am said to be of spongy consistency, weighing in at one hundred and fifty-five pounds (formally I was one hundred and sixty-two), and measuring, still, six feet in length." [29]

The American writer, Philip Roth, narrated this account of a middle-aged man who woke up one morning to discover that he had become a breast, in a novel of the same name. His newly formed body included a long pink nipple, seventeen lactiferous openings, and several seven inch antennae.

The man had been having an affair with a beautiful younger woman. Although his initial passions had waned, he tried to maintain an affectionate but reserved relationship with her. Above all, he wanted to avoid the grinding *"burden of dependence"* and the *"deception, placation and dominance"* of marriage. He had been through a *"lacerating divorce"* and had just terminated a five year psychoanalysis.

As he lay in hospital, helpless in a bra-like hammock, he recalled his friend, *"Pleasure-giving Claire"*, his envy and strange desires to be the breast he had so often suckled. Yet, for him, *the breast*, was much more than a part of the body. It was the actual practice of feeding, caring, loving, sustaining, providing, stimulating and pleasure-giving. The story of this man's metamorphosis is really the narration of his successful attack, and consequent self-punishment, on all that Claire could and did do for him. He attacked her function by taking over her function, and by grotesquely parodying the relationship that existed or might have existed between them.

Roth's fiction illustrates a common fact. Many individuals hate the sense of needing or depending upon another, and will do all they can to subvert or destroy dependency. By dependency I mean an appreciation of need, the taking of food and gratitude for being fed.

No-one can avoid being dependent, but at some point everyone tries to begrudge the experience, because dependency involves an awareness of love-hate, guilt, loss and grief. The dependent person attacks these painful feelings in himself by blaming others. The resultant onslaughts range from a transient grumpiness in the presence of a parent (or spouse or anyone who has, or might be trying to provide something) to a defiant negativity.

Attacks on dependency equal attacks on the breast. They inevitably feature a contemptuous dismissal and triumphal overtaking of the functions of the envied object of desire. Melanie Klein observed these features in a patient of hers who had just had a major professional success. This woman dreamed that she was riding on a magic carpet which allowed her to peer into a room where a cow was munching on an endless trip of blanket. The dream announced her wish to triumph over her need for Klein and the psychoanalytic relationship. The carpet, and her riding high, meant that she had the magic power, the ability to soar and outstrip a therapist whom she had derisively relegated to the role of a cow.

> *"She associated that the endless strip of blanket represented an endless stream of words, and it occurred to her that these were all the words I had ever said in the analysis and which I now had to swallow. The strip of blanket was a hit at the wooliness and worthlessness of my interpretation. Here we see the full devaluation of the primal object, significantly represented by the cow, as well as the grievance against the mother who had not fed her satisfactorily."* [30]

Klein's patient and Kepesh, Roth's protagonist, sought to deny need, get fed and express ingratitude simultaneously. As with many children adults their reveries led them to believe that they had become all powerful and the source of everything. For them, *"I am nothing!"* reversed to *"I am everything!"*, *"I am empty!"* to " *I am full!"*, and " *I am impotent!"* to *"I am omnipotent"*. In these circumstances dependency stops being an issue because people feel they can have whatever they want whenever they want it. They have become the breast!

* * * * *

The denial of ambivalence, loss and guilt often occur together. So do the angry possession of, triumph over and contempt for the feeding person. Melanie Klein called this combined assault on internal and external reality the *manic defense*. The manic defense, really a manic attack, is a forceful means of averting hurt and asserting superiority. The triumphant feelings reek of rivalry and revenge, while the contempt serves to denigrate care and containment so there is nothing to miss or suffer guilt about. This combination of self-protection and subversion can vary in intensity from an overbearing arrogance to a manic psychosis. The difference is one of degree, not of kind.

The manic defense is probably the most common systematic way of attacking the breast, whether in the family, in psychotherapy or elsewhere. This state of mind activates both virulent envy and devastating greed. The manic adult or child believes he has an absolute right to devour attention, emotions, devotion, activities and assets. Any lapse, even the smallest lapse, is a terrible threat because it may expose the hollowness of the omnipotence and the persistence of need. This state of continuous feasting over others' time and energy has been termed the *manic feast*. It is the closest that most people get to unrestrained cannibalism. *Manic feasting* can leave its victims drained and skeletonized and confirms Abraham's description of oral sadistic savagery.

The manic state, like the phenomena that encompass the *Nirvana Principle*, signals another point at which envy and narcissism converge. Each presents a different side of the same coin. The manic individual hides his wounds by assuming a position of God-like exuberance which allows him to take and give with reckless abandon. He aims to control and caricature care. Should this fail, he can burst into an even greater frenzy or flip over into a suicidal retreat. Either possibility entails an all-consuming rage with external providers.

These providers include people and places which have supplied, or might supply and replenish feelings of inner worth, fullness and fulfilment. Whether a relative or stranger, a home or country, they are linked with good experiences, with food and with feeding. Therefore, people and places, in themselves, can signify 'the breast' and can be treated as such. Yet, they differ from a cornucopia or soda fountain because they are not automatically on tap and do require some care in return. Occasionally mothers do need a rest and even a house does need a coat of paint every few years. Otherwise it stops being a good house. That is why the manic person so ruthlessly attacks his human and non-human environment. Even the slightest demand calls into question his own goodness and reminds him of his own limitations. So he adheres to the role of a tyrannical child. The breast must not have any life of its own. It solely exists to serve his wishes, or it will be destroyed.

Although most children do not behave this way all the time, some adults do, especially in relation to each other. The profligate lover, or Don Juan, is a well known character with an impetuous and insatiable craving for women. Greedy for love, he seeks them out like an addict scrounging for a fix. And like an addict he is never satisfied with what he gets. He is ever on the lookout for more alluring, exciting and self-sacrificing partners. Any hint that the woman might have her own needs, make demands, feel hurt, or have interests of her own provides a pretext for angry rejection. No-one is good enough to assuage his emptiness or withstand his destructiveness. At best he turns from one to the other to avoid their harm and his guilt. Otherwise his basic attitude is drain, deceive and discard.

The 'Don Juan,' a charming 'Dracula', preys on the emotions of his victims and aims to insert himself inside them in order to totally possess their vitality. His actions may have a sexual motif, but they have little to do with sex. They are a vengeful vampirization of the female body and soul for what it holds and allegedly withholds. He is not just a greedy man, but a very envious one, who believes he has the right to take what he can get and give false hopes, broken promises and bad dreams in return. Possessiveness is his way of spitefully spoiling a woman's autonomy. He wants to make sure that she can't use and make use of her own qualities and capacities as she sees fit. The woman must remain at his beck and call. His pride depends on her subservience to him, and her worthlessness to others. [31]

Basically I have been describing a man who maintains that women deceptively keep their goodies for themselves, a view not limited to Don Juans. It is typical of people with a tendency to falsely attribute greed. They take for granted that providers prefer to feed themselves and hurt those who depend on them. They also assume that if these providers are not keeping things for themselves, then they must be diverting the goods to others. This assumption connects envy with jealousy and fuels the wish for revenge. It is rooted in children's ideas that if mommy isn't available, then she must be caring for daddy, or sister or brother, and that there are always undeserving, grasping interlopers about who are ready and able to steal her affections.

The imagined rival is a much more serious threat than a real one. He or she is a provocative self-creation. I refer to an image that feeds false beliefs about infidelity and sustains severe hostility in states of 'morbid', 'pathological', 'delusional', or 'insane' jealousy. On these occasions people insist that their partners, and certain named or unnamed third parties want to rob them of everything, taunt, tantalise, outrage, strip them of self-respect, spoil their lives and leave them loveless, hopeless and despairing. These accusations often duplicate deeply felt, overwhelmingly dangerous, guilt-ridden desires. [32]

It only takes some minor event, 'a last straw', to precipitate the violent expulsion and re-location of the destructive impulses in a friend or relative. The effect is comparable to a 'Don Juan' who suddenly reproaches his companion for meanness and duplicity, or an 'Othello' who denounces his spouse for lechery and treachery. In fact, this phenomenon has been termed, *The Othello Syndrome*. It denotes a murderous obsession with the alleged infidelity of a spouse. [33]

On close examination the imagined rival is not necessarily an intruding outsider, but the original partner, the focus of envious enmity, not for being bad, but for being good. This feature helps to distinguish jealous rivalry from envious rivalry. As I have previously pointed out, jealousy involves a triangular relationship. Here the hatreds head toward the challenger and may bypass the real loved one. Hence the issues are love lost, love denied or love called into question. On the other hand, envy is bilateral. These hatreds go directly to the primary person, often a provider seen as an adversary. Therefore in delusional jealousy or envious rivalry the underlying issues are narcissistic rage, impotence and dependency. (34)

* * * * *

Deadly rivalries can also embrace a place or setting as happened with an acquaintance whose family owned a sheep ranch in Australia. It provided a regular income plus a treasure trove of stories about the Australian outback. Yet, the man hated the place and never missed an opportunity to denigrate sheep, farms, the 'Wild West' or Australia. His unceasing antagonism was a barely concealed brew of greed, envy and jealousy. The greed grew from a belief that he had never got his due. Although he had received substantial sums over the years, he personally felt cheated and deprived. He blamed the ranch for this, and his family too. He liked to upset his parents with bitter asides that the property was too big, too grand, too far away and not worth a visit. But his malice boiled over whenever his father waxed nostalgic about the hardships and excitement of the old days. Such memories engaged both envious and jealousy rivalry. The envy arose from a sense that the ranch was an extension of his father's strength and wealth, qualities which he could never equal and which his father always held over him. The jealousy followed his conviction that the land was a literal rival for his father's affection. No matter what he did, the 'old man' would always find lush pastures and streams more interesting. So as far as he was concerned, a sheep spread had usurped his place, and he longed to eradicate its power and prestige.

Attacks on the land and those who till it are a basic ingredient of recorded history. The Old Testament relates that Abimelech, King of the Philistines, was displeased when Isaac cultivated Gerar, the area in Israel between Gaza and Beer-sheba:

> *"Isaac sowed in that land and reaped a hundredfold the same year. The LORD blessed him and the man grew richer and richer until he was very wealthy: he acquired flocks and herds, and a large household, so that the Philistines envied him. And the Philistines stopped up all the wells which his father's servants had dug in the days of his father Abraham, filling them with earth. And Abimelech said to Isaac, "Go away from us, for you have become too big for us."* [35]

Several millennia later American and European farmers face less dangerous, but no less malevolent gibes for making their farmyards the 'breadbaskets of the world'. Press reports like *"Jaguars in the farmyards"* have aroused such resentment that farm union officials have been moved to publicly complain that their members are: *".....getting fed up at the growing national sport of biting the hand that feeds you."* [36]

People and places attract hostility because they are specific providers and containers, good objects, or bad as the case may be, upon whom we are all dependent. In combination they yield generalizations like 'the mother-land', which can become a passionate focus of feeling, like a mother. [37] Yet, whether concrete or abstract, a body or a symbol, these entities are a part of the ultimate dimension of the breast which is reality itself.

* * * * *

The creation of reality begins with the first tentative steps to locate and conceptualize the source of supply, a task which continues throughout one's life. Initially reality comprises basic experiences such as warmth and fullness, or roughness and tension, as well as the act of experiencing these things. Or, it is a part of the mother-baby body such as the mouth or nipple, and the aptitude to perceive, remember and appreciate these organs. However, as the one matures, reality grows too and encompasses, for example, material things, human relationships and physical qualities as well as the contents and functions of the mind.

The American psychologist, George Miller, points out that *"the main intellectual accomplishment of the nervous system is the world itself."* [38] This 'world' is a picture of things, a conjectural model derived from multiple interactions in and between oneself and others. By others I include both the human and non-human environments. First the interactions center around food and feeding. But they soon branch out in many other directions. The result is a dynamic structure of perceptions, memories, feelings, expectations and skills which themselves have the capacity to become sustaining and containing, or not. [39]

An infant's early relationship with *breast-reality* determines his world-view, which, in turn, determines his relationship to life. A sense that *"life is good"* or *"the world's O.K."* reflects a positive world-view. The opposite sense that *"life is bad"* or *"the whole world's horrible"* reflects a negative model. These attitudes are not static. Many internal or external events tilt the balance one way or the other. There are occasions when reality is so intolerable that it becomes and literally feels like a *bad breast*. Then people deflect their hatred to consciousness itself, or space, or time, or, more prosaically, the weather. They want to flee from these things or fight them. Concurrently they will also try to establish new realities by flying to the sunshine during winter or by revelling in comforting day-dreams.

The re-evaluation and annihilation of reality is very clear during a psychotic or quasi psychotic episode. Then the very fabric of existence is at stake. Anything indicative of feeding or caring, and any links with food or care, may become the focus of savage attack. The links are crucial because they are reminders of the pain and suffering which mother and father, under the guise of 'life' has inflicted and still seems to be inflicting, on a hapless soul.

Typical links include perception and the perceptual apparatus, representing the desire and capacity to take things in (the symbolic equivalent of the mouth). They also include communication, words, thoughts and emotions, representing the intermediary between child and parents (the symbolic equivalent of the nipple or teat). Finally the links encompass states of mind and understanding, representing the parental container full of digested or undigested experiences (the symbolic equivalent of the bosom and its contents). [40] Collectively these elements equal the *mouth-nipple-breast* connection which the contented person cherishes in contrast to the distraught person who solely wants to deny, subvert or smash them to smithereens.

In a seminal paper entitled, *Attacks on Linking*, the British psychoanalyst, Wilfred Bion, illustrated how these attacks may be reactivated, especially during psychoanalysis. The patient may feel compelled to repeat a hurtful relationship with an unresponsive, non-containing mother, or a very envied one. Bion comments:

> *"Attacks on the link, therefore, are synonymous with attacks on the analyst's, and originally the mother's, peace of mind. The capacity to introject is transformed by the patient's envy and hate into greed devouring the patient's psyche; similarly, peace of mind becomes hostile indifference."* [41]

* * * * *

Time was the essential issue for a middle aged teacher who consulted me after a suicide attempt. During the first months of treatment she was diligent and punctual. Rarely coming a moment too early, or tarrying a moment too late, her depression lifted and she went back to work. But the picture was too good to be true, as the summer holiday break dramatically proved.

A changed woman resumed sessions, someone who cast aside fastidious facades and appeared for her appointments minutes, sometimes hours early. Later on in the therapy, she would act like a thief and seize any excuse, a sudden memory, a last minute dream, a broken shoe to stay on and on. Occasionally she apologized. Yet the very next time she would beg and whine to stay longer, or refuse to leave. I felt as if I had to push her out of the room, whereupon she would dawdle on the stairs and hang around the street in front of my office.

In addition, he dressed differently. Previously the lady was prim and proper. Now she wore tight sweaters and short skirts, and doused herself in such heavy perfume that I felt faint from the fumes. Alternatively she would arrive bruised and scratched, with a torn shirt and dirty tights, screaming about suicide. Then she wouldn't turn up for a week, leaving me shattered about what happened to her.

I thought: *"She wants to give me a good time, but if she can't, she'll give me a hard time, a very hard time".* My intuition was right. She associated seductiveness with lust, and lust with being *"a good time girl".* She really was trying to show me what she wanted from me – a good time, lots of time, all my time. And if she couldn't have it, then she would corrupt and disrupt my time and timing.

She hated the idea that I might have time for someone else, or keep time for myself. As the Christmas break approached, she became more disruptive, more seductive, more difficult. She intended to fill me with desire, or fear, or rage, so I could have no time in my mind for anyone else. This was her jealous revenge for my 'two-timing her' during the holiday.

Time, the time of sessions, my mental time were the links between her and me. The more she wanted me, the more she subjected these links to an unceasing barrage of greedy, envious and jealous attacks. Her mouth was insatiable for time. It never got enough. Almost in passing she recalled that her parents were farmers. They got up early and went to bed early. They never seemed to have any time for her, or if they did, they preferred to spend it with her two sisters. As a child she felt that outings were 'stolen time'.

The therapy sessions and the flow of time were my nipples and the milk that flowed through them. Her aims were ruthless control and abject contempt. Sometimes she talked so much that the sessions were deluged with ideas. On other occasions she maintained a sullen silence so that time soured and our work wasted.

Then there were different silences, akin to a calm, deathly quietness, with slow breathing and little movement for hours on end. It seemed she remained suspended in time, as if she had returned to an intrauterine state when there was no intermediary between her and me, and time was endless.

That's what she wanted, endless time, and me. I was the breast, a cornucopia of time, the source of everything her parents had denied her. Towards the end of the treatment, she apologized for all the upheavals and hassles. She knew she was difficult. Long ago she had sworn to herself that some day someone would give her all the time she had never had as a child. But if the person reneged, or if it didn't work out, then she was determined to destroy time once and for all.

* * * * *

For the teacher the destruction of time equalled the destruction of reality, which, from her point of view, didn't sustain her, nor contain her hurts. Others vented their rage on different aspects of the breast. Kepesh attacked *the function* (a dependent relationship); Don Juan, *the person* (a girlfriend); King Abimelech, *a place or setting* (the land of Gerar) and a psychotic patient, *the inner world* (a state of mind). Previously I have described attacks on the breast as *an experience, a part of the body, a material thing, a product* and *a quality or accomplishment.* Each aspect is a separate but related mode of feeding and caring. Each can become a source of power and strength, or, can arouse great longing and terrible antagonism.

Bruno Bettelheim was struck by the extent to which the boys at the Orthogenic School in Chicago treated the breast as an extremely powerful object, something to be feared and desired.

> *"A riddle they repeatedly, with envious preoccupation, asked exemplifies this: "What is the strongest thing in the world?"*
>
> *They never failed to supply the answer: "A brassiere, because it holds two huge mountains and a milk factory."* [42]

This raises the question, is there a difference in the degree of desire, or quality of hate that emanates from boys or girls, men and women, towards the breast?

Both males and females need love, security, stimulation and the relief of pain. But until relatively recently it usually has been the woman who did the nurturing, for social and anatomical reasons. Perhaps it is easier for girls to pass from childhood dependency to adult activity since they know that in giving up the breast (mother) they will also be gaining the breast (motherhood). For boys the knowledge that they will never develop a bosom, nor produce milk, nor suckle the young, compounds the loss of childhood.

Men resent the lack of a breast no less than women rue the lack of a penis. They feel deprived of a tangible means to feed and be fed as well as an overt sign of desirability. In fantasy they assume that all women have to do is turn on some magical tap inside themselves, while they have to spend a lifetime accumulating capital and possessions. Moreover, they suspect that women can always suck on their own breasts, but that they will remain dependent on females for food. These assumptions breed an intense hostility that contributes to male wishes to dress like women, act like women, become women and, of course, totally subjugate them.

From their perspective women suffer for being the object of such hostility, both from men, and from other women who envy their abilities. This helps to explain female preoccupations with reducing or increasing the size of the breast. The former has to do with diminishing others' greedy and envious fascination with their organ. The latter is concerned with power and the use the breast to triumph over maternal and fraternal rivals. Silicon implants extend this obsession with large bosoms. Thus, some women experience their desires through the need to be desired, and express their antagonisms by putting their bust on a pedestal.

Yet, it is not the size of the breast that counts, but the capacity for care, which can be as strongly developed in men, as it remains undeveloped in women. The teacher who attacked time, blamed her mother in particular. When she came to see me she was in despair not only because the world didn't sustain her, but because she couldn't sustain her students. Years ago Freud conveyed the larger dimension of her dilemma very well:

> *"The reproach against the Mother which goes back the furthest is that she gave the child too little milk – which is construed against her as a lack of love ... the child's avidity for its earliest nourishment is altogether insatiable and it never gets over the pain of losing its Mother's breast...."* (43)

Chapter 5

Suffocation of the Mother – Womb Envy

The womb has long been considered to be an extremely dangerous organ. Around 400 B.C. the philosopher Democritus advised Hippocrates that: "*...the womb was the origin of six hundred evils and innumerable catastrophes.*" [1]

This view has permeated civilized thought right down to modern times. The famous Persian physician, Haly Abbas (? - 994 A.D.), compared the womb to a "*wild animal longing for semen*", [2] and the sixteenth century French writer, Jean Liebaut declared:

> *"The uterus has naturally an incredible desire to conceive and to procreate. Thus it is anxious to have virile semen, desirous of taking it, drawing it in, sucking it, and retaining it."* [3]

More recently a gynaecologist was overheard, after performing an emergency hysterectomy, and holding the newly detached uterus aloft:

Ah yes, I am (pleased). Another small victory in Man's unending battle against the womb." [4]

By 'womb' the doctor might well have added the labia, the clitoris and the vagina - the entrance, the signal and the passageway to the dark interior of a woman's body which, together with the breasts, comprise the essentials of feminine endowment. Variously called a centre of creativity or a furnace of carnality, a biological powerhouse or a suffocating mother, the womb is the focus of both dread and desire. The latter, like a lilting Lorelei, urges a return to the beginnings of life, to a state of weightless warmth and blissful envelopment. Wilhelm Tell narrated these feelings in, *Song of the Fisherboy*. There a voice from the depth of a *"clear smiling lake"* calls forth:

> "*.......a melody,*
> *Flowing and soft,*
> *And sweet as when angels are singing aloft...*
> *With me thou must go, I charm the young shepherd,*
> *I lure him below."* [5]

Tell's poem refers to a shepherd, or boy, but the wishes might equally apply to a shepherdess, or girl. They concern everyone who recalls the delights of the breast and seeks, with varying degrees of desperation, to discover and rediscover the entrance and passageway to Mother's body. Therefore, the initial conception of the womb is a magical interior, a conjunction of body and breast which carries the expectation of continuous, effortless pleasure experienced as warmth, softness, fullness and satisfaction. Yet, unlike the breast, this organ cannot be seen or grasped, nor can its goods be felt or tasted. It is an infolding rather than an outfolding of the body, something dark and secret, readily transformed by the mind into a trap, a lure, whose siren-call is a *"hiss from the abyss"* threatening to drain and devour, dissolve and destroy whomever or whatever might enter. [6] This dreaded tomb is a greedy womb, a creature imbued with the very cravings that have been directed towards it. Just as the bosom can appear like a cornucopia or a crocodile, depending on mood, and circumstances, the depths of a woman can seem like a cavern of contentment or a chamber of horrors. Such a fathomless hell contains hideous perils, as Tell also described in his ballad, *The Diver:*

> *"Salamander-snake-dragon-vast reptiles that dwell*
> *In the deep, coil'd about the grim jaws of their hell."* [7]

These lines convey universal fears that the womb/woman is not only hungry for semen, the male fluid, but also for the penis, the male member. Lizards, snakes and reptiles represent maleness, the male members which have been bitten off and captured. Such phantasies lay the basis for intense anxieties that either the penis has been devoured and digested, or that it has been trapped and incorporated so the womb becomes a cave filled with the organs of any man with whom the woman has had a relationship. There they lurk, sinister guardians of the treasures within.

But the womb threatens more than maleness. Pride and self respect are as vulnerable to a woman's real or imagined demands as the vitality and viability of the penis. Indeed, incessant worries about emotional weakness and psychic disintegration invariably surface as doubts about physical prowess: *"Am I big enough? Can I give enough?" Will I cope enough, or will I be swallowed up and lost inside her?"*

Greed sustains the impression that the vagina/womb/woman can never be satisfied. This includes the actual greed of a mother, for example, who never gets enough because she rarely gives enough, and the projected greed of infants and children of either sex who invade their parents with screaming mouths and flailing arms. Rebuff arouses revenge followed by *"the perils of the deep".* [8] These perils encompass both rapaciousness and oblivion. Rapaciousness leads to a terror of being torn apart, as by sharks in the sea. Oblivion conjures forth fears of falling apart, of dissolving in intrauterine waters as might occur during a period of regressive withdrawal. The accompanying experience of ego-loss or loss of identity has been commonly compared to 'mental castration'. [9]

* * * * *

The wish to return to the womb is only one of the hundreds of 'evils and catastrophes' that have been attributed to it. Generally these dangers comprise disease, dementia and demonic possession. They reflect a litany of fear and hatred of *"the mysterious capacity that woman's bodies have of creating babies out of food and what men give them."* [10]

What other organ can nurture, but also create and produce concretely what men (and some women) can only make metaphorically? The womb is the core of female potency. It is a part of the body that is perfectly placed to be idealized and envied for feeding and breeding, for loving and being made love to. Although it tends to receive a lot of the ardour and anger that may be initially directed to the breast (which helps to explain the oral origins of genital passions), the womb is not a passive organ. [11] On the contrary, in recent decades, old epithets like 'furnace or powerhouse of carnality' have gained new meanings as sex research reveals that woman have an almost inexhaustible capacity for orgasms, and feminist writers like Kate Millett proclaim that the sexual performance of woman are naturally stronger than men. [12] So we are faced with a situation where modish myths of female dominance and newborn enmities about womb power echo ancient fears and begin to erode the previously preeminent 'dangers of male supremacy'. [13]

Many peoples have believed that the womb has a will, even a life of its own. It can be lustful or rejecting, angry or depressed. It can decide to reside in the pelvis or the belly or the throat, or sometimes outside of the body altogether. In other words, it can be a separate animate creature like a frog that happens to be housed inside a woman and make women sick when aroused. [14]

Three thousand years ago the Egyptians blamed the womb or uterus for a vast array of complaints ranging from physical illnesses to hysteria. The term 'hysteria' comes from the Greek word *hystera* meaning uterus. 'Globus hystericus', or inability to swallow, was often ascribed to the uterus rising to the throat. To overcome the problem women were advised to repeat, *"Womb high, womb low, get back to the old place that God sent you. In the name of God, the Father, the Son...." and to make the sign of the cross three times.* (15)

The Egyptians thought that the emotional excesses and bizarre physical manifestations of hysteria were solely a disorder of women, a view that persisted, with a few notable exceptions, until the 1600's. (16) Their attitude was to placate or punish the womb in order to make it know its proper place. Fumigation with fragrant and powerful substances was a popular prescription. The *Papyrus Ebers,* an important medical text, recommended that:

> *"The dry excrement of men is placed on frankincense, and the woman is fumigated therewith; let the fume thereof enter into her vulva."* (17)

Similar treatments prevailed during the Greco-Roman period when hysteria was considered to be a constriction, a *suffocation of the womb* or *suffocation of the mother.* (18) But theories about the womb and the role of women changed radically with the writing of St. Augustine and other Christian theologians. They affirmed that female maladies, in particular hysteria, were caused by an *"alliance with unholy powers"*, typically, *"seduction by the devil"*, and hysterical women were equated with witches. However, the organized persecution of them did not begin in earnest until the ninth century when Charlemagne, emperor of the Holy Roman Empire, decreed the death penalty for:

> *".......all who in any way evoked the devil, compounded love-philters, afflicted either man or woman with barrenness, troubled the atmosphere, excited tempests, destroyed the fruits of the earth, dried up the milk of cows, or tormented their fellow-creatures with sores and diseases."* (19)

Charlemagne's decree signifies an abhorrence and hostility towards woman's powers, their bodies, their functions, their products and their pleasures that culminated in 1494 with the publication of *Malleus Maleficarum* also known as *The Witches Hammer.* [20] The impact of this work was immediate and long lasting. It became an international 'best seller' and an established authority by which untold numbers of women were tortured and executed *"ad majorem Dei gloriam"* over the next couple of centuries. [21]

The book purports to define witchcraft, to describe witches and their methods, and then to detail the steps to be taken in prosecuting them. It contends that women are greedy for sex and they can only be gratified by copulating with the devil. Lust is their hallmark and if thwarted in any way, they will "deprive man of his virile member".

> *"We have already shown that they can take away the male organ, not indeed by actually despoiling the human body of it, but by concealing it with some glamour (enchantment) ......And of this we shall instance a few examples.*
>
> *In the town of Ratisbon, a certain young man who had an intrigue with a girl, wishing to leave her, lost his member; that is to say, some glamour was cast over it so that he could see or touch nothing but his smooth body. In his worry over this he went to a tavern to drink wine; and after he had sat there for a while he got into conversation with another woman who was there, and told her the cause of his sadness, explaining everything, and demonstrating in his body that it was so."* [22]

The *Malleus* indicts women for being deceptive and carnal, castrating and evil. It argues that their intelligence is poor, their memories are weak and their passions are inordinate. Their chief symptoms are envy and jealousy.

> *"What else is woman but a foe to friendship, an unescapable punishment, a necessary evil, a natural temptation, a desirable*

calamity, a domestic danger, a delectable detriment, an evil of nature, painted with fair colours!" [23]

This picture is the mirror image of age old antagonisms towards women and their powers of production and reproduction that continue to surface via religious fundamentalism, radical puritanism and kindred public and private attitudes. It reflects intense desires to disparage and debunk that 'vessel which bears all things', including its capacity to receive, to conceive, to delight, to suffer and to bear fruit. It expresses the spirit of malice insinuated within the body of another. [24]

* * * * *

Why was the *Malleus* so influential? As an expose, it was part of a widespread reaction to the rebirth of science and the renewal of art and literature that occurred during the Renaissance. Many people were trapped between their hunger for knowledge and beauty (exemplified by the female form) and theological condemnation. They could only admit these hungers, aside from act upon them, at the price of burning guilt. Consequently, they perceived the object of their desires, particularly women, as provocative and extremely dangerous. The *Malleus* helped men (and women) to deny their own guilt ridden impulses and locate them elsewhere – in the vagina and uterus seen as *"lousy with lust"*. The devils were disembodied desires which could indeed bedevil by arousing intolerable anguish. Therefore the private parts of women became what people feared most in themselves.

It is likely that the young man from Ratisbon who claimed he had been deprived of his member was suffering from impotency. He couldn't get it up because he felt guilty about seducing the girl and then wanting to abandon her. He experienced this as if she had attacked him. If he chose (as many did) to blame her for frustrating him, and for sexual intrigues (that is, for his needing her as a sexual partner in the first place), then he could wreak a revenge which, in the circumstances of the day, put her life in mortal danger.

But the *Malleus* did more than absolve guilt. It was a basic text in attacking women unleashed by the church in its struggle with the forces of the Renaissance. The tome illuminates a thousand year history of envious and jealous rivalry with femininity, barely held in check by the capacity of the church to 'elevate spiritual motherhood' and 'devalue real motherhood'. [25] It remains of interest because it exploded on the world like a volcano through which the deepest detestations that men harbour towards women were able to flow.

Heinrich Kramer and James Sprenger were the Dominican monks who had been commissioned by Pope Innocent VIII to write the book and strike out at 'deluded souls'. The alleged delusions (*"many persons of both sexes......have abandoned themselves to devils, incubi and succubi"*) were metaphors meaning that many persons began to believe that goodness resides in women, that they are life renewing and ecstatic and are desirable in their own right. [26] These beliefs conflicted with dogmas that the church was the source of goodness and light, the fountainhead of spiritual and temporal truth, the urobolic union of male and female, big, embracing and all sustaining. [27]

The challenge, akin to that of Galileo in the next century, called forth massive envious retribution. Reputations were ruined, bodies were burned. Perhaps the most sinister result was that women's minds and bodies were undermined by constant attributions of evil – envious attacks which transformed them from victims to victimizers. I refer here, of course, to the operation of projective identification and the ways that the envied object can appear as the envier, the persecuted person as persecuting. Old women were favorite objects for this because, like Gericault's, *A Mad Woman with the Mania of Envy,* they appeared to embody the life begrudging spite of their accusers.

It is likely that in many instances the accused women were bitter and bizarre, which made it all the easier for them to become the focus of others' malevolent projections. Ironically, the bitterness can be seen as a realistic reaction to life circumstances involving severe sexual deprivation and frustration. I especially refer to the untold number of nuns who, having renounced physical relations, were subsequently accused of wanting it.

The most vicious onslaughts were aimed at the female genitalia, said to be in league with the devil. The accusations operated like Bacon's poisonous 'ejaculations and irradiations'. No wonder the vagina and uterus became dreaded objects! They were treated as combined evil eyes and envious mouths, organs infected by the deviltry of their accusers.

The idea of the vagina as a malevolent mouth, a genital Korba Khobee, did not arise with Pope Innocent VIII or the authors of the *Malleus*. Institutionalized hatreds simply allowed them to give vent to their own simmering suspicions. Countless boys and men are shocked to discover that women do not possess a penis, but others are more upset to learn that women have an extra orifice which enables them to take things in and get extra satisfactions. (28). It is noteworthy that in many languages the folds of skin which encircle the entranceway to the mouth and vagina have the same name – *labia*, or *lips*.

For children and adults who remain preoccupied with oral issues, this lack of a third passageway is a great disappointment, and a source of enmity which heralds various attempts to abuse, spoil, stuff up, mutilate or otherwise destroy the organ, or its equivalents, just as happened during the inquisition.

However, vagina envy is not limited to men. It is a powerful impulse in girls and women who fear that their genitals are too small and inadequate. Malicious rage follows comparisons and conclusions that they will not be able to get or give food and love to the same extent as others. (29).

Jealous rivalry also contributes to the ill will. Wife versus mistress, mother versus daughter, it is hardly necessary to detail the bad tempered, vituperative behavior that can be aroused by third party threats to love and emotional preeminence. The third party may be perceived as a sex organ. On a large scale this took place during the late middle ages. The Mother church identified the Renaissance with sensuality and seemed to treat non-virgins as debased vaginas, temporal competitors to its own spiritual openings and openness.

Certainly the *Malleus* and subsequent mania were frequently used by women to persecute other women. In England Elizabeth I made witchcraft a capital crime in 1562. A year later Mary Queen of Scots did the same. By the late 1600's this public savagery had crossed the Atlantic, although it had begun to ease in Europe. Women were prominent accusers in the New England witch trials. These currents continue today in various forms such as 'Satanic Ritual Abuse' and 'Alien Abduction,' which are a few of the examples that Elaine Showalter has detailed in her book *Hystories: Hysterical Epidemics and Modern Culture.* (30)

While the vocabulary has changed,'pollution,' 'abuse,' and 'alien' having replaced 'devils' and 'succubi', the intention is similar, to define and denigrate women as wicked walking wombs. The men and women who instigate these actions might conceal their envies and jealousies, but they would agree with many of the views I have cited, that the womb is:

choking, constricting and dissolving (an experience);

an evil eye, an envious mouth, a dark, castrating interior (a part of the body);

a wild animal, a frog, a furnace (an animate or inanimate thing);

a trap, a tomb, an abyss, a well, the sea, the deepest depths (a place or setting);

draining, devouring, lustful, hysterical, poisonous, sinful and inciting (qualities, capacities and characteristics); and

a siren, a Salome, a witch or a prostitute (a mythical or real woman);

These representations contribute to the conception of the bad womb.

In contrast, the longed for good womb is a sense of:

floating, melting, enveloping warmth or effortless, delicious pleasure and ecstatic ebbs and flows (an experience);

sweet lips, an exciting mouth, a bountiful breast, a dark, fruitful interior (a part of the body);

a pear, a purse, a house, a powerhouse (an animate or inanimate thing);

a tunnel of love, a cavern of contentment (a place or setting);

receptive, conceptive, creative, nourishing, renewing, sheltering, energizing and mysterious (qualities, capacities and characteristics); and

the 'Virgin Mary', a mother (a mythical or real woman). (31)

* * * * *

Mystery, the dark secrets, the miracle of life, created de novo from within a tiny pear shaped chamber are properties which have been especially valued and envied. Women are a center of mystery and a keeper of mysteries which men spend which of their lives trying to discover, debunk, emulate and prove worthy of knowing.

Margaret Mead has described several South Seas tribal societies in which men have appropriated mystery and claim, through the playing of the sacred flute, to guard the secrets of life. The essential activities of the tribe revolve around the making, learning and ceremonial playing of the flute, tasks from which women are excluded. This allows the men to compensate themselves for a basic inferiority within a tribe that reveres fertility, and to overcome feelings that their real roles are uncertain, ill-defined, and possibly unnecessary.

"Equipped with various mysterious noise-making instruments, whose potency rests upon their actual form's being unknown to those who hear the sounds – that is, the women and children must never know that they are really bamboo tubes, or hollow logs, or bits of elliptoid wood whirled on strings – they can get the male children away from the women, brand them as incomplete, and themselves turn boys into men. Women, it is true, make human beings, but only men can make men." (32)

This attitude and the underlying implications are remarkably similar to that of the United States Marine Corps. It also claims to take boys and make men of them. In Mead's tribes a crocodile figure *"represents the men's group and (the initiates) come out new-born at the other end".* [33] In the Marines, boot camp is the magic crocodile or incubator which turns raw recruits into warriors. [34]

Soldiers and military matters are the direct rivals of peace, procreation and motherhood. They not only transform boys to men, but creation to destruction. [35] This envious spoiling of creativity, and usurping of female functions, have been well portrayed by John Milton in *Paradise Lost:* Satan envies God. He wants to spoil Heaven and take it over, but he fails. Then Satan and all the other fallen angels decide to construct Hell as a rival to Heaven. They assume the powers of death in lieu of the forces of life and forever seek to destroy what God has created. [36]

Mother Earth, a highly gifted but uneducated, black woman from the slums of Trinidad, saw these satanic powers in her Son, or the Male Principle, born from her womb. Son coveted his mother's power of creation. And it came to pass that the Race of the Son became *"the Race of the Whites, the Race of Science and Death. They were created by the Mother for Her Son because of his continued interference with Nature."* [37]

In 1973, at the age of thirty nine, she turned her back on modern society and retreated into the bush with her husband, children and various acolytes. [38] She feared that 'the Son', that is, maleness, white people, aimed to steal the power of procreation,*"through a technology of robots, computers, 'tissue' (test-tube) babies, and sex change operations."* [38]

Mead, the Marines, Mother Earth, all demonstrate various attempts to emulate, control and take over female functions and products, a project motivated by envy and awe. Male pride is very much an issue here, to do with the constant sense of having to prove oneself in the face of women 'who only have to be themselves for things to grow naturally inside them'. The ensuing 'anything you can do I can do better attitude' in conjunction with spiteful putdowns or physical threats is a 'manic assault' on female prowess. It conveys contempt; triumph over the need for care or for sex; and greedy control over powerful but frightening forces.

Men also dress and behave like women for non-malicious reasons, to avoid loss and make good real or imagined damage done to them. In a male oriented, competitive culture this is not an easy task and the opportunity to emulate women may be totally proscribed or limited to a few ceremonial occasions. The result may be a resurgence of vengeful rage for all the pain suffered in trying to be feminine.

The experience of women is not dissimilar. They have a sense of biological and social insecurity heightened by envious and jealous rivalries with mother, sisters and familial surrogates. But they are innately closer to the figures whom they wish to harm as well as emulate. Therefore the pattern of violence is different, more likely to be inner rather than outer directed. As in sterility, this leads to the negation of function. Seemingly an attack on the self, it inevitably embraces a vicious onslaught on an 'internalized other'. For one patient of mine this 'other' was her mother. She used to gloat:

> *"I may be barren, but so is the woman my mother wanted to be when she decided to live inside me."*

She also liked to provoke strangers to beat her up. They were her wrath. She was her mother. The masochism was a chimera. She hated power of women. In the rest of the chapter I shall trace the ambivalent intentions of boys and girls, men and women, towards four major areas of female potency: *menstruation, fertility, pregnancy and childbirth.*

* * * * *

Menstruation

There are records of male horror and fascination with menstruation in practically every society. [39] Albertus Magnus, a thirteenth century medical scholar, noted in his book, *The Secrets of Women:*

> *"Menstruating women carried with them a poison that could kill an infant in its cradle."* [40]

More recent observers have asserted that menstrual blood can *"turn wine into vinegar"*, *"cause mayonnaise to curdle"* and make *"the very flowers in the fields lose their aroma"*, aside from doing terrible things to the male member. [41] Many restrictions and taboos on menstruating women confirm these fears and the basic ideas that menstruation is dirty, damaging, contaminating, castrating and a sign of castration as well as a punishment for sin. [42]

Yet, men have maintained the deepest interest in womb-blood as a life giving magical potion and the essence of female reproductive power. They admire and begrudge the fact that girls have a clear-cut signal of biological maturity and a natural means of self-purification.

In Australia the male members of various aboriginal tribes go to extraordinary lengths to replicate menstruation at puberty. They practice ritual *subincision.* This involves cutting a slit along the entire under surface of the penis and leaving an opening called a 'vulva', 'vagina' or 'penis-womb.

> *"....As soon as ever (the novice) was in position another man sat astride of his body, grasped the penis and put the urethra on the stretch. The operator then approached and quickly, with a stone knife, laid open the urethra from below......When all was over the (newly initiated) were led to one side while they squatted over shields into which the blood was allowed to drain......and from which it is emptied into the centre of a fire which is made for the purpose...As a result of the operation.......micturation is always performed in a squatting position."* [43]

The vital issue is not simply the original wound, but subsequent reopenings of it to produce blood called 'woman' or 'milk'. This represents menstruation and fertility. It is used to ritually anoint and paint the body in the rainbow-serpent ceremony when *"a vaginal father replaces the phallic mother"*. [44]

The Indians of New Guinea have different methods of inducing male menstruation. They stuff a razor sharp leaf up and down the nostril, or scrape the tongue with it. [45] These activities are an important means of self-purification and an essential precursor to playing the sacred flute, a secret rite which embodies creativity and fertility. Interestingly, most of the women know all about the secrets, but they pretend to know otherwise.

> *"The women take the attitude that as they have everything of importance – the babies, the pigs, the gardens – they will let the men have their flutes and their ceremonies if it makes them feel satisfied."* [46]

Although overt displays of male menstruation are uncommon in Western society, Bruno Bettelheim has described the intense desire of teenage boys to possess female features and to mimic the menses. One small group of boys and girls at the Orthogenic School decided that:

> *"The boys would cut their index fingers every month and mix their blood with that of the menses."* [47]

I could cite other examples where boys and men have wounded themselves or covertly suffered recurrent accidents or internal hemorrhages for the same purpose. [48] It is possible that these practices are much more frequent than is generally realized.

Women share traditional beliefs that they are unclean and contaminating during the menses. In popular parlance they often refer to the menstrual period as 'the curse', a term which implies much more than 'a nuisance'. [49] In the late 1960's a couple of ethnographers interviewed women in a French village about menstruation and attendant dangers. There was some divergence of opinion about whether a menstruating woman could make a barrel of salt pork go off, but one person averred:

> *"Oh, boy! Once I caused the entire barrel to go bad. It's true. I wasn't thinking at all. I just went in there. And when I came back later for some more bacon, it was all green."* (50)

Such convictions undoubtedly contribute to the emotional distress and physical pain that can accompany the menses. They also contribute to modern preoccupations with pads, tampons, medications and other means to soak up, clean up or stop the menstrual flow. (51) Yet, until relatively recently there was a countervailing view that menstruation was a natural means of purification which should not be impeded. In this century Finnish countryfolk bled onto their clothes and argued that it was harmful to use pads because:

> *"Women are cleaned of evil and dirt during their monthlies ; so that the cleaning will be unimpeded, the genitals must not be stopped up with a cloth or a pad."* (52)

'Evil', 'dirty', 'bad', 'unhealthy' are concepts which hark back to the *Malleus* and long before. They reflect fear, ignorance, superstition, observation and malicious insinuation. (53) But I think these views persist so tenaciously because women want them and use them to protect themselves against envy of their biological potency and pride. They intend to convince others that this tangible evidence of fertility and reproductive power is really disgusting and dangerous. Then they hope that men (and female rivals) will be less inclined to take it over and attack it – an effective defense.

* * * * *

Fertility

The grenvious eye does not threaten one biological function, rather the entire capacity to bring forth bread from the earth, babies from the body or ideas from the mind. Together they represent the good, creative breast and womb which give and sustain life. In agrarian societies these activities are so highly prized that they may be given Divine status, to which men wholly aspire.

Man the creator painted caves, built huts and made myths. Collectively the myths are 'spiritual storehouses'. They insure against spiritual starvation while the priests and shamen who service them play the same role with the soul as women perform with the body. Both renew and give birth to life.

The earliest habitations followed the female form. Many buildings still do. The architect and psychologist, Olivier Marc, has observed the dwellings of African tribesmen:

> *"Their houses look like slightly attenuated pouches, each with a vertical slit along one side. Seen from a certain angle, they reminded me of enormous breasts pointing up towards the sky. But even more striking than the shape was the entrance, a thick-lipped slit, the only decorated element of the structure. I was then convinced that the interior model which had presided over the birth of this form had been a mother's womb, seen from the inside. These houses were wombs."* (54)

The earliest paintings had to do with food and fertility. They are often found in caves that can only be approached with the greatest difficulty, down *"long, narrow, slippery corridors"*, or *"through a manhole below which a river runs."* (55) Bettelheim suggests that the artists deliberately picked womb-like interiors. In this way they not only depicted the animals, and showed where they came into being, but also made themselves and their fellow tribesmen experience the process of procreation and birth. (56)

In the progression from agrarian to industrial to post-industrial cultures the same impulses to recreate procreation and its setting remain very strong, but expressed with increasing degrees of abstraction. Magic leads to myth to religion to science to cosmic speculation, 'the big bang.' Cave figures lead to representational art to abstract expressionism, 'black on black.'

This trend is not universally satisfying. While the symbolic expression of womb dramas pervades art, literature and other disciplines, people crave their literal re-enactment. Visitors to the futuristic Israel Museum in Jerusalem return and may be reborn as they pass through a long corridor before entering the central chamber containing the Torah scroll and other treasures. Users of the curved passageways of the TWA terminal at Kennedy airport in New York have a similar opportunity. [57]

In contrast, the films of Stephen Spielberg allow onlookers to relive and relieve their horror of the female interior by identifying with the hero, Indiana Jones. In *Raiders of the Lost Ark* he hacks his way through the jungle (pubic hair), negotiates a secret tunnel (vagina) and discovers the treasure room (womb). In *Indiana Jones and the Temple of Doom* the mise en scene is the villain's palace. A comparable sequence occurs. Only Jones can overcome the terrible dangers: spears, darts, poison, pitfalls, tarantulas, crushing stones, and so forth.

The 'passage with knives' or 'passage with biting insects' represents the dreaded *vagina dentata* or vagina with teeth. This is one of the earliest and most tenacious phantasies of a woman's insides and accounts for untold incidents of male and female impotency. Many men won't enter a woman, or even come near one, for fear that their penises will be chewed, mangled or poisoned. Moreover, many women won't let men enter them, because they also fear their bodies are damaging. If intercourse took place, they would be left with an intolerable sense of guilt. One reasons for the immense popularity of Spielberg's films is that they demonstrate the possibility of complete invulnerability to the vagina with teeth, indeed, to the bad, retaliating womb.

Ceremonies of the sacred flute, cave paintings, astronomical speculation or entertaining cinemas may celebrate fertility, or not, depending on whether they respect female prowess or debase it. The aggressive response, indicating envy instead of awe, is overtly and covertly destructive to a woman's body, abilities, pride, social position or life-opportunities. As in a manic attack, it doesn't just seek to emulate women, but to control and triumph over them.

Spielberg's films do not enhance femininity. They treat women as mildly inconvenient sexual toys or frightening, hateful objects. The overbearing arrogance of the hero more than compensates for feared female or male inferiorities. No doubt this is another reason why the films have been so successful. However, there is a change in *Indiana Jones*. The hero depends on his female accomplice to escape from the dangerous chamber with mangling spikes and walls. She partially portrays the good helpful womb. At least Spielberg hints that such an entity exists.

* * * * *

Since the sixties, there have also been useful changes in the psychological literature. Previously female capacities and accomplishments were not taken seriously. Women were seen as extensions of men. The wish to emulate them was frequently interpreted as 'a defense against Oedipal wishes', or 'a sign of inadequate masculinity' or 'an urge to obtain a superior penis', rather than as a positive desire in its own right. (58) With certain individuals these views may or may not be correct. When applied indiscriminately, they are begrudging and disparaging, and, as far as women are concerned, confirm the need for a wary eye towards others' interest in their minds and bodies.

The traditional safeguards include amulets and talismans and occasional visits to a priest, rabbi, shaman or doctor. Among oriental Jews it is still fashionable to wear amulets in order to promote fertility, ensure pregnancy, assist delivery and generally avert the evil eye. Distinguished Kabbalists used to write special handbooks on amulet making. For a childless woman, for example, suitable texts would include:

"There shall not be male or female barren." Deuteronomy 7, 14.

"And the Lord remembered Sarah....And Sarah conceived." Genesis 21, 1-2. [59]

The magic is a protection against the ill will of female friends and relatives, not just men. These hostilities are especially dangerous because they have a nasty tendency to boomerang back against the perpetrators. The Argentine psychoanalyst, Marie Langer, points out that women who simmer with envious anger towards their own fertile mothers are likely candidates for sterility. [60] Projective processes lead them to feel that their own insides have been attacked and laid waste by extremely hostile internal and external figures, the proverbial, 'evil witch'. [61] Moreover, *"the fear resulting from hatred of the fertile mother"* prevents them from having good creative persons to take after. No wonder that spasms or anaesthesia of the entire genital apparatus may precede or accompany sterility. Yet, the malicious glee that spiteful daughters derive from preventing their parents from becoming grandparents barely compensates for the self-inflicted emotional and physical damage. [62]

Langer discusses a young girl who was able to overcome the fear and hatred that centered on her envied mother. Before beginning analysis, the girl had had several abortions and had twice tried to kill herself, first by taking poison and later by drowning. She had been terrified that her mother was trying to poison her. During the course of the treatment she tried to become pregnant and eventually succeeded. Just after the conception she had a dream:

"She is in the cellar of her childhood home. Everything is full of dust and there are dead cockroaches hanging from the ceiling. One falls down. It disgusts but does not horrify her. She calmly starts cleaning the place." [63]

The dream depicts a daughter who feels capable of restoring her own and her mother's womb (the cellar), and the children she had killed inside her mother and her self (the dead roaches, the abortions). Langer adds that by doing this she is able to overcome her guilt and fear of the past and prepare her womb for a new and fruitful pregnancy. [64]

* * * * *

Pregnancy

The worst fear that can afflict a woman is that her insides will be robbed and destroyed. [65] This is the female equivalent of castration anxiety. It is a deep sense of dread that encompasses the breast, the body, the womb and all the babies contained therein, past, present and future. They represent food, parents, life and the continuity of life. [66]

Children at play demonstrate these fears and the wishes that lay behind them. Hanna Segal has described one little girl who was "*preoccupied with pregnancies*". [67] During one session she started to smear glue on the floor. This turned out to be her 'sick' or vomit by which she hoped to spoil Segal's insides and prevent her from having new babies. Later she was frightened to come back because the same might happen to her.

In the same vein Melanie Klein narrated the story of 'Erna', a six year old who was obsessed by brutal phantasies of cutting, tearing and burning. These led to an extraordinary inhibition of learning whereby "*arithmetic and writing symbolized violent sadistic attacks on her mother's body and her father's penis,*" as well as the babies contained therein. [68]

Simple observation of children's activities confirm such intentions. Girls and boys do treat their 'Cindys', houses, cars, trains, and now, male dolls, with unbearable cruelty. As most parents can attest, a new toy may only last a few minutes before it is soiled and broken. On the other hand, gentle play harbours loving, reparative feelings. A near inconsolable grief may ensue if a favorite play thing is damaged. Klein comments:

> *"...beneath the little girl's ever recurring desire for dolls there lies a need for consolation and reassurance. The possession of her dolls is a proof that she had not been robbed of her children by her mother,that she has not had her body destroyed by her and that she is able to have children."* (69)

Attacks on the pregnant body extend to caves, houses and any life-filled interior structure up to and including the mind. That is why we react with particular horror when a malicious man or woman desecrates a house or cuts up pictures in a museum.

In the last chapter I discussed two patients who systematically interfered with my mental life. They loathed my thoughts, to them, mental babies as well as psychic food, and the mind womb which carried them. These persons repeatedly refused me the time and space to develop my ideas. They engaged in a variety of anxiety provoking activities designed to abort my creative processes. Consequently I noticed that my interpretations rarely grew to term. Either I would blurt them out prematurely (suffer a psychic miscarriage) or remain unheeded (be a bearer of stillborn messages). Their attacks illustrate another dimension of 'the negative therapeutic reaction'.

Psychotherapy involves hard labour, as does most creative endeavour that must emerge from a dark internal space. Artists and writers often remark that they feel like a woman making a child. Their finished product only comes forth after a prolonged confinement and difficult delivery. (70) In his *Diaries* the director, Peter Hall, refers to a conversation with Harold Pinter. He was trying to beget a new work. Pinter told him: *"I think I might be pregnant."*

Hall chuckled to himself: "This is great news. A play is on the way." (71)

Similarly, Mr. Tatsuro Toyoda, president of a joint General Motors-Toyota car venture, exclaimed after the first of a new generation of Novas came off the assembly line: *"I feel like an expectant father. I am not sure what to do. Pat it on the hood or pass out cigars."* (72)

Few artists do not suffer long labours. Mozart, however, could create whole symphonies in his head and transcribe them note perfect onto paper. In Peter Shaffer'S play *Amadeus,* Salieri opens a portfolio of Mozart's original scores. His eyes fall on the first pages of the *29th Symphony.* He is astounded to discover that they are not copies, there are no corrections of any kind. He exclaims: *"It was puzzling - then suddenly alarming. What was evident was that Mozart was simply transcribing music - completely finished in his head. And finished as most music is never finished..."* [73] This passage casts further light on Salieri's mischief. He hated Mozart with a passion perhaps only equalled by a woman who produces deformed or stillborn babies while her sister or neighbor gives birth to child after healthy child.

* * * * *

Aggressive onslaughts on the pregnant person and the child-to-be are commonplace, and include include neglect, assault and malicious rivalry. Indeed it is well known that expectant fathers often begin affairs during their wives' pregnancies and can become so engrossed in their own activities that they become oblivious to their partner's needs. [74] The competitive element is clearest in *couvade,* the custom and ritual by which the father-to-be takes over the dress, activities and physical symptoms of his pregnant wife. [75] Originally conceived in the mid 1800's to denote primitive tribal practices, couvade appears to be a general phenomenon. [76]

Based on a study of one hundred English fathers, Brian Jackson asserts that approximately one half went through couvade. In America he suggests the figure is even higher. [77] Jackson has described a cluster of couvade signals, the most prominent of which are a heightened interest in pets and physical fitness. For example, he observed one man who became obsessed with a newly purchased dog:

> *"He was continually kissing it on the nose, nursing it, holding it close and staring into its eyes. He spoke to it in baby talk, and kept telling it, ' You're such a baby."* [78]

Another joined a health club and was forever weighing himself and sipping carrot juice. He used to explain that he was keeping fit for the baby. On the other hand, several men related a variety of physical symptoms including abdominal pain, back pain, 'a feeling of fullness in my stomach', broken sleep patterns, strange cravings for food and drink and marked weight gain:

> *"I've put on three quarters of a stone since Sally got pregnant. I'm keeping up with her all right."* (79)

Cuddling canines has a distinctly malicious edge when it detracts from the varied needs of the pregnant woman and puts her and the baby at a disadvantage to a dog. The envious father resents both his wife's condition and the special care and attention she requires. To him the pregnancy is a narcissistic wound which arouses strong desires to steal the limelight and ruin her health and happiness. Simultaneously he may feel intensely jealous of the fetus for seeming to appropriate his rightful love and pleasures. As one father put it:

> *"It's not a bun in the oven she's got. We've got a bloody Christmas turkey."* (80)

This turkey was an unwelcome intruder who came between the man and his mate as well as the idea of a great greedy feast from which he had been and would continue to be excluded. Far from sharing in a joyous occasion, the predominance of envy and jealousy alienated him from his future child. It is not too farfetched to think that in using words like 'bloody Christmas turkey', he wanted to bludgeon the baby and eat it, a spiteful deed that incorporates the regressive wish to become the infant-inside-mother and regain all his 'lost' real or and imagined comforts. (81)

* * * * *

Childbirth

The alternative to being the baby is having the baby. Couvade demonstrates the extraordinary lengths to which many fathers may go to capture attention and foster phantasies of impregnation. But this holds true for other men as well, heterosexual and homosexual. Anal intercourse, fellatio, constipation, abdominal distention and ruminations about intestinal tumours have all preceded or accompanied strong desires for anal or umbilical births. [(82)]

Recently a scientist confided to me that he had wanted to conceive a child in his abdomen for years, long before his marriage. He remembered that as a youth he used to daydream about babies growing in his tummy and being born by Caesarean section. He had worked out all the details. Now he was getting worried because his once distant phantasies were becoming technically feasible. [(83)]

Test tube babies, cloning, gene splicing and robotics are kindred achievements which indicates that 'Mother Earth's' fearsome predictions about the race of males taking over female generative powers cannot be taken lightly. [(84)] As far back as 1818, Mary Shelley anticipated many of these same issues in *Frankenstein.* She depicted a scientist who was obsessed with making life. He exalted,

> *"After days and nights of incredible labour and fatigue, I succeeded in discovering the cause of generation and life; nay, more, I became myself capable of bestowing animation upon lifeless matter."* [(85)]

The protagonist, Dr. Victor Frankenstein, thought he had brought forth a blessing. In fact he had created a monster and revealed a dilemma which has haunted us ever since. The monster has to do with a creature starved of love but imbued with the destructive impulses of its creator. The dilemma has to do with the ethics of imitating or interfering with natural processes. Procedures to redress sterility, produce drugs or automate hazardous and dehumanizing work may be developed with the best of intentions but still unleash terrible dangers. Fears about them underlie the longstanding debate about the 'new science of conception' and several generations of monster and sci-fi films. [86].

Doctors have not only tried to replicate life, but the womb as well. A former teacher of mine used to refer to the incubators in his premature baby unit as, *"a womb with a view".* [87] He was a kind man who respected babies and their mothers. Indeed it would be unjust and incorrect to suggest that the scientific community has a malicious mentality. Whether a particular practice is harmful, or not, has to be judged within a multiplicity of contexts, social, historical, technological, psychological and so forth. Nowhere is this more true than in the drama of childbirth, an event burdened by pain and flanked by benevolence and sadism. Until the late Victorian era, childbirth was a leading cause of death in women and few efforts were spared, no matter how gruesome, to save the life of the mother. [88] Notable among these was the development of the use of forceps.

Forceps were invented by members of the Chamberlen family, a London dynasty of male midwives, in the late sixteenth century. They tried to keep the invention secret, but by the 1730's the news had leaked out and new improved models were being developed. [89] Forceps were especially useful in prolonged deliveries, when the infant got stuck in the pelvis. Prior to forceps the only recourse to losing the mother was to kill the child and pick it out of the womb piece by piece. [90] But, a forceps delivery, especially without anaesthesia, was a fearsome business. The vagina and uterus were frequently torn by incompetent or impatient attendants and the resultant mortality rate was high. As late as 1920 certain urban practitioners were known as 'forceps fiends' and their abuses led to restrictions on home deliveries. [91]

Antisepsis became a major area of obstetrical concern in 1847 when Semmelweis published his momentous discovery that the simple use of disinfectants markedly reduced maternal infections. Previously both doctors and midwives barely thought of washing their hands. They would poke around the vagina and cervix with hands covered in dirt and pus. Moreover, both home and hospital were breeding grounds for the most virulent organisms. Few women would deliver without a transient fever (called "weed" or "milk fever) and many died from massive infection (the dreaded "childbed fever"). (92) All too often a hospital confinement was akin to a death sentence. (93) Yet Semmelweis was generally ignored and antisepsis did not begin in earnest until three decades later when the Germans and French obstetricians adopted Lister's work with Carbolic acid (phenol). Subsequently a rigorous asepsis became the norm and septic deaths a rarity. (94)

In current practice women in labour suffer from overscrupulous cleanliness. They are scrubbed, shaved and purged, a routine which many find upsetting and degrading. Yet, it is only the first part of a ritual by which their condition becomes medicalized and responsibility for their body and its function is more or less taken out of their hands. (95) Peter Lomas points out that:

> *"Much that is done in the name of medical necessity has the consequence of preventing the mother from regarding herself as a mature human being, from participating actively and fully in the birth, from loving and caring for her baby, and from taking an uninhibited and triumphant joy in the occasion."* (96)

Lomas adds that the convention of segregating the mother and transferring the significance of the procedures away from her is very similar to couvade. But in this instance it is the doctor who takes over rather than the husband. The directly destructive components of this control are manifest in excessive surgery, notably in episiotomy and hysterectomy.

Episiotomy is the cutting, usually with a pair of scissors, of the tissue at the base of the vagina during the second stage of labour. Originally described in 1742, it has become a popular means of avoiding vaginal tears, facilitating forceps deliveries and protecting the fetus from a prolonged labour. But many midwives and doctors question its validity. [97] Serious tears of any kind are infrequent and the operation itself carries significant risk of pain, scaring and fistula formation between the vagina and anus. [98] According to a survey of 1,800 mothers done by the British National Childbirth Trust, *"In every situation we looked at, those with (natural) lacerations suffered less than those with an episiotomy."* [99]

Consultant obstetrician, Yehudi Gordon, has called the episiotomy, *"the commonest invasive procedure performed during the lifetime of a woman"*, and Derek Llewelyn Jones writing in *Fundamentals of Obstetrics and Gynaecology* declares:

> *"...(it is) one of the least considered and most painful operations performed on the human female.....far too many women leave hospital with the memory of perineal pain, which they aver was far worse than the pain of parturition."* [100]

Two hundred years after its inception the suitability of this procedure still requires substantiation. [101] Similar questions becloud the hysterectomy, the partial or total removal of the womb usually done later in a woman's life. Many practitioners also believe that this operation is performed far too frequently and with little consideration of the severe emotional sequelae. [102] The general medical attitude seems to be that women should *"be happy to have a potentially cancer-bearing organ removed."* [103]

* * * * *

The loss of control, pain and humiliation that accompanies antisepsis, and the cutting, scaring and scooping out that occur during forceps, episiotomy and other surgical procedures come ominously close to fulfilling women's worst fears, that their bodies will be invaded, robbed and destroyed. In large measure this accounts for the dread that precedes childbirth and the depression that follows it.

The classical psychoanalytic view is that women equate childbirth with castration because it provides the penultimate proof that they are not male. [104]. On the contrary childbirth is the climax of feminine biological achievement. If castration takes place, it results from the way that help becomes hurt during the hard work from conception to birth. I distinguish three major reasons for this transformation. The first is social and medical inertia. Traditions, no matter how damaging, die slowly. [105] The second has to do with the traumatization of the attendants in the face of suffering and death. Doctors, midwives and relatives will go to almost any length to prevent the loss of mother and child, and avoid their own horrific fear and guilt if they cannot to do so. The third factor is envy: of female creativity, happiness, active accomplishment and last, but not least, her suffering. [106] This leads me to conclude that procedures like episiotomy, which remain questionable, but are nevertheless, widely performed, are a highly structured defense against guilt as well as the manifestation of institutionalized envy. By this I mean that spiteful, begrudging, destructive wishes towards women are hidden within respected societal practices that allow sadism to be indulged with a minimum of personal responsibility. But there are times when the underlying contempt does emerge, as in the claims of Ian Donald, Professor of Midwifery at Glasgow: *"There is not much difference after all between a foetus in utero and a submarine at sea."* [107]

Deep rooted, non-medical, social and religious customs also express comparable antagonisms. Among many tribes and cultures women are treated like pariahs, instead of celebrated, after childbirth. Churching was widely practiced among Anglicans and Catholics until the twentieth century. It is a form of religious decontamination that gave a woman permission to re-enter society. But it also conveyed the view that a new mother is 'unclean' and a source of evil. [108] In Germany, for example, people used to believe that a new mother could contaminate a well, or cause a house to burn down, if she entered it before the churching ceremony had taken place. [109]

With noteworthy exceptions, women generally tend to accept the treatment meted out to them during pregnancy and childbirth in a detached, stoical, long suffering, almost masochistic manner. Given the extent of their physical and emotional vulnerability, this stance is hardly remarkable. It is a stratagem of self-sacrifice designed to protect themselves and their forthcoming child from external dangers and internal conflict. The latter may surface as a puerperal breakdown when dread of internal enviers, experienced as condemning, attacking mother and sister figures, becomes overwhelming, especially if it coincides with actual rejection or damage. (110) Then all the complicated propitiation gestures, the shaving, the enemas, the anaesthesia, the exhausted if not meek compliance with doctors who cut her body and nurses who remove her baby go for naught and the woman is left with her own momentary but terrible fragility within a world that looks upon creativity, whether in art, science or females, with ambivalent fascination. (111)

Childbirth, and the other major areas of female potency, indicate that the womb is more than a part of the body, a thing, a quality, an experience, or a person. The womb encompasses both the idea and actuality of a function, a product and universal reality.

Menstruation, fertility, pregnancy, childbirth and creativity are positive functions which contribute to the concept of the *good womb.*

War, ritual bleeding, sterility, couvade, and medical mania convey the opposite. They are negating, mutilating activities which signify the *destroying and destroyed womb.*

The products of the good womb include *rich blood, healthy babies, books, plays, sculptures, symphonies and life-enhancing innovations,* while the foul womb yields *bad blood, dead babies, deformities, monsters, roaches and robots.*

Both wombs, fair and foul, connote universal realities ranging from the *deepest depths to celestial abodes, from human consciousness to cosmic consciousness, from heaven to hell.* Each bears some responsibility for the generative powers generally attributed to the womb, the uroboros, the origin of all things, which is neither entirely female nor entirely male.

At a time, however, when umbilical pregnancies and intelligent robots are a distinct possibility, it is worth recalling that the human species derives from the body of women, not the rib of Adam, nor the head of Zeus. (112). As *Mother Earth* would be quick to point out, these myths contain the seeds of hubris, a distinct overstepping of bounds, to compensate for a feared inferior biology. (113)

In contrast, a five year old boy conveyed his acceptance and wondrous belief in the continuity of life. He hoped that his pregnant mother would give birth to a girl, and added:

> *"...then she will have babies, and her babies will have babies, and then it goes on forever".* (114)

Chapter 6

Penis Greed

Penis Greed is an insatiable desire for the male member and all the perks and privileges that seem to accompany it.

"I know it's not true, but I'm like a lot of men. Even when we know better, we feel deep down that ' the bigger your cock, the more of a man you are'." STEVE [1]

"When one has it, one has everything, one feels protected, nothing can touch you...one is what one is, and the others can only follow you and admire you.......it is absolute power." IDA [2]

"What have you been doing all summer?"
"Growing a penis! " BRENDA [3]

These preoccupations with the penis extend from the anatomical organ to far reaching concerns about strength, power, authority, virility, ambition, energy and enterprise, which account for Carl Jung's trenchant remark, *"the penis is only a phallic symbol".* [4]

The longing for male qualities, functions and status, *the phallus,* features in many cultures, but in this century Freud drew special attention to phallic wishes during the course of describing the development of female sexuality. He observed that at a certain stage in their lives the physical interests of children shift away from the mouth and anus to the genitals. Then the little girl discovers what she lacks and passionately desires the missing part:

> *"The discovery that she is castrated is a turning-point in a girl's growth......Her self-love is mortified by the comparison with the boy's far superior equipment."* [5]

> *"She makes her judgment and her decision in a flash. She has seen it and knows that she is without it and wants to have it."* [6]

Freud called the sudden shocking awareness of absent maleness and the wish to overcome it, *penis envy.* Related to the *castration complex* or the *masculine complex,* this term (and attendant assumptions) has achieved a prominent place in the psychological literature and popular parlance. [7] But I believe it is a misnomer, and as generally used, perpetuates several misconceptions.

The classical concept of *penis envy* has little to do with envy. On the contrary it conveys intense admiration, emulation and identification for all things masculine. It is a wish, first for a penis, then for a penis in intercourse, and finally for a penis substitute, such as, a baby. [8]

An admixture of resentful, raging, spiteful, spoiling, begrudging, belittling attitudes and actions towards men, maleness and male organs certainly does exist. This is appropriately called *penis envy* and can be expressed by the penis as well as towards it. I shall soon discuss this complex in considerable detail, but it was not an essential part of Freud's initial formulations.

The early analysts also believed that *penis envy,* or what I call, *penis greed,* was essentially a biologically determined feature of females which condemns them to spend much of their life trying to regain something they had been born without. Karl Abraham stated confidently that most women want to be men:

> *"...we come across this wish in all products of the unconscious, especially in dreams and neurotic symptoms. The extraordinary frequency of these observations suggests that the wish is one common to and occurring in all women."* (9)

Freud put the issue more succinctly, *"Anatomy is destiny."* (10) This epigram is based on one by Napoleon. He too spent much of his life trying to overcome an accident of birth. Potency and power are not issues limited to the female sex. Most boys and men are obsessed with being bigger, stronger and more powerful than others, even if they have to conquer the world. This is an expression of *the small penis complex* or *the Napoleon syndrome.* As with girls who may be struck with admiration and awe upon observing the male member, boys also describe feelings of bewilderment and wonder when comparing themselves to sibs, friends or parents. (11) A friend of mine still trembles with shock and surprise when he recalls his Father urinating. Physically he is tall and strong, but he longs to be 'macho' like his Dad. No matter how much work he does, or how many women he sleeps with, *"becoming a man is the continuing battle of my life."*

Small penis people take various positions. Some emphasize their smallness or inadequacies in order to take advantage of pity and put others to shame. Woody Allen does this in many of his films. Then greed is tempered by aggression. Allen follows the traditions of Yiddish literature where many a saying pokes fun at the man (or woman) who makes himself appear smaller, weaker, more inadequate than he really is:

"Mach sich not azoi Klein
-- du bist not azoi grois!"
(Don't make yourself so small
-- you're not that big!) (12)

In *Annie Hall*, Allen plays his typical role, the *shlemíl* on the make. (13) He decides to remake Annie (Diane Keaton) in his image and convinces her to see a therapist. On her return from the first session he asks her how it went:

"So, I told her about the family and about my feelings towards men.....then she mentioned about penis envy. Did you know about that?"

"Me? I'm one of the few males who suffers from that!" (14)

Allen exaggerates. He is one of many men who long to be big. His *'envy'* reveals a voracious appetite for phallic power. Children and adults of both sexes harbour kindred desires, not just for a penis, or phallus, but for a magical member, an idealized penis and for the person who possesses it.

Victorian women were noted for their lofty views of the men they married. In a book addressed to the women of England in 1842, Mrs. Sarah Ellis proclaimed:

It is essential to recognize..."the superiority of your husband simply as a man.......In the character of a noble, enlightened and truly good man, there is a power and a sublimity so nearly approaching what we believe to be the nature and capacity of angels, that...no language can describe the degree of admiration and respect which the contemplation of such a character must excite." (15)

Female fascination for the super man remains unabated. In 1982 the genre of romantic fiction alone saw worldwide sales of 250 million books. [16] The basic plot involves a young, inexperienced girl who meets, marries and tames a tough, sophisticated, successful (but often vulnerable) older man. The same theme reappears in popular magazines like *Playgirl* which aim to provide *"a smorgasbord of everything wonderfully male"*.

In addition to lots of muscular full frontal nudes, a typical issue features articles about rugged loners like playwright Sam Shepard who *"....exudes the unmistakable scent of sexual gunpowder"* or electrifying, unpredictable actors like Mel Gibson, *"a complex and divided man running at full speed."* [17] *Playgirl* permits its readership to see, feel, even taste virility. The latter comes conveniently packaged as multicoloured heart-shaped pills and elongated capsules ('Magnum', 'Triple Strength', 'Fast One') in ads for 'Continuous Action Stimulants'. [18]

Male phantasies focus on prowess, the penis which is two feet long, hard as steel, and can go all night. [19] Myths of superpotency leap from ancient legends (Hercules, Achilles, Sampson) to contemporary comics. The character of *Superman*, *"faster than a speeding bullet, more powerful than a locomotive,"* was created by two seventeen year old boys in 1933. [20] And *Clark Kent* is less than a leap from the macho heroes of Ernest Hemingway, Norman Mailer, Yukio Mishima, D. H. Lawrence, Henry Miller and Harold Robbins. [21] Their tales are cravings which ricochet through the dreams of untold readers, *"endlessly searching, sensing, expanding, probing, penetrating, throbbing, wilting and wanting more."* [22]

* * * * *

Why is there such a tendency to put the penis on a pedestal, to value and overvalue maleness? First, like the womb, the penis is the heir to the breast. Much of the passionate love and hate originally directed to Mother and her body becomes redirected to Father and his organ. As Segal points out:

> *"Klein's earlier view of penis envy as autonomous.......is supplanted by the more radical hypothesis that the primary origin of excessive penis envy must be sought in the infant's envy of the breast."* [23]

In their minds' eyes both boys and girls tend to transform the penis into a richer source of food, pleasure and stimulation. They imbue it with the power to satisfy all desires and turn to it with devastating voraciousness whenever they feel hungry and deprived, or are deprived such as during weaning, separation and illness.

I am not just describing a phantasy. In actuality, fathers and husbands are often considered superior providers. Women may prepare food, but men grow, trap or rear it, and gain the glory for culinary expertise. Traditionally the most famous cooks in Europe and other gastronomic centers have been men. From Taillevent to contemporaries Michele Guerard, Paul Bocuse, Robert Carrier and Kenneth Lo, male chefs have been able to command public attention and commensurable fees. [24]

The male product has also been likened to superior milk – a rich, condensed cream. High caste Hindus aver that a single drop of semen takes forty days and forty drops of blood to make, although a careful attention to diet speeds things up. There is a reservoir in the head with a capacity of just under seven ounces. A good store of quality semen/cream guarantees health and well being. [25]

It follows that many people prefer fellatio to any other genital activity. This practice gives undisguised expression to the ideal of the feeding phallus and subsumes the wish to suck, chew, bite, swallow and retain the penis or its products in the mouth, or other parts. [26]

'Colin' is a fifty year old businessman whose obsession, whose driving force, is *"big pricks"*. He is constantly on the go and has become a connoisseur of haunts and hideaways all over Europe where he seeks out men who possess the largest organs. He aims to see and suck on them. But he has another and even more compelling obsession, jewellery shops. He can spend hours searching for gems, the right gems, especially diamonds and rubies. As with big 'pricks', he becomes mesmerized by the sight of large jewels. In fact he will make any excuse to look at and fondle them. This led to his entering therapy. He had begun to spend so much time and money in these shops, that his family and business were in jeopardy. During the course of the treatment he had a frightening but vivid vision of jewels embedded in the walls of the consulting room:

> *"I could hardly believe it, they looked so real. They were everywhere, bigs ones, little ones, and even as I thought of them they grow brighter, more magnificent. But what surprised me the most was their shape, their cut. I couldn't get out of my mind that they looked like tits and then like pricks, tits and pricks over and over, all ending in sparkling points of light."* (27)

These gems were brilliant teats, nipples, thumbs, concentrations of desire. Colin transformed cravings for an engorged nipple into passions for a huge penis. In his mind they looked alike and were alike, a conjunction noted by the Dutch analyst, August Stärcke, who asserted in 1921 that children are dependent on a penis-like organ of their mother and often experience weaning as a castration. (28)

Interestingly, the penis and nipple do not only look alike, but share similar functions. They engorge when stimulated, yield life-giving fluids and link one person to another. A big penis, like a big nipple, means a big link. (29) This is especially important for men like Colin who feel uncertain about their own ability to retain deep personal connections. (30)

The intense desires of one twenty-five year old woman illustrates the primitive quality of some phallic linking. For her the penis represented an umbilical cord, and the male - female relationship was a form of umbilical attachment. She desperately desired to possess a penis, that is, be masculine in order to be able to plug into and attach herself to her mother (or vice versa). She saw sexual relations as nourishment, and stated: *"My concept of my genitals is a means to attach."* [31]

* * * * *

The penis, indeed, epitomizes attachment. Paradoxically, it also represents detachment, that is, the possibility of separating from the breast in order to establish a distinct sense of self. At a time when children want to differentiate themselves from their mother, and gain a greater degree of control over their lives, boys possess positive proof that their body is different. Therefore it is easier for them to conclude that they are different. Unlike girls whose external genitals develop at a later date, they have an organ to see, feel, exhibit and play with. [32] The advantage is self-assertion. The disadvantage is ever present fears of being taken over and submerged in and into women, nature, *the eternal female.* [33]

> *"......the whole process of becoming masculine is at risk in the little boy from the day of birth on; his still-to-be-created masculinity is endangered by the primary, profound, primeval oneness with mother, a blissful experience that serves, buried but active in the core of one's identity, as a focus that, throughout life, can attract one to regress back to that primitive oneness."* [34]

This is one aspect of several dilemmas which boys and girls both share: how to recognize their body type (biological identity), while gaining a sense of their sexuality (gender identity) and maintaining themselves as separate human beings (personal identity). The struggle begins at birth and has as much to do with parental attitudes as the child's own biological endowment and psychological development. [35] The penis that little girls miss is the freedom from maternal domination and the ability to control their own bodies and lives. Not surprisingly they pine for a magic wand, an alternative organ which feeds yet supersedes dependency. Most want a penis not to be a man, but to be a woman. [36]

In general girls find gender identity an easier task than boys because they and their mothers share the same kind of body. So they can keep the body image which follows close emotional ties. Boys face a more complicated endeavour in that they have to develop a new body and self image, that is, dis-identify with their mothers, not feel like a woman, and at the same time retain their basic maternal connections. [37]

The wish for exaggerated male powers, especially before boys have established a separate awareness of themselves as individuals, is an attempt to solve the conflict between remaining tied to mother (and thereby being like her) and growing up (identifying with dad). The lack of adequate differentiation from mother and mothering can be a great danger both to sexual identity and personal integrity. The subsequent surfeit of femininity contributes to castration fears, which also may be perpetuated by a clinging and self-seeking mother in conjunction with a weak, inaccessible father. Of course, the other factor is a father who is so hostile to his son that he doesn't permit an alliance to develop, or allow him to work through filial rivalries. So the boy may feel forced for his own survival to remain in a stifling relationship with his mother. In either case, the outcome may be a person who demonstrates sudden outbursts of desperate activity (a grasping at maleness) punctuated by long periods of passive withdrawal.

Female fears are not dissimilar, but revolve around *wounded womanhood* which can encompass everything from damaged insides to damaged pride. When the emotional pain is too great the girl may repudiate her sex and replace it with a masculine veneer. Then the wish is not to have the phallus, but to be the phallus. [38]

* * * * *

When the issues of attachment and detachment, or nourishment and autonomy, become less urgent, people turn to the penis for a third, compelling reason: to express, to complement their sensual pleasures and procreative powers. In Freudian theory this begins around the ages of three to five, with the *phallic* or *primary masculine phase*, during which children become very interested in their genital, really phallic functions. (Freud postulated that true awareness of female genitals functions did not occur until adolescence.) In fact many observers note that genital wishes, if not activities, occur from early infancy.

During childhood boys take pride in their penis. They fondle and play with it incessantly, while also showing it off and competing with playmates about who can urinate higher and farther. This is the forerunner of later rivalries about who can hit the most home runs, kick the longest goals, throw the biggest spear or make the most money.

Freud assumed that girls had similar wishes, but were frustrated because they were born without a male member. The only recourse they have is to transform their wish for a penis into love for their father and a wish for a baby.

These views have always attracted considerable controversy. Ernest Jones, one of the 'founding fathers' of psycho-analysis, strongly disagreed with Freud and considered his model excessively *phallo-centric.* [(39)]. He agreed with Melanie Klein that a girl wants to take a penis into her body in order to make a child, rather than have a child to replace a missing penis. [(40)]

For most people the male member is a means to an end, rather than an end in itself. [(41)] It enhances survival (attachment), psychological achievement (detachment) and biological achievement (procreation and pleasure). Yet, there is one area where the phallus may be an end in itself, the social sphere, where possession of male parts and qualities can ensure special privilege and power. [(42)] Although now under challenge in Western countries, 'mankind' has lived in male dominated families, tribes, cultures and societies for several millennia, and continues to do so. Within these social contexts the phallus symbolizes superiority and reflects patriarchal concerns. In part the value of maleness lies in these multiple reflections seemingly independent of time and place. [(43)]

By the 1980's advertisements for large corporations like Crest Hotels International began to announce that women, who look and work like men, can qualify for the prerogatives that men have long learned to take for granted. A particular two page spread offered a profile of a businesswoman wearing short hair, a leather watchband and little makeup. She could have been unisex if a simple string of pearls were removed from her dark, turtleneck sweater. In big bold type, the left hand page proclaimed:

"I've finally found a hotel that treats me like a man." [44]

The text explained that this patron would be treated with respect and dignity. In the restaurant she would not be fobbed off with 'a table behind a pillar or near the door of the kitchen'. In the bar she would not have to take a briefcase 'to prove all I want is a drink'. Crest promised to maintain a 'friendly and businesslike attitude' and that professional persons will know what is meant.

What is implied is that an hotel chain should serve, as do other institutions, the phallic cravings of the public. The Crest ads illustrate and perpetuate a basic aspect of *penis greed:* an insatiable *desire for* the experiences, objects, products, qualities, functions, person and settings that contribute to erotic satisfaction and self-inflation. [45]

* * * * *

The complement of *penis greed* is the *greedy penis,* an organ that thrusts its way into things in order to control, possess, propagate, dominate, devour or destroy them. This is not desire for, but *desire by* the phallus: active power, raw ambition, hungers honed by assertion and strength. The *greedy penis* is both defensive and aggressive, a shield and a sword.

The former President of the United States, Lyndon Johnson, used to brag about his ability to bully or buy fellow politicians. In referring to colleagues he would openly exclaim, *"I have his pecker in my pocket."* [46] Johnson was not just referring to his voracious appetite for power, nor providing examples of phallic cannibalism. The 'peckers' were hostages, tangible protection against feared rivalries and insecurities. [47]

Compulsive promiscuity, combat, work, sport or body building may all serve a similar function: to assuage persecutory fears (others are out to get you), depressive dread (you will hurt loved ones), covert femininity, homosexuality, organ inferiority, masturbatory conflict, narcissistic fragility, shame, guilt and humiliation.

Often the penis, or more specifically the phallus, is not strong enough to sustain the weight of ambitions, or to avoid inner doubts. Then tragedy may strike as happened with Mark Thompson, a nineteen year old snooker prodigy who had won three major tournaments and had found himself a financial sponsor. He killed himself.

> *"Mark's irrational fear was that his cue would be damaged and, like a broken spell, the magic of his playing would be lost... He was married to his cue."* [48]

I think Mark also feared becoming too potent. He had already vanquished his father and friends. Castration anxiety (a damaged cue) was magnified by possession anxiety (a cue that damaged). [49] In this instance Mark was not strong enough to carry the guilt that accompanied his victories. Consequently, the phallus that men and women seek is not an ordinary organ, or skill, but an all powerful weapon that can grant every wish, and destroy every danger, including guilt.

Anais Nin recalls the first time a boy hurt her at school. In her book, *Cities of the Interior,* she speaks through Lilian, a girl who aspired to invincibility by assuming the mantle of her brother. :

> *"I don't remember what he did. But I wept. And he laughed at me. Do you know what I did? I went home and dressed in my brother's suit. I tried to feel as the boy felt. Naturally as I put*

on the suit I felt I was putting on a costume of strength......I thought that to be a boy meant one did not suffer." [50]

Later Lilian decides to be a warrior, a Joan of Arc, riding and fighting side by side with men. She demands the sword, for her, not just the end to pain, but the means to be herself. In this Nin speaks for the many members of her sex for whom maleness, and the glorification of maleness, gives them the freedom to assert feelings, desires, indeed, their very existence.

Nin's views coincide with a singer I know who is very proud of her deep, booming Wagnerian voice. Her songs are spears hurtling through the farthest recesses of a room, or a mind. She aims to be heard and be feted around the world:

"As a child I liked to watch my father pee. I was very envious of him. But, I didn't want to have a big penis like he had, no, not that, I was envious of the loud noise, the big splash he made when he peed into the bowl. Then I could only make a little stream. But when I grew up, I knew things would be different. I would make a big splash too." [51]

For other women profanities are their forbidden parts, open angers flashing against a closed chorus of maternal furies:*"Fuck you!", "Screw you!", "Get stuffed!"* [52] Similarly, the poet Sylvia Plath used words as weapons to slash through extremes of rage and remorse. Her writings let live a torrent of *"desires to mingle with road crews, sailors and soldiers, barroom regulars....to sleep in open fields, to travel west, to walk freely at night."* They were her exploits, her wild tales, her 'perfect male counterparts'. Meanwhile, Plath was a warrior, a literary Amazon, riding the libraries and collegiate fetes, who, in mid-life, died by her own hand, her words having filtered an excess of love and hatred of phallic forces. [53]

* * * * *

The Greeks believed the Amazons were a race of women who loved to fight and perform the deeds of men. They lived during the bronze age, about 3000 to 1000 B.C.E., some say around the black sea in modern Turkey (Scythia), while others connect them with Crete (the Minoans) and various Aegean Islands. [54]

Their name derives from the Greek, *amazos,* without a breast. Hippocrates described the copper instrument used by Scythian Amazons to burn off the right breast of baby girls so that it wouldn't stand out when the girls matured and be in the way of throwing the javelin or shooting arrows.

At home they spent most of the year hunting, riding, breeding horses and training for war. They favoured the cavalry for they were excellent equestrians. The less physically able were farmers. Otherwise they loathed domestic work which they left to menfolk whom they humiliated and enslaved except in the spring when they slept with neighboring tribesmen in order to get pregnant. In general the men had no political or civic freedoms and were not allowed to carry arms lest they *"become presumptuous and rise up against women"*. [55]

This view of the ancient Amazons has to be treated with care as it originates from the Dorian Greeks, the progenitors of Western patriarchal civilization. The Dorians were the mortal enemies of their matriarchal, gynecocratic predecessors, possibly identifiable with their Hittite, Minoan and Mycenaean rivals. Nevertheless sufficient evidence exists to sustain the picture of powerful female predominant tribes who ruled large areas of the near east. These bronze age peoples are a model for women who aggrandize the perks and possessions of men while scorning maleness and subordinating male companions. [56] They sought land, horses, cattle, glory, political power, military prowess, and physical fitness. [57] Modern Amazons are remarkably similar in their likes and dislikes. Some are 'deadlier than males' (female terrorists); others 'pump iron' (body builders) and many reject men (militant lesbians). [58]

* * * * *

The damage done by *penis greed* is the consequence of tearing, gnawing, invading desires, initially for the breast, and then for mother, her body, the goods inside her. And, as I mentioned before, the counterpart of *penis greed* is the *greedy penis*. Both are desires held by members of either sex. While initially directed to the mother, they soon extend to father, his body and parts. The penis embodies all of these aims as well as the means to obtain them. The first penis is a tooth. Only later does it become a penis. Many children and adults never reach this developmental point. Their phallic savagery remains rooted in oral sadism. [(59)]

The *Phallus Dentatus*, or the penis with teeth, is a dreaded object, often equated with piranhas, sharks, snakes, alligators and rats. All of these animals denote rapacious aggression and are synonymous with 'tooth and claw' rivalries. Lyndon Johnson, for example, believed he had to maintain a macho facade because he reigned in a city, Washington, *"with enemies everywhere, with sharks swimming out there waiting for any sign of weakness."* [(60)]

The Bible yields an early record of the *Phallus Dentatus* used as a willful weapon by a subject people:

> *"The Lord said to Moses and Aaron,*
>
> *"When Pharaoh speaks to you and says, 'Produce your marvel', you shall say to Aaron, 'Take your rod and cast it down before Pharaoh,' It shall turn into a serpent."*
>
> *So Moses and Aaron came before Pharaoh and did just as the Lord had commanded: Aaron cast down his rod in the presence of Pharaoh and his courtiers, and it turned into a serpent.*
>
> *Then Pharaoh, for his part, summoned the wise men and sorcerers; and the Egyptian magicians, in turn, did the same with their spells:*
>
> *Each cast down his rod, and they turned into serpents. But Aaron's rod swallowed their rods."* [(61)]

Aboriginal women still use a magical tooth phallus either to make black magic or conjure forth love. The Australian Luritja cut their pubic hair and braid it into a long string to which they attach the teeth of a kangaroo rat. Then they smear it with blood drawn from their vagina. They believe the string can penetrate the earth, then the sky, and finally the heart of their victim. When evil is intended it becomes a snake eating the vital parts. For love they use a sharpened 'pointing bone'. (62)

Aboriginals put the bite on their victims for vengeance as well as frustrated desire. The same can happen in more civilized places, like a London suburb. In the late 1970's the newspapers covered the antics of a middle aged builder who put twenty rats into the house of a girlfriend and cut up her cat. He claimed he still loved her, but was obsessed with revenge because she had jilted him.

The rats nested in her oven and settee, crawled through the curtains, chewed through electric wires, left droppings all over and multiplied exceedingly. These rodents ('furry penes with teeth') were more than extensions of phallic greed. They were the vengeful expression of his envy and jealousy, phallic creatures that despoiled her insides and threatened her loved ones. He aimed to cut her connections and blow her circuits. If he couldn't have her, no one would, nor would she ever enjoy peace and quiet again. (63)

Phallic passions rarely convey pure lust or greed. More commonly they involve spite and possessive control. In this instance a lover felt rattled, and resorted to rats to get back at the woman he blamed for his misfortune. Others blame the phallus itself for their sense of unjust deprivation and wounded pride. Freud observed that girls get furious for not having or being given a phallus and blame their mothers. (64) Karl Abraham elaborated that girls not only feel disadvantaged, but they believe that they have been robbed and seek revenge on whomever was responsible, the depriving mother and the privileged father. In response:

"...two reactions occur which are closely associated with each other: a hostile feeling against the other person associated with the impulse to deprive him (or her) of what he possesses." (65)

* * * * *

Penis envy is the vengeful union of kindred impulses – spiteful hostility and begrudging deprivation. It may or may not coincide with the wish to be male. Abraham distinguished between two kinds of reactions to the awareness of the phallus, *wish fulfillment* and *revenge*. The wish fulfillment type of person is primarily concerned with possession. (*"I am the fortunate possessor of a penis and exercise the male function."*) The revenge type is overwhelmed with malice. (*"I want to cut up your parts and throw them to the dogs."*) (66) The former has to do with *penis greed*, the latter with *penis envy*.

When the wish coincides with the hatred, it may be more appropriate to speak of *penis grenvy*, that is, the combination of greed and envy, 'thraldom and enmity', about phallic functions. This is a frequent state because greed and envy remain intimately associated and are usually expressed concurrently. (67) Thus, ostentatious maleness, as in certain 'fortunate possessors', not only reflects greedy aggrandizement, but murderous attacks on parental activities and pride. (*"If I have it, then you can't!" I'm the biggest, you're a nothing!"*)

The question still arises, why is there such a degree of enmity, little girls towards their mothers, the builder to his girlfriend, over the phallus, or the lack of it? The answer takes us back to basic issues of dependency and assertion. The child who hates her mother for not being given a penis is also a child who hates her mother for not being given the breast, that is, a source of absolute satisfaction. (68) Obviously a penis which takes the place of the breast is something extraordinarily valuable in and of itself, and subject to all the desires and hatreds originally directed to the breast. In the mind of the child the phallus exists within the mother, and without, in the shape of father, his parts, or those of kindred relatives and friends – male cornucopias, all providing continuous comforts.

Such intense desires and hatreds do not only assail girls. They are just as prevalent among boys, who, after all, suffer similar conflicts. *Penis envy* is not sex restricted. Small penis problems, for example, demonstrate that far into later life men can remain preoccupied with feeding frustrations transferred from their mothers and wives onto their own organ. [69] Alternatively, a phallic breast may inspire awe and terror. One person recalled that he had gradually reconciled himself to the fact that other boys and men had larger organs and could pee farther and higher. But even as an adult he remained tormented by the memory of a wet nurse who had inadvertently sprayed his face with a huge spurt of milk from her nipple. From that point on he felt that women had a powerful advantage over him. [70]

But the ability to make a big splash is not necessarily the advantage that women want. Like men, they seek access to their mothers' love and the secrets of that love as contained in the original treasure trove, her body. The penis is envied not only for taking the place of the breast, but for giving access to it. The organ is an alleged commanding key to realizing all embracing desires for melting, effortless, warmth feelings, an prebirth state of bliss. As Sandor Ferenczi pointed out, the sex act itself *"......is the finest form of transitory regression......the expression of the striving to return to the mother's womb."* [71]

Otto Rank proposed that the most painful wound is the trauma of birth and that the rest of one's life is taken up with rediscovering, if not replacing, this lost Garden of Eden. [72] In a very real sense every step forward from weaning to walking to adult autonomy evokes the trauma of birth and the wish to redress the pain of separation. The phallus, by which I mean the penis and attendant maleness, embodies this wish and the means to achieve it. [73] Perhaps that is why devotees have worshipped it as God, or have tried to be the God they worship as in Hindu Tantric rites where the goal is to remain in perpetual and ecstatic intercourse with oneself. [74]

The very importance of the phallus means that the absence of it, even a relative absence, is an intolerable affront. The child feels bereft of care, the adult of love. Both want to return to a special place that forever excludes them. This dilemma is especially acute during early childhood (*the phallic phase*) and adolescence when the demands for self-assertion conflict with needs for self-assurance, and when children fear they lack the organs, capacities and privileges necessary to retain the past or attain the future.

The absent phallus arouses anguished rage directed towards:

1) its presence in others;

2) its possession by others;

3) others who want it; and

4) itself for being absent.

Thus, a boy consumed by *penis envy* might hate his father's (idealized) penis, his father for possessing such a penis and maleness, other men for the same reason, his mother for having access to this maleness as well as for her own authority, women in general (for being the object of his or others desires) and his own phallus (for its inadequacies). Similarly, a girl might be tormented by her mother's prowess and happiness (at possessing her father), her father (for existing), his organ (always idealized), other men (for the same reason), other women (for their desires) and herself for only possessing a clitoris (for organ inferiority). [75]

* * * * *

The complement of *penis envy* is the *envious penis,* all the traits and functions of maleness which have been denigrated but incorporated and turned against the world. This is not hatred of, but hatred by a malicious phallus. Like the *greedy penis*, its aims are defensive and aggressive, to avoid torment, doubt, deprivation and wreak revenge.

The male rapist embodies the *envious penis*. He deploys his organ like an evil eye, to pry and invade, to inflict fear and instill pain. The 'Beast of Belgravia' was only sixteen when he terrorized women throughout a prosperous part of London. When arrested he claimed to have committed the rapes because he was "*jealous*" (i.e. envious) of the women's wealth and boasted:

> *"They have everything and I have nothing. They are not so good now they have been raped by a black boy!"* (76)

The degree of horror and disgust that rape engenders confirms a crime far worse than theft. Rape is a manic attack, an extension of the most destructive intentions to dirty and dominate the body of another. As the young man stated, he wanted to do more than steal, he wanted to blacken his victims, destroy their goodness, make them feel hopeless and helpless. The same holds true for the builder. Each rat was a rape which defiled his girlfriend and triumphed over her pleasures and prospects.

The female hysteric is the counterpart of the male rapist, a woman who takes over the phallus and disruptively thrusts herself into the lives of others. She's the reality described in the *Malleus*, *"a desirable calamity, a domestic danger"* whose impassioned eyes provoke desires, but soon give 'short thrift' and 'cut you down to size'. (77)

This is an apt description of the patient whose shrieks assaulted and intransigence confounded me. She made me the breast that couldn't feed, the womb that couldn't conceive and 'the prick' that couldn't penetrate. With a fixed stare that looked daggers and radiated resentment, she liked to declaim:

> *"I'm so powerful, I can go anywhere, do anything, no-one can handle me......I think of being a rapist, forcing myself into every mind.....I want to expand and take over space....take over time.....take over people."* (78)

So many sessions were rapes, of me, by her. She allowed me no voice or even thoughts, no way to touch her, nor hope to stop her. She was a woman bewitched by phallic forces who yearned to become the instrument for my destruction. With screams, yells and shit in the post she threatened to blow me up and cut me down. She was a self trying to embody teeth, turds and knives.

On the deepest level I was the hated phallus which had access to mothers and the hated mother who was impenetrable to her. During an insightful moment she casually remarked that the reason she got angry was that "*men can enter women, but women can't*". She wanted to get inside people like men, otherwise no one would get inside her. Anyway, she recalled, no-one could get through to her mom, she was unavailable, always putting on powder. "*My mom was a beautiful brick wall.*"

This conflict with her mother was never resolved, maybe mitigated. The active hate conveyed her hurt and also preempted feared critical condemnations. She rarely acknowledged wrongdoing, but tended to treat me like the law which added another dimension to her rage. [79] Otherwise many meetings were punctuated by withdrawal and derision. She didn't feel anything and I couldn't help her. Men were 'wankers', I was stupid, and there were lots of therapists who could do a much better job.

The unfeeling attitude reflected a state of emotional frigidity and sexual uncertainty. She aspired to keep me a weak and impotent. Then I couldn't challenge her masculine fronts or feminine daydreams.[80] Infidelity was a stick to batter my ego, while promiscuity a promise of insatiable appetites replayed by a female 'Don Juan'. [81] The dragon of jealousy lurked along with envy. She hated men who got through to Moms, but she feared Mom for her wanting a man. My weakness was proof that I wasn't worth having, and vindication that she, like her mom, was invincible.

* * * * *

The female hysteric takes oral issues onto a sexual battlefield. In addition gender and personal conflicts, often in conjunction with social oppression and economic upheaval, have all proved capable of catalyzing endless rounds of bloodletting. The Amazons erupted with the double, sometimes single battle axe (*pelekus and sagaris*), the bow and arrow, sword, lance, javelin and spears with 'broad iron heads'. Yet their aggression did not necessarily betoken envy. It encompassed the political and religious struggles and violence typical of their age. (82) And, it reflected the bitter wrath of their enemies. Nevertheless, their unremitting hostility: the malign extent of their cruelty, the pervasive mutilation of male children, and systematic denigration of menfolk regardless of circumstances went beyond the bounds of reactive revenge. It exudes guilt ridden fears (it is likely that many loved the men they made love to, but mistreated), and inherent hatreds.

The Greeks, who enshrined their Amazonian rivals among the Furies, used a multitude of epithets to describe their endowments:

> *"man-murdering; man-hating; flesh-devouring; living without men; striving against men; war-lustful; slayer of men; man-subduing; dauntless, fearless; man-destroying; fighting with men; man-slaying; murderous; hurtful to men; and bringing pain to men."* (83)

The Amazons were also devotees of Cybele, the great fecund mother goddess, whose murderous orgiastic rites continued long after the female warrior tribes had formally been defeated. (84) During Roman times the Galloi (priests of Cybele) used to parade through the capital wearing strange clothes and chanting to the music of cymbals, tambourines, flutes and horns, very much as the disciples of Hare Krishna do today. (85)

The Cybele demanded absolute obedience. On 24 March of the year, *dies sanguinis* (the day of blood), all the novitiates would whirl dervishlike and ritually slash themselves before the temple. Then when the religious frenzy was at its peak, they would fling off their clothes and cut off their privates with a consecrated stone knife. (86)

> *".......the flood of orgiastic emotion even spread to the onlookers and they, too, castrated themselves. With their genitals in their hands, the worshippers ran through the streets and threw them into some house, from which they then received women's clothing, according to custom."* [87]

Once the liturgy was over, the worshippers left their genitals and male clothes in the bridal chamber of the Cybele. A ceremonial death presaged a symbolic rebirth. [88] After being anointed, the new priests would dress and be addressed solely as women. Many became mendicants pervading the countryside with ecstatic dancing, scourgings and millennial prophecies. [89]

Such Cybelen practices continued to break out in Roman times and afterwards. A castrated Phrygian, converted to Christianity, founded the sect of Montanism whose devotions included an ecstatic readiness for martyrdom. And, as late as the eighteenth century, the Russian sect of Scoptzes introduced ceremonial castration in their liturgy. [90]

These Cybelen rites reflect perverse tendencies in both men and women including inordinate desire and extreme fear of the opposite sex. [91] The hostilities that lay behind these tendencies are still prevalent. Bruno Bettelheim recalls an incident near the Orthogenic Institute in Chicago. A teenage girl was walking with her counsellor and a friend in a public park one day when she saw a man urinating. He turned and exposed himself to her, whereupon she gleefully exclaimed, *"He'll cut off his penis and throw it at us."* [92]

* * * * *

Ritual mutilation in order to placate terrifying female forces has an ancient tradition. Many initiation rites conclude with the sacrificial offering of blood, teeth and foreskins to mother figures. There exists considerable evidence that male and female circumcision serves the same function. Among various peoples the mother may swallow the foreskin or proudly hang it around her neck. Alternatively, it may be buried in the ground (mother earth) as a sign of birth and rebirth. Certainly circumcision is often instigated if not actually performed by women. (93)

Aggressive reactions to female attacks can also be traced to antiquity. The *Bible* forbids a woman to help her husband in a fight if this leads her to grab the opponent by the testicles. Should she do so,"*then you shall cut off her hand*". (94) The *Assyrians Laws* were equally severe in this matter:

> *"If a woman has crushed a man's testicle in an affray, one of her fingers shall be cut off; and if although a physician has bound it up, the second testicle is affected with it and becomes inflamed or if she has crushed the second testicle in the affray, both of her (breasts or nipples) shall be torn off."* (95)

Presumably the *Book of Deuteronomy* and the *Assyrian Laws* would not have taken the trouble to proscribe such assaults unless they were a common occurrence. The phallus itself came to symbolize the 'Rod of Law' and authority of the state. By extrapolation in patriarchal societies, any attack on the phallus or male genitals could be and was taken to be equivalent to an attack on the state itself.

The Romans used replicas as power charms, the *fascina,* to ward off and counterattack evil influences, especially from the opposite sex. Later a horn, a finger or even a gesture served the same purpose, as I discussed in chapter 2, on the evil eye. The law ordained subordination of women is simply an extension of these practices.

Male brutality is not only a response to physical injury and psychic insults. It encompasses the whole range of vengeful rage towards women for possessing masculine in addition to feminine prowess. According to Kleinian psychology the phallic woman is the *combined parent*; 'the breast with knives, a body with guns'; the mother who spares no rod while spoiling herself; the wife who wields the sword to dominate her mate; and in general, any woman who seems to usurp strength, power and privilege. These images refer to the child's idea of the mother with father's penis inside her or attached to her. These combined female/male figures are terrifyingly dangerous, and, in various guises, provide the gist of many horror movies.

Queen Christina of Sweden (1626-89) has been called 'the first great phallic woman in modern history'. (96) Her father, Gustavus II Adolphus, wanted a son and she was brought up to become a proficient male. Indeed, she used to refer to herself as a 'Nordic Amazon'. Later a capable coquette, she remained extremely competitive with men and her main relationship with them was rivalry or ownership. This included the French philosopher and mathematician, René Descartes.

The Queen was obsessed with the fact that a master of logic and rationality existed outside her grasp. Eventually, like a spider to a fly, she sent an admiral and ship to get him. Descartes must have been flattered for he returned to the Swedish Court in the dead of winter to commence duties as court scholar and personal savant. Unfortunately he was a frail man who was soon overwhelmed by incessant demands like early morning discourses and late night dinners. Less than five months after his arrival, he caught a cold and died. Her triumph was complete. She had physically, if not intellectually outlasted him, while he was buried in a plot for unbaptized children. (97)

Christina carried on with religious and political intrigues. Too often the results were devastating and her ambitions were thwarted. She was trapped by incompatible body, gender, personal and social claims. The denial of femaleness and the conquest of maleness were basic attempts to resolve these conflicts. (98)

The seduction of Descartes echoes the demise of the Assyrian general in Hebbel's drama about Judith, 'the virgin widow.' (99) Her first husband was 'paralyzed on the bridal night by a mysterious anxiety' and never touched her. She remains a maiden until the day that Holofernes lays siege to her city. Judith decides to save the citizens by using her beauty ('Like belladonna, it brings madness and death') to arouse his desires. He responds and deflowers her, whereupon she rages and cuts off his head. (100)

Freud's view was that the beheading represented castration and that patriotism concealed a woman's revenge for losing her virginity. He related the story to the dream of a young woman who hated her husband for entering her body. She wanted to tear off his penis and keep it for herself.

"Behind this envy for the penis, there comes to light the woman's hostile bitterness against the man, which never completely disappears in the relations between the sexes, and which is clearly indicated in the strivings and in the literary productions of 'emancipated' women." [101]

This person, like Judith or Christina was not threatened by loss of virginity, but loss of identity, and the besieged city was not the body, but the soul. For most women the initial intercourse is a welcome event which confirms their creative potential and status as adults. Similarly, childbirth is a major achievement. Yet, the British psychoanalyst, Peter Lomas, has described the conflicts evoked in one woman who suffers a puerperal psychosis:

"....it is clear that a woman who has a great envy of men and to whom the baby that grows within her symbolizes the penis she has longed for, will feel childbirth as a castration and a loss." [102]

* * * * *

A state of begrudging hostility towards men essentially disguises but also reflects underlying conflicts about feminine functions and a confused sense of self. All this originates in profound hatred and contempt towards the mother exacerbated by painful relations with father or other males. [103] These issues were especially clear with Christina who suffered a rejecting, probably murderous mother and an adoring, but oppressive father. [104] The ensuing difficulty is not just that Christina, or other women with comparable upbringings, become male-wishing, or male-hating, but that the interplay of their internal and external conflicts prevents them from becoming male-sustaining, that is, capable of sustaining a mutually satisfactory relationship with men or effective male 'strivings'. The latter encompasses a wide range of activities that may be culturally determined or self defined as 'masculine'. Many women excel in politics, business, warfare, sports, scholarship or kindred areas. These achievements are not necessarily based on the active hatred of men nor depreciation of femininity. But the woman with the phallus soon arouses the envious eye of other women who cannot use or appreciate their own assets. Hence *penis envy* is a frequent feature of hostile relationships among women.

Equally intense antagonisms predominate in men who may be threatened by female revenge, but even more by female accomplishments. Hell hath no fury like a man who feels 'hard done' by a female competitor. As far as he is concerned, 'it's unfair' that women possess the phallus ('business acumen') as well as the breast and womb ('female charms'). 'Unfairness' conceals gnawing anguish and shattered self-esteem, hugely magnified in societies where men are expected, or themselves expect, to 'work, play and fight hard' while their wives or womenfolk keep to the kitchen.

In relations with women, male *penis envy* or *jealousy* (when 'the girl with a gun' is seen as a dangerous interloper for the attention of other men or women) tends to surface as nagging resentment, something to which a successful politician like the British Prime Minister, Margaret Thatcher ('The Iron Maiden') is continually subject. Thus, her former defense minister publicly commented:

> *"I don't think that the way in which she conducts business would have been tolerated sometimes had she been a man because she uses her feminine charms......She doesn't argue her position through logically and intellectually in the way that intelligent men would do."* [105]

Geraldine Ferraro had to endure more vicious attacks during the United States Presidential election in 1984. Carping led to character assassination and then to backstabbing onslaughts on her family and finances. The many attempts to ruin her reputation, and thereafter her life, followed envious tensions provoked by her strength, wealth, position and thrusting ambition. (106)

Sports stars, business executives and, in general, working women accrue resentment and actual abuse for the same reason. (107) Ultimately this encourages primitive attacks on women, rape and murder, not for their being female, but for their being male. The African Nandi peoples take this attitude to literal extremes. They resent women possessing a penis like organ (the clitoris) in addition to breasts and womb and practice clitoridectomy. One village chief explained:

> *"We are Nandi. We don't want such a hanging down thing in our women." (108)*

Men hate authority, fame, status, strength and 'hanging down things' in women, but especially in other men. Since success is an erection and 'power is the ultimate aphrodisiac', the sight of either arouses malicious comparison and a terrible awareness of failure. (109) This explains the pain excited by men like the Kennedys and reactions like prideful inflation and envious deflation. (110) With men the *envious penis* is a weapons system that can *"shoot down whatever's up, and blow up whatever's down".* (111)

Hitler's weapons included the extended salute which exemplified both the *envious and jealous penis*. This gesture aimed to humiliate the opposition and to prove that his prowess was more powerful than anyone else's. Once it was noted that Hitler invited a young woman to his room. He stuck out his arm in a Nazi salute and boomed:

> *"I can hold my arm like that for two solid hours. I never feel tired......my arm is like granite – rigid and unbending, but,*

Goring can't stand it. He has to drop his arm after half an hour of this salute. He's flabby, but I am hard. [112]

These rivalries are not unrelated to Teutonic attentions to mighty swords and gigantic guns or *"the cataclysmic ecstasy of violence".* [113] Such passions preoccupied a student whom I helped. One day he reported a disturbing dream, that he was having anal intercourse with a stranger. After the man had entered him, his own anus turned to glass which shattered and cut the other's penis to shreds. His thoughts led to gay magazines and then to a play about Mary Barnes, a woman whom I had helped. [114] I replied that I was the stranger and the dream had to do with his *penis greed and envy and jealousy.* He craved my knowledge, the sharp edge of intellect which would make him invincible like Siegfried or Woton. Yet as soon as he heard me, he felt like an asshole and proceeded to soil my ideas and cut them to shreds. He had a glass ass because his feelings were fragile. His envy turned love to hate which shattered under pressure of hunger and rage. Then he was terrified I would return the rancor.

The man calmed and brought up Plato. Plato desired young boys. He was a young boy vis-à-vis me. I shook my head and said he was the Plato who wanted to screw me because he felt superior and wanted to take over my ties to other therapists and sources of knowledge. He calmed, but again blew up, screaming that the room was too light and accusing me of controlling the level of lighting. I pointed out that lighting had to do with enlightenment. He resented the degree of my enlightenment and bitterly resented the degree to which I was in charge of his. The moment before, I had given too much. That made him feel guilty. Usually, however, I gave too little. That meant I was selfish and stingy.

A smile broke across his face:

"You know, I can see me mum. She never fed me enough. I remember wanting to cut up her tits with a carving knife." [115]

The smile signalled a hint of recognition that the roots of his phallic desires and shattering hostilities ran deep indeed, from virility to feeding, from the head to the heart. [116] For him, as everyone, the penis holds diverse, often divergent, degrees of meaning. They include:

the breast, nipple, tooth, thumb, clitoris, any strong, extensible limb or muscle (parts of the body);

searching, probing, throbbing, thrusting, expanding, exploding, electrifying excitements and annihilating satisfactions (experiences);

snakes, sharks, rats, tigers, horses, whips, rods, spears, swords, guns, any big, wild, powerful, penetrating, overwhelming animal or thing (animate or inanimate objects);

brother, father, husband, God, Superman, Superwoman, Joan of Arc, Queen Christina, Mrs. Thatcher, combined parents, complete parental persecutors (persons);

milk, cream, sperm, babies, water, fire, warriors, cars, cocaine, 'continuous action stimulants' (products);

procreation, pleasure, hunting, riding, raping, sport, body building, business, politics, war (activities);

strength, stamina, size, assertion, ambition, authority, virility, prowess, power, privilege, unstoppability (qualities and characteristics);

pedestals, towers, New York, Houston, Cape Kennedy (places or settings); and

Father Heaven, patriarchal society, Mount Olympus, storms, thunder, lightning, enlightenment, the intellect, rationality (outer reality, states of mind versus peace of mind and states of peace).

All of these features comprise the phallus and denotes a hierarchy of hurt and hope. The hurts encompass the *bad penis,* an organ and entity which ravishes life. In contrast the *good penis* is loving and reparative. Like the womb, it gives hope, makes babies and affirms the continuity of life. (117)

John Donne confirmed the latter, the loving penis, in his poem, "To his Mistres Going to Bed." His words set forth the wish to explore a woman's body (called America) and thence the mysteries of the world and beyond, without damage, but with awesome discovery:

"*.......Before, behind, between, above, below.*
O my America! my new-found-land,
My kingdome, safeliest when with one
man man'd ....
How blest am I in this discovering thee!
To enter in these bonds, is to be
free...." (118)

PART 3:

THE IMPACT OF MALICE

Inter-and Intra-Generational Conflict

Chapter 7

Witches, Giants and Scary Parents

Traditionally the witch is a withered old woman with bony hands, humpy back and sharp tipped teeth, who preys on the blood and flesh of boys and girls. She dresses in black because she is a creature of the night shrieking with delight as her owlish eyes discover a tender baby or chaste young girl. [1] Jocular caricatures of long nosed ladies with magic hats and black cats astride flying broomsticks bolster beliefs that untold women possess vast powers of occult destruction. [2]

The legendary counterpart of the wicked witch is not the warlock, but the killer giant, whose huge size and and fearsome strength conveys elemental forces given over to rampant evil. Dante described the Archfiend lying in the lowest depths of the Inferno as *'un gigante,'* while Milton's Satan *'extended long and large'* both in body and possessions - hordes of fallen angels who could change size and sex to perpetrate malice. [3] Giants abound in myth and folklore from Cornwall to China and are usually well equipped with savage teeth, loud voices, rough hair and extra eyes as well as clubs, hammers, swords and, nowadays, guns. [4]

Witches and giants are not only products of rampant imaginations, the childs' eye view of parents, or their parents' scary constructions, but they actually touch upon archaic and not so archaic memories of childhood and child care. According to the psychohistorian, Lloyd deMause, this is a nightmarish succession of parent child relations where:

> *"......the further back in history one goes, the lower the level of child care, and the more likely children are to be abandoned, beaten, terrorized and sexually abused."* [5]

The witch represents the cruelly rejecting, depriving, devouring, treacherous mother, more concerned with her own looks, feelings and needs, than her child's. She is a woman greedy for food, envious of youth and jealous of love, the *'Cruella DeVil'* of contemporary cinema, the *'malign crone'* of our forbears who could bring down misfortune by a curse or a glance.

In fact mothers have commonly put unwanted children out to die and there are many references to infanticide from antiquity onwards. In ancient Greece and Rome children were thrown into rivers, flung into cesspits, potted in jars or simply left exposed by the roadside *"a prey for birds, food for wild beast to rend."* [6] As recently as 1890, abandoned babies were a common sight in London streets, lying dead in the gutters and dung heaps. [7]

Even when they were not left to die, vast numbers of newborn babies used to be passed into the hands of wet nurses to be suckled. Disease or neglect led many to perish before they were handed back after two to five years. In the interim they rarely saw their biological parents. [8] This custom was an effective shield against passionate involvement with offspring who probably would not have reached adulthood anyway. And if anyone need be blamed, it could be the nurse, just as the unsuccessful midwife might be accused of witchcraft. [9]

But by the 18th century the practice began to diminish even before improved sanitation made motherhood less problematic. It became more common for children to enter their parent's emotional life, to be prayed with, and sometimes played with. Closer contact led to new methods to curb anticipated greedy demands and wicked behaviour. Psychic assaults replaced infanticide and physical abuse. The child was a mind to be filled with frightening figures in order to engender compliance.

For Europeans, Bluebeard, werewolves and Napoleon Bonaparte were valued additions to an arsenal of images that included "*gorgons and ghosts, witches, giants and Jews,*" as well as a tyrannical God who held aberrant youngsters "*over the pit of hell, much as one holds a spider, or some loathsome insect, over the fire.*" In addition, both Europeans and Americans were obsessed with '*boogiemen,*' that is, black people. Typically in 1882 one little girl was told to behave herself otherwise a "*horrible little Black Man...(who) was hidden in the room to catch her the moment she left her bed or made the slightest noise.*" [10]

In modern times it is hard to tell whether the levels of child abuse, physical and psychic, are on the decline, as DeMause contends, are remaining the same, or are actually increasing. Until relatively recently the battered baby and the battering parent were taboo topics. Now increasing public attention means that the number of known child abuse cases appears to escalate all the time. [11] One can hardly open a newspaper in the United States or Europe without encountering a child murder or sexual assault, aside from more numerous, but less obvious examples of mental and bodily cruelty. In Britain alone the estimated number of children murdered by their parents or caretakers ranges from five to twenty five per week. [12]

I intend to begin the chapters on the influence of envy, greed and jealousy with a study of the *Persecuting Parent*, an adult who hates and attacks children. In so doing I hope to redress the prevalent view that in the relations between parents and children resentments invariably flow from sons to fathers or daughters to mothers. In truth there exists a balance of terror, albeit mitigated by the tender feelings that young and old hold for each other. While children certainly crave the breast and begrudge womb and phallic powers, parents are also assailed by terrible tensions for which they often blame their offspring. These concern their own inadequacies in the face of life renewed, but especially, in an age of narcissism, the special attentions which children demand, but which mothers and fathers prefer to keep for themselves. Thus, even before Oedipus becomes an issue, parents may feel deprived of love and life, and seek mortal revenge. [13] Considering the relative size and strength of adults in comparison to infants, it is no wonder that these antagonisms tend to be denied, but located in other worlds at other times and places.

* * * * *

The Malevolent Mother

Malevolent mothers are scary, a point which folk and fairy tales make with the utmost clarity. The story of *Hansel and Gretel* provides one of the finest descriptions of their grenvious, cannibalistic personae. Different versions exist in many countries, but all have similar features. The Brothers Grimm acquaint us with a poor woodcutter who lives at the edge of a big forest with his son and daughter and wife (their step-mother). A famine hits the land and there is not enough food to go around. The woman tells her husband not to worry. They'll take the children far out into forest and leave them. Then, *"they won't find the way back home and we'll be rid of them."* [14]

The man protests, but his wife, ever concerned with her own needs, prevails. So, after several false starts, the young boy and girl are dumped in the forest to die of starvation. Forlorn and frightened they decide to follow a little white bird. It brings them to a lovely house with walls of bread, roof of cake and windows of pure sugar. The children are delighted, but it's a trap. Suddenly the door opens and an aged, decrepit crone creeps out and invites them in. She pretends to be kind. Really she is:

> *".......an evil witch who lay in wait for children and had only built the little bread house to lure them her way. When a child fell into her power she would kill it, cook it and eat it, and that was a day of feasting for her."* [15]

On the next day the old woman locks the boy in a shed and forces his sister to help her fatten him for the kill. Eventually she prepares the oven to roast them both, but Gretel plays a trick and pushes the crone into the oven instead, whereupon *"the godless witch burned miserably to death."* (16)

The villains in this story are a step-mother and a witch. They represent two aspects of the same person, the bad mother, who is usually transformed into a combination of one or more step-mothers, witches and mothers-in-law so it is safer to hate her and get revenge, at least in the world of make-believe. The bad mother may be a monstrous creation of the child's own projected impulses. But all too often the negative view coincides with one or more aspects of real maternal destructiveness. A 1999 report by the British NSPCC (National Society for Prevention of Cruelty to Children) seems to serve as a coda to Grimm tales It surveyed twenty five years of child abuse and concluded that mothers perpetrate 33% of child murders. (17)

Hansel and Gretel feared hunger and abandonment. What they overlooked was the likelihood of being eaten themselves. Many mothers regard their infants as 'food objects'. It is a common experience to see a woman kiss a baby on the behind and exclaim with delight, *"Oh, you look good enough to eat."* Sometimes this is not a joke. (18)

The desired food is more than milk. The baby is a breast which flows with love towards those who care for it. Battered babies and children have parents who reverse the roles. They insist that their offspring look after them, and get enraged if this doesn't happen. One woman who severely injured her child commented:

> *"I have never felt loved all my life. When the baby was born, I thought he would love me. When he cried, it meant he didn't love me. So I hit him."* (19)

Hansel and Gretel were brutalized by their 'step' mother, a common feature of many folktales. Their story is a parable about an emotional famine. The children are burdened with a mother who begrudges love while resenting their youth, their vitality and above all the affection they draw from their father. He loves them but is a *schlemíl,* he can't protect them from her devouring jealousy. So the children have to rely on ingenuity as occurs in many families where emotional strength and shrewdness are keys to survival.

The fatal trap is narcissistic seduction, while the intent is self-aggrandizement. The malicious mother enchants children with false hopes, and inflated promises – candy floss, while forcing them to feed her pride and self-esteem. Bertram Karon has described several such women in his book on the psychotherapy of schizophrenia. One lived off her son's artistic talents. From his childhood onwards she hoarded his paintings to show off to her friends. He begged her permission to retain them, but she refused, saying she was only keeping them for his sake. She used the attention and praise the paintings provoked to feed her ego, and his worthlessness. On the surface she tried to help him, but deep down she was a vicious rival. This wasn't a relationship from which he could easily extricate himself. He felt totally dependent, and we can be assured that if he hadn't go along with her, she would have pushed him away to 'roast in hell'. [20]

R. D. Laing has portrayed his childhood in comparable terms. He was an only child in a bleak, pleasureless house with a mother who was either *"in a decline"* or deeply possessive of his psychic life. When he was little she snatched away his favoured toy horse, and burned it because *"he was getting too close to it."* An Aunt observed that she *"burned up with envy and jealousy,"* and would destroy anything he got attached to. Later in life, after he had left home and had become a famous psychiatrist, he discovered that his mother had acquired a tiny figurine which she called *"Ronald"* or *"Ronnie."* She enjoyed sticking pins into its heart in order to make him have a heart attack. [21]

* * * * *

A mother's rage can extend to an unborn child. 'Kate' had yet to give birth to the child inside her, yet she feared her fetus was a dangerous rival, 'a thing' nibbling away inside her just like the bug in *The Very Hungry Caterpillar.* [22]

Although continuing to eat, drink and smoke excessively, she was aware that the baby might be damaged by a rapid weight gain (no room for the womb) and nicotine (poison). She also worried that the fetus was too close to her back passage where *"a lot of heavy shit goes down"*, in other words, her own shitty feelings.

Kate herself had been premature and still resented her mother for cheating on womb time. So the pregnancy stirred up enormous appetites which she preferred to deny and bury in her body in the form of 'galloping leukemia' or 'Aids'. The 'galloping leukemia' was an uncontrollable group of cells which she imagined would suddenly proliferate and savage everything before them. But 'Aids' was the most terrifying prospect. It meant she would waste away and was an unjust desert for being greedy.

Who was to blame? Kate fingered her husband and baby. The bigger she got the more 'it' got in the way. Once she was crossing the street and a car whizzed by. Her husband pulled her back onto the pavement by pulling her tummy. She was indignant. How dare he try to save the baby before her. She felt ignored and the incident confirmed the unwelcome prospect of a newborn baby occupying the center of familial attention. Moreover, it brought to mind many memories of her own parents who were "*always busy, always having all the fun while I was just a pudding.*"

The worst conflicts were between Kate's determination to nurture and protect the fetus and her wish to compete with or destroy 'it'. The competition was for food, love and attention. She enjoyed musing about the clothes, the dinners, the holidays and the thousand other things that she could chose as soon as the baby was born. Then she would be preeminent again. In this respect she was like her mother and thought her children would be like her, proving themselves at others' expense while setting the stage for the transmission of envy and jealousy from one generation to the next.

As the psychoanalyst Leslie Farber points out in his book *lying, despair, jealousy, envy, sex, suicide, drugs, and the good life*:

"In a house (with narcissistic mothering) where envy is in the air, the child need but look, listen, and breathe to be instructed in consolation and counterattack.......If he accepts the conditions offered him and agrees to be instructed by the example of his elders, thus will their envy breed his own." [23]

* * * * *

Maternal destructiveness is also a defense against maternal destructiveness. Many women contemplate killing themselves, or their children, in order to avoid the wrath of their mothers. Joseph Rheingold has detailed the death wishes of mothers towards their children. He notes that it is not unusual for women to give birth and then beg their mothers not to kill them. [24]

In terms of a three generational model of mother-child relations, suicide, sterility, miscarriage and madness do not only stem from the upward flow of envy and jealousy, the young towards the old, and consequent reflections and refractions, but the downward deluge, the extremes of spite and vengeance by mothers who abhor their daughters' femininity and abominate their social successes. [25]

The sacrifice of children in order to propitiate the mother's mother has been practiced from antiquity onwards. Aside from literal abandonment, examples include the the transfer of care to alternative parents and filicide. The latter has been recorded in the annals of the Irish Celts, Gauls, Scandinavians and many middle eastern peoples. Inscriptions which identify the victims as the first-born sons of noble families have been traced to Jericho 9,000 years ago. [26] Even now when boys and girls play *London Bridge is Falling Down,* and catch the child at the end of the game, they are acting out a sacrifice to a river goddess. [27]

Of course, conflicts between new mothers and old do not begin with pregnancy or motherhood. They reach far back into childhood when the first hints of sexual maturity arouse envious rivalries, mother to daughter and vice versa. And the same hostilities extend far forward into adulthood when disparagements of childbearing become critiques of child rearing.

For the little girl the wicked witch is the mom who refuses her make-up or jewellery or clothes, and won't let her grow up. The tales of the Brothers Grimm are replete with spiteful step-mothers, jealous mothers and begrudging mothers-in-law who curse, suffocate or poison their daughters as in *Snow White* , defame and condemn them to death as in *The Twelve Brothers*, or put impossible conditions on their meeting men as in *The Six Servants* : [28]

> *"Long ago there lived an old queen who was a sorceress and her daughter was the most beautiful maiden under the sun. But the old queen's one idea was to lure people to their destruction, and when a suitor came she would say that any man wanting to marry her daughter must first perform a task, or his life would be forfeit.* [29]

The queen was merciless. Untold men met a terrible fate while the poor girl was left unmarried and seething. Finally a prince who had heard of the challenge accomplished the tasks with the help of six magic servants. Even then the queen intervened with the slander, *"He's not good enough for you,"* and tried to recapture the daughter and murder her husband.

The Hollywood story of actress Joan Crawford and her adopted daughter, Christina, falls into the same category. Both in the cinema and at home, this mother played the modern sorceress and malicious Queen. Her wand was self-seeking infatuation and scornful detachment. At a wave it could turn Christina into a little princess at a film opening or exile her to a convent run like a penal colony, for kissing a boy. The older Crawford was surreally envious and ruthlessly disruptive of her daughter's youth, sexuality, prospects, in fact, her entire personality. [30]

Crawford was not untypical. Many contemporary mothers, like the proverbial wicked witch, are adept at dramatic interventions:

disrupting weddings, inducing chaos and generally ruining the happiness of their daughters and sons-in-law, or sons and daughters-in-law. These mother are not adverse to casting spells, summoned from hearts fermenting with fury. These include seducing the groom, fighting the guests and dying from heart attacks.

* * * * *

Perhaps the most formidable feature of witches is their fondness for transforming victims into witches. In modern terms this attaching malice to others. A common occurrence during the times of the *Malleus*, it is still a significant event as was dramatized during a sensational trial in Livorno, Italy, in 1983. (31)

The defendant was Carol Compton, a twenty one year old Scottish nanny who was accused of fire-raising and trying to murder a little girl in her care. The main witness was the girl's aged grandmother who publicly claimed Ms. Compton was a witch. Signora Cecchini explained that the nanny possessed special powers and practiced black magic. When she was about plates fell of the walls and fires started without explanation. (32)

The Italian press covered the trial under banner headlines, "*The Witch Defends Herself*" and did not hesitate to quote elderly spectators such as a faith healer who hissed: "*That girl is possessed by demons. She comes from Britain.*" (33) But the testimonies of the grandmother and her daughter-in-law (the girl's mother) were eventually refuted by a previous nanny who said the two women had made life hell for herself and Ms. Compton. As for the fires, the electricity in the house was overloaded and the wiring was terrible. Anyway, the old granny used to leave burning fag ends about. A few days later Carol Compton was acquitted.

By reading between the lines, and with some extrapolation, it appears that the Cecchini household was one where three generations of women exploited and resented the nannies that came into their midst. The nannies, in turn, became the projective foci and receptacles for the malign tensions that the Grandmother, mother, and little girl bore towards each other.

As for the little girl, it is not too farfetched to think that she enjoyed the extra attention, but used the nanny as a scapegoat for naughty antics (breaking the occasional plate?) and as an unloved surrogate for a mother or grandmother who misused her.

In the end Ms. Compton managed to return to Britain alive and well. She was lucky to have obtained outside support which confirmed her perceptions and challenged the family. Otherwise she might have succumbed to her allotted role and agreed to bear the family's enmities (the overloaded circuits) and punishments too.

* * * * *

A special interest of the malign enchantress is to transform boys into girls. In *Hansel and Gretel* it was not by chance that the old crone chose the boy to lock up and fatten for the kill. Crones and hags embody ancient fears of possessive, castrating mothers who appropriates their sons' phallic powers. Similar suspicions poison relations with wives, daughters and women in general. In the ensuing struggles either the men manage to retain their identities (and facilities), or the women wind up with the broomsticks. Then the victims become unsexed, bitter, vengeful people – like witches.

Not surprisingly, many men are terrified of their mothers, who have been variously described as whirlpools, hurricanes, tornadoes and typhoons or, from the animal world, treacherous cats, dogs and snakes. [34]

One middle aged writer confirmed these epithets during the course of recalling life long feelings of isolation and panic in the face of women. He grew up in New York in a household of feminists. His mother was dominating and oppressive. She seemed to have treated his father as an inferior species and married solely to get a son.

With a frustrating panache she enjoyed exhibiting her nude body while he was on the toilet or she in the bath. Yet, she avoided kissing, hugging, or other physical contact. Forever exciting, she belittled male bodies, said sex was dirty and males unacceptable. Her general attitude was that the penis and testicles were messy. The female genitals were much *"neater"*. [35]

Unlike this person, Robert Stoller depicts a woman who was more subtle, yet more devastating in her assault on her son's body, gender and personal identities. She created a transsexual. [36]

Mrs. C came into therapy after being scolded by neighbours for dressing her son as a girl. She herself appeared slim, boyish and perky, but felt she was "*a nothing, a cipher, a mirage.*" [37]

Her own mother had been an "*empty woman*" whose lasting endowment was *"great envy, rage and guilt"*, while her father was an alcoholic with personalities ranging from happy and affectionate to violent and oversexed. She had two brothers who were the favourites in a family that believed that males were superior, females inferior.

Feeling no place as a tomboy or woman, Mrs. C saw herself as a 'neuter.' Yet she married and was happy when she got pregnant. Her child was a son, which gave her a tremendous sense of *"well-being"*. Mothering was an addiction. She cared for him constantly, rarely letting him out of her sight or touch. His body was hers. In the meanwhile she hated her husband and he agreed to stay out of the way.

As time passed, Mrs C. feel in love with her son's penis, which she called *"the phallus of her flesh,"* her rebirth. She recalled:

> *"In regard to boys' penises, I was very put out that God didn't give me one of those. This started when I was four or five. I kidded myself and probably thought that maybe I would have one eventually. I can remember at night when I would say my prayers that I would wake up a boy the next morning......"* [38]

Stoller concludes that Mrs. C was a bisexual mother with severe*"envy and anger"* (grenvy) towards males. By means of unlimited physical contact and other intimacies she promoted a form of pathological symbiotic identification between her son and herself.

Her son was solely allowed to exist as 'his mother's feminized phallus.' As far as she was concerned he was her, not him, and existed mainly to cure her of emptiness. What she denied was her hatred of him as a male, and separate person. Should he have tried to separate, to be himself, she would have wreaked revenge. [39]

Neither Mrs. C. nor the writer's mother would be unfamiliar to the ancients who would be quick to see in their destructive styles many aspects of the Amazonian queens and the great mother goddess, Cybele. [40] Her consort was Attis, a devotee and lover, both a man and a boy. His sufferings were seductions quite similar to those I have just described. The writer was warned that if he used his penis for pleasure it would fall off. Cybele imposed a vow of chastity on Attis. His life was hers. His potential was hers. She foretold he would die if he loved a woman, that is, grew up, asserted his manhood, and separated from her. The prophecy emanated from her boundless desires.

A difficult wedding led to death and resurrection. Attis prepared to marry the daughter of King Midas. Cybele found out and tried to prevent the marriage by using her head to break down the walls of the city. They had been closed for the wedding feast. When Attis observed this, he went mad and cut off his genitals under a spruce tree. Then 'the Great Mother' anointed his penis and buried it, whereupon violets sprang up from the site and surrounded the tree with their beauty. [41]

Ovid related a poignant variation. Attis promised to remain pure and virtuous. But he broke his vow and took to himself a lovely young maiden. When Cybele found out she killed her, whereupon Attis went mad, hacked at his body and castrated himself with the words:

> *"Pereant partes quae nocuere mihi."*
>
> *(There, take these genitals–you caused trouble enough on their account.")* [42]

The Attic myths feature madness and self-mutilation instigated by a jealous older woman, 'the Great Mother'. But some versions linked

Attis with Adonis, a youth of extraordinary beauty, who was loved by a goddess and killed by a boar at the behest of a jealous older man, Zeus, 'the Great Father'. [43]

* * * * *

The Brutal Father

Zeus was the son of a Giant, the grandson of a Titan, and the chief of a multitude of fierce patriarchal deities introduced by the Dorians when they conquered Greece about 1,200 B.C.E. Although imbued with wisdom and beneficence, he commonly displayed despotic power for selfish ends, and was capable of the basest passions and frailties. In various myths he was described and appeared as jealous, cruel, spiteful, vengeful, deceitful, lascivious, rapacious and cowardly. [44]

Zeus and his father, Cronus (Saturn), and his father's father, Uranus are models for brutal fathers (to a small child, dreaded Giants) which appear in every culture at every time. Kin to Goliath, Gargantua and now, Rambo, they are huge, powerful, bestial creatures with enormous appetites and terrible tempers. [45]

In the domain of folklore these Giants can be traced to Norse, Welsh, Cornish and Appalachian legends where ogres with huge hammers or clubs threaten to crush babies and boys, while in England they proclaimed:

Fee, fau, fum
I smell the blood of an English man, (or, Earthly man;)
Be he alive, or be he dead,
I'll grind his bones to make my bread. (or, Off goes his head.) [46]

The English ogre spawned dozens of tales all to do with an unlikely young man who climbs a tree or a magic stalk to vanquish a killer. Yet the original story of *Jack and the Beanstalk* is far more complicated and horrific than the watered down accounts that appear in children's books. According to the version researched by Iona and Peter Opie for, *The Classic Fairy Tales,* Jack is the "*indolent, careless and extravagant* " child of a poor widow, who accuses him of bringing them both *"to beggary and ruin."* (47)

It transpires that Jack's father was a rich man who was good and kind. Unfortunately he came to the attention of a Giant who lived some miles away. This person was:

> *".....altogether as wicked as your father was good: he was in his heart envious, covetous, and cruel; but he had the art of concealing these vices. He was poor, and wished to enrich himself at any rate."* (48)

Eventually Jack realizes that he has to fight the monster in order to destroy a murderer and regain the family's treasures. But he is frightened. Only the threat of starvation and his mother's nagging force him to climb the beanstalk and seek out the Giant. Then there begins a series of encounters with the flesh eating figure (*"Fee, fau, fum. Wife, I smell fresh meat"*) which ends years later with him killing the killer and changing from a surely youth into a *"dutiful and obedient son,"* aside from a strong, honourable and prosperous man.

Jack's Giant shares the characteristics of the Gods. He is large and powerful, totally unprincipled and lives in a mansion (castle) high in the sky (Olympus). And, in common with so many deities and devils, he enjoys the flesh of human beings. The paintings by Goya and Rubens of Saturn devouring his son would not do him an injustice. (50)

These Gods – Giants, Titans, dragons, dinosaurs, ogres and ghouls represent the dangerous, self-centered father. He is the man who lords it over his wife and children, and begrudges their needs while cannibalizing his family's emotional and material resources. The story of Jack concerns such a family where the father, perhaps akin to a contemporary alcoholic or philanderer, has battered the babies, drained the wife and abandoned them all to stew in their juices. The story also explains why, because he is '*envious, covetous and cruel.*'

The envy focuses on the newborn child who has privileged access to his mother's body, and is preordained to surpass his father in strength and character. A farmer once told me:

> *"I was delighted when my son was born. Yet, when I held him in my arms for the first time, I was seized by a sudden, overpowering impulse to smash his little body against the ground and to stamp on it. This thought made me terribly upset. Then I realized how envious I felt towards the baby. All he had to do was open his mouth, and he was fed. I had to work damn hard. His whole life lay before him. Much of mine was past. He had a father who loved him. My dad had died years before.* [51]

Covetousness is incessant greed, the desire to compete with the child for food, attention and love both to assuage emptiness and overcome envy. Paradoxically it arises from a feeling of detachment from the sublime riches that the birth of a child confers on both father and mother. In Jack's case the Giant attacked his family not long after his birth. Similar dangers threatened the farmer's month old son at a time when his father couldn't get enough food or sex. Indeed, the baby boy became a food object. The farmer said he often thought of cooking him like a chicken in his microwave oven, probably to make up for a painful lack of attention.

This man's cruelties also encompass envy and jealousy, the hatred aroused by a third person's challenge to preeminence in the family. Whether the wife will be honoured or destroyed depends on the balance of forces, ranging from delight with the birth to fury at her taking a lover, the baby.

The wicked Giant had stolen a hen and a harp, that is, his mother's capacity to feed her young and maintain her peace of mind. Jack's task was to restore his mother's health and happiness, the family fortunes, and punish the giant, cut a bad father down to size. In order to accomplish this he had to sell a cow – get rid of childish dependency and sow some seeds – discover his own strength and potency [52] It was an extended struggle, not only because it takes time for a boy to become a man, but also because the Giant embodied his own wicked impulses which he had to conquer in himself. Only then could he make amends to his mother and regain her confidence.

Yet, there is more to this tale than vicious attacks on abundance and love. The Giant also damaged a mother's procreative powers. He killed her husband, the source of seeds for future life, and nearly destroyed the woman and her offspring. Almost an entire generation had to pass before her son's maturity (the magic beans) renewed the possibility of progress.

The Giant was a changeling, the personification of good turned bad, He was a father who disappeared in order to prevent babies being born. And, as Jack discovered, he was an ogre who confined children to a dungeon and ate them at his convenience. These elements are echoes of many legends, especially Grecian beliefs about the creation of the cosmos and the relations between men and women.

* * * * *

First there was Gaea, 'the deep-breasted earth'. She conceived Uranus, 'the sky crowned with stars', and made him her consort and ruler of the Titans. But he feared that their children would rise up against him, so he sealed them in the depths of the earth (the dungeon, a state of unbornness). Gaea mourned, then instigated Cronus, her youngest son, to attack Uranus with a sickle drawn from her bosom. Cronus obliged. He waited till his father slept, then hacked off his genitals and threw them into the sea. [53]

Subsequently Cronus led the generation of Giants. But he also feared that his children would supplant him, so he swallowed them (infanticidal cannibalism) as soon as they were born. His wife, despairing that all her progeny would disappear, sought the help of Gaea. Together they arranged to substitute a stone wrapped in swaddling clothes for Zeus, the next baby. Cronus swallowed the ruse and lived to be overthrown by his son when he grew to manhood. Not surprisingly, the adult Zeus dreaded that the same would happen to him. [54]

Father-son conflicts carried on through several generations of mortals and led directly to the tragedy of Oedipus, which was brought about by a curse on a King who had seduced a boy. Tantalus was a first generation mortal, the son of Zeus and the great grandchild of Uranus. He tried to serve his son, Pelops, to the Gods in a pie. They took exception and brought Pelops back to life. In angry retribution the Gods condemned Tantalus to a life of endless 'tantalizing' frustrations.[55] Afterwards Pelops, whose kingdom was the seat of the ancient Olympic games, became a key figure in the unfolding of the Oedipus saga as well as that great narration of sibling intrigue, the *Oresteia.* [56]

These tales tell of the damage inflicted by men, but provoked by women and aroused by prophets. Their prophecies were correct. All men tend to be supplanted by the fruit of a woman's womb, children who naturally grow older and stronger while their parents grow older and weaker. My own son seriously explained this dilemma when he started school:

> *"You know Daddy, I am going to grow up, but you are going to grow down.* [57]

Interestingly, the Greeks did not overemphasise the conflicts between father and son. Even in *Oedipus* the prevailing issue is the relationship between a mother and her son. [58] The men were much more concerned with the direct threats that women posed, in the guise of maternal Furies, or female warriors, to their flesh and blood and pride, an obvious consequence of the Dorian conquest of matriarchal, female ruling (gynecocratic) predecessors. Having taken over their power, authority, assets and maleness, they feared Amazonian counterattacks. Thus the Athenian national hero was Theseus whose definitive defeat of Queen Hippolyte appeared to preclude the possibility of female reconquests.

* * * * *

For the ancient Greeks, strategic avoidance was the counterpart of confrontation. They created a male oriented culture which celebrated pederasty and subordinated women. [59] To our eyes pederasty signifies the sexual desire of adult men for young boys and is considered extremely odious. However, in Greece in the period 750 -300 B.C.E., it was a socially sanctioned form of higher education whereby a man of good intellect and breeding endeavoured to impart *aretë*– ' the driving force of a man's skill, power and character' – to a pubescent boy. [60]

> *"The bloom of a twelve-year-old boy is desirable, but at thirteen he is much more delightful. Sweeter still is the flower of love that blossoms at fourteen, and its charm increases at fifteen. Sixteen is the divine age."* [61]

The Danish psychoanalyst, Thorkil Vanggaard, who has studied the practice in great detail, points out that pederastic intercourse was a sacred act. It was publicly celebrated and steeped in solemnity and honour. This relationship, called *paiderastia* by Vanggaard, was a form of phallic transference which had little to do with homosexuality per se, and nothing to do with effeminacy, quite the opposite. Vanggaard notes: "*......the aim (was) to make of the boy a man with strength, a sense of duty, eloquence, cleverness, generosity, courage and other noble virtues.*" [62]

Both the older man, the *erastës*, and his younger lover, the *erömenos*, were aggressively male in dress and demeanour. Unlike contemporary 'butch' figures, they were expected to marry and produce children. Those who didn't were ridiculed and punished. [63]

In a larger sense, the idealization of the older man-pubescent boy relationship can be seen as a cultural necessity. Besides male-female combat, *paiderastia* served to minimize the inherent and inherited conflicts between generations of which the Greeks were well aware. After all their myths described them in gruesome detail. As far as they were concerned it was better to bed a boy a than to kill him. Presumably they also realized that it is possible to allay overt envy by treating someone as a narcissistic extension of oneself. An adult who could impart himself to a handsome youth, and be honoured as well, was less likely to dwell on his own inadequate or fading assets. (64) Similarly, a boy who was chosen by a distinguished man, held a sure way to gain style and grow big, thereby minimizing the doubts and discords of adolescence. (65)

The fact that *paiderastia* was not a private erotic enterprise indicates the importance of the custom to Athenian society, indeed, to the state. Solon, the famous law giver who lived about 600 B.C.E, laid down strict rules for paiderastic relations. (66) It took place openly with the consent of the boy's family and under the supervision of responsible authorities. In Crete, for example, the formalities were comparable to marriage by capture. When a Cretan nobleman wanted to educate a particular boy as his *erömenos,* he would let the family know in advance that he intended to capture him at such and such a time and place. If the family considered him to be a worthy suitor, they allowed this to happen. Then a big party was held to commemorate the event, not unlike a contemporary confirmation or Bar Mitzvah celebration. (67) Certainly the parents kept themselves well informed about the new relationship and felt hurt if it went wrong. Aristophanes joked about this in his play, *The Birds*, when a father complains about his son's *erastës:*

> *"Well, this is a fine state of affairs, you damned desperado! You meet my son just as he comes out of the gymnasium, all fresh from the bath, and you don't kiss him, you don't say a word to him, you don't hug him, you don't feel his balls! And yet you're supposed to be a friend of ours!"* (68)

After partaking of a man's love and returning home, the boy was granted the title, *klënós*, meaning famous. In addition he was accorded special privileges including distinguished dress and marks of public respect which he retained for life. These honours were given because the young adult had attained *aretë*, which, for the Dorians, was the greatest distinction that can befit a man. [69]

* * * * *

There exists considerable evidence that *paiderastia* was a part of ordinary Grecian life. Abundant legends indicate it was also a common practice on Mount Olympus. [70] Since these legends (told and retold, lost and discovered, discovered and rediscovered over thousands of years) mediated the relationships between man and man, and ultimately, man and society, *paiderastia* and its aftermath have to be important factors in the way that modern man has come to perceive himself. [71]

King Pelops played a leading role in many of the most crucial myths. He achieved the title of *klënós* after being the lover of Poseidon, God of the sea. In later life Pelops called upon Poseidon for help in order to gain the hand of a princess whose father always destroyed her suitors. With Poseidon's help Pelops gained a wife and mother of the House of Pelops, whose malevolent intrigues led to the *Oresteia* and several generations of infanticide, fratricide and matricide. [72]

But Pelops had other wives, one of whom produced a beloved and favoured son, Chrysippus, acclaimed for his extraordinary gifts and beauty. During the course of a visit with Pelops, Laius, the King of Thebes, fell desperately in love with him. Without asking Pelops' permission, Laius abducted the boy and took him as his *erömenos*. The enraged Pelops cursed his colleague and all his kin, an action which precipitated the tragedy of Oedipus. [73]

Laius' crime was not simply untamable desire, but a greedy eye for a luscious youth which broke all bounds and violated sacred social and moral conventions. The curse was that his children and children's children would do likewise. Laius tried to avoid this fate by refusing to produce further offspring, but his wife, Jocasta, tricked him by getting him drunk and forcing herself upon him. So, Laius himself became a victim of what the Greeks feared most, overweening female sexuality and ambition. (74)

Having been warned by the oracle that his baby would kill him, Laius prepared for murder. He arranged for the male-child to be exposed on a mountain with its ankles pierced by pins (hence the name Oedipus, meaning swollen foot). The boy should have died, as did the many unwanted children who were left on hillsides in antiquity, but Oedipus was rescued by a shepherd and adopted by the childless King and Queen of Corinth.

Laius the King is a paradigm of 'the bad father'. He is a weak, selfish, dishonest man, unsure of his sexuality, but consumed with anger. To cover his wounds and conceal his defects he inflates himself in every which way. This swollen self is not just a sign of hubris, but of pathological hatred, of life and love. No wonder he raped the son of a friend. Having been abandoned by his father at an early age, he can't stand the love between Pelops and Chrysippus, nor the grace revealed in another's body. (75)

Later he feared his own son would do what he had done, and would have done to any child, no matter what the provocation: abandon, neglect, torture and kill him. How extraordinary it was that Freud ignored his role in the drama that followed. (76)

The mythological Oedipus was not a vengeful son. Far from perpetuating a terrible curse, he fled from Corinth as soon as he heard of it, in order to protect the parents he loved. On the road to Thebes he was assailed by a stranger whom he only killed in self-defense. He did not know that the man was Laius. (77)

Upon arriving at Thebes he discovered that the city was being terrorized by the *Sphinx*, a female monster, who strangled and ate anyone who couldn't answer a riddle: *"What is it that walks on four legs in the morning, on two at noon, and on three in the evening?"* (78) Undaunted, Oedipus gave the correct reply: It is a human, who first crawls on all fours, then walks upright and, in old age, needs an extra stick. In other words he asserted his identity in the face of female tyranny. In response the *Sphinx* threw herself off a cliff (went into a terminal depression) and Oedipus was offered the throne of Thebes. What he didn't realize was that his mother, Jocasta, was part of the package.

The ensuing marriage worked well. The couple produced four healthy children and Oedipus became a wise and capable ruler. Then a plague struck the city. A blind prophet proclaimed that the disaster was a curse, a consequence of the murder of Laius. It could only be overcome if the murderer was driven away. Oedipus swore to find him but Jocasta begged him to desist. She had discovered the truth about Laius and herself and preferred 'to let sleeping dogs lay'. But her son and husband ploughed on and, after a ruthless investigation discovered the murderer was himself. (79)

The issues appear to be incest and parricide. Once the secrets were revealed Jocasta hung herself. She declaimed guilt and shame, and we can assume she feared the envy of women and the vengeance of men for having loved and honoured a patricide. (80) In the meanwhile Oedipus thought of suicide, but he decided to gouge out his eyes and go into exile, suitable punishments for his crimes. But are they? He had sought to save his parents, not kill one and sleep with the other. The slain man was a stranger, someone who had tried to kill him twice before. Moreover, Jocasta knew all about the curse, yet persisted in marriage to a younger man. Perhaps the *Sphinx* was one of her incarnations.

The classical view is that Oedipus was hounded by remorseless fate (uncontrollable libidinal impulses) to attack his father and possess his mother. And the sequelae, disgrace, mutilation, exile and regressive dependency, were unavoidable. This is a fate all men share in phantasy, if not in actuality. Others have argued that the self-blinding was an act of cowardice. It represented the wish not to see what had taken place nor experience appropriate guilt and sorrow, again a typical human reaction. (81)

In *Oedipus at Colonus* Sophocles points out that the legend was far from a tragedy. Although the course of his life was 'not quite to be envied', Oedipus emerged with honour and dignity. [82] After extremes of success and suffering, he became and was seen as a seer. Paradoxically it was his very act of self-immolation that made this possible. It extirpated eyes, too greedy for their own good, and expiated an 'I', grown beyond all bounds. Simultaneously, Oedipus appeased Thebes and protected himself from a higher fate, not his personal desires, but *Phthonos Theon*, envy of the Gods, who saw his success as a personal challenge to their prerogatives. After all, if you kill your father and marry his wife, sire his children and rule his domain, there are few other conventions you can't break. This clarifies the nature of Pelops' curse. Not only were Oedipus and his kin destined to violate all moral rules, but they were also condemned to be destroyed by the envy and jealousy that the breaking of these rules would arouse. Still it took the Gods (Laius', Pelops', paternal envy) seventeen years to wake up to the fact and apply their evil eyes (the plague) to his life. By blinding himself Oedipus renounced his omnipotence and freed himself from the continuing fear of divine revenge.

Pelops' curse passed over Oedipus and in some respects he overcame it. He was not destroyed by libidinal impulses (his greed) nor by the hands of his father or his children (their envy). However, his recovery remained incomplete. Although we never learn whether his sons took lovers, he felt they had disowned and dishonoured him, something he could not forgive. When they turned to him for help, he denounced them and perpetuated the curse by refusing his blessing and condemning them to fratricidal strife. In his eyes they never achieved *aretë*. [83]

* * * * *

Like mediaeval fantasies of courtly love, *paiderastia* was less pure in practice than in theory. By the third century B.C.E. it had long been debased and carnality, or the greedy penis, was less often a metaphor than an aim in itself, as we can see in the relationship between Socrates and his young disciple Alcibiades. Once Alcibiades arrived at a dinner party to discover Socrates sharing a couch with his host. According to Plato he scowled,

"You would move heaven and earth to sit next to the best-looking person in the room!"

Socrates retorted,

> *"My love for that fellow is always landing me in trouble. Ever since I feel for him, I have not been allowed even to glance at a good-looking boy, far less talk to one. He gets jealous straight away."* (84)

The ensuing relationship of father to child was transformed during periods of Roman and Christian hegemony. An imperious patriarchal authority became the norm. Over the next millennium, the predominant fears of children and adults shifted from oral devouring and womb destroying giants and Gods to phallic fathers preoccupied with political and sexual aggrandizement. It became the practice for men to be seen and treated as 'Lords and Masters' who needed to wield firm hands and stout rods to control unruly wives and children. If paternal regimes were authoritarian and status seeking, then 'this was needed to maintain the natural order of things' and to triumph over children's 'inordinate rivalries and hostilities'.

The idea that children were basically sinful arose from the unrestrained tendency of parents to treat them as the projective foci of their own lost wishes or unrealized malice. In other words children weren't children, separate beings, rather sorrowful mirrors of their parents' and parents' parents' unwelcome feelings or, within the social climate of the time, destroyed subjectivity. This included neediness, pain, rebelliousness, assertiveness and, of course, rage. The resultant frightening, hated figure can be called *'the Childish Monster.'* (85) This figure is a subjective perception. In technical terms it is based on the transference relationship whereby his or her parents 'see' him as a bad aspect of themselves or of others, in their past or present.

Such 'Childish Monsters' help to account for countless number of boys and girls who were rejected and injured, or simply killed, often by fathers, but also by mothers, for misbehaving, or just for existing. Since the parents couldn't tolerate, or even acknowledge their own childlike experiences, there was no way that they would allow 'this child' to live in the outside world either. Needless to say this is a problem still seeking a solution.

> *The view of children as inherently bad was augmented by widely read homilies which warned "Against Wilful Rebellion and told about ".......the mischief and wickedness when the subjects unnaturally do rebel against their prince."* (86)

By the sixteenth century there exists considerable evidence of a fierce determination on the parts of elders and superiors to break the will of children, possibly because of a covert, and not so covert, struggle among adult citizens to assert their own will. John Robinson, the first paster of the Pilgrim Fathers in Holland only reflected current ideas when he asserted:

> *"Surely there is in all children ..... a stubbornness, and stoutness of mind arising from natural pride, which must in the first place be broken and beaten down."* (87)

Similarly the training of children was commonly equated with the breaking-in of young horses or hunting dogs. As Lawrence Stone points out in his study of *The Family, Sex and Marriage: In England 1500-1800*, "*the characteristic equipment of the schoolmaster was not so much a book as a rod or a bundle of birch twigs*"' (88)

On Chartres Cathedral porch the emblem of Grammar is a master threatening two children with a scourge. And by the next century flogging became routine for boys and girls regardless of rank or age, whether at school or at work. In London the heads of the most distinguished public schools, Dr. Busby of Westminster and Dr. Gill of St. Pauls, were notorious for their savagery while at Oxford and Cambridge Universities the *'colleges freely used physical punishments......either by public whippings in the hall or over a barrel in the buttery, or else by putting them in stocks in the hall'.* [89] A lot of this violence carried an overtly envious tinge as Samuel Pepys noted in his *Diaries:*

> *"Pelham Humphrey......was admitted Gentleman of the Chapel Royal in 1666, and distinguished himself so much as to excite the envy of his instructor, who (eventually) died of discontent at his pupil's excelling himself."* [90]

A malicious preoccupation with discipline prevailed in most parts of Europe and America. This was most carefully documented in accounts of the childhood of the King of France, Louis XIII, son and heir of Henri IV. The child was treated as if he possessed, in the most generous supply, all the sins of his fathers, from envy to obstinacy. He got his first whipping at the age of two and these continued until he became King at the age of nine. Usually his nurse beat him with with a switch or birch as soon as he woke up. The favoured place was his behind.

> *"The whippings increased in frequency when he was three, and on one occasion his father whipped him himself when in a rage with his son. As he grew older, his nurse could not control him, and the child was held down by soldiers while she beat him. At the age of ten, he still had nightmares of being whipped, and the threats to whip him only stopped at the age of thirteen, not long before his marriage."* [91]

Paradoxically the strict subordination of children was the result of greater interest in them bought about by the Reformation and, in

Catholic Europe, the Counter Reformation. Children were charged with corruption and sin (principally pride and disobedience) just as women had been accused of witchcraft two hundred years previously, and they were threatened with similar punishments. The doctrine of the 'Original Sins of the Young' became the heir to possession by 'incubi and succubi. While women had been dismissed for being 'lousy with lust', boys and girls, 'Childish Monsters,' were condemned for being 'suffused with insolence.' or worse, as 'changelings.' (92)

The Protestant reformer, John Calvin, was so concerned that he demanded the death penalty for disobedient children, a precept that was turned into legislation in America. Although only a handful of children were ever executed for this crime, the Connecticut judiciary was authorized in 1642 to jail a child upon complaint from his parents about *'any stubborn or rebellious carriage'.* And Massachusetts imposed capital punishment in 1646 for any child over sixteen who *'shall curse or smite their natural father or mother'* , or even refuse to obey their orders. (93)

By Victorian times these extreme measures were replaced, or at least ameliorated, by more sophisticated techniques of paternal control, such as psychic assault. Moreover perceptions of children changed. While still possessed of the devil, it was a devil less charged with religious reprobation. Concomitantly old ideas about innocence returned to the fore. Fathers remained authoritarian and overbearing, but aloofness eroded over-involvement. The Victorian father enjoyed an Olympian stance, but was himself controlled by being placed on a pedestal. Therefore he could be feared and hated at a distance. (94)

The corporal focus of parent-child conflict in Victorian times was child sexuality, especially masturbation. While this conflict was most acute between fathers and son, there remained a special destructive element in the relations between fathers and daughters that often surfaced in the emotional disabilities of the filial generation. In either case the tyrannical father was partly displaying anxieties about his own potency, and partly acting under pressure from intense jealousy and envy about his children's abundant sexual energies. These issues are universal and more than evident today, although in the 19th century it was the sexuality that was suppressed, while in the present parents prefer to forget the hurt and sheer malice that adolescents can and do provoke. [95]

An oppressive, exploitative father often acting together with a self-seeking, resentful mother comprise the "*Monstrous Parent*", an actual persecutor. He and she tend to fill their offspring with pernicious projections (pride, insolence, sexuality, envy) and then attack them for possessing a 'bad disposition'. Essentially such people treat their children as toilets, convenient receptacles for their own denied, guilt-ridden impulses (deviltries). 'Monstrous Parents' can be very dangerous because they often disguise their preexistent (subjective) perceptions by citing minor transgressions, to which they respond excessively and inappropriately. [96]

A Polish Rabbi has provided a vivid illustration of the actual mechanism employed to attribute sin, pathological projective identification. He used to beat the young students who sat shivering in his classroom with leather thongs. After demanding that they pull down their pants and lie across a wooden bench, he would carefully recite:

> *"In every person there is a Good Spirit and an Evil Spirit. The Good Spirit has its own dwelling-place – which is the head. So has the Evil Spirit – and that is the place where you get the whipping."* [97]

The projections are clear. The Rabbi sees good in the head and bad in the bum, although there is no inherent reason for goodness or its opposite to reside in any particular region of the body. The element of identification comes in when he not only locates, but equates badness or 'The Evil Spirit' with the behind. And the pathological aspect of all this resides in his treating the students as 'Childish Monsters,' frightening figures and convenient receptacles for his own denied wilful, resentful, sensual self. By getting rid of the evil spirits which are very much his own, he is essentially expressing his envy of everything that young men have which he doesn't.

The students, in turn, are relatively powerless to oppose the attributions of their teacher. After all he is the authority and strong views backed up by violent deeds always have an penetrating impact. Inevitably many of them will succumb to the belief that their backsides, aside from other parts, are full of evil and deserve punishment.

* * * * *

This same process was institutionalized by the nineteenth century German physician and pedagogue, Daniel Gottlieb Schreber, whose views and writings on child-rearing were extremely influential during his lifetime and for a long time thereafter, up to and including the Nazi era. Schreber believed that children were naturally 'weak', 'soft' and 'rotten', and that their 'daemonic' defects were the cause of 'moral decay' in society as a whole. He warned against "ill-temper, morose or sulky forms of mind" in young children and compared these moods to *"life-endangering daemons"* which had to be rooted out like rotten weeds. (98) The same held true for older children. One had to be constantly on guard against and crush any *"ignoble, immoral or depressive emotions"* such as might be manifested through defiance and disobedience. Moreover:

".......one has to feel out the rotten spots by means of intense help; otherwise they eat away and the roots get so strong that this process will continue indefinitely." (99)

The solutions that Schreber advocated included beatings, starvation, and, in particular, complicated leather or metal contraptions, that were placed around the child's head or back or in order to force him to sit, lie or stand straight. For Schreber straight posture was identical with moral straightness or virtue. Should the boy or girl lapse, then these devices would press against the body and produce extreme discomfort or suffocation. [100] They have the same purpose as the bundle of birch twigs, in Italy called a 'fascio,' which is used to enforce absolute compliance in supposedly truculent children. Such devices have come to symbolize the political movement known as fascism.

* * * * *

Donald Duck and other Walt Disney cartoons convey similar concerns and solutions. Again and again Uncle Donald (and sometimes Aunt Daisy), accuse their nephews and nieces of harbouring their own greedy, irascible feelings. These attributions ostensibly explain and excuse their subsequent punitive behaviour, which is often extremely nasty. Thus, in *Donald's Happy Birthday* Huey, Dewey and Louie make a great effort to earn some money to buy their uncle a present. But he makes them put it in a bank. Still, wanting to get him a box of cigars, they 'borrow' the money. Donald finds out, calls them greedy no-good thieves, and sadistically forces them to smoke all the cigars, something he wanted to do himself. [101]

In truth the films often provide two perspectives, an objective study of a obdurate, angry, tyrannical adult or couple, which I call, the 'Monstrous Parent' (O), and a subjective impression of the same threatening person(s) from the point of view of their children or allegedly hapless victims. Melanie Klein and her colleagues have included such individuals under the rubric of 'the Combined Parent.' I would call him or her the 'Parental Monster' (S). To keep in mind the distinctions between the two terms I have added the letters (O), which stands for objectively real, and from the point of view of the child, refers to actual persecutors. Meanwhile (S) stands for subjectively real and includes the projective biases of the children in the child-parent dyad and triad. [102]

The latter is a focus of hatred turned against the hater, arising from overpowering phantasies of both parents locked in continual pleasurable (oral, anal, genital) exchanges. 'The Parental Monster" (S) is a mother imbued with traits of the father, and father imbued with traits of the mother, simultaneously attacked and transformed by the child's envy, greed and jealousy into a single terrifying figure. Such images help to explain, although they do not necessarily excuse, the vicious behaviour of children towards their elders.

In this chapter I deliberately emphasized the concrete reality of malevolent mothers and the brutal fathers, people transformed from helpers to hurters under sway of breast, womb or phallic forces. But the picture I presented was incomplete. We have to add the predominant phantasies of the angry child which can exaggerate parents' badness and negate their goodness. The fact that Laius was cruel to Oedipus does not mean that Freud's 'Oedipal' formulations are incorrect. Sons and daughters can and do harbour murderous intentions towards their parents or caretakers no matter how well or poorly they are treated. What is important is to place these feelings within the larger context of parent-child transactions. This helps to distinguish reasoned revenge, for example, from sheer malevolence.

With regard to the latter, each side frequently uses the other as a focus of pernicious projections and a dumping ground for 'sin'. But these very actions, the filling of persons or things with badness, and their subsequent metamorphosis, essentially define envy. So we are basically considering the flow of envy or other elements of malice from one generation to the next.

The envious child is 'The Monstrous Child' (O), the vengeful enemy of older people and established traditions, no less than 'The Monstrous Parent' (O) is an adult who demonizes youth. [103] Samuel Butler, for one, specifically referred to such children in his late Victorian novel, *Erewhon.* He envisioned a time when all infants signed a birth contract stipulating that their parents were not responsible for bringing them into the world and apologizing in advance for intentionally and treacherously setting about to *"pester and plague"* them. [104]

Butler articulated fears extending from pre-history to the present that children are mortally dangerous to their parents. These fears encompass dual perspectives, objective conclusions that boys surpass their fathers, and girls their mothers, whether as a fact of nature, or to repay the hurts they actually suffered, and subjective impressions of children as 'little devils'. The latter arise from the overpowering phantasies of parents. The resultant, terrifying, hated figure is 'The Childish Monster'(S). This is a fantastic image, which can overcome adults just as 'The Parental Monster' (S) can overcome children.

'Monstrous Children' (O) and 'Childish Monsters' (S) together with 'Monstrous Parents' (O) and 'Parental Monsters' (S) comprise a matrix of malice that affects all families. Sigmund Freud was the first of several investigators who have described different aspects of this matrix under the rubric of The Oedipus Complex (Freud), The Electra Complex (Jung), The Early Oedipus Complex (Klein) and The Laius Complex (Devereux). [105] Although the psychological literature abounds with examples of child-parent Oedipal conflicts, it is relatively rare for these exchanges to be seen within the larger matrix of parent - child relations, that is, the edifice of reciprocating hurts and hopes.

* * * * *

A colleague has told me about two separate dreams which he and his son had on the same morning. 'Dr R' dreamed about a fight among himself, his son, and an older man. It was a 'pea fight' which he started by throwing green peas at the others. While this was going on, his son was dreaming about being attacked by *"a Daddy-long-legs"*, a black bug with a long body but no legs. It had attached itself to his leg and begun to suck his blood and *"put in something that would make me sick"*. These dreams occurred at a time when the boy was doing well at school, but his father was pushing him to do more homework (prep), and had himself just bought a computer.

In discussing the dreams together the father thought that the older man represented his own successful father. Throwing peas had to do with the wish to pee both on his father's accomplishments and his son for doing well at school and 'getting up in the world'. R laughed when he thought of 'green peas' because he immediately connected green with *"green with envy"*. So he concluded that dream conveyed a multigenerational envious putdown.

The boy, who was psychologically quite astute, concurred and added that he thought his Dad's dream had been precipitated by rivalry, for he had recently been beating him at golf. In thinking about his own dream he related the bug to his Dad's bugging him about doing more 'prep' as well as computer bugs. He was amused by his Dad's interest in computers and thought he was on his way to becoming a computer bug, that is, an adept. He himself had been bitten by the computer bug long before and resented the purchase of a new machine that wasn't specifically for him. So he had been secretly hoping that the computer would be spoiled by bugs, that is, problems and errors.

R's son realized that his dream was about revenge, his own wish to get back at his Dad, and his fear that his Dad would get back at him. He suggested that the 'Daddy-long-legs' without legs represented his father without a penis, that is, without all his skills and expensive equipment. R was delighted with the interpretation and reminded the boy that the previous week he had half-jokingly called him a *"blood sucker"* for demanding a rise in his weekly allowance. All these recriminations recurred in the dream but had been put into the bug which appeared as a castrated, blood sucking, little shit. This bad bug was a memory, a fear and a wish. It was a retaliatory figure who threatened to attack this dreamer's leg/phallus and punish him for his own envious, vengeful thoughts. [106]

* * * * *

Morton Schatzman deciphered a different relationship where a man, an eminent German judge, was persecuted by mental and physical phenomena which he did not know and could not accept. It transpired that these were memories of the painful disciplines his father had inflicted on him. I refer to the case of Daniel Paul Schreber, the son of the pedagogue. [107]

At the age of sixty-one Daniel Paul published *Memoirs of My Nervous Illness* an account of the experiences and thoughts he had suffered during a fourteen year career as a diagnosed paranoid. He described the murder of his soul brought about by mysterious rays, writings, sensations, pressures, influences and miracles. [108]

According to Schatzman, and also the American psychoanalyst, William Niederland, these 'miracles' were almost exact representations of the father's practices as distilled from the voluminous writings of a pedant with divine pretensions. 'Compression miracles', for example, were directly related to the Screbersche Geraldhalter (Schreber's straight-holder) and Kopfhalter (head-holder). The former was an iron crossbar fastened to the table to force children to sit straight. It pressed against the child's collar bones and shoulders. The child could not lean against the bar for long without experiencing extreme discomfort. [109] As for the Kopfhalter, it was a strap clamped to the child's hair and his underwear which pulled and tore the hair if the head was not held absolutely straight. Father Schreber admitted that it had "*a certain stiffening effect.*" [110]

* * * * *

The two relationships I have been describing contain many elements of Laial and Oedipal conflicts, or, to put it another way, matrices of malice aroused both by the Laius and Oedipus Complexes. However, Dr. R. and his son were able to acknowledge their antagonisms and talk to each other because their rivalry and vindictiveness occurred within a larger context of affection and respect. The older Schreber professed love but practiced hate. His son was confused. Freud thought that his 'delusions' masked a homosexual attachment, that is, hidden love, toward his father. [111] Given his upbringing, it is more likely that they harboured unrequited hatred toward a father who refused to permit overt or covert filial antagonisms while demanding absolute obedience.

The extreme passions unleashed by parents towards children, or children to parents, are never resolved by their assuming an subterranean existence. At best potential explosions are put off till another time. What does happen is that the desire for life and wellsprings of love tend to intersect and mitigate curses, furies and complexes. Otherwise, we all would inhabit worlds solely determined by ancient or recent hurts. Nevertheless there are many instances where excessive envy or actual abuse overwhelm loving capacities and leave children and adults at the mercy of their destructive impulses, and those of others.

The younger Schreber was probably so resentful about the way he had been treated that he could not remember what he needed to remember, because to do so would have released a flood of the very feelings he had been taught not to feel. Instead they remained underground until outer circumstances in conjunction with inner pressures precipitated their chaotic release. [112] Such events are notable features of many lives, especially during adolescence or middle age when intense desires and enmities reassert themselves. Although Freud spoke about an earlier dissolution of the Oedipus Complex by taking parent figures into oneself and identifying with them, it is more accurate to say that the complexities of intergenerational love/hate/fear/guilt do not dissolve, but divert, inwardly, as he described, and outwardly in the case of myth and folklore. [113]

The boy who slays the Evil Giant also has to dispose of the Wicked Witch. Similarly the girl who overcomes a fearsome Queen also has to account for dreaded beasts. Both in dream and actuality, witches and giants are complementary creatures, cruel, self-centered, begrudging and usurping vitality and youth no less than male and female powers. Witches and giants embody the 'Monstrous Parent,' parental figures created by the imagination of the child and the misdeeds of the adult.

In every generation both children and parents need to assert themselves, yet avoid being beguiled, destroyed, or transformed into 'Complete Monstrous Persecutors' (objectively and subjectively), and trappped in the realms they rule.

In these tasks son Schreber became hopelessly lost, while son 'R' seems on the right track. Much earlier the Greek Titans, Giants and Gods were total failures while Oedipus had some success. Despite the dangers and difficulties, the stories of Jack the Giant Killer and Hansel and Gretel demonstrate that it is possible make progress, a point a patient of mine made when she decided to come off her pedestal, step out of fairy tales, and, as she put it, *"confront envy and jealousy, my parents' legacy and my own".*

Chapter 8

It's Not Fair

"Now Israel loved Joseph more than all his children, because he was the son of his old age; and he made him a coat of many colours.....And his brethren envied him......And when they saw him afar off, they conspired against him to slay him. And they said to one another, 'Behold, this dreamer cometh. Come now therefore, and let us slay him, and cast him into some pit, and we shall say, some evil beast hath devoured him; and we shall see what will become of his dreams.' " [1]

The story of Joseph, indeed, much of *Genesis,* is a discourse on sibling rivalry. The biblical origins of Western civilization touch Adam and Eve, Cain and Abel, Sarah and Hagar, Isaac and Ishmael, Jacob and Esau, and, in greatest detail, Joseph and his brothers. When they saw how much Jacob adored his eldest son, they were speechless with hatred, an animosity inflamed by Joseph's vivid dreams of preeminence, which he took pleasure to report. The *evil beast* was the spirit of malicious vengeance aroused by paternal favoritism and fraternal pride. [2]

The pattern was repeated in Egypt when Joseph's superior talents led to recognition and promotion by a new master, but also led to the unrequited desire and enmity of others, notably his master's wife. The woman attempted to seduce him. When he resisted her advances, she slandered him before her husband who had him imprisoned. (3) This episode has remarkable similarities to the Egyptian narrative, "Tale of Two Brothers", an account of sibling intrigue and conflict, which Bruno Bettelheim has called, the world's oldest fairy tale. (4) Preserved in a papyrus manuscript, it can be dated to 1225 B.C.E., but is undoubtedly older. Subsequently the legend has taken on close to eight hundred different versions. It concerns an older man and his younger brother, their bitter struggles and eventual reconciliation, all fomented by the wife of one who tries to seduce and thereby impugn the honour of the other. (5)

According to separate Hebrew and Egyptian descriptions the woman made herself the the center of a jealous storm, yet the protagonists strove to retain connections to their common stream – family and fraternal bonds. In these tales the woman symbolizes the interloper, the outsider, or more likely, the aggrieved brother or sister, who rues the loss of real or imagined rights, and wishes to assume ones he or she never had. It is interesting that the word that describes the ensuing intense, competitive, combative behaviour, *rivalry,* stems from the Latin root, rivalis, meaning *"having rights to the same stream."* So the original word implies sharing, based on joint inheritance or interests, while in actual usage, the word denotes aggression, the heir to feelings of unjust deprivation or simply greedy aggrandizement.

* * * * *

The Greek legends emphasize dual perspectives with both Gods and mortals striving *"to break the bounds of the brook."* Tantalus did this when he served his son in a pie, and Pelops did likewise when he murdered an accomplice during the course of gaining the hand of the beautiful, but guarded Hippodamia. (6) The deed did not go down well with Hermes (Mercury) the youth's father, who noted a challenge to his divine prerogatives. So he condemned the descendants of Pelops to repeat the fratricidal excesses of their father and grandfather. In the meanwhile Pelops himself was doomed to be the victim of equally devastating conflicts by colleagues such as Laius, who stole his favourite son, and Hippodamia, who orchestrated the boy's death.

This curse and antecedent actions proved to be the common source for ***Oedipus Rex*** and the ***Oresteia***, two blood filled streams of inter- and intra- generational ambition, pride, fear, malice, guilt and revenge. However, those who discuss these dramas usually stress the inter- generational features, that is, the conflicts between father and son or mother and daughter. Consequently sibling conflicts whether in the Greek myths or elsewhere tend to be seen through 'Oedipal' filters. (7) While it is clear that parents and children vie with each other for food, power and preeminence with a demonic intensity, and treat each other with extra-generational abandon (parents expecting their children to parent them or children seeing their parents as children), nonetheless, the sibling bond has a life of its own, which isn't just a pale reflection of earlier struggles. (8)

Parents frequently treat their children, and children their parents, as sibs, that is, compatriots sharing the same stream, either of love or hate. This may be especially evident during times of marital conflict when parents expect their children to take sides in their convoluted feuds, or during pregnancy or after childbirth. Many men have commented that they wanted to welcome a newborn child, but found the task too difficult because they simultaneously saw the baby as an intruder, like a younger brother or sister. (9) Similarly Peter Lomas has described a woman who suffered a prolonged depression after the birth of a son because he reminded her of a hated brother. (10)

In Latin America fathers, along with the displaced child, commonly share a state of severe physical decline known as *chipil* when a new baby arrives. This condition is a post-weaning syndrome that is generally due to protein and calorie deficiency following withdrawal of the breast, but it is popularly explained on the basis of intense envy (extreme discontent) toward the new foetus. No matter how proud the man may be, or pleased by the prospect of future economic contributions, he knows that he will be sharing his wife with a rival for love. [11]

On other occasions the discontent may flare up directly via angry, rejecting behaviour, or indirectly by encouraging one child to bully another. In this way some adults get their offspring to dramatize their own competitive instincts. In one family the older kids tried to poison and set fire to the younger ones, while the mother seemed oblivious to what was going on. Her therapist noted:

> *"The older siblings were acting out mother's (only slightly) unconscious wish to be rid of the younger children–a rather drastic form of maternal rejection."* [12]

Oedipus himself recognized sibling issues when commenting on his relationship with his daughters:

> *"These luckless two*
> *Were given birth by her who gave birth to me.*
> -----
> *(Chorus) These then are daughters:*
> *they are also –*
> -----
> *Sisters: yes, their father's sisters ....."* [13]

By the same token, Oedipus could have pointed out that he was the brother of his sons. Consequently their quarrels did not only encompass father to son, but also brother to brother as had been foretold by Pelops' curse. As the eldest 'son', Polyneices held the right to the throne of Thebes. But after Oedipus become an outcast, the throne was seized by the youngest one, not Polyneices, the next in line. While trying to effect a reconciliation their sister, Ismene, decried the 'ancient curse' and the way it enthralled their 'pitiful family:

".....then some fury put it in their hearts–
O pitiful again!–to itch for power:
For seizure of prerogative and throne;
And it was the younger and the less mature
Who stripped his elder brother, Polyneices,
Of place and kinship, and then banished him." (14)

According to Euripides, Polyneices had earlier confronted this treachery and deplored the fact that his brother had broken his agreement to share the throne, year by year, on the understanding that each would have his turn, and neither would engage in 'hatred or envy' with the other. (15) Both turned to Oedipus for support towards the end of his life, but he turned a deaf ear to their pleas and reminded them, somewhat unjustly, that for lack of '*a little word from that fine pair, out I went, like a beggar, to wander forever!'* (16) Although dying with honour, Oedipus rebuffed all attempts to stop the impending fratricides. His last act was to *"abominate and disown"* Polyneices and to foreclose the male line that had emanated from Laius:

" *....you shall die*
By your own brother's hand, and you shall kill
The brother who banished you. For this I pray. (17)

While this was happening the malediction was working its way through the other stream. Ostensibly, the *Oresteia* concerns the period from the fall of Troy to the trial of Orestes for killing his mother. (18) Actually it is a tragedy that reaches from Tantalus to Pelops and extends through an additional three generations of violent discord. By Hippodamia Pelops had several children including two sons, Atreus and Thyestes. By another wife he had Chrysippus whom he especially loved. If the conflict with Laius were not enough, Hippodamia became enraged by the favour shown to the son of another wife and arranged for her own sons to kill him. Presumably they envied the boy's good fortune and were jealous of the attention that their father, like Jacob, gave one among many. So they were more than willing to do the dirty work. [19]

Revenge and counter revenge continued through the next generation. The children of Atreus included Agamemnon and Menaleus, the husband of Helen, whose abduction precipitated the Trojan war. The children of Thyestes included Aegisthus, who killed Atreus and Agamemnon, after his triumphant return from Troy,.

Ultimately Orestes, Agamemnon's son, completed the blood feud by slaying his mother, Clytemnestra, and his uncle, her lover, Aegisthus. He was goaded to the matricide by his sister, Electra, who retained a fanatical devotion to the memory of her father and equally obsessive hostility to her mother. [20] It is said she remained the driving force behind his actions. However the abiding legacy of these events is not *The Electra Complex* – the alleged universal wish of a girl to kill her mother and love her father. [21] Rather, the *Oresteia* exemplifies the social fact and legendary curse that the sibling rivalries (intra-generational strife) of the parents may be replayed with devastating consequences through the inter- generational struggles of their children, and children's children. [22]

* * * * *

One essential theme unites all the contributors to sibling strife – **It's not fair!** This is an argument, more a war cry, that runs from Cain and Abel to the *Oresteia*, or, in the late 20th century, the TV series, *Dynasty.* [23] The perceived presence or absence of 'fairness' provokes or mitigates the resentments that lurk in all peoples concerning food, love, beauty, attention, privilege, power, that is, breast, womb or phallic possessions – the common streams.

Malice appears when fairness disappears, a fact confirmed by the angry child at times of separation and loss or, coincidentally, parental indifference. But one event stands out, the birth of a new sibling. The newcomer arouses the most acute reactions because the birth (or the sudden presence of a new child, as in certain step-families) announces a state of permanent deprivation coupled with an acute blow to self-esteem. The dethroned sib (or father) is no longer first and foremost in his mother's life. [24]

A sense of 'fairness' or proto-morality begins with wide eyed comparisons between what one has and what the newcomer is getting. The initial reaction is to exaggerate and then belittle both baby and mother, her breast, caring, feeding, caressing, lots of time; 'its' demands; and the growing relationship between them. Thus the *evil eye* awakens even before words or deeds can formulate and communicate the extent of one's discontent.

Phyllis Greenacre has described states of intractable jealousy in women, *The Medea Complex,* which she relates to extreme feelings of anxiety and envy often suffered in childhood upon the birth of a new brother or sister. For one sixteen month old girl the trauma was the sight of of a new-born baby at her mother's breast which filled her with unspoken, unspeakable and uncontainable oral aggression. [25]

Another psychoanalyst, Gerhart Piers sees the same situation in terms of guilt. This arises from the simple logic: *"The other gets more than me. I must take it away from him or kill him."* Piers remarks that the murderous resentment is fueled by feelings of extreme helplessness and impotence. The child assumes that all adults will behave like his parents who suddenly and unjustly withdraw their favours and direct them elsewhere. The resultant feelings of raging inferiority and guilt may then extend to all authorities or symbols of authority like Kings and institutions, or 'The State.' In the minds of the discontented, they all stand tried and convicted for favoritism, regardless of what they have or have not done. [26]

In the face of such intense hatred, mere reassurance does not work. As the paediatrician, Penelope Leach, put it:

> *"How would you like it if your husband arrived home with an additional wife, explaining that she was someone for you to play with."* [27]

The displaced children (and adults) tend to take their revenge on themselves (for unlovableness), the mother (for unfairness) and the new sib (for intrusion). The 'self' destruction frequently appears in the form of depression and regression, aside from conditions like *chipil* or *couvade*. We all have seen youngsters who become sulky and demanding once a sister or brother has been born, or cry remorselessly, wet their bed and go off their food.

On the other hand attacks on the mother may be surprisingly direct. A friend has told me how his two and a half year old daughter got very upset upon seeing her new brother being fed. The little girl got a knife from the kitchen, went up to her mother, and started to make wild slicing motions at her breasts. When asked why, the child replied:

> *"I want to cut off your breast, want to cut it off, stamp on it, on the floor, want to make a big mess of it."* (28)

The actor Randy Quaid recalls *"pangs of jealousy"* the moment he saw brother Dennis in a little bassinet. Until then, he had been the only child and was used to getting all the attention. He recalls anger watching his mother nursing him, but his strongest feeling was jealousy. This followed because he was put into the hands of a nanny and no longer had the ready access to his mother that he had previously known. (29)

The combination of envious deprivation and jealous exclusion can be an immediate flashpoint, or it can simmer for decades. Quaid hated the fact that Dennis remained the baby of the family and got preferential treatment. So he enjoyed being the older and stronger one who could *"beat the hell out of him and make his life miserable for the first sixteen years. It gave me a nice thrill."* (30)

The hatreds that new siblings evoke frequently extend to older sibs and parents. A thirteen year old North London girl was arrested after she set fire to the cots of her baby brother and sister. When questioned by neighbours about what had happened, she remarked, "...

they're gone, they're history." Previously that day she had written is her diary, *"Mummy is going to die tonight."*[31]

Grown-ups can also kill their entire family for similar reasons. One twenty four year old Milanese man strangled his mother and shot his father and younger brother in their beds because his parents thought he was *'stupid'* and his brother was *'the favourite.'*[32]

This violence affects all social classes. A scion of the English aristocracy, Lady Elizabeth Longford revealed how she caught her eldest daughter, Antonia (later Mrs Harold Pinter) in the act of smothering her baby brother Thomas. [33] Comparable episodes told by friends or relatives explain why most parents worry about the reception a new baby will get, all the more so with step-children. For them the new arrival is not only a threat in its own right, but tangible proof of the love which their own mother or father has given to another, and, by implication, withdrawn from them. All too often the step-parent feels second best too. A young woman anticipated problems marrying a man with three daughters. But she hadn't thought her step-children would continue to be '*spiteful, hostile and unpleasant'* long after she had made great efforts to be nice to them. Perhaps the last straw was when her own child was born:

> *"...the girls were downright cruel to him, putting salt, oil and mustard in his bottle and deliberately sticking nappy pins in his legs to make him cry."*[34]

The child psychiatrist, Donald Winnicott, has written about his work with a two year old girl nicknamed, 'the Piggle', who suffered nightmares, sleep disturbance, multiple illnesses and malicious destructive regressive behaviour, really the whole range of reactions, after the birth of a sister, seven months previously. Her parents said she had become extremely jealous and very greedy, constantly demanding to suck her mother's breasts in place of the baby. The Piggle called these breasts 'yams'. Often her mother seemed unable to cope with the intensity of her wish to suck on her 'yams', which her daughter likened to lollipops. The desire alternated with malicious rejection. When offered she might grab them or retort: *"No, I want to spoil them. I want to spoil your things."* [35]

For months the Piggle remained confused and chaotic. Her envious attacks were never entirely blocked by greed, while the greed only rekindled envy and intolerable, tormenting feelings of guilt. One moment she might seem calm, and then suddenly turn on her mother and hiss: *"Pity your yams have no milk in them."* [36] Her parents themselves felt confused and hurt. Her mother remembered:

> *"When I say good night to her she often buttons up my cardigan so that my yams don't get 'dirty and dead'. She has been very preoccupied with 'dead' lately. I said once: 'Soon your yams will grow.' She replied; 'And yours will die'."* [37]

Significantly, the Piggle was less aggressive to her sister than to her parents or to herself. She could be extremely mean and spiteful, but also solicitous and loving. A lot depended on whether the baby took her toys or not: *"Yes, I hate her very much only when she takes my toys away."* [38]

I think 'toys' means 'all the good things that mommy and daddy have'. When this happened, in fact or phantasy, her sister became 'black', that is, bad and blackened by her messy anger. Otherwise the Piggle was able to overcome some of the pain of losing her mother by identifying with her and playing the mommy with her sister. [39]

* * * * *

The birth of a sib is a peak 'unfair experience', but in every family there are many events which signify 'loss of the breast' and may feel just as unfair, or more so. They can roughly be categorized as *absences* or *intrusions*. The absences include the tangible loss of a parent through divorce, death, hospitalization, job induced separation, prolonged holiday; or the near equivalent via sickness or indifference; or excessive attention paid to another child. The author Nancy Friday links her rivalry with her eldest sister to such passive persecutions, that is, torture by endless emptiness:

> *"I couldn't get my mother's attention no matter what I did. No matter how many laurels I won, I was terrified of being left out......."* (40)

The active persecutions include both the absence of goodness and the presence of meanness, as with a narcissistic mother who alternates indifference with rivalry and denigration, or a Schreber-like father who fills his children with malicious projections, but some more than others. (41)

I have already discussed a major intrusion, a new baby. But the sudden appearance of a new step-parent, or friend or relative such as an elderly grannie who moves in and takes up a lot of the family's time and attention may be equally devastating. The intruder occasions loss and is an obvious person to blame. Mom herself may be seen as an unwelcome interloper when Dad (or an older sib) takes on the maternal role (to replace a mother preoccupied with other things, for example), or the infant just prefers him. And according to the circumstances, a child may be most furious for a new baby coming between him and his father, rather than between him and his mother. (42)

Of course, when there are a number of children in the family, the most common intrusions stem from the claims of other sibs, younger or older. Sigmund Freud, for example, in a letter to his friend Wilhelm Fliess noted that his daughter Anna (Annerl) was not at all pleased when her sister ate the family's store of apples:

> *"Recently Annerl complained that Mathilde had eaten all the apples and demanded that her belly be slit open (as happened to the wolf in the fairy tale of the little goat). She is turning into a charming child."* (43)

Whether a particular absence or intrusion, or as is more often the case, an extended sequence of absences and intrusions, is bearable or not does not only depend on the events themselves, but the subjective impact on the parents and sibs. Some children have a remarkable ability to brush off hurts and seek out support from the larger family or social circle. Others have a low hate/ high love/ high stimulation threshold. They hoard hurts like squirrels garner nuts, yet seem obtuse to the ordinary give and take, kiss and make up exchanges that are effective in children with high love/ low hate capacities. The latter may be lucky and have parents who notice their needs and respond accordingly. If not, trivial events will seem like terrible misdeeds, and the resulting resentments will turn their parents and sibs into persecutors, the focus of fights, both in the outside world, and psychic spheres, for years to come. (44)

* * * * *

'Joan' is a middle aged woman who has told me about battles with her sister which she still relishes. Once, in their late teens, they went into a pastry shop in Evanston, Illinois. They only had a small amount of money with them, barely enough for coffee and one cake. She wanted to leave, but her sister's eyes lit up in front of the cream cakes, the big ones with beautiful glazes and icings. *"That's how she was, blind greedy!"* So they sat down and the waitress came over with a large selection of cakes on a trolley. Her sister seemed mesmerized by a white, sticky cake. No sooner was it on her plate than she dived into it, totally oblivious to anything else. But Joan noticed that the trolley had become stuck on a bit of carpet which began to sway as the waitress tugged on it. A few moments elapsed before it finally tipped over and spewed cakes all over:

> *"I could have done something, but decided not to. The white cream and yellow icing went all over the table, rugs, my sister, the waitress It was hysterically funny. I laughed so much I*

cried. But the waitress was in tears and my sister, who finally noticed what had happened, began to cry too. In the end she felt guilty, and couldn't finish her cake. And there wasn't even any money for a tip." [45]

At the time Joan was triumphant, thinking that once again her sister had been caught out by greed and had to take the can. She could have stopped the trolley from tipping over, but didn't. She enjoyed watching the show and seeing everyone's embarrassment. For her the event was a great victory over family persecutors, a sister who '*got in the way*' and a busy mother in the guise of a waitress who provided food, but little else.

Joan was not unaware that inaction, where action is called for, is a powerful form of attack and a superb way of expressing envy and jealousy. The others get hurt, but it is easy to avoid blame. This attack and ensuing '*hysterical laughter*' constituted a manic defense against 'the unfairness' of continuing neediness, and against guilt for the countless subtle ways she continued to run down family rivals and subvert their expected counterattacks.

Manic-type defenses involving denial, self-inflation and the contemptuous denigration of envied objects are basic manoeuvres in sibling battles for the breast. Melanie Klein recalls one woman who intensely admired and coveted a shapely dress her mother had worn when she was a child, and at a time her elder sister was courting. She could barely control her rage. In later life she did better by maintaining a pervasive air of intellectual superiority. [46]

Klein's patient was the envier, but many children and adults act in strangely convoluted ways, not just to disguise their enmity, but to avoid the hatred that privilege and accusations of unfairness attract. Among the aborigine tribes of Central Australia mothers try to minimize *Cain jealousy* by eating every second baby and sharing the feast with the older child. [47] Here the mother regresses in the face of sibling cannibalism and becomes the deprived next in line while simultaneously deflecting the impulses away from herself. Alternatively, when a baby is born to certain Guatemala Indians, they beat a chicken to death against the body of previous child. The ritual serves to express and absorb the hostility that would otherwise be directed against the neonate, and probably the mother as well. [48]

* * * * *

Concealment, appeasement and negative assertion are other means to restrain passions aroused by 'relative deprivation', 'social proximity' and any other summons to sibling strife. A lot of times the issue is happiness. An article in the *The New York Times* points out that many couples hasten to hide their happiness, or feign unhappiness, in order to avoid the ill looks and sour thoughts of friends and colleagues who refuse to believe that people can be happy after a long marriage. [49] Similarly, within pairs of sisters or brothers, good fortune can lead one of the pair to *'play down everything good that ever happened.'*

Concealment often coincides with negative assertion. A sib may not only chose to 'hide goodies' from another, but also counter attack by 'running her life by a different set of rules' or 'becoming everything the other isn't' in order to make a favoured brother or sister feel bad. Sibling rivalries tend to enhance the process of individuation both from parents and other sibs. The feared or hated sib becomes a contrary model for doing well, or poorly, but certainly differently. The hope is to 'outshine them all'. Typically the eldest of two very pretty and capable girls became so 'pissed off' by the younger's social and intellectual achievements, that at age sixteen, and against all expectations, she ran away with a Hoover salesman and had three kids by the time she was twenty. A friend remarked, *"At least she had made her mark".* [51]

This story echoes with that of Sarah and Hagar, where one woman was pretty, but the other fertile, and the countless rivalries, within families and without, over female potency, including breast size, body shape, physical attractiveness, number of children and overall creativity. In the biblical tale Sarah was a great beauty, but unable to obey the injunction, *'be fruitful and multiply.'* Accordingly she gave her Egyptian maidservant to her husband Abraham, for under ancient

Middle Eastern codes, a wife was obliged to provide a concubine if she hadn't born a child within a stipulated number of years [52] However, as soon as Hagar conceived, she became contemptuous of Sarah and began to slander her, allegedly saying:

> *"My mistress Sarah is not inwardly as she appears outwardly. She pretends to be a woman of piety, but she is not, as she has prevented conception in order to preserve her beauty."* [53]

The words reveal an envious triumph and the preparation to take over another's place. But Hagar's mistress did not collapse. Instead Sarah, no doubt replete with envy herself and alarmed at the threat to her preeminence, treated Hagar harshly and forced her to flee to the desert. There she gave birth to a son, Ishmael. Later Hagar returned and submitted to Sarah's torments. But eventually she had to flee again, after Sarah bore Isaac and became extremely distressed at the sight of Ishmael playing with him.

The Bible indicates that Ishmael was reconciled with Abraham, and Isaac, at the time of their father's death, although the descendants of these two brothers, the Jews and Arabs remain antagonists. It is not inconceivable that their feuds continue to reflect the bitter hatreds that passed between their respective mothers some thousands of years ago.[54]

* * * * *

Folklore and fairy tales provide many variations of Sarah and Hagar sagas. Perhaps the best known and best liked is *Cinderella*, which was first written down in China during the ninth century A.D. [55] Like the biblical narrative, it concerns vicious rivalries over physical appearance, feminine functions and social status, with a younger sister as the servant and elder sisters/mother as the mistress. But maturation and morality are added complications. Cinderella is not quite a woman. She has to battle her own reluctance to come of age as well as bad tempered, evil siblings. Yet there are good reasons for her sisters to feel threatened. Cinderella is an unrealized, yet real sexual threat. But she also embodies purity, virginity and virtue. (56)

Bettelheim compares Cinderella to Jacob's Joseph. Although his father lavished love, Joseph ended up like the ash girl, abused and debased by his siblings and turned into a slave. He too has a miraculous escape and ends up surpassing his superiors. Bettelheim concludes that both stories have almost equal appeals to boys and girls because all children identify with heroes or heroines who suffer from sibling rivalry and vanquish their persecutors. (57)

The Brothers Grimm gave more details about the happy outcome. In some versions of the story, and after Cinderella married the handsome Prince, pigeons attacked the cruel sisters and plucked out their eyes. (58) The action was not only a victor's revenge, but also a precaution, related to the ancient, but still popular custom of veiling brides. The unstated purpose is to avoid maleficent onlookers.

Even now fears of the *Evil Eye* are not necessarily misplaced. In real life losers' reprisals frequently surpass the sororal viciousness of Grimms' characters. In 1959 American headlines screamed, *"Co-Ed Chopped in Envy......"*, after an attractive twenty year old college student had been butchered with an axe. The culprit was her former roommate, a plain, chubby girl who apparently filled with fury at the sight of her prettier friend. (59)

Similarly, grannies have been known to make a sordid spectacle in order to establish pride of place. A daughter recalls that her mother and mother-in-law were at permanent yule loggerheads, fighting continuously to see who would be the most helpful grandmother. (60) In my own family, the Passover holiday raised kindred conflicts. Two powerful elderly ladies contested gefilte fish and grandchildren. Envious assertions about who made the best food and produced the brightest kids, and jealous asides about who was the most loved, recapitulated earlier struggles for feminine supremacy. Generations of children were treated like potential lovers whose words and deeds signaled degrees of desirability. We tried to be fair, but inevitably failed. At some Seders, the ritual meals which commemorate the exodus of the Jews from

Egypt, there clearly was 'a better fish'. And, even when this was not the case, neutral statements could and were taken as hints of preference. Praise was a weapon that made one smile and the other depressed. The winner would repeat it over and over, while the loser revelled in headaches, shortness of breath and hands over heart which made everyone aware that she would soon be dead. Guilt sliced through the celebrants like a scimitar leaving wounds which took years to heal.

These grannie conflicts illustrate underlying patterns based on parental and sibling bonds. The latter is more likely when the two women are of similar age, but as I have previously discussed, sibling rivalries may mimic inter- generational conflicts, or the reverse. Cinderella had to fight both her mother and sisters, although each of the protagonists had their own axes to grind. These included the prospect of remaining an ashgirl as well as fears of reverting from a princess (or Queen) to a dirty, debased, that is, an unloved and unwanted woman. As for the grannies they were appalled that their opposite number might predominate and were obsessed with being relegated to the scrapheap, representing death.

The Cinderella scenario presumes a triangular relationship where one side is a woman who needs to possess a man and ward off rivals in order to confirm her female identity. However, many women describe a different triangle where their most impelling concern is to maintain close, supportive bonds. Indeed, the opposite of sibling rivalry is sibling closeness and cooperation. It is not uncommon for sibs to form an alliance with each other that lasts throughout their lives. (61) In these relationships the greatest threat comes from the feared loss of a sister or sisterly companion:

> *'I get very jealous when some man goes off with a woman "best friend" of mine. Because I feel that woman is an almost sister, and I don't want to lose her."* (62)

Interestingly, this person was also intrigued by men whom she could treat like her *'big sister Meg'*, or whose ex-girlfriends reminded her of Meg. She even enjoyed getting one up on her sister and 'sisters' when men switched allegiances to her. In contrast H.G. Wells observed that his relationship with fellow writer, Rebecca West, remained impossibly tempestuous, because of her elder sisters "*blind hysterical opposition*" to attention and support for anyone other than themselves.(63)

Another famous trio, the Mitford sisters, created a secret language called *"Honnish"* along with special games and rituals in order to fight common enemies including their nanny and brother. The latter aroused a separate organization, the *"League Against Tom."* (64) Perhaps the Mitfords saw Tom as an intruder and threat to their sororal solidarity a la Wells. More likely they resented the 'unfair' privileges that accrued to a male sibling in the aristocratic patriarchal culture of their youth. Such considerations led Freud to develop the ideas of penis envy and the castration complex :

> *"We have learned from the analysis of many neurotic women that they go through an early age in which they envy their brothers their sign of masculinity and feel at a disadvantage and humiliated because of the lack of it (actually because of its diminished size) in themselves."* (65)
>
> *"They feel themselves unfairly treated."* (66)

Freud concentrated on organ inferiority. In truth, many little girls focus on the physical equipment of their brother(s). which is an observation, not a conjecture. A neighbour I know was astounded by his three year old's fascination with penes,

> *"I want to be a boy. I want to be like Solly. I want to have a willy too. Look I can pee like Solly."* (67)

Usually, however, the rivalry is not for the organ per se, but for what the organ represents or can obtain, particularly the attention or favours of mother. This little girl flew into a rage whenever her mother hugged Solly, her elder brother. Here physical strength and masculine prowess has become unconsciously translated into attractive strength, that is, degree of desirability. (68) Coincidentally, I am also familiar with another family where the accusations of the younger sister concentrate on unfair privileges and perks, often to do with age, rather than physical characteristics. She insists "it's not fair" because her brother *"eats more, goes to bed later, gets more pocket money, gets hit less, has a better computer, takes control of the telly, 'is always butting in on my business' and' bosses me about.'"* Moreover, the girl complained that her brother had *'bigger legs'.* (69)

If the sex of these siblings were reversed, the narcissistic wounds would hurt just as much. Whether the ensuing resentments point to the penis seems to depend on several factors: birth order, age, gender, cultural expectations and specific family dynamics. Thus, masculinity may become the issue solely because the new baby is a male child who appropriates mother, specifically her breast and nipple. (71) And if the parents are inordinately proud of the baby just because he is male, then the penis itself is more likely to become the center of everything hateful. To the dethroned child, the over invested organ may seem identical to both the intruder and the absent object, that is, love, lovableness, warmth, nourishment, fullness and that which fills. This phantasy is a short step from the thought that the boy baby has somehow stolen the nipple and grafted it onto himself for his personal, exclusive use. (71)

Although Freud emphasized the pale and bitter looks of the aggrieved sister, the displaced brother often feels no less unfairly treated. True, he can down and see he has a penis, yet from from his point of view, he has a less useful member, one that has has lost its magic to cajole attention and aggrandize love. In these circumstances the boy's response may be to withdraw, or attack, but especially to compete for preeminence. In comparison to a younger or favoured brother, he may not be the hottest model, but like Avis to Hertz, he can try harder. The resultant rivalries, over strength, stamina, virility, authority, prowess and power, among a multitude of overtly phallic preoccupations, tend to take on a life of their own. Nonetheless, original objectives, pride of place and parental esteem, will never be completely obscured. They often emerge later in life through the strivings of men who meet, and sometimes buy, the public eye.

* * * * *

A good endowment is no defense against fraternal strife, it may simply serve to raise the stakes. The anguish of writer Gore Vidal has been ascribed to his*"absurd good looks, detachment and elegant ease,"* which *"prompts his peers to consider their own defects – and fall into uncontrolled envy."* [72] Not one to conceal or appease, at any given moment Vidal is sure to be trading invective with some member of America's political or literary establishment. Having successfully skirmished with Robert Kennedy, Richard Nixon, William F. Buckley, Jr. and Truman Capote, Vidal's thirty year war of words with fellow novelist Norman Mailer, culminated in a fist fight at a publisher's party. Mailer, an equally vain and contentious man, had apparently likened him to *"an old Jew."* After the dust had settled, Vidal quipped, *"Poor Norman, once again words failed him."* [73]

Like two old codgers locked in a room, Vidal and Mailer will continue to snipe until they take their last breaths, and probably long afterwards with the help of future generations of students and critics who remain fascinated by the essential qualities of their antagonisms. Certainly success did not diminish their vanity or personal insecurities. While referring to himself, the photographer Cecil Beaton explained the difficulty. Fame and fortune do not bring contentment, all that happens is that other talented, accomplished people intrude into one's life, and it becomes harder to avoid being overshadowed.

At the age of fifty eight Beaton made a long list of artists he envied. These included Graham Sutherland, John Betjeman, Noel Coward, John Osborne, Lawrence Olivier and Truman Capote. And after reading an article by Eveyln Waugh, he delighted in thoughts of:

"....gouging out his eyes with a pencil, then his nose and mouth and finally destroying his whole head before getting gleefully into my bath." (74)

Beaton claimed that he was not against talent, only talent which brought success, especially for people from modest social backgrounds. As an inveterate snob, that was unbearable. (75) However he also hated effortless honours, because he had worked very hard to inflate himself. In his view natural aristocrats and their 'hangers-on' only needed to stretch out their hands to pick up the plums. That was unfair! (76)

Just as Beaton suffered from a corroding discontent, he loved to inspire it in others, by name dropping, and other affectations all of which demonstrate the strategic importance of snobbery. Yet, when a knighthood finally did arrive, he was not satisfied. Like a younger brother caught in the trap of primogeniture, Beaton never felt he could catch up with past injustices nor overcome the differences between aristocratic friends and himself.

Billy Carter, the younger brother of Jimmy, the former President of the United States has led a less accomplished, but equally painful life, having had to endure noxious comparisons with successful sibs (or their substitutes) as well as extreme disparities between how he was and how he wanted to be. He compensated by negative assertion - public drunkenness, financial scandal and self-parodying appearances. In this respect he was not unlike the girl who married a Hoover salesman. At the end of the Carter era, the Chicago columnist, Joan Beck, noted:

"How sad to be a Billy Carter, psychologically caught in a good brother-bad brother bind, unable to live his underachieving life in backwater peace and privacy because he can't escape from the edges of the spotlight focussed on his overachieving brother." (77)

Billy exemplifies the person for whom destructive achievements assume the same significance as positive ones. Since he couldn't be the best boy in the world, he would be the worst, a phenomenon Herbert Rosenfeld has termed, 'destructive narcissism.' (78) This is a form of inverse snobbery that transforms shame into pride, and self-misery into a weapon to attack the identity of hated competitors. Having relinquished ambition, Billy exacted a terrible revenge. (79) By playing the' black sheep,' he seems to have set out to shame and embarrass his brother and family. (80)

Although this scenario is not uncommon, it is remarkable that a similar theme and variation has been played out by another southern boy made good, Bill Clinton, President of the United States during the 1990's. His nemesis was not a blood brother, rather a boy from a almost identical poor, rural Arkansas background, Cliff Jackson. They met when the two were students at Oxford University during the 60's. A mutual friend noted that *"when Bill was in the room he was the center of attention, (but) Cliff was a maverick, a sort of scratchy, prickly person (who) didn't have the acumen to make people feel comfortable."*

Both men were fiercely competitive, from sports to politics. But Bill prospered, and Cliff did not, so the latter man has spent much of life trying to run his former rival down. In that he has come close to success. Jackson was responsible for tipping off reporters about the President's draft record, about his obsession with woman and deception and corruption. Like Billy Carter, his revenge, has been to ruin, or at least attempt to ruin a colleague's career. (81)

* * * * *

Cecil Beaton, Bill Carter, Cliff Jackson, and others, all demonstrate the intransigence of envy. Fraternal jealousies, where the ostensible object is love, not power or privilege, concern triangular relationships, where the aim is to humiliate and annihilate the rival. Age is no barrier as indicated by reports like *"Three Dancing Pensioners in Jealous Tango".* (82) This story concerns a seventy one year old ex-army captain who became enraged when his regular ballroom dancing partner, a sixty four year old widow, dropped him for a new escort. He replied by attacking his seventy three year old rival's car, cutting the brake hose, putting water in the petrol tank and puncturing the radiator. [83]

In modern myths the excluded third party may be a computer. The film, *Electric Dreams*, describes a young architect who falls a love with a pretty cellist and courts her with the help of his computer. But the machine becomes jealous and acts like a Fury until it finally understands that love is unselfish and destroys itself. [84]

While these rivalries feature in untold tales, both before and beyond the ancient Greeks to the Brothers Grimm, few accounts convey the absolute rage and unremitting viciousness of fraternal strife as well as the Disney cartoons, *Tom and Jerry*. Tom, of course, is the tough old cat. Jerry is the tiny mouse who has to rely on ratlike cunning and total ruthlessness to get his way.

In *Polka Dot Puss* Tom pretends to be sick and sneaks special privileges from a sympathetic housekeeper. Jerry wreaks revenge by painting spots on Tom's face and using 'measles' as an excuse to administer sadistic treatments. [85] In *The Hollywood Bowl* Tom is the center of attention conducting an orchestra, but Jerry wants a piece of the action. During the ensuing fracas, first one is on top, and then the other, but Jerry triumphs and Tom is wiped out. [86]

The conflicts are objective and subjective. To Jerry, Tom is an actual persecutor, and an imaginary one, full of his own malicious wishes. As someone bigger and stronger, Tom embodies both parents and older siblings, 'complete monstrous parents and siblings.' This gains Jerry immediate sympathy and creates the tension which can only be resolved when Tom gets his comeuppance.

To Tom, Jerry is also an actual persecutor, and an imaginary one. As someone smaller and more diabolical, Jerry embodies both children and younger siblings, 'complete monstrous children and siblings.' In this way Disney creates a countervailing tension and sympathy for a harassed Tom which can only be resolved when Jerry gets hurt or at least deflated, such as in *Polka Dot Puss*. In the end he comes down with measles too.

These cartoons are a study in persecution. And for their audience, children and adults, they are a focus of vicarious retribution. At any given moment either Tom or Jerry may be chopped, knifed, stung, shot, crushed, flattened, drowned, bounced, bombed, burned, chased, smacked, slapped and shattered. [87]

Fortunately for both protagonists and onlookers, the damage doesn't stick and in several episodes hate turns to remorse. [88] Thus, Tom and Jerry hold a mirror to 'real life' where brothers 'fight like cats and dogs' or rather cats and mice, but also make up and make good teams, whether fighting external enemies or engaged in creative projects like the Wright brothers, Warner brothers, Smothers brothers, Smith Brothers and Brothers Grimm. After all, they come from the same stream.

Randy Quaid concluded that the best thing about having a brother is *"….having another man you are really close to, somebody you feel understands."* But Quaid only came to this realization after the traumas of childhood injustice had *"pretty much passed".* [89] Other men do this through triangular relations where the point of the intrigue is not to capture a woman or dispose of a rival, but to establish and maintain fraternal closeness.

The psychoanalyst Robert Robertiello describes a 'glorious phantasy' *"of going down on the guy who'd stolen a woman"* from him. [90] The man was bearded and black, an alter ego, a narcissistic self-image filtered through the body of another male. Here the third party was not an intruder but a necessary extension of himself, an animus containing elements of an external character and his own needs. As with the woman who sought sororal bonds, the greatest threat is not rivalry but the lack of rivalry, not the presence, but the absence of fraternal figures against whom one can measure and discover oneself. Anything less seems unfair.

A male or female companion may serve as a mirror and seem like a persecutor because he or she establishes boundaries and prevents the vainglorious overstepping of bounds that brought down characters as diverse as Agamemnon, Oedipus, the Amazonian Queens, Queen Christina or Tom and Jerry. In this sense brothers and sisters are necessary interlopers in the lives of parents and siblings, if they enable them to avoid the curse of hubris, and the fate of the House of Pelops.

While fulfilling this role sibling companions tend to be hated because they dethrone ambitions and deflate expectations. Yet, as the Quaids and others make clear, even after such hatreds, they can also focus the deepest affections. This occurs when they reflate lost hopes, contain bad dreams and provide much needed excitement and pleasure. So sibs or friends, can reestablish justice both by bounding excessive pride and binding intolerable absences along with all the grievances that might otherwise flow. (91)

* * * * *

I would like to conclude this chapter on siblings, and the previous one on parent-child relations, with a brief account of a happily married middle aged professional woman who began psychoanalysis because of depression and work inhibition. (92) The problems that emerged during the final phase of her analysis recapitulate many of the themes I have been discussing.

Having worked through triangular rivalries with her brother and father, and penis grenvy, she seemed ready to conclude the treatment. But before this could happen, a frightful residue of unresolved craziness burst out. She became obsessed with ideas that her husband was unfaithful and her brother was interfering in her analysis, a delusional state similar to the 'Othello Syndrome.' Although these disturbing thoughts gradually receded, she was left feeling very fragile, and worried about a small wart that had appeared on the crown of her head. She associated it with *"warts on the brain"* and growing a penis.

One day she met a friend at a party, a spinster who suffered from *alopecia nervosa,* that is, anxious loss of hair. (93) The party itself had been lots of fun, like a carnival, with dancing and balloons to bring home. But the patchy bald woman upset her. Afterwards she had a dream which featured a repulsive growth right next to her wart. In the dream she thought, *"And the little wart as well!"* She had not expected to suffer from both.

The puzzling images slowly revealed their secrets. In the analysis the woman connected the growth with her friend's baldness, with cancer of the womb and breast, and with a spoilt balloon losing its air. Simultaneously she recalled a dead sister with beautiful hair whom she had envied, terribly. Having no husband, or children, or parents, her friend was like this sister who had lost her life at an early age.

All these connections helped, but her torments persisted until she came across a Spanish proverb about ringworm:

> *"If envy were ringworm, how many ringwormy people would there be in the world!"* (94)

Of course, she thought, ringworm is a growth which invades the skin. Then everything fell into place and she experienced enormous relief. The*"wart on her brain"* was envy which like ringworm or cancer, invaded all her relationships and activities. The dream thought, *"And the little wart as well,"* equaled an earlier, unconscious realization that she had greed and envy on the brain. She wanted everything for herself, the breast, the womb, babies, all manner of feminine success, and the penis, phallic achievements as well, while also begrudging her sibs and parents the same.

In this world of invasive rivalry her friend represented both her sister and Mother. (95) Hanna Segal, her analyst, pointed out, for this woman penis grenvy and sibling rivalry were secondary to breast and womb grenvy, intense desires and malice really directed at and concerned with her mother, and her mother's body, the spoilt balloons. (96) As for her dead little sister, and anyone like her, she needed them, both to feed her vanity, and to use as a dustbin for her own shitty, sooty feelings. In this sense this story is a version of *Cinderella*, but with a different ending. Here the older girl (the step-sister) comes up trumps while Cinderella remains with the ashes.

In fact this person wanted everything and hated everybody.

Segal comments:

> *"She envied men their penis and the love of the woman; she envied mothers their new babies; feeding mothers their breasts; married women their husbands; but she also envied the unmarried women their time, free of family or financial worries, and sometimes their greater professional success."* (97)

Because of these feelings, all she did or had, marriage, children, professional skills, joie de vivre, was spoilt by guilt which surfaced as depression and difficulties at work. And the successes she did manage, which weren't inconsiderable, added to her troubles. (98) These only began to lift after she understood the dream and acknowledged the dark side of herself. As for the wart, it dried up and fell off of its own accord.

The Politics of Malice

Chapter 9

The Politics of Malice

The politics of malice is the transformation of envy, greed and jealousy from personal events to social processes. I refer to the myriad ways that people seek to amplify and conceal their animosities and desires, and do this through social, economic and political policies, as well as accompanying rituals, customs, laws and organizational practices. For the envier this is an opportunity to enlarge the scope of envy, while evading responsibility for the consequences. For those affected it appears that ill-will is emanating from an institution, or society itself, which helps to explain ancient preoccupations with 'Phthonos Theon,' Envy of the Gods.

'Institutionalized envy' is the expression of spite, grudge, vengeance and venom by corporate bodies, political parties and other established entities. [1] The ensuing damage may be done directly through the representatives of these institutions, or indirectly via the implications of their basic ideas. This does not mean that institutions are inherently vicious, nor that all the damage perpetrated by them has to do with envy. As with individuals, the ill-effects of institutional actions may be assertive, defensive or functional. However, envy must be considered when the impact of these actions on individual citizens or clients is harmful, and contradicts stated intentions, such as to educate the young, disseminate information, create wealth or redress injustice.

The British journalist, Paul Johnson, has documented the extent to which the trade unions tread on their members because of *"fear of the free play of brains, the consciousness of inferiority, the hatred of the energetic and the successful...."* [2] In a similar vein an article in the *London Standard* assails gossip columnists who malign ministers and asks why jockeys or tennis players are entitled to huge fees, but not businessmen or politicians:

> *"I'll tell you why. Because the second-raters, who cannot cut their mustard, tell the yarn that those who excel them have done it fraudulently, unjustly, and without earning the money they are paid."* [3]

Governments themselves tend to be uncommonly interested in personal wealth. In the former African kingdom of Dahomey, a commoner who used too many leaves on the roof of his hut suffered the loss of a limb, while the German National Socialist party came to power under Hitler with promises to limit incomes to 1000 marks per year and eliminate unearned earnings. [4] In 1986 Burma passed a law enabling the cabinet to investigate the well-to-do. Those who had attained a certain degree of property were automatically suspect of tax evasion, bribery and corruption, and liable to ten years in prison. [5] A law like this is ominously close to the spirit of Nemesis, the Greek Goddess who attacked the prideful and rich, deploying devices like public ridicule and ostracism. [6] In all of these examples "*envy is the negative unifying force* " which connects private hates with the public will. [7]

The *New Yorker* cartoon illustrates 'institutionalized greed.' [8] A massive, overblown building, the headquarters, perhaps, of a business or government, dominates everything and everyone with windows like huge prying eyes and an imposing entranceway and supporting pillars, its mouth and teeth, all too ready to gobble up whomsoever dares approach. The architecture signifies the structure of a voracious, insatiable organization, preoccupied with growth and bigness for its own sake. Such bigness not only denotes the greedy aggrandizement of function and privilege, but narcissistic inflation, the wish to crush the independence and ego of clients and competitors. Hence the cartoon is correct to display lust (excessive desire) and envy (malicious denigration), which helps to explain why so many people feel enraged by the quality of bigness. [9]

'Institutionalized jealousy' can be seen in threesomes involving an individual and two organizations, or an organization and two individuals. Disloyalty is the keyword indicating the lack of perceived commitment as well as the threat of vengeful retaliation. A husband or wife who works for a large corporation and spends more time with his or her spouse than on company business may be irrationally liable to such accusations. Alternatively Lee Iacocca, former President of the Ford Motor Company, has depicted the tangible hostility that prevented Ford executives from having anything to do with rival car makers, especially General Motors. As Henry Ford once snarled at him, *"You're talking to too many people outside."* [10]

Jealousy, as envy and greed, may also be embedded in longstanding customs. Primogeniture is the principle whereby the eldest son inherits everything and other siblings little or nothing. Among the English property-owning classes, it was an essential tradition, which guaranteed bitter acrimony between first born sons and their younger brothers. (11) Among fifteenth century Turks the absence of primogeniture meant that battles for succession invariably ended in a blood bath. This was institutionalized by Muhammad II who issued the Law of Fratricide. It decreed that future Sultans, upon attaining the throne, should immediately execute all their brothers. Achmet I, however, tried to be kinder. He declared that male claimants should not be killed, simply locked in a small house, called the Cage, until their time might come, decades later. (12)

* * * * *

The malice I have been describing begins in the form of intra-psychic impulses attracted to primal organs such as the breast, and their reflections and refractions. These quickly progress to inter- personal events carried out by parents and children, brothers and sisters. In this section of the book on the institutionalization of envy, greed and jealousy, I intend to demonstrate the many ways that these basic impulses and events can and do coalesce into pernicious, collective policies. Unless checked by beneficent forces, the end results range from minor personal tragedies to global wars.

In 1921 Freud provided an extremely illuminating analysis of the transformation of individual to group enmity during the course of discussing the *'herd instinct.'* (13) He observed that a '*'herd instinct'* or sense of group solidarity develops when an older child suffers the birth of a sibling or is sent to nursery school and has to compete for love and attention with other children, Intense envy and jealousy arise. The child would like to get rid of the rivals and keep his parents and teachers to himself. But he knows that new sibs or children are also loved, and if he did this, he would damage his own interests. Instead, he identifies with the other boys and girls and they with him. All more or less tacitly agree to give up their individual claims in return for collective fair play, that is, equal treatment for all. Then the loud, implacable howls, *"it's not fair,"* no longer refer to personal desires, but to others' transgressions of the rule, *"there will be no favourites."*

The emergence of group feeling or mass emotion in conjunction with the submergence of personal rancour occurs in an almost endless variety of settings from nursery schools to teen fan clubs to professional societies and political parties. As a member of a therapeutic community led by a charismatic psychiatrist, I noticed the intense tension and hostility that the group as a whole felt and expressed when anyone tried to get too close to the leader. *"Too much"* revolved around an unspoken consensus about what was *"fair"* or *"just."* I myself rarely admitted to feeling personally aggrieved, but I certainly participated in group decisions to chastise and sometimes ostracize offenders.

Freud commented about this phenomenon:

> *"What appears in society in the shape of Gemeingeist, esprit de corps, 'group spirit', etc., does not belie its derivation from what was originally envy. No one must want to put himself forward, everyone must be the same and have the same. Social justice means that we deny ourselves many things so that others may have to do without them as well, or, what is the same thing, may not be able to ask for them. This demand for equality is the root of social conscience and the sense of duty."* (14)

Herd transactions are popular because they allow negative feelings to be disguised, yet also acted upon. But even more useful, they appear to reverse hostility into positively-toned ties of mutual support and solidarity. Therefore the shame and guilt provoked by envy, greed and jealousy can be denied, while the participants bask in self-righteous identification with the common good. The same incentives contribute to the power of tribalism, nationalism, religious fundamentalism, such as Islamic Jihad, and many all-encompassing ideologies. (15)

However, a group is not simply an amalgam of individual interests, but it has a life of its own, and a capacity to coerce people, who may be inadvertent members, to concede certain passions and deny others. Thus, a Christian born in Germany during the first half of the twentieth century, may not have felt personal hostility towards Jews. But in order to survive as a citizen in a Nazi state, he would have had to malign them, or be endangered himself.

There exists a continual flow of feelings from the individual to the group and back the other way. In the latter circumstances the group projections may be so strong as to force people to feel what they don't feel. Or, in the case of men and women accepted as 'leaders', the return flow replenishes and amplifies hostilities which they had put into the group in the first place. (16) This is an advantage of leadership. It gives people a sounding board, and sometimes a deadly opportunity for carrying out personal malice. (17) Helmut Schoeck points out that Freud's theories of the *'herd instinct'* and the *'leadership principle'* provide an astonishingly accurate picture of Nazi Germany under Adolph Hitler. (18) The same holds true for Iran under the Ayatollah Khomeini, as in many other countries and organizations under the sway of autocrats. (19) The institutional infrastructure may do the dirty work, but behind faceless mandarins and impenetrable group processes, there lies personal praxis, that is, the specific actions of strong willed, aggrandizing, hate filled personalities.

* * * * *

It is possible to trace the impact of individuals on all areas of social and institutional life, although specific instances are often obscured because of deliberate concealment or organizational muddles. Politics provides a good starting point for the little man who wants to become big. Reinhold Hensch, for example, was the deputy head of the Nazi SS in charge of the campaign to exterminate Jews, gypsies and other *"enemies of the Nazi state."* (20) Before the war he was a journalist for a Frankfurt newspaper, had a Jewish girlfriend, and was a member both of the communist and Nazi parties. A colleague described him as *"not especially brilliant."'* [21] Hensch began his climb to power by accepting the post of press advisor. At the time he seemed to be frightened by Nazi policies, but claimed he had no choice for he wasn't especially clever and came from a undistinguished background. [22] He envied his colleagues, especially Jewish ones, who were better off. Comparing himself to them, Hensch felt his prospects were poor, yet he wanted power and money. He wanted to be *'a somebody'* :

> *"That's why I joined the Nazis four or five years ago when they first started rolling. And now I have a party membership card with a very low number and I am going to be somebody! The clever and well-born and well-connected people will be too fastidious, or not flexible enough, or not willing to do the dirty work. That's when I'll come into my own. Mark my word, you'll hear about me now."* [23]

Hensch's views are not dissimilar from those of his Führer, Adolph Hitler, and Hitler's opponent, Joseph Stalin, both of whom mobilized their states for total war. The quest was power and the motivation, grenvy. To begin, neither man represented unstoppable or even potent historical forces. They were guided by *"personal prejudices of the crudest kind and by their own arbitrary visions."* [24] In Russia Hitler's aims were narrowly and ruthlessly acquisitive. After *"cleansing"* the Crimea of Slavs and Jews, he intended to turn it into a gigantic spa, a sexual pleasure ground for ex servicemen. [25] Stalin, on the other hand, was less of a plunderer, but just as greedy, for power, land and especially, revenge. After the war he redirected his enmities against former colleagues and comrades, using the mechanisms of state to choreograph insatiable show trials and executions. [26]

These dictators were able to maintain a political stranglehold by total control of the press and media. In this they were aided by journalists like Hensch. Stalin also made use of the officially sanctioned practice of anonymous denunciation, a hangover from the days of the

Tsar. [27] It meant that anyone could send poison pen letters to the newspapers or other authorities which were often acted upon without further investigation. In Stalin's time unsigned slanders led directly to Siberia, and were an important means of control by terror. No-one was safe from the noxious gaze of a neighbour. [28]

In other countries the wish to *"pull a person down a peg or two", "knock him off his pedestal"* and *"pull the rug from under"* has long been the province of gossip columnists and yellow journalists acting on behalf of a readership voracious for smut. In England the writer, Richard Ingrams, made a success of *Private Eye*, a small magazine which quickly became the anti-establishment's establishment's evil eye. [29] His alter ego, gossip columnist, Nigel Dempster, insists that he is a defender of the public: *"It is my great joy to show that the privileged are not what they seem,"* and employs a host of informants to dig up embarrassing and derogatory items about famous people. [30] Friends remark he has a memory like an elephant, often directed to those who have snubbed him, and *"is given to wild hatreds."* [31] Dempster himself rationalizes the hurts he purveys by referring to his *"tremendous curiosity"* and *"a great urge to tell."* [32] In fact he embodies a long tradition of muckraking whose American compatriots have included Mark Twain, Sinclair Lewis, H. L. Mencken, Bob Woodword and Carl Bernstein. While Dempster quips that his job is to pull the plug on *"Fairyland,"* their targets had more to do with politics and business. And their envy surfaced as moral indignation. [33] In that sense, envy may have a positive function, as part of a system of checks and balances. In a free society, when one part becomes overblown, it is likely that 'the fourth estate' will blow the whistle.

In a massive book on bribery, John Noonan, Jr. points out that in the 1970's alone, 43 American mayors, 60 legislators and 260 sheriffs and policemen were indicted for corruption, not to mention four governors and a former Vice President, Spiro T. Agnew. [34] In a related study of corporate greed, Morton Mintz, a reporter for *The Washington Post,* comments on the disastrous decision by executives of the A. H. Robbins Company to market a faulty intrauterine device,

The Dalkon Shield. [35] Approximately 90,000 women suffered major complications from which most would never recover:

> *"The human being who would not harm you on an individual, face-to-face basis, who is charitable, civic-minded, loving, and devout, would wound or kill you from behind the corporate veil."* [36]

The trade union counterpart of the ill-natured businessman can be seen in the person of Bill Geddes, former branch chairman of the National Union of Public Employees at Hammersmith Hospital, London. During the years that he pursued vendettas against *'rich bastards'*, *' private medicine'* and *'capitalism,'* the hospital was plagued by an unending series of unofficial strikes, wildcat strikes and selective withdrawals of services. Another steward declared: [37]

> *"I shut the works down on several occasions because it was a nice day and I wanted to go fishing.....I did not want the other fellows to have more money in their pay packets than I did."* [38]

For these officials the issues had partly to do with morality and partly with legality. Geddes thought workers were good and capitalists bad, beliefs which rationalized absolute attacks on the 'the system', that is, inequality. He did not seem to be too concerned with equity, or fairness, a concept which underpins most systems of law. The second chap was more concerned with fairness, rather than right and wrong. For him, an increase in happiness (fishing) did not balance a loss of income. He used the idea that income differentials were *'unfair'* to cover envy of his mates superior capacity for work. So he took the law into his own hands.

* * * * *

Envy, and the fear of envy, are intimately connected with the principles and practice of morality, ethics, law and justice. Thus, Bertrand Russell declaimed morality was a masquerade for misery, and H. L. Mencken averred that excessive moral zeal served solely to punish happiness and to bring people down to the same *"stupid, cowardly and chronically unhappy"* level. [39] The effects of such zeal can be traced quite closely through the life and career of Anthony Comstock, a vengeful, evangelical man who was personally responsible for virulent moral purification campaigns in the United States during the late 1800's as well as anti obscenity statutes which censored the literary and artistic tastes of Americans from 1873 until 1959. [40]

Comstock suffered a tumultuous childhood and during his teens was obsessed with masturbation, which he thought would lead to suicide. Around the onset of the Civil War he became *"an inspired member of the YMCA"* and enlisted the organization to propound his views of the dangers of erotic books and pictures which he believed, were *"...a moral vultures which steal upon our youth, silently striking their terrible talons into their vitals."* [41]

Informers, spies, entrapment and mail tampering were all part of his plan to ferret out evil doers. Although opposed by people who feared the loss of constitutional freedoms, Comstock was aided by business leaders and industrialists such as J. P. Morgan who believed that sexual permissiveness detracted from workers' efficiency. [42] In 1873 he persuaded Congress to pass a federal bill prohibiting obscene materials from the post. President Grant added a rider appointing him a special anti-obscenity agent of the Post Office. Two months later the New York legislature granted his own organization, 'The Society for the Suppression of Vice', police powers including the right to carry guns. [43] In the ensuing decades, Comstock and his Society terrorized publishers and arrested hundreds of citizens caught with questionable literature. Fifteen women accused of immorality chose to kill themselves rather than face the humiliation of a public trial. [44] Towards the end of his life the crusader boasted that he had:

".......convicted persons enough to fill a passenger train of sixty-one coaches, sixty coaches containing sixty passengers each, and the sixty-first almost full. I have destroyed 160 tons of obscene literature." [45]

Comstock was a modern incarnation of a mediaeval witch hunter. Armed with an Act, a mid Victorian version of the *Malleus Maleficarum*, he deployed fellow inquisitors amidst a public ready, if not willing, to be preyed upon. Like Kramer and Sprenger, he internalized the prevalent hysteria of his time, magnified it through frustrated desire and envious torment and reinserted the whole lot into the body politic. In response the law became an organ overlooking the happiness of unsuspecting citizens, while the courts and police became rods of ruination. This situation is not unique in American history.

In the twentieth century J. Edgar Hoover of the Federal Bureau of Investigation, Harry Anslinger of the Federal Bureau of Narcotics and Joseph McCarthy of the House Un-American Activities Committee all put their personal prejudices and perverse ambitions towards the same ends. [46] Each of these organizations became an agent of the evil eye, first exaggerating, then denigrating and finally destroying whomever and whatever was caught in its gaze. I am not describing a simple abuse of power. On the contrary I refer to the transformation of a state service, under the impact of private intentions and public perceptions, into a rapacious, malevolent monster capable of inducing states of near chaos and panic in ordinary citizens, aside from actively spoiling their lives.

* * * * *

An investigative agency or a House committee may or may not convey extreme examples of institutive violence, but one does not have to look far afield to discover extremes of greed and envy in the everyday practices of government and professional bodies. Having related such actions to individual interests, I now wish to trace their impact on specific targets beginning with wealth and prosperity.

Gossip columnists, glossy magazines and, of course, radio and TV, expend great efforts to arouse desires and inflate personalities. Usually the celebration of avarice occurs in conjunction with advertising which is potent means of creating new needs, and changing old ones.(47) The ad agency, N. W. Ayer, had astounding success in persuading people of all economic brackets to buy diamonds on the basis that, *"A Diamond is Forever".* (48) In fact the gems can be shattered, chipped, discoloured and very easily lose value. Nonetheless the slogan led to a massive boom in engagement rings in the United States and Japan (where they were previously unknown) and fueled speculation which greatly increased the fortunes of the De Beers cartel at the expense of individual owners. (49)

Gullibility and vanity are certainly not limited to the diamond exchange. Brokers maintain that *'fear and greed rule the stock market'* while the motto of Goldman Sachs, one of the largest investment banks in the United States, is: *"Long-term greedy, not short-term greedy,"* a statement which both denies and asserts the importance of extravagant financial desires. (50) The stock market itself often behaves like a roller coaster with manic managers all too willing to give *"the punters a flutter".* Should they get sick or fall off, become insolvent, well, that is their business. The experts concentrate on oiling the wheels and producing the highs. Covert contempt for the cogs in the wheel and the system as a whole remains unacknowledged.

Michael Milken and Ivan Boesky have been two of the greatest experts in milking 'the system' for huge cash flows. Milken invented 'junk bonds', high yielding loans based not on what a company has done, but what it might do in the future. (51) Boesky, nicknamed, *"Piggy"*, because of an insatiable appetite for speculative stocks, used and abused corporate trading to parlay a modest inheritance into a gigantic fortune. (52)

Boesky was proud both of his financial success and his greed. He liked to flaunt his wealth, connections and arrogance. (53) Thus, while meeting with business students, he assured them that 'greed is good' :

> *"I want you to know that. I think greed is healthy. You can be greedy and still feel good about yourself."* [54]

Boesky's greed and his ability to manipulate a business or political system for personal purposes, are not unique. At the same time that Boesky was learning his business, on the other side of the world, Imelda Marcos, the wife of the former President of the Philippines, was amassing money and goods to a scale that might have made even Boesky wince. She used and abused her position to obtain, among a multitude of things, 3,000 pairs of shoes, 68 pairs of gloves and five shelves of Gucci handbags, all with their pricetags still attached. After visiting her palace, U.S. Congressman, Stephen Solarz, remarked: *"Compared to Imelda, Marie Antoinette was a bag lady."* [55]

Subsequently, avarice at the service of vanity, led to Boesky's undoing. In one of the most spectacular scandals the American business community ever encountered, he was indicted and convicted for dealing with insider information. Flamboyant to the end, he paid the largest fine ($100,000,000) ever imposed (at the time of conviction). Meanwhile, Imelda Marcos has been indicted by the Philippines government. [56] Milken did not share the same public opprobrium, although he did serve a term in jail and pay a huge fine. Perhaps this was because he chose to live on a modest scale, and unlike Boesky, avoided rubbing so many noses in his success. [57] In fact, many bankers and businessmen consider Milken to be a financial genius who has helped to revolutionize and revitalize the American business system.

* * * * *

Like corporate raiders, many other businessmen and professionals share the wish to ravish the public and bite the hand that feeds them, perhaps none more so than members of the American bar. Two thirds of the world's lawyers live in the United States and they are increasing at a rapid rate. [58] In Washington D.C., where one in every twenty-five men, women and children is a lawyer, jurists draw up the laws which assure them more work and the need for more laws. Should they be stumped for jobs, graduates can and do spend their time dreaming up new ways to sue. The American Bar Association calls the practice *"imaginative lawyering."* [59] Sharp attorneys know it as *"looking for the deep pocket"* and often advertise their availability. One went on television wearing a straw hat, playing a banjo badly. His punchline was: *"I need the money for banjo lessons".* [60]

In consequence the legal system can act like a predator instead of a protector. A deluge of suits guarantees long delays, while certain cases become so convoluted that they may never be concluded. [63] On various occasions the former Chief Justice of the Supreme Court, Warren Burger, has warned:

> *"The truth is that we may be on our way to a society overrun by hordes of lawyers, hungry as locusts, and brigades of judges in numbers never before contemplated.....The United States legal system is too costly, too painful, too destructive and too inefficient for a truly civilized people."* [61]

Although America has always been a litigious society, the current rash of writs began with malpractice suits against the medical profession in the 1960's. Doctors were an obvious target, being both idealized and resented for their skills and high fees and sense of superiority which sometimes covered incompetence. Then the focus extended to airlines, big business, and finally, government agencies at all levels. [62] Tens of thousands of patients have won malpractice awards worth hundreds of thousands to millions of dollars each. [63] In related litigation a fat man who had a heart attack after starting his lawn mower was awarded $1.8 million from the retailer and a contestant for the 'World's Strongest Man' received $1 million for a knee which buckled after he ran a 40-yard dash with a fridge strapped to the top of his back. [64] Perhaps the most audacious claim was made by a failed suicide against the New York City Transit Authority. He persuaded a jury to grant him $650 thousand for injuries received after he had deliberately jumped in front of a train. [65]

Under the American system, lawyers receive a high percentage of the final settlement, and unsuccessful litigants do not have to pay defense costs. So there is little risk in having a go at the 'fat cats'. All of the suits I have described contain elements of redistributive and retributive 'justice'. The redistribution is clear, from the haves to the have nots, or, at least, to those who want more. For clients and counsel the 'fattest cats' tend to be the insurance companies seen as big, dominating businesses with endless resources, like overblown parents. The angry, spurious, spoiling quality of the claims denotes envious retribution. The law allows anyone with a grudge to wreak revenge for having a raw deal or for simply being less successful, as used to be the case with practitioners of the law in comparison to their fraternal medical colleagues. Not surprisingly, a popular car sticker reads: "*Become a doctor, support a lawyer.*" [66]

Greed aside, it is not difficult to discern envious malice expressed through legal channels. It leads to the extreme disruption of a person's private and professional life on the basis of allegations that go beyond the bounds of reasonable responsibility. For example, in identical circumstances, psychiatrists can be sued for prescribing drugs, and for not prescribing drugs. [67] Whether the individual mounts a successful defense, or not, the secondary social effects of such applications of the law tend to be spoiling and generally negative. Unfounded claims against doctors have precipitated a huge increase in insurance premiums, unnecessary diagnostic tests (with associated morbidity), higher medical fees, and the partial withdrawal of medical cover. Therefore the quality of care goes down, a typical envious influence.[68]

Worst still, these actions corrode the quality of life for everyone. Doctors, for example, have begun to strike back at lawyers. In Brunswick, Georgia they have refused to deliver the babies of women lawyers or lawyers' wives. One explained: "*This is a desperate measure that I have decided upon......my pulse rate goes to about 160 every time I see a lawyer's letter in the mail."* (69)

Furthermore, sky-high personal injury and liability awards have curtailed social welfare and recreational services, because business organizations and municipalities can't afford, or even obtain the necessary insurance protection. In at least fifty California cities parks, playgrounds and swimming pools have had to close, and in Minnesota, a nativity play, had to be cancelled because of an exorbitant insurance demand for protection against injury by Mary's donkey. (70) The theatre world seems especially vulnerable. Even if not overwhelmed by excessive insurance or labour claims, producers remain liable according to the dictum: "*Where there's a hit, there's a writ.*"

* * * * *

In America litigation takes the place of taxation to promote the levelling of economic and social differences. Other countries are less reticent to use taxation policies for this purpose, itself a means of propounding and propitiating envy. Very high marginal rates of tax led many Britons to become 'tax exiles' during the last Labour government in the 1960's and 1970's. Tim Rice, the lyricist for *Jesus Christ Superstar* and *Evita,* refused to leave, and paid the price, a tax of £2258 on weekly royalties of £2884, plus a tax of £183 on a weekly investment income of £192. (71) During the same period wealthy Swedish citizens were assessed at a rate of over 100%. (72)

The Swedes use the term, *"royal Swedish envy"* , to give some idea of their consuming interest in friends' and neighbours' riches, an interest institutionalized by a statutory right to examine each others' tax returns. (73) Together with confiscatory tax rates this right promotes the collective at the expense of the individual and exemplifies Freud's views on the *'herd instinct'* whereby personal distinction succumbs to social similarity.

Americans are much more secretive about their tax returns, yet between 1923 and 1953, in the state of Wisconsin, anyone could inspect the detailed return of a fellow citizen, and even after this law was modified, a fee of one dollar enabled the curious or envious to learn the total tax another had paid. (74) In Switzerland, however, many people chose to turn this policy of social control through public exposure on its head. The Social Democratic Party of Wolhusen used to publish a compete list with the names, assets and incomes of all the residents in this small town near Lucerne. Schoolchildren sold it from door to door. Subsequently it was found that various citizens had falsely expanded their assets and income, either to obtain credit or marry off daughters into better families. (75) In the end, they managed to counterattack the perpetrators of malicious gossip by inflating themselves and adding to the envy that their detractors suffered.

The limitation of personal wealth by the state serves a multitude of purposes ranging from paying for war to preserving privilege or providing benefits. (76) This can be accomplished through direct and indirect taxation or legalized plunder as illustrated by the *muru raid* of the New Zealand Maori peoples.

The word *muru* literally means plunder, more specifically, to plunder the property of those who have transgressed community norms, such as having more than others. Then one's neighbours can descend with savage howls and carry off anything desirable. There would be no resistance, for this would not only have provoked injury, but excluded the victim from taking part in raids on others. (77) Unrestrained attacks on rich peasants by the Russian and Chinese governments under the direction of Stalin and Mao indicate a similar plundering. Such activities embody greed and envy when they aggrandize the state or state agencies at the expense of individual citizens and promote social disharmony and fiscal drag.

The popular *BBC* comedy series, *Yes Prime Minister*, further illuminates the force of government greed. In one program the Prime Minister tells Sir Humphrey Appleby, the Head of the Civil Service, that there is some extra money in the kitty and proposes to reduce taxation and return small amounts *'to the people'*. Sir Humphrey reacts with total horror, explaining that it is *'our'* money and *'we'* (i.e. him, the civil service, the government) *'need it'.* Anyway, one must never give it back to *'them', 'they'* wouldn't know how to use it. *'We'* know best.[78]

The envious aspects of plunder lurk in the moral fervour of the tax collector and the intellectual posturing of politicians and civil servants. The former can and do wield investigative and punitive powers which, in the United States, have led many ordinary citizens, not just cheats, to fear the Internal Revenue Service more than the F.B.I. In America people become palpably and irrationally nervous as the April 15th deadline for filing tax returns approaches. The date itself is like an evil eye. It is not unusual to see cartoons in the papers which depict an mean looking person looking over a taxpayer's shoulder, with the caption, *'Be honest; envy is watching you."* [79]

On the other hand populist officials tend to be obsessed with redistribution and social engineering at the expense of economic expansion and individual incentive. Helmut Schoeck points out that many of those who devised and implemented excessive fiscal measures in the name of fairness or egalitarianism also demonstrate excessive anxiety and guilt about their own wealth or background. This may serve the useful function of arousing much needed sympathy for the underprivileged, but it also accounts for a tendency to attribute too much envy to them as well. [80] Punitive taxation then becomes a means of placating the alleged envy of the lower classes while using their actual and presumed poverty as an excuse to attack the upper classes, specifically, those whom the policy makers see and resent as superiors. Put succinctly, the economist E. J. Mishan concludes that the purpose of progressive taxation and welfare economics is to prevent people from feeling bad:

> *"Ideally, of course, the tax should suffice to cover all the initial and subsequent claims necessary to placate everybody in the lower-income groups, and the stronger is this envy of others, the heavier must be the tax."* [81]

Interestingly several studies indicate that lower income groups are more concerned with making money than soaking the rich. Except for certain legislators most men and women, regardless of circumstances, do not believe that high tax rates are just or fair. [82] The economics of envy is a version of the zero sum game where one person's gain is another's loss. Those who play insist on a small pie equally distributed rather than a bigger pie unsymmetrically sliced.[88] As one might expect from policies based on attacking rather than enhancing prosperity, economic activity declines, innovation suffocates and politics becomes more repressive. [83]

The opposite policy is that people should be allowed to keep a large slice of the wealth they create and that this encourages economic activity and wealth for everyone. Under the influence of 'supply-side' economists in the United States tax rates have been slashed since 1981.[84]

* * * * *

The British anthropologist and psychoanalyst, Roger Money-Kyrle, has specifically focussed on the fears and expectations in countries with *laissez-faire* economic systems. [85] Although offering excellent opportunities for growth, *laissez-faire* suffers from periodic oscillations in the money supply and a tendency towards unlimited capital accumulation. Unless corrected these defects interfere with achievable goals such as "*the greatest good for the greatest number*". Over the past century it became obvious that the corrections involved a degree of graduated taxation and pump priming during slumps. However, these measures aroused tremendous anxiety and antagonism among the well-to-do, often, as Money-Kyrle points out, because of delusional beliefs about the nature of wealth and how it might be stolen. Thus, they have tended to equate the starving masses with real and imaginary siblings or children who threatened to drain money, that is, life milk from their bodies and *"from the mother-banks from which they drew their sustenance."* Therefore the wealthy perceived the necessary changes as lethal sacrifices and resisted accordingly. [86]

The impoverished victims of the economic cycle drew different conclusions. They thought that rich people possessed endless resources, but that they chose to starve the working classes, their needy children, in order to keep everything for themselves. It is notable that, these views of evil parents spitefully begrudging inexhaustible goodness often originated in middle or upper class intellectuals with their own axes to grind.

Karl Marx, for example, came from an affluent professional background. He married into an upper class Prussian family. His brother-in-law was Ferdinand Westphalen, the Prussian Minister of the Interior, and he was supported by wealthy relatives and friends throughout his life. (87)

Marx's meticulous critiques of capitalism covered inexhaustible hatreds which had little to do with direct observation. Marx did not know manual workers and never set foot in a factory. His descriptions of alienation, debasement and exploitation subsumed projections of personal phantasies and familial torments which could hardly fail to strike a note, given conditions at the time. (88) When taken up by the downtrodden, or those who felt that way, his prescriptions, *"spoil the despoilers"*, *"expropriate the expropriators,"* as well as the hopeless hopes of radical millennialism, *"to all according to their needs,"* *"the classless society"*, gave intellectual justifications for attacks on capital, in phantasy, parental good fortune. (89) Politically Marx it seems that acted like Comstock to exult envy through violence and insinuate group oppression, in this instance, *"the dictatorship of the proletariat,"* as the central feature of individual life. (90)

Money-Kyrle points out that the wealth which Marx and kindred followers have fought so hard to control, or destroy, can be divided into three distinct categories. These are: 1) necessities - food, clothes, housing; 2) luxuries - the things we want because others have them; and 3) non-transferable commodities - beauty, intelligence, a good education, a stately home, a distinguished heredity. (91) Although all are important, non-transferable qualities and possessions are the ones most desired and most envied, because they are unique in themselves and convey a crushing sense of superiority. Considerations like these led Ralph Waldo Emerson to quip that for the fortunate few envy "*is the tax which all distinction must pay.*"[92]

In fact this tax tends to be levied on necessities first, and then luxuries, if, for no other reason, that institutions as well as people prefer to redirect their hatred of non-transferable commodities to less obvious items in order to avoid appearing deficient. [93] Moreover, it is easier to assert that man is what he owns and exploit envy-as-greed by grabbing, or destroying, goods and possessions, than by attacking intangible signs of supremacy. [94]

Sumptuary laws, that is, the regulation of luxury, have a varied and venerable history. The Roman *Lex Didia* (143 B.C.E.) declared harsh punishments for both the guests and givers of extravagant meals. Alternatively, prohibitions might suddenly descend on choice morsels like shrews or mussels. In the twelfth century Richard the Lionhearted restricted the Crusaders' extravagant use of furs and later Charles V forbade long pointed shoes. [95] Similar decrees raged throughout the middle ages often connected with fanatical forms of religious egalitarianism. Noted clerics demanded that no one should have more than his neighbour and pressed for legal restraints on consumption. Doctors too were attacked for charging high fees and urged to practice for free. [96]

All embracing restrictions on luxury did not begin to disappear until the eighteenth century when free-market economies took hold in Europe and America. Even now, legal remnants remain, exemplified by special taxes on powerful cars or splendid houses. The actual yield from sumptuary penalties has always been very small in comparison to other revenues. Nonetheless they attempt to satisfy almost universal pressures to punish the better-off. [97]

To avoid the wrath of friends, or the state, it is not uncommon to deny goods, or hide them under the mattress. This is a classic defense which is rather more difficult when the bed is grand and the bedroom is even grander. Alternative tactics include sop behaviour and aggressive counter measures like conspicuous consumption which fends off envy by flaunting wealth. Often the two coincide which happens when the extremely rich appease communal ill-will by massive acts of charity. In

Roman times such people paid for a day at the games. Presumably the sight of slaves being torn apart by lions deflected the baser impulses of the crowd. Nowadays they endow hospitals and universities or foundations for cancer research. Yet, the intentions remain the same, to buy gratitude and assert unassailable superiority. The latter has to do with the subtle process of converting wealth into style and status.

* * * * *

Status is a non transferable blend of position and prestige in contrast to class which denotes wealth and power. These social states may complement each other, but it is not uncommon for the newly rich to have little status, or for prestigious people to have little money. As early as 1805 John Adams pointed out that the rewards of status are *"the esteem and admiration of others (while) the punishments are neglect and contempt."* (98) He might have added that the ostentatious display of stylish dress or snobby speech aside from municipal munificence can and does transform status distinctions into effective weapons of social warfare. Envious broadsides can then be countered by superior firepower – self-inflation and other-deflation. This holds true both for the privileged proud and those who would emulate them.

Status competition avoids the cruder forms of class conflict, although indignant combatants still growl that *"one side gets the sugar while the other gets the shit."* (99) Inevitably displays of wealth evolve into displays of style. Good taste and flair confer status and, when used precisely, leave as many wounds as raw riches and power. In contemporary Los Angeles, possession of a Russian wolfhound is said to yield special benefits. Showy and expensive, the dog acts like a *fascinum* to absorb envy and protect its master. Those who cannot afford such distinctive magic, or are disinclined to own a Borzoi, can rent one for $100 per week. (100)

Designer jeans serve the same function, to allow the wearer to slip into the non transferable commodities of Gloria Vanderbilt or Calvin Klein. The illusion is transparent, yet highly effective, as evinced by the huge demand for these products and the palpable bitterness of men and women who can't obtain or fit into them. Here fashion serves schadenfreude. The 'haves' feel elevated while the 'have-nots' suffer contempt. In the meanwhile the 'real Vanderbilt's' tend to wear comfortable, but scruffy old clothes on informal occasions. They do not have to dress to impress and intuitively know that the paramount mode of status seeking is mockery of status seeking. It has not escaped notice that members of the upper crust frequently prefer mongrels, Volkswagens and old, threadbare carpets. (101) 'Old', moreover, implies 'effortless' which confirms preeminence and simultaneously deflects envy on to social inferiors who look like characters from the TV series, *Dallas or Dynasty.*

Mass marketing and consumerism gives everyone a chance to possess valuable commodities while perpetuating the belief that it is possible to transfer non-transferable qualities from one person to the other. It is another, typically American form of social levelling and a potent defense against mass envy and greed. Even welfare recipients feel less inclined to head for the barricades when they can afford stylish jeans and ghetto blasters.

When institutionalized defenses are not available, or when they do not provide adequate protection, then unsharable assets remain prey to personal acrimony and collective assault. This usually involves multiple displacements from: 1) the individual to the group; from 2) one part of the group (i.e. a particular social class) to another; and from 3) high status items to basic necessities.

During the French Revolution the inchoate anger of the mob, was primarily concerned with the availability of bread. Month by month, even week by week, the presence or absence of certain Parisian uprisings directly coincided with the ups and downs of the bread price. (102) The mob or *menu peuple* only became a revolutionary force when organized and used by specific members of the bourgeoisie to attack the standing and privileges of the aristocracy. (103) In this instance the displacements ranged from enraged intellectuals to hungry craftsman, from the middle and upper middle classes to the lower orders and from cake to bread. The envy that fueled the blood bath flowed from upstairs to downstairs and then back upstairs again.

The historian, Eric Hobsbawm, points out that the *menu people* were not overcome with egalitarian impulses, nor did they want to join or do away with the wealthier classes. (104) They knew that the destruction of fine palaces or carriages or clothes could not help them. On the contrary upper class extravagances meant work for them. What they wanted was a ransom, a fear induced tangible improvement in their lives so they could carry on as before. Their violent moments could not have continued except for motivations and a leadership imposed from without and concerned with issues not of their making.(105)

* * * * *

Revolution is the institutionalization of envious attacks on non-transferable commodities displaced onto wealth and power. If successful, a brief period of ecstatic camaraderie will break out, for it appears that greed itself, as personified by the possessing class, the privileged parents, has been destroyed. After the high, however, comes the low, brought about by the reality of the damage done and difficulty in restoring revered values. In a well known cycle of spite and backstabbing, old comrades behave like Greek Furies, blaming each other for betraying 'the cause', while simultaneously finding scapegoats for their own sense of guilt. (106) The final acts include divine punishment, the reign of terror, and the reestablishment of the old hereditary structure with new faces, as has occurred in twentieth century Romania and North Korea.

Revolutionaries do not always take care to conceal their hatred for intrinsic signs of superiority, that is, talents and accomplishments which confer strength and status. This is especially true in less developed countries where exceptional individuals are more easily singled out. In October 1964 *The New York Times* reported that units of the Congolese People's Republic had captured a young teacher just home after a year's training course at the University of Oregon. Before beheading him, the rebel leader shouted:

"You're an intellectual, aren't you? You have even been to America, our greatest enemy. You are too smart. You are an enemy of the revolution." [107]

In some countries this same process of malicious vengeance can and does extend generations into the future. At various times the People's Republic of China has openly discriminated against the children and grandchildren of families ranked as 'rich peasants', even though their only 'sins' comprised a mildly distinguished pedigree. Approximately 30 million citizens have been forced into a subordinate, sub-human category labeled: *"bad class background".* In consequence, they get low wages, poor education and inadequate medical treatment. Their political activities are restricted and they remain frequent targets of verbal and physical abuse. [108] All this occurs regardless of ability or need in order to maintain egalitarian principles in a society permeated by *"the red-eyed disease."* [109]

Yet, overt attacks on talent and pedigree are hardly limited to the third world. The British Labour Party presided over the virtual dismemberment of the state educational system in the 1960's and '70's. Their professed intention was to enhance educational opportunities for all by doing away with the private sector (the elite public schools). But the background to the debate were acrimonious arguments about wealth and privileges in Britain. The Labourites were levelers. They not only opposed the snobbish emulation of public schools (exclusive uniforms, single sex education, careful selection, 'old boys' networks), but the differentiation of students according to educational ability. Accordingly they abolished 11+ exams and state grammar schools (academic secondary schools) and established a comprehensive system of mixed ability education. [110]

The effects were remarkable. The hated public schools gained a new lease on life gradually taking over the function of the old grammar schools. Having relinquished dreary habits like fagging, they quickly responded to parental wishes for reasonable discipline and academic excellence. However, the high fees they charged essentially equalled a special tax on ambition as well as achievement.

At the same time the state sector showed progressive signs of deterioration. Both students and teachers suffered a lack of resources and the loss of standards. Government inspectors regularly reported that the ablest children were *"not always sufficiently challenged"* and the less bright were not getting the right lessons. (111) And indiscipline was rife. Pupils sprayed graffiti, while instructors went on strike.

One statistic stands out. The number of working class children entering university has slumped by over 50% from the late sixties to the mid eighties. (112) This is a surprising result, or was it? The answer should be yes, for the comprehensive system was ostensibly initiated to promote the prospects of workers' children. Yet, it must be no, for the impetus for the changes initiated by the Labour government was envy, of wealth, of status, but especially of intelligence, from where ever it came. (113) Envy is a major factor whenever the negative effects of institutional policies contradict apparent aims. In this instance the envious intent was not to enrich the educational pie, but to destroy it.

* * * * *

In reviewing the long arm of the state, I have been considering greedy, malicious attacks on wealth, or non-transferable qualities which confer and reflect prosperity, like learning and culture. The many political, legal, business and educational examples I have cited basically comprise institutionalized attacks on the breast. I now intend to focus on similar assaults on the womb, or, generative feelings and functions.

The Dalkon Shield disaster was more than an unfortunate corporate hiccup. By mid-1985 twenty one women had died, thirteen thousand were infertile and hundreds more had given birth to damaged children. Morton Mintz claimed that this was the consequence of *"a few men with little on their mind but megabucks".* (114) But it is unlikely that financial greed was the sole factor. Court testimony demonstrates that company scientists knew that the intrauterine device was flawed at least six months before it went on the market. (115) The story of the shield is entirely consistent with the covert contempt for female fertility, pregnancy and childbirth which I have described in my chapter on Womb Envy. Ritual bleeding, couvade, test tube babies, episiotomy and hysterectomy all employ established customs and procedures to challenge the creative preeminences of women and, out of animosity, to inflict substantial damage on their minds and bodies. The violence marketed by the Robbins Company did no less.

Femininity is a key issue in J. P. Hartley's utopian novel, *Facial Justice.* (116) Hartley describes an entire society organized to eliminate beauty and the accompanying sins of parenthood and happiness. These features are despicable in themselves, and because they are arouse enmity in others. The government, ruled by a dictator like 'Big Brother' in *Nineteen Eighty-four,* is obsessively concerned with uniformity. (117) Therefore, the worst sin is not envy, but exciting envy, and the most disruptive elements are pretty girls known as' Alphas'. At a certain age every Alpha is morally obliged to go to an 'Equalization (Faces) Centre' for surgical alteration into a 'Beta' or standard face. Similarly 'Gammas' or ugly girls must undergo a Beta upgrade. The object is to eradicate envy, called 'Bad Egg' or simply 'Bad E', by destroying everything enviable, an act which is, of course, the essence of envy.

The main character is a spirited Alpha named Jael who refuses disfigurement. She even resists complaints from the 'Ministry for Face Equality' that her long eyelashes cause other women sleepless nights. Eventually her brother Joab, a civil servant, admonishes her:

> *"You have a right to nothing that is liable to cause Envy in the heart of a fellow-delinquent (citizen).. Our constitution and way of life are based on it."* (118)

Jael disagrees and at a later point rebuffs her sibling rival with clever queries as to whether he would like to have his brains lowered.(119) Here she retorts:

> *"I know that Envy is the worst thing possible, but don't you think that there is another side to it – in my case. Don't you think that when people see me looking pretty, it makes them feel more cheerful?"* [120]

Jael underestimates the degree of hatred that a pretty face and accompanying cheerfulness may provoke. They remind people what they don't have and can't feel, particularly the actuality and echoes of the good breast and inviting interiors full of sexual delights. These are all emotional impossibilities in societies devoted to the absolute control of thoughts and feelings. [121] In fact the members of many cultures are threatened by happy women, and treat them accordingly, as demonstrated by the *Malleus*, The Society for Suppression of Vice, Ayatollah Khomeinism and puritan revivalists in America.

Alternatively people of both sexes try to gain the happiness that they think women possess by turning to substances like 'happy pills'. The use of drugs is akin to a manic attack on female feelings which aims to bypass the source and aggrandize the goods. Thus the euphoria induced by heroin has been described as "*instant bliss*" not unlike the experience of an infant after a feed or an adult after intercourse. [122] But the original destructive impulses, essentially to shit on women, do not disappear as indicated by the terrible ways that addicts degrade themselves and the organized persecution of drug users by civil authorities. The latter often behave like the 'face police' in Hartley's novel. [123]

Certainly, Jael's pleasure in her person did not deter Joab, who replied:

> *"Cheerfulness is all right in its place, but if it excites a single twinge of Bad E, then it must be stamped out."* [124]

Towards the end of the novel we learn that Jael suffers a prearranged accident. While in hospital, and before regaining consciousness, she is given a Beta face to satisfy the dreaded dictator, who, it transpires, is an ugly old woman.

* * * * *

While also concerned with the political exploitation of envy, Orwell's 'Big Brother' presents the force of phallic aggrandizement and the raw exercise of power. He embodies a party disconcertingly close to contemporary establishments whose virility lies in the ability to see all, know all and dominate all. I refer to the corporate entities parodied by the *New Yorker* cartoon as well as paternalistic, authoritarian governments.

The 'Big' in 'Big Brother' catches the worrisome element in masculine assertive cultures to do with the inflation of institutional strength, size, assertion, ambition, prowess and privilege. One can see this at work in the business community where certain companies become 'King of the Castle' and everyone else, 'the dirty rascal'. Similarly many commentators have lambasted the British trade union movement and its political counterpart, the Labour Party, for becoming 'too big for their britches'. Here 'big' means 'overweening' and 'omnipotent' as in the excessive pride and arrogant exertions which have transformed libertarian aims into collectivist policies and practices. (125)

Paul Johnson has written at length about Australia, an apparently wide-open, free-enterprise country which celebrates maleness with curious abandon. (126) His surface impressions embrace hard nosed businessmen, militant miners, strident radicals and raucous sportsmen swilling beer and thumping tables. Even the playgrounds resound with aggressive little ditties like:

"Boys are strong – like King Kong.
Girls are weak – chuck 'em in the creek." (127)

This macho bombast hides reflex uncertainties about the degree of independence and power people really have. Unlike American pioneers who fled an oppressive State, the early Australians remained wholly dependent on that power, England, the home government, for support. [128] And even after these bonds were broken, the citizenry had to rely on another country, the United States, for external protection while turning to public sector services to satisfy internal needs. Consequently the Australian national image of rugged self-sufficiency conceals a complex network of sustaining relationships.

As a myth, 'the tough, self-reliant Australian,' exemplifies the institutionalized denial of dependency, and serves to fend off and express the envious resentments that multiple dependencies arouse. I say fend off because the hostilities involved appear to be displaced from outside powers to national agencies, from national agencies to social class and from all concerned to wives and mothers. The women get the worst deal because they tend to be hated for being themselves and for representing the parental powers (i.e. government departments) who indeed often behave like 'Big Brother'. [129] These antagonisms can be seen in the ritual avoidance and casual contempt that accompany Australian attitudes towards women. Otherwise the simple act of denying their importance is tantamount to annihilating their existence.[130]

The overbearing maleness that makes up such an important part of the Australian character, and the American too, is a variation of the manic attack on female functions. But it also serves as a sword and shield in the ceaseless struggle for power between 'men' and 'men' or, more significantly, 'male' institutions and 'men'.

Almost two thousand years ago Plutarch noted that ostracism was an effective device that enabled the Greeks to *"cut down to size and expel from time to time whoever of the citizens excels in reputation or power, relieving their envy rather than their fear"*. [131] Similarly comic writers like Aristophanes, who were the overlookers and muckrakers of their time, used satire to topple the high and mighty and make them rejoin the crowd. [132] The modern media continues public traditions of phallic rivalry by training its 'big guns' on 'highfliers' who grow too big too quickly.

In the 1980's tennis star John McEnroe was a special target. When he finally lost at Wimbledon the British press jumped for joy. An editorial in *The Times*, arguably the voice of the establishment, chortled:

"At Wimbledon we like our sure losers.......When John McEnroe returns here next year he may find that many of his problems with the press and people of Britain are behind him." [133]

No longer strongest and fastest, McEnroe was freed by *The Times* from threats to spoil his success with further slices of critical exposure. Comparable attacks on people who rise above the herd are so common as to be almost unnoticeable. This has not been the case with the 'Big Bang', or the abrupt removal of restraints on competition in London financial circles in 1986. [134] Desperate for talented traders, many banks and investment brokers offered huge salaries and even larger lump sums ("the golden hello") to gain needed staff. Among the new dealers, often ambitious young men in the mid or late 20's, the size of the financial package became a prime virility symbol and sparked off murderous resentments among older dealers who had been passed by. [135] Their thoughts simmered in City's (financial district) hallways (*"It's not fair!"*) and surfaced through the verbal deluge of like minded journalists and politicians.

The *Spectator* railed against financial 'whiz kids' calling them:

"...unnervingly young and unpardonably well paid.

You can see them most evenings in the smarter trattorias and brasseries.......(and) hear them, braying at the top of their voices." [136]

Meanwhile, Denis Healey, a senior Labour M.P. and former cabinet minister, provided a derisive counterpoint with warnings about:

> *"...the sort of young men of 26 or 27 who crack bottles of champagne on the floor of the stock exchange before they dawdle into their Porsches."* (137)

Probably the *Observer* made the most dangerous thrust by encouraging the government to flex its bureaucratic muscles and impose a special tax on 'highflying' earnings. In fact this wasn't done, but Robin Leigh-Pemberton, the Governor of the Bank of England, was so concerned about the ferocity of the offensive that he felt obliged to defend the new specialists and their premium wages. He argued that if Britain wanted to play in the big leagues, then it had to pay big bucks.

Big bucks or, lots of money, is especially angry-making when it supports a flamboyant masculinity. It took Porsches, champagne and smart trattorias, not just high salaries, to provoke Denis Healey and the *Spectator* to a state of critical rage. The same happened a few years earlier when explosive outbursts against the phallic fervour of John De Lorean destroyed a new sports car and his career. De Lorean had been an extremely successful executive with the General Motors Corporation. Although over fifty, he exuded vigorous good looks and confidence. And his pretty young wife complemented a fast, flash life-style very much like the sleek gull-winged car he proposed to build. Having left General Motors, he convinced the Northern Ireland Development Agency to put up tens of millions of pounds towards the cost of bringing the car into production, in conjunction with his own designs, patents and development work. Within two years a factory was built near Belfast and by the fall of 1981 the first cars were ready for sale. He seemed to have achieved an industrial miracle as well as to be driving towards a personal fortune. (138)

Then Nemesis struck. A severe downturn in the car market meant that dealers refused to place anticipated orders or pay for cars already brought. Concomitantly the British government held up payments of £10 million in compensation for attacks by the IRA. In the preceding months the factory had been firebombed over 140 times, aside from many attempts to intimidate executives with sniper fire. But this was only the beginning. After receiving some good publicity about the car, the company, and De Lorean personally, were overwhelmed with allegations of financial malfeasance. These were made, in particular, by two disgruntled employees, aided and abetted by members of parliament and various newspapers.

In consequence the company collapsed. The British government withdrew support and various bankers refused further credit. Other institutions behaved like howling Furies taking bigger and bigger bites out of De Lorean's rapidly fading reputation and activities. In Parliament he was accused of being *"an American conman,"* while in the United States he was indicted for cocaine dealing, a charge subsequently disproved. Essentially De Lorean paid the price of overreaching others and overstepping bounds. The public ridiculed him and business colleagues shunned his company.

De Lorean's macho displays transformed into stylistic arrays attracted a bevy of criminal charges and civil suits like so many like evil eyes. He may not have been an innocent, but he was acquitted of fraud and racketeering in two major trials. [139] Eventually *The Times* acknowledged that his basic 'malfeasance' included the fact that he and his investors stood to do very well financially if the project succeeded. The newspaper pointed out that this placed both De Lorean and government agencies in a 'Catch 22' situation. If the project failed, then they were fools for supporting him, and he was a 'conman.' If the project thrived, then they should have made a better deal, and he was a 'conniver.' But perhaps his worse 'crime' had to do with successfully building a sports car in Belfast, which most civil servants thought could never be done. His punishment was to see his stature and status ruined by the forces of social hatred.

Chapter 10

Anarchy and Vandalism

> *"Everyone, arise! With your arms and your hearts, with the pen and the word, with the knife and the gun, with the curse and the irony, with adultery and pillage, with poisoning and fire. Let's make the war against civilization."* [1]

These words embolden the Political Will of Jean-Paul Sartre which he dedicated to his *"anarchist friends, unjustly ignored."* [2] Sartre condemned property, wealth, family, religion and government, which were, for him, all sources of oppression and called for revolutionary subversion, equated with knifing the rich and destroying all bourgeois institutions. Brutus and Spartacus were his heroes, men who were not afraid to burn down castles and dip their hands in the blood of their masters. [3]

Sartre's exhortation corresponds with long traditions of individual attacks on the State, its institutions, representatives and values. In 1891 the Italian anarchist, Errico Malatesta, declaimed the State was a political, legal, judicial, military and financial framework for controlling people and robbing them of their personal freedom. [4]

Since it acts by force, the police, it needs to be opposed by force, the insurrectionist. Others have believed that the State, and state agencies, are tyrannies which needs to be destroyed simply because they exist. In this sense an anarchist is a person who maintains a narrow, malevolent view of Society and whose destructive impulses are supported by political theories. In contrast a vandal acts inchoately to loose his *"blood-dimmed tide"* onto the world. (5)

Anarchy derives from the Greek words *an archos* meaning, 'without a rule.' Hurled derisively against the Levellers during the English civil war and the Enragés of the French revolution, it was first used as a term of abuse. (6) Subsequently the English non-conformist minister, William Godwin, and the French printer and socialist leader, Pierre-Joseph Proudhon, developed the positive elements of anarchist thought to do with justice, egalitarianism, decentralization and mutual aid. Godwin argued that government was evil, but individuals were naturally benevolent. If left to themselves, they could spontaneously organize their affairs for the good of all. He advocated an economic system based on the principle *'from each according to their means, to each according to their needs.'* (7) Proudhon emphasized freedom and equality. While rejecting the centralized state and accompanying political activity, he envisioned a new society where there were *"No more parties, no more authority, absolute liberty of man and citizen."*(8)

In spite of these high ideals, and possibly because of them, the theories of Godwin and Proudhon were superseded by demands for revolutionary violence which indelibly linked anarchy with bombs and blood. There were several reasons for this development. Arguably, their model for social change was insufficient, and ill suited to the conditions which it purported to correct. More important, it aroused impossible expectations, 'a second coming', which led to dashed hopes and murderous frustrations. Most important, it built a superstructure of virtue atop an infrastructure of hatred. When ill-winds (external adversity, internal conflict) blew, the social pleasantries toppled exposing the underlying destructiveness. Comparable events happen when individuals rely on idealization to overcome murderous inner tensions. Once they lose faith in absolute love, or absolute beauty, or absolute justice, then any degree of violence is justified to retain their beliefs [9]

Proudhon was followed by a Russian nobleman turned agitator, Mikhail Bakunin, whose ringing declaration, *"the passion for destruction is also a creative urge"* has dominated the mainstream of anarchist thought and practice, as well as peripheral political currents, since the mid nineteenth century. [10] Called a pan-destructionist because of his millennial insistence on sweeping away all existing social institutions, Bakunin proclaimed violent revolution was a necessary prelude to the construction of a free and peaceful society. In fact he exemplifies the person who needs a theory to release chaos and rationalize murder. His disciples did likewise, particularly Nechaïeff, who established the firm foundations of modern terrorism with the doctrine, *"propaganda of the deed"*. His specialty was spectacular assassinations of government officials. [11]

Contemporary terrorists, belonging to groups like Action Directe, Baader-Meinhof or the Aum sect, shoot computers and gas commuters for kindred reasons, that is, to gain the attention and support of *"the masses"*, while demonstrating the vulnerability of *"the system"*. [12] Although the overt aim may be to destroy a hated organization, an underlying intention is to inflate the ego or self-esteem of the destroyer. The two functions go hand in hand and illustrate the phenomenon of 'destructive narcissism.' This impulse to destroy, to take pride in destruction, to become famous for cruelty and death-dealing at the expense of everything else, becomes especially strong when a person, especially a 'committed' person, feels alienated from society and at odds with his positive ideals. In other words, it occurs at a time when an activist despaïrs of his 'all-powerful' abilities to save the world. [13] A devastating loss in inner worth ensues, which, destructive narcissism, the idealization of venom and violence, tries to overcome.

The destructionist approach involves a psychic reversal of cherished values. Good becomes bad, and badness becomes exalted, as has happened with many 'freedom-fighters'. Though the rhetoric may continue, and the comrades may still talk about truth, love, peace, equality, these become distant goals relegated to an indeterminate future. Instead, murder, sabotage, and subversion replace them in immediate importance and destructive achievements take over as essential springs of praise. Herbert Rosenfeld observed:

> *"The destructiveness ......appears often highly organized, as if one were dealing with a powerful gang dominated by a leader, who controls all the members of the gang to see that they support one another in making the criminal destructive work more effective and powerful...."* (14)

* * * * *

In the previous chapter I showed how and why and the State and its institutions attack the individual. In this chapter I will show how and why the individual attacks the State: its ideals, organisations and agents. As we have just seen, the terrorist is one such person. The vandal is another, someone who takes pleasure, and gains a sense of inner worth from gratuitous attacks on the fabric of civilization, citizens or things, the malignity of the deed. Hilaire Belloc warned about young tearaways in his *Cautionary Tales*:

> *"John Vavasour de Quentin Jones*
> *Was very fond of throwing stones*
> *At horses, people, and passing trains,*
> *And especially at window panes."* (15)

De Quentin Jones was not a lower class, but an upper class lout whose *"favorite form of Play* " was *"the sound of broken glass"*. He acted alone (and came to a bitter end). Others act alone, or in gangs, but with the discharge of envy, experienced as resentment, foremost in their minds. Recurrent vandalism, far more than anarchy, is a pervasive feature of modern life. No school can be built in New

York City without taking into account an inevitable spate of broken windows and arson.[16] Meanwhile in England, at least £25 million of random damage is done each year to schools, railways and, more recently, farms. [17] One terrorized man explained:

> *"Farming here has got to the stage that when we sow a crop they ride motor-cycles over it. When it's growing they playing it, and if it gets ripe, they set fire to it."* [18]

In common usage vandalism refers to any senseless spoilage, but originally the term was applied to the willful despoiling of cultural assets, particularly works of art. In 1794 Bishop Henri Grégoire of Blois named such atrocities after the Vandals, a Germanic tribe who sacked Rome in 455 C. E. After two weeks in the city they carried off a mass of loot and burned what they couldn't carry. Actually, various German scholars contend that the Vandals did not behave with ruthless abandon. [19] Nonetheless, the term has stuck. Vandalism gained a fearful reputation which also implies savage greed, more typical of envy, and inverted snobbery, because vandals tend to attack things 'over their head', and feel superior for having done so.

* * * * *

The center of attention for the vandal, often a 'rebel without a cause', and the anarchist, an individual whose grudges breed theories, is society. But the emphasis may be different. The former concentrates on products and values, park benches and paintings, while the latter looks to the whole: revolutionary upheaval. Yet their symbolic interests are comparable, the cornucopias of life and rods of authority.

In this respect Sartre's position was prodigious. He announced wealth was death, just as Proudhon had once declared, *"Property is theft."* [20] Both embraced the war cry of the zero sum game, no-one should have more than his neighbour. Sartre, however, as an existentialist turned 'Nemesist', began to begrudge life. If he could not possess the whole pie (health, happiness, intellectual treasure troves), there would be no pie.

It is interesting to compare Sartre in his old age with the financier, J. P. Morgan. He used his resources to hire young girls to suckle him. Even in his dotage Morgan enjoyed the breast. Sartre reverted to the opposite extreme. He regressed to the position of an envious, negative child.

Oppressed by sickness, Sartre strongly identified with 'the wretched of the earth'. For him the bourgeoisie took on the role of the evil, depriving source of supply, against whom the proletariat (himself, the wretched) would take revenge. (21) He advised select workers to ransack the rich, to break into their homes in the middle of the night, strangle the occupants, rifle the jewel boxes and burn down the buildings. Moreover, at New Year's eve, or kindred festivities, he proclaimed pastry chefs and serving staff should infiltrate their parties and poison the sweet trays so *"one hundred or one thousand wealthy people will cease to exist."* (22) And the same should happen at gift shops. They should:

> *"...poison the champagne, (and) if this is possible, the rare wines, the gloves, the cakes, the ices, and the creams."* (23)

Once these goodies went, then the rest of the country would follow: crops, churches, government offices and commercial centers. The point was not just to attack the wells of plenty, but to destroy life itself, so that *"in all things joy will be born out of the excesses of evil."* (24)

It would be easy to dismiss Sartre's statements as the rantings of a deranged philosopher. Yet, he was one of the foremost writers, thinkers and activists of the twentieth century, and has continued to be treated as such right up to and after his death. (25) Sartre lived by words and demanded that they should be taken seriously. The position he asserted in his Political Will was consistent with decades of polemics, during which time he had been on close terms with anarchists, Maoists, Leninists, Stalinists, situationalists and, towards the end of his life, the Baader-Meinhof gang. [26] Sartre's thoughts provided intellectual ammunition for the actions of individuals as diverse as the Red Brigade and the Khmer Rouge. Verbally they were the essential elements in a powerful projection system:

> *"I am throwing this seed into the heart of all those who suffer, and let's begin! You will not escape this insurrection. I hope it will start right away."* [27]

His echoes haunt the headlines. In Paris youths claiming to be members of the Anarchist Autonome movement raged through the most expensive shopping streets looting and wrecking the luxury shops. [28] In London a band of self-proclaimed anarchists staged armed raids on supermarkets in order to buy weapons and bombs for *"attacks upon institutions of our society."* Others, like Roland Lee, of the Animal Liberation Front, or Ffred Ffrancis, of the Welsh Language Society, have attacked a pig farm in Bristol (burned), the Cancer Research Campaign in London (defaced), Welsh holiday cottages (burned) and television transmitters (blown up). [29] On previous occasions a group called, The Angry Brigade, bombed a fashionable boutique and a BBC van the night before the Miss World contest in order to destroy the *"spectacle"* of consumerism:

> *"Brothers and Sisters, what are your real desires? Sit in the drugstore, look distant, empty, bored, drinking some tasteless coffee? or perhaps BLOW IT UP OR BURN IT DOWN."* [30]

This communique emphasized the issue of boredom, or the absence of a basic 'foodstuff', adequate stimulation. Here the protagonists blame 'society' for their feeling bored and propose an exciting remedy. Explosions express the wish to grab the excitement that others get and to retaliate for 'inadequate mothering', that is, understimulation. [31] For these very reasons the British Prime Minister has been violently blamed both for unemployment, as if she were an evil woman who deliberately starved her children of necessary stimulation, and for starting the war with Argentina, that is, for giving them too much. [32] In the same vein attacks on *"consumer spectacles"* reflect envious hostility towards others who are or have been stimulated too much or too little (when the stimulation is painful) in comparison with the disgruntled spectators. [33]

* * * * *

In the United States the Counter Culture of the 1960's and '70's overshadowed the looting and rioting that was directed against consumer targets. The equivalent of Angry Brigades was at work (the Weathermen, for example), but spontaneous outbursts in the black ghettos did most of the overt damage. [34] Conversely, the 'flower people', the cultural revolutionaries, the 'free university freaks', tried to overcome the rigid morals and mores of the 50's with provocative changes in attitudes and lifestyles often based on libertarian principles. [35] At best their idealism led to innovative social experiments which challenged the success oriented materialism of their parents. At worse their aggressive anti-consumerism became an excuse for grenvious assaults on the goods and services they supposedly rejected.

Both the benevolence and malevolence of the '60's surfaced in the shape of the Diggers, a loose convergence of dropouts and activists who set up shop in San Francisco in 1966 to care for homeless, drug damaged kids. Within a short time they managed to establish soup kitchens, a legal aid service, the Haight-Ashbury free medical clinic and a store, the Free Frame of Reference. [36]

The Diggers named themselves after a 17th century group of impoverished Englishmen who tried to become masters of their own economic fate by digging and planting the common land. The original 'Diggers' advocated communal living and political equality. Although destroyed by local opposition, these people laid down the principles of self-help and mutual aid, as well as hostility to property and authority, which were later taken up by Godwin, Proudhon, Kropotkin and others. [37]

By 1967 the San Francisco Diggers were overwhelmed by the sheer numbers of young runaways who flocked to the city from all over the country. Out of money and resources, they shut down, only to reopen a year later, angrier, but better organized. They published a manifesto, "The Post-Competitive, Comparative Game of a Free City" which asserted: *"Every brother should have what he needs to do his thing."* [38] To accomplish this the group tried to establish a 'liberated zone', a 'free city' complete with free food, medicine, music and even 'free money'. [39] But they never resolved the vital question, where do all the 'free things' come from? The Diggers and their program remained dependent on the very society they despised. A subversive logic led to theft (*"the necessary thievery and plunder of a rancid State"*) and intimidation, the shakedown of pop groups and psychedelic shopkeepers, aside from the general public. [40]

> *"By now we all have guns, know how to use them, know our enemy, and are ready to defend. We know that we ain't gonna take no more shit. So its about time we carried ourselves a little heavier and got down to the business of creating free cities within the urban environments of the western world."* [41]

Emotionally the Diggers' propaganda, and deeds, constituted a manic attack on their California cornucopia. Good intentions got lost amid greed for the fruit and contempt for the source. Yet they were not able to undermine society, nor triumph over a pervasive pop culture. Within a few years the Diggers themselves dissolved, victims of violent posturing, a last grasp at self-importance, as well as changing fashions. [42] Significantly, the same tendencies continue to appear and reappear in different guises, devoid of theory. I refer to the many ways that individuals assault 'the system' through welfare abuse or computer hacking, essentially different varieties of economic or electronic vandalism.

* * * * *

Most men and women who 'cheat the system' while on welfare do not necessarily see themselves as anarchists, even though they may be attacking the 'nipple of state materialism'. These claimants assert, often correctly, that the state cheats them, so they have every reason to get back at it. But in so doing, they deplete the pool of money available for legitimate claimants, and spoil their chance to be helped without being demeaned. For example, so many 'fraudsters' flooded into the seaside town of Newquay, Cornwall, that it became known as the 'Costa del Dole', and local youngsters could not claim social security benefits without attracting opprobrium. [43]

As 'electronic breasts' full of valuable data, computers are also vulnerable to operators who attack both hardware and software, the package and the contents. Machines have been shot, blown up, urinated on and disabled with knives or keys. [44] In a celebrated incident the employee of an insurance company acted like the Angry Brigade because he was bored. Over a period of two years he repeatedly sabotaged the disk drives of a Burroughs B3500. It turned out that every time the engineers were called, he became the center of attention and excitement, a heady brew. [45]

In addition there are 'hackers' who systematically assail the data banks. They act for for thrills as well as for profit – to enter forbidden places and gain access to piles of information. In this regard they are just like children who would worm their way into their mothers' bodies in order to hack out the goodies. Greed may be the motivation, as with the embezzler who diverts electronic funds, or the diddler who steals trade secrets or proprietary programs. [46] However, the malicious hacker does not stop at theft. He tends to take after the burglar who breaks into a house, turns on the taps, and smears shit on the wall.

Such a person despoils data with 'Trojan horses,' 'logic bombs' and 'viruses.' These are special sets of instructions which when inserted into software make it malfunction, either immediately, or at some time in the future. (47) They can also be used to infect computer networks ('bulletin boards'), which as a Manhattan computer consultant put it, is like *"poisoning the candy in the supermarket on Halloween."* (48)

'Trojans' and 'logic bombs', which can easily blow a program to 'bits', are to the hacker what plastic explosive is to the terrorist. They enable him to ravage the computer and simultaneously deprecate the parent organization.

* * * * *

The targets of the subverting, vandalizing attacks I have been considering – riches, sweets, crops, supermarkets, data banks, drugstores or welfarè – symbolize the female side of society. Since their feeding, containing, stimulating features overlap with generative, life promoting functions, one might expect that vandalism would reach deep into the body of the motherland, the womb of all things as well of the breast. Clearly this is the case.

"Ecological rape" has become a byword for individual onslaughts on beautiful, fertile places, while inventive organizations remain prey to corporate sharks. (49) Similarly disaffected students have been known to vent their spleen on artistic centers by spraying museums and slashing paintings. The person who mutilates a Rembrandt or a Madonna and Child illustrates the original meaning of 'vandal'.

For many, the 'hated object' is the institution of motherhood. Filial vandalism has to do with injuring the product of another woman's happiness and love. Helmut Schoeck has described a middle aged spinster who suddenly pushed a friend's baby and pram into the Isar river in Munich. (50) Afterwards the murderer said she had been overcome by envy of the new mother's good feelings. It would be safe to say that this woman was also enraged by evidence of her friend's fertility, and maternity. Not infrequently newspapers report analogous deeds by babysitters or family acquaintances, culprits who may be men or women, respectable or outcast.

In the quiet town of Westbury, England, a fifty year old teacher, described as a cold, lonely divorcee, butchered the wife and child of a colleague. Aside from jealousy, it became clear at the trial that the woman's motive was *"envy over a happy family enjoying a new baby".* (51) Similarly, twenty year old Bruce Lee set fire to over two dozen men, women and children, because he thought they were members of happy families. (52) Lee was the epileptic son of a prostitute who had been *"kicked from pillar to post."* Had he entertained political yearnings, revolutionaries might have applauded a 'heroic contribution to the struggle against bourgeois marriage'. In fact he acted gratuitously.

Ultimately, these impulses touch traitors, citizens who vandalize their own state. The abhorrence they attract not only arises from raids on national sovereignty, but from their inevitable tendency to undermine the creative capacity of a country to care for its citizens and renew its environment. In this sense traitors are maternal moles with evil intentions. (53)

* * * * *

Power provides the primary targets for radical leaders like Bakunin, Kropotkin and Marx. They instinctively directed their insurrectionist eyes and vocal teeth towards the exercise of authority. Thus, the 1882 Anarchist International avowed:

> *"Our ruler is our enemy. We Anarchists, i.e., men without any rulers, fight against all those who have usurped any power..... our enemy is the State, whether monarchical, oligarchical, or democratic.....Our enemy is every thought of authority, whether men call it God or devil....."* (54)

The manifesto condemns officialdom – landowners, factory chiefs, priests, judges and Heads of State – all representatives of a collective patriarchy responsible for oppressing the young (the weak and helpless, *"the proletariat"*) and exploiting femaleness (production and reproduction, *"the means of production"*) [55] Later insurrectionists equated the State with a greedy penis (*"the ant-eater proboscis"*), a legal organ able to thrust itself *"into every corner"*' in order to perpetuate privilege. [56]

Yet, for all his attacks on big government, Bakunin was not averse to power. In 1864 he founded the International Brotherhood, a secret, close-knit society composed of conspirators who would initiate and lead the revolution. Likewise Marx, first a friend and finally a bitter enemy of Bakunin, was totally preoccupied with political intrigues and the control of men. [57] Almost without exception his colleagues and acquaintances recalled:

> *"....his overriding characteristic is boundless ambition and thirst for power...he is very jealous of his authority as leader (and is) an absolute ruler (who) tolerates no opposition."* [58]

> *...the aim of all his endeavors was personal domination... with a shameless impudence worthy of Napoleon."* [59]

Bakunin, Marx and their followers were not contradictory in their attitude towards governmental power. In the guise of stripping the State of strength, they sought to garner it for themselves. Thus the rod of authority can pass from the individual to the collective and back again in a multitude of ways. In the last chapter I described institutions and political parties whose virility lay in their capacity to dominate individuals. Here I am describing the opposite course, individuals who commit their skills to emasculate society and take over command.

* * * * *

The aggrandizement of power is not limited to the political arena. Like successful hunters, computer hackers devote untold ingenuity to tracking, slaying and redirecting programs for their own use. Here the issue is not plunder, rather the wish to be big, that is, to take on the qualities of the experts, or computer, or the company itself. As one college student remarked, hacking *"....is a game. It is a chance to show you are clever."* [60] Security analysts, however, insist a lot more than games are at stake. They think every programmer is a potential *"cracksman"* :

> *"Telling a programmer that a computer system is safe from penetration is like waving a red flag in front of a bull."* [61]

Having cracked the code, the hacker can leave 'trap doors', passwords like 'Joshua', so vividly depicted in the film *War Games.* [62] These allow future access to computers and computer networks as well as the opportunity to lay down logic bombs which can be used in fraternal strife with other hackers or hobbyists. Richard Streeter, a CBS executive, discovered this to his detriment while checking electronic bulletin boards for new programs. He came across one called EGABTR which promised to improve the efficiency of his graphic displays. Intrigued, he copied it onto his hard disk and tried it out. Within seconds *"Arf, Arf! Got You!"* flashed on his screen. Streeter discovered what *"Got You!"* meant when he tried to retrieve other data. Nothing was there! EGABTR had effectively destroyed all nine hundred programs and documents contained in his storage system. [63]

'Worms' and 'viruses' damage the data and software. The worm is a program which can wriggle through large computer networks and take over idle power for exceptional uses. But worms also allow hackers to enhance their capacities at others' expense or to play Robin Hood by 'donating' computer time and information *"to the masses"*. Alternatively malign mutants are able to burrow through data bases leaving massive memory gaps.

Viruses are infectious data destroyers that can spread like the plague, replicate with ease, and contaminate a whole system *"for revenge"* or *"just for the fun of it."* (64) Not surprisingly, instigators of such trap doors, trojan horses, worms and viruses have done formidable damage. (65) The De Paul University in Chicago central computer suffered one breakdown after another because teen-age cracksmen broke in and deleted parts of its operating system. Similarly, Los Angeles high school students took joy rides through the research data of doctorate candidates. More alarming, members of the 414's, a Milwaukee group named after the telephone area code for eastern Wisconsin, mucked around the mainframes of over sixty institutions including the Los Alamos nuclear-weapons research facility in New Mexico and the Sloan-Kettering Cancer Centre in New York. (66)

By the mid 1980's the U. S. National Security Agency was regularly warning allied countries about the consequences of political malcontents sabotaging their computer systems. Not long afterwards, a Parisian programmer and a New York writer produced a 'techno-thriller' call *Softwar*. It was based on the idea of injecting a logic bomb into the Soviet computer network that was so powerful it would *"wipe out everything but the graffiti in the Kremlin's men's room."* (67)

* * * * *

The 414's and related 'rebels with theories' aim at the electronic analogues of institutional power and illustrate the narcissistic analogues of envy. At one and the same time they propose to tear down 'the system' and boost themselves. These are the two aspects to these manoeuvres. The latter operates according to the popular refrain: *"Anything you can do, I can do better.* (68)

The same holds true with reckless programmers, or, for that matter, political vandals, whose driving force is the wounding awareness of their own frailty juxtaposed to the virility of 'the state machine'. These people are always trying to 'beat the system' but are never satisfied by what they achieve. They remain prey to others' accomplishments, their own doubts, the absence of praise, and ever escalating rivalries. In other words I am describing an escalating degree of mental pain, more specifically narcissistic wounds.

When this pain becomes too great, the person may stop trying to hurt others by outdoing them and ally himself with negative wishes. So we can see why destructive narcissism is the converse side of self inflation. Although the destructionist still registers qualities like strength, size, prowess, authority or staying power, he attaches them to violence and devastation.

Such hatreds allow us to look at the phenomenon of destructive narcissism from yet another angle. With Billy Carter the overt issue concerned a bad brother-good brother problem. Since he could not occupy the identify of the good boy, he decided to make a career of being the bad boy. In other words he got stuck in his destructive identifications.

In this chapter we saw how destructiveness follows the loss of positive ideals and idealized self-images. If the anarchist cannot save the world, then he will destroy it. This conundrum, in turn, has to do with overcoming intolerable despair at the loss of positive identifications (the ideals).

Now we can appreciate that the destructiveness illustrated in these two previous examples are closely related to the hurts aroused by self deflation. The affected person tries to overcome the deflation, that is, the collapse of his narcissistic structure, by reinflating himself, really by reinventing him (or her) self, through hate and violence. If he can't be an angel, then he will be a devil. If she can't be 'beneficence,' then 'she will be maleficence.'

Consequently these individuals prefer regicide to reign, and plastique to logic bombs. Instead of trying to reform or surpass the system, they want to smash it and everything connected with it. Many rationales may be given. Radical ideologues, for example, often proclaim computers are tools of capitalist oppression:

> *"Computers are the favorite instrument of the powerful. They are used to classify, control and to repress."* (69)

This is part of a public statement by a French terrorist group called CLODO which is slang for *"tramp"* and also an acronym for words which roughly translate: *"Committee for the Liquidation and Misappropriation of Computers."* [70] In Europe there have been dozens of direct assaults on computer installations by guerrillas armed with weapons ranging from Molotov cocktails to submachine guns. [71] Members of the Red Brigade have carried out a large proportion of these raids. After one explosion at the Motor Vehicle Ministry, so many files were obliterated that the Italian government didn't know who owned cars or trucks, or had licenses to drive them, for almost two years.

Computers announce the complexity and power as well as the grandiosity and pomposity of the organizations that use them. In the early '80's young Swiss anarchists bypassed electronics and vented their spleen straight at the Zurich opera house, for them the overstuffed structure of overbearing burghers. [72] Calling themselves *Die Unzufriedenen – The Dissatisfied,* they charged a gala performance with eggs and paint after which they burned cars and looted luxury shops for several days. [73] *The Dissatisfied* came from a pool of apprentices, unskilled workers and disgruntled students. They saw themselves as losers in a society where success equalled virility, and reacted accordingly. If they couldn't compete, that is, join the rat race, they would destroy it.

Similar sentiments have motivated the Hell's Angels a motorcycle club founded in Fontana, southern California, in 1950. Many of its adherents have come from the ranks of disaffected mechanics and service station attendants. One commented:

"We were all losers. We were unhappy and we wanted to have other people be unhappy. We did anything evil that any of us could think of to do." [74]

During the early years, the club members favored violent brawling, often taking over small towns for bouts of weekend hell-raising. Later they moved into racketeering. Their ironic self-description is instructive, *"Hell's Angel's"* or Angel's from Hell, as opposed to more obvious epithets like Satan's Commandos or the California Devils. It implies that on some level they wanted to be Angels, that is, beings who were widely known for good works, or within a California context, worldly accomplishment. Since this avenue appeared to be blocked, they aimed for wickedness and infamy, that is, to become the 'biggest baddies on the block'.

* * * * *

The perverse longing for notoriety, the counterpart of fame, characterizes the destructive narcissist. Really, the term is a misnomer, since all narcissism is destructive. However, the difference is between a personal and interpersonal strategy that builds pride at the expense of others (by inducing inferiority, inadequacy, shame, and so forth) and one that seeks celebrity by annihilating others (or society and its symbols).(75) The latter exults in power, and tries to procure a place in history (or, at the very least, the minds of colleagues) by outrageous acts, not just the murder of men, but attacks on the pillars of civilization. (76)

In ancient times the Greek Herostratos grasped renown by burning the temple of Artemis at Ephesus, then one of the wonders of the world. (77) The Ephesians responded by banning the mention of his name. This would be more difficult in present circumstances when news of comparable crimes can flash around the world in minutes. It is not insignificant that soon after shooting President Reagan, John Hinckley demanded to know how he was shown on television. For similar reasons urban rioters often race home to watch 'the box' after *"an evening's entertainment"* smashing and burning about the streets.(78) Indeed, when the coverage is inadequate dedicated terrorists are quick to complain about *"a conspiracy of silence"*. More likely the media is suffering from overkill. (79)

Riots are concentrated outbursts of 'macho' rage which otherwise can take the form of gratuitous defacements of powerful vehicles or any large public edifice. Thus a Porsche or BMW left out in the open is in constant danger of receiving progressive scratchmarks right along the paintwork. This process seems to have achieved its ultimate expression in the New York subway system where graffiti covers the carriages inside and out, and the stations as well. [80] Far from being a new native artform, as some critics have claimed, the chaotic iconography proclaims an unrelenting antagonism to the society which built the system, and the trains, symbols of the ceaseless energies searching, sensing, throbbing and probing the deep, dark tunnels of the city. As for the passengers, they are the victims of a host of spray figures, a multiplicity of evil eyes designed to pass on the fears and hatreds which 'have-nots' direct to 'haves' in order 'to be big'. It is impossible to ride the subway without feelings assaulted by these 'eyes' and their scrawled accompaniments:

> *"Kill!" "Destroy!" "Off that!" "Off everything!" "I'm the meanest!" "I'm the greatest!"* [81]

Both the ikons and words are envious ejections screaming *"Screw you,"* but *"Look at me!"* which indicate they originate in destructive phallicists with an eye for trouble. [82] The object of the sprayers, no less than the 414's, CLODO and other hell raisers is the societal phallus. I refer to authority and power incarnated in the structure of the State and its values and institutions, always seen by those who attack them as oppressive and exploitative.

* * * * *

The questions arises, do governments and organizations 'have it coming to them' for being cruel and tyrannical, or are they phantoms created by and victimized for the malicious impulses of their attackers? The answer is not clear cut. In actuality, almost anything that a person can imagine has been done at some point at some place in the name of some society. In this century alone, the realities of Nazi Germany, Stalinist Russia, Maoist China, or for that matter, two global wars, have strained the bounds of iniquity. And even within 'advanced Western countries' there remain pockets of poverty that would not be unfamiliar to a Victorian workman.

All too frequently the same holds true with cultural conventions. During the post world war decades the American anthropologist, Jules Henry, reconnoitred his own country. In *Culture Against Man*, and other studies, he documented schools that imparted stupidity, no less than mental hospitals that perpetuated madness and families which prevented their children from growing up. [83] Interestingly there exists a word that denotes a situation when a person feels persecuted, but isn't. I refer to *paranoia*. Yet there doesn't exist a word for the actual predicament of being persecuted, while not recognizing the fact nor responding accordingly. Nor are there words to denote the wide variety of in- between states.

In practice institutions, and the societies which support them, contain elements of good and bad, danger and deliverance. At one extreme there are social systems which require resistance, yet overwhelm the opposition by ruthless repression. They are objective persecutors and may be termed 'Monstrous Societies' or 'Monstrous Cultures.' They have the same relationship to their citizens that actual parental persecutors ('Monstrous Parents') have to their children. Like Jael in *Facial Justice* the victims of 'Monstrous Cultures' not only have to conform, but they have to accept whatever harm may be inflicted on them in the name of society without challenging or even thinking about what has been done to them. [84]

In the last chapter I pointed out that the ill-effects of institutionalized malice include redistributive and retributive starvation as well as systematic attacks on feminine and masculine accomplishments. Perhaps worse, is that 'Monstrous Societies' leave little room for projective processes to take place, that is, to serve, like parents, as useful containers for people's envy and greed. They are already so terrifying, that their victims remain speechless, even when confronted with what has been done to them.

Paradoxically countries and cultures which are reasonably beneficent, are more likely to be perceived as monstrously evil. This is a consequence of not being totally oppressive. Citizens are allowed to hate, and express their hates, without being immediately whisked off to jail. But in addition to being the focus of pernicious projections, these societies also become a receptacle for idealized expectations, especially during periods of social change. Since actual events never coincide with impossible goals, such as 'eliminating poverty within a generation' or 'equal health and happiness for everyone', society itself, or 'the system' gets the blame for being savage, pitiless, child destructive and so forth.

* * * * *

At the other extreme the 'Societal Monster' or 'Cultural Monster' is a political entity or cultural institution transformed into a blood sucking savage by the angry thoughts of its citizens. It is a subjective reality, a creature created in the minds of the hard-done-by which uses bad features to mirror malevolence while burying good bits beneath bitterness. The 'Societal Monster' is the social counterpart of the 'Parental Monster." Like Sartre's 'bourgeoisie', it embodies the Wicked Witch and Killer Giant all rolled up into one horrific, all-powerful persecutor.

The Angry Brigade, the White Panthers and kindred spirits have all provided abundant descriptions of society qua demon based on attributions of inner impulses and distortions of external realities:

> *"The politicians, the leaders, the rich, the big bosses, are in command.... THEY control. WE, THE PEOPLE, SUFFER....THEY have polluted the world....THEY shoved garbage from the media down our throats. THEY made us absurd sexual caricatures... THEY killed, napalmed, turned us into soap, mutilated us, raped us."* (85)

"THE RULERS OF OUR PLANET ARE TOTALLY CORRUPT. THE RULERS OF OUR PLANET ARE TOTALLY INSANE." [86]

These statements make monsters from grains of truth. For sure some rulers are corrupt, and others may be 'insane', but exaggerated leaps from the specific to the general across time and place simply perpetrate the states of mind: paranoia, despair, paralytic hopelessness, that precede 'the facts'. Similarly the use of WE and THEY provides a mechanism for splitting good from bad and pinning the bad on societal figures, representing the state. [87] Thus, THEY are greedy (rich, exploitative), envious (polluting, garbage shoving), jealous (commanding, controlling), vindictive (mutilating, napalming) and perverted (raping, caricature making, sexually brutalizing). In the meanwhile WE, mere citizens, are brutalized, unloved (mere functions of a production process) and totally justified in violent revenge.

The 'Societal Monster' has all the characteristics of a THEY and continues to be portrayed in innumerable hideous shapes and sizes. European anarchists seem to prefer the image of a jackbooted soldier holding a gun to the head of a quivering comrade, while in '60's America, the pig became the favored symbol of avaricious authority. [88] Contemporary effigies include a robotic teacher wielding an iron rod over *US*, long suffering students, as appeared in the anarchist journal, *Black Flag*: [89]

The pedagogic oppression posed by this robot is probably, though not necessarily, the product of perverse perception. If social facts coincide with rampant hatred, then it is more appropriate to speak of the 'Monstrous Society'. This term includes people acting on behalf of the larger cultural or political establishment, the agents, as well as the whole system itself. Typically teachers take on the role of 'Monstrous Parents' when serving in loco parentis to unwilling students, but turn into 'Monstrous Society'. while trying to civilize unruly students.

The basic elements in these dramas include the actual behavior and imaginary threats posed by both sides. Unwilling students use their teachers, just like in other circumstances, unwilling citizens use the State, as a mirror and receptacle for their personal antagonisms. Unruly people do the same. But, in addition, they actively mobilize the imagination of the authorities who then, not only respond to the way things are, but also to their own exaggerated fears and guilts. The projection of these feelings onto and into individuals often 'justifies' an escalating spiral of violent oppression. This process peaked at the 1968 Democratic Presidential Convention in Chicago. A small number of agitators and a large gathering of students precipitated a political crisis by provocative, but essentially harmless demonstrations which engaged the phantasies of the-powers-that-be. At one of the meetings a pretty coed walked naked carrying the head of a pig on a platter. Many others smoked dope or chanted anti-war slogans. These actions aroused such passions that the arena became a war zone with armed police brutalizing the demonstrators. Thereby they appeared to demonstrate that Mayor Daley, the Democratic candidate, and indeed, *'the whole rotten system'* was really rotten. More to the point, the youngsters, and some of their older mentors, created the facts they needed in order to convey the hurts they felt in the first place. [90] This left them in no doubt that both 'the pigs' and politicians had it coming to them.

* * * * *

The demonized or 'Citizen Monster' is the counterpart of the state or institution that attracts hostility. He or she is an individual who becomes the projective focus of collective fears and seems to embody everything that his compatriots hate in themselves. In America in the '60's this included unrestrained sensuous qualities, Dionysian reveries, that clashed with outspoken moral and materialistic values. Anyone with long hair and beards, or unkempt feminine features, was immediately suspect and often lumped with 'beatniks', 'hippies', ''weirdos' or 'homos'. Onlookers 'saw' them as incubi and succubi out to infiltrate their homes and neighbourhood with drugs, sex and communism. At one and the same time they were condemned for being oversexed, castrated and castrating. Yet, their alleged unremitting enmity to the American way of life reflected the hostility hurled in their direction. This made them an even greater menace, and called forth even greater retribution.

The Michigan poet and publicist, John Sinclair, was one of many white, middle class dropouts demonized for non-conformity. After a stint at Wayne State University, he founded an artists' workshop for kindred souls and became a spiritual leader of the Detroit-Ann Arbor psychedelic/ Rock and Roll community. His lifestyle led to a lot of adverse attention from local law enforcement agencies, and Sinclair's defiant decision to form the White Panther Party for the propagation of *"Rock and Roll, Dope, and Fucking in the Streets."* (91) He explained:

> *"Our program is cultural revolution through a total assault on culture.......art, music, newspapers, books, posters, our clothing, our homes, the way we walk and talk, the way our hair grows, the way we smoke dope, and fuck and sleep and eat – it's all one message, and the message is FREEDOM."* (92)

Sinclair was eventually arrested and imprisoned for ten years for possessing two marijuana cigarettes. (93) The draconian sentence undoubtedly reflected 'the politics of gesture' and his ability to get under the skin and agitate the minds of city and state authorities through the interplay of outlandish, he would say 'revolutionary', words, sounds and images. [94] It is likely that he had the same emotional impact in '68 as pictures of truculent students still produce today: [95]

The student with squinting eyes, gnashing teeth and bristling appearance seems to be especially designed to send shivers through the most hardened robot, or bourgeoisie. But if he didn't exist, he would be invented, for he compliments the oppressive pedagogue. Whether the result is fight or flight, such a fearsome person or 'Citizen Monster' is a phantom that reflects and stirs up preexistent conflicts in his family or society.

On the other hand, the 'Monstrous Citizen' relies on deeds, not phantasies, to attack the establishment. Like the filial persecutor who vandalizes adults, the 'Monstrous Citizen' cuts his teeth on public figures and everything they represent. He is a tangible, not an imaginary malcontent. Hate mailers, for example, frequent the 'fourth estate'. In England, a Mr. George Richards, of Poole, Dorset, made it his life's work to bombard journalists with the news that they were *"pitiable imbeciles."* Finally words failed him and he resorted to sending toilet seats to chosen columnists. [96]

More often than not the 'Citizen Monster and 'Monstrous Citizen' are one and the same person. I am describing the point where objective persecution and subjective perception meet. The early John Sinclair was mostly a nightmare in the minds of local police, but once he started to retaliate, he became much more than a long haired spaced out 'freak'. The later Sinclair was a revolutionary propagandist who managed the band, M. C. 5., and was involved in subversive activities throughout the Detroit area. [94] Similarly, the Angry Brigadists exploded bombs and images outside courthouses, and inside politicians. Therefore, the term 'Complete Persecuting Citizen' more accurately describes their impact, and that of the modern terrorist, on society.

* * * * *

The key word is 'Monster', indicating a subjective fact, 'an observer created reality'. In this chapter on the individual against society, and the previous one on society against the individual, I have tried to explore the subtle, and not so subtle ways that either side (the instigator, the subject) brings together fear and hatred, actuality and phantasy in order to justify its attacks on the other (the victim, the object). Superficially it appears that the instigator is quite separate from his victim, but on closer examination, we can see that the two are linked. Like the relation between the envier to the envied, there exist many points of confluence. This leads to alliances which encompass at least two distinct parts: There is an actual person in conjunction with the malevolent phantasies that the authorities have projected on to him. And, secondly, there is an actual society or institution in conjunction with the malevolent phantasies that its citizens have projected onto it. The projected phantasies may have little to do with the object, the target, or may be called forth by foci of similarity to the very things that the aggressor hates in himself. In any case each side, subject and object, individual and society, remains a dreaded part of the other, which goes some way to explain the intransigence of social conflict.

Thus, the 'Complete Persecuting Citizen' is a man or woman who plays on the imagination of the State in order to get a response which transforms all sides into monsters: the individual in the eyes of authority: and the authorities in the eyes of the individual. But the effects often extend to the individual's perception of himself and the government's view of itself. If these transformations do not stick, then the citizen may remain a nuisance or persecutor, but someone to be dealt with appropriately, without panic or unnecessary aggression.

From the point of view of ordinary people the 'Complete Persecuting Citizen' becomes demonic not just by acting hurtfully, but by forcing itself into their minds, and coercing them from within. Again, without this internal interaction, citizens would still suffer, yet they would not remain incapacitated by political or institutional tyrannies.

These processes feed a matrix of malice which can escalate out of control or wind down when touched by reparative reactions. At their worst, they recapitulate timeless family dramas when the Oedipal son confronts the Laial father – the conjunction of subjective states and objective events played to a massive audience where all the world's the stage.

Chapter 11a

National Pride

The politics of malice culminates in the expression of extreme antagonisms among institutions, cultures and nation-states. These hatreds effectively submerge and simultaneously reinforce the enmities of individual citizens. Over two thousand years ago the Greek orator Lysias narrated the rage that Sparta 'felt' towards its prosperous Corinthian allies, while in this century the French economist, Eugène Raiga, emphasized that whole countries are capable of mutual envy and jealousy and that they mimic the tensions that exist among people.[1]

What does it mean when a politician or journalist states that a nation or country 'feels' hurt, or angry, or vengeful? Is this a tangible phenomenon, or metaphor, or projection perhaps of the speaker's own emotional state? Certainly countries often appear to behave as they are said to feel. Egypt under Nasser took over the Suez canal to assert 'independence' and 'avenge humiliations' by Britain and France. Similarly Argentina under Galtieri invaded the Falklands to regain 'pride' and confirm its 'superiority' over Britain and fellow Latin countries.

More often than not these feelings comprise the 'unarticulated premises' which lay behind public policies. They originate from above, national leaders, with all their blind and not so blind interests and prejudices; and, in recent times, from below, a citizenry whose passions can be aroused and channelled by the powers of mass communication.

Previously, the feelings of the populace were less significant than those of their leaders because the people were expected, indeed, forced to feel and do what their rulers, the patresfamilias, desired. Thus the dynastic wars of the Middle Ages were like extended family quarrels and the fratricidal carnage that followed was fueled by the private greed of six Renaissance Popes. (2)

The modern concept of a state as an independent entity began to emerge from the 16th century with the writings of Niccolò Machiavelli and Jean Bodin. (3) Whereas Machiavelli focussed on the strength and craftiness of the Prince, or head of state, Bodin presaged the idea of 'the divine right of kings' – the state and its ruler were one. Consequently the emotional predilections for good or bad, of kings or premiers necessarily became political issues. In the 20th century a comparable strain of vengeful autocracy has characterized the regimes of Josef Stalin and Adolf Hitler as well as the 'personalismo' of Gamal Abdel Nasser and Fidel Castro. (4)

In contrast the philosopher Jean Jacques Rousseau argued that the state derived its authority from the general will of the governed. (5) The implication of his work and that of subsequent thinkers was that people did not owe allegiance to a particular individual, but to a national body. Here we have a nascent definition of nationalism, arguably the most important collective force in modern history. Citizens could and did direct elemental feelings towards their cultural, linguistic and political community, that is, their nation or state. (6)

Emotionally the power of this community or 'body politic' is much more than the sum of its individual parts. Since its members are linked by bonds of common interests, physical closeness and rapid communication, it can and does function like a large crowd and volatile person, all in one. Wild enthusiasms and passionate hatreds tend to brew up at short notice and spread like wildfire with ever increasing intensity. Not surprisingly, patriotic assemblies can be notoriously fickle and irrational. [7]

The national crowd is a Freudian herd where, as Elias Canetti has pointed out, all become equal, no distinctions count, even of sex. [8] People press together, they make contact, they gain comfort by merging within the same political body. This allows them to surrender to the common good as well as the gravest evils. Too often the latter results from raising national esteem at the expense of others. [9]

This entity has a life of its own, separate from that of its constituent interests. Sovereign status means it is a 'national actor', one unit among the family of nations and field of supranational relations. [10] Fellow 'players', rich and poor, big and powerful or small and weak frequently use terms like *"poisonous", "filthy", "licentious" and "regicidal"* (Germany about Serbia, pre 1914) or *"evil", "dangerous" and "dominating"* (America about Russia, post 1945) to describe each other. [11] Other words, *"imperialist", "plunderer" and "warmonger"*, are part of an international verbal armory deployed by young, undeveloped countries to denigrate older, industrialized ones. Thus, individual states, acting cohesively, if not coherently, appear to display the whole range of sensitivities, insecurities and resentments that characterize children and adults.

I am describing a phenomenon amply evidenced by the diaries, memoirs, biographies, personal accounts and theoretical constructions of national leaders and commentators as well as ordinary citizens. Having imbued the state with intense emotional forces, often at the expense of depleting themselves of the same, all members of the community discover a vested interest in turning their beliefs into concrete realities. Consequently the state, can be seen as an external tableau replete with internal dramas. Diplomacy is the focal point where much of the 'lost' envy, greed and jealousy may be found. In fact, some states essentially exist in an extrasocietal form, that is, through foreign relations. [12] Relative to their own shaky inner structures, they prefer to accumulate international kudos by lambasting richer countries for *'consumerism'* and other *'transgressions'*. [13]

* * * * *

There have been many moments when sheer greed has been elevated to the status of a national obsession. (14) Spain of the conquistadors and Belgium under King Leopold provide only two examples of the ruthless despoliation of human and material resources by Europeans and non- Europeans alike. In the past century Russia starved the Ukraine, China devoured its peasants, and Germany ravished most of Europe. (15) The Nazi longing for land has been satirized by the comedian, Mel Brooks, in his film, *To Be Or Not to Be*. In one skit Brooks plays Hitler looking over a map of the continent while claiming to be a man of peace. Suddenly, he switches tune and starts a frenzied song about taking *"…. a piece of France, a piece of Denmark, a piece of Russia…."* (16) I am told that this is an old joke often applied to any country which ostentatiously covets the territory of another.

Greed, however, is not the privilege of single nations. In the 1970's a transnational cartel of oil producing countries (O.P.E.C.) suddenly quadrupled the price of oil, *"a pivotal event"* which effectively held the rest of the world over a barrel. (17) Among the many ramifications, the traditional flow of envy from East to West and South to North reversed. The United States and Western Europe began to deeply resent the wealth of Arab and African oil producers, and especially disliked becoming dependent on 'lesser powers' for energy resources.

As with children to parents, a noxious sense of dependency, or, lack of economic autonomy, is a key issue that determines the degree of hate of that one country (their leaders and citizens) feels towards another. Prior to World War Two, Britain and France attracted the most opprobrium for being colonial powers, that is, keeping or seeming to keep smaller, less developed territories in a state of economic and political subservience. (18) After the war the old animosities continued to fester, but the United States, as the predominant economic power, became the prime target of international abuse. From Latin America to southeast Asia and northern Europe, old and new nations alike blamed American affluence for their 'poverty', 'backwardness', 'chaos' or 'unhappiness'. South of the border, both right and left wing commentators on "dependence and underdevelopment" popularized the simple message:

> *"We are poor because the United States is rich; the United States is rich because it exploits us; let's fight against the United States."* [19]

The most common forum for this fight is the United Nations where the United States, and its Western allies, face a near deluge of denigration, before select committees and the General Assembly. Typically the head of one Indian delegation, the Maharaja of Jammu and Kashmir, denounced the *"colonial denudation"* of the East and the *"vulgar affluence"* of the West. [20] Similarly Western delegates like Professor René Dumont of France have provided reports which literally accuse the 'consuming countries' of cannibalism.

> *"Last year, in over-consuming meat which wasted the cereals which could have saved them, we ate the little children of the Sahel, of Ethiopia, and of Bangladesh. And this year, we are continuing to do the same thing, with the same appetite."* [21]

These denunciations extend from bread and butter to fertility. At one conference on population control the American delegation brought up the relation between over population and poverty. But even countries which agreed with the equation vilified America for daring to criticize the one thing that they could do which Americans didn't, make lots of babies. [22] They seemed to fear reflections of their own cupidity, in the guise of womb envy. The perverse extension of the right of unlimited fecundity, is the right to ecological rape. At another meeting on the human environment, Brazil insisted it had a right to ruin the rain forests. Any attempt to prevent this was a conspiracy of 'haves' to keep the 'have-nots' down and out. Here the Brazilians attributed greed in order to hide grenvy. [23]

* * * * *

The rhetoric of resentment, whether deployed by Brazil or a new state, is essentially a British contribution. It is the language of Fabian socialism applied to the international arena. [24] When India assails the *"arrogance of the affluent nations"*, she is using words which originate with Beatrice and Sidney Webb and their colleagues at the London School of Economics. [25] This demonstrates that it is possible to trace the flow of indignation from the individual to the group to society as a whole. By the 1950's the Webbs, were they alive, could truthfully claim that a large chunk of the world lived under regimes fashioned by their Victorian instincts. This also meant that while no longer an economic superpower, Britain was able to retain considerable political influence by conferring sovereign status on its class struggles. [26]

These supranational resentments do not always remain on the level of *"jaw, jaw"*. They can escalate into terrorist attacks on the "fatherland' (or 'motherland', depending on the predominant phantasy) and finally flash into full scale wars between a larger power, and a subordinate people. The latter always feels and sometimes is oppressed by the other nation which tends to be equated equated with '*a complete monster*' or '*a complete persecuting parent*.' This fusion of projected (greedy, envious) and perceived (exploitative) realities justifies the ensuing violence. Thus, in 1987, the speaker of the Iranian parliament, Hashemi Rafsanjani, asserted that Lebanese and Iranians were justified to take hostages and commit other acts of terror because they were "so ignored and so oppressed" by the United States, *"the great Satan."* [27]

Lloyd deMause contends the basic cause of open warfare is the pervasive group feeling, 'through war we (a nation) will be born'. In evidence he cites extensive references to specific experiences – a collective sense of *"choking"*, *"drowning"*, and *"suffocating"* leading to an *"inexorable sliding"* and *"breaking out"* – that tend to precede the onset of hostilities. DeMause can be criticized for taking metaphorical imagery too literally, although his conclusions are backed-up by a plethora of material taken from the intentional comments and unintended asides of leaders and other national prime movers. [28]

In referring to the American revolution, Samuel Adams spoke of *"the child Independence...now struggling for birth."* [29] Here, and in general, 'independence' or 'self-determination' denotes the struggle against smallness and servility, feelings which are common both to individuals and countries. [30] Despite the realities, colonial America, for example, was treated by Britain as an inconvenient child, the most tenacious antagonisms stem from envious beliefs that dependencies or nascent nations can never have as much or be as good as their parent country. [31]

Even after achieving independence some countries nourish the old hatreds by sponsoring or directly engaging in international terrorism. [32] But the usual response is ingratitude, succinctly described by the Aleksandr Solzhenitsyn in a speech to American trade unionists:

> *"The United States of America has long shown itself to be the most magnanimous, the most generous country in the world...... Who helps the most and unselfishly?*
>
> *And what do we hear in reply? Reproaches, curses, "Yankee Go Home." American cultural centers are burned, and the representatives of the Third World jump on tables to vote against the United States."* [33]

Ingratitude debases benevolence. It attempts to overcome relative inadequacy and inferiority (that is, envious tension) by denying goodness and by asserting help is harm. Thus Tanzania regularly excoriates the very countries which keep it afloat, while Western observers note that the more aid Egypt gets from America, the more critical and resentful Egyptians become. [34] Paradoxically the combination of Russo-American rivalry and post 60's affluence, seems to have created the conditions whereby sovereign nations, as opposed to private recipients, can thumb their noses at donor countries, yet continue to get increasing amounts of economic and military assistance. [35]

Ingratitude, however, is not limited to the Third World. In response to the American Marshall Plan various European countries acted like the angry Dervish in Handelsman's "Story of the Envious Man". While economically prostrate, some rejected it out of hand claiming it was a cruel charade instigated by a selfish power in order to enslave the world. Others accepted and used the aid well, yet major factions maintained a murmur of discontent. Although tempered by admiration, similar enmities remain a potent factor in Europe today. Anti-American prejudice is rarely far below the surface. At Cliveden, one of the most exclusive hotels in England, Americans have been singled out for surly service. (36) And at the 1985 Edinburgh Festival American tourists were openly abused in the quality, not the gutter press. (37)

The journalist, Thomas Friedman, comments on these very processes in his article. "American Power and an Envious, Angry World." The every fact of American dominance leads allies like France to hobnob with Iraq and Serbia, while complaining about America, *"The Capital of Global Arrogance"* The latter may act like global vandals directly, or indirectly by empowering angry young men or women to cut America down to size. Friedman notes that this is what happened in 1993 when Ramzi Yousef, who 'had no political program or ideology other than hating Israel and America,' was commissioned to blow up the World Trade Centre in New York. (38)

What Friedman describes is not unrelated to a plethora of envious and jealous rivalries between small states seeking to enjoy special relations with larger ones, or between superpowers for the support of smaller powers. This is a problem compounded at the end of the twentieth century by globalization, instantaneous communication (world wide web, e-mail, mobile phones) and the escalating break-up of large states into smaller units. (39) The scenario is not dissimilar from that of a child who plays off one parent against the other. Alternatively two small countries may fight for the favour of a larger one. (40)

* * * * *

The British cartoonist, Low, has depicted the problems of ingratitude in the person of an aging, Britannia being ousted from her home (i.e. former colonies) by a gleeful trio of newly independent countries. With packed bags at her feet, she clutches a copy of Freud in her hands. The caption reads:

> *"I wonder why children never want Grandma to depart through the front door but always long to kick her down the back stairs?"* (41)

The answer to Low's query is that the children want to triumph over Grandma. During decolonization, the kick in the pants was the repetitive claim that the colonial past was all bad and that former rulers were only rapacious exploiters. When combined with the denial of need and millennial promises of a glittering future, these hostilities were always part of a manic attack on dependency, the urge to rubbish Grandma and Grandpa alike.

Some, but not all of the newborn nations acted this way. For those who did, the premise: *I'm big, you're dung"* was an omnipotent attempt to erase old humiliations, often aided and abetted, in a world of power politics, by potential new patrons. Countries like China, conveyed the same message by retreating behind 'bamboo curtains'. Yet, it only took a few flowers to blossom internally, or a peek at Western accomplishments, to set off a national attack of the 'red eyed disease'. I refer both to the cultural revolution of the '60's and the unrest of the '80's which culminated in the fall of General Secretary, Hu Yaobang, for *"bourgeois liberalism"*. (42)

According to Chairman Deng *"self-reliance"* was what mattered.(43) Hu had been too taken by Western ideas. The feared consequence was that *"luan"* or chaos would overwhelm the country. But chaos results from envy. The *"luan"* Hu's opponents feared was the projection of their own fragmenting rage towards Hu personally, and to the larger world of Western learning particularly, into China as a whole. Therefore, the political upheaval represented a belated attempt to contain and express the feelings that flowed from growing Chinese participation in the global village. [44] This participation aggravated a collective 'inferiority complex' related to China's relative lack of power as well as wealth. Typically Chinese leaders assert superiority when they wish to conceal their 'third world' standards from first world countries.

The concept of a 'third world' was coined during the cold war by the French sociologist Alfred Sauvy. He utilized, of course, the French experience:

> *"....for this Third World, ignored and exploited and despised exactly as the Third Estate was before the Revolution, would also like to become something."* [45]

'Third worldness' quickly became an ideological weapon in the hands of Asians and Africans jostling for position. For them *"something"* meant more than independence. It signified political and military prowess. Whatever they had, or didn't have materially, they could identify with the ability to wage war or soar into space. The 'implicit premise' was that a mighty fatherland took precedence over an ample motherland. In other words phallic strivings overcame empty tummies, which led agricultural economies to turn to steel mills and socialist countries to erect missiles but neglect wheat.

* * * * *

The rush for bigness makes pride the national phallus, and policy the passion to cut others down to size. More than one United Nations delegate has noted:

> *"There is a kind of Freudian element in this, an anger on the part of the newly independent countries at the old colonial father."* [46]

These angers are both Oedipal and Laial in underlying intent, as can be seen in the emotionally charged interplay between the United States and Castro's Cuba or post-Samoza Nicaragua. Here an older superpower overreacts because of a threatened curse (chaotic upheaval), while a revolutionary regime tries to cripple a giant and take over his wealth (prenationalized facilities). (47) The result is a nightmare which does not create, but greatly exaggerates preexistent geopolitical miseries.

Moreover, in this example, the smaller combatants have skilfully managed to play on the fears of their feared persecutor by becoming clients of a rival superpower. This complicates the matrix of suspicion and hate by evoking fratricidal strife. Significantly, the Soviet Union and the United States cannot easily extricate themselves from such conflicts, even if they wanted to do so. In the first place they themselves began their national lives through revolutionary patricide. I refer to the overthrow of the governments of Czar Nicholas II and King George III. In consequence many of their citizens identify with emergent states, seen as successful parricides.

Secondly, and more important, both countries remain committed to policies of phallic supremacy. This includes imperial thrusts around the world and into space. For proof one needs look no further than the huge sums the two Titans, and subsequently other countries like India and Pakistan, devote to enormous rockets with a high *"thrust-to-weight ratio, soft lay down and deep penetration"*. (47)

In America the Boeing Corporation regularly appeals to phallic pride in order to get the funding for bigger and better missiles. In one appropriation battle Boeing engineers constructed comparative models of Russian and American missiles. They painted the American ones painted blue and the Russian ones red. The military took these models to Congressional hearings where they argued:

"But, Senator, how do you feel when America has these small blue missiles and Russia has these great big red missiles?" (48)

The arguments were successful, but it would be wrong to suppose that the issues were simply sexual. From America's point of view the missiles confer grandeur, righteousness and an essential superiority over other nations. A gigantic rocket program has allowed the Russians or Pakistanis or Indians to draw similar conclusions about their system. In all of these countries the missiles serve a rampant nationalism.

* * * * *

Nationalism is not the expression of a loving devotion to national interests or the well-deserved respect that comes from collective accomplishments. On the contrary it conveys fanatical patriotism: mass identification with narrow, excessive, unreasoning, boastful beliefs in the right and might of one's country over all. Nationalism is to the state what narcissism is to the individual. It is a form of national narcissism, the expression of a perverted or pathological 'self'-absorption and pride.

Nationalism allows individuals to use the group, and groups to use the state, to paper over problems of wealth and power by grandiose schemes and gestures. An aggressive nationalism is the political equivalent of envious self assertion. One might expect this to be particularly acute during rapid periods of tribal, religious, cultural or technological change. And indeed, since the 18th century, nationalism has become an essential channel for the mass expression of malevolence.

Nationalistic preoccupations with size (bigness), shape (borders and boundaries), inner content (racial purity) and outer appearance (prestige) mirror narcissistic concerns. The attendant rivalries have often fueled open warfare, although sporting competitions increasingly channel a lot of the aggression. The Olympic Games or World Cup demonstrate international quests for glory. However, sudden or unexpected losses can equally demonstrate a national brittleness which can bring a country to its knees and kindle bitter cries for revenge. [49]

In the relations among states, self-inflation and other-deflation reflect the rapacious hunger for honour, status, splendour, eminence and supereminence. These actions also serve to deflect the murderous rage that follows national humiliations on the playing or killing fields. After World War One the French believed that Germany had willed 'The Great War' not just to undermine her power, but to destroy her greatness. (50) In fact France's economic and demographic decline could hardly keep pace with the bluster and braggadocio designed to conceal it. The country was awash with weird racial theories. Dr. Edgar Bérillon 'discovered' that the reason Germans smelled so bad and shat so much was because their intestines were nine feet longer than other humans. (51) But Anglo-Saxons fared no better. The novelist François Mauriac echoed popular opinion when he wrote:

> *"I do not understand and I do not like the English except when they are dead."* (52)

Having defaced their rivals with vulgar abuse, the French returned to the attack by exalting themselves. At the Versailles peace conference, they were reluctant to permit the use of the English language. It was not sufficiently refined, a position consistent with French views on culture or 'civilization'. Since coining the term in 1776, they thought they owned it, and deserved to remain its official keepers. Yet, in 1927 France spent less on higher education than on feeding cavalry horses.

The French were not alone in using arrogant attitudes to conceal envious onslaughts. Among Europeans peoples, fraternal putdowns remain familiar and popular such as: *"Italians are thieves,"* "*Finns carry knives* ," *"all French are snotty"*, and *"Germans all swagger."* But these generalizations are a pale shadow of the patronizing pose of the colonial powers, especially since the 18th century. Armed with technological might and organizational success, they began to believe that their own social practices and values were totally superior to the 'unintelligible barbarities' found elsewhere.

The British, for example, maintained a sense of superiority that was so dense as to be almost impenetrable. In relation to their colonial 'children' in America, this precluded knowledge and promoted a fatal underestimation of the strength of 'rabble' feelings. (53) Towards the end of the revolution, during the peace negotiations, John Adams concluded:

> *"The pride and vanity of that nation is a disease; it is a delirium; it has been flattered and inflamed so long by themselves and others that it perverts everything."* (54)

As the historian Barbara Tuchman notes, it is not irrelevant that two centuries later, the United States was 'afflicted' by the same 'disease' vis a vis the Vietnamese.

* * * * *

The delirium of disdain is not a European or American invention, nor solely a feature of a colonial mentality. In 1986 Prime Minister Yasuhiro Nakasone created a storm by asserting that Japan is far more intelligent than America because America contains large numbers of low level *"blacks, Puerto Ricans and Mexicans."* Nakasone's views were consistent with opinion polls that agreed: *"Japanese society is superior to others."* (55)

Japanese hubris, like British imperialism and other expressions of national pride, are inner as well as outer directed. All aim to master social tensions by promoting mass identification with an omnipotent state. In conjunction with self-inflation, the xenophobic denigration of foreigners is a necessary element in the process of deflecting hate from the 'body politic' to another body. In India the British defined their task, 'the white man's burden', in terms of taming a *"grossly ignorant population,steeped in idolatrous superstition, unenergetic, fatalistic, and indifferent to the evils of life."* (56) In essence a civilian and military elite projected widespread fears about 'the baser classes' onto a rich but alien culture. Meanwhile an impoverished citizenry aped authority and seized the opportunity to boost itself at others' expense. Of considerable importance, we can see in these practices some of the origins of institutionalized racism. Although not as new as modern nationalism, it serves the same purpose and is just as perverse. Many aspects of racism (whether allied with nationalist fervour or not) are both a defense against and expression of envy.

For almost a century, the lowest, least educated, uncultivated Englishman thought that he was superior to the highest Brahmin. Yet, the Indians themselves had maintained a rigid caste system for over 2,000 years. The light skinned descendents of the Aryan invaders treated the darker Dasas whom they conquered as inferior, and products of mixed Aryan and Dasa marriages as extremely inferior. All sides discriminated against the non-caste 'untouchables'. (57) Similarly, ethnic pride was and remains a powerful emotional current among Muslim peoples. It is impossible to comprehend current Arab-Jewish, indeed Arab-Western conflicts without taking into account the enforced subservience of non-Muslim peoples, 'the dhimmis', and the psychic wounds, still unhealed, that followed the abolition of 'dhimmi' status by the late Ottoman sultans. (58)

The 'dhimmis' included Jews, Christians, Armenians, Druses and Copts, but not pagans, who remained roughly equivalent to 'untouchables'. The 'dhimmi' was a second class citizen, tolerated, but subject to a Koranic poll tax and many other disadvantages. These included the requirement to wear special clothes or badges, the prohibition from bearing arms or riding horses and inequality before the law. No matter what his accomplishments, every Muslim could feel superior to a 'dhimmi', and could abuse him as he saw fit. (59)

For the Arab world the end of Islamic ascendency announced by the enfranchisement of 'dhimmis' and rule by foreigners reversed the proper order of things, just like the discoveries of Galileo shocked a Catholic Europe. But it was only one of a series of painful religious, cultural and political upheavals which fueled a nationalistic fury. The establishment of the State of Israel was a particular blow, for it called into question the preeminent basis of Islamic religion and honour. [60] As an oriental writer put it:

> *"That a land Arabized by jihad should have been lost to a dhimmi people by the beneficiaries of the dhimmi condition during 13 centuries is considered as a catastrophe of cosmic dimensions."* [61]

The Arab response to Zionism, or a resurgent Jewish nationalism, and the challenge of Western technology, was threefold, all encompassed in the personalismo and policies of the Egyptian leader, Gamal Abdel Nasser. [62] Nasser fused his very being, his hopes, fears, humiliations and hates with that of Egypt and the Egyptian people. [63] In so doing he activated a resurgent Arab nationalism, the politics of grandeur, the rhetoric of revenge, that became known as Nasserism, and blew like the sirocco throughout the Middle East.

The political scientist, P. J. Vatikiotis points out that Nasser fused personal with national humiliation and projected both onto the international stage. He developed an highly personal, charismatic style of leadership, a 'Modern Pharaonism' through which he sought a perfect rapport with the Egyptian, thence Arab masses. By means of the 'leadership principle' Egyptian, thence Arab nationalism became equivalent to Nasserism, and vice versa. However, even his mesmeric speeches could not conceal the ever increasing gap between victories declared and realities lived. [64] Gradually a national narcissism which emphasized positive glories changed into a militant nationalism which gloried in destruction and death.

On the national level, the jingoist face of Nasser illustrates the flip side of self-inflation. As the flow of frustration and envy increased, the wish for grandeur evolved into a hatred of life and the idealization of violence. This process parallels the transformation of human hubris into destructive narcissism: the glorification of death in lieu of the love of life. As Herbert Rosenfeld perceived: "the destructive aspects of the self (that) are idealized and submitted to." [65]

Similarly, the state, like the individual, can forget constructive goals and try to regain influence and prestige through terrorism abroad and despotism at home. Once slogans are facile and accomplishments languish, only renewal through war may appear possible. Thus, the refrain of an aggressive Victorian music hall song was:

"We don't want to fight,
but, by Jingo if we do,
We've got the ships, we've got the men,
We've got the money too." (66)

* * * * *

Nasser's ululations echoed Egypt's historic theme: *"Death and Resurrection, Resurrection and Death."* (67) But few countries has demonstrated the craving for wealth, the aggrandizement of power, the arrogance of pride concealing terrible fragility, the exultation in death and the rebirth of a nation transformed from envier to envied, as well as Nazi Germany. So I shall conclude the chapter by reviewing the progress of the German state from the nineteenth to the end of the twentieth century.

Although the German people had a long, often distinguished history, modern Germany did not become a unified country until 1871. Previously it had been divided into dozens of kingdoms, duchies, principalities, free cities and bishoprics, and, for generations, there had been no national currency or industry. Kant claimed the only common characteristic of Germans was their *"pedantic inclination to classify themselves in relation to other citizens according to a system of rank and prerogatives."* (68) Nevertheless, German artists and intellectuals maintained a mystical longing for *Das deutsche Vaterland* (The German Fatherland) and celebrated their shortcomings with rousing calls to German greatness. (69) Around 1810 Adam Müller declared: *"Everything that is great, everything that is thorough, everything that is enduring in European institutions is German."* [70] This closely followed Johann Fichte's stirring *Addresses to the German Nation* which proclaimed that Germans were a unique, primal people ('Urvolk'):

> *"To have character and to be German undoubtedly mean the same...All comparisons between the German and non-German are null and void...We are the chosen people. Chosen by God... with a moral right to fulfill our destiny by every means of cunning and force."* [71]

As the century wore on Fichte's words seemed to be matched by German achievements. Europe was astounded, and increasingly alarmed, by her industrial development, technological resourcefulness and artistic fecundity, besides her political progress under the Iron Chancellor, Otto von Bismarck [72] Yet, Germany did not get the respect she thought was her due, especially from France, who continued to patronize her as a barbarian upstart. Germany responded to her neighbour's envy and her own uncertainties with a mixture of over-confidence and arrogance, sentimentality and ignorance. [73] Many politicians throughout the German speaking world stressed that mankind was divided into Aryans and apemen, and the French were among the latter. Interestingly this view was later repeated by Adolf Hitler in *Mein Kampf.* He lumped the French with the Jews, and blamed both for being *"obsessed with negroid ideas...and world domination".* [74]

By the turn of the century Germany sported a blatant if not so innocent sense of national superiority which did not endear her to the rest of Europe. [75] The ensuing 'Great War' has been termed the war of Ottoman succession, the war of Austro-Hungarian succession and the war against German domination. It could even by termed the war of sibling rivalry in as much as many of the contending royals were direct descendents of Queen Victoria, and bitter rivals. [76] In truth it was all of these, but more. The war was the first great clash of regional nationalisms, a world civil war which waxed hot and cold until 1945, and is still going on, as evidenced by the nationalist upheavals in Eastern Europe and the former Soviet Union in the 1980's, and the aftermath in the Balkans in the 1990's.

All the participants in the Great War believed that self-righteous pride gave them the right to pursue grandiose ambitions, none more so than Germany. Her unexpected defeat was more than a humiliation. It was a narcissistic disaster for a country who perceived its 'volk' as 'übermenschen' long before the Nazis came to power. (77) The national loss of self-esteem was compounded by her refusal to face facts, specifically the negative and positive features of the peace settlement known as the Treaty of Versailles. Derisively dismissed as 'the Diktat of Versailles', 'the Treaty of Shame' or 'the Treaty of Treason', many of the terms were indeed punitive and vindictive. The Germans were unfairly blamed for everything that had happened and made to pay crushing reparations, most infuriatingly to her boastful neighbours. Nonetheless, Versailles allowed Germany to retain the essential gains she had made under Bismarck. Had she accepted the terms it is likely that a resurgent Germany would have become the dominant force in Europe within a generation. (78) Instead she set about the undermine the treaty, which led to the chaotic inflation of the 1920's, a further blow to the national will, and the racist refusal to allow Germans to live under Slav rule. (79)

In the years that followed, Germany, that is, her people and institutions, crescendoed hostilities that were more than reactions to political or economic events. They reflected a 'destiny' seeped in the songs of Wotan and Siegfried and a propensity for vengeance that covered hundred of years. (80) In 1808, for example, the dramatist Heinrich von Kleist wrote *Michael Kohlhaas*, one of the greatest renditions of the revenge motif in world literature. (81) The story describes damaged pride and its aftermath, insatiable aggression, of a kind that flowed through schoolchildren both before and after Versailles:

"We'll redden the iron with blood
With hangman's blood
With Frenchmen's blood
Oh sweet day of Revenge!" [82]

All this aggression coincided with an endless envy, outwardly at the Allied Powers, and inwardly at Jews, socialists, and other non-Aryans who appeared to do well (during economic chaos) by *"sucking the life-blood of the German soul."* The result was a fury just waiting to be unleashed, an extremity of rage that fueled the transformation of a pompous Teutonic narcissism into a world destroying, vengeful nationalism.

* * * * *

Germany embodied the lust for revenge and exultation in war in the person of Adolf Hitler, a man who began his career at the behest of the German General Staff. He was one of a number of demagogues employed to spread militant nationalism among the masses. Joseph Goebbels likened him to a kind child and a clever cat, but especially to a roaring lion, *"great and gigantic."* [83] And, after a single visit, the British statesman, David Lloyd George, called him the *"George Washington of Germany.......a national hero who reigns over the heart and mind of Germany."* [84]

This was a heart and mind that that effectively engaged its wish to be led with Hitler's wish to lead ('Führerprinzip'). People from all walks of life made him the 'Volksgeist', the mystical link between Volk and State, who would dominate Germany as Germany intended to dominate the world. Hitler believed he was the new Barbarossa (King of Germany and Emperor of the Holy Roman Empire 1155-1190) who would rescue a tortured and divided country and establish a mighty Reich. And indeed, it did not take long after the Nazis took power for Hitler to be portrayed and seen as the symbol and personification of national unity, national community, and greatness. Thus, in fall of 1933 banner headlines proclaimed, *"Today Hitler is the Whole of Germany."* [85]

Towards these end, Hitler was the beneficiary of the talents of Joseph Goebbels, whose propaganda ministry fabricated images of the Nazi dictator as a simple man, *'close to the people,'* a man *'toiling for his people while others slept,'* but also as a great hero and saviour, not a dictator, but an almighty Führer who was the executor of the people's will. *"We see in him the symbol of indestructible life-force of the German nation, which is Adolf Hitler has acquired living shape."* [86]

Towards these ends, Hitler was the beneficiary of *"an enormous, destructive tidal wave in the ebb and flow of the generations"* released after the shame and hunger of the war years and disorder of the nineteen twenties. The young flocked to the Youth Cohort while many older citizens joined the Free Corps ('Freikorps'), the greatest single source of Nazi personnel and spirit. Hitler, in turn, supplied abundant hatred. According to many observers, that was his main energy. Goebbels recorded one of Hitler's 'best' epigrams in his diary.:

> *"For our struggle, God gave us His abundant blessing. His most beautiful gift was the hate of our enemies, whom we too hate with all our heart."* [87]

Meanwhile, the diplomat, Harold Nicolson, noted that he had never met a man *"capable of generating so terrific a condensation of envy, vituperation, and malice."* [88] This energy nourished Hitler's passion for bigness, his insatiable ambition to becoming the source of all things and wield the mightiest sword. [89] He was convinced that Germany needed to conquer and control vast areas of Eastern Europe in order to provide 'Lebensraum' or living space. Hitler envisioned vast territories connected by canals and autobahns stretching to the Crimea (*"our Riviera"*) and the Caucasus. [90] The Ukraine, in particular, was to become the German breadbasket, a feeding ground, a complementary 'motherland', devoid of Jews and other *"unclean"* peoples.. Hitler was quite clear what would happen to the "the ridiculous hundred million Slavs." They would be transferred to "pig-pens" without "hygiene cleanliness". If not killed off, they would essentially serve as slave drones for their German masters who would live in "marvelous buildings and handsome farms." [91] This was to be ethnic cleansing on a grand scale, in some ways similar to the British policy of transporting undesirables to Australia in the 18th and 19th century. The philosopher, Jeremy Bentham, argued that:

> *".....the subject-matter of (the) experiment was.... a particularly commodious one; a set of 'animae viles', a sort of excrementitious mass, that could be projected, and accordingly was projected–projected, and as it should seem purposely–as far out of sight as possible."* [92]

Hitler's obsession with 'living space' was not new. For decades the German government had stressed that the Ukraine was to Germany what Africa (and Australia) was to England. But Hitler gave 'lebensraum' a personal, deadly significance because, according to the American historian, Ralph Binion, he associated the 'the push toward the east' with his own maternal traumas. [93]

Hitler's mother, Klara, had three children all of whom died in quick succession before Adolf was born. Therefore, as an infant, he was over indulged as well as suffused with his mother's constant worries *"lest she lose him"*. [94] The ensuing symbiotic relation between mother and child was severely tested by the birth of two more children (one of whom died), her widowhood and his mother's final illness from breast cancer during his late teens. Hitler nursed her day and night, while she was attended by a Jewish doctor named Bloch, who undertook an expensive, toxic treatment with iodoform, a liquid spray that burned through the skin like mustard gas. Ostensibly Hitler concurred with the treatment. However, he seems to have developed a burning hatred for *"the Jew "* who had killed his mother, and then all Jews: *"the Jewish cancer, the Jewish poison, the Jewish profiteer."* This simmered until he himself was overcome by mustard gas in 1918. [95] After a diagnosed hysterical breakdown, he emerged from a two day trance determined to restore Germany (*"the motherland"*) and avenge her defeat (*"his mother's death"*) by killing the Jews (*"his mother's killer"* and *"blood poisoner"* of the entire German nation). [96]

As Führer, Hitler's personal abomination of Jews would have made life extremely difficult for them, no matter what the circumstances. But he was able to institutionalize his genocidal intentions because his hatreds coincided with those of the nation as a whole. Germany had a long, vicious history of European, but especially German anti-semitism.

The Harvard political scientist, Daniel Goldhagen, has documented in, *Hitler's Willing Executioners,* that 'eliminationist anti-semitism' in Germany can be specifically traced over hundreds of years. In particular he demonstrates the relationship between these intentions and the attitude of mediaeval Christendom, which represented the Jews as *'self willed agents of evil."* [97]

Subsequently, the Reformation yielded the legacy of Martin Luther, whose extreme antagonism towards Jews was widely known. Luther, who was one of Hitler's special heros, advocated the total annihilation of Jews and everything about them. His program, which Hitler appears to have meticulously carried out, was set forth in 1543:

> *"First, to set fire to their synagogues or schools."*
>
> *Second, I advise that their houses also be razed and destroyed.*
>
> *Third, I advise that all their prayer books and Talmudic writings, in which such adultery, lies, cursing and blasphemy are taught, be taken from them.*
>
> *Fourth, I advise that their Rabbis be forbidden to teach henceforth on pain of loss of life and limb.*
>
> *Fifth, I advise that safe-conduct on the highways be abolished completely for the Jews.*

Sixth, I advise that......all cash and treasure of silver and gold be taken from them.

Seventh, Let whosoever can, throw brimstone and pitch upon them....and if this not be enough, let them be driven like mad dogs out of the land." (98)

Was it only an accident of history that Hitler launched his first major pogrom, known as 'Kristallnacht', on the night of 9 November 1938, Luther's birthday? In her book, *The Origins of Satan*, Elaine Pagels, demonstrates that the process of demonizing Jews, so conclusively institutionalized by the Reformation, was displaced from the early Christians' fight with Rome as embodied in the new Testament. (99)

While it is true that Hitler and the National Socialist party and policies exaggerated a two-thousand year old Christian tradition of Jew-hatred, it would be wrong to conclude that the were acting on behalf of Christianity. Nor were the Nazis pagans, although they appeared to idealize old Teutonic rites and rituals. The psychoanalyst, Richard Rubenstein, concludes that the Nazis were satanic anti-Christians, who hated God and wanted to invert all religious standards. (100) It is possible that if the Nazis had won the war in Europe, the killing of the Jews would have been a prelude to the mass murder of Christians and related institutions. In terms of Nazi ideology, these were rivals who could not be tolerated.

One can speculate that in order to implement their agenda, the Nazis would forced their followers to see Christians as 'agents of evil,' like the Jews. if so, Hitler may also have 'benefited' from a long history of Satanic 'anti-Christianity' in Europe.

Goldhagen maintains that demonic perceptual changes, in conjunction with an intense economic and racial rivalry with a people long seen as inferior, helped to transform a national consensus on assimilating or uprooting Jews (by mass emigration) into one of exterminating them. He argues that:

> *"The inescapable truth is that regarding Jews, German political culture had evolved to the point where an enormous number of ordinary, representative Germans became.....Hitler's willing executioners."* [101]

Hitler did not begin with genocide. His first impulses were a land grab in the east and racial purification at home. The 'land-grab' only turned into a 'Jew-kill' after he realized that the war against Russia was lost. This dashed his hopes for an endless supply of food (a reunion with Klara !?) as well as his overweening pride in an army of *"magnificent blond beasts, roaming wantonly in search of prey and victory"*. These were the 'Übermenschen' or Supermen who would create a New Order that would dominate Europe with their tanks and rockets, but especially their iron will. [102]

The 'Übermenschen', of course, embodied Hitler's own omnipotence, an omnipotence which protected him from feeling weak or being conscious of weakness. I refer to a terrifying state of non-omnipotence, which included, one might imagine, any lingering doubts or regrets he may have had about his 'mother' and 'fatherland'.

An essential feature of such a psychological structure is that the non-omnipotent elements of the personality have to be ruthlessly denied. As far as Hitler was concerned, anything less than total denial threatened to implode the myth of an all-powerful-people ('Urvolk,' 'Übermenschen') and their leader (Führer).

The non-omnipotent elements included need, desire, sorrow, fear, and guilt - in other words, basic human feelings. Experienced as totally bad, these *'deviltries,'* had to be located elsewhere. What better than to attribute them to a people both feared and hated, a role that Jews filled in abundance. Thus, they were feared for being different (dirty, unclean, amoral, immoral, immigrant bolsheviks) and for being similar (the chosen people, socialist, capitalist assimilationists). Moreover, they were hated for appearing weak (more deserving victims during a period of rapid social change) and for being strong (more successful in business and the professions).

I am describing a primitive, psychotic system of social relations which depends on the continued denial and projection of despised elements in order to maintain itself. This process provides an operational definition of envy. Hitler and his followers acted as a 'complete persecuting society' by directing raw envy towards Jews as well as gypsies, communists, mental patients, homosexuals and others who were also feared and despised. In consequence these people were seen and treated as *'vermin,'* as an *'excremental mass'* that had to be defecated and destroyed. (103)

The Nazis referred to Auschwitz as the *'anus mundi.'* Like the other death camps, it was the places where the process of evacuation took place. Indeed, as Rubenstein notes, in German folk-culture the Devil, depicted as a Jew or Lord of the Jews, invariably exudes a faecal odor. (104) The gas Cyclon B was chosen to be the means of transforming Devils into dirt. interestingly, Cyclon B is a conjugate of Cyclon A, which was used as an insecticide.

The *'excremental mass'* literally emerged as a mass of bodies covered from top to bottom with faeces. Surviving witnesses of the gas chambers observed that the final act of those who died by gassing was involuntary defecation. It may be that the major accomplishment of Hitler and his National Socialist regime was to actualize envy. Instead of envy being a look which spoils anything in its line of sight, it literally became an action which turned 'gold' (that is, worthwhile peoples) into 'shit'

Once this strategy no longer worked, or his favoured dumping grounds no longer existed, Hitler was left with a state of mind replete with the very elements he could not endure. So he embraced the one state he really loved, a state of death.

Similarly for the Third Reich, the battle of Stalingrad and the beachheads at Normandy, coming from the East as well as the West, were more than defeats. They decimated a military machine and tradition that was, for the country, its manhood, its *"marching forest"*, its symbol of potency and respect. Both ordinary citizens and their leaders lost a sense of grandeur and community, a feeling of authority and uprightness that had previously filled their hearts with *"a deep and mysterious delight"* and rationalized an absolute assurance of racial, cultural and political superiority. [105] Once this was lost all they had left was a sense of dread, an awareness of fragility and, like Hitler, a wish for death. [106]

* * * * *

The idealization of death has been a recurrent theme in German history. Throughout the Nazi era, it flew on the wings of Hitler's pronouncements and National Socialist policies. As a result *Thanatos* came to life through the agency of the State. But the destructive nationalism of Nazi Germany also represented the millennial wish for a last battle, an Armageddon, whereby torrential violence would bring salvation. In this regard the Germans have succeeded beyond the wildest dreams of Versailles. Helped by the competing nationalisms of the United States and the former Soviet Union, they have rebuilt a wealthy and strong country which has become a model member of the United Nations. German politicians now reluctantly expend considerable effort warding off attacks by less prosperous and powerful peoples. The former Chancellor, Herr Helmut Schmidt, gave the reason for this state of affairs. He blamed envy for the continued, and as he believed, unjustified criticisms of the Federal Republic:

> *"If the Germans were economically weak, and the destiny of the German worker like the average European levels, and if inflation and unemployment were as high as in Italy or Britain; many critics would cease to be so interested in the Germans."* [107]

Herr Schmidt added that Germany had become a substitute for others' *"internal enemies"*. What a twist of fate for the heir to a government which had previously laid its inner problems on the rest of the world.

With the unification of East and West Germany, it seemed that the German experience demonstrates that a country whose citizens enjoy 'the blessings of a late birth" and are not ground down by hunger or hate no longer need rely on the politics of pride, nor a thirst for vengeance. [108] Subsequent outbreaks of virulent racism against Turks, Gypsies, Jews and other foreigners indicates that this conclusion is still uncertain.

Perhaps the greatest irony of the post war period is that while fascist impulses in Germany may have subsided, these same tendencies have begun to resurface in the United States and Britain, the allied victors. Since the advent of the Internet, groups like the Aryan Nation in the United States and Combat 18 in England have spewed forth violent messages which have been taken up by disaffected youth. At the same time vicious video games have become popular ('Doom,' 'Blood ll') and 'goth-rock' or 'shock-rock' singers like Marilyn Manson, who took the name of a psychopathic killer. One song, "Antichrist Superstar," intones,*"The time has come it is quite clear, our antichrist is almost here,"* while another advocates *"grenades and guns."* [109].

On the 20th of April 1999 these lyrics were made all too real by two American teenagers who methodically murdered over a dozen students at the Columbine High School in Littleton, Colorado. They also tried to blow up the school before killing themselves. [110] Calling themselves the 'Trenchcoat Mafia,' they wore Nazi gear, sang Nazi songs, and idealized Hitler. The two boys, who had signalled their intentions months beforehand, both on the Internet and with fellow members of their gang, were obsessed with 'isolation, rage and the apocalypse' and talked incessantly about 'mutilations and decapitations.' Their targets were 'jocks,' (successful athletes) and others at the school whom they had come to loathe, indeed, the Columbine High itself. The day they chose for the carnage was not an accident. It was the anniversary of Hitler's birthday.

The incident illustrates how the same forces which affect a society, and which lead to murderous attacks on their own citizenry, as well as other countries, can reemerge in individuals, often in distant continents and generations later. Similarly the violence which captures the vandal or solitary activist can resurface as violent group or political processes. Objectively and subjectively the 'complete persecutor' evolves from a person to group to a whole country, and then back to the person again. The dynamics of destructive narcissism provides the common thread. The two students apparently came from well-to do families, but they felt they were failures and became increasingly estranged from their parents and fellow students. At a certain point they denied they could become or wanted to become good students or athletes and identified with the forces of hate and destruction. Through death, like Hitler, they gained endless notoriety, and have since become 'the biggest baddies on their block.'

Chapter 11b

The Psychology of Muslim Terrorism

Joseph H. Berke & Stanley Schneider

While taking into account cultural, religious and nationalistic factors, underlying psychological conflicts are the major considerations when trying to understand violence and terrorism. Familial and social issues may seem to predominate. But these are an outgrowth of personality and psychological substrates, which on a group basis, can lead to very dangerous policies and actions.

Destructive nationalism, for example, culminates in the mobilisation of state policy and mass action for murderous ends. It is a point where envy and narcissism converge, when the forces of hate replace the possibilities of life, and an imperfect society becomes a near perfect persecutor. The British historian Elie Kedourie echoes this point is his classic work on the subject:

> *"Nationalism looks inwardly, away from and beyond the imperfect world. And this contempt of things as they are, of the world as it is, ultimately becomes a rejection of life, and a love of death."* [1]

Alan Dershowitz, Professor of Law at Harvard University, has taken a psychologically sophisticated approach in trying to understand why terrorism has become more widespread and epidemic. By terrorism we mean direct violent attacks on civilians in order to provoke fear and demoralization in the general civilian population, in order to bring about social and political changes as the attackers may wish.

Dershowitz believes that countries around the world have been afraid to confront terrorists and terrorism and have, therefore, caused an internalization and internationalization of terrorism. [2] In consequence the Western way of life (culture, values etc.) has become a martyr on the terrorist agenda. Western ideals and philosophy have become hostage to radical Muslim terror and, more importantly, the fear of terror. People are afraid to ride buses, the underground, or to fly. Airports have become armed camps oftentimes holding innocent passengers at bay for hours of security checks. Besides the inordinate amount of time and monetary expense, the fear of terror because of these necessary precautions increases manifold.

As the millennium approached, it clearly become the turn of the wounded pride of the Muslim world to manifest these destructive influences, in the form of a *jihad,* against multiple aspects of Western civilization. In fact *jihad* against infidels (Jews, Christians, Americans, Druse, other Muslims) has been going on for decades. Westerners have preferred to turn a blind eye towards these attacks, but the strikes against the Twin Towers of New York's World Trade Center on 11 September 2001 (9/11 in popular parlance), or in the London underground on 7 July 2005 (7/7), made the *jihadist* rage impossible to ignore.

Jihad means striving, struggle or effort. [3] For many Muslims, especially in the Sufi order, this refers to an inner struggle which they must make against personal immoral, destructive tendencies which can be called, the inner 'infidel.' Nonetheless, within Islam there has always been a *jihadist* faction which locates the 'hated other' or infidel as an external force or person, and wages war against it. Thus, during the early years of Islam there were a series of assassinations of Muslim leaders including Ali, the son-in-law of Mohammed. This led to a major schism between the followers of Ali, who considered him to be the rightful successor to Mohammed, and those who did not. The latter became known as Sunnis, and the former as Shi'ites. The Sunnis (meaning: course of conduct, tradition) are the predominant sect and have persecuted the Shi'ites as nonbelievers, while both sects, as we have previously discussed, have acted viciously towards Christians and Jews. [4, 5] Or, from another point of view, the two sides harbor deep fears of illegitimacy and inferiority. These have fuelled both a deadly internecine conflict, and have been displaced onto substitute others, the [external] infidels, whom they believe they have to dominate or destroy, just as they wish to eliminate alien parts of themselves.

Why is it important to detail a brief history of Islamic conflicts? Because by doing so, it is possible to understand the escalating Muslim attacks on each other, or on the West. These attacks are both bilateral and trilateral.

Bilateral conflict denotes envious comparison and wounded pride, encapsulated as a consuming rage towards the other, commingled with an eviscerating self-hatred. From the 19th century onwards, the Muslim world has been tantalized by the vision of Western accomplishment and affluence. But the more that Arab and non-Arab people have tried to imitate the West, the more impoverished they seem to have become, while modernisation itself has been treated as a severe threat to their religious and cultural values.

This view has become more prominent since the rise of a radical, puritan, Islamic movement called Wahhabism in the eighteenth century. It was named after its founder, Muhammad ibn Abd al-Wahhab (1703-87), an Arabian theologian, who launched a campaign of purification and Islamic renewal. [6] Wahhabism has become a significant aspect of Islam ever since the Wahhabi cause was embraced and promoted by the Saudi rulers of central and eastern Arabia. Subsequently Wahhabist and kindred ideas have fueled the philosophy of the Egyptian thinker and activist, Sayyid Qutb (1906-1966) whom many consider to be the father of modern Islamist fundamentalism, and the Saudi terrorist leader, Osama Bin Laden.

Their followers rail against the West for humiliating, exploiting, oppressing, and generally degrading Islam by its physical and scientific advances. In particular, they hate Jews and Zionists, whom they see as representing western values and as America's advance guard, and for having successfully established a modern state in what many Moslem's see as their heartland. In response the Ayatollah Khomeini designated the United States as 'the Great Satan,' and Israel as 'the little Satan.' But what is this devil, this Satan?' As the Islamic scholar, Bernard Lewis points-out, the Koran describes Satan as "the insidious tempter who whispers in the hearts of men." [7] This is the essential feature of Satan, he is not necessarily a conqueror, nor an exploiter. First and foremost he is a tempter, an entity who seduces the unwary with promises of sexual license, political freedom, material plenty and technological wizardry.

When these promises remain unfilled, or are unfulfillable, then hope turns to hatred, and the effect of temptation is to arouse intense greed and envy. These two feelings feed on each other. Frustrated greed leads to implacable envy, while overwhelming envy stirs up unbearable longings for dashed desires. In consequence the tempted is trapped in an escalating spiral of excitement, hunger, rage, and revenge. Vengefulness is the response to a sense of self, transformed from superiority to inferiority, from significance to insignificance. [8]

Now we can see why the end of Islamic ascendancy and the enfranchisement of 'dhimmis', as we previously discussed was such a blow to Moslem mentality. Unlike Weimar Germany where damaged pride was predominant, for Moslems 'the catastrophe' of Western culture, meant that they were relegated to an intolerable loss of status, an endless inferiority.[9] This, to a large extent, they blamed on the ravages of colonialism and continuing colonial depredations.[10]

It now seemed that Satan, 'the great tempter,' had gained a foothold from within their midst. The point of Wahhabism or Islamic fundamentalism is to destroy Satan. We can see this very clearly when Bin Laden announces that terrorist attacks are the way to get American troops (with their attendant temptations: Western values, equality of women, Western dress etc.) out of the 'holyland,,' that is, Saudi Arabia.

Similarly, groups like Islamic Jihad have deliberately targeted Western tourists in Egypt and Jews in Jerusalem. In order to avoid temptation, the tempted (Moslems) attack the tempters (Westerners, Jews). These events begin with the denial of personal temptation (inner libidinal impulses) and the reliance on projective processes to evacuate these impulses and to identify them with degraded others. Thus, for example, Western women are seen as whores, and Jews as Nazis and as greedy pigs and foul smelling apes (as described in the Koran). [11]

Although the Koran specifically forbids attacks on civilians, in the current conflict fundamentalist *jihadists* encourage woman and children to blow themselves up on buses, restaurants, dance halls, anywhere where 'infidels' congregate. This method appears to replicate the work of the 12th and 13th century 'assassins,' although these killers usually attacked political leaders and tried to avoid collateral damage including themselves. It is not without a considerable degree of irony that one of the rationales for encouraging young men to blow themselves up is the conviction that they will go straight to heaven and enjoy the company of seventy two black eyed virgins, in other words, unlimited libidinal delights. [12] Hence terrorist attacks on the tempters are encouraged by appeals to higher temptation. [13]

The turmoil released in the Middle East and elsewhere by Islamic terrorism may stress bilateral strikes on Satanic tempters. But *jihadist* ideology has another and not so hidden agenda: political power. We refer to the intention of tyrannical states (which currently describes most Islamic regimes) to maintain power or terrorist groups to gain power. This introduces a third element in the equation, terrorist and terrorized. We refer to the instigator of the terrorism. In practice, most bilateral attacks are instigated by others. Thus we can say that trilateral terrorism sustains bilateral destruction. [14, 15]

The vast majority of terrorist attacks are triangular and include the instigator (such as Iran), the terrorists (such as Hezbollah, funded by Iran) and the terrorized (such as Israel). The excuse may be religious, but a deeper purpose is to keep tyrannical regimes in power. To accomplish this, the instigator stirs up chaos in others in order to obscure economic privation and political repression at home. Israel is a soft target because, as Bernard Lewis points out, grievance towards Israel is the only passion that can be safely expressed in many Muslim countries. [16]

Similarly the PLO under Yassir Arafat, and afterwards, has instigated a plethora of Kamikaze strikes on Israelis, tourists and non-Jewish workers in Israel. [17] The ostensible reason is to regain 'lost' territory. However, the underlying triangular functions of such attacks are multi-determined: by the PLO's determination to maintain power; by the determination of the Husseini family (the largest of the seven main family clans in Arab Palestine of which Arafat was a prominent member) to maintain its position and privileges; by the intention of Saadam Hussein (who paid the families of every suicide bomber $25,000) to gain prestige and divert attention from his regime; and by the resolve of other countries who funded Arafat (i.e. Libya, Iran, Syria, Egypt and Saudi Arabia) to keep the pot boiling in Israel in order to keep the heat away from themselves. [18] It is important to note that third party instigators are rarely killed or injured in suicide attacks.

One of the main effects of these attacks is to stir up anti-Jewish sentiment in Muslim and non-Muslim countries around the world. Thus the official website of the Palestinian Authority (PA) published large excerpts from the *Protocols of the Elders of Zion*, a 19th century Tsarist forgery, which purports to detail a Jewish conspiracy to take over the world [19] This book has subsequently been widely distributed throughout Asia and the Middle East. The *Protocols* have led to the general belief among Muslims that Jews personify evil. Such beliefs are reinforced by sermons of prominent preachers like Sheikh Ibrahim Mudaires that are broadcast live every Friday from mosques under the control of the PA and on PA television. A common theme calls for Allah to wreak vengeance on the Jews and Americans. [20]

Typically, on 13 May 2005 Sheik Mudaires declaimed at the Sheik Ijlin Mosque in Gaza:

> *"Allah has tormented us with the people most hostile to the believers' – the Jews... With the establishment of the State of*

Israel, the entire Islamic nation was lost, because Israel is a cancer spreading through the body of the Islamic nation, and because Jews are a virus resembling AIDS, from which the entire world suffers...You will find that the Jews are behind all the civil strife in this world. The Jews are behind the suffering of the nations...Listen to the Prophet Muhammad, who tells you about the evil end that awaits Jews. The stones and trees will want the Muslims to finish off every Jew...We have ruled the world before, and by Allah, the day will come when we rule the world again." [21]

As we see here the forces of envious (bilateral) and jealous (triangular) hatred, as embodied in this instance in quasi-Nazi propaganda, can lie dormant for decades, only to slowly sprout in individuals, groups, and whole cultures, from the fertile soil of mass inferiority, humiliation and resentment. [22]

The Swiss psychologist, Arno Gruen argues that: "The source of aggression and destructiveness lies in our culture, not in the individual. And everything that reinforces the fragmentation of our personality and closes-off access to our inner world contributes to the creation and growth of our destructive drives." [23] This is an interesting paradigm that places the cultural and social context as the impetus in molding the innate personality and psychological structures. If the cultural environment advocates terrorism and murderous violence, then the personality of the terrorist becomes fragmented and disjointed and this cuts-off parts of the inner world. These would be the innate and socially sanctioned morals and mores. Moreover, the cultural influence blocks any moral value system and only enhances and develops the skewed murderous side which now becomes the dominant mode of the personality.

Despite the cultural and religious brainwashing to which Muslim terrorists are subjected, one would think that the underlying moral views of the greater society, which include proscription against murder, would somehow subsume societal conformity. Yet, the extremism is so intense, there is a shutting down of emotional, empathic and ethical awareness.

This could be Gruen's idea of fragmentation or Robert Stoller's novel interpretation of perversion. We know from Freud's work on mourning, that there is a strong connection between love and hate. Freud saw that within the hate there was a strong identification and ambivalence mixed with an erotic cathexis. [24] Stoller took Freud's ideas one step further and 'modernized' them: he added the concepts of revenge and power. "One moves from victim to victor, from passive object of others' hostility and power to the director, ruler; one's tormentors in turn will be one's victims." [25]

In our scheme of understanding, the Muslim terrorist, indoctrinated in mosques by imams who preach hate and fundamentalistic ideology, is swept up by an erotic surge of emotion that fuels hostility, murderous rage and a sadistic urge to conquer and be all-powerful. This libidinal excitement is a temptation that hangs in-the-air and becomes transformed and displaced as violent feelings which run amok amid erotic urges which are then expressed as extreme sadistic expressions of terrorism.

Once hatred is engendered, then: "The primary aim of one consumed by hatred is to destroy its object...An extreme form of hatred demands the physical elimination of the object and may be expressed in murder or in a radical devaluation of the object that may generalize in the form of a symbolic destruction of all objects." [26] This sounds reminiscent of Freud's idea that "hate comes into operation on this substitutive object, abusing it, debasing it, making it suffer and deriving sadistic satisfaction from its suffering." [27] Otto Kernberg maintains that rage reactions may be a response leading to an "activation of all-bad, persecutory object relationships." [28] This means that the internal world of the terrorist is replete with persecutory all-bad objects because the good objects have been repressed and displaced by religious and cultural indoctrination.

Two experts in the field of political psychology, Robert Robins and Jerrold Post remarked that once religion becomes enmeshed with politics, the end-result can only be extremism: "Aggression is required to defend against the world of unbelief." [29] The enemy of the religion, ideology or political belief is viewed as an aggressor for railing against the beliefs of the believer. This situation, in turn, legitimises aggression as a norm and correct form of response. Even more so, if the aggressive response fails to come, there can be a revolt against the belief system which leaves the believer with an extreme form of guilt and self-deprecation. The only way out is aggression against the infidel. Robins and Post note that: "Society sets sharp limits on the expression of anger, and religion often serves as a socially sanctioned umbrella under which it may be expressed...For many devout Muslims, the humiliating defeat...at the hands of the Jews was God's punishment for the corruption of Islam and its abandonment of the tenets of the Qur'an." [30]

Muslim terrorists, because of the fundamentalistic religious and cultural indoctrination and brainwashing do not have a perceived internal conflict. [31] They utilize primitive defenses such as denial, splitting and projective identification in order to remove from themselves any possibilities of internal emotional turmoil or conflict. By cutting-off any connection to their identification with societal mores, they can allow their selves to be driven by primal, primitive instinctual drives. This raw and unbridled aggression, which may have been tempered during their growing-up period, washes away through external moral cleansing, and rebounds them to the instinctual, libidinal phase of early childhood.

In Nazi Germany, politicians hungry for power, manipulated a primitive system of social relations. This depended on the continual denial and projection of despised elements in order to advance and perpetuate their personal status. It would seem that Muslim political and religious leaders (they often occupy the same position) utilize a similar technique by attributing parts of peoples' inner world (the feared 'inner infidel') to others (Jews, Christians, Americans, Westerners). These external others literally become 'the infidel,' the forces of greed, exploitation, sickness and suffering, aside from suppressed female sexuality, that Muslims hate in and about themselves. Once these projections stick, they believe they have the right to denigrate infidels (Jews, for example, depicted as degenerate apes, Western women as dirty whores), to subjugate them (as dhimmis) or destroy them.

> *"All spears should be directed at the Jews, at the enemies of Allah, (who) has described them as apes and pigs, calf worshipers, idol worshipers....whoever can fight them with his weapons, should go out (to do so) with machine-guns, swords and knives... whoever can fight them with his hands, should go out... This is our destiny.... The Jews have exposed their fangs. Nothing will deter them except the colour of their filthy people's blood."* [32]

The German sociologist Wolfgang Sofsky wrote an immensely important book on a study of cruelty and a system of absolute power built on systematic extreme violence. In his analysis of 'absolute power,' Sofsky differentiates between terror and violence: "Terror is meant to intimidate, to crush resistance, to spread fear. It comes to an end when the last opponent has been eliminated and the peace of the grave holds dominion. Violence, however, remains an instrument of suppression, a means to an end. Once that end has been reached and the regime's power consolidated, despotisms make do with arbitrary, lawless rule, shifting pragmatically among punishment, incentive, and reward." [33]

For Osama Bin Laden, the al-Qaeda leader, we would surmise that the 'infidel' was not only a despised Jew or Westerner, although as a youth he seems to have frequented the clubs and bars of Beirut, but any fellow Muslim who did not accord with his Wahhabist world-view. He himself was born to a wealthy Yemenite builder with close ties to the Saudi royal family. His father married at least ten times and had many concubines. He is said to have fathered fifty-four children. Some accounts say that Osama was the seventeenth son, others that he was the last of twenty-five sons, and was born to his father's tenth wife, who was reportedly of Syrian descent. On the other hand it is also said that Osama was the product of one of his fathers concubines, a situation which left him with considerable sadness. [34]

Who really is Osama Bin Laden? Is he a Yemenite, Saudi or Syrian, legitimate or illegitimate, a boy who was loved or ignored? These are pertinent questions for a man who has become one of the world's foremost terrorists. Is it possible that by anchoring himself in Wahhabist ideology, and by externalising doubts disguised as "dreaded others", he was able to overcome a fearsome inferiority and a terrorizing state of triangular conflict? These must have included internecine battles between his mother and his brothers' mothers, his bothers and semi sisters, no less than an intense power struggle with his own father and uncles over who possessed what. What we do know is that Osama Bin Laden possesses a powerful will, a ruthless cunning, and the wish to take the place of the ruling elite of the 'holy' Saudi Kingdom.

Like others who have taken advantage of an enormous tidal wave in the ebb and flow of conflicting cultures, Bin Laden has been able to actualize murderous intentions on a world stage. But without his family's wealth and connections he might not have been able to be educated, gain a wife (he has several including his mother's niece, also a Syrian), and father over twenty-four children. Instead he would have shared the hopelessness of so many fellow Muslims stuck in shanty towns and refugee camps throughout the Middle East and Asia. They also want wives, children, careers, and most important, a sense of empowerment. The alternative is endless bitterness and envious hatreds because they can't get what they have been promised. Then their leaders direct, rather manipulate, the ensuing destructiveness away from themselves and onto to the alleged sources of their frustration: Americans, Jews, Christians, Westerners, etc. All this exemplifies, as Herbert Rosenfeld pointed out, libidinal narcissism, the rage that results from not being able to have what one wants. [35]

But as Rosenfeld also describes, when the frustration becomes too intense, when their inner rage becomes too great, they may stop wanting the goods and chattels of contemporary culture, and fall in love with death and destruction. As we previously pointed out, this is what Rosenfeld called destructive narcissism. [36] We think this phenomenon lies behind the mentality of the suicide bomber and idealisation of the *shahid* or martyr. His or her greatest joy becomes the maximum havoc that they can inflict on infidels (or even fellow Muslims, hundreds of whom were killed in the attack on the Twin Towers, or in suicide bombings in Israel, Iraq, Pakistan and elsewhere).

Freud's theoretical formulations see the instinct or drive as needing to eliminate the state of tension via a discharge of this pent-up energy. [37] When Freud utilizes the word *trieb*, there is a form of 'pressure' involved; something is forcing the instinct to explode into discharge. Freud moved from a theoretical framework stressing the influence of sexual instincts to a model that framed the instinctual entanglement in other terms: a life and death instinct. In reality what Freud conceptualized was a combination of a somatic (i.e. sexual) instinct state and a biological force (life – death). For our purposes, in terrorism there seems to be a need for a release – possibly of a sexual or erotic type and also a strong death drive that eliminates totally the desire for the life instinct. In the Muslim tradition, the radical Islamic theology promises a multitude of virgins awaiting the martyr in a 'Heaven.'

When Freud discussed eros or thanatos (life and death instincts) as two opposites, it was formulated as a polarity: an 'either' /'or' theoretical idea. One chooses either life or death. One cannot choose life by deciding on death. Yet, the terrorist sees a type of absolutism or extreme in that by willing to die, he/she is choosing a desirous life in heaven and ensuring a beautiful life for those left behind because of the sacrifice for advancing Islam's values. There is no containing function operating here but rather a primitive discharge of libidinal tension. The libidinal excitement overloads the emotional system. It has to exit as a release of tension, a discharge. The release of these pent-up emotionally charged primitive libidinal feelings can be expressed as psychotically charged fragmentation or be transformed into thanatos, the death instinct.

For our purposes, Melanie Klein's concept of 'sadism' helps our formulations regarding the psychology of Muslim terrorism: "...sadism is at its height, I have found that all the pre-genital stages and the genital stage as well are cathected in rapid succession. What then happens is that the libido gradually consolidates its position by its struggle with the destructive instinctual drives." [38] The terrorist, through years of ideological indoctrination, has a collapsing of developmental stages and in a fused primitive mode is pressured by strong instinctual urges that become expressed sadistically. In Klein's formulations, this sadism has now developed into a life-death struggle: "...the vicious circle dominated by the death-instinct, in which aggression gives raise to anxiety and anxiety reinforces aggression can be broken by the libidinal forces when these have gained in strength; in the early stages of development, the life-instinct has to exert its power to the utmost in order to maintain itself against the death-instinct. But this very necessity stimulates sexual development." [39]

A typical example is Hasan Abu Zaid, who blew himself up in October 2005, outside a felafel stand in Hadera, Israel, killing five people and injuring thirty others. Before doing so, he explained to his mother: "I want a place in heaven and to marry the 70 virgins who are promised to me in the Koran." [40] Similarly, a terrorist who attacked a residential compound in Saudi Arabia shouted to his contact on his mobile phone just before blowing himself up: One second to the maidens of paradise." [41] We now have sadism blended with the death instinct with a sexual under/overtone.

Whereas Freud discussed instincts and drives as independently operating forces, and Klein referred to instincts in terms of object representations, that is, personal relationships, the psychoanalyst, Wilfred Bion emphasised, "the polarization between narcissism and what he refers to as 'social-ism.'" [42] He explained that if the individual is narcissistically enmeshed within a love (*L*) mode (and this happens in an ideological indoctrination and brainwashing) then hatred (*H*) would be directed outside towards a group whom he would view as: wrong, unfair, hateful and would need to be rebuffed and rejected. If the *L* is so strong then the *H*, as polarity, must be equally as strong. This fuels primitive defenses in order to protect the self from intrusion from the outside. Bion would say that the other, the group is extruded (*H*). [43] An "increase of narcissistic intensity would be accompanied by narrowing of the *emotions*, up to the point in which only one emotion, such as *love* or *hate*, can be experienced." [44] We see a shutting-down of choice, understanding and willingness to interact at a shared level – this is the mind of the terrorist. The container-contained function is completely dominated by sadism and envy, and cannot emerge as a viable desire or necessity. This does not allow a container *K* to develop.

As Rafael López-Corvo, a Venezuelan psychoanalyst who compiled a dictionary of Bion's work, has written, instead one gets "...a nameless terror, a kind of container-contained provision that Bion represents as –*K*. This condition becomes very serious when the breast not only is unable to neutralize the wish to die, but removes the wish to live, represented again by Bion as (minus) container-contained and qualified as a without-ness... [45] In Bion's words: "...it is a 'super' ego. It is an envious assertion of moral superiority without any morals." [46]

Typically, a Gaza resident, Wafa al-Biss, aged twenty-one, was caught with twenty pounds of high explosives hidden in her underwear. She intended to explode this at a hospital in Beersheba (where she was being treated after suffering severe burns to her face and body in an 'accident'). The attack only failed because when she tried to detonate the explosive, it failed to go off. During a TV interview she cried:

> *"My dream was to become a martyr (shahid). I believe in death... since I was a little girl I wanted to carry out an attack."* [47]

One has to place al-Biss's wish within the context of Palestinian television, newspapers, and text books, which teach children as young as six years old that the greatest aim of their life should be to become a *shahid.* [48] The Palestinian media celebrate parents who send their own children off to be killed. It gives them and their offspring enormous prestige. One mother whose seventeen year old son blew up five Israeli teenagers along with himself explained:

> *"How (could I encourage this)? Because I love my son and want to chose what is best for him."* [49]

Osama Bin Laden conveyed a kindred message when he postured against American troops hunting for him in Afghanistan:

"This place may be bombed. And we may be killed. We love death. The U.S. loves life. That is the big difference between us." [50]

Many Muslims argue that Western Intellectuals miss the point. *Shahada* (Martyrdom) is not about death, but about life. It is about the myriad delights that will befall the *shahid* in the afterlife. 51 But who are they to describe the afterlife? That is the province of mystics. Clearly anything else is a combination of lies and disinformation designed to mislead the vulnerable. In this regard the Saudi journalist, Sa'ad Al Sowayan, writes that his country has been flooded by tape cassettes which advocate *jihad* by enphasizing the sexual rewards awaiting the martyr in paradise. He points out that these tapes are particularly aimed at tempting teenagers who can find no sexual release in conservative Arab societies. He adds:

"So should we not consider sexual suppression as one of the factors leading to such deviation? Listen carefully to what these religious cassettes convey...They have converted this world to a filthy and mythical place and the Hereafter into a fabled utopia..." [52]

There are Muslim voices that contest the forces of death and destruction that currently flow like a Tsunami through Muslim societies. We refer to the writer Fuad Ajami, the psychiatrist Wafa Sultan, or to the commentator Nonie Darwish, who was born in Cairo and raised in the Gaza strip. Herself the daughter of the Fedayeen leader, Mustafa Hafaz, Darwish moved to the USA in the late 1970's along with "the usual baggage and prejudice from a Middle East upbringing: fear of Jews, of government, of speaking my own mind." [(53)] But after a while she began to question her ingrained assumptions.

"To admit one's flaws and mistakes, to correct and repent is inconceivable...in Muslim culture. To acknowledge one's

shortcomings before first blaming others would bring deep shame and dishonor not only to the individual but to his or her entire family...If the mistake is a cultural taboo, one's reputation may be scarred for life and the perpetrator might end up brutally punished.

In Arab society...there was no reward for loving humanity, striving to improve oneself...Many aimed only to please brutal dictators, currying favor and wealth at the expense of their fellow Arabs....in Friday's prayers at the mosque, no one mentioned the common sin of wronging one's neighbor, of stepping on him in a rush to self-promotion. Evil was always out there, never in here.

No one can deny the current sad state of Middle Eastern society. Terrorism flourishes in every Muslim country, poisoning the world. War and genocide have ravaged communities of Muslims and non-Muslims in the Sudan, Algeria, Iraq and Kuwait, and the list goes on. Terrorists burn churches...behead Jews, destroy Buddha temples, and weaken economies – and the Arab media react with deafening silence.

The once-great Nile Valley lies amid pollution and garbage... poor citizens must bribe government officials to survive. And yet, the media focus on the destruction of Israel. In this manner, they shift the blame for societal problems to an outside force...a useful enemy that Arabs blame for everything." (54)

Wafa Sultan came to even more robust conclusions after seeing her Professor at the University of Aleppo medical school (northern Syria) gunned down in front of her class by members of the Muslim Brotherhood. She presented her views in a debate with a fundamentalist Egyptian cleric which was transmitted on Al-Jazeera TV (Qatar) in February 2006.

"The clash we are witnessing around the world is not a clash of religions, or a clash of civilisations. It is a clash between two

opposites, between two eras. It is a clash between a mentality that belongs to the Middle Ages and another mentality that belongs to the 21st century. It is a clash between civilization and backwardness, between the civilized and the primitive, between barbarity and rationality."

"Only the Muslims defend their beliefs by burning down down churches, killing people, and destroying embassies. This path will not yield any results. The Muslims must ask themselves what they can do for humankind, before they demand that humankind respect them." [(55)]

Nonie Darwish framed her views after considerable contacts with Jewish people in the States. She was particularly impressed by the celebration of Yom Kippur, 'The Day of Atonement,' an organised form of self-examination and repentance. From another point of view, Yom Kippur represents an occasion to acknowledge reality, the reality of recognising the damaging things that a person has actively or passively done during the course of the year. The capacity to face such reality, to accept shame and blame, and to grieve for everyone who has been hurt, provides a means to overcoming the 'psychosis' of hate on a micro- and on a macro-human scale, in the individual, and in an entire culture. [56]

Both Darwish and Sultan demonstrate that it is possible to tame the perverse feelings that contribute to the terrorist mentality, by dialogue and a spirit of tolerance. Towards this end Darwish has helped to establish a website, *www.arabsforIsrael.com*, where Arabs and Muslims from many countries are able to express their support for Israel as well as the United States. She also hosts her own website, *www.NonieDarwish.com*, and lists a dozen other kindred sites. She contends that Israel's hand has been extended towards the Arabs for a long time, and that it should not be ignored.

The corollary of Darwish and Sultan's argument is that the pressures of revenge, humiliation, inferiority or illegitimacy lose their power to intimidate, once ordinary Muslims gain a voice. They intend to show that there is a strong reparative streak in Islam even at a time when the *Jihadist* mentality appears to be on the ascendancy. We would suggest that this dilemma is related to attempts to overcome, as well as to continually resist, the state of inner conflict which Melanie Klein has called the depressive position. [57]

The term denotes the point in human development when people begin to integrate feelings of love and hate. The alternative to to maintain a near total division between subjective states of love and hate, and the focus of such states, the 'hated object' and the 'idealized object.' Such splitting is accomplished by the psychological mechanisms of denial and projection and/or projective identification. [58]

Whether unconsciously determined or not, in order to gain or maintain political power, the belief systems of the *jihadists* seem to exemplify these mechanisms, Thus, on one hand, they widely disseminate the *Protocols of the Elders of Zion,* in order to prove a Jewish conspiracy to take over the world. [59] And, on the other hand, Sheik Mudaires, among others, publicly asserts, *"(Moslems) have ruled the world before, and by Allah, the day will come when we will rule..... America, Britain, and the entire world."* [60] In considering these words one must not underestimate the power of projective processes.

This point particularly relates to the transformation and displacement of violent urges into an erotic discharge of terrorist activity. Similarly an 'unexplainable' violence that has erupted over the last few years in educational systems around the world. Often times, this violence and murder occur in schools, such as Columbine High, where a student runs amok and shoots fellow classmates and teachers. Various theoreticians have tried to understand what prompted this sudden 'break with reality.' What causes someone to lose all constraints and controls and pursue a murderous rage? Stuart Twemlow, a psychiatrist and psychoanalyst has written extensively on this subject. While Twemlow feels that no one model can adequately explain such a major reversal in character, he has chosen to deal with school violence, unlike terrorist acts which are premeditated and deliberately chosen to intimidate, emasculate and destroy any remnants of disagreement or differing ideology. Terrorism means that there is no room for accommodation or compromise.

This kindred to what U. S. President George W. Bush has called "theocratic terror." [61] The indoctrination of fundamentalistic beliefs does not permit a maturation of the instinctual urges into a socially modifiable and coherent whole. Rather it fosters a regression back to early pre-oedipal strivings and longings, or to the sadism and envy that Klein described, as well as the erotic longings and early sexual awakenings Stoller has focussed on. In other words, the victimizer functions at a very early, primitive and regressed emotional level. Bion tried to tie-together all these parts with a micro (individual) v. macro (society) paradigm. The narcissistic investment in self does not move towards a merger with the group. Rather, it denudes the individual of psychic energy that could and should move him forward. Such is the mindset of the terrorist.

PART 4:
THE RESOLUTION OF MALICE

Chapter 12

On Resolving Envy, Greed & Jealousy

Envy, greed and jealousy are the negative constituents of character and culture. They are the dark forces, the basic relations of the *'yetzah harah'*, what the Kabbalah calls the evil impulse. Frequently represented as the guile of the viper, the crunch of the shark or the sting of the jellyfish, these impulses can exert a bitter tyranny over perception and feeling, indeed, all areas of human endeavour.

In the first chapters I showed how they afflict the eye, really the 'I', a process which leads to obsessive comparisons, an oppressive hyper-awareness of the qualities, traits, capacities, accomplishments and relationships of others. In response envious tensions both create and replace inner emptinesses and arouse hostilities which, when projected, turn the outer world into a threatening hell, replete with imagined as well as actual persecutors.

Malice tyrannizes the inner world by taking up too much of it. Greed feeds envy, envy breeds jealousy, and jealousy reflects self-hate. On an individual level this leads to extremely destructive relations between or within generations – parents versus children and siblings versus siblings. In the latter chapters I have traced the same patterns, self-inflation and other-deflation, direct or narcissistic aggressions, to the interplay between citizens and society. Ultimately these impulses, seemingly far removed from individual intention, emerge on the international scene in the form of combative nationalisms.

However in exploring these issues, it is important to recognize that the tragedy of human existence cannot always be explained by nor simply reduced to envy, greed or jealousy. They only comprise one part of an emotional lattice which also include the life essential elements of love: gratitude, generosity and compassion. The positive and negative components of this lattice are in a constant dynamic relationship with each other. Problems arise when the relative balance of love and hate shifts so that hate predominates. This occurs both when benevolence weakens or malevolence strengthens.

Guilt especially weakens benevolence. It is very hard for a person to maintain good feelings yet simultaneously suffer mental agony for damaging the object of these feelings. The paradox is that the intensity of guilt is directly related to the degree of positive concern in the first place. The net effect may be a determined attempt to diminish the torment, first, by the denial of affection and second, via the vehement condemnation, not of oneself for greed or resentment, but of others for seeming to provoke it.

The writer, Arthur Koestler, has described why he became a communist and egalitarian. [1] He could not stand feeling privileged at a time of family crisis. Apparently his father was an inventor whose plans were always going wrong:

> *"I suffered a pang of guilt whenever they bought me books or toys. This continued later on, when every suit I bought for myself meant so much less to send home. Simultaneously, I developed a strong dislike of the obviously rich; not because they could afford to buy things (envy plays a much smaller part in social conflict than is generally assumed) but because they were able to do so without a guilty conscience. Thus I projected a personal predicament onto the structure of society at large."* [2]

Koestler denied hating the rich because they are rich, although his wish to emulate them, even to a small degree, obviously stirred up a lot of tension in himself. It may be difficult to distinguish between a hatred aroused by guilt and a hatred aroused by envy. However afflicted, people aim to discharge the resulting turmoil by eradicating outside sources. Often a vicious spiral ensues whereby envy provokes guilt and guilt evokes envy. In this instance Koestler loathed *"the rich"* for their guilt-free enjoyment of life. One suspects that beneath his anguish there existed a hint of envy, and more than a hint of greed. As for the idea that *"the rich"* do not suffer guilt, we can assume that that is a projection of Koestler's imagination. (3) Others have blamed *"the poor"* for identical reasons.

Koestler admitted that he evacuated his *"personal predicament"* onto the political landscape. For similar reasons 'the politics of envy' tends to merge with 'the politics of guilt', a process clearly observable during the 1987 British general election. The campaign was portrayed by the press as *"Labour's moral crusade vs Tory consumer power".* According to *The Sunday Times* Labour sought to brand Thatcherism as the *"politics of self-interest"* and promote itself as *"the party of standards, fairness and decency."* (4) Squeezing the rich was a concurrent theme so that everyone could have the *"freedom to enjoy a fair share of national resources."* (5)

Giving everyone a fair share by equalizing income represents the egalitarian answer to the existence of malice and the predicament of evil. But there do exist alternate ways to curb the 'yetzah harah' and relieve human suffering. Altogether the proposed solutions encompass three basic strategies: 1) annihilate malice; 2) ignore malice; or 3) overcome the life subverting elements of malice by enhancing life sustaining feelings.

* * * * *

The first category concerns egalitarianism, or the attempt to get rid of ill-will and bad conscience by deriding desire and destroying the objects of such desire, not only money and goods, but intangible qualities and unique experiences. [6] Examples abound of privileged peoples who have tried to assuage their own discomfort by minimizing the wealth or opportunities of others. Typically an American doctoral candidate seriously advocated a ministry of culture in order to assure his fellow citizens had *"equal sensory experiences of aesthetic objects."* [7] For him cultural engineering was the means to overcome an "*oppressive class background*", that is, a wealthy family and distinctive education. He believed that when everyone saw the same, then he could shed the shame and guilt of being special.

This relates to the difficulty in discussing egalitarianism. It is a highly charged issue, all the more because it has been invested with utopian hopes for absolute fairness and justice since ancient times. Those who criticize the theory or practice, or point out its destructive roots, are liable to be dismissed as right wing, or fascist. Conversely, it is hard to demonstrate the positive side of egalitarianism, or advocate it, without being labeled socialist, communist, or, 'ultra-leftist'. In fact, economic levelling comprised an integral part of National Socialist policy and a tyrannical elitism was a major feature of the egalitarian regimes of Chairman Mao and the Cambodian dictator Pol Pot.

The function of egalitarianism has to be seen within a particular social context. During times of famine or other kind of collective threat, the equal distribution of scarce resources is a great advantage. In these circumstances the egalitarian ideal reflects a generosity of spirit and may be essential for group survival.

Yet, during most other occasions, the tenacious demand for total social, economic and political equality is a chimera. In fact, it is worse than a chimera, because egalitarian actions secretly serve to arouse and express the very resentments they are supposed to suppress. Many observers have noted that these policies create social tensions which are divisive and dangerous. Groups founded on egalitarian ideals, such as the Israel Kibbutzim, have been only able to survive by departing from these ideals. [8] Otherwise the equal allocation of food, shelter, clothing or other opportunities has to be maintained by force as in Russia, China or Cuba. [9]

* * * * *

Where egalitarianism is the aim, social levelling provides the means. levelling is the process of reducing wealth, power, knowledge, qualities, even sensations to a lower common denominator. Whether enforced by public humiliation, legal sanction or physical brutality, an active levelling trivializes standards and corrupts and spoils what is good in the name of equality.

I have already described the effects of levelling on the English educational system. [10] The Deputy Foreign Minister Anatoli Adamischin has confirmed a similar, deadening impact, in the Soviet Union:

> *"Levelling takes away all creativity. People just don't work if they are just going to end up on the same level as everyone else."* [11]

As for the United States, the journalist, William Manchester, believes that Vietnam and Watergate afflicted Americans with the wish to level on all levels. [12] He sees this process at work in excessive informality, the aggressive use of nicknames, unisex clothes and the vanishing bijoux of excellence:

> *"In short, we are expected to look down on those above us, and up to those beneath us. Since superiority is in itself suspect, everyone tries to look like, talk like, and be like everyone else...... Doubtless this comforts those in whose breasts lurk the gnawing (and usually justified) hunch that they really are inferior."* [13]

Levelling appears to reduce differences. The underlying assumption is that if everyone were equal, then no-one would have anything to be envious about. But the reality is more complicated. Envy begins in the eye of the envier, not with the envied object. Even if we all looked alike, spoke alike, ate alike or dressed alike, we could still imagine that the neighbour next door enjoyed his porridge better, or for that matter, had a better time in bed. Paradoxically attempts to breed conformity, yield hostility. People may seek solidarity during times of stress, but their hearts lie with distinction, not similarity.

The motto of the French revolution, *liberté, égalité, fraternité,* highlights the difficulties in reconciling social ideals with concrete truths. Egalitarian policies do not necessarily promote social fraternity. Quite the opposite, they invite invidious comparisons and social sclerosis. Individually this depresses talent, achievement and ultimately, equity – equality of opportunity. During the 'cultural revolution' rampant levelling led to the absurd situation whereby the Chinese were not allowed to say what professional or business position they occupied. They could only be introduced as*"a responsible person of a department concerned"* without any inkling of what exactly they did. [14]

Internationally, the development economist Peter Bauer has convincingly argued that *"the unholy grail of economic equality"*, is a form of sop behaviour which is more likely to depress living standards, at home and abroad, than enhance them. [15] Moreover Bauer points out that there exists irreparable conflicts between the pursuit of equality and the pursuit of liberty. Neither people nor countries willingly submit to the redistribution of wealth in the name of 'fairness'. And as Stalin demonstrated in the 1920's collectivism is often a ruse for despotic sharing. [16]

Except in rare instances of non-coercive agreement, it appears that the equalization of resources always coincides with an inequality of power. In financial terms a decrease in wage differentials means an increase in power differentials. The former Conservative Minister, Sir Keith Joseph, has reasoned:

"The inequality of power is far more menacing than inequality of money. Inequality of money is constantly subject to change: money

is made or lost. But inequalities of power, such as must exist in an egalitarian society, continually erode the rule of law so that, even in societies which are supposed to be democratic and constitutional, the rule of law becomes weak or non-existent" [17]

> *Inevitably there arise leaders, elites, parties or states who force similitude on others, like the mythical Procrustus or contemporary Big Brothers.* [18]

* * * * *

Procrustean politics are essentially paternalistic. An egalitarian leadership does not believe that citizens are naturally endowed for *"life, liberty and the pursuit of happiness."* 'Freedom' or 'liberty' solely consists of economic security, that is, the right to be well clothed, housed and well fed. This implies that life is a gift from the government, a gift which can be given or taken away depending on whether the citizenry fits in (has the right race or class background) and behaves (attends party functions), or not. [19]

Ultimately, egalitarianism leads to the idealization of the state. The contradiction is that when people try to solve the problems of life by imbuing the state or party or collective with omnipotent maternal (and paternal) powers, their greed and envy tends to turn towards these entities too. Then the state has to use its powers not just to coerce equality, but to prevent its 'free', albeit dependent, citizens from attacking it. Such threats evoke a seductive, rejecting attitude, like that of a certain parents who rage when is their seductions don't work, and suddenly become rejecting and mean spirited. In other words I am describing a mechanism by which the omnipotent nationalism of both communist and fascist (national socialist) countries can turn from pride for providing (basic necessities) to persecuting and withholding (basic necessities).

All this appears to be a far cry from the egalitarian millennialism of the early Christians who responded to misery by elevating the lowly, and idealizing the afterlife. Jesus, when asked by his disciples which of them was the greater replied, *"the least among you all is the one who will be great."* (Luke 9, 48) Cyprian (c. 200-258 C.E.) who was the bishop of Carthage, commented that *"by His reply He cut off all rivalry. He tore out and broke away every cause and material of gnawing envy."*[20]

Meanwhile pagan philosophers tried to solve the problem of envy by retiring to a world where only a philosophical elite mattered.[21] Iambulus postulated one of the the first political utopias, an island off the coast of Arabia where all men were equal. The highest values were given to unity and harmony. Jealousy, pride and civil strife could not occur, because marriage was not allowed. Men shared the common possession of woman and children and there was enough food for everyone. The lifespan was a 150 years, after which the men were obliged to kill themselves. [22]

Earlier, in the *Politics*, Aristotle had discussed the ideas of Phaleas, a Chalcedonian thinker, who proposed equalizing the property of all citizens. Aristotle himself did not believe that the levelling of wealth would end theft. But he thought it might help to eliminate minor crime and to prevent civil disturbance. Otherwise he wrote that human nature suffers the defect of never being satisfied. Ones' wants just get bigger and bigger. [23]

The egalitarian tradition continued throughout the middle ages, an inheritance from Greek and Roman notions of the 'State of Nature' whereby all men were equal in status and wealth, and had to right to share possessions, even wives. [24] These beliefs, combined with the exhortations of Christian and political dissenters, nourished the English Peasants Revolt of 1381, and the Anabaptists, the Taborites and Ranters, among a host of radical groups. [25] For them, liberation concurred with the Last Judgment – a day of vengeance of the poor as well as a time of final but equal sharing of God's gifts. [26]

Related themes have suffused the repeated refrains of insurrectionists ranging from fifteenth century Czech anarcho-communists to contemporary students who quote the pan-destructionist hopes of Mikhail Bakunin and the utopian dreams of Leo Tolstoy. [27] All his life the Count searched for a little green stick buried by the road at the edge of ravine in the Zakaz Forest. It was a very special stick:

> *"....whereupon was written the message which could destroy all evil in men and give them universal welfare."* [28]

Tolstoy intended that his millennial message would free men from chaos, disorder, license, waste, arbitrariness and uncertainty as well as presage an era of health and happiness. Yet it is likely that he, and others who preach impossible ends while denying inherent hatreds, have made the opposite reaction more likely. Ideal goals lead to endless frustration and exaggerate the hostilities which are no longer supposed to be present, all under the guise of creating *"a new heaven and a new earth."* [29]

* * * * *

The concept of luck provides an altogether different means to minimize malice. It doesn't seek to deny envy, but to ignore it. Luck is the benign leveler. It removes the personal responsibility that contributes to feelings of inferiority and envy. With good luck, or bad, whatever has happened appears to be outside of human control. [30]

Luck is a superbly efficient social sanctioned device to rationalize inadequacy, incompetence, poor judgment and, in general, dissimilar skills, traits or resources. By giving the illusion of absolute equality, luck allows the envier to carry on without suffering a loss of status or becoming overwhelmed by hatred. Conversely by claiming luck, a person can accept success without having to dread others' reactions. No doubt this explains the perennial popularity of games of chance as well as the immediate propensity to refer to luck when faced with good fortune.

There is a well-authenticated story about a gang of men repairing a road on the outskirts of London. They were forced to scatter by the loud hooting of an approaching Rolls Royce. When the chauffeur-driven car drew close, one of the labourers spat at it, a second threw a stone and the third shouted an obscenity. But as the car passed, its sole passenger wound down a window, put out his head and yelled:

> *"You stupid gits – it's me, Charlie. How d'you think I got this lot then? Won it on the pools, didn't I ?"* (31)

Upon hearing this, all three men dropped their shovels, raised their arms and began to cheer. Their rancour vanished as soon as they realized that Charlie had obtained the Rolls by chance, rather than by acquired privilege or inherited wealth. In fact they were pleased, for they assumed that if 'lady luck' could smile on him, she could smile on them too.

The large number of common expressions involving involving good luck, bad luck, states of luck or wishes about luck demonstrate the importance of the concept of luck or chance or fate in normal social intercourse. Hence *"in luck"* and *"luck out"* convey good fortune, while *"out of luck"* and *"down on one's luck"* assert the opposite, misfortune. Concurrently *"to try one's luck"* means to do something without being sure of the outcome and *"to push one's luck"* implies the same but with an added element of extra, perhaps unnecessary risk.

The English language has an ample vocabulary of words and expressions that signify a state of being or mind which is independent of individual effort or intervention. English speaking peoples, just by using this vocabulary, are able to diminish the impact of actual or anticipated envy in human relations. Other peoples are not so fortunate. The German language, for example, has only one word, *'glück'*, to indicate both happiness and luck. Consequently, it is easier for an American or Englishman to avoid being hated for the happiness that comes from a *"lucky win"* than a German whose *"glücky"* contentment might equally stem from hard work and enviable talent. (32)

Societies which have no words, indeed, no concept of luck, fate or "*'the blind goddess' Fortune*" lack social softeners. Their members feel extremely vulnerable to envy and black magic and remain obsessed with counteracting the evil eye. I have previously mentioned the Navaho Indians, a tribe frequently idealized by young people because of its egalitarian practices. For them the absence of *"luck"* inhibits achievement because the Navaho believe that fellow Indians can only prosper at each others' expense. In consequence their cultural norms must emphasize sharing in order to avoid continual bloodshed.

Similarly, the Siriono of Bolivia rarely eat the animals they kill, while various Polynesian islanders always refuse the fish they catch. As with the Navaho, the persistent presence of hostile eyes never allows the hunters to have *"a lucky shot"* or the fishermen to *"hit the jackpot."* with their spears. Comparable cultures which lack a 'lucky' strategy of envy avoidance, remain vulnerable to the demands of the zero sum game and the constraints imposed by envy. [33]

* * * * *

The third means of dealing with malice is radically different. It does not try to depose the negative side of existence, as in egalitarianism or luck, but to enhance positive feelings. This redresses the emotional balance between omnipotent destructive forces and life sustaining ones and makes it possible to accept the central role that envy, greed and jealousy play in human affairs.

However, before proceeding, it is important to note that even pernicious impulses can and do have salutary psychic and social effects. Envious tension, for example, generates anxiety and contributes to an emotional tone which is a necessary stimulus to action. The physical equivalents are ongoing states of muscular and sensory stimulation. Without a state of ambient tension people would be so relaxed they could not breathe. And it is well known that children born without the capacity to feel pain lie in mortal danger.

Almost 2500 years ago Aristophanes dramatized the dilemma of too much versus too little envy in his play called *Wealth.* [34] The plot was simple. The ruler of Olympus, Zeus, had become envious of the God Wealth. So he blinded him. In consequence wealth and virtue became unevenly distributed. Some people got a lot, while others got none at all. But later, as part of a utopian solution, Wealth regained his sight. Still there were problems. 'Poverty' claimed:

> *"If Wealth were to see again and to share himself out equally, no one of men would bother with any craft or skill."* (35)

In other words, a modicum of envy is an essential impetus for change. If everyone had as much as they needed and wanted, there would be little incentive to do anything. People would all live in a state of bliss perhaps akin to a 'heroin high'. Concomitantly, envy and jealousy help to avoid regimentation and excite diversity. Without the wish to shift these tensions, our social structures might remain rigid and static. Therefore we can say that exists a positive side to malice, just as there can be a negative side to excessive goodness. (36)

It is noteworthy that envy can thwart innovation, or stimulate it. Equally, envy may provoke the abuse of power, or help to tame it. As we have seen in chapter nine, the yellow press and assorted hordes of gossip mongers, muckrakers and muckraking politicians, all serve as part of a complicated system of checks and balances. They make it difficult for one group or institution to gain power at the expense of others. In a free society, envy allows people to exercise mutual and spontaneous supervision over each other. If there were no envy, or, if societal persecutors, that is, political dictators or institutional tyrants, overwhelmed its free expression, then the tentative exploration of the thresholds of social tolerance could not occur. Thus we are faced with the paradox that man's success as a creative, social being depends on his capacity to constrain his malevolence, yet the same propensities set the tone for his social life. Helmut Schoeck has neatly summarized the issue:

> *"We are thus confronted by an antimony, an irreconcilable contradiction: envy is an extremely anti-social and destructive*

emotional state, but it is, at the same time, the most completely socially oriented. And without universal consideration of at least a potential or imaginary envy in others, there could not be the automatic social controls upon which all association is based." (37)

The capacity to cope with this contradiction depends on the degree of malignity and the extent to which love is able to modify the overall emotional matrix. Thus Geoffrey Chaucer, having asserted in "The Parson's Tale", that *"envy is the worst sin that is"*, also reminded us:

"The remedy for Envy is to love God, your neighbour, and your enemy." (38)

Interestingly, Wilfred Bion points out that the love of a parent or child toward each other may not be noticed because envy, rivalry and hate obscure it. But Bion insists that *"hate would not exist if love were not present."* (39) These views seem to contradict Freud's dictum that hate is older than love.

* * * * *

The conflict between love and hate, good and evil is one of mankind's oldest and deepest concerns. The book of Job teaches that it is possible for inherent goodness (Job's belief in God's righteousness) to overcome the vengeful inclination (the test of outer adversity and inner aggression). In the meanwhile the Greek poet Pindar declared that beneficent looks counteract destructive ones and urged people *"to look harmony"* on each other. (40)

In his classic study on *Europe's Inner Demons* Norman Cohn observed that the widely feared black or evil witches were often successfully opposed by beneficent or white witches. Essentially these were good spirits and protective guardians whose origins lie in a pre-

Christian, pagan world view that has existed for thousands of years. In Sicily the spirits were known as *"ladies from outside", "ladies of the home", "beautiful ladies"*, or simply, *"ladies."* [41] And the Brothers Grimm immortalized these kind, female figures in the tale of "Briar-Rose", or "The Sleeping Beauty." [42]

As we all know, the girl's parents, a king and queen, were overcome with joy on the birth of their daughter. They ordered a great feast and invited the wise-women of the land to give their blessings. But one, ominously called Maleficence in various versions, was left out. Subsequently, she burst into the celebrations and, in a paroxysm of spite, laid a death-curse on the child. However, one of the women, Beneficence, was able to intervene, for she had not yet given her blessing. Although the she could not entirely undo the curse, she was able to ameliorate it: *"But it shall not be death the princess falls into, only a deep sleep lasting a hundred years."* [43] True enough, a hundred years later, a handsome prince found the princess, kissed her lips, and woke her up. So the curse was broken and, the tale confirms that in spite of evil, beneficence can prevail. [44]

The existence of black and white witches, good and bad spirits, coincides with profound perceptions that most mothers have good and bad moments. They may be loving and loved, but hunger, discomfort or actual mistreatment can quickly change them into someone hateful and hated. Folk-tales such as "Briar-Rose" describe collective fears of starvation and death at the breasts of unsatisfying, malicious, self-centered women. Conversely happy outcomes convey collective hopes that the spirit of the loving mother will rule, even if she is not always immediately present. It was in this vein that Melanie Klein commented:

> *"In the last analysis the image of the loved parents is preserved in the unconscious mind as the most precious possession, for it guards its possessor against the pain of utter desolation."* [45]

Notice that Klein refers to *"parents"*, not just mothers. In doing so she emphasizes the importance of a good relationship with father.

He too must be loving and loved in order to guard against *"desolation"*, a word which means more than hunger and loss. It refers to a sense of utter ruin that follows when destructive impulses, inherent or reactive, get out of control and there does not appear to be sufficient love or good-will about to redress the subsequent damage. Otherwise truly murderous and quite tender feelings can coexist in the same person and same family to a remarkable degree. Much depends on the preserved image of the good parent and reciprocated love which is then available to overcome ill-will. (46)

* * * * *

An exchange between myself and a patient, an artist, well illustrates the capacity to dissolve malice. This person had been enjoying a particularly good period of work. After being told that I would have to change the time of a session and miss another, he came to our next meeting in a very angry mood bitterly complaining that his creativity had left him. Moreover, a woman who reminded him of his former wife had begun to pursue him. From many previous discussions I knew that any such woman represented his own jealous, hysterical self. So I replied that he was being chased by his own furious feelings towards me for changing a session, stealing his creativity and leaving him adrift, excluded and unwanted. The man concurred and his mood lifted. He began to talk about his sister who had just written to him from far away. He realized how much he liked her. Again I related his thoughts to myself. It was clear that when I helped him to understand his bad temper, he realized how much he liked and valued me, both for myself and as a reminder of his own 'good parents'.

Then, he suddenly sat up and exclaimed:

> *"I see horrible little things, they seem to be melting, dissolving away in some warm medium, a pleasant warm medium. They are scrunched up little bits with little faces on them, evil little imps. They remind me of mosquito larva in a barrel of rain water.*

As he was talking the combination of melting imps and mosquito larvae evoked images in my mind of primitive blood sucking creatures turning friendly. I told him I thought the warm pleasant fluid represented the power of his warmth and affection to melt and transform his envious stings, greedy bites and jealous fears, everything that had been aroused by the sudden separation and attendant assumption that I was away enjoying myself at his expense. He smiled and replied:

> *"Yes, it's true. But you know they don't disappear. They just become smaller, and much less menacing. I shall try to put them into my work."*

On the following day the man was unusually relaxed and confident. He said a great burst of energy had been released, and that he felt wonderful. Instead of holding back out of fear, he had been able to put the creatures' potential to good use. Once they had dissolved in the warm water, his negativity did likewise and he had been able to maintain a positive frame of mind and feel closer to me. (47)

The basic ingredients of the warm medium were gratitude, generosity and loving consideration or empathetic compassion. Gratitude has to do with the appreciation of goodness in others, and oneself, and is the antithesis of envy. It is closely linked with early gratifying experiences at the breast and subsequent satisfying relations with relatives and friends. (48)

The pleasures that gratifications provide lead directly to the esteem that gratitude conveys. In fact the intimate bonds between these two life-sustaining experiences reach right down to their etymological roots. In English both terms stem from the Latin 'gratus' meaning pleasing. 'Gratus', in turn, supports the concept of grace, an inner state of good will, charm, decency and favour, which averts the evil eye.

In Greek mythology the three sister goddesses known as the Graces were celebrated for filling life with brilliance, joy and vigour, that is, for making life worthwhile. (49) Interestingly, the Greek word 'charites', also denotes these deities as well as 'feelings of gratitude.' (50)

Perhaps the absence of gratitude best highlights the fundamental importance of gratitude for humane relations. The great Athenian orator Demosthenes observed that it is a disaster for the entire state if envy is stronger than gratitude for services rendered:

"Envy is a disease whereas gratitude has a place among the Gods." [51]

Contemporary critics are no less scathing when confronting the presence of ingratitude, the converse of thankful appreciation and the emotional equivalent of envy. The American clergyman, W. C. Bennett, once noted: *"Blessed is he who expects no gratitude, for he shall not be disappointed."* [52]

Possibly this cynicism reflects the attitude in certain business circles where thank-you notes after a dinner party are only considered appropriate for people *"who cannot deal with being imperious."* But the absence of gratitude does not always rest lightly. In America a man came close to winning a lawsuit against his girlfriend because she did not make love with him after he had taken her out to dinner fifty times. A simple 'thank-you', or less ambiguous 'no thank-you', might have spared her heavy legal expenses. [53]

Generosity reflects the spirit of gratitude. The grateful person is able to take in and assimilate everything from good feelings to good thoughts, aside from tangible items like food or books. This means he or she can build up an inner storehouse of enriching experiences all of which helps to counter greed and transform the world into a much more friendly, giving, stimulating place. The drama of a woman who was taken to dinner fifty times and who still did not respond with kindness shows what can happen when generosity sustained by a firm sense of self-worth is missing. [54]

The third element of love, empathetic compassion, has to do with the capacity to see other persons in their own right, not as extensions of oneself. It allows one to sympathetically consider what others are doing without jealously assuming that the outcome of their acting in their own interests will be a catastrophe for oneself. These three elements comprised the warm medium that allowed my patient to dissipate his venom and transform energies that had been locked up as hatred into great bursts of creative affection. His gratitude flowed from understanding. The understanding released a generous flow of good feelings. And both his gratitude and generosity allowed him to accept that I had needs unrelated to him, that I had to change the schedule for my sake, not to specifically hurt him, or attack our relationship.

* * * * *

The acceptance of reality is itself an essential first step in the process of healing, or reparation, which enables people to sustain generosity and gratitude. Bertrand Russell, wrote in *The Conquest of Happiness*:

> *"Merely to realize the causes of one's own envious feelings is to take a long step towards curing them."* (55)

This kind of open acceptance brings malice down to earth. Envy, greed and jealousy no longer seem so powerful, or impossible to counter. Moreover, the realization of hate also involves the liberation of love. Both sides, love and hate, tend to be buried and retrieved together. When retrieved, love can become a helper, an emotional ally, whether to assess damage done (that is, to face reality) or to withstand painful feelings of remorse. Without such love, or powerful positive impetuses, we would all remain stuck, like the King's soldiers and King's men who couldn't put Humpty Dumpty back together again.

The acknowledgement of destructive aims and impulses has been institutionalized by many cultures and religions. Jewish people, for example, devote an entire day, Yom Kippur, or The Day of Atonement, to the ritual acknowledgement of individual and collective wrong thinking or wrong doing. The service for Yom Kippur includes the powerful prayer, *"Al Chate"*

"We confess our sins and bring them to the light of our own recognition and of God's forgiveness. By confession we may become clean. By forgiveness we may become free. O God, release us from the burden of our failure. Do not let our past imprison us. Renew us.

For the sin we have committed before You

...by over-eating and drinking.

...by hurting others

....by envy

...by betraying trust

...by false pride

...by despising You....

For all these sins, Forgiving God, forgive us, pardon us, grant us atonement." (56)

The second step in the reparative process is reparation, literally, re-pairation, a re-pairing, a bringing together of broken bits. In order to abjure ill-will, it is not sufficient to acknowledge the injured object. Whether animate or inanimate, a person or a relationship, one has to do take whatever action may be necessary to repair, restore, renew, recreate and redeem it. It appears that no amount of damage cannot be repaired. Even if the original object has been smashed to smithereens, or killed, the reparative process can go on, both in the outside world, and inwardly.

According to Klein reparation is never complete, rather it is an active process of striving towards completeness, whether of the head or heart or entire being. It is intimately related to the Kabbalistic concept of 'Tikkun.'

The poet and Kabbalist, Pinchas Sadeh, has described what the process, *Tikkun Ha-Lev*, or Restoration of the Heart, has meant for him:

> *"This evening, while I was still engrossed in thought on a certain topic, a thought entered my mind regarding 'repair of the heart.'*
>
> *A few years ago, when I edited a book of the writings of Rabbi Nachman of Breslov, I chose to call it Tikkun Ha-Lev, repair of the heart. I thought that the meaning of the name, simple in itself, was absolutely clear to me. But I am thinking that perhaps only now its meaning is becoming clear to me.*
>
> *...Time, fate, life and death – all these powerful forces prevent the possibility of repairing that which is broken. If so, what is possible?*
>
> *What remains for man to do, after all? What can save and rescue the things that are smashed? Maybe only – and even this only through tremendous effort, through difficult struggle, through great pain – this; repairing the heart.* "[57]

The despair in this refrain echoes with that of Pinchas Sadeh about the difficulty, even impossibility, of effecting a repair. I think the sentiments are so moving because they are so elemental. How can one put together a loved one, loved ones, after we have hurt them? And how strong are our reparative capacities, really equal to our life forces, when, to quote Dr. R. D. Laing, *"the dreadful has already happened?"* Surely this is the case with Humpty Dumpty. For he is not an ordinary creature. Rather he embodies the cosmic egg, the primal contents and container of all.

The same sequence can affect an entire people. In the last chapter I discussed the Germans' views of Jews, views which culminated in the Holocaust. Like my patient, the Germans had previously denied responsibility for their actions, and saw themselves as the aggrieved party, threatened by hostile forces from within and without. However, this attitude changed after the second world war. Under the leadership of Konrad Adenhauer (1949-1963), the Federal Republic (West Germany) faced up to what it had done and decided to make reparations both to individual Jews and to Israel, as representative of millions of murdered Jews. By 1987 about $25 billion has been paid out, and it is likely that this figure will increase to over $30 billion by the end of the century. Although these monies hardly compensate for the stupendous loss of life, they do represent a genuine desire to come to terms with the crimes of the Nazi era, and have brought about a remarkable restoration of relations between the Federal Republic and the Jewish State. [58]

As we can see from these examples, reparation not only affects the damaged object, but the subject as well. It brings together warring factions and restores the balance between love and hate. In other words it effects a process of at-one-ment. Like Oedipus at Colonus, the damager no longer need feel that he *"violates the ground from whence he came."*

The healing or re-integration takes place on three levels: Firstly, the injured person or thing revives. And once he has been put back together, he ceases to be a victim or a victimizer. He is no longer someone or something that has been tyrannized by malice. Moreover, he is able to avoid the danger of becoming a tyrannizer himself, a new source of guilt and hatred.

At the same time reparation relieves the maledoer, whether a single person or an entire nation, of negative tensions. So it doesn't need to restrain its energies for fear of destructive consequences. Instead they can be released for constructive purposes while admiration and emulation take the place of resentment and withdrawal.

Thirdly, reparation transforms the relations between envier and envied, between subject and object. It enables both parties to give up entrenched fears and to discover areas of common interest.

The simple acceptance of damage done accompanied by ungrudging efforts to put things right signals an increased capacity for gratitude, generosity and compassion. These feelings, in turn, tilt the love/hate lattice towards positive ends and strengthens benevolence. By the same token the failure of reparation has the same effect as an excess of malice. It tilts the lattice the other way towards destructive ends and the triumph of death over life.

This whole cycle of love and hate emerged in the person of a man whom I knew at the Arbours Crisis Centre in London. [59] He had been severely wounded during the course of prolonged conflicts with an ostensibly loving, but tyrannical family as well as his own inner demons. When his negativity predominated, he often affected a posture of psychotic withdrawal. As far as he was concerned the world was dead, and so was he, all of which terrified his parents. On the other hand, he could also be warmly playful and communicative, reparative efforts which were usually rebuffed by the very same people who were urging him to get better. Then the negativity would return with a vengeance.

Sometimes I was able to follow these emotional swings by his use of words. During up periods he would doodle incessantly, emphasizing, in particular, the word, EVIL. He liked to write and draw EVIL every which way. One day he cornered me in the kitchen and exclaimed:

"You know, Joe. EVIL spelled the other way is LIVE."

I had never previously thought of the reverse spelling of the word. Upon reflection, I observed that by playing with words one could turn evil to live, good to bad, not unlike the ancient Gods who could transform Furies into Eumenides or 'kindly ones'. He nodded in agreement. Yes, he knew it was possible to turn bad to good, to transcend evil. That's why he doodled. It helped him to overcome terrible *"urges"*. When EVIL returned, his rage gained the upper hand. But when LIVE appeared, his tension disappeared and the world became OK again.

"Joe, That's why I write. When I can't get away from EVIL, everything feels real bad inside. But when I change it 'round, to LIVE, then I feel good. I have to do this, Joe, turn EVIL to LIVE, and keep it there. For me, it's a matter of life and death." [60]

PART 5
ENDNOTES

Endnotes

Elaborations, Commentaries and Source Notes

INTRODUCTION

1) Lewis Carroll, *Alice's Adventures in Wonderland AND Through the Looking-Glass*, Penguin Classics, 1998, p. 132.

2) R. D. Laing, "The Mystification of Experience", *The Politics of Experience*, Pantheon Books, New York, 1967, p. 49. This chapter was originally published under the title of "Violence and Love", in the *Journal of Existentialism*, Vol. V, No. 20, 1965.

3) *American Journal of Sociology*, (1947-1985);

Rural Sociology, Vols. 1-20 (1936-1955);

The British Journal of Sociology, (1949-1959);

American Anthropologist and the Memoirs of the American Anthropological Association, 1949-1958;

Southwestern Journal of Anthropology, Vols. 1-20 (1945-1964)

Helmut Schoeck pointed out this remarkable gap, or should one say refusal to look envy in the eye, in his book *Envy: A Theory of Social Behavior*, Harcourt, Brace & World, New York, 1966, p.9.

4) Ashley Montagu, *The Nature of Human Aggression*, Oxford University Press, London, 1976.

Erich Fromm, *The Anatomy of Human Destructiveness*, Holt, Rinehart and Winston, New York, 1973.

5) Geoffrey Chaucer "The Parson's Tale" in *Canterbury Tales*, trans. by Nevill Coghill, Penguin Books, London , 1982, p. 506.

Chaucer continues: "Envy is sorrow at the prosperity of others and Joy in their hurt........And is flatly against the Holy Ghost, source of Bounty. Backbiting and grumbling are the Devil's Paternoster."

Interestingly, Chaucer described seven sins including: Pride, Envy, Anger, Accidie, Avarice, Gluttony and Lechery. On closer examination the seven sins reduce to three, envy, greed and jealousy. Of these envy is the most prominent. It includes pride (hubris, hateful self-inflation), anger ('a wicked will to vengeance') and accidie (vengeful passivity). Greed comprises avarice, gluttony and lechery. And jealousy touches upon lechery and anger.

6) Thomas Aquinas (1225? - 1274)

7) Quoted from an editorial in *The New York Times*, "Pyongyang as Outlaw", and republished in *The International Herald Tribune*, 18 January 1988, p. 6.

8) Barry Rubin, "The Triumph of the 'Old Middle East,' *MERIA Journal*, Vol, 6, No, 2, June 2002, pp 2 & 7.

9) Ian Buruma, "Homeland insecurity." *FT Magazine*, No. 114, 16-17 July 2005, PP. 22-25.

10) "The State of Islam, " *Daily Telegraph*, 1 August 2005, pp. 15-28.

CHAPTER 1

1) "The witchcraft or sorcery of the evil eye is recognized by the Church as one of the Devil's weapons ... it is said that a person known to have the evil eye 'has an eye infected by the Devil'". Peter Walcot, *Envy and the Greeks*, op. cit., pp 87-88.

The contemporary Italian novelist, Alberto Moravia, concurs: "A person who has the evil eye does harm without any motive at all, haphazard, scattering disaster as a water sprinkler scatters water. There's no rhyme or reason about it." Jack Shamash, "Warding off an evil eye," *The Times*, 13 March 1999, p.19

2) Joshua Trachtenberg, *Jewish Magic and Superstition: A Study in Folk Religion*, Atheneum, New York, 1970, p.56.

Moreover, in Jewish legends, the Angel of Death is depicted as having many eyes. Rivka Ulmer, *The Evil Eye in the Bible and Rabbinic Literature*, Ktav Publishing, New Jersey, 1994.

3) To the Greeks, the Furies were dramatic representations of the evil eye, and therefore, of envy. They were figures of absolute horror, as Aeschylus makes clear in his play, *The Furies*. Ibid., p.60

4) Jean Louis Andre Theodore Gericault (1791-1824) was a forerunner of the French Romantic movement. His most famous work is entitled, *Raft of the Medusa* (1817) which depicts the cannibalistic survivors of a shipwreck. His treatment of envy is part of a series of paintings on the theme of insanity.

5) There exists hundreds of proverbs on the subject of envy, many of which are similar in different countries. Dr. Helmut Schoeck quotes from a number of Russian proverbs including:

"Envy turns a blade of grass into a palm tree."

"In the eye of the envious man, a toadstool becomes a palm tree."

"The envious eye makes elephants of midges".

Helmut Schoeck, *Envy: A Theory of Social Behaviour*, op. cit., pp 20-21

6) Ibid., pp 20-21

7) Edward S. Gifford, Jr., *The Evil Eye: Studies in the Folklore of Vision*, The MacMillan Co., New York, 1958, pp 3-4.

8) Martin Delrio, a Jesuit of Louvain, wrote in 1603: "Fascination is a power derived from a pact with the devil, who, when the so-called fascinator looks at another with evil intent, or praises, by means known to himself, infects with evil the person at whom he looks." Ibid., p.15.

9) Ibid., pp 6-9.

10) Other names for the evil eye include *innochiatura* (Corsica), *mauvais oeil* (France), *mal ojo* (Spain), *böse Blick* (Germany), *booze blik* (Holland), *zte oko* (Poland), *skjoertunge* (Norway), *ondt oje* (Denmark), *cronachadt* (Scotland), *droch-shuil* (Ireland), *aghashi* (Iran), *paterak* (Armenia), *szeniveres* (Hungary), *l'ain* (Morocco) *ayenat* (Ethiopia), *drishtidosham* (India) and *hassad (Egypt).*

11) One does not have to appear evil to be a *jettatura.* The evil inherent in the *mal occhio* is inherent and may occur spontaneously and outside voluntary control. This view is consistent with the view that envy is natural and inherent in everyone.

12) Edward Gifford quotes from an Italian describing the difficulties that beset Pope Pius IX: "Now, if he hasn't the jettatura, what is it that makes everything turn out at cross purposes with him? For my part, I don't wonder the workmen at the Column in the Piazza di Spagna refused to work the other day in raising it, unless the Pope stayed away." Ibid., pp 16-17.

13) "Vilde worme, thou wast ore-look'd even in thy birth." William Shakespeare, *Merry Wives of Windsor,* Act 5, Sc. 5, L. 81 *The Complete Pelican Shakespeare: The Comedies and the Romances* edited by Alfred Harbage, Penguin Books, London, 1969, p.318.

To overlook also has come to mean: to ignore, or to look down upon. These meanings also are indicative of envy, for the envious person is someone who ignores others' achievements and looks down on his superiors. See: *Oxford Universal Dictionary*, 3rd Edition, Oxford, 1933, p.1404.

Such events remain common occurences, as the popular presss delights in reporting. Typically the *Sun* newspaper reported thst an RSPCA worker had put the 'evil eye' on dogs he did not like. His intense stares drove them into frenzies so that they had to be destroyed. John Scott, "Evil Eyes," *The Sun*, 10 July 1990, pp. 1-2.

14) According to the *Oxford Universal Dictionary*, to blink can mean to turn milk sour. To put blinkers on is to ignore many aspects of reality, or to hoodwink. These definitions are also consistent with envy. Ibid., p.190.

See also Edward S. Gifford, Jr., *The Evil Eye: Studies in the Folklore of Vision*, op. cit., p.6.

15) Ibid., p.21.

16) Jonathan Mirsky, "Get rich - but not too fast," *The Times*, 21 March 1985, p. 16.

In this vein, my ten year old daughter, commented at the time of buying a rabbit: "I don't want one with pink eyes. Reminds me of a 'wear rabbit'." Deborah Berke, personal communication, 27 April 1985.

Her remark demonstrates the projection of destructive impulses into the eyes of another, whether the green-eyed monsters in Othello, the reddened eyes of an angry Chinese, the blood-shot eyes of a gangster, or the pink eyes of a rabbit.

17) In reminiscing about his childhood the English writer Laurie Lee has vividly described the appearance of a deaf-mute beggar said to be possessed of the evil eye: "He had soft-boiled eyes of unusual power which filled every soul with disquiet. It was said he could ruin a girl with a glance and take the manhood away from a man, or scramble your brains, turn bacon green, and affect other domestic disorders." Laurie Lee, *Cider With Rosie*, Penguin Books, London, 1959, p. 35.

18) Edward S. Gifford, Jr., *The Evil Eye: Studies in the Folklore of Vision*, op. cit., p. 17-18.

19) Elias Canetti, *Crowds and Power*, Victor Gollancz Ltd., London, 1962, p. 262.

Psychologically, the 'dead' who envy the living refers to the dead parts of the self which retain the capacity to terrorize the live parts, (in other words, an intra psychic phenomenon) and to the projection of these dead parts into a corpse, or part of a corpse, like the eye.

20) Yuri Olesha, *Envy*, op. cit., p.2.

21) A comparable process of projection helps to explain why many primitive peoples 'see' danger everywhere. In such cultures the envier, or *fascinator,* can easily become *fascinated*, or bewitched, or bedeviled, by the things he envies. All this is experienced on a level of supernatural magic and is exceptionally frightening.

22) Helmut Schoeck, *Envy: A Theory of Social Behaviour*, op. cit., p. 2.

23) *Miguel de Unamuno, Abel Sanchez: The History of a Passion,* translated by Anthony Kerrigan, Gateway Editions, Chicago, 1956, p.103.

Foster quotes from many writers to document his view that praise can be very unwelcome in peasant as well as urban societies because it arouses and it is seen as an expression of envy.

Edward Banfield on South Italy: ".. one of the most interesting superstitions is the belief that invidious comment, even though made to flatter, will bring harm to the one who is put in an enviable light." *The Moral Basis of a Backward Society,* Glencoe Free Press, 1958, p.144.

Horace Miner on Timbuctoo, Mali: ".. the belief that compliments from non-intimates bring evil upon those praised. People therefore tend to avoid direct compliments and fear those directed to them". *The Primitive City of Timbuctoo,* Princeton Univ. Press, 1953, p.103.

Sania Hamady on the Arab world: "... some compliments which, even if well intended, are considered portentous. Laudatory expressions may attract the contrary of what they propose to say, because envy may be mixed with them. That is why a mother is not simply told that her son is handsome and healthy, or a proprietor that his house is splendid. It is feared that the son might fall sick and the house might burn." *Temperament and Character of the Arabs*, Twayne, New York, 1960, p.166.

George M. Foster, "The Anatomy of Envy: A Study in Symbolic Behavior", op. cit., p.172.

24) Peter Walcot, *Envy and the Greeks*, op. cit. ,pp. 25-26.

"But in general, throughout the Homeric poems, we hear of the envy of the gods merely in vague statements which reflect the pessimism of Homeric man, but do not add up to anything like a theory of divine envy directed against the powerful."

25) Ibid., p.31.

26) Pindar, lyric poet, 518-438 B.C.E.

Aeschylus, Athenian tragedian, 525/4 - 456 B.C.E.

Herodotus, historian, c.484 - c.420 B.C.E.

27) Ibid., p.34. Aeschylus, *Agamemnon*, verses 468-70.

Peter Walcot comments that for the Greeks a basic dilemma was how to achieve success without attracting too much envy, which invited resentment, malice and displeasure of the Gods. In *Agamemnon* the chorus chooses 'prosperity without envy' but as Walcot points out, it is doubtful that this option existed, especially for the Greeks, who were a people obsessed by envy.

28) Ibid., p.34. *Agamemnon* verse 947.

29) Euripides, Athenian tragedian, c485- - c406 B.C.E.

Plutarch, biographer and essayist, c45 - c125 C.E.

Walcot states, "In Euripides', *Suppliant Women*, Theseus claims there are three groups of citizens, the rich, the poor, and those in the middle. What does he say of the second class? The have-nots, those who lack the essentials of life, are motivated by envy and release 'evil stings' on those who have (verses 240-242)." Ibid., p.35.

Discussing Plutarch, Walcot writes, "The 'suffering soul' affects the body, and envy (phthonos), sinking naturally into the soul more than any other emotion, fills the body too with wickedness. When those consumed by such envy fix their glance on someone, their eyes, being very near, draw from the soul the wickedness and strike a man down like poisoned arrows." Ibid., p.82.

30) Ibid., pp. 47-48.

31) Ibid., p.82

32) Heliodorus was the author of the longest Greek novel to survive, the *Aethiopica*. He lived in the second half of the 3rd century A.D.

Ibid., p.83

33) Plutarch was quoted by Samuel Reynolds, who edited Bacon's essays.

Plutarch also comments: "... how is it possible that the only cast or regard of the eye should transmit any noisance or hurt into the body of another?" The answer is that 'envy filleth the body with an untoward and bad disposition; when therefore they who be infected with envy do cast their eyes upon others, and so shoot their venomous rays, like unto poisoned darts upon them, if such a chance to be wounded or hurt thereby whom they look upon and wistly behold, I see no strange thing not a matter incredible." *Symposiaques*, Bk. 5, Question 7.

Francis Bacon, "Of Envy" in *The Essays or Counsels, Civil and Moral*, op. cit., p.62.

34) Ibid., p.56.

35) Ibid., p. 64

Bacon's view reflects the long held belief that vision was the result of rays emitted by the eye which bounce back from the perceived object to the viewer, somewhat like radar.

36) Ibid., p.56.

Shining stars and planets have long been associated with heavenly 'eyes'. By the psychological mechanism of projection it is easy to attribute 'evil influences' or 'evil aspects' to these distant eyes, just as the early Greeks did with their Olympian Gods.

37) Personal communication, January 1986.

For this young man, the breasts (the desired objects) and the eyes (the desiring objects) were one.

38) Mishle Yehoshua, from R. Alcalay, *Words of the Wise*, Masada Press, Israel, p.131.

39) Pindar, *Pythian Odes*, 8, verses 71-72 and 67-69, quoted in Peter Walcot, *Envy and the Greeks*, op. cit., p. 80.

40) Ibid., p. 56.

41) Immanuel Kant, *Metaphysik der Sitten*, op. cit., p. 36.

42) H. Schoeck quotes the proverb, "No sooner is envy born than he consorts with the hangman and the gallows." Ibid., p.22.

43) In England, the assizes are court sessions held to try civil and criminal cases, in this case in Lewes.

44) I am indebted to the barrister, Peter Marsh, who brought this crime to my attention and provided details of the case for me.

Haigh pleaded not guilty on grounds of insanity, but he was convicted and executed at Wandsworth Prison in August 1949.

45) The psychoanalyst, Hanna Segal, points out that when envy is turned inwards it attacks the psychic representations of 'the good object', such as the feeding mother. This can lead to an impoverishment of the ego and even more intense envy. She comments: "This gives rise to a painful vicious circle. The more the good internal object is destroyed, the more impoverished the ego feels, and this in turn increases envy."

Segal adds: "The projection of envy into the (internal) object gives rise to an envious superego. The over-severe superego which Freud describes as the basis of psychical disturbance, often turns out on analysis to be an envious superego. That is, its attacks are directed not only against the individual's aggression, but also, and even predominantly, against the individual's progressive and creative capacities." Hanna Segal, *Klein*, Fontana Modern Masters, London, 1979, p.143.

46) Other sayings include:

"Envy will eat nothing but its own heart."

"Envy brings suffering to the envious man."

"Envy flogs itself."

Helmut Schoeck, *Envy: A Theory of Social Behaviour*, op. cit., p.32.

47) For example, the Greek orator and teacher, Isocrates (436-338 B.C.E.), wrote at length about envy which he considered a disease and scourge of mankind. Walcot comments: "In the *Antidosis* Isocrates reports .. some men have been made so savage by envy and want and are so hostile that they are at war not with wickedness but with prosperity; they hate not only the best men but also the noblest of activities; they sympathize with men who are wicked and destroy, if they can, those whom they envy." (15, 141-142) Peter Walcot, *Envy and the Greeks*, op. cit., p.72-72.

In the contemporary thought the same message comes through. In one sequence of the popular cartoon, "Hagar the Horrible", the scribe asks Hagar, "For my records, what illnesses have you had?" Hagar thinks, "Lemme see, Black Plague...Evil Eye...Demon Possession...Spells." The scribe replies, "I'll just put down "regular childhood diseases"."

Dik Browne, "Hagar the Horrible", *The Sun*, 9 September 1983, p. 32.

48) The internalized envier may also be a psychic representation of an envious, but dissociated part of the envying person, that is, of himself. Then the envier is a part of himself, turned against himself, and the person is both the envier and the object of his own envy - the envied. These occasions are extremely threatening and tend to evoke the greatest defensive response by the envied person.

49) Debra Weiner, "Under the Gaze of the Evil Eye", *International Herald Tribune*, 17 September 1982, p. 10W.

50) In considering the three categories of responses by the envied person, I am referring to someone who, consciously or unconsciously, is aware of being envied and feels

threatened by this. I would not suggest that an envied person always responds in these ways. There are many instances when someone is aware of being envied, but does not feel threatened and simply ignores it.

51) Discussed by David Ward Tresemer in, *Fear of Success*, Plenum Press, New York, 1977, pp. 66-67.

52) Ibid., p.67.

53) In Mexico Williams wrote, *The Streetcar Named Desire*, Ibid., p. 67.

54) Gifford describes a conversation between the English novelist, Edward Bulwer-Lytton, and an intelligent, well-informed, upper class Italian woman: which well illustrates this point:

"My God, that man," she whispered, tremblingly. "His look fell full upon me. Something dreadful will certainly happen. The last time he looked upon my husband, it was at cards, and he lost half his income at a sitting; his ill-luck was miraculous. The Count met my little boy in the gardens, and the poor child broke his arm that evening. Oh, what shall I do? Something dreadful will certainly happen." Quoted by Edward S. Gifford, Jr., *The Evil Eye: Studies in the Folklore of Vision*, op. cit., p.18.

55) The use of self-inflation to deflate others is a typical envious technique which I will discuss in length in the next chapter. But Mozart also directly denigrated those around him with foul language and scurrilous actions.

56) Edward S. Gifford, Jr., *The Evil Eye: Studies in the Folklore of Vision*, op. cit., p.9.

The press often documents accounts of people who were seemingly damaged by 'the evil eye'. In one instance a West Indian woman suffered from severe depression and herself became a killer after a relationship with a man who took charge of her body and "she was scared not to follow. Scratches on her body she put down to the evil eye." Heather Mills, "Killer was 'influenced by evil eye' ", *The Daily Telegraph*, 25 June 1986, p. 3.

57) Posy Simmonds, "Black Looks", *The Guardian*, 24 January 1983, p. 10.

58) When fifteen year old high jumper Deborah Marti, Britain's youngest prospect for the Los Angeles Olympic games, was questioned about the reaction of school friends to her successes, she replied: "I think they are jealous...I tend to withdraw from them." For her, social isolation was the price of professional success. Doug Ibbotson, "Murray's jumpers have high hopes", *The Daily Telegraph*, 25 April 1984, p. 31.

59) David Ward Tresemer, *Fear of Success*, op. cit., pp. 32-33

Horner is particularly concerned with the psychological barriers to success in women. The data for Horner's study was collected in 1964 and analyzed for her doctoral dissertation in 1968. This material was supplemented by further studies in 1972.

60) Helmut Schoeck, *Envy: A Theory of Social Behaviour*, op. cit. pp. 29-30.

61) The rapacious wish to drain and devour an object may inadvertently spoil it. The net effect of such a greedy attack is the same as a purely envious one. Or, the spoiling may be intrinsic to a combined envious and greedy attack, as with the devouring and defiling which characterizes 'grenvy'.

62) The French-Swiss doctor and depth psychologist, Paul Tournier, has written at length about the fear of envy, an attitude which he calls, 'false guilt feelings'. This seems comparable with what I describe as the state of uncalled for guilt about being envied.

Tournier comments: "A certain sense of guilt is a corollary of any privilege even when the privilege is deserved."

Tournier doesn't explain why this has to be the case. I think it has a lot to do with the cultural context in which the guilty person lives (an envy ridden or envy arousing society) as well as with the tendency of the envied person to identify with the envier. Paul Tournier, *Guilt and Grace*, Hodder & Stoughton, London, 1962, p.14

Quoted by Helmut Schoeck in *Envy: A Theory of Social Behaviour*, op. cit., p.259.

63) This is a widespread, pervasive belief system based on magical ideas of 'grenvy'. It is a feature of many ancient or tribal societies, as well as the early state of mind of the infant. These beliefs have influences modern social and political ideologies both in 'developed' cultures and subcultures and in 'underdeveloped' countries.

64) Ray Connolly, "The Winged Wonder, *Evening Standard*, 6 April 1979, Page 21.

65) John Vinocur, "W. Germans Rethink Status Symbols: Some Even Have No More Stars in Their Eyes", *International Herald Tribune*, 26-27 May 1979, pp 1-2.

According to one physician in Kiel, the only kind of Mercedes that did not embarrass him was 'one that's 10 years old, rusted to the guts and driven by punk rockers or immigrant workers from Turkey."

66) Helmut Schoeck, *Envy: A Theory of Social Behaviour*, op. cit. ,pp. 30-31.

See A.R. Homber, *Nomads of the Long Bow, The Siriono of Eastern Bolivia*, Smithsonian Institution: Institute of Social Anthropology Publication, No. 10, Washington D.C., 1950.

Schoeck comments that Allan Holmberg, the American anthropologist who did the field work, eventually adopted the practice of eating alone. This may have reflected his wish to share their customs, but may also indicate the power of envious intimidation.

No doubt this also explains the widespread conscious and unconscious resistance to census taking in all societies, or the specification of wealth. Typically, Mrs. Seward Johnson, the heiress of the baby powder fortune, refused to have her picture taken at Sotheby's when she spent the highest price ever paid at an auction for a piece of furniture. Mrs. Johnson begged the press: "Please, no photographs. I don't want people to recognize me when I go around. I have many enemies–I think they envy me." Geraldine Norman, "The fine art of marrying well", *The Times*, 28 December 1983, p. 8.

67) The reluctance to be noticed covers all manner of privileges. It is a common practice for boys at Eton, the famous English public school, to hide the fact they they are Etonians in order to avoid public hostility. As one boy put it, "Etonians don't like to admit they're Etonians. You like people to ask. You never offer. If you meet somebody and you sense that you oughtn't to tell them you're at Eton, you just keep quiet." A teacher at the school said he does likewise. "If I'm asked where I teach, I very often say Windsor. It's not that I'm ashamed, but sometimes it overawes people." Graham Turner, "The New Etonians", *The Sunday Telegraph*, 5 July 1981, pp. 8-9.

68) Helmut Schoeck, *Envy: A Theory of Social Behaviour*, op. cit., pp. 88-89.

The pressure to conform arises for several reasons including the rear of envy, the desire to be part of group identity, social responsibility or political reality. Each may reinforce or negate the other. Thus, students at a secondary school may refuse to do well academically both because to do so would not be in keeping with their peer culture and also because it would subject them to the envious hostility of their classmates. The same holds true for workers in a factory or office.

Schoeck notes a study of conformity in Norway and France by Stanley Milgram. Milgram found that there is considerable pressure in both countries to conform to the group norm more so in Norway. This was conveyed by the phrases, "Skal du strikke deg ut?" and 'Voulez-vous vous faire remarquer?" both of which are said critically and roughly mean, "Don't show off!" (Literally, "Are you trying to show off?")

Schoeck concludes, "What, then, is basically feared by the man who, against his better judgement, conforms to the group, is verbal reprisal, a reproach for wanting to be better, more knowledgeable, cunning and observant than the group. In other words, an expression of envy of his particular abilities, his individuality and his self-assurance." Ibid., pp. 80-83.

69) Ostracism was the Athenian practice of temporary banishment from the State. The name of the individual proposed for banishment was scratched on a piece of broken pot, the *ostrakon*. This was a form of voting paper. A majority of 6,000 votes could send a man into exile for ten years.

According to Peter Walcot, non political considerations, trust or mistrust, like or dislike (i.e. irrational and intensely subjective issues) were often paramount. He believes that ostracism was "a piece of democratic machinery almost ideally contrived to cater for widespread envy, since it allows envy to be expressed legitimately and it does not have too devastating a consequence for the victim, just ten years of exile but without, however, the loss of citizenship or property." Peter Walcot, *Envy and the Greeks*, op. cit., p.54.

Viewed in this light, ostracism was both an expression of envy and a defense against it. Now ostracism refers to any expulsion or rejection from a group by general consent.

70) Socrates, Athenian philosopher and teacher, 470? - 399 B.C.E

Walcot points out that Plato (Socrates' student) believed that he was the victim of envy. Plato wrote in the *Apology* that Socrates was confident that his condemnation was the result of the 'slander and envy of the many'. Ibid., p.67.

71) According to a report in the Chinese newspaper, *The People's Daily*, fear of being 'sent to Coventry' is widespread. Many individuals are reluctant to be singled out as 'model workers' for fear of being ridiculed and ostracized by their workmates. The report added that the situation had improved in comparison with previous years when soldiers and workers were scorned as toadies for saving a boy from drowning. Quoted in *The Times*, 17 February, 1982, p.8.

72) Apparently the Coventry Family Practice Committee reprimanded and fined Mr. Summerfield on a technicality. Mr. Clemons, the secretary of the local dental committee said that Summerfield had not done anything illegal. He simply ran a large practice and had seven associates working for him (all of whom earned a higher than average wage): "He was a workaholic and opened his surgery at 8 a.m. working through until 8 p.m. He did not close for holidays and was open six days a week." However,"his work was not considered to be tidy enough and it was the paperwork in his practice which brought this to light and resulted in disciplinary hearings." Mr. Summerfield was fined £5,000. On appeal Dr. Gerald Vaughan, the Minister for Health, reduced the fine to £600.

James O'Brien, "12-Hour day NHS dentist earned £1M in 10 years", *Daily Telegraph*, 17 February 1982, p.17.

73) While describing life at the court of Charles II, Samuel Pepys wrote: "I do find that it is a troublesome thing for a man of any condition at the Court to carry himself even, and without contracting envy or envyers; and that much discretion and dissimulation is necessary to do it." Samuel Pepys, *The Diary of Samuel Pepys*, Vol. 1., Everyman's Library, J. N. Dent & Son, Ltd., London, 1927, p. 360.

74) George M. Foster, "The Anatomy of Envy: A Study in Symbolic Behavior", op. cit., p.172.

The *Talmud* is the major collection of writings which constitute the Jewish civil and religious law.

Certain ecologists often give similar admonitions about the extravagant use of natural resources. Amory Lovins, of Friends of the Earth put it this way: "If you ask me, it'd be a little short of disastrous for us to discover a source of clean, cheap abundant energy because of what we would do with it. We ought to be looking for energy sources that are adequate for our needs, but that won't give us the excesses of concentrated energy with which we could do mischief to the earth or to each other." Quoted in an article by Bertram Wolfe, "The Perfect Energy Resource? A Hopeless Search", *International Herald Tribune*, 9 February 1982, p.4.

Behind this admonition there lurks a general distrust of any society with abundant energy supplies, whether oil, or drive and ambition. Lovins seems to be worried about greed, as well as envy. Why assume abundance inevitably leads to 'mischief'? Warnings like this may also serve as an expression of envy, as well as a defense against it.

75) George Foster emphasizes the defensive nature of modesty. He points out that in small town America, families that are significantly wealthier than others often manifest a standard of living (home, dress, activities) that is greatly below what they could afford. But if the same families move to a big city, where they are not constantly exposed to the eyes of their neighbors, they tend to be much less inhibited about their life style. George M. Foster, "The Anatomy of Envy: A Study in Symbolic Behavior", op.cit., p.177.

76) Editorial, quoted in the International Herald Tribune, 22 February 1982, p.4.

77) There exists a world over-supply of false bad news. This has been amply documented by Julian Simon, Professor of Economics and Business Administration at the University of Illinois, Urbana. In an article on the subject he documents the conclusion that: "Bad news about population growth, natural resources and the environment that is based on flimsy evidence or no evidence at all is published widely in the face of contradictory evidence." Julian L. Simon, *"Resources, Population, Environment: An Oversupply of False Bad News,"* Science, Vol. 208, 27 June 1980, pp. 1431-1432.

78) Envy does not just preoccupy English public school boys and their teachers. Dr. John Rae, the former Headmaster of Westminster School, and former Chairman of the Headmasters Conference, has described the difficulties he faced in becoming a public figure.

"So deeply engrained is the English public school taboo against pushing oneself forward and in favour of calculating self-effacement, that the headmaster whose name becomes too familiar is regarded as something of a cad ("brazen" was the adjective one elder statesman of the Headmasters Conference used to describe me)." John Rae, "Success", *Punch*, 11 March 1981, p.383.

79) Edmund Leach, "Envy and the English Sickness", *The Listener*, 26 March 1970, p.409.

Similarly, a calculated self-effacement has long been observed in the Chinese character. It includes self-deprecation, excessive humility and great modesty (at least in front of strangers). As Helmut Schoeck points out, this was all part of a carefully institutionalized attitude to envy. Helmut Schoeck, *Envy: A Theory of Social Behaviour*, op. cit., pp. 54-55.

80) Francis Bacon, "Of Envy" in *The Essays or Counsels, Civil and Moral*, op. cit., p.59.

Bacon believed that 'pity' was particularly useful for politicians. He advised them to arouse pity, if not by asceticism, then by continually lamenting their toilsome existence, and would have agreed with the *Washington Post's* assessment of "humble-origins chic."

81) This person envied my life in all its aspects. He deliberately used his open wounds to make himself pitiable, not to gain help, or disarm my envy of him, but to actively and

maliciously attack me, by arousing pain and discomfort inside me, especially through pity. All this was really a part of a life-long project. While his cancer, and the effects of it, were terrible blows, they also served as welcome additions to a devastating emotional armamentarium.

82) Just as European peoples continue to exclaim, "Knock on wood," or wear silver or gold crucifixes or stars of David to stave off misfortune, contemporary Moslems say, "May God protect us from the Evil Eye when it envies," and wear a turquoise stone or bead representing the eye of Horus (Middle East) or a bronze replica of the hand of Fatima (North Africa) around their necks.

In poor neighborhoods of Cairo many families still make red handprints with sheep blood above the door of their homes to keep away the Evil Eye. Debra Weiner, "Under the Gaze of the Evil Eye", op. cit., p. 10W.

In modern Italy even the horses and cattle get blue beads to wear around their necks. R. W. Apple, "Apulia", *International Herald Tribune*, 26 July 1985, p. 8.

Similarly, in a modern Mother and Baby unit for religious Jews in North London, every cot contains a piece of laminated paper with a pictiure of an open hand and Hebrew charms against the evil eye. Shamash, op. cit., p. 19

83) "Thou man, son of his god,

The Eye which hath looked upon thee for harm,

The Eye which hath looked upon thee for evil ...

May Ba'u smite it with flax

May Gunura smite it with a great oar,

Like rain which is let fall from heaven,

Directed unto earth

So may Ea, king of the Deep, remove it from thy body."

Edward S. Gifford, Jr., *The Evil Eye: Studies in the Folklore of Vision,* op. cit., p.54

84) The abbreviated form of the eye of Horus appears on medical prescription as 'Rx'. This is taken to mean, recipe, but also refers to a benevolent eye watching over the compounding of medicaments. Ibid., p.67.

85) Ibid., p.68. The divine eye did not just serve as protection against the evil eye. It also was said to have direct beneficent powers, as did many amulets and talismans. Hence they often served a dual purpose, to ward off bad luck ('the evil eye', envy), and to bring good luck. Ibid., pp. 67-68.

86) *Fascinum* meant both fascination by the evil eye, and the counter charm. Eventually it came to mean phallus because the phallus was the most common countercharm. Gifford points out that the original double significance of the word has persisted. "Dunglison's medical dictionary of 1874 defines *fascinum* as the penis, while the Gould medical dictionary of 1874 defines the same word as the belief in the evil eye." Ibid., p.71.

87) St. Augustine related and was horrified by the rural custom of combating the evil eye by placing a huge carved phallus in a wagon which was drawn through the grain fields and the town during the spring festival of the fertility god. Ibid., p.71.

88) The Greeks and Romans also used to divert the evil eye by making amulets that embodied envy, or the envious 'eye' itself, which were then attacked in terrible ways. Walcot describes one such agate amulet: "Obv. Naked man standing in front, head turned

to left, hands crossed on chest. A large snake coils round his whole body, its head striking at the back of the man's head. The man is assailed by various creatures; a bird pecks at his eyes, a scorpion attacks the crown of his head, another has his phallus, a third his left knee, while a centipede fastens its pincers into each elbow. The tortured figure personifies Envy, and the stone is an amulet to protect against the evil eye." Peter Walcot, *Envy and the Greeks*, op. cit., p.85.

89) Horns may be more proper than phalli, but they are pagan in origin and have a long history. The horns of a cow have been particularly favored.

The horseshoe, a common talisman on the outside of a house or barn, was nailed with its prongs pointing upwards (like horns) so that the good luck wouldn't run out. Simultaneously it served as a defense against evil eye.

90) Edward S. Gifford, Jr., *The Evil Eye: Studies in the Folklore of Vision*, op. cit., p.73

Other peoples invoke the names of Gods or other powers for the same reason, or simple words asking for protection have taken on a magical significance. Thus Jewish people say: "Kayn ayn horeh" when something good happens or is desired. This means, "Let not the evil eye behold it."

91) Ibid., p.90.

The hand has always figured prominently in gestures and amulets concerning the evil eye. It symbolizes the power of the Gods, or God. Hand amulets can be found in Etruscan tombs and continue to be widely worn in the Maghreb, and by oriental Jews. This hand pendent is called a hasa and is associated with the Kabbala.

92) Saliva is the favored body product in averting the evil eye, but urine and the milk of a prostitute have also been considered highly effective. Ibid., pp. 62-66.

Spitting three times in a time honored gesture and was mentioned frequently in Greek and Roman writings. It is part of the customs of many peoples. Recently on a trip to the United States I discussed measures to avert the evil eye with my uncle, Sam Auspitz. In his youth in Hungary he clearly recalls the custom of spitting three times in front of a stranger, or spitting on one's finger and touching the centre of the forehead three times, or of pulling one's ear three times.

93) Ibid., p.62.

94) George M. Foster, "The Anatomy of Envy: A Study in Symbolic Behavior", op. cit., p.177

Inciting pride and arrogance may also be an expression of envy. When Agamemnon returned from Troy, Clytemnestra sought revenge for the death of Iphigenia. She also sought to protect herself from Agamemnon's jealousy (because of her relationship with Aegisthus) and envy (for her rule). Moreover she herself was envious of his success and jealous of his relationship with Cassandra. She chose to greet her husband with a fulsome praise and concomitant advice not to fear envy: "Who feareth envy, feareth to be great."

Clytemnestra hoped to destroy him by arousing the *Envy of the Gods (Phthonos Theon)*. Agamemnon was rightly wary. Her advice was good, but in the context of his homecoming, it was venomous.

Aeschylus, *The Agamemnon*, Translated by Gilbert Murray, George Allen & Unwin Ltd., London, 1925, verse 939, p.40.

95) Irenaus Eibl - Eibesfeldt, *Love and Hate*, tr. G. Stachan, Methuen, London, pp. 185-186.

Professor Eibesfeldt is an ethologist in the tradition of Konrad Lorenz. He comments that the successful hunter feels honored when his elders urinate on him. I wonder whether this isn't an example of the reversal and denial of the process of self-abasement.

96) Foster points out that a sop may be psychologically discomforting. This is "indicated by the frequency with which it takes the form of a humorous 'booby prize'. As in other sensitive situations, humor is called in to gloss over what might otherwise be a more painful experience."

George M. Foster, "The Anatomy of Envy: A Study in Symbolic Behaviour", op. cit., p.177.

97) The distress and anger evinced by a child who does not receive a favor is also a response to a disappointed expectation, not just envy. But the point remains why is this practice so widespread, if ostensibly unnecessary. I have observed my own children become extremely anxious if they did not have the right number, variety and quality of favors to give to their guests after a party. Their anxiety indicated a latent fear of envy, an echo of their own experience when (rarely) they came home empty handed after attending parties of their friends.

98) The ritual giving of presents to visitors who admire your possessions, or to family and friends after a long trip or holiday, the tip to a person who brings good news, the throwing of the bridal bouquet, the small prizes awarded to the losers of competitions, the postcard with, *"Having a wonderful time, wish you were here."* are further examples of sop behavior. The greeting can serve as an expression of a desire to share, and is disarming. After all, if a holidaymaker or traveller takes the trouble to wish you were with him, you are less likely to wish him ill. Similarly if someone gives you what you admire, or a token present that symbolizes what you admire, you are less likely to wish to do him harm. This practice is universal.

99) "It is the jealousy of the dead that that the living fear most, and they try to propitiate them with everything they need for their journey to the land of the dead, so that they may go far off and never return to harm and torment the living. The spirits of the dead send disease, or bring it with them; they have power over the increase of game and crops, and a hundred ways of meddling with life. Passionately and continually they seek to get hold of the living." Elias Canetti, *Crowds and Power*, op. cit., p. 262.

100) George M. Foster, "The Anatomy of Envy: A Study in Symbolic Behaviour", op. cit., p. 179.

101) Charitable customs in many countries convey a mixture of gratitude, fear and hatred. Foster suggests that "the Boxing Day custom of giving presents to servants and tradesmen on the day after Christmas is certainly sop behaviour, symbolic sharing of the good fortune of the privileged classes." Ibid., p.179.

Innumerable examples could be cited where charitable acts are done grudgingly and with a primary wish to buy off the hatred of the sick, poor, or unfortunate.

102) Handelsman "The Story of the Envious Man and of him that was envied", *Punch*, 5 March 1980, p.368. Reproduced by permission.

CHAPTER 2

1) Yuri Olesha, *Envy,* Anchor Books, Doubleday & Co, Garden City, N. Y., 1967.

2) Ibid., pp. 78-79.

3) William Shakespeare, *The Tragedy of Othello*, Pocket Books, New York, 1957.

4) "O, you are well tuned now!

But I'll set down the pegs that make this music,

As honest as I am" Ibid., Act 2 Sc 1, Lines 231-34.

5) Ibid., Act 2 Sc 1, Line 340.

6) Othello declares:

"O, now for ever

Farewell the tranquil mind! farewell content!"

Ibid., Act 3 Sc 3, Lines 392-3.

7) Ibid., Act 2 Sc 3, Lines 358-64

8) "Make the Moor thank me, love me, reward me

For making him egregiously an ass

And practising upon his peace and quiet

Even to madness." Ibid., Act 2 Sc 1, Lines 336-39.

9) Peter Shaffer, *Amadeus*, Andre Deutsch, London, 1980. *Amadeus* was the first produced at the National Theatre in London in 1979. My discussion of the relationship between Salieri and Mozart is based on Shaffer's fictionalized dramatization of their biographies. Unless otherwise indicated my quotations are from the first edition of the play by Andre Deutsch.

Salieri's envious hatred of Mozart had been previously portrayed by the Russian writer, Alexander Pushkin, in *Mozart and Salieri*, completed in 1830. Alexander Pushkin. *Mozart and Salieri: The Little Tragedies*, trans. by Anthony Wood, Angel, Books, London, 1982. This work was later the basis for an opera by Rimsky-Korsakov.

Some biographers dispute the story of Mozart's poverty, loss of status and alleged poisoning by Salieri. See: Francis Carr, *Mozart and Constanze*, Franklin Watts, New York, 1986. Another theory is that Mozart was poisoned by the Freemasons because he revealed their secret ceremonies and signs. Richard Morrison, "Who Killed Mozart?" *The Sunday Times Magazine*, 29 July 1990, p52.

10) The historical Salieri was a more prolific composer and powerful person than Shaffer indicates. He composed about 40 operas over a period of 35 years and his pupils included Beethoven and Schubert. David Stevens, "For Salieri, Signs of a Revival", *International Herald Tribune*, 15 April 1987, pp. 1 & 8.

11) Envy usually operates in secrecy because it is such a fearful and shameful passion, and is all the more effective for not being recognized for what it is. Herman Melville discusses this in novel, *Billy Budd*, when he comments on the malice directed towards Budd, a sailor, by John Cleggart, his master-at-arms: ".... did ever anybody seriously confess to envy? Something there is in it universally felt to be more shameful than even felonious crime. And not only does everybody disown it but the better sort are inclined to incredulity when it is in earnest imputed to an intelligent man. But since its lodgement is in the heart not the brain, no degree of intellect supplies a guarantee against it. *The Portable Melville*, ed. J. Leyda, New York, 1952, p. 677.

12) Fate also intervened on behalf of Iago to help him 'prove' Desdemona's infidelity to Othello. Desdemona accidentally dropped the special handkerchief that Othello had given to her. It was found by Emilia, Iago's wife, who innocently gave it to Iago. He then dropped it where Othello's adjunct, Cassio, could find it and eventually incriminate himself.

13) One of Mozart's biographers comments on the hornet's nest of feelings that Emperor Joseph stirred up by commissioning an opera in German. The following quote is taken from the programme to the production of *Amadeus* at Her Majesty's Theatre, London 1981:

"Joseph II formed the plan .... of alienating taste from Italian operas by supporting German Singspiele and singers .... He accordingly assembled the best singers and commissioned a German opera from Mozart. For these virtuosi he wrote the well-known and well-loved Singspiele, *The Flight from the Seraglio* in 1782. It created a widespread sensation; and the cunning Italians soon saw that such a mind could endanger their foreign tinklings. Envy now awoke with all the sharpness of Italian poison!"

Franz Xaver Niemtschek, *Mozart*, 1808.

14) Many references confirm Salieri's malevolence :

"Salieri was Chapelmaster to the Court, a clever shrewd man, possessed of what Bacon called crooked wisdom; he was backed by .... a cabal not easily put down." Michael Kelly, *Reminiscences*, 1826.

"An intriguer .... There can be no question of Salieri's malevolent interference with the success of his Austrian colleagues. His fine musicianship told him to concentrate his malice on Mozart, whose lamentable fate was due in no small degree to the Italian's machinations." P. H. Lang, *Music in Western Civilization*, 1941.

Quotes from *Amadeus*, programme guide, op. cit.

15) Peter Shaffer, *Amadeus*, op. cit, pp. 94-95.

16) The realization that envy is stimulated by comparisons with others which leave the envious person feeling inferior and worthless was noted by the philosopher, Francis Bacon, in his essay, *On Envy*, in 1612.

"... envy is ever joined with the comparing of a man's self: and whence there is no comparison, no envy; and therefore kings are not envied but by kings." F. Bacon, *The Essays of Counsels, Civil and Moral*, ed. S. H. Reynolds, The Clarendon Press, Oxford 1890, p. 58.

17) Yuri Olesha, *Envy*, op. cit. p. 79.

18) William Shakespeare, *The Tragedy of Othello*, Act 3 Sc 3, Lines 500-502 & 505.

Of course, it was an envious frenzy too. It is in the nature of envy to arouse jealousy, as well as envy, in another.

19) John Milton vividly depicted the nature of envious revenge in the person of Satan in *Paradise Lost:*

"Who first seduced them to that foul revolt?

Th'infernal serpeant! He it was, whose guile,

Stirred up with envy and revenge, deceived

The mother of mankind ....'

Satan – so call him now.".

John Milton, *Paradise Lost*, Book IX, quoted by Helmut Schoeck, *Envy, A Theory of Social Behaviour*, Harcourt, Brace & World, Inc., New York, 1966, pp. 156-157.

20) Peter Shaffer, *Amadeus*, op. cit., p. 67.

21) *The Times*, London, 19 August 1981, p. 4.

22) William Shakespeare, *The Tragedy of Othello*, Act 3 Sc 3, Lines 182 & 184-186.

A begrudging envy sustains both racism and vandalism:

In Norwich, England, a young man who received a ten year jail sentence for fire bombing the home of a Chinese family commented: "I do not like the Chinese because they have more money and cars than anyone else." Quoted in "Ten years for Race Attack", *The Times*, 9 January 1982, p. 3.

In the wealthy Kensington area of London, during one night alone, a tire-slasher did £10,000 of damage to Porsches and Jaguars, completely ignoring the tires of cheaper cars. A police spokesman commented: "It would appear that he has some kind of grudge against rich people. We think this is going to continue in the future if he is not caught." Quoted in "£10,000 grudge", *The Standard*, London, 1 February 1985, p. 9. And in April 1983, anarchist stickers which flooded the prosperous Camden Town area of London proclaimed: "Filthy Rich Bastards. Go Drown in your Jacuzzis."

Similarly, Moslem clerics have attacked a fellow Moslem for winning £18 million on the lottery quoting the Koran that such winnings are, "abominations and Satanic devices." Frank Corless and Patrick Mulchrone. "Moslem's jackpot angers Mosque leaders." *Daily Mirror*, 14 December 1994, pp.1 & 5.

23) Aristides, " A Few Kind Words for Envy," *American Scholar*, Autumn 1989, p. 495.

24) Heather Mills, "Banker 'killed because he looked rich'", *The Daily Telegraph*, 7 January 1986, p. 3; and Heather Mills, "Life for man who killed rich stranger", *The Daily Telegraph*, 14 January 1986, p. 3.

25) The motivation of the thief or arsonist are complex and not solely, nor necessarily to do with greedy or envy. In the case of the thief, revenge, a way of life, deprivation and other factors contribute, although one is ultimately left with the question, "Why steal?".

In the case of the arsonist even more complicated psychological issues may be at work. Envy itself has been described as a fiery burning consuming, corroding feeling. The envy motivated arsonist, as I described, wished to destroy the object of his envy, the house, and to externalize and thereby locate, his consuming destructiveness elsewhere. Therein lay his satisfaction.

26) *Time*, 3 November 1952.

27) Dr. Helmut Schoeck points out that the 'envy-oriented politician' is someone who ".... begrudges others their personal or material assets, being as a rule almost more intent on their destruction than on their acquisition." Helmut Schoeck, *Envy, A Theory of Social Behaviour*, op. cit., p. 19.

Dr. Schoeck also quotes the American journalist, H.L. Mencken, on the politics of envy: "Puritanism is represented as a lofty sort of obedience to God's law. Democracy is depicted as brotherhood, even as altruism. All such notions are in error. There is only one honest impulse at the bottom of Puritanism, and that is the impulse to punish the man with a superior capacity for happiness - to bring him down to the miserable level of 'good' men, i.e. stupid, cowardly and chronically unhappy men. And there is only one sound argument for democracy, and this is the argument that it is a crime for any man to hold himself out as better than other men, and, above all, a most heinous crime for him to prove it ..." Ibid., p.193-194, taken from: *The Vintage Mencken*, ed. Alistair Cooke, New York, 1956, pp. 75-77.

28) The novelist, Oliver Knox, who joined the British (Tory) Centre for Policy Studies in 1984, succinctly explained his political philosophy: "Tory greed over Socialist envy." "Hitting the road", *The Times*, 29 August 1984, p. 8.

29) Betty Joseph points out that intense grenvious impulses essentially characterize the personality of non-criminal 'psychopathic' people. In referring to one young man in particular she commented: ".......he approaches his objects with an attitude of extreme greed and stealing (which)......lead immediately to feelings of intense envy of the object's capacity to satisfy him." Betty Joseph, "Some Characteristics of the Psychopathic Personality", *Int. J. Psycho-Anal.*, Vol. 41, 1960, pp. 526-531.

30) Newspapers provide abundant evidence of this sort of crime. A typical article describes how thieves broke into an expensive house and did extensive damage by slashing the wallpaper, painting and furniture with knives and by pouring paint and paint stripper over clothing, carpets, chairs and the hi-fi. "House Wrecked", *The Daily Telegraph*, 25 April 1984, p. 14.

31) "Envy can fuse with greed, making for a wish to exhaust the object entirely, not only in order to possess all its goodness but also to deplete the object purposefully so that it no longer contains anything enviable." Hanna Segal, *Introduction to the Work of Melanie Klein*, The Hogarth Press, London, 1975, p. 41.

32) People who harbor envious grievances can often point to some basis in fact to justify their obsession. But if you explore matters a bit further you usually find that they are quite selective in their perception, minimizing what they have, and exaggerating what others have. In other words, their grievances are basically irrational are rooted in ingratitude which their frustrated greed served to mask.

See discussion on greed and delusional hatred by Joan Riviere in her essay, "Hate, Greed and Aggression" in *Love, Hate & Reparation* by Melanie Klein and Joan Riviere, The Hogarth Press, London, 1967, pp 26-30.

33) Jilly Cooper in "Jilly Cooper vs the Green Eyed Monster", *The Sunday Times*, 25 April 1971, p. 36.

34) The bilateral orientation of envy and greed does not expect or want any reciprocity. For the envious or greedy person, reciprocity is retribution

35) Robert Bringle's research about the predisposition to jealousy indicates that it is strongest in persons who "self-deprecating and dogmatic and who view themselves as unhappy, anxious and externally controlled." Quoted from: Gordon Clanton, "Frontiers of Jealousy Research", *Alternative Lifestyles*, Vol. 4, No. 3, August 1981, p. 263.

36) The girl recalled: "I felt it burning. I felt I was on fire....(Now) I suffer discomfort and pain almost all the time and due to the injuries on my chest I will not be able to breast-feed my baby which was something I would have liked to have done." (The girl had subsequently become pregnant by another man.) Paul Stokes, "Acid attack 'disfigured girl for life' ", *The Daily Telegraph*, 21 October 1986, p. 3.

37) Peter Walcot, *Envy and the Greeks*, Aris & Phillips Ltd. Warminster, England, 1978, p. 2.

38) Ibid., p. 69

39) Ibid., P. 3

40) Until 1981 article 587 of the Italian penal code allowed betrayed wives and cuckolded husbands to literally get away with murder. This law, now amended, prescribed a greatly reduced penalty for crimes of passion. Sometimes the honor-killers' could walk out of the courtroom freely - amid the rapturous applause of the spectators. Report by Leslie Child, "Italians lose their license to kill'", *The Sunday Telegraph*, 26 July 1981 p. 2.

Gordon Clanton points out that jealousy can go in and out of fashion."Prior to about 1966 most people (in the United States) viewed jealousy as a natural evidence of love and as good for marriage. Beginning in the late 1960's, many people have come to see jealousy as evidence of a defect in the personality of the jealous person (such as low self-esteem) and as bad for relationships." Gordon Clanton, "Frontiers of Jealousy Research", op. cit., p. 264. Similarly, John Leo, writing in *Time* magazine in the mid 1980's, discusses the evolution of various fashions and theories of jealousy: In the 1950's jealousy was treated as a healthy expression of sexual love. In the 1960's jealousy was seen as a pathological obstacle to sexual freedom. By 1980 he claims three views have vied for attention: 1) Sociobiological - Jealousy is evolutionary and adaptive. The person who chases of a rival enhances his chance of getting his genes into the next generation; 2) Sexual Revolutionary - Jealousy is a hang-up, a lamentable hangover from days when men claimed proprietary rights over women; and 3) Feminist - Male jealousy is part of the structure of patriarchy, i.e. control and domination, which keeps women in line. John Leo, "Battling the Green-Eyed Monster", *Time*, 25 November 1985, p. 39.

41) William Collins and World Publishing Co., Inc, New York, 1974, p. 755.

42) Cooper, op. cit. p.36.

43) The journalist, Irma Kurtz, has correctly itemized envious attacks on female qualities. Once, in the 1960's she found herself at a party next to an "aging lady of fashion" when a pretty young girl strode into the room. Kurtz observed the immediate eruption of outrage from the older woman who hissed: "Do you see those eyelashes? I'd kill for those eyelashes." Irma Kurtz, "Envy", *The Sunday Times Magazine*, 22 February 1987, p. 42.

Kurtz also takes care to distinguish between envy and jealousy. As she puts it, "Jealousy fights duels. Envy poisons the soup." Ibid., p. 42.

44) William Shakespeare, op. cit., Act 3 Sc 3, Lines 191-3.

45) Sigmund Freud, "Some Neurotic Mechanisms in Jealousy, Paranoia and Homosexuality" in *Standard Edition of the Complete Psychological Works of Freud,* ed. J. Strachey, Hogarth Press, London, 1968, Vol. 18, pp. 221-232.

46) The psychoanalyst, Joan Riviere provides a thorough discussion of morbid jealousy in her paper, "Jealousy as a Mechanism of Defense", *Int. J. Psycho-Anal.*, Vol 13, 1932, pp. 414-424.

47) Joan Riviere thinks that Othello wished to blacken Desdemona's name by accusations of infidelity and in that way overcome his own sense of guilt for abducting her.

"It is the cause, it is the cause, my soul' - the old tradition has it that with these words the actor spoke to his own image in a mirror, which he contrasts in the next breath with Desdemona's "whiter skin". Does not Othello's blackness, also seemingly irrelevant, sum up in one symbol the whole story of his guilt, doubt, anxiety and his mode of defense against them? Iago the envious is but his alter ego. He cannot endure the evil in himself. He must make Desdemona black instead". Ibid., p. 424.

48) The writer Philip Howard has cited the phrase, "I don't envy anyone with money these days." as an example of a 'reversible', a word or phrase that mean the opposite of what they say. *The Times*, 14 July 1980.

49) I refer to an advertisement about the exclusive New York hotel, the Waldorf Astoria:".... if you've never been a Waldorf guest, you could unthinkingly, believe it to be expensive ... The admiration (if not envy) of the folks back home is included in the room rate." *The New York Times*, 7 December 1961, p. 29.

50) Helmut Schoeck points out that the sociologist W. G. Runciman demands ''uninhibited reference group choice' in regard to all inequalities in order to maximize social justice. Schoeck, *Envy: A Theory of Social Behavior*, op. cit., p. 209.

51) *The Sunday Times*, 11 September 1977.

52) Sometimes envy is mistaken for the context in which it occurs: 'social proximity', or 'invidious proximity', a term employed by the American historian, David M. Potter in *People of Plenty: Economic Abundance and the American Character*, Chicago, 1954, pp 102.

53) The philosopher Immanuel Kant, pointed out in his late work, *The Metaphysics of Morals*, that envy denies intrinsic worth, even if it is there:

"Envy .... is a disinclination to see our own good overshadowed by the good of others, because we take its measure not from its intrinsic worth, but by comparison with the good of others and then go on to symbolize evaluation."

Immanuel Kant, *Metaphysik der Sitten*, in Sämtliche Werke, ed. K. Vorlander, Vol 3, 4th Edition, Leipzig, 1922, p. 316. Translation by H. Schoeck.

The advertisement seeks to arouse this experience by implying that old equipment, old working conditions, and old methods are no good in comparison to what Vickers has to offer. This overlooks the intrinsic worth of previous work and conditions.

54) Quoted by Schoeck, op. cit. p. 209. See W.G. Runciman, *Relative Deprivation and Social Justice: A Study of Attitudes to Social Inequality in Twentieth Century England*, Routledge & Kegan Paul, London, 1966.

55) Similar feelings might well be aroused by an advert for Charnos black lingerie in the Christmas 1986 issue of *Harrods Magazine*. Entitled, "Envy. One of the Seven Deadly Sins", it shows a beautiful model clothed in Charnos lingerie lying on green silk sheets. Here "Envy" is used synonymously with intensity and desire, i.e., the ad arouses intense desire and also indicates that anyone who wore Charnos would be highly desirable, like the model. But the green background gives a hint that other emotions might also be involved, in this instance, that such intense desires might conceal or give rise to equally intense hatreds, as Irma Kurtz's aging ladies of fashion might feel. *Harrods Magazine*, London, Christmas 1986, pp. 94-95.

56) Resentment, indignation and frustration can all arouse envy because the actual injustice or deprivation reverberates with imagined hurts, especially with someone 'who has a chip on his shoulder'. Then the person may misperceive outer events as inner events and react with enhanced fear and rage.

Actual deprivation and frustration can kindle and rekindle feelins of weakness and inferiority, especially in people with low self-esteem. This can lead to ill-will and rage, far out of proportion to the precipitating event. For all these reasons resentment, indignation and deprivation are associated, but not identical with envy.

57) Bertrand Russell, clearly distinguished between envy and admiration in his book, *The Conquest of Happiness*. He pointed out that of all the characteristics of human nature, envy is the most unfortunate because the envious person does not only "wish to inflict misfortune and (will) do so whenever he can with impunity, but he is also rendered unhappy by envy ... Fortunately, however, there is in human nature a compensating passion, namely that of admiration. Whoever wishes to increase human happiness must wish to increase admiration and decrease envy." *The Conquest of Happiness*, Unwin Paperbacks, London 1978, p. 66.

58) Søren Kierkegaard (1813-1855), Danish philosopher and theologian.

59) Emulation is often equated with envy. The two phenomena are quite distinct, and generally opposite in content. To emulate is to wish to be like someone, to identify with them out of admiration. Emulation is not spiteful, self-seeking, begrudging or malicious, as is envy. Emulation does not seek to hurt the rival, just equal or surpass. However, when emulation is thwarted, then the rivalry may become malicious.

60) The Fisons Company placed a similar envy arousing advertisement entitled "Make Your Neighbour Green with Envy" in the London *Daily Telegraph Magazine*, 20 May 1979. It shows a view of the garden of two adjacent houses. The house on the left is freshly painted and has a brilliant green lawn. The house on the right is dull and has a lawn that is yellow and half dead. The owner of this house can be seen looking over the fence at his neighbor's lush attractive lawn accomplished by the use of Fisons products. The ad calls for the man to emulate his neighbor and use Fisons products in order to get a better lawn. Yet, the ad literally suggests that anyone who uses Fisons products opens himself to envious destructive attacks by his neighbors with the result that his lush green lawn would soon become yellow and sick!

61) Elkan Allan, "Best loot guide?', *The Times*, 25 July 1981, p. 8.

62) Jean Cuisenier points out that in Catholic countries there is an abundant iconography of envy, one of the seven deadly sins. In the *Miroir de vie et de Mort*, a miniature shows a large tree with seven roots, each taking the shape of a snake, and ending in the figure of a woman. The sixth, *radix invidiae*, carries a beast in her breast. Cuisenier comments, "We recognize here the tree of evil of the 12th century theologians, where vices are at the roots and the roots are at the same time the seven heads of the Apocalypse's dragon".

From discussion to paper by George M. Foster, "The Anatomy of Envy: A Study in Symbolic Behaviour", *Current Anthropology*, Vol. 13, No. 2, April 1972, p. 189.

The car sticker is mentioned in: David Ward Tresemer, *Fear of Success*, Plenum Press, New York, 1977, p. 21.

CHAPTER 3

1) Immanuel Kant, *Metaphysik der Sitten*, op. cit., p.36.

Quoted by Helmut Schoeck, *Envy: A Theory of Social Behaviour,* op. cit., p.166.

2) "Hate, as a relation to objects, is older than love. It derives from the narcissistic ego's primordial repudiation of the external world with its out-pouring of stimuli".

Sigmund Freud, "Instincts and their Vicissitudes", *S.E.*, Vol.14, Hogarth Press, London, 1957, p.139

3) "Introjection and projection are first experienced purely in terms of phantasy (mental representation of an instinct) and are specifically concerned with pleasure and pain, gratification and frustration, good and bad. As the child grows older, images and imagos become the foci of introjection and projection aside from sensations, instinctual desires and emotions."

Joseph Berke, "Primitive Mental Mechanisms: A Study of Introjection, Projection and Identification", 1982, unpublished paper, pp. 1-2.

4) Freud explicitly discussed the issue of a death instinct in a number of papers including, "Beyond the Pleasure Principle", *S.E.* Vol. 18, 1920; "The Economic Problem of Masochism", *S.E.* Vol. 19, 1924; and "Analysis Terminable and Interminable". *S.E.* Vol. 23, 1937.

5) Melanie Klein, "Envy and Gratitude" in *Envy and Gratitude and Other Works 1946-1963,* The Hogarth Press, London, 1975. This work was originally published as a separate volume, *Envy and Gratitude: A Study of Unconscious Sources*, Tavistock Publications Ltd., London, 1957.

6) Entropy is the degree of randomness in a system. The struggle between life and death forces can be seen in terms of the increase or decrease of entropy in a human

system. Order, integration, and an upward energy flow is akin to a negative entropic reaction (order increases). Disorder, fragmentation and a downward spiral of energy is akin to a positive entropic reaction (order decreases). Recent work in physics indicates that randomness or chaos is a fundamental property of the universe, and therefore, of human life too. Paul Davies, *The Cosmic Blueprint*, Heinemann, London, 1987.

7) Bruno Bettelheim argues that 'instinct' is an erroneous translation of *trieb,* the term Freud used. 'Impulse' is much closer to the meaning of the concept. Bettelheim further points out that if Freud had meant 'instinct', he would have used the specific word, *instinkt.*

Bruno Bettelheim, *Freud and Man's Soul,* Chatto & Windus, London, 1983, pp. 103-106.

8) This may explain Melanie Klein's view that the 'death instinct' is partially projected and partially converted into aggression and directed against persecutors (anything felt to be threatening).

9) Walter G. Joffe, "A Critical Review of the Status of the Envy Concept", *Int. J. Psycho-Anal.,* Vol. 50, No. 4, 1969, p. 537.

10) Ibid., p.544.

11) Sigmund Freud, "Instincts and their Vicissitudes", op. cit., p.138.

12) Charles Brenner, "The Psychoanalytic Concept of Aggression", *Int. J. Psycho-Anal.,* Vol. 52, No. 2, 1971, p.138.

While stating that aggression does not have a somatic source, Brenner did conclude that psychological evidence alone is acceptable evidence to support 'the concept of aggression as an instinctual drive'.

Ibid., p.143.

13) In "Beyond the Pleasure Principle" Freud clearly indicated that he believed the 'death instinct' involved the whole organism. See especially pages 49 & 50. In this respect Freud's view was different from that of Melanie Klein who believed that the 'death instinct' referred to the ego.

14) The infant researcher, Louis W. Sander, has a home movie which shows an eight day old baby who clearly prefers father to mother. "What delights Sander is the sensibility of the infant, a quality not generally associated with newborns. In light of a host of similar observations, partly made possible by the innovative use of videotape, scientists are revising a long-held belief that newborns are passive creatures waiting for the world to imprint its wisdom on them. From at least the moment of birth, infants are enormously responsive." Richard M, Restak, "Newborn Knowledge", *Science/82,* Vol. 3, No. 1, 1982, pp. 59-60.

See also: Bruno Bettelheim, "The World of the Newborn" in *The Empty Fortress: Infantile Autism and the Birth of the Self,* The Free Press, Macmillan Publishing Co, New York, 1967, pp 14-21, and Rudolph Schaffer, *Mothering,* Fontana/Open Books, London, 1977.

15) "As an example of the fight for rank among animals, the farmyard pecking order has recently been much discussed. The rankling impulse in envy would appear to be an analogy on the one hand with the merciless and irrevocable classification of an individual in the precise rank ascribed to it within such an animal society, on the other hand with the possibility every animal has of moving up to a higher rank by engaging in a fight for it." Edward Baumgarten, *"Versuch über mogliche Fortschritte im theoretischen und praktischen Umgang mit Macht",* Studium Generale, 4th year, 1951, pp. 540-58.

16) Adrian Berry, "Animal skinheads", *The Daily Telegraph,* 3 October 1983, p. 14.

17) Aeschylus, *Agamemnon*, translated by Gilbert Murray, George Allen & Unwin, Ltd., London, 1925, verses 832-837, p.35.

18) Milan Kundera, *The Book of Laughter and Forgetting*, trans. H. Heim, King Penguin, Penguin Books, London, 1985, pp. 119-154.

19) Ibid., p. 121.

20) Ibid., p. 123.

21) "The pleasure principle seems actually to serve the death instincts." Sigmund Freud, "Beyond the Pleasure Principle", op. cit. p.63.

22) "Aggression and libido bear similar relations to the pleasure principle. In general, discharge is associated with pleasure; lack of discharge, with unpleasure."

Charles Brenner, "The Psychoanalytic Concept of Aggression", op. cit., p.143.

23) Bertrand Russell, *The Conquest of Happiness*, op. cit., p.66.

24) Helmut Schoeck, *Envy: A Theory of Social Behaviour*, op. cit., p.8.

25) Leslie Farber, "The Faces of Envy" in *lying, despair, jealousy, envy, sex, suicide, drugs, and the good life*, Basic Books, Inc., New York, 1976, p.36.

26) George M. Foster, "The Anatomy of Envy: A Study in Symbolic Behavior", op. cit., p.184.

Foster states: ".... a very important part of the explanation lies in the fact that in feeling guilt, shame, pride, greed, anger and other similar emotions, a person is not necessarily comparing himself to another or evaluating his performance against that of another with respect to some quality or characteristic." Ibid., p. 184.

Foster also quotes from Harry Stack Sullivan who was one of the first contemporary psychiatrists to clearly differentiate envy from jealousy. Sullivan pointed out that to admit to envy was to admit to inferiority:

"... we find that the people who are much at the mercy of envy have learned to appraise themselves as unsatisfactory - that is. as inadequate human beings." Harry Stack Sullivan, *Clinical Studies in Psychiatry*, W.W. Norton, New York, 1956, p.129.

27) Melanie Klein, "Envy and Gratitude", *Envy and Gratitude and Other Works 1946-1963*, op. cit., p. 181.

28) It is so obvious that envy is an impediment to learning that it is surprising that more has not been written on the subject. The psychoanalyst, Leslie Farber has commented on the relation between envy and learning, both in terms of his own inability to take in the gist of lecture from someone he envied, and in general. Leslie Farber, "The Faces of Envy", op. cit., pp36-37, 40.

29) "Envy, in its inhibition of both relation and learning, invariably feeds on itself. Out of envy, the child may abandon the acquisition of a given skill that might repair the imbalance between him and the envied person -whether it be a parent or another child -resorting instead to some uncomfortable display of self-assertion. Ibid., pp. 43-44.

30) M. Klein, "Envy and Gratitude", *Envy and Gratitude and Other Works 1946-1963*, op. cit., pp.183-185 & 221-230.

See also: Herbert Rosenfeld, "Negative Therapeutic Reaction" in *Tactics and Techniques in Psychoanalytic Therapy: Volume 11 Countertransference* ed. Peter Giovacchini, Jason Aronson, New York, 1975, p. 221.

31) M. Klein, op. cit. pp. 194-195.

32) "Excessive envy, an expression of destructive impulses, interferes with the primal split between the good and bad breast, and the building up of a good (internal) object cannot sufficiently be achieved. Thus the basis is not laid for a fully developed and integrated adult personality; for the later differentiation between good and bad is disturbed in various connections. In so far as this disturbance of development is due to excessive envy, it derives from the prevalence, in the earliest stages, of paranoid and schizoid mechanisms which, according to my hypothesis, form the basis of schizophrenia." Melanie Klein, "Envy and Gratitude", *Envy and Gratitude and Other Works 1946-1963*, op. cit., p.192.

33) The scapegoat ceremony is described in the Bible, *Leviticus*, chapter 16, verses 7-10. See also Edward Whitmont's discussion of the scapegoat in *Return of the Goddess: Femininity, Aggression and the Modern Grail Quest*, Routledge and Kegan Paul, London, 1983, pp. 105-120.

34) Francis Bacon, "Of Envy", op. cit., p.64.

These 'ejaculations or irradiations' are essentially envious projectiles. The English psychoanalyst, Dr. Wilfred R. Bion, considers envious projectiles to be what he terms, 'beta-elements'. These are concrete, hostile, bits of thought, objects that can be evacuated or used for a kind of thinking that depends on the manipulations of what are felt to be things in themselves as if to substitute such manipulation for words or ideas."

Wilfred R. Bion, *Learning from Experience,* reprinted in *Seven Servants: Four Works by Wilfred R. Bion,* Jason Aronson, New York, 1977, p.6.

35) Francis Bacon, "Of Envy", op. cit., p.64.

Malicious projective identification can also seem like black magic, hence terms like 'bewitch', 'fascinate' and 'overlook,'

36) Edward S. Gifford, Jr., *The Evil Eye: Studies in the Folklore of Vision*, op. cit., p.20.

37) Joseph Berke, "Primitive Mental Mechanisms: A Study of Introjection, Projection and Identification", op. cit., pp.7-8.

38) Bion has commented on the effect of envy on thinking. It can precipitate a regression from symbolic thinking ('alpha functioning') to concrete thought ('beta-functioning') comparable to the action of projective identification. "Envy aroused by a breast (i.e. a feeding person) that provides love, understanding, experience and wisdom, poses a problem that is solved by the destruction of alpha-function. This makes breast and infant appear inanimate with consequent guiltiness, fear of suicide and fear of murder, past, present and impending."

Wilfred R. Bion, *Learning from Experience*, op. cit., p.11.

39) Hanna Segal, *Klein*, Fontana Modern Masters, Fontana, London 1979, p.143.

40) W. Clifford M. Scott,"Self-Envy and Envy of Dreams and Dreaming" in *Remembering Sleep and Dreams, Int. Rev. Psycho-Anal.*, Vol. 2, Part 3, 1975, pp. 335-336.

41) Ibid., pp. 336-337.

42) The young man was not a patient of mine. I only knew about him through what the woman told me about him.

43) Hanna Segal points out that in "Envy and Gratitude", Melanie Klein does not specifically link envy and narcissism, but the intimate relation between envy and narcissism is clearly implied. Certainly Segal connects the two concepts. Hanna Segal, "Some Clinical Implications of Melanie Klein's Work: Emergence from Narcissism", *Int. J. Psycho-Anal.*, Vol. 64, No. 3, 1983, pp. 270-271.

44) The American psychoanalyst, Otto Kernberg, distinguishes between what he calls 'normal narcissism' based on self-love and 'pathological narcissism' based on self-hate. See: "Why Some People Can't Love" an interview of Otto Kernberg by Linda Wolfe in *Psychology Today,* June 1978, pp.55-59. Also, Otto Kernberg, *Borderline Conditions and Pathological Narcissism,* Jason Aronson, New York, 1975.

45) I am describing the process of projective identification. The envier projectively identifies his victim with shit, to utterly rubbish and destroy him. The narcissist projectively identifies his 'victim' with himself, to prevent him from having any life of his own and to transform him into an extension of the narcissist's own adored self. Of course, the extended transaction also involves introjection and introjective identification in that the narcissist desperately wants to take in whatever will feed his self-inflation, and identify with another who has already been identified with his ego-ideal.

46) By partner I mean the object of narcissistic attention.

47) Hanna Segal, *Introduction to the Work of Melanie Klein,* op. cit., pp.44-45.

48) In narcissistic states the absence or presence of vanity can arouse intense anxiety and depression, made worse because the subject cannot comment on his dilemma without arousing intolerable shame. This is a classical, double-bind, no-win situation, often associated with mental breakdown.

49) The British psychoanalyst, Herbert Rosenfeld, has stressed the links between destructive narcissism and envy. See: Herbert Rosenfeld, "A Clinical Approach to the Psychoanalytic Theory of the Life and Death Instincts : An Investigation into the Aggressive Aspects of Narcissism", *Int. J. Psycho-Anal.,* Vol. 52, Part 1, 1971, pp.169-178.

50) In discussing *The Oresteia,* Melanie Klein quotes from Gilbert Murray's definition of hubris: "Hubris ... is followed by Dike, Justice, which reestablishes (bounds and order). This rhythm-Hubris-Dike, Pride and its fall, Sin and Chastisement --is the commonest burden of those philosophical lyrics which are characteristic of Greek tragedy...."

Melanie Klein, "Some Reflections on 'The Oresteia'", *Envy & Gratitude and other Works 1946-1963,* op. cit, p. 280.

51) Lee Harvey Oswald shot and killed John Kennedy, President of the United States, in Dallas, Texas, in 1963.

Sirhan Sirhan shot and killed, Robert Kennedy, Vice-President of the United States, in Los Angeles, California, in 1968.

Mark Chapman shot and killed John Lennon, singer, composer, 'pop-star'. in New York, in 1980.

The dilemma of contemporary American narcissism is discussed by Christopher Lasch in, *The Culture of Narcissism: American Life in an Age of Diminishing Expectations,* W.W. Norton & Co., New York, 1978.

52) My comments about the Kennedys and John Lennon are confirmed in many books and articles. About the Kennedys, see, for example: Garry Wills, *The Kennedy Imprisonment: A Meditation on Power,* Little, Brown & Co., Boston, 1982.

About Lennon, see: Thomson Prentice, "Lennon: The rebellious voice of a generation", *Now,* 12 December 1980, pp.19-21.

53) The terrible extent to which fame attracts nemesis and ill-will has been documented by Celia Brayfield in her book *Glitter: The Truth about Fame*, Chatto & Windus, London, 1985.

54) Joan Riviere points out that where unconscious defenses against emptiness, hatred and death are based on greed, a lack of goods or goodness arouses an intolerable sense of insecurity because the person not only feels empty or 'no-good', but constantly feels he has been robbed by others with whom he compares himself. Joan Riviere, "Hate, Greed and Aggression", in *Love, Hate & Reparation,* by Melanie Klein and Joan Riviere, The Hogarth Press, London, 1957, pp.26-28.

55) The narcissism of the child may be a defense against envy, an expression of envy and a defense against depression, among various considerations.

56) The omnipotence of a child of narcissistic parents is partially a learned response, a variation of 'identification with the aggressor'. On the other hand the omnipotence of the aggressively narcissistic child is an expression of contempt.

57) "In the narcissistic states where the libidinal aspects predominate destructiveness becomes apparent as soon as the omnipotent self-idealization is threatened by contact with an object which is perceived as separate from the self .... In analysis one observes that when the patient's feelings of resentment and revenge at being robbed of his omnipotent narcissism diminishes, envy is consciously experienced, since it is then that he becomes aware of the analyst as a valuable external person."

Herbert Rosenfeld, "A Clinical Approach to the Psychoanalytic Theory of the Life and Death Instincts : An Investigation into the Aggressive Aspects of Narcissism", op. cit., p.173.

58) "Flaw in narcissistically perceived reality" is a term employed by the American psychoanalyst, Heinz Kohut, to denote what calls forth the "archaic rage of the narcissistically vulnerable" person.

Heinz Kohut, "Thoughts on Narcissism and Narcissistic Rage" in *Psychoanalytic Study of the Child,* Vol. 27, Quadrangle, New York, 1972, p.386.

In his discussion of narcissistic rage, Kohut does not relate it to envy. However, he attributes many qualities and characteristics to narcissistic rage which are almost identical to my description of envy, that is, its spiteful, begrudging, vindictive, fanatical, uncompromising, unforgiving qualities. This leads me to believe that he is, in fact, describing envy.

59) The story of *Snow White* appears in many versions throughout Europe and other continents as well. My quotes are from the tale collected by the Brothers Grimm:

Jacob and Wilhelm Grimm, *Selected Tales,* translated by David Luke, Penguin Classics, London, 1982, p.74.

60) Ibid., p.74.

61) Ibid., p.75.

62) Ibid., p.75.

63) *The Nirvana Principle* is a term suggested by the English psychoanalyst, Barbara Low, and adopted by Freud in order to signify ... "the tendency of the psychical apparatus to reduce the quantity of excitation in itself, whether of internal or of external origin, to zero – or, failing that, to as low a level as possible."

J. Laplanche and J.-B. Pontalis, *The Language of Psycho Analysis,* The Hogarth Press, London, 1973, p.272.

Freud directly connected the *Nirvana Principle* with the death instinct in his paper on, "The Economic Problem of Masochism", op. cit., p.160.

CHAPTER 4

1) Certainly, the newborn infant, indeed, many children and adults, do not readily differentiate between what they want, what they feel and where the feelings come from. From their point of view they create the breast in order to satisfy their own needs, and the breast is identical with whatever they experience. It does not matter that an outside observer might think otherwise.

2) Merell Middlemore, who was one of the first doctors to systematically study the suckling mother-child relationship, described many of these early physical and emotional experiences under the heading of 'suckling satisfaction'. Merell Middlemore, *The Nursing Couple*, Hamish Hamilton Medical Books, London, 1941.

3) Jonathan Miller, *States of Mind*, British Broadcasting Corporation, London, 1983, p.255.

4) The need for adequate stimulation remains throughout one's life. Thus, a project supported by Age Research (Bristol, England) showed that a lack of stimulation can lead to incontinence among the elderly, and that the effects of incontinence can be alleviated, and even totally overcome, by stimulating the old folks in meaningful ways. "Memory jog for health in old age", *The Times*, 16 April 1986, p. 3.

5) Sigmund Freud, "Instincts and their Vicissitudes", op. cit., p.138.

6) The image of a mother destroying her infant by feeding agitation was evoked by Bruno Bettelheim in his discussion of the Holocaust. Bettelheim likened the destructive mother to a provider of 'black milk', that is, the milk of death. He commented: "When one is forced to drink black milk, from dawn to dusk, whether in the death camps of Nazi Germany, or while lying in a possibly luxurious crib, but there subjected to the unconscious death wishes of what overtly may be a conscientious mother - in either situation, a living soul has death for a master. Bruno Bettelheim, *Surviving the Holocaust*, Flamingo Books, Fontana Paperbacks, London, 1986, p. 103.

7) Merell Middlemore emphasizes the importance of the mother's emotional attitude on the mental as well as physical development of the child. A hostile, frightened state of mind, often evinced by rough or clumsy handling, will get through and attack the child just as if she were providing poisoned milk. Merell Middlemore, *The Nursing Couple*, op. cit., pp. 111-121.

8) I don't think it is necessary for me to discuss the relative merits of breast versus bottle feeding. What matters most is the feeding, caring relationship. The bosom/nipple or bottle/teat can be satisfactory or unsatisfactory as part of the larger process of bonding between mother and child.

9) In discussing the problem of unsatisfied sucklings(inert and/or irritable babies) Merell Middlemore provides an excellent description of the containing mother: "They did not complain of the long feeds, and were patient and gentle with the babies-more patient than the nurses who attended them...." Merell Middlemore, *The Nursing Couple*, op. cit., p. 80.

10) The mental representation or image of the breast is an 'internal object' to which people relate just as much as to an external object. The concept of the 'internal object' has been discussed at length by Melanie Klein and her colleagues, and from another perspective by psychologist, Professor George Miller. See his discussion of an 'internal representation' in his dialogue with Jonathan Miller, "The Background to Modern Psychology" in Jonathan Miller, *States of Mind*, op. cit., pp 12-29.

11) While commenting on comparable issues, Merell Middlemore also points out that aside from being self-absorbed, many mothers have specific physical and mental

difficulties in feeding their babies. These include an active fear or dislike of breast feeding, a poorly constructed breast (congested, balloon-shaped breasts with flat nipples), excessive sensitivity the baby's sucking, inadequate supply of milk and depression or other mental disturbances. (All of these may or may not be associated with narcissistic mothering.) Merell Middlemore, *The Nursing Couple*, op. cit., pp. 69, 73, 91, 95-97.

12) The statue of Diana of Ephesus depicts a large, succulent woman with arms outstretched and with a plethora of breasts covering the top half of her body. Plate 35, Diana of Ephesus in Erich Neumann, *The Great Mother: An Analysis of the Archetype*, Bollingen Series XLVII, Pantheon Books, New York, 1963.

13) The Mosque of El Jazzar is located in Acre, Israel. It was completed in 1781 by Ahmed el-Jazzar who was noted for his cruelty. Any workman who made the slightest mistake was buried alive. This indicates his desire to create the perfect woman, not unlike Diana of Ephesus.

The breast covered courtyard is dominated by a tall minaret. Arguably this represents the potent phallus of el-Jazzar dominating his domain. It is often noted how much Arab men wish to possess and dominate their women.

I am thankful to Helen Silman for bringing this Mosque to my attention.

14) *Forum*, Vol. 17., No. 10, October 1984, p. 117.

15) Merell Middlemore states that with this little girl the feeding difficulties arose entirely in the child. The mother had successfully nursed an elder child and wanted to nurse this one. Moreover there was plenty of milk. "The point is that although she (the girl) had never sucked the breast properly, still less 'attacked' it, she entertained very fierce fantasies of biting." Merell Middlemore, *The Nursing Couple*, op. cit., pp. 189-190.

16) Joseph Rheingold, *The Fear of Being a Woman: A Theory of Maternal Destructiveness*, Grune & Stratton, New York, 1964, p. 136.

17) *Everything You Always Wanted to Know About Sex but Were Afraid to Ask*, United Artists, 1972, directed by Woody Allen, produced by Charles Joffe.

18) David Sapsted, "Dancer's 60in breasts 'gave me whiplash.' *Daily Telegraph*, 3 July 1998, p. 3.

19) Melanie Klein, "Early Stages of the Oedipus Conflict and of Super-Ego Formation" in *The Psycho-Analysis of Children*, The Hogarth Press, London, 1975, p.128.

20) Ioan Lewis is Professor of Anthropology at the London School of Economics. Personal communication, June 1983.

21) Karl Abraham, "A Short Study of the Development of the Libido, viewed in the Light of Mental Disorders" in *Selected Papers on Psychoanalysis*, The Hogarth Press, London, 1973, p.488.

22) I am indebted to Thomas T. S. Hayley, the former editor of the *International Journal of Psycho-Analysis*, who has made available to me an article he wrote on "Khoba Khobee" for a symposium on envy and jealousy. It is based on anthropological field work he had done in Assam. Khoba and Khobee are male and female demons who sprang forth from the mouth of the Hindu Goddess, Parbati, the wife of Shiva. According to myth, Shiva used to live by begging. His wife hated the taunts of other Gods and Goddesses and nagged him to take up cultivation instead. Shiva did this but with such skill and enthusiasm, that Parbati felt alone and abandoned.

"Finally she went out herself to see what he was doing, when she saw his magnificent crops, in her unbounded astonished admiration she exclaimed, "Uh, Ah".

At this two terrible beings Khoba and Khobee came forth from Parbati's mouth. They were male and female joined together. They rushed through the crops burning them up." Thomas T. S. Hayley, "Khoba Khobee", unpublished article.

23) "....if a man is good and does or says things of good intent, the backbiter will turn all this goodness upside down to his own shrewd intent. Or if other men speak good of a man, then the backbiter will say that he is very good, but will point to someone else who is better, and will thus disparage he whom other men praise." Quoted by Klein in *Envy & Gratitude*, op. cit. p. 41.

24) Edmund Spenser (1552-1599?). The passage was also quoted by Melanie Klein, Ibid.,. pp.40-41.

25) John Walsh, "Fear and loathing in L'Escargot", *ES* (*The Evening Standard Magazine*), December 1987, pp. 54-58.

26) "I have seen babies as young as three weeks interrupt their sucking for a short time to play with the mother's breast or to look towards her face. I have also observed that young infants - even as early as in the second month - would in wakeful periods after feeding lie on the mother's lap, look up at her, listen to her voice and respond to it by their facial expression; it was like a loving conversation between mother and baby. Such behavior implies that gratification is as much related to the object which gives the food as to the food itself". Melanie Klein, "On Observing the Behavior of Young Infants" in *Developments in Psycho-Analysis,* edited by Joan Riviere, The Hogarth Press, London, 1952, p. 239.

27) "...early infantile splitting processes related both to confusional anxieties and oral sadistic envy constitute one of the fixation points of hypochondriacal states. The ego seems unable to work through the confusional state in the mental apparatus. It constantly projects the confusional state, including the internal objects and parts of the self, such as oral sadism, into external objects which are immediately re-introjected into the body and body organs." Herbert Rosenfeld, "The Psychopathology of Hypochondriasis" in *Psychotic States*, op. cit., p.199.

28) In considering the ways that human qualities, capacities and characteristics can represent the breast, the second century Clement of Alexandria often referred to Logos as "the milk of God the Father". For the Greeks, Logos meant the power of reason. For Christian Theologians it meant the creative, sustaining spirit of God as revealed in Jesus. The product of this Logos can be seen in a prayer which begins with, "Lead us, holy Shepherd of rational sheep..." and ends with, "......source of heavenly milk from the bride's sweet breasts which are the graces of thy Sophia. As it is pressed out, the babes with tender mouths are nourished, filled with the dewey spirit of thy Logos-nipple." Quoted by Edmund Leach, "The big fish in the biblical wilderness', *Int. Rev. Psycho-Anal.*, Vol. 13, part 2, 1986, p. 140.

29) Philip Roth, *The Breast,* Jonathan Cape, London, 1973, p.12-13.

30) Melanie Klein, "Envy and Gratitude", *Envy and Gratitude and Other Works 1946-1963*, op. cit., pp. 207-208.

31) Vampires, werewolves and other draining creatures so beloved by film makers and their audiences illustrate archetypal desires towards anyone in the role of source of supply, especially women. The horrific fate of the victims does not simply consist in their drained, cadaverous look, indicating the effects of unrestrained greed, but especially in their loss of will and transmutation into an agent of the devil, indicating the effects of envy.

32) The basic wish is to rob and destroy mother's insides so she cannot feed herself, or anyone else. See the discussion of morbid jealousy by the psychoanalyst, Joan Riviere,

in her paper, "Jealousy as a Mechanism of Defense", *Int. J. Psycho-Anal.*, Vol 13, 1932, pp.414-424.

33) See: John Todd & Kenneth Dewhurst, "The Othello Syndrome: A Study in the Psychopathology of Sexual Jealousy", *The Journal of Nervous and Mental Disease*, Vol. 122, No.4, October 1955, pp. 267-277.

Also, "The Othello Syndrome" in *Some Uncommon Psychiatric Symptoms*, edited by M. O. Enoch, W. H. Trethowan and J. C. Barker., Wright & Son, Bristol, 1967, pp.25-40.

34) There are exceptions to this rule. An obvious one occurs where envy and jealousy occur together and neither predominates. Then the third party may be hated for intruding (jealousy) and hated for being good enough to warrant affection (envy). Similarly the primary partner may be hated for loving another (jealousy) and hated for being lovable (envy).

Alternatively the envier may direct his hatred to a third party in order to disguise the enmity and make it appear less shameful. In this instance jealousy masks envy.

35) *Genesis*, chapter 26, lines 12-16. *The Torah: A Modern Commentary*, Union of Hebrew Congregations, New York, 1981, pp. 180-181.

36) Mr. Roy Watsdon, director general of the (U.K.) National Farmers' Union, told Lincolnshire farmers at Woodhall Spa. *The Daily Telegraph*, London, 9 January 1982, p.3.

37) The many ways in which a physical environment can be seen, treated and attacked as 'the breast' has also been illustrated by Julia Segal in: "Mother, Sex and Envy in a Children's Story", *Int. Rev. Psycho-Anal.*, Vol. 6, 1979, pp. 483-497.

Similar issues sustain 'the greens' and other environmentalists determined to protect natural beauty from the grenvious ravages of man. Sometimes, however, the reasons for these attacks are not obvious. Why, for example, do Californians so often deface their environment by destroying great trees, wrecking coastlines, and so forth? Is it simply envy? Long ago the naturalist Henry David Thoreau argued that anger about the awesome beauty of mother-nature, that is, a sense of personal diminution in comparison to nature, led Californians to want to mutilate it, so they wouldn't feel so inferior. Essentially Thoreau was commenting on the narcissistic nature of the attack and, in not so many words, he was linking envious malice with narcissistic vulnerability. See discussion by Kevin Starr in *Americans and the California Dream 1850-1915*, Oxford University Press, Oxford, 1973, p. 418.

38) Dr. George Miller in Jonathan Miller, *States of the Mind*, op. cit., pp. 27-28.

39) 'Reality' is a conjectural model based on the uniquely human capacity to define experience, anticipate experience (and behavior), formulate responses and make corrections according to whatever happens. See discussion between Jonathan Miller and George Miller, Ibid., pp.14-28.

40) I use the term symbolic equivalent rather than symbol to denote the fact that during a period of regression elements of reality may lose their symbolic, 'just like', quality and, as far as the regressed person is concerned, become identical to the object they are meant to symbolize. See: Hanna Segal, "Notes on Symbol Formation", *Int. J. Psycho-Anal.*, Vol. 38, 1957, pp.391-397.

41) Wilfred Bion, "Attacks on Linking", *Int. J. Psycho-Anal.*, Vol. 40, 1959, p.313.

42) Bettelheim added: "Girls never seemed interested in the riddle, but the preadolescent emotionally disturbed boys nearly always were fascinated by it." Bruno Bettelheim, *Symbolic Wounds*, Thames & Hudson, London, 1955, pp.36-37.

43) Sigmund Freud, "New Introductory Lectures in Psycho-Analysis", *S. E.*, Vol. 32, op. cit., p.122.

CHAPTER 5

!) Quoted by John Williams in, "An essay on the utility of sea bathing......especially in nervous, scrophulous, bilious and cutaneous complaints" in, *Three Hundred Years of Psychiatry 1535-1860,* edited by Richard Hunter and Ida Macalpine, Oxford University Press, London, 1963, p. 223.

2) Ilza Veith, *Hysteria: The History of a Disease,* University of Chicago Press, Chicago, 1965, p. 96.

3) Jean Liebaut, *Thresor des remedes secretes pour les maladies des femmes,* Paris, 1597, p. 529, quoted by Edward Shorter in, *A History of Woman's Bodies,* Penguin Books, London, 1982, p. 13.

4) Quoted by Maggie Scarf in her review of *Medical and Psychological Interfaces, Vol. 1: Sexual and Reproductive Aspects of Woman's Health Care,* edited by Malkah Notman and Carol Nadelson in *The New York Times Book Review,* 31 December 1978, p. 11.

5) Wilhelm Tell, "Song of the Fisherboy", translated by Theodore Martin, quoted by Karen Horney, "The Dread of Women", in *Psychoanalysis and Male Sexuality,* edited by Henrik Ruitenbeek, College and University Press, New Haven, Conn., 1966, p. 84.

6) "A kiss is a hiss from the abyss", R. D. Laing, personal communication, 1966.

7) Wilhelm Tell, quoted by Karen Horney, "The Dread of Women", op cit., p. 84.

In this ballad Tell compares entering a woman to leaping into a dangerous whirlpool which sucks all into its depths, ".....and cleaves through the ocean a path that seems winding in darkness to hell."

8) "I think it is probable that the masculine dread of the woman (the mother) or of the female genital is more deep-seated, weighs more heavily and is usually more energetically repressed than the dread of the man (father)....." Karen Horney, ibid., p. 88.

9) "Horney's (1923) belief that men's fear of women and dread of the vulva derive from the boy's fear of loss of self-esteem because his penis is not large enough to satisfy his mother and his subsequent fear as a man of being sucked in or engulfed during intercourse should not be taken too literally, but rather in terms of the pull of the wish-fear for reunion with the mother and re-engulfment by her." Ruth and Theodor Lidz, "Male Menstruation: A Ritual Alternative to the Oedipal Transition", *Int. J. Psycho-Anal.*, Vol. 58, 1977, p. 27.

Similarly, Neil Maizel points out that the 'mental castration' that accompanies intercourse, or the wish to repose inside mother, is essentially a feared inability to become separate and independent. Neil Maizel, "Self-Envy, the Womb and the Nature of Goodness", *Int. J. Psycho-Anal.*, Vol. 66, 1985, p. 186.

10) Joan Riviere, "Hate, Greed and Aggression", op. cit., p. 32.

11) "Excessive envy interferes with adequate oral gratification and so acts as a stimulus towards the intensification of genital desires and trends. This implies that the infant turns too early towards genital gratification, with the consequence that the oral relation becomes genitalized and the genital trends become too much coloured by oral grievances

and anxieties." Melanie Klein, "Envy and Gratitude", *Envy and Gratitude and Other Works 1946-1963*, op. cit., p. 195.

12) Before the widespread availability of contraceptives, both ingrained prudery and the social consequences of unwanted pregnancy cast a chill over women's sexual responsiveness. Subsequently the work of sexologists like Masters and Johnson shed new light on female orgasmic potential, so much so, that some feminists began to taunt men for their sexual inferiority. Thus Mary Jane Sherfey wrote: "Theoretically, a woman could go on having orgasms indefinitely if physical exhaustion did not intervene." And Kate Millett concluded: "While the male's sexual potential is limited, the female's appears to be biologically nearly inexhaustible." Quoted by Christopher Lasch, *The Culture of Narcissism: American Life in an Age of Diminishing Expectations*, op. cit., pp. 193-194.

13) While discussing penis envy, Judd Marmor points out that as women become more valued and privileged in Western society, then they will become relatively more hated, and "unconscious manifestations of penis envy will begin to diminish, and those of women envy will begin to increase." Judd Marmor, "Changing Patterns of Femininity: Psychoanalytic Implications", in Jean Baker Miller (ed.), *Psychoanalysis and Women*, Penguin Books, 1974, pp. 230-232.

14) This view was common among the European peasantry.

"Some people thought of the uterus as a frog "with many legs that is supposed to stay in the body, because you have to die when the colic (or frog) creeps out of your throat." According to one account from the Tirol, a woman became ill on a pilgrimage and lay down on the grass. "Scarcely was she asleep when the uterus, and the attaching ligaments crept out of her mouth into a brook, swam around, and crawled back inside. When she awakened she was healed.""

Edward Shorter, *A History of Women's Bodies,* op. cit., p. 287.

15) Ibid., p. 287.

16) By the 1600's the English physician, Edward Jordon, and the French physician, Carolus Piso, affirmed that hysteria was caused by perturbations of the brain and could afflict men as well as women. Ilza Veith, *Hysteria: The History of a Disease,* op. cit., pp. 120-129.

17) Ibid., p.5.

Veith comments: "Although the medicinal use of highly unappetizing substances was far from uncommon in ancient Egypt, this particular prescription suggests deliberate choice. The implication of gratifying the uterus with discharges from the opposite sex cannot be disregarded."

18) Ibid., pp. 22-31.

The idea of the womb being constricted or suffocated was related to observations of female disorders such as prolapsed uterus. It is important to note that in spite of views about hysteria that we would consider to be bizarre, many physicians, from Egyptians to Romans, related hysterical symptoms to sexual abstinence or frustration, a much more accurate assessment of the problem.

19) Jules Garinet, *Historie de la magic en France,* Foulon, Paris, 1818, p. 29, quoted by Ilza Veith, ibid., p. 57.

20) Heinrich Kramer and James Sprenger, *Malleus Maleficarum,* translated with an introduction, bibliography and notes by Montague Summers, Pushkin Press, London, 1951.

21) In many cities in Germany alone "the average number of executions for this pretended crime (witchcraft) was six hundred annually, or two every day, if we leave out the Sundays, when it is to be supposed that even this madness refrained from its work."

Charles Mackay, *Memoirs of Extraordinary Popular Delusions,* Richard Bentley, London, 1841, p. 463, quoted by Ilza Veith, *Hysteria: The History of a Disease,* op. cit., pp. 60-61.

22) *Malleus,* op. cit., p. 119, quoted by Ilza Veith, ibid., p. 64.

23) Ibid., p. 43, quoted by Ilza Veith, ibid., p. 63.

24) The Celts had a particular fear of hags and witches that threatened travelers with 'women's spells'. Therefore 'Journey Prayers' became popular, to be said before embarking on a trip. A typical journey prayer asked for protection against: "The woman in her knee, at her evil eye, with her spleen, with her envy." Quoted by Anne Ross, "The Divine Hag of the Pagan Celts", in Venetia Newall (ed.), *The Witch Figure*, Routledge and Kegan Paul, 1973.

25) Phyllis Chesler points out that the tendency of men in religion "to devalue real motherhood and elevate spiritual motherhood as much as they do" is further proof of their pervasive "uterus envy". Quoted by Janet Chase-Marshall in "Who's Afraid of Phyllis Chesler?", *Human Behavior,* September 1978, p. 55.

26) *Malleus,* op. cit., p. xix, quoted by Ilza Veith, *Hysteria: The History of a Disease,* op. cit., p. 59.

27) The *uroboros* is "the symbol of the psychic state of the beginning, of the original situation in which man's consciousness and ego were still small and undeveloped. As symbol of the origin and of the opposites contained in it, the uroboros is the "Great Round," in which positive and negative, male and female elements....intermingle." Erich Neumann, *The Great Mother,* op. cit., p. 18.

In other words the uroboros symbolizes the 'womb of all things'.

28) "It vexes me that women have two openings in the lower part of their bodies, while men have only one. I envy them that." Comment by thirty year old male patient quoted by Felix Boehm in, "The Femininity Complex in Men", in *Psychoanalysis and Male Sexuality,* edited by H. Ruitenbeek, op. cit., p. 128.

29) "The girl's nature as biologically conditioned gives her the desire to receive, to take into herself; she feels or knows that her genital is too small for her father's penis and this makes her react to her own genital wishes with direct anxiety: she dreads that if her wishes were fulfilled, she herself or her genital would be destroyed." Karen Horney, "The Dread of Women", op. cit. p. 91.

30) Elaine Showalter, *Hystories, Hysterical Epidemics and Modern Cilture,* Columbia University Press, New York, 1997.

31) The inclusion of the 'Virgin Mary' as an example of the 'good womb' is based on the idealization of its non-use for heterosexual reproduction and pleasure. Mary symbolizes receptivity to spiritual powers, but her physical prowess, is that of the the 'Madonna' also has to do with feeding, the 'good breast' incarnate, as well as reproduction. One sees this split particularly strongly in Catholic countries like Mexico where the womb as a person is divided according to its idealized loving, feeding, caring qualities, the 'Madonna', and its denigrated, carnal function, the 'Whore'. See discussion by Phyllis Chesler, *Women and Madness,* Doubleday & Co., New York, 1952, pp. 22-24.

32) Margaret Mead, *Male and Female,* Victor Gollancz, London, 1950, pp. 102-103.

Mead adds: "Behind the cult lies the myth that is some way all of this was stolen from the women; sometimes women were killed to get it. Men owed their manhood to a theft and a theatrical mime, which would fall to the ground in a moment as mere dust and ashes if its true constituents were known. A shaky structure, protected by endless taboos and precautions, enforced by the women's name in Iatmul, by fluttery fear for their child-bearing qualities in Arapesh, by good-humored indulgence of male vanity in Tchambuli, and by blows and buffets and the various reversed identification of flute and women in Mundugumor, it survives only as long as every one keeps the rules....the missionary who shows the flutes to the women has broken the culture successfully." Ibid., p. 103.

33) Ibid., p 103.

34) The Marines and other military organizations have many other features of male motherhood. Not only does the military preserve and enhance the idea of mystery or military secrecy, but it perpetuates dependency. Members of the organization, and their families, remain dependent on it for their every need, as on a feeding breast.

35) Soldiers destroy what mothers create. It is worth noting that women can be soldiers as well as men.

36) John Milton, *Paradise Lost,* Books I & II.

See also discussion by Melanie Klein in "Envy and Gratitude", *Envy and Gratitude and Other Works 1946-1963,* op. cit., p. 202.

37) Roland Littlewood, *Pathology and Identity in Northeast Trinidad,* D. Phil. thesis. Chapter 5, para VIII, subsequently published as, *Pathology and Identity, Cambridge U. Press, 1993.*

'Rastas' refers to the followers of the Rastifaris, an Afro-Caribbean religious and political movement.

38) In the ensuing years a community of upwards of two dozen followers (at any one time) was established in the bush. These were usually black Trinidadian men who sometimes brought their girlfriends and children "to come and 'Plant for the Nation'".

Roland Littlewood, "The Imitation of Madness: The Influence of Psychopathology upon Culture", *Soc. Sci. Med.,* Vol. 19, No. 7, 1984, pp. 710-712.

39) Edward Shorter, *A History of Women's Bodies,* op. cit., p. 287.

See also: Penelope Shuttle and Peter Redgrove, *The Wise Wound: Menstruation and Everywoman,* V. Gollancz, London, 1978, and Paula Weidegar, *Menstruation and Menopause: The Physiology and Psychology, the Myth and the Reality,* Alfred Knopf, New York, 1976.

40) Edward Shorter, ibid., p. 287.

41) Ibid., pp. 287-288.

42) Ruth and Theodor Lidz, "Male Menstruation", op. cit., pp. 23-25.

43) B. Spencer and F.J. Gillen, *The Native Tribes of Central Australia,* MacMillan & Co., London, 1899, quoted by Bruno Bettelheim in *Symbolic Wounds: Puberty Rites and the Envious Male,* op. cit., p. 174.

44) G. Roheim, *The Eternal Ones of the Dream,* International Universities Press, New York, 1945, p. 165.

45) Ruth and Theodor Lidz, "Male Menstruation", op. cit., pp. 18-24.

46) Ibid., p. 20.

The authors add: However, the women believe, as much as do the men, that the group's well-being and the fertility of the women, pigs and soil, as well as the growth and maturation of the children, depend on the mediation of the ancestor spirits who must be summoned and placated, if not controlled and satisfied, by the rituals the men carry out." Ibid., p.20

47) Bruno Bettelheim, *Symbolic Wounds: Puberty Rites and the Envious Male*, op. cit., p. 30.

Many of the boys felt "cheated" or "gyped" that girls had vaginas and they didn't. Some repeatedly complained, "She thinks she is something special because she has a vagina," or "Why can't I have a vagina?" Ibid., p. 34.

48) Felix Boehm, "The Femininity Complex in Men", op. cit. p. 128.

49) Penelope Shuttle and Peter Redgrove, *The Wise Wound: Menstruation and Everywoman*, op. cit., p. 52.

50) Lucieene Roubin, *Chambrettes des Provencaux*, Plon, Paris, 1970, p. 157, quoted by Shorter, *A History of Women's Bodies*, op. cit., p. 288.

51) Pre-menstrual tension (PMT) has become a recognized medical syndrome and an important defense for women on trial. Thus, a woman who pleaded PMT was freed after running down her lover with a car. Recently, however, this defense has been challenged as a defense both by the law and feminists who feel that women should not use biology to avoid equal responsibility (with men) for their actions. Sheila Duncan, "No defence for crime", *The Sunday Times*, 27 January 1985, p. 36.

52) Pelkonen, *Begurtshilfe Finnland*, [31], pp. 17-18, quoted by Edward Shorter, op. cit., p. 261.

"Even in more advanced areas of Europe like Switzerland, the custom of letting the menses flow unhampered persisted until quite recently. A Swiss woman recalled her girlhood in the 1890's: 'At most, underpants were worn only in the coldest winter. People called them unhealthy, and said the body has to get air. Nobody even thought about washing there.'" Ibid., p. 261.

53) Shuttle and Redgrove discuss at length the widespread tendency in many cultures to equate menstruating women with witches, demons, and assorted evil beings. Penelope Shuttle and Peter Redgrove, *The Wise Wound: Menstruation and Everywoman*, op. cit., pp. 197-224.

54) Olivier Marc, *Psychology of the House*, Thames and Hudson, London, 1977, p. 13. Marc documents his views with photographs of dwellings from many countries.

55) G. R. Levy, *The Gate of Horn*, Faber and Faber, London, 1946, discussed by Bettelheim, *Symbolic Wounds*, op. cit., p. 147.

56) Bruno Bettelheim, Ibid.., p. 147.

57) These curved passageways lead to and from a large round centre of connections. The traveler both returns to the womb and is reborn during the course of 'taking off'.

Generally, women don't share the modern obsession with abstraction. It may be a truism, but it is useful to note that when one possesses a body capable of concrete fulfillments, there is less need to engage in abstract expressions. The British critic, George Steiner, infers that, "women find purely speculative, purely abstract, life-distancing pursuits somehow "childish", that women are rooted in an adult "realism" about the weight and presence of the given world." George Steiner, "Chess" the cruelist game", *The Sunday Times*, 9 September 1984.

58) See: Daniel Jaffe, "The Masculine Envy of Woman's Procreative Function", *J. Amer. Psychoanal. Assoc.*, Vol. 16, 1968, pp. 521-548; also Felix Boehm "The Femininity Complex in Men", op. cit. p. 131.

59) Lea Mindel, "May Heaven Protect Us", *Jewish Chronicle Magazine*, 8 June 1979, p. 55.

60) Marie Langer, "Sterility and Envy", *Int. J. Psycho-Anal.*, Vol. 39, 1958, pp. 139 -143.

61) Peter Lomas, notes that "there exists a vast mythology surrounding female beings who do not take kindly to the event of childbirth; namely, witches. Witches are said to cause sterility, abortion, and to steal, kill or eat newborn babies". Peter Lomas, "Ritualistic elements in the management of childbirth", *Brit. J. Med. Psychol.*, Vol. 9, 1966, p. 210.

62) Langer, "Sterility and Envy", op. cit. p. 139.

Langer adds: "...the sterile or infertile woman sets up different barriers against the incorporation of the penis, semen or foetus, and defends herself by different means according to her personality structure. The understanding of paranoid and depressive anxieties, together with the concept of envy as the central factor, enables us to grasp the meaning and the psychosomatic mechanisms of many fertility disorders." Langer includes among these fertility disorders defloration fears, vaginismus, frigidity, spasm of the fallopian tubes, the expulsion of semen and miscarriage. Ibid., p. 142.

63) Ibid., p. 140.

64) Ibid., p. 140.

65) Melanie Klein, "The Effects of Early Anxiety-Situations on the Sexual Development of the Girl", *The Psycho-Analysis of Children,* The Hogarth Press, London, 1975, pp. 194-195.

66) A typical unconscious equation of the inner contents of a woman's body is: *breast = faeces = penises = babies.*

67) Hanna Segal, *Introduction to the Work of Melanie Klein,* op. cit., pp. 28-29.

68) Melanie Klein, "An Obsessional Neurosis in a Six-Year-Old Girl", *The Psycho-Analysis of Children,* The Hogarth Press, London, 1975, pp. 56-57.

"In her unconscious these activities were equated with tearing, cutting up or burning her mother's body, together with the children it contained, and castrating her father. Reading, too, in consequence of the symbolic equation of her mother's body with books, had come to mean a violent removal of substances, children, etc. from the insides of her mother. " Ibid., p. 57.

69) Melanie Klein, "The Significance of Early Anxiety Situations in the Development of the Ego", *The Psycho-Analysis of Children,* op. cit., pp. 182.

"Moreover, by nursing and dressing her dolls, with whom she identifies herself, she obtains proof that she had a loving mother, and thus lessens her fear of being abandoned and left homeless and motherless. This purpose is also served to some extent by other games which are played by children of both sexes, as, for instance, games of furnishing houses and traveling, both of which spring from the desire to find a new home - in the final resort, to rediscover their mother." Ibid., p. 182.

70) "Men's desire for female functions comes openly to expression in painters and writers, who feel they give birth to their works like a woman in labour after a long pregnancy. All artists in whatever medium work through the feminine side of their personalities; this is because works of art are essentially formed and created inside the

mind of the maker, and are hardly at all dependent on external circumstances." Joan Riviere, "Hate, Greed and Aggression", op. cit., p. 32.

What Riviere says equally applies to female artists and writers.

71) Peter Hall, *Peter Hall's Diaries,* edited by John Goodwin, Hamish Hamilton, London, 1983, p. 113.

72) "Toyota and GM Present: The Nova", *International Herald Tribune,* 20 December 1984, p. 11.

73) Shaffer adds through the mouth of Salieri: "...I was staring through the cage of those meticulous strokes at an Absolute Beauty!...Capisco. I know my fate. Smashed, Smashed down – the Palace of Sound! Now for the first time I feel my emptiness, as Adam felt his nakedness." Peter Shaffer, *Amadeus,* op. cit., pp. 65-67.

74) I have referred to the pregnant *person,* rather than *woman,* to encompass symbolic as well as actual pregnancies.

Direct assaults involve verbal and physical abuse up to and including murder. "Marital difficulties, abortion wishes, mutilation fantasies, and criticism of the childless woman are amongst the manifestations of pregnancy envy." Kato van Leewen, "Pregnancy Envy in the Male", *Int. J. Psycho-Anal.,* Vol. 47, 1966, p. 323.

75) *Couvade* comes from the French, meaning to broode, or to hatch. The term was coined by the anthropologist, Sir Edward Taylor, to denote the practice by which, on the birth of a child, the father is also put to bed and treated as if he were physically affected by the birth. Many primitive peoples have a word, 'manchildbed', for the place in which this happens. Taylor also used couvade to mean this special bed. Anthropologists have described variations of this practice in South American, Polynesian, African and Indian life.

76) Peter Lomas has described various theories of couvade, positive and negative. On the positive side Sir James Frazier (*The Golden Bough*) believed that couvade was a form of sympathetic magic designed to mitigate the birth pains and transfer them to the father, and Arnold Van Gennep saw it as a 'rite of passage'. Others have taken a more ominous view of couvade. J. Bachofen thought that "the husband imitates childbirth in order to gain rights over the child which previously belonged to the woman......it is an attempt on the part of the male to oppose the authority and influence of the woman." Theodor Reik viewed couvade as a form of protective magic, an attempt to ward off devils who might attack the woman and fetus, devils representing the man's own projected hostility.

Peter Lomas, "Ritualistic elements in the management of childbirth", op. cit., pp. 208 - 209.

77) Brian Jackson, *Fatherhood,* George Allen and Unwin, London, 1984, p. 56.

78) Ibid., p. 55.

Jackson quotes another man who used to chat to his pet: "Won't you wonder what's happened when you don't get all this attention any more?" Ibid., p. 55.

79) In Britain one stone is a unit of weight equal to fourteen pounds. Ibid. p. 56.

80) Ibid., p. 57.

81) Joan Raphael-Leff considers the problems of the angry father-to-be (whom she calls, 'the renouncer') in her paper, "Facilitators & Regulators: Participators & Renouncers: mothers' and fathers' orientations towards pregnancy and parenthood", *J. Psychosomatic Obstetrics & Gynecology,* Vol. 4, 1985, pp. 176-178.

82) Felix Boehm has written about a patient who was tortured by fears of cancer of the stomach, caecum and kidneys. During the course of his analysis he associated: "Recently

it has occurred to me that possibly these difficulties are connected with an unconscious idea of anal birth. Perhaps my attitude to my other symptoms is like that of a woman during gestation." Felix Boehm, "The Femininity Complex in Men", op. cit. p. 135.

83) Gail Vines, "Test-Tube Embryos", in the "Inside Science" section, *New Scientist*, 19 November 1987, p. 4. See also: Dick Teresi and Kathleen McAuliffe, "Male Pregnancy", *Omni*, Vol. 8, No. 3, December 1985, pp. 51-56 & 118.

84) "When you talk about cloning and babies in test tubes, you are talking about repressed male uterus envy." Phyllis Chesler quoted by Jane Chase-Marshall, op. cit., p. 55.

85) Mary Wollstonecraft Shelley, *Frankenstein*, Gibbings & Co., London, 1897.

Frankenstein, adds: "A new species would bless me as its creator and source; many happy and excellent natures would owe their being to me. No father could claim the gratitude of his child so completely as I should deserve theirs." Ibid., pp. 50 & 52.

86) Otto Friedrich, "The New Origins of Life: How the science of conception brings hope to childless couples", *Time*, 10 September 1984, pp. 34-43.

87) Dr. Lewis Fraad, Professor of Pediatrics, Albert Einstein College of Medicine, Bronx, New York. Personal communication, 1963.

88) Edward Shorter, op. cit., pp. 98-99.

By the 1930's, at a time when maternal mortality had been greatly diminished, the emphasis changed from saving the life of the mother to preserving the life and health of the baby. Ibid., p. 139.

89) Ibid., p.84.

90) Ibid., p. 84.

91) Ibid., pp. 152-153.

92) Ibid., pp. 103-114.

93) Shorter raises the interesting question, why were infections less likely at home than at hospital. He thinks the answer is that " many women had become more or less immune to their own dirt." Ibid., p. 128.

94) By the turn of the century a mother ran more risk from infection at home than in hospital. Ibid., pp. 132-133.

95) Peter Lomas, "Ritualistic elements in the management of childbirth", op. cit. p. 211.

96) Ibid., p. 212.

97) Jan Dansig, "Scissor-happy?", *The Times Health Supplement*, London, 29 January 1982, p.12.

Edward Shorter, *A History of Women's Bodies*, pp. 171 -173

"By the 1970's a mother birthing anywhere in Western society would have a good chance of an episiotomy: 65% in Ontario, 64% in a Wuppertal hospital in Germany, 70% to 90% in a London Hospital, 60% among first mothers around Brighton." Ibid, p. 172.

98) "In 16,000 births from 1911 to 1929 in Sursee County, Switzerland, only 9 percent of the mothers had appreciable tears. In 10,000 deliveries in the Jena University Hospital just before the Second World War, only 6 percent of the mothers tore (seven times as many first mothers as multiparas). The conservative doctors at the Chicago Maternity Centre found in the early 1930's that 6 percent of mothers were likely to tear: the 3

percent on whom they did episiotomies, and an additional 3 percent who did not have the procedure. Thus, if no intervention took place, perhaps one woman in fifteen would have an unpleasant tear." Edward Shorter, ibid., p. 171.

After episiotomy, dyspareunia (pain on intercourse) was suffered by nine out of ten women and was directly attributable to the scar according to a study from King's College Hospital. Jan Dansig, "Scissor- happy?", op. cit. p. 12.

99) Ibid. p.12.

100) Derek Llewelyn Jones, *Fundamentals of Obstetrics and Gynaecology,* Vol. 1, Faber & Co., London, 1982. Quoted by Jan Dansig, "Scissor-happy?", op. cit., p. 12.

The views of Gordon and Jones echoes those of midwife Juliet Willmott. "I am very sorry that some doctors and midwives have become so 'scissors-happy' lately." If there is no fetal distress, there is , "no need to hurry the birth of the baby." Juliet Willmottt, "Too Many Episiotomies", *Midwives Chronicle,* February 1980, p. 46, quoted by Edward Shorter, *A History of Woman's Bodies,* op. cit., p. 172.

101) Jan Dansig, "Scissor-happy?", op. cit. p. 12.

"We are beginning to discover the sometimes long-term emotional and destructive effects of doctors treating women as if they were merely containers to be opened and relieved of their contents, and of concentrating their attention on a bag of muscle and a birth canal instead of relating and caring for the person of whom the uterus and vagina is a part." Shiela Kitzinger of the National Childbirth Trust. Quoted by Jan Dansig, ibid., p. 12.

102) In the United States women undergo surgery much more often than men, and the most common operation is a hysterectomy. "A survey of 27 million hospital admissions across the country found that 11 of the 20 most frequently performed surgical procedures were exclusively for women. None of the top 20 were operations performed only on men. Total hysterectomy accounted for an average 3.89 hospital admissions per 1000 women. The second most common procedure for women was Caesarean section, followed by diagnostic dilation and curettage, which involves scraping the lining of the uterus." in "Women Outpace Men in Operations", *International Herald Tribune,* 15 November 1984, p. 7.

In the United Kingdom, approximately 50,000 hysterectomies are performed per year. Suzie Hayman, "10 times better", *Forum,* Vol. 17, No. 10, October 1984, pp. 25-29.

103) I quote from an editorial by Aileen Dickins, formerly Consultant in Obstetric and Gynaecological Surgery at University College Hospital, London, "Uterine ligaments and the treatment of prolapse", *Journal of the Royal Society of Medicine,* Vol. 77, May 1984, p. 355.

The view of the uterus as a cancer container coincides with the view of the fetus as a tumor. During my first weeks of medical training I was accosted by a surgeon with the question, "What is the most common tumor?" Neither I nor my colleagues were able to supply the required answer. The surgeon then impatiently retorted, "A fetus, of course!". Both views may be narrowly correct, but they overlook and denigrate the reality of both womb and baby to a woman.

104) Sigmund Freud, Karl Abraham, and Helen Deutsch all expressed the view that childbirth is equated with castration in the minds of women. Peter Lomas points out that this does women an injustice. "This is not to say that feelings of castration and loss do not have place in the mind of many parturient mothers, especially those with a marked masculine identification, but that such feelings have received exclusive attention in the past and consequently the success of childbirth, which may itself be envied, has not been given much thought." Peter Lomas, "Dread of envy as an aetiological factor in puerperal breakdown", *Brit. J. Med. Psychol.,* Vol. 33, 1960, pp.108-109.

105) This is especially the case with the practice of female circumcision, an injurious, mutilating procedure which involves the excision of the entire clitoris, the labia minora and the inner fleshy layers of the labia majora. In conjunction with these excisions, the walls of the vulva are usually stiched together leaving a tiny matchstick opening (infibulation). Female or pharonic circumcision dates back to antiquity but its origins are obscure. Africans say it curbs "aggressive female sexuality" and the operation is celebrated as a rite of passage. Although told it makes them a woman, circumcized girls suffer a near total absence of sexual feeling. It makes intercourse as well as childbirth much more difficult and is associated with a host of gynecological and obstetrical difficulties. (Infibulated women often have to be surgically opened up to allow the baby to pass, before being sewn up again.) Still female circumcision is widely practiced throughout much of Northern Africa.

Hanny Lightfoot-Klein, "Pharonic Circumcision of Females in the Sudan", *Medicine and Law*, Vol. 2, 1983, pp. 353-360.

Blaine Harden, "Female Circumcision: A Norm in Africa", *International Herald Tribune*, 29 July 1985, p.1.

106) Childbirth is an occasion when women are not only the center of attention, but also take over the active role in the family in comparison to men who are relegated to the passive position. This is a source of considerable fear and resentment among men.

Men also resent the suffering women go through as though they have a superior means to relieve themselves of guilt.

107) Quoted by Ann Oakley in her book, *The Captured Womb: A History of the Medical Care of Pregnant Women*, Blackwell, Oxford, 1984.

108) Edward Shorter believes that religious taboos like churching provide "the most consistent evidence of a male disposition to believe women's bodies dangerous to society." Edward Shorter, *A History of Women's Bodies*, op. cit., pp.288-289.

The practice has its origins in the *Old Testament*. "According to *Leviticus* 12: 2-8, a woman shall be unclean for seven days after the birth of a boy, and for fourteen days after the birth of a girl. For a further thirty-three days in the case of a boy, and sixty-six days for a girl, she shall not enter the sanctuary. Finally she shall make offerings to the priest at the door of the tabernacle, when she shall be 'cleansed from the issue of her blood.'" Edward Shorter, ibid., p. 289.

A friend of mine was brought up in the Church of Scotland and has not personally undergone churching, but she thinks that the modern equivalent is the post natal examination.

109) Ibid., p. 289.

110) Peter Lomas, "Dread of envy as an aetiological factor in puerperal breakdown", op. cit., pp. 105-109.

111) Peter Lomas, "Ritualistic elements in the management of childbirth", op. cit., pp. 212-213. The anesthesia, for example, may not simply be desired to relieve pain, but to deny feelings, and inhibit active participation in an event which the woman feels is liable to attract envious attention.

The converse of attenuating creativity, and, in particular, childbirth, is to celebrate it, as the American artist, Judy Chicago, has done through *The Birth Project*. This consists of nearly 100 needlework creations done by dozens of volunteers from around the United States. It is based on drawings and paintings by Judy Chicago of women at term and giving birth. Leslie Bennetts, "Judy Chicago: 100 Needlework Creations Make up Artist's 'Birth Project' ", *International Herald Tribune*, 15 April 1985, p. 18.

112) "So the Lord God cast a deep sleep upon the man; and, while he slept, He took one of his ribs and closed up the flesh at that spot. And the Lord God fashioned the rib that he had taken from the man into a woman; and He brought her to the man. Then the man said, "This one at last/ Is bone of my bones / And flesh of my flesh. / This one shall be called Woman, / For from man was she taken." Genesis, chapter 2, verses 21-23, *The Torah: A Modern Commentary*, op. cit. p. 30.

In Greek mythology Athene was born, "fully armed and brandishing a sharp javelin" from the head of Zeus. "At the sight all the Immortals were struck with astonishment and filled with awe." *New Larousse Encyclopedia of Mythology*, Introduction by Robert Graves, Paul Hamlyn, London, 1969, p. 108.

113) The American psychoanalyst, Gregory Zilboorg asserts that "it was man who perceived himself biologically inferior, and it was this sense of inferiority and concomitant hostility that led to the phenomenon of *couvade* - neurotic, hostile identification with the mother.......it is not penis-envy on the part of the woman, but woman-envy on the part of the man, that is psychologically older and therefore more fundamental." Gregory Zilboorg, "Masculine and Feminine: Some Biological and Cultural Aspects", *Psychiatry*, Vol. 7, 1944, p. 290.

114) Melanie Klein, Melanie Klein, "Envy and Gratitude", *Envy and Gratitude and Other Works 1946-1963*, op. cit., p. 203.

The words of this boy echo with those of my daughter. About the age of seven she came up to me and quite spontaneously proclaimed: "You know Daddy, one day, I will have a baby, and she will have a baby, and then she will have a baby, and it will never stop."

Deborah Berke, personal communication, 1982.

CHAPTER 6

1) A male informant quoted in, Alexandra Penny, *How to Make Love to a Man*, Papermac, London, 1981, pp. 29- 30.

2) A female informant quoted by Maria Torok, "The Significance of Penis Envy in Women" in, Janine Chasseguet-Smirgel, *Female Sexuality*, University of Michigan Press, Ann Arbor, 1970, p. 139.

Another woman asserted: "I don't know why I have this feeling......but it has always been like this for me. As though, only man was fit to fulfill himself, to have opinions, to go always further. And everything to him is so naturally easy......nothing, nothing can stop him." Ibid., p. 139.

3) Philip Roth, *Goodbye Columbus*, Andre Deutsch, London, 1959, p. 128.

4) Charles Rycroft, *A Critical Dictionary of Psychoanalysis*, op. cit. p. 113.

Phallus refers to an idea or image of the penis. It denotes both the physical and symbolic qualities of maleness.

5) Sigmund Freud, "Femininity", in *New Introductory Lectures on Psycho-Analysis*, *S.E.*, Vol. 22, p. 126.

6) Sigmund Freud, "Some Psychical Consequences of the Anatomical Distinction between the Sexes", *S.E.*, Vol. 19, p. 252.

7) In classical psychoanalytic theory it is the girl or female who suffers from penis envy, that is, the resentful awareness of an organ absence which she tries to deny or

remedy. In contrast the boy or male suffers from the castration complex, that is, a complex array of feelings centering around castration anxiety, the fear he will lose what he has. In the popular genre, *penis envy* and *castration complex* are often used synonymously. And, as I go on to explain and illustrate in this chapter, they may be suffered by members of either sex.

8) "Penis envy originates in the discovery of the anatomical distinction between the sexes: the little girl feels deprived in relation to the boy and wishes to possess a penis as he does (castration complex). Subsequently, in the course of the Oedipal phase, penis envy takes on two secondary forms: first, the wish to acquire a penis within oneself (principally in the shape of the desire to have a child) and, secondly, the wish to enjoy the penis in coitus." J. Laplanche and J-B. Pontalis, *The Language of Psycho-Analysis*, op. cit. p. 303.

9) Karl Abraham, "Manifestations of the Female Castration Complex", in *Selected Papers on Psycho-Analysis*, The Hogarth Press, London, 1973, p. 338.

10) Sigmund Freud, "The Dissolution of the Oedipus Complex", *S.E.*, Vol.19, p. 178.

11) Phyllis Greenacre, "Penis Awe and its Relation to Penis Envy", in *Drives, Affects and Behavior*, R. M. Loewenstein (Ed.), Volume 1, *Contributions to the Theory and Practice of Psychoanalysis and its Applications*, International Universities Press, New York, 1960, pp. 176 -190.

Greenacre coined the term *penis awe* in order to denote the state of mind and emotions aroused in a girl upon seeing 1) the adult penis, flaccid or erect; 2) sexual intercourse; 3) others boys exhibiting themselves; 4) chance encounters with other men urinating or masturbating.

Penis awe involves intense admiration, shock, fear, veneration, a feeling of strangeness and aggression, but much less than in *penis envy.* Greenacre clearly distinguishes *penis awe* from *penis envy.* Her view is much closer to a strong overwhelming wish for or submission to the phallus and to what I call *penis greed.*

Dinora Pines reiterates this in her recent review of *Early Female Development* (MTP Press, 1982). "Undoubtedly penis awe, or penis wish, a term that I believe is more appropriate than that of penis envy, plays a part in the little girl's development." *Int. J. Psycho-Anal*, Vol. 65, 1984, p. 237.

12) Popular Yiddish saying translated by Rabbi Hugo Gryn.

13) A *shlemil* is Yiddish for an insecure, neurotic, weakish man, a foolish bungler who can't 'get it right' or 'get it up'. It affectionately describes a *putz*, literally a stupid *prick.*

14) Woody Allen, *Annie Hall*, screenplay in *Four Films of Woody Allen*, Faber and Faber, London, 1983, p. 61.

15) Quoted from John W. Dodds, *The Age of Paradox: A Biography of England 1841-1851*, London, 1953, p. 72 in Reay Tannahill, *Sex in History*, Abacus, London, 1981, pp. 333-334.

16) Minette Marrin, "A Bandwagon Named Desire", *Observer*, 19 February 1984, Weekend page.

17) David Thomson, "Sam Shepard: An American Original", *Playgirl*, Vol. XII, No. 7, December 1984, p. 18.

18) Ads for stimulants like "Amphetrazine" and "Fast One" appear to appeal to the desire for consumable maleness. *Playgirl*, Vol. XII, No. 7, December 1984, pp. 100, 109.

19) Bernie Zilbergeld, *Male Sexuality,* Bantam Books, New York, 1981, p. 23.

20) Jerry Siegal and Joe Shuster elaborated the wish to be super men, while they were high school students in Cleveland, Ohio. But it wasn't until 1938, that Action Comics took Superman aboard. The models for Superman and his alter ego, Clark Kent, included Tarzan, Buck Rogers and Flash Gordon.

Dennis Dooley and Gary Engle (Eds.), *Superman at Fifty: The Persistence of the Legend,* Octavia Press, Cleveland, 1987.

21) Zilbergeld illustrates the phantasy model of masculinity with quotes from many of these writers. Their works emphasize explosive performance, total control, inexhaustibility and invulnerability. Like the romantic novelists their works sell in the hundreds of millions. Bernie Zilbergeld, *Male Sexuality,* op. cit., pp. 23-69.

22) Gay Talese, *Thy Neighbor's Wife,* Collins, London, 1980, p. 116.

In his book Talese is refers to D.H. Lawrence's, *Lady Chatterley's Lover,* which he considers to be a masterly 'phallic novel'. "Lawrence probes the sensitivity and psychological detachment that man often feels towards his penis– it does indeed seem to have a will of its own, an ego beyond size, and is frequently embarrassing because of its needs, infatuations and unpredictable nature." p. 115.

23) Numerous psychoanalysts have commented on the oral origins of phallic desires (and hatreds.) Thus, in referring to the development of Klein's views, Segal concludes: "Penis envy is also deeply influenced by the more primitive envy of the breast. The infant may turn away in hatred from the envied breast to an idealized penis, which in turn becomes a carrier of the original envy of the breast. Hanna Segal, *Klein,* op. cit., p. 142.

24) Although there have been many noteworthy female chefs and writers about food, men predominate in the profession. This is only partially explained by the limited public roles allowed to women in different eras and cultures. For example, even today the art of pastry making is almost totally the domain of men.

Guillaume Tirel dit Taillevent was "queux de bouche" (prince's cook) to Philippe de Valois (1349), then cook to Duc de Normandie (1361) and "first cook" to King Charles V (1381). His book, *Le Viandier,* (1375) was the first completely preserved French cookery work. *Food and Drink Through the Ages: 2500 B.C. to 1937 A.D.,* Maggs Bros Ltd., London, 1937, p. 18.

I am indebted to the writer, Adrian Bailey, for various references and very useful perspectives.

25) From G. Morris Carstairs, *The Twice-Born. A Study of a Community of High-Caste Hindus,* London, 1957, pp. 83-84 discussed in Reay Tannahill, *Sex in History,* op. cit. p. 327.

26) The unconscious phantasies that underlie fellatio are over-determined, that is, they may include oral desires (for magical feedings) as well as ideas of oral impregnation, vengeful castration, and change of sexual identity. See Otto Fenichel, *The Psychoanalytic Theory of Neurosis,* W.W. Norton & Co., New York, 1945, p.229.

27) This account represents the condensation of several separate cases reported to me by colleagues. The essential theme and outline of events which I describe accurately reflects the material presented to me.

28) August Stärcke was the first psychoanalyst to emphatically emphasize that the experience of suckling, and that the cessation of suckling associated with the withdrawal of the breast/nipple, was the basis for the experience of castration.

"We have therefore to look for an infantile situation of universal occurrence in which a penis-like part of the body is taken from another person, given to the child as his own (a situation with which are associated pleasurable sensations), and then taken away from the child causing 'pain' (*Unlust*). This situation can be none other than that of the child at the breast." August Stärcke, "The Castration Complex", *Int. J. Psycho-Anal,* Vol. 2, 1921, p. 182.

Freud also argued that the strong feelings that the child has about the penis have powerful oral-erotic roots "....for when suckling has come to an end, the penis also becomes heir of the mother's nipple." Sigmund Freud, "Anxiety and Instinctual Life", in *New Introductory Lectures on Psycho-Analysis,* op. cit., p. 101.

29) Bion believed that the primitive breast or penis is the prototype for all links with reality. This includes states of mind, emotions, verbal and non-verbal communication and understanding. Wilfred Bion, "Attacks on Linking", op. cit., pp 308-312.

30) Géza Róheim, "Aphrodite or the Woman with a Penis" in *The Panic of the Gods and other essays,* Harper Torchbooks, New York, 1972, pp. 177-178. When a male child is born to the Somali people, the parents are careful to cut the umbilical cord so as to leave as much of it possible. Then they stretch it for they believe that the longer the cord is, the longer the penis will be. It may be that these people believe that the longer the penis the stronger the connection between Mother and son.

31) Laila Karme, "The Penis as Umbilical Cord", *Psychoanalytic Quarterly,* Vol. 47, 1978, p. 428.

32) Karen Horney, "On the Genesis of the Castration Complex in Women", *Int. J. Psycho-Anal.,* Vol. 5, 1924, pp. 51-54.

Horney pointed out that all these capacities put girls at a considerable narcissistic disadvantage, that is, they felt less able, valuable and important when they saw what boys could do. She quotes from a female patient: "If I might ask a gift from Providence it would be to be able just for once to urinate like a man. For then I should know how I really am made." p. 52. I think by this the woman means that only then she would really feel herself.

33) In his book, *The Prisoner of Sex,* Norman Mailer acidly calls "the eternal feminine", the "Great Bitch", something to be ceaselessly opposed, subdued and conquered. Peter Schwenger, *Phallic Critiques: Masculinity and Twentieth-Century Literature,* Routledge & Kegan Paul, London, 1984, p 17.

Mailer's choice of words indicates the degree of fear and anger involved in this struggle.

34) Robert Stoller, *The Transsexual Experiment,* Hogarth Press, London, 1975, quoted by Thomas Ryan in, "The Roots of Masculinity" in, *The Sexuality of Man,* edited by Andy Metcalf and Martin Humphries, Pluto Press, London, 1985, p. 26.

35) "I think it can be shown that the sense of being a female develops out of the same roots (parental attitudes and ascription of sex, genitalia, and a biological force) as that of being a male, and that this core gender identity persists throughout life as unalterably in women as in men." Robert Stoller, *Sex and Gender: Volume 1 The Development of Masculinity and Femininity,* Maresfield Reprints, London, 1984, p. 52.

36) In recognizing a wish for a separate identity, one assumes that the child has the freedom to have such a wish and act upon it within the framework of family dynamics. Many girls grow up within a family where one or both parents want them to be boys so that the desire for a penis can represent an attempt to placate and please the parents, not establish a separate sense of self.

37) See also: R. R. Greenson, "Dis-identifying from the Mother: Its Special Importance for the Boy", *Int. J. Psycho-Anal.,* Vol. 49., 1968, pp. 370 -374.

38) In other words girls turn to masculinity when they despair about their own femininity, a conclusion drawn by Karen Horney, Joan Riviere and many others. See: Joan Riviere, "Hate, Greed and Aggression", op. cit. pp. 32-34.

39) Charles Rycroft, *A Critical Dictionary of Psychoanalysis*, op. cit., pp. 117-118.

40) Ernest Jones, "The Phallic Phase", in *Papers on Psycho-Analysis*, The Beacon Press, Boston, 1961, p. 474.

41) Stoller stresses that girls are not castrated versions of boys. He adds: "If Freud had worked with a woman without a vagina, I think he would have seen that the only thing a woman wants more than a penis is a vagina. It is only when a woman has normal genitalia that she can afford the luxury of wishing she had a penis." Robert Stoller, *Sex and Gender*, op. cit., p. 51.

42) The American psychoanalyst, Clara Thompson, emphasized that longings for the phallus had to do with female wishes to overcome an ingrained sense of inferiority brought about by cultural constraints, that is, by their living in male dominated societies. See: Clara Thompson, " "Penis Envy" in Women", in *Psychoanalysis and Women*, edited by Jean Baker Miller, Penguin Books, London, 1974, pp. 51-57.

43) The British social psychologist, Marie Jahoda, queries why Freud took such a strong stance about women not having a penis. She points out that Freud had no personal bias against women, quite the contrary. She concludes that he "unwittingly succumbed to the prevailing cultural stereotype of women, mistaking their historical role for the essence of femininity." Marie Jahoda, *Freud and the Dilemmas of Psychology*, The Hogarth Press, London, 1977, pp. 86-87.

44) *The Sunday Times Magazine*, 23 December 1984, pp. 30-31.

45) *Penis Greed* (Desire for the phallus) includes, of course, cannibalism. Many peoples literally ate their enemies and thereby believed they had gained their powers. Alternatively the hunting, preparation and eating of phallic foods has always been popular. These include vegetables that look like a phallus (asparagus) or extracts from phallic animals (Rhinoceros horn, Bull's blood, snake flesh) or meat, in general.

In the Far East tiger meat has become popular: "Tiger meat has been selling in Taiwan recently at $30 per kilo because some people believe it can increase virility." *International Herald Tribune*, 15-16 December 1984, p. 4.

46) David Halberstam, *The Best and the Brightest*, Barrie & Jenkins, London, 1972, p. 434.

47) It is said that Johnson would hold business meeting in his bathroom or pool while naked. Presumably he sought to demonstrate that he had the largest organ and to intimidate those present. His activities exemplifies greed for and greed by the penis. He was constantly trying to accumulate more and more riches, power and privileges (greed for). Concomitantly he used his wealth and position to force himself on and into others, often to possess, dominate or destroy them (greed by).

48) Yvonne Roberts, "The Tragedy of Mark Thompson", *The Sunday Times*, London, 23 December 1984, p. 23.

49) The psychoanalyst, Andrea Sabbadini, has coined the term 'possession anxiety' in relation to the fears that arise from using the phallus as opposed to fears that arise from losing it. Andrea Sabbadini, "Possession Anxiety: The Other Side of the Castration Complex", *Brit. J. Psychoth.*, Vol. 3., No. 1, Fall 1986.

I think possession anxiety is related to depressive dread brought about by the deployment of strengths and capacities to injure others.

50) Anais Nin, *Cities of the Interior,* distributed by the Phoenix Box Shop, New York, 1959, quoted by Phyllis Chesler, *Women and Madness,* op. cit., p. 4.

51) Personal communication, 1978.

52) Psychologist, Harriet Lerner, comments: "Expressions of anger are not only encouraged in boys and men, but may be glorified to pathological extremes......In contrast, women have been denied the forthright expression of even healthy and realistic anger.......To express anger--especially if one does so openly, directly--makes a woman *unladylike, unfeminine, unmaternal* --and sexually unattractive." Quoted by Carol Tavris in, *Anger: The Misunderstood Emotion,* Simon and Schuster, New York, p. 181.

53) In her journals Plath asserts: "I will not submit to having my life fingered by my husband, enclosed in a circle of his activity....I must have a legitimate field of my own." Yet six years after marrying the poet Ted Hughes she speaks of him in glowing terms as "the buried male muse and god creator risen to be my mate". *The Journals of Sylvia Plath,* quoted in book review by Anne Schrieber in, *International Herald Tribune,* 7 May 1982, p. 18.

54) Bernice Schultz Engle, "The Amazons in Ancient Greece", *Psychoanalytic Quarterly,* Vol. 11, 1942, pp. 512-514, 518 -521.

Engle comments: "Several modern historians have attempted to identify the Amazons with various tribes or classes of people such as the Hittites or armed priestesses. Other writers believe that knowledge for positive conclusions is lacking. A few dismiss the Amazons as mere fairy-tale creatures. But serious critics of Greek mythology like Bachofen, Weigert and Turel have emphasized the psychological importance to classical Greek civilization of Amazonian legends whether Amazons actually existed or not." Ibid., p. 512.

In contrast Walcot thinks the Amazons were "fantasy creatures, the type of predatory woman or domina; they are everything a woman ought not to be.....and illustrate the appalling consequences of woman usurping what is properly man's role." Peter Walcot, "Greek Attitudes Towards Women: The Mythological Evidence", *Greek & Rome,* Vol. XXX1, No. 1, April 1984, p. 42.

55) Engle, op. cit., pp. 514-515.

56) Ibid., pp. 542-548.

Engle concludes that the Amazons were 'originally Eurasian people with large numbers of women in their bands who first developed the mobile economic use of horseback riding.' Amazonian invasions aroused fears of domination by the Cretan matriarchy as well as Mycenæan gynecocracy (rule by women). Theseus was the great national hero of Dorian Greece who saved Athens from being overrun by the Amazonian tribes and finally conquered them. Interestingly he is said to have fathered a son by the Amazonian queen, and also taken on many Amazonian traits. Ibid., pp 536-538.

59) Theseus's victory was celebrated throughout Greek art and literature. The famous orator Lysias wrote: "They (the Amazons) were accounted men for their high courage rather than as women for their sex, so much did they seem to excel men....They had become the *rulers of many nations* and hearing of our country, how great it was, and moved by *greed of glory* they mustered the bravest nations and marched against us. Having met with valiant men they found their spirit was now like their sex; the repute they got was the reverse of the former.....They stood alone in failing to learn from their mistakes and so to be better advised in their future actions. They would not return home and report their own misfortunes and our ancestors' valor. So they perished on the spot, were punished for their folly.....So these women, in unjust *greed for others' land,* justly lost their own." (my italics) Lysias, *Epitaph,* ii, 4. Trans. by W. R. M. Lamb, Putnam, New York, 1930, quoted by Engle, Ibid., pp. 538.

58) Caroline Moorehead, "Deadlier than the male", *The Times*, 16 January 1985, p. 13.

Moorehead details the large number of women who have become terrorist activists and leaders. "Groups led by women tend to be tougher than those led by men and, once captured, few women have cooperated." Various women cited included: Angela Davis, Leila Khaled, Bernardine Dohrn, the Price sisters and Fusako Shigenobu.

Rose Rouse, "Pumping iron-maidens", *The Sunday Times*, 23 December 1984, p. 38.

Certainly male fears and female hopes for feminine hegemony did not die with the famous victory of Theseus at Athens, or of the Greeks over the Persians. Engle notes: "Historians celebrate the importance of the Greek defeat of the Persians. No doubt much fear of the Persian threat went back to the old fear of Cretan and Amazonian domination. One important connection has not elsewhere been noted. Soon after the battle of Salamis, Athenian art and literature began to emphasize the victories of Theseus over the Amazons.....in that battle one of Xerxes' allies was the Carian queen Artemesia whose valiant deeds brought from Xerxes the remark that his women allies had acted like men, his men aides like women. Athenians after that battle offered the immense reward of 10,000 drachmas for the capture of Artemesia alive 'so great was the indignity that a woman should make war against Athens'. (Herodotus: *History*, Dutton, New York, 1912 ed., viii, 88; 93)

59) Ernest Jones, "The Phallic Phase", op. cit., p. 463.

60) David Halberstam, *The Best and the Brightest*, op. cit. pp. 433-434.

61) Exodus, Chapter 7, verses 8 -12, *The Torah: A Modern Commentary*, op. cit., pp. 422-423.

Here 'serpent' is the translation of the Hebrew word, 'tanin'. A more appropriate translation would be crocodile. Ibid., p. 424.

62) Géza Róheim, *Psychoanalysis and Anthropology: Culture, Personality and the Unconscious*, International Universities Press, New York, 1973, pp.130-131, 141-142.

63) "Rats wrecked home on 'lovers revenge raid'", *The Daily Telegraph*, 7 February 1979, p. 7.

64) "Girls hold their mother responsible for their lack of a penis and do not forgive her for being thus put at a disadvantage."

Sigmund Freud, *New Introductory Lectures on Psycho-Analysis*, quoted by Walter Joffe in, "A Critical Review of the Status of the Envy Concept", op. cit., p. 535.

65) "Karl Abraham, "Manifestations of the Female Castration Complex", op. cit., p. 340.

Abraham emphasized that narcissistic injury was a major factor in the girl's angry response.

66) Ibid., p. 348.

67) In her paper on "Penis Awe' Phyllis Greenacre points out that Freud was aware that girls can have simultaneous but opposing reactions to the phallus. She quotes from his 1918 paper on "The Taboo on Virginity": "It is interesting now to find that psychoanalysts come across women in whom the two contrary attitudes -thraldom and enmity-both come to expression and remain in close association." Phyllis Greenacre, op. cit. p. 189.

The Standard Edition of Freud's work provides slightly different nuances in its translation of this passage: "It is interesting that in one's capacity as analyst one can meet with women in whom the opposed reactions of bondage and hostility both find expression and remain intimately associated with each other." *S.E.*, Vol. 11, p. 208.

68) Klein commented that "a number of factors contribute to penis-envy", but of these, oral issues play a central role: "I wish to consider the woman's penis-envy mainly in so far as it is of oral origin. As we know, under the dominance of oral desires, the penis is equated with the breast (Abraham) and in my experience the woman's penis-envy can be traced back to envy of the mother's breast. I have found that if the penis-envy of women is analyzed on these lines, we can see that its root lies in the earliest relation to the mother, in the fundamental envy of the mother's breast, and in the destructive feelings allied with it." Melanie Klein, "Envy and Gratitude", *Envy and Gratitude and Other Works 1946-1963*, op. cit., pp. 199-200.

69) John Todd and his colleagues have provided several examples of men who were obsessed by the idea that their penes were too small, that they couldn't satisfy their wives and that their wives were being unfaithful to them. All this is closely associated with morbid jealousy, and related, as I have previously discussed, to envious rage towards the female companion. We may surmise that these men harboured deep resentments towards their mothers whom they felt didn't give them enough and to whom they were unfaithful. These issues were repressed and at a much later date reenacted with their wives, but in an inverted form. (The wish to seek revenge because the wives weren't giving enough, i.e. the idea that their breasts were too small or they were keeping everything for themselves, was denied and transformed into fears of their wives' revenge because the men weren't giving enough. The wives' alleged unfaithfulness then justified the men's original murderous intentions arising not just out of frustration, but of envy.)

John Todd, J. R. M. Mackie and Kenneth Dewhurst, "Real or Imaginary Hypophallism", *Brit. J. Psychiat.*, Vol. 119, No. 550, September 1971, pp. 315-318.

70) This is a good example of *breast awe*. Felix Boehm, "The Femininity Complex in Men", op. cit., pp. 133-134.

71) Ferenczi adds: "The purpose of the sex act is an attempt on the part of the ego to return to mother's womb.... where there is no such painful disharmony between ego and environment as characterizes existence in the external world." Sandor Ferenczi, *Thalassa: A Theory of Genitality*, The Norton Library, W.W. Norton & Co., New York, 1968, pp.18-19.

72) Patrick Mullahy, "The Theories of Otto Rank", in *Oedipus: Myth and Complex*, Evergreen Books, Grove Press, New York, 1955, pp. 162-168.

73) "The phallus is the very mark of human desire; it is the expression of the wish for what is absent, for reunion (initially with the mother)." Juliet Mitchell, *Psychoanalysis and Feminism*, Allen Lane, London, 1974, p. 395.

74) Reay Tannahill, *Sex in History*, op. cit., pp. 208-213.

Tantric devotees claim that their practices are simply a means to an end, the achievement of a higher state of consciousness. To western eyes they are akin to phallic rituals that used to be extensively practiced in European and Near Eastern countries. For example, ancient stone lingams can still be found in England and Ireland. Non tantric phallic worship includes fetishistic masturbation and various states of auto-annihilation as described under the rubric of the *Nirvana Principle*.

75) In various writings Freud emphasized that the clitoris was an inferior organ, in size, function and general capacities to the penis. See for example: Sigmund Freud, "Some Psychical Consequences of the Anatomical Differences between the Sexes", op. cit., pp. 253 -256. Numerous studies now contest this view.

Although " the female organ is minute compared with the male organ....the size of its nerves...and nerve endings....compare strikingly with the same provision for the male. Indeed.....the glans of the clitoris is demonstrably richer in nerves than the male glans, for the two stems of the dorsalis clitoris are relatively three to four times as large as the equivalent of the penis...." Quoted from: R. L. Dickenson, *Human Sexual Anatomy,* 2nd edition, Williams and Wilkens, Baltimore, 1949; Judd Marmor, ibid., p. 232.

76) "Belgravia Rapist only 16", *The Daily Telegraph,* London, 26 July 1984, p. 3.

77) *Malleus,* op. cit., p.43, quoted by Ilza Veith, *Hysteria: The History of a Disease,* op. cit., p.63. By 'reality' I mean that many woman, through their demeanour, embody and justify imputations of wickedness.

78) Abraham has pointed out that in some women a fixed stare is equivalent to an erection., and has the same purpose as exhibiting a penis has with men. These women hope to scare people with their look just as they are scared by maleness (or their own feminine impulses). Karl Abraham, "Manifestations of the Female Castration Complex", op. cit., pp 352-353.

79) The phallus can represent a guilty conscience seen as 'the rod of authority' and more specifically 'male oppression'. Feminists like Germaine Greer believe this justifies active struggles to overcome all representatives of such authority: "What oppression lays upon us is not responsibility but guilt. The revolutionary woman must know her enemies, the doctors, psychiatrists, health visitors, priests, marriage counsellors, policemen, magistrates and genteel reformers, all the authoritarians and dogmatists who flock about her with warnings and advice." Germaine Greer, *The Female Eunuch,* MacGibbon & Kee, London, 1970, pp. 19-20.

This same phallus (the paternal judge) may conceal a maternal executioner. This 'Terrible Mother' conscience appears in a multitude of legends, the Hebrew *Lilith,* the Roman *Lamia,* the German *Brunhild.* In particular it is associated with the Greek figure of *Hecate* with her demands for human sacrifice.

Cirlot comments: "There is a certain quality of the virile about her (Brunhild), as there is about Hecate, the 'accursed huntress'. The overcoming of the threat which Lilith constitutes finds its symbolic expression in the trial of Hercules in which he triumphs over the Amazons." J. E. Cirlot, *A Dictionary of Symbols,* trans. by J. Sage, Routledge & Kegan Paul, London, 1962, p. 180.

80) Her unfeeling unresponsiveness demonstrates the passive aggressive assault in addition to active hostile attacks (screams, physical threats, etc). This is characteristic of the 'Snow Maiden' approach which prefers psychic damage (painful humiliations) to physical threats. In other words if she felt nothing, then I hadn't touched her, penetrated her, or had a relationship with her. From her point of view my impotence and her omnipotence remained intact.

Abraham describes a variety of such assaults including frigidity, kleptomania, vaginismus, marriage dread and parthenogenesis ('immaculate conceptions'). Karl Abraham, "Manifestations of the Female Castration Complex", op. cit., pp. 354-362.

Jones pointed out that the lack of feelings is also a defense against a sense of unendurable privation. One might add that it is also an attempt to placate the 'Terrible Mother' (persecutory envious and jealous internal maternal imago) by renouncing sexual feelings ('the permanent extinction of sexual pleasure'.) Jones called this state of self-castration *aphanisis.* Ernest Jones, "The Early Development of Female Sexuality", *Papers on Psycho-Analysis,* The Beacon Press, Boston, 1961, pp. 440-446.

81) The female 'Don Juan' exhausts lovers and therapists like her male counterpart preys on women. Her seductiveness is a partner to his charm, an instrument for the

vengeful vampirization and of the penis and maleness. Her pride depends on the ability to dominate, humiliate and rubbish men.

82) "In her admirable article on Cybele, Edith Weigart ("The Cult and Mythology of the Magna Mater from the Standpoint of Psychoanalysis", *Psychiatry, I*, 1938, pp. 347-378) has pointed out how tenaciously the mother cults persisted in Asia Minor and Greece, how deeply the worshippers of the Great Mother feared loss of fertility and death. They were concerned with birth and with conservation of their resources; they dreaded commercial and military expansion. Matriarchal influences predominated.

83) Ibid., pp. 517-518.

The original Greek reads respectively: deianeira; styganor; kreobotos; anandros; anitaneira; mnesimache; androphonos; androdamas; megathumos; androleteira, amometos; andromache; androktonos; and androdaiktos.

84) According to Heschyius, *kubelis* (Cybelis) is a synonym for *pelekus* or axe. Cybele, also known as the *Magna Mater* or Great Mother, was revered by the Amazons. Detailed studies of the Cybelic cults and the Amazons show many points of contact, if not similarity. Both favored the axe and the horse and both depreciated men. Cybelic temples gave the Amazons sanctuary. Ibid., p. 523.

See also: Maarten Vermaseren, *Cybele and Attis: The Myth and the Cult*, Thames and Hudson, London, 1977.

85) Reay Tannahill, *Sex in History*, op. cit., pp. 107, 237-238.

86) The rites of the Cybele are relatively well known. The novitiates could be both men and women. Women novitiates cut off one or both breasts. "Still, mutilation of the men was much more severe than that of women; in the male the primary sex characteristics were sacrificed, in the female the secondary." Bruno Bettelheim, *Symbolic Wounds: Puberty Rites and the Envious Male*, op. cit., p. 157.

87) Edith Weigart, "The Cult and Mythology of the Magna Mater from the Standpoint of Psychoanalysis", op. cit., p. 353.

88) "In spite of cauterisation with boiling oil, many died of the castration wounds." Ibid., p.353.

The Romans invented a castration clamp to reduce the mortality rate. "The penis was drawn through the oval ring to keep it out of harm's way, while the scrotum and testes were pulled through between the arms of the clamp.....when everything was locked in position.....It took only a single stroke of the knife to cut away scrotum and testes, and the cut edges were then either sewn up or cauterized. Reay Tannahill, *Sex in History*, op. cit., p. 237.

89) After being anointed, the priests wore long hair which they offered to the goddess from time to time. They also took many other measures to feminize their bodies. Latin and Greek writers usually spoke of them in the feminine gender. Ibid., p. 353.

Weigart points out "from this form of religious exercise, arose the concept of fanaticism (from fanum-sanctuary).These "fanatici" of Cybele were in the thralls of the goddess, her "famuli," they were excluded from the masculine struggle for life." Ibid., p. 353.

90) Ibid., p. 354.

91) Bruno Bettelheim, *Symbolic Wounds: Puberty Rites and the Envious Male*, op. cit., p. 157.

92) Ibid. pp. 157-158.

93) Bettelheim contests Freud's theory that circumcision has to do with a "phylogenetic memory trace" of the jealous father. He says there is little evidence to support this while there is a large body of myth, legend and social practices to indicate that castration in the service of the great maternal deities, as the price of grace, was widespread. "These myths, when considered with the revenge like postcircumcision behaviour that is found among some tribes today, support the idea that circumcision may have originated with women and been taken over only later by men." Bruno Bettelheim, "Circumcision Imposed by Women", Ibid., pp 159-164.

See also: Robert Hobson, "Psychological Aspects of Circumcision", *Journal of Analytical Psychology*, Vol. 6, No. 1, 1961, pp. 5-33; and Hanny Lightfoot-Klein, "Pharonic Circumcision of Females in the Sudan", op. cit., p. 355-358.

Among Jews circumcision is a ritual obligation for all male infants on the eighth day after birth. (Genesis 17:11-12). According to the biblical account it was originally performed by Abraham on himself at the age of ninety nine at divine behest. But rabbinic legend suggests it was known before. In fact the procedure dates back to prehistoric times. *Encyclopedia Judaica*, Keter Publishing House, Jerusalem, 1972, Vol. 5, pp. 567-575.

It is possible that circumcision was originally a ritual sacrifice to appease the fertility Goddesses in the transformation of the tribe of Abraham from a matriarchal cult to a patriarchal religion.

I am reminded of an incident with a Jewish colleague. His first son had just been born and he was considering the *bris* (ritual circumcision) on the eighth day. In large measure he thought the practice was atavistic and brutal, but he was wavering, and had just decided to go through with it when he received a telegram from his mother, "Remember the eighth day!" This so frightened and infuriated him that he changed his mind, but he was left with considerable unease. His mother continued to bitterly criticize him.

94) The Harkavy translation of the Bible adds some interesting nuances: "11 When men strive together one with another, and the wife of the one draweth near for to deliver her husband out of the hand of him that smiteth him, and putteth forth her hand, and taketh him by the secrets: 12 Then thou shalt cut off her hand, thine eyes shall not pity *her.*" *Deuteronomy* in, *The Pentateuch* from *The Twenty-Four Books of the Old Testament*, Vol. 1, translated by Alexander Harkavy, Hebrew Publishing Co., New York, 1926, p. 331.

Subsequent commentaries de-emphasized the punishment. According to the *Babylonian Talmud* (Tractate: "Baba Kamma") only a monetary fine was meant, but only when the woman had other means to save her husband. The monetary compensation was in lieu of 'eye for eye, tooth for tooth', or in this instance, as Rabbi Hugo Gryn has pointed out, "a testicle for a testicle". Personal communication, May 1985.

95) G. R. Driver and John C. Miles, Middle Assyrian Laws in, *The Assyrian Laws*, Oxford, 1935, para. 8, quoted by Reay Tannahill, *Sex in History*, op. cit., p. 58.

96) Karl Stern, *The Flight from Women*, George Allen and Unwin, London, 1966, p. 97.

97) Ibid., pp. 97-98.

98) At birth Christina was hairy, yelled loudly and was covered with a caul which enveloped most of her body. All this in conjunction with wishful thinking led the midwives to proclaim that the baby was a boy and precipitated celebrations about the birth of a male heir. This was but one of many discordant impingements on the girl's development. See: Georgina Masson, *Queen Christina*, Secker & Warburg, London, 1968; and Barbara Cartland, *The Outrageous Queen: A Biography of Christina of Sweden*, Frederick Muller Ltd., London, 1956.

99) Friedrich Hebbel, *Judith und Holofernes*, discussed by Sigmund Freud in, "The Taboo of Virginity", op. cit., p. 207-208.

100) Ibid., p. 207.

101) Ibid., p. 205. By *envy* Freud means desire. So *envy for the penis* exemplifies what I term *penis greed* tempered by *hostile bitterness*, that is, *penis envy.*

102) Peter Lomas, "Dread of envy as an aetiological factor in puerperal breakdown", op. cit., p. 110.

One could add that childbirth provides conclusive proof that a woman is a woman, not a man, as some women wish to be.

103) Moulton provides several examples of women whose 'typical penis envy' covered a multitude of disturbed family relations. Ruth Moulton, "A Survey and Reevaluation of the Concept of Penis Envy", *Psychoanalysis and Women,* edited by Jean Baker Miller, Penguin Books, London, 1974, pp.251-254.

104) In spite of her travails and scandals, it must be noted that Christina was a courageous politician and person. She effected a number of significant reforms during her reign, especially in education, and refused to be dragooned into militaristic policies. In later life she was a benefactor of music, art and literature. *Encyclopedia Britannica*, 15th edition, 1974.

105) Nicolas Comfort, "Thatcher Uses Female Charm Says Nott", *The Daily Telegraph*, 26 January 1985, p. 36.

106) Geraldine Ferraro was the Democratic candidate for the Vice-Presidency. This was the first time that a woman ran for such high office in the United States. Her phallic 'possessions' included a successful husband, a further focus of envy and jealousy.

107) Phyllis Chesler comments on the male anxieties and aggression aroused by women who engage in activities or take on male roles or qualities. She quotes from a 1971 New York Times report on Billie Jean King: "Billie Jean King, the country's most successful woman athletic star, says she is never offended by people who tell her she plays tennis just like a man. But she has become increasingly irritated by people who ask her when she is going to settle down and attend to a home and family." Phyllis Chesler, *Women and Madness*, op. cit., p. 265.

Subsequently King was subject to an extensive campaign of slander and character abuse in the press. Similar attacks had been made on tennis champion Martina Navratilova for her determined, aggressive, fast, powerful play, as well as her life style which include fast cars and a big estate in Virginia.

108) F. Bryk, *Die Beschneidung bei Mann und Weib,* Gustav Feller, Neubrandenburg, 1931, p. 56, quoted by Bruno Bettelheim, *Symbolic Wounds: Puberty Rites and the Envious Male*, op. cit., p. 254. Bettelheim adds that while envious revenge may be a contributing factor, he thinks it is not the major motive behind the Nandi's mutilation of girls. He thinks it arises from more positive desires such as the wish to gain control of their female sex functions.

109) This quip has been attributed to Henry Kissinger.

110) Otto Fenichel concluded that boys suffer the same castration fears as girls, and may react in the same way with wish fulfillment or vindictive behaviour. He states that the former covers deep feelings of inferiority and wounded pride while the latter has to do with murderous rage towards whomever may be held responsible (usually parents) for masculine inadequacies.

Otto Fenichel, *The Psychoanalytic Theory of Neurosis*, op. cit., p. 495.

111) An advert by the American McDonnell-Douglas Corporation exemplifies envious rivalry. It proudly proclaims the virtues of a new weapons system which can destroy the enemy (in this case, the masculine prowess of the USSR) wherever it may be. Helen Caldicott, *Missile Envy*, William Morrow & Co., New York, 1984, p. 297.

112) Ibid., p. 297.

113) Description of World War 2 by American General George Patton. Ibid., p. 297.

114) See: Mary Barnes & Joseph Berke, *Mary Barnes: Two Accounts of a Journey Through Madness*, Penguin Books, London, 1982.

The stageplay, *Mary Barnes*, was adapted from the book by David Edgar and performed in London at the Royal Court Theatre in 1979. The man was angry because a friend of his had seen the play twice and had remarked about my being depicted by a brilliant character.

115) Personal communication. As many men, this person was overwhelmed by severe conflicts between body, gender and personal identities. He had great difficulty in separating himself from his love/hate relationship with his mother. Sometimes this struggle seemed too much and he tried to avoid it by identifying with her. Then his personal identity was at greatest risk and his *penis envy* rose accordingly.

116) Hanna Segal has also described a situation where intense *penis envy* led a male patient to dream of anal intercourse. Ostensibly Segal represented the potent, successful father whom the man hated out of envy and jealousy and the analysis represented the paternal potency under attack. Hanna Segal, *Introduction to the Work of Melanie Klein*, op. cit. pp. 42-43.

As the treatment proceeded, issues of maternal potency began to predominate. The man launched desperate attacks on Segal representing the phallic breasts, again demonstrating the close connections between the penis and the breast.

117) Melanie Klein points out that the *good penis* not only expresses but helps to overcome aggression. This helps a man to obtain a sense of security in himself, adds to his creativity in other areas and adds to his masculine sense of achievement. Melanie Klein, "Love, Guilt and Reparation", op. cit., p. 73.

118) John Donne, *The Complete Poetry and Prose of John Donne & The Complete Poetry of William Blake*, The Modern Library, Random House, New York, 1941, pp. 84-85.

CHAPTER 7

1) The ancient Romans described a terrifying night creature which they called a *strix* from the Greek word meaning to screech. Like an owl and hawk combined, the *strix* was a woman by day and ravenous bird by night who flew through the air on amorous, murderous or cannibalistic missions. The *strix* lay the basis for innumerable popular legends. Norman Cohn, *Europe's Inner Demons*, Paladin Books, London, 1976, pp. 206 -224.

2) John Widdowson, "The Witch as a Frightening and Threatening Figure" in *The Witch Figure*, edited by Venetia Newall, Routledge & Kegan Paul, London, 1973, pp. 200-220.

3) Aligheri Dante, *Inferno*, Canto 34, l. 30; John Milton, *Paradise Lost*, Book I, l. 777 quoted by Beatrice White, "Cain's Kin", in *The Witch Figure*, edited by Venetia Newall, op. cit., p. 189.

4) Iona & Peter Opie, *The Classic* Fairy *Tales*, Paladin Books, London, 1980, pp. 58-63.

5) Lloyd DeMause, "The Evolution of Childhood", in *The History of Childhood,* edited by Lloyd DeMause, The Psychohistory press, New York, 1974, p. 1.

6) Ibid., p. 25.

7) Ibid., p. 29.

8) "Robert Pemell complained in 1653 of the practice of "both high and low ladies of farming out their babies to irresponsible women in the country," and as late as 1780 the police chief of Paris estimated that of 21,000 children born each year in his city, 17,000 were sent into the country to be wet-nursed, 2,000 or 3,000 were placed in nursery homes, 700 were wet-nursed at home and only 700 were nursed by their mothers." Ibid., p.35.

9) One aspect of this feared involvement had to do with excessive grief and guilt following the deaths of multiple offspring. This reaction was mitigated but not eliminated when such deaths were expected.

10) Venetia Newall, "The Jew as Witch Figure", in *The Witch Figure*, edited by Venetia Newall, op. cit., pp. 95-124.

Rhoda White, *From Infancy to Womanhood: A Book of Instructions for Young Mothers*, London, 1882, p. 31, quoted in Lloyd DeMause, "The Evolution of Childhood", op. cit. p. 12 - 13.

11) There exists an enormous literature on child abuse ranging from physical injury, physical neglect and failure to thrive to mental cruelty. In Britain the National Society for the Prevention of Cruelty to Children (NSPCC) has documented the increasing number of reported cases:

Angela Skinner and Raymond Castle, *78 battered children: a retrospective study*, NSPCC, London, 1969.

Susan Creighton, *Child Victims of Physical Abuse, 1976*, NSPCC, London.

Susan Creighton, *Trends in Child Abuse*, NSPCC, London, 1984.

Gavin Bell, "Child Sex abuse cases doubled last year, NSPCC survey shows", *The Times*, 22 March 1986, p. 4.

The same holds true for other countries. In a typical late '80's report, Istat, the Italian statistical centre, reported a big increase in reported rape and abuse cases. Roger Boyes, "Italian rape and child abuse increase", *The Times*, 2 January 1988, p. 7.

12) Susan Creighton, "Child Abuse Deaths", *NSPCC Information Briefing No.* 5, NSPCC, London, 1985.

"The Victims who can't fight back", *The Times*, 31 March 1986, p. 10.

Clare Garner, " More than 100 children die of abuse and neglect every year," *The Independent*, 15 March 1999, p. 5.

13) I do not think that every instance of child abuse can be simply reduced to parental malice. Much depends on the capacity of the parents to support each other, or not; the character of the child; the personality of the parents; their own background (often violent and deprived); their capacity to contain their own infantile feelings, or not; and so forth. Nevertheless, when an adult who feels worthless and empty faces a child being cared for by another, or demanding attention himself, the narcissistic rage, itself an extension of envious forces, often becomes uncontrollable. See:

Joan Court, "Battering Parents", *Social Work*, Vol. 26, No. 1, January 1969.

Jean Moore & Beryl Day, "Family Interaction Associated with Abuse of Children Over 5 Years of Age", *Child Abuse and Neglect*, the International Journal, The Pergamon Press, 1979.

Christine Smakowska,"Marital Problems and Family Violence", *NSPCC Information Briefing No. 7*, NSPCC, London, 1985.

14) "Hansel and Gretel" in Jacob and Wilhelm Grimm, *Selected Tales*, op. cit., p.56.

15) Ibid., p. 60.

16) Ibid., p. 61.

17) Joseph Rheingold gives many examples of maternal destructiveness in his chapters on "Parental Cruelty" and "The Filicidal Impulse" in *The Fear of Being a Woman: A Theory of Maternal Destructiveness*, op. cit. pp. 1-84.

The 1999 NSPCC report was featured by Clare Garner, op. cit. p.5.

18) The point of eating human meat is to incorporate and take over the other's vital essence. So the wish behind eating a baby's behind, or other parts, may be to incorporate youth and new life, just as the wicked Queen in "Snow White" tried to eat the young girls liver and lungs both to destroy her and to take over her youthful beauty, exuberance, sexuality, potential, etc. When envy predominates over greed, the primary purpose is destructive.

19) Lloyd deMause, "The Evolution of Childhood", op. cit., p. 7.

20) Bertram Karon and Gary VandenBos, *Psychotherapy of Schizophrenia: Treatment of Choice*, Jason Aronson, New York, 1981, pp. 118-119.

21) R. D. Laing, *In the Psychiatrist's Chair*, interview by Dr. Anthony Clare, BBC Radio 4, 14 July 1985.

See also: R. D. Laing, *The Facts of Life*, Pantheon Books, New York, 1976, pp. 3-6.

22) Eric Carle, *The Very Hungry Caterpillar*, Hamish Hamilton, London, 1970.

23 op. cit., p. 44.

I added the point in parentheses about narcissistic motheirng, as it always evokes envious hostility.

24) Joseph Rheingold, *The Mother, Anxiety, and Death: The Catastrophic Death Complex*, Boston, 1967.

25) Peter Lomas has detailed how the 'dread of envy' can be a casual factor in puerperal breakdown, that is, an acute psychosis after the birth of a child. He shows that the wish to abandon or kill a newborn baby was not necessarily aroused by hostility to the child, but by the urgent need to placate a feared and fearful grandmother. See: Peter Lomas, "Dread of Envy as an aetiological factor in puerperal breakdown, op. cit., p. 108.

26) Plutarch documented Carthaginian child sacrifice: "......with full knowledge and understanding they themselves offered up their own children, and those who had no children would buy little ones from poor people and cut their throats as if they were so many lambs or young birds; meanwhile the mother stood by without a tear or moan; but should she utter a single moan or let fall a single tear, she had to forfeit the money, and her child was sacrificed nevertheless.." Plutarch, *Moralia*, Frank Babbitt trans., London, 1928, p. 493.

27) Henry Bett, *Nursery Rhymes and Tales: Their Origin and History*, New York, 1924, p. 35,

28) Jacob and Wilhelm Grimm, *Selected Tales,* op. cit., pp. 77-81; pp. 114-115; pp. 178-183.

29) Ibid., p. 178.

30) Christina Crawford, *Mommie Dearest,* Hart-David, London, 1979. The book was also made into a film with the same title starring Faye Dunaway as Joan Crawford and directed by Frank Perry (MGM).

While Christina Crawford was not an impartial observer, many of her stories were collaborated by people who knew the family. Even late in her life, Joan Crawford tried to take over her daughter's life and roles. Once Christina, an aspiring actress in a TV soap opera, was rushed to hospital with gynecological problems. Her mother immediately stood in for her playing love scenes with a man thirty years her junior.

31) Leslie Childe, "'Supernatural Trail' of girl in witch trial", *The Daily Telegraph,* 14 December 1983, p. 3.

32) Leslie Childe, "Enter an exorcist at the witch trial", *The Daily Telegraph* , 15 December 1983, p. 17.

33) Ibid., p. 17.

The trial obviously evoked powerful feelings among the spectators. The healer, a tiny old woman dressed in black and carrying a wooden crucifix, appeared daily at the back of the courtroom. At one stage she tried to grab Ms. Compton but was taken away by the police. She explained: "I had a dream in which the Devil came to me and told me that Carol Compton and her mother are possessed by an 18th-century spirit. That spirit has given them the power of fire." She added the Devil had told her to cleanse Carol of her demon. Ibid. p. 17.

34) The encircling snake represents clinging vines, possessive arms and dominating, insatiable women. And because the snake devours its object whole, it also has been associated with mothers' devouring breasts, eyes, mouths, vaginas, wombs and psyches. Finally because the snake gets into things, it has been linked with the female phallus, which 'knows what is going on'. See: Philip Slater, *The Glory of Hera: Greek Mythology and the Greek Family,* Beacon Press, Boston, 1968, pp. 80-97.

35) Daniel Jaffe, "The Masculine Envy of Woman's Procreative Function", op. cit., pp. 534-541.

36) Robert Stoller, *Sex and Gender,* op. cit., pp. 108-125.

37) The boy was 5 years old when she came into therapy. She had been dressing him as a girl since he was 11 months old. At this point Mrs. C. also had a daughter who was 11 years old. Ibid., p. 109.

38) That was until she was nine or ten years old. Afterwards she enjoyed normal girls' activities. Ibid., p. 301

However, the onset of menarche, and development of breasts was extremely traumatic. It ended her hopes of becoming a boy. Ibid., p. 113.

39) Ibid., p. 120.

40) In her destructive aspects Cybele is not unlike the Indian goddess, Kali

John Carroll points out that the male Indian fear of females has a lot to do with the practice of totally indulgent mothering till about aged five followed by exposure to a constraining and critical male environment. Since the Indian father remains distant from his son in early childhood, the boy is deprived of crucial identifications that would allow him to overcome fears of the ever present, dominating, all powering mother.

John Carroll, *Guilt: The Grey Eminence Behind Character, History & Culture,* Routledge & Kegan Paul, London, 1985, p. 61.

41) Edith Weigart, "The Cult and Mythology of the Magna Mater from the Standpoint of Psychoanalysis:, op. cit., p. 357.

In this narration, Attis's bride mourns him with the Great Mother, binds him in soft wrappings, and kills herself by cutting off her breasts. An almond tree then grows up on the burial ground.

42) Ovid, *Metamorphoses, X* (A. Riese edition), pp. 103-105, quoted by Weigart, Ibid., p.357.

The Latin translation is a paraphrase according to Arnobius. Ibid., p. 537.

According to Andrea Sabbadini, a more literal translation would be: "Let the parts that damage me, die."

43) Betty Radice, *Who's Who in the Ancient World,* Penguin Books, London, 1984, pp. 48-49.

Adonis was a vegetation God born of incest between father and daughter. He was loved by Aphrodite (Venus). His name is semitic, meaning 'Lord' (Hebrew: Adonai) and was commonly associated with the Babylonian, Thammuz, beloved of Ishtar. Both loved beautiful mother goddesses and were torn to pieces by angry fathers in revenge. Both are also associated with nature cults of death and rebirth.

See also: *New Larousse Encyclopedia of Mythology,* Paul Hamlyn, London, 1969, p. 150, and Edith Weigart, "The Cult and Mythology of the Magna Mater from the Standpoint of Psychoanalysis:, op. cit., pp. 357-358.

44) Zeus was Lord of the sky, of wind and rain, thunder and lightning. Like Jupiter, his Roman counterpart, he was omnipotent, omniscient and the supreme authority, the upholder of law, but law based on might, not morality. *New Larousse Encyclopedia of Mythology,* op. cit., p. 98, pp 85-198.

45) Rambo is the character created by Sylvester Stallone, the incarnation of American omnipotence and vengeance.

46) Iona & Peter Opie, *The Classic Fairy Stories,* op. cit., pp. 58-82, especially pp. 58-59, 78-79.

47) "Jack and the Bean-Stalk", Ibid., p. 214.

Jack and his mother are close to starvation and, as a last chance, he is sent to sell their cow. The lad exchanges it for colored beans which, when he returns, his mother flings into the garden. Overnight a huge beanstalk grows right through the clouds. The widow forbids him to climb it, but to no avail. Jack sets out and eventually comes to a strange, barren land. He is frightened and fears he will die, but walks on and soon meets an old lady, not a witch, but a good woman, who tells him the truth about his background. So in this account we not only see a clash between the good and bad father, but between the good and bad mother (seen as critical and nagging).

48) Ibid., p. 217.

50) These paintings are in the Prado Museum, Madrid, Spain. They are reproduced in many books including, Norman Cohn, *Europe's Inner Demons,* op. cit. plates 7 & 8.

51) Personal communication, 1975.

52) It is interesting that the central actions takes place in a mansion far away in the sky. The location serves several purposes, both to emphasize the father's character, aloof, 'all-

high', distant, and to distance the action from down to earth dramas, where cannibalistic fathers and vengeful sons are extremely frightening.

The Giant's wife embodies a bit of the bad mother, that colludes with the wicked father to devour, terrorize and generally oppress the children. But she has some good qualities as she helps Jack confront her husband. The wife may also represent small bits of goodness in the Giant himself. After all, after killing the father, that is changing from a good to bad person. he did feel remorse.

53) *New Larousse Encyclopedia of Mythology,* op. cit., pp. 87-93.

54) Zeus was often at a loss in the presence of a maternal goddesses. When Metis, his first wife and goddess of wisdom, became pregnant, he swallowed her whole, thus incorporating wisdom and child bearing capacities. Eventually Athene sprang forth from his head. Zeus also renounced Thetis because it was predicted that any child of theirs would dethrone him. He arranged for her to be married to a mortal. Ibid., p. 99.

55) Tantalus was King of Siplos in Lydia, an ancient kingdom now part of modern Turkey opposite Greece. In punishment for dismembering and serving his son to the Gods he was made to stand in water up to his chin and suffer terrible thirst and hunger in the presence of food and drink which just moved out of his reach when he tried to take them. Betty Radice, *Who's Who in the Ancient World,* op. cit., p. 232.

56) Pelops was King of Elis, an ancient kingdom on the Western side of the Peloponnesus peninsula, named after him.

The *Orestia* was written by Aeschylus and is the only surviving trilogy in Greek drama which survives from antiquity. It describes a bloody chain of ambition, hubris, murder and revenge.

57) Joshua Berke, personal communication, 1976.

James Joyce essentially commented on this very point in his novel, *Ulysses.* "The son unborn mars beauty; born he brings pain, divides attention, increases care...his growth is his father's decline, his youth his father's envy." Quoted by John Ross in "Oedipus Revisited: Laius and the 'Laius Complex'", *Psychoanalytic Study of the Child,* Vol. 37, Yale University Press, New Haven, 1982, p. 169.

58) In his study of Greek mythology and family structure, Philip Slater observes: "....the father-son conflict is but a tiny episode, while the prevailing situation is one of father-absence and mother-son marriage. Philip Slater, *The Glory of Hera: Greek Mythology and the Greek Family,* op. cit., p. 135.

59) Different studies provide divergent views about the lot of women in ancient Greece. Many comment on their lack of legal, political and religious rights and how women were relegated to domestic toil. Others point out that in various city states the women had extensive rights. In Sparta the girls were trained like the young men in discus and spear throwing and were expected to attend the games and festivals. Women could and did become influential administrators. See:

Reay Tannahill, *Sex in History,* op. cit., pp. 82-87.

Thorkil Vanggaard, *Phallós: A Symbol and its History in the Male World,* International Universities Press, New York, 1972, p. 45.

60) The Dorians supervised the upbringing of boys with an intensity and severity that was admired throughout Greece. The emphasis was on the development of *aretë,* an ideal of nobility which has no precise equivalent in English. It is close to the old norse idea of *hamingja. Aretë* embodied physical strength, marital prowess, courage, integrity, clarity of thought, stamina, honesty and adherence to duty. *Aretë* was synonymous with honor, fame, and distinction as well as aristocracy and fine breeding. Ibid., pp. 34-35.

61) Straton, *Anthologica Palatinus,* XII, 4, quoted by Reay Tannahill, *Sex in History,* op. cit., p. 75.

62) Vanggaard comments: "Since the erotic pleasure was subordinated to a more important aim this was a genuinely symbolic act, the aim being to make of the boy a man with strength, a sense of duty, eloquence, cleverness, generosity, courage and other noble virtues." He compares this with the actions of New Guinea natives. The Kiwai Papuan when selecting wood for a harpoon, will press his phallus against the trunk of the chosen tree in order to impart straightness, strength and great power of penetration. Thorkil Vanggaard, *Phallós: A Symbol and its History in the Male World,* op. cit., pp. 12-13.

63) Ibid., pp. 43-44.

Paiderastia was akin to the upbringing of North American plains Indians or of Japanese before World War 2. It emphasized lofty ideals, immense demands, merciless severity and produced warriors of great skill and tenacity. *The Sacred Band of Thebes* consisted of pairs of lovers fighting side by side, and was the backbone of the Theban army that conquered the Spartans of Leuctra in 371 B.C.E. *The Sacred Band* remained unconquered until 338 B.C.E. when it was overcome by Philip of Macedonia at Cheironeia. All 300 of its members were killed and lay on the battlefield pair by pair. Ibid., p. 41; Reay Tannahill, *Sex in History,* op. cit., pp. 79-80.

The role of the erömenos came to and end when the boy reached adolescence as was signified by the first growth of beard. The erastës or older lover was usually in his 30's.

64) In Plato's *Symposium,* Phaedrus says: "I for my part am at a loss to say what greater blessing a man can have in earliest youth than an honourable love, or a lover than an honourable favourite." Quoted by Thorkil Vanggaard, *Phallós: A Symbol and its History in the Male World,* op. cit., p. 40.

65) The status of the *erastai,* or older lovers, was on a par with the boy's father. They could and were held responsible for the conduct of the *erömenos* and shared his honor and dishonor. After the paiderastic relationship was concluded the older man continued to have special relationship with his *erömenos,* perhaps akin to that of a Godfather or favored uncle, and could be called upon for help when needed. Ibid., p. 37.

66) Thorkil Vanggaard, *Phallós: A Symbol and its History in the Male World,* op. cit., p.26.

Slaves were forbidden to be taken as lovers because they were considered unworthy. They were also forbidden to rub boys with oil at the gymnasia because this practice often heralded the onset on a paiderastic relationship.

The physical erotic element in *paiderastia* was certainly present. Men and boys tended to meet at the gymnasia where the boys competed in sport naked except for the oil on their body and fine strings that protectively tied the foreskin back over the glans of the penis. Reay Tannahill, *Sex in History,* op. cit., p.78.

67) The German scholar E. Bethe has summarized the Dorian ideas about male upbringing: "The qualities of the man, his heroism, his arete, are in some way transmitted to the beloved boy through love. Therefore it is society's view that skillful and competent men ought to love boys; the state even exerts pressure on them to do so......it was an honour for a boy to have found an honourable lover and be ceremoniously united with him, an honour which in Crete was celebrated in public by the family." E. Bethe, *Die DorischeKnabenliebe, ihre Ethik und ihre Idee,* Rheinishces Museum für Philologie, Neue Folge, 1907, p. 457, quoted by Thorkil Vanggaard, Ibid., p. 43.

68) Aristophanes, *The Birds,* Ls. 137-142, quoted by Reay Tannahill, *Sex in History,* op. cit., p. 78.

69) Thorkil Vanggaard, *Phallós: A Symbol and its History in the Male World,* op. cit., pp. 40 &43.

70) Ibid., pp. 26-27.

71) I refer, in particular, to the narcissistic, as well as homoerotic, components of paiderastia.

72) Pelops needed help to gain the hand of Hippodameia, the daughter of King Oenomaus, who demanded that all her suitors stake their lives in a chariot race. Many suitors had lost their lives. Pelops managed to bribe, Myrtilus, the King's charioteer, to loosen a wheel, so the King lost the race. Later Pelops murdered Myrtilus in order to get rid of an embarrassing accomplice. But the father of Myrtilus was Hermes (Mercury) who was enraged by Pelops's action. In revenge he placed a curse on Pelops and his House. I shall discuss many of the consequences of this curse in the next chapter on sibling rivalry.

73) The Laius-Chrysippus legend was well known in the fifth and fourth centuries B.C.E. and formed the basis for several tragedies all since lost. These include *Laius* by Aeschylus and *Chrysippus* by Euripides, plays known because of references to them in other works.

74) Presumably Jocasta realized Laius's fears. So in getting pregnant she was getting back at him for his homosexuality, misogyny and overall indifference to the needs of a woman. As far as the Greeks were concerned this was all part of the war between the sexes. John Ross, "Oedipus Revisited: Laius and the 'Laius Complex'", *Psychoanalytic Study of the Child,* op. cit., pp. 177-178.

75) Ross comments: "If the anachronisms can be pardoned, Laius's misdeeds and delusions can be taken as "evidence" of: disturbances in gender identity and sexual orientation, problems with impulse control; unmodulated aggressivity; cognitive and intellectual impairment; and pathological narcissism." John Ross, "Oedipus Revisited Laius and the 'Laius Complex'", *Psychoanalytic Study of the Child,* op. cit., p. 177.

Laius himself had been abandoned and persecuted as a child. His father, Labdacus, the ruling King of Thebes, died when he was one year old. He was left in the care of his mother. Later he was forced to flee Thebes and wander about Greece, when his uncle usurped the throne. Ibid., p. 177.

76) Ross strongly makes this point and adds that the same was true for all but a handful of analytic authors after Freud. Ibid., p. 174.

77) As presented, Oedipus was a virtuous young man, perhaps too much so. Having learned from a drunken friend that Queen Merope and King Polybus are not his real parents, he flees Corinth. One might think he would discuss the matter with them and even be inclined to stay, for if the news were true, then he would be safe in his adopted home. The failure to do so may have been a dramatic necessity, but it also indicates the existence of unconscious forces related to his severed past and uncertain present.

78) Betty Radice, *Who's Who in the Ancient World,* op. cit., p. 225.

The Sphinx had the body of a lion and a human head. It originated in Egypt where it was considered either female or male, but came to Greece via the Near East and then was always considered to be female. In Kleinian terms, the Sphinx can be seen as a 'pre-oedipal' combined parent figure.

79) Sophocles, *Oedipus Rex,* trans. by Albert Cook, in, *Ten Greek Plays,* edited by L. R. Lind, Riverside Editions, Houghton Mifflin Co., Cambridge, Mass., 1957, pp.111-154.

Teiresias was the blind prophet who foretold the problem and only told the truth after Oedipus threatened him. The quality of his blindness seemed to be associated with wisdom.

Jocasta clearly understands the situation before Oedipus. She tries to convince Oedipus not to proceed with his investigations for several reasons: conceal her infidelities, protect Oedipus, and continue the relationship which allowed her to remain Queen and maintain her female powers and ambitions.

80) The struggle for preeminence between Laius and Jocasta, Jocasta and Oedipus, Oedipus and Creon (Jocasta's brother) reflected the continuing conflict about matriarchal versus patriarchal authority, and the gradual shift to a system of patriarchal authority. Jocasta's reign symbolized continuing matriarchal power, after a time when she had ostensibly accepted male domination by concurring in his attempts to destroy Oedipus at birth.

81) Rollo May, "Guilt and Awareness" in, *Man and Society,* edited by Roger W. Smith, Anchor Books, Doubleday & Co., New York, 1971, pp. 171-184.

John Steiner, "Turning a Blind Eye: The Cover Up for Oedipus, *Int. Rev. Psycho-Anal.*, Vol. 12, 1985, pp. 161-172.

82) Sophocles, *Oedipus at Colonus,* trans. by Robert Fitzgerald, in, *Greek Tragedies,* edited by David Grene and Richmond Lattimore, Phoenix Books, The Univ. of Chicago Press, Chicago, Illinois, 1960, L. 144.

83) Oedipus to his son, Polyneices:

"Now go! For I abominate and disown you!
You utter scoundrel! Go with the malediction
I here pronounce for you: that you shall never
Master your native land by force of arms,
Nor ever see your home again in Argos,
The land below the hill; but you shall die
By your own brother's hand, and you shall kill
The brother who banished you. For this I pray." Ibid., L's 1383-1390

84) Plato, *Symposium,* 213 d, quoted by Reay Tannahill, op. cit., pp.76-77.

85) Lloyd DeMause provides many examples of the transference relationship between parent to child (which he calls, 'the reversal reaction') in his chapter on "The Evolution of Childhood, in *The History of Childhood,* edited by Lloyd deMause, op. cit., pp. 6-21.

86) The extended 'Homily Against Wilful Rebellion' seems to have been the basis for a passage in Shakespeare's, *King Lear,* when Gloucester speaks to his bastard son, Edmund, about familial and social conflict. *Certain Sermons or Homilies,* 1817 edition, p. 541, quoted by G. K. Hunter in his introduction to, *King Lear,* Penguin Books, London, 1972, p. 40.

Hunter points out that behind this homily and the passage from *Lear,* there lies a passage in Mark:

"Now the brother shall betray the brother to death and the father the son; and children shall rise up against their parents and shall cause them to be put to death......

but he that shall endure unto the end, the same shall be saved." 13. 12-13

87) Robinson added, "Children should not know, if it could be kept from them, that they have a will of their own, but in their parents' keeping." P. Greven, *Child-Rearing Concepts, 1628-1861,* Itasca, 1973, pp. 13-14, quoted by Lawrence Stone, *The Family, Sex and Marriage In England 1500-1800,* Weidenfeld and Nicolson, London, 1977, pp. 162-163.

88) Ibid., p. 163.

89) Dr. Busby was known to the boys as 'flog-em' Busby.

Dr. Gill used to have 'whipping-fits'. They were not unusual. Indentured apprentices suffered the same fate as students, that is, they were often exposed to limitless sadism by their masters. Stone points out that the bolder spirits sometimes sued their masters for assault. These suits reveal a female apprentice who was stripped naked, strung up by her thumbs and given twenty-one lashes and a boy who was flogged, salted and held naked to a fire. Ibid., pp. 163-167.

90) In this instance the choleric anger did not just injure the envied object, but the envier as well. Pepys went on to relate that the student succeeded his teacher as "Master of the Children; but his career was very short; for he deceased at Windsor, 14 July 1674." Samuel Pepys, *The Diary of Samuel Pepys, Volume 2,* J. M. Dent & Sons, London, 1906, p. 381.

91) Lawrence Stone, *The Family, Sex and Marriage In England 1500-1800,* op. cit. p. 169.

See also: Elizabeth W. Marvick, "Childhood History and Decisions of State: The Case of Louis XIII" in *The New Psychohistory,* edited by Lloyd deMause, The Psychohistory Press, New York, 1975, pp. 199-244.

92) Lawrence Stone, *The Family, Sex and Marriage In England 1500-1800,* op. cit. p. 174.

Children who cried too much or who were too demanding were in danger of being considered 'changelings'. The *Malleus* comments that you can recognize changelings because they "always howl most piteously and even if four or five mothers are set on to suckle them, they never grow". Quoted by Lloyd deMause, "The Evolution of Childhood", in *The History of Childhood,* edited by Lloyd deMause, op. cit., p. 10

93) Ibid., p. 175.

See: L. L. Schüking, *The Puritan Family,* New York, 1970, p. 73; R.H. Bremner, *Children and Youth in America*, Cambridge, Mass., 1970, I, pp. 37-38; and A.W. Calhoun, *A Social History of the American Family from Colonial Times to the Present*, New York, 1945, I, pp. 47, 120-121.

94) Stephen Kern, "Explosive Intimacy: Psychodynamics of the Victorian Family" in *The New Psychohistory,* edited by Lloyd deMause, The Psychohistory Press, New York, 1975, pp. 39-44.

95) *Press Bulletin: News from Marriage Guidance,* The National Marriage Guidance Council, England, 29 March 1985.

The bulletin reports on the difficulties that parents have with sexually active teenagers. A mother and teacher said, "We couldn't cope with the idea of our daughter making love in our house. Apart from it setting a bad example to our younger children, we couldn't handle the thought of it and said 'no'."

Another father commented, "I will not let my sons and daughters sleep with their friends in my house. It's not morally right. I would be very embarrassed if the parents of my son's girlfriends felt that when she was a guest in our house we would let them sleep together. And I would expect the same from my friends."

96) During Victorian times Ambriose Tardieu, professor of legal medicine at the University of Paris, and dean of the Faculty of Medicine, charted the horrendous abuse of children in France, including physical torture and sexual assault. His seminal paper was: "Etude médico-légale sur les sérvices et mauvais traitments exercés sur des infants" (A Medico-legal Study of Cruelty and Brutal Treatment Inflicted on Children). Tardieu noted that parents who torture children inevitably claimed they were merely exercising their parental rights in order to curb the child of his or her "bad disposition". Discussed by Jeffrey Masson in *The Assault on Truth: Freud's Suppression of the Seduction Theory*, Penguin Books, London, 1985, pp. 15, 18-25.

In the 20th century the Swiss analyst, Alice Miller, has documented and publicized the problems of child abuse, in particular, the sexual abuse of children, in *Du Sollst nicht merken* (1981), published in English as *Thou Shalt Not Be Aware*, Pluto Press, London, 1985.

97) Shmarya Levin, *Childhood in Exile*, New York, 1929, pp. 58-59, quoted by Lloyd deMause, "The Evolution of Childhood", in *The History of Childhood,* edited by Lloyd deMause, op. cit., p. 10.

98) Morton Schatzman, *Soul Murder: Persecution in the Family*, Random House, New York, 1973, p. 142.

99) Daniel Gottlieb Schreber, *Kallipädie oder Erziehung zur Schönheit durch naturgetreue und ghleichmässige Förderung normaler Körperbildung* (Education Toward Beauty by Natural and Balanced Furtherance of Normal Body Growth), Fleischer, Leipzig, 1858, p. 241, quoted by Morton Schatzman, *Soul Murder: Persecution in the Family*, op. cit., pp. 142-142.

At another point Schreber asserts, "In the case of nearly every child, however, even the most well-brought up, there are sometimes surprising manifestations of defiance and rebelliousness....a vestige of innate barbarity which leads the developing self-confidence astray.....This could be caused by anything--the most important thing is that the disobedience should be crushed to the point of regaining complete submission, using corporal punishment if necessary." Ibid., jacket quote.

100) Ibid. p. 39-52.

101) *Donald's Happy Birthday*, Directed by Jack Hannah, Distributed by RKO Pictures, 194_ .

The major theme in this and many other Disney cartoons is that children are naturally naughty, and therefore have to be controlled and punished. However Disney's cartoons have some redeeming features. The parent characters often discover their mistakes after the damage has been done and acknowledge shame and guilt.

102) Melanie Klein, "Early Stages of the Oedipus Conflict and Superego Formation", in Melanie Klein, *The Psycho-Analysis of Children*, op. cit., pp. 131-132.

Joseph Berke, "Differentiation of the Pre-Genital Phase from the Genital Phase of the Early Oedipus Complex", unpublished paper, pp. 3-4.

103) Christopher Lasch, for one, has pointed out that attacks on the past, including past values, traditions, and teachings are equivalent to Oedipal attacks by the child towards his parents. Christopher Lasch, *The Culture of Narcissism*, op. cit., pp. 150-151.

104) Discussed by Stephen Kern, "Explosive Intimacy: Psychodynamics of the Victorian Family" in *The New Psychohistory*, edited by Lloyd deMause, op. cit. pp. 40-141.

Erewhon was published in 1872. By 1901 Butler published *Erewhon Revisited* which envisioned a father-son relationship based on love, not only enmity.

105) *The Oedipus Complex* - Sigmund Freud, "A Special Type of Choice of Object Made by Men", *S.E.* Vol. X1, pp.163 - 176.

The Electra Complex - Carl Jung, "Versuch einer Darstellung der psychoanalytischen Theorie", *Jahrbuch für psychoanalytische und psychopathologische Forschungen*, 1913, V, 370. (Trans: *The Theory of Psycho-Analysis*, New York, 1915)

The Early Oedipus Complex - Melanie Klein, "Some Theoretical Conclusions regarding the Emotional Life of the Infant" in *Envy and Gratitude and Other Works*, op. cit., pp.61-93.

The Laius Complex - G. Devereux, "Why Oedipus Killed Laius, A Note on the Complementary Oedipus Complex in Greek Drama", *Int. J. Psycho-Anal.*, Vol. 34, 1953, pp. 132-141.

106) There are many other features of the dreams that could have been mentioned, for example, the appearance of a black bug, indicating the degree to which the boy had turned his father into something evil, shitty, and devalued and his fear that the father/bug would inject the badness back into him. All this provides further examples of the intrapsychic operations of malicious projective identification, that is, internal envy and the internalized envier.

107) Morton Schatzman, *Soul Murder: Persecution in the Family*, op. cit.

108) Daniel Paul Schreber, *Denkwürdigkeiten eines Nervenkrankan*, Oswald Mutze, Leipzig, 1903. Translated and edited by Ida Macalpine and Richard Hunter, *Memoirs of My Nervous Illness*, Dawson & Son Ltd., London, 1955.

This book provided the basis for an extended study of paranoia and psychosis by Sigmund Freud, "Psycho-Analytic Notes upon an Autobiographical Account of a Case of Paranoia (Dementia Paranoides)", *S.E. XII*, pp. 9-82.

Historians of psychiatry, Macalpine and Hunter commented: "Schreber is now the most frequently quoted patient in psychiatry." *Memoirs of My Mental Illness*, op. cit. p. 8.

William Niederland, *The Schreber Case: Psychoanalytic Profile of a Paranoid Personality*, expanded edition, The Analytic Press, Lawrence Erlbaum Associates, Publishers, Hillsdale, New Jersey, 1984.

109) Father Schreber recalled: "I had a Geraldhalter manufactured which proved its worth time and time again with my own children......."

A further advantage was that the instrument prevented the child from crossing his legs. Shoulders straps ensured that he did not "toss and turn."

Daniel Gottlieb Schreber, *Kallipädie oder Erziehung zur Schönheit durch naturgetreue und ghleichmässige Förderung normaler Körperbildung*, op. cit., p. 203, quoted by Morton Schatzman, *Soul Murder: Persecution in the Family*, op. cit., p. 46.

110) Ibid., Daniel Gottlieb Schreber, pp. 198-199, Schatzman, p. 49.

111) Sigmund Freud, "Psycho-Analytic Notes upon an Autobiographical Account of a Case of Paranoia (Dementia Paranoides)", op. cit., pp. 9-82.

112) Niederland points out that Daniel Paul's first 'breakdown' occurred at a time when he had been "called upon to become a member of the *Reichstag*, that is, a rebellious son in opposition to the awe-inspiring Bismarck. When, nine years later, he was called upon to take a father's place by becoming the presiding judge of the superior court, he again

fell ill, and this time for good." William Niederland, *The Schreber Case: Psychoanalytic Profile of a Paranoid Personality*, op. cit., p. 41.

113) Sigmund Freud, "The Dissolution of the Oedipus Complex", op. cit., pp. 176-177.

CHAPTER 8

1) *Genesis*, chapter 37, verses 3, 11, 18, 19 & 20, *The Twenty-Four Books of the Old Testament*, Vol. 1, trans. by Andrew Harkavy, Hebrew Publishing Company, New York, 1926, pp. 62-63.

2) The hostilities were fueled by the fact that Jacob (Israel) used Joseph, and Joseph allowed himself to be used, to keep track of the brothers. Ibid., verses 1,13 &14.

Although later rabbinic commentaries cited Joseph as the embodiment of filial love and family loyalty, they also criticized him and his father for favoritism and hubris. The rabbis, as the biblical scribes, were keenly aware of the events that provoke fratricidal strife. According to Moslem tradition similar warnings were aired after Joseph told Jacob about his dream. Jacob replied: "O my son! tell not they vision to thy brethren, lest they plot against thee: for Satan is the manifest foe of man." *Koran,* Sura X11: 4 (2-19, Joseph, Peace Be on Him), quoted in *The Torah: A Modern Commentary,* op. cit., p. 248.

3) *Encyclopedia Judaica,* Vol. 10, op. cit., pp. 202-203.

4) Bruno Bettelheim, *The Uses of Enchantment: The Meaning and Importance of Fairy Tales*, Thames & Hudson, London, 1976, p. 91.

5) See: the story of the brothers Anup and Bata, discussed by Patrick Mullahy in *Oedipus: Myth and Complex,* op. cit., pp. 90-93.

6) Myrtilus was the accomplice and charioteer who helped Pelops will the race against Hippodamia's father, Oenomaus, by removing the pins from the wheels of his chariot. It is said that Pelops drowned Myrtilus, instead of paying him, in order to hide the deed. But other versions state that Pelops killed Myrtilus to prevent the promised payment which included the right to share his intended bride.

Later Pelops tried to appease the ghost of Myrtilus by paying him great honors, but the curse remained for several generations until the purification of Orestes.

7) Typically Mullahy views the ancient struggle between the younger Anup and older Bata for Bata's wife in straightforward Oedipal terms. The older brother equals the father, the wife equals the mother. The rivalry between the brothers concerns the incestuous object and all the different episodes are repetitions of one fundamental situation, that of the son who seeks to overthrow the father and take possession of his wife. A careful reading of the myth does not necessarily deny this, but demonstrates that the siblings relationships are much richer and more complex than this interpretation encompasses. Ibid., pp.90-93.

8) This point has been made in various studies of sibling relationships including:

Stephen Bank & Michael Kahn, *The Sibling Bond*, Basic Books, New York, 1982, pp. 197-201.

Leslie Pepitone, review of, *The Sibling Bond*, in *Am. J. Orthopsych.*, Vol. 54, No. 2, April 1984.

Judy Dunn, "Sibling Relationships in Early Childhood", *Child Development*, Vol. 54, 1983, pp. 787-811.

9) The psychiatrist Robert Robertiello has commented about a former patient whose wife was pregnant: "He dreamed he destroyed the fetus. It was so awful he came to me for help. He and his wife were very close. What was agonizing was juggling the idea of feeling competitive with the unborn child and loving him at the same time. On top of that, breaking up of the exclusive union he had with his wife–even if the intruder was his own child–rearoused memories of rivalries with his brothers and sisters." Discussed in Nancy Friday, *Jealousy*, William Morrow & Co., New York, 1985, p. 352.

10) Peter Lomas, "Dread of envy as an aetiological factor in puerperal breakdown", op. cit., pp. 107-108.

11) George Foster, "The Anatomy of Envy: A Study in Symbolic Behavior", op. cit., pp. 174 & 193.

12) Stephen Bank & Michael Kahn, *The Sibling Bond*, op. cit., p. 204.

Incidents such as this are commonly reported in the daily press. For example, "Boy, 5, started fire that killed sister", *Guardian*, 8 may 1985, p. 3. The boy had started several other fires at his home before the fatal one on a New Year's Day. The police noted that his mother showed a marked lack of control amounting to indifference. Although there might be a related issue of phallic excitement, after the event the boy was put into a children's home, but showed no further interest in starting fires.

13) Sophocles, *Oedipus at Colonus*, op. cit. Ls 532-535.

His daughters were Antigone and Ismene. Oedipus, of course, recognized the situation of having children who were also siblings within the context of acknowledging an incestuous union with his wife. Nonetheless, he was also articulating a pervasive unconscious experience, not simply of incestuous union, but of seeing and treating children as sibs.

14) Oedipus's second son and younger brother of Polyneices (and Oedipus) was Eteocles.

Ibid., Ls 371-376.

15) Euripides, *Phoenician Women*, Ls 469, 476-480, discussed by Peter Walcot, *Envy and the Greeks*, op. cit., pp. 61-62.

16) Sophocles, *Oedipus at Colonus*, op. cit. Ls 444-445.

17) Ibid., Ls 1387-1389.

18) Aeschylus' *Oresteia*, includes three plays: *Agamemnon, The Libation Bearers* and *The Eumenides*. See, Aeschylus, *The Oresteia*, trans. by Robert Fagles, Penguin Books, London, 1983.

19) The two boys were exiled to a neighbouring city state where Atreus eventually succeeded to the throne. Not surprisingly contention followed them. Thyestes seduced his brother's wife and stole the ram with golden fleece which had been a special present from Hermes (whom as you will recall, had inflicted the curse in the first place). Later he arranged for a son of Atreus to kill his father. The plot almost succeeded, but Atreus managed to dispatch the young man first. Soon afterwards he realized who the assailant had been. To avenge himself, Atreus pretended to forgive his brother and invited him and his family to a great feast. During the festivities and in the manner of his grandfather, he served up the bodies of Thyestes' sons. When this happened, it is said that the sun hid from the sky in order not to cast light on such a crime.

20) In *The Eumenides* Orestes also points that he loved his father dearly and thirsted for revenge. Yet, Electra is generally seen as the provoker. Orestes' action demonstrates the degree to which one sibling will act out the malice of another.

21) Jung developed the idea of the *Electra Complex* to denote the feminine counterpart of the Oedipus Complex, that is, a girl or woman's (often unconscious) fixation on her father coupled with underlying, murderous jealousy towards her mother.

Freud, however, did not believe in the analogy. He insisted that only boys were beset by the "fateful combination" of love for one parent and simultaneous murderous rejection of the other. J. Laplanche and J-B. Pontalis, *The Language of Psycho-Analysis*, op. cit., p. 152.

22) The *Oresteia* concludes with the trial of Orestes for matricide, an act which embodies the horror of several generations of familial strife. Orestes defended himself stating that he had been spurred on to kill his mother by Apollo, but the Furies (the ghosts of his mother in combination with his own sense of guilt) were thirsty for revenge. They argued that unless Orestes was punished then "every man will find a way to act at his own caprice; over and over in time to come, parents shall await the deathstroke at their children's hands."

In the end the jury of twelve Athenian citizens deadlocked, but Athene, acting as the presiding judge, cast the deciding vote for mercy and acquittal. However, she took care to placate the Furies by offering them a powerful role for good in the family, "No household shall be prosperous without your will." In so doing the Furies (angry figures) became the Eumenides (the benevolent ones) and Orestes achieved atonement and absolution for his deeds. But the question of sibling intrigues remained.

Aeschylus, *The Eumenides*, trans. by Richard Lattimore, in *Greek Tragedies: Volume 3*, edited by David Greene and Richard Lattimore, Phoenix Books, University of Chicago Press, Chicago, 1963, Ls 494-498 & 895.

In the 20th century there have been a number of similar, well publicized, albeit less profound, dynastic struggles. One engaged the extended family of the late billionaire John Paul Getty and involved murderous quarrels among Getty's sons and grandchildren for control of the assets of the Getty Oil Company. The result could have been the demise of Texaco, the 8th largest corporation in the United States. Alexander Chancellor, "The Getty squabbles that brought down a giant", *The Independent*, 16 April 1987, p. 8.

23) *Dynasty* is a Richard and Esther Shapiro TV Production in association with Aaron Spelling Productions, Inc., 1987.

24) Melanie Klein points out that the trauma of the birth of a new sibling may exist long before the sib is conceived. The existing child tends to imagine that mother's breasts and body are full of babies. So attacks on sibs can begin with attacks on mother's threatening breasts and body, experienced as real or imagined babies. All this is aroused by anticipated (inevitably coexistent) deprivation, frustration and envious and jealous hurt. See the case of Richard as discussed by Hanna Segal, *Klein*, op. cit. pp. 157-158.

25) Phyllis Greenacre, *Trauma, Growth, and Personality*, The Hogarth Press, London, 1953, p. 233. The jealousy Greenacre describes is akin to 'delusional' or 'pathological' jealousy which I have previously discussed under the rubric of 'The Othello Syndrome'.

26) Gerhart Piers and Milton Singer, *Shame and Guilt: A Psychoanalytical and Cultural Study*, Thomas Publishers, Springfield, Ill., 1953, p. 23f.

27) Quoted by Mary Kenny in, "Mary Kenny's Week", *Sunday Telegraph*, 23 September 1984, p. 15.

28) Personal communication, 1985.

29) "We had this awful old nanny, Miss Box. Mother was always sending me out of the room to Miss Box, which upset me. I got Miss Box, the ultimate hag, and he got Mom." Quoted from "Everybody and his Brother', compiled by Jean Penn, *Playboy*, January 1986, p. 194.

30) Ibid, p. 194.

Quaid adds: "The meanest thing I ever did to him was hitting him so hard once, he didn't speak to me for four days. He told on me, of course. I was about fourteen then. The meanest thing he ever did to me was becoming successful."

31) Michael Horsnell, "Girl, 13, denies twin murders,"*The Times*, 30 January 1991, p.8.

32) "Son Kills 3 Out of Hate", *Daily Telegraph*, 23 March 1981, p. 5.

33) Mary Kenny, "Mary Kenny's Week", *Sunday Telegraph*, 23 September 1984, p. 15.

34) Elizabeth Hodder, *The Step-Parents' Handbook*, Sphere Books, London, 1985, p.46.

35) D. W. Winnicott, *The Piggle: An Account of the Psychoanalytic Treatment of a Little Girl*, edited by Ishak Ramzy, Penguin Books, London,1980, p.52.

36) Ibid., p. 64.

37) Ibid., p. 64

38) Ibid., p. 103.

39) Towards the end of the therapy, her mother wrote to Winnicott: "Gabrielle (the Piggle) is very close to Susan (the sister), handles her with great circumspection, cajoles her, is often the mediator between her and us. We are struck by how often she will try and get her way by deflecting Susan's attention or by some inventiveness, rather than by direct attack, though sometimes she is miserably, and helplessly, consumed by jealousy. The other day, in the middle of a fierce fight, she suddenly kissed Susan and said: "But I like you." This is very different from Susan, who alternatively looks up to Gabrielle fervently, and ruthlessly wants to destroy her superiority." Ibid., p. 177.

40) Quoted by John Leo in, "Battling the Green-Eyed Monster", *Time*, 25 November 1985, p. 39.

41) In this instance the absence of projections, or the ability to avoid malicious projections by the parent, may constitute 'the good breast'.

42) In the Cambridge study of the developing child, it became clear that many first born children become very jealous of any intrusions between them and their father. One firmly told her mother (about baby Ronnie), "Daddy is not Ronnie's daddy." Another mother reported, "She minds him (father) holding him (baby) much more than when I do. I think she takes me and him (baby) for granted." Judy Dunn, *Sisters and Brothers*, Fontana Paperbacks, London, 1984, p. 88.

43) *The Complete Letters of Sigmund Freud to Wilhelm Fliess*, edited by Jeffrey Masson, The Belknap Press of Harvard University Press, Cambridge, Mass., 1985, 23 February 1898.

44) I have already described how a parent can be an objective persecutor (*the monstrous parent*) and subjective persecutor (*the parental monster*) to a child. In the same vein one sibling can very much appear and be a persecutor to another. The child (or adult) who actually attacks a sibling can be called and is very much *a monstrous sibling* . On the other hand, the child (or adult) who has been transformed into an envious, greedy and jealous monster by a sibling who exaggerates what he sees and projects his own malicious intentions onto the other can be called *the sibling monster*. The combination of both is *the complete sibling monster*, an extremely frightening figure and the product of one sibling's perceptions, imaginings and projections about another.

45) Personal communication, 1984.

46) Her spoiling side tended to be denied and was projectively identified with her sister whom she considered to be severely neurotic. Melanie Klein, "Envy and Gratitude", *Envy and Gratitude and Other Works 1946-1963*, op. cit. pp. 209-210.

47) The displacement of the breast from mother to new baby serves the older child too. J. D. Suttie comments: "Not only can the child go on "eating the mother," but she even lets it *"....eat the younger baby."* J. D. Suttie, *The Origins of Love and Hate*, Paul, French Trubner & Co., London, 1935, p. 110, quoted by H. Schoeck, *Envy: A Theory of Social Behaviour*, op. cit., p.69.

48) B. D. Paul, "Symbolic Sibling Rivalry in a Guatemalan Indian Village", *American Anthropologist*, Vol. 52, 1950, pp. 205-218.

In contrast Bettelheim comments on the way that the parents of the great German poet Johann Wolfgang von Goethe dealt with his sibling rivalry. Goethe's earliest memory was of tossing his toy dishes out of the window and rejoicing that they shattered. After this he threw out his mother's crockery as well. Freud later said that the toy dishes represented Goethe's new brother and the wish to get rid of him, while smashing the mother's dishes represented his fear and hostility to the thought that she would not be able to feed him and the new sib too. Although Bettelheim does not disagree with this, he thinks that the most important aspect of the story was the fact that his parents did not get frightened or angry and punitive about the incident, as one might expect. Instead they accepted it. Therefore Goethe was able to work out his resentments and grow up to have a good relationship with his brother. By implication there are times when a child must be allowed to be destructive. See: Megan Rosenfeld, "Too Old to Play, Bettelheim Still Scolds Parents", *International Herald Tribune*, 11 April 1986, p. 20.

49) Letty Cottin Pogrebin, "Couples who hide their happiness", *New York Times*, 1 September 1983, p. C2.

50) Nancy Friday, *Jealousy*, op. cit., pp. 157-171.

51) Sue Arnold, "Girls with green eyes", *The Observer*, 21 August 1983, p. 22.

Kindred events among brothers are well illustrated in the biography of the American academic John Wideman. He came from a poor Black family, but managed to become an accomplished athlete and scholar, and later a writer, University professor and good family man. In contrast his brother became a thief, marauder, junkie and drug dealer who eventually wound up serving a life prison sentence for murder. John Wideman, *Brothers and Keepers*, Allison & Busby, London, 1985.

52) Some authorities quote ten years. The concubine who was used for the purpose of procreation gained a special status. Under Mesopotamian law, the concubine who bore the child of her master could be punished but not sold. Other codes stressed the obligation of the wife to provide a concubine who could never be sold. *Encyclopedia Judaica*, Vol. 7, op. cit., pp. 1074-1075.

53) Ibid., p. 1076.

54) *Encyclopedia Judaica*, Vol. 9, op. cit., p. 82.

55) As a story, *Cinderella* already had a long history before it was written down, not only in China, but in many countries. For the earliest Chinese version see: Arthur Waley, "Chinese Cinderella Story", *Folk-Lore*, Vol. 58, 1947.

56) For an extended discussion of the Cinderella story and its relation to other fairy tales see: Bruno Bettelheim, " Cinderella", *The Uses of Enchantment: The Meaning and Importance of Fairy Tales*, Thames and Hudson, London, 1976, pp. 236-277.

David Luke, "Introduction", in Jacob and Wilhelm Grimm, *Selected Tales*, op. cit., pp. 39-41.

57) Bruno Bettelheim," Cinderella", *The Uses of Enchantment: The Meaning and Importance of Fairy Tales*, op. cit., pp. 239-239.

58) Edward Gifford, *The Evil Eye: Studies in the Folklore of Vision*, op. cit., p. 35.

59) At her pretrial hearing the girl stated that her motive was envy and jealousy. Although her former roommate was not a raving beauty, she was a distinctly more attractive person. Helmut Schoeck, *Envy: A Theory of Social Behaviour*, op. cit., p. 107.

60) Jilly Cooper, "Watch your step at Exmas", *The Sunday Times*, 20 December 1981, p. 26.

61) Dale and Lynne Spender, who were both trained as teachers and eventually became writers, have described this outcome.

Dale (the eldest, by a couple of years): "We've always been immensely close and although she can make me cross sometimes, I have no recollection of jealousy or serious rivalry. As kids we complemented each other.....We've decided that if we live to 70 we'll retire together and smoke, drink and eat ourselves to death."

Lynne: "I haven't taken on feminism in the way Dale has...but it's played a vital part in guiding me to do what I want.......Of course, I do wonder sometimes if I would have worked harder at my marriage if Dale hadn't been there, reinforcing my feelings that (housework) was not fair.....So here I am in my early forties, on my own with two kids, feeling great about life...I suppose without support from Dale it might have looked very different."

Angela Neustatter, "Women of Letters", *The Sunday Times Magazine*, 1 November 1987, pp. 13-16.

62) The informant is thirty-two year old woman with two sisters. Brigid McConville, *Sisters: Love and Conflict within the Lifelong Bond*, Pan Books, London, 1985, p. 48.

63) "The elder sister, I am convinced, was distorted by a suppressed jealousy - not for me, but for physical love. She adored her sister and also now hated her."

"And whatever we two did, whatever arrangements we made, was spoilt for Rebecca by the relentless and indiscriminating disapproval of her home. They would not let her find any pride in my position and success; they expressed horror and disgust at any effort we made to face things out together. They forced upon us idiotic lies and pretenses...."

H. G. Wells, *H. G. Wells in Love*, Faber & Faber, London, 1984, extract published in the *Sunday Telegraph*, 9 September 1984, p. 12.

64) Jessica Mitford, *Hons and Rebels*, Gollancz, London, 1960, discussed by Brigid McConville, *Sisters: Love and Conflict within the Lifelong Bond*, op. cit., pp. 26-28.

65) Sigmund Freud, "The Taboo of Virginity", *S.E.*, Vol. 11, p. 204.

66) Sigmund Freud, "On the Sexual Theories of Children", *S.E.*, Vol. 9, p. 218.

67) Personal communication, 1985.

68) Bank and Kahn describe another situation where parental favoritism, and sororal resentment, was brought about by fraternal weakness. Consequently over-protective parents were constantly admonishing: "Don't be so tough with your brother, be careful!" Stephen Bank and Michael Kahn, *The Sibling Bond*, op. cit., p. 203.

69) Personal communication, 1985.

Interestingly, in both examples the elder brothers tended to get on well with their younger sisters in spite of severe provocations. In this family, the brother's main complaints had to do with presents (hers were more spontaneous); school (she got off easier); attention (she got more - something hotly denied by his sister); parents (more sympathetic to her - again hotly denied) and privileges (girls get more -a point of agreement).

70) Ruth Moulton points out that sibling rivalry may simply enhance a preexisting state of envy based on general frustration of early childhood needs: "This exacerbation of envy may occur with the birth of a new baby or the existence of a preferred child. If the rival is a male, of course, envy is apt to be focussed on the penis as the reason for the preference." Ruth Moulton, "A Survey and Reevaluation of the Concept of Penis Envy", in *Psychoanalysis and Women,* edited by Jean Baker Miller, op. cit., pp. 243-244.

71) Jules Glenn has described the difficulties faced by a three year old girl who suffered from severe fecal retention after the birth of baby brother. The parents doted on him and the mother described the baby as a 'ball buster'. When the girl did have bowel movements, they were in the shape of large, hard, fecal masses as big as baseballs. Glenn comments that the girl's 'penis envy' was clearly established long before classical psychoanalytic theory would allow. Jules Glenn, "Psychoanalysis of a Constipated Girl: Clinical Observations during the Fourth and Fifth Years", paper presented at the Panel on the Psychology of Women: Infancy and Early Childhood, at the May 1974 meetings of the American Psychoanalytic Association.

72) Henry Porter, Gore and gall", *The Sunday Times*, 5 August 1984, p. 7.

73) Ibid., p. 7.

74) Hugo Vickers, *Cecil Beaton: The Authorized Biography,* Weidenfeld & Nicolson, London, 1985, p. 454.

75) As Beaton exemplifies, snobbery is essentially a form of narcissistic inflation serving to express and defend against envy.

76) An exasperated Beaton used to snipe: "Whereas Freddie Ashton can dream away in his summer house or blink at the ceiling and eventually be rewarded with pomp and ceremony, Sir Lawrence (Olivier) can booze away and be out of the running for an age, only to be surprised by the arrival of a messenger bringing him the greatest good news of a personal nature." Ibid., p. 454.

77) Joan Beck, *The Chicago Tribune,* 30 January 1980, quoted by Stephen Bank and Michael Kahn, in *The Sibling Bond,* op. cit., p. 229.

78) Rosenfeld is referring to the idealization of the omnipotent, destructive sides of the self. In other words the person identifies with the force of his own envy and luxuriates in vicious attacks on positive libidinal ties. Herbert Rosenfeld, "A clinical approach to the psychoanalytic theory of the life and death instincts: an investigation into the aggressive aspects of narcissism.", *Int. J. Psycho-Anal.*, Vol. 52, Part 2, 1971, pp. 169-177.

79) In their discussion of the conflict between the Carter brothers, Bank and Kahn point out that Billy also had reason to be angry with his brother. When given the chance to manage the family business when his brother was Governor of Georgia, he had done well. But the opportunity had been pulled out from under him when his brother became President and the business was put in a blind trust. Billy did try to buy the business, but was turned down, the final turn of the screw which effectively robbed him of a positive identity. Stephen Bank and Michael Kahn, *The Sibling Bond,* op. cit., pp. 229-231.

80) In a paper on shame and envy I point out that shame and envy act in tandem and shaming can be a devastating form of envious revenge. Joseph Berke, "Shame and Envy", *Brit. J. Psychoth.*, Vol. 2, No. 4, 1986, pp. 262-270.

81) Laura Blumenfeld, "Bill Clinton's Nemesis, Or Rancorous Remains Of an Old Friendship," *International Herald Tribune,* 31 December 1993, p.1

82) "Three Dancing Pensions in Jealous Tango", *Daily Telegraph,* 16 June 1981, p. 3.

83) The plot was eventually discovered and the former captain was fined and given a suspended jail term.

84) *Electric Dreams*, starring Lenny Dohlen and Virginia Madsen, Virgin Video, Virgin Films, 1985, VVP 064.

85) *Tom and Jerry, Polka Dot Puss,* Directed by William Hanna and Joseph Barbera, produced by Fred Quimby, released by MGM, February 1949.

86) *Tom and Jerry, The Hollywood Bowl,* Directed by William Hanna and Joseph Barbera, produced by Fred Quimby, released by MGM, September 1950.

87) All the Tom and Jerry cartoons vary in their degree of violence, but they reach a pinnacle of persecution and retribution in *Yankee Doodle Mouse*, Directed by William Hanna and Joseph Barbera, produced by Fred Quimby, released by MGM, 1944. Here both Tom and Jerry are engaged in a continuous battle that is relentless in its viciousness. As often happens, Tom is almost about to gain the upper hand, when he stupidly blasts himself off into space, instead of Jerry. For the younger audience this fulfills the wish to punish the parent (or older sib) and mitigates the impact of parental sadism.

Objective confirmation of the events described in these cartoons can be seen in a study published in *The Journal of Child Maltreatment* in 2005. Based on a representative national survey of 2030 children, it found that 35% had been 'hit or attacked' by a sibling in the previous year. Of these, 13% had been injured. Katy Butlan, "A Hidden World of Sibling Violence," *The New York Times* selection, published in *The Daily Telegraph*, London, 9 March 2006, p. 5.

87) *Heavenly Puss* features a repentant Tom. After the usual chase, he injures himself and dreams of going to Heaven. But he can't get in because he has spent his whole life tormenting mice. His only chance is to get a letter of forgiveness from Jerry, otherwise he will be consigned to Hell. Jerry holds out, then relents. Tom rushes back, but it is too late. He falls to a fiery fate, only to awake and discover his tail simmering by the fireplace. This time he doesn't blame Jerry, but gives him a kiss. The mouse is surprised and delighted. *Tom and Jerry, Heavenly Puss,* Directed by William Hanna and Joseph Barbera, produced by Fred Quimby, released by MGM, 1949.

By the same token 65% of children interviewed in the previous study had apparently not been hit or attacked. Ibid. p. 5

89) Jean Penn, "Everybody and His Brother", op. cit., p.196.

Brother Dennis came to believe that childhood fights, like when Randy tortured him, ultimately cemented their relationship. "I think the brothers who can fight with each other are the closest, as long as you never let it get so bad that you walk away and say "I'll never talk to you again."" Ibid., p. 196.

Like with Tom and Jerry, to fight is right, but to destroy is wrong.

90) The quote itself is by Nancy Friday from prior interviews and a discussion with Robertiello who is considering various aspects of his homosexual attraction to certain men within a context of male-male rivalries. Nancy Friday, *Jealousy,* op. cit., pp. 347-352.

91) Technically we can say that the 'good enough sib' bounds narcissistic inflation (which acts as a magnet for outside aggression) and envious deflation (which is the

expression of inner discontent) brought about by pervading feelings of breast, womb or phallic inadequacy and inferiority (the absences).

92) The analyst was Hanna Segal who discusses the case in: Hanna Segal, *Introduction to the Work of Melanie Klein*, op. cit., pp. 47-53.

Segal comments: "She worked in an academic profession and, though successful in her career, she found recurring blocks in relation to the more creative and rewarding research aspects of her work." Ibid., p. 47.

93) Her friend was also a middle aged woman who had suffered the loss of both parents in childhood. She herself connected the patches of baldness with this fact.

94) Quoted by Hanna Segal. Ibid., p. 50.

95) The woman displaced many feelings from and part aspects of her mother onto an image of her dead sister. The psychic connections became evident when she associated the balloons which had lost their air with her dead sister (i.e.someone who has lost the breath of life) and later with her mother's body and breasts.

96) Her friend's name was Joan. Sometimes she made slips of the tongue and called her Jean. Jean was the name of a pretty young woman who had just had a baby, that is, become a mother. Ibid., pp. 50-51.

97) Ibid., p. 51.

98) Segal emphasizes that she associated any bit of feminine or masculine achievement with the operation of her envy and greed, and then felt very guilty. But the worst feelings arose when she began to realize how she continued to use her resources and accomplishments to stimulate envy in others, for this reminded her of how she had spoiled (and to her mind) killed her younger sister by filling her full of envious projections. Moreover, it reminded her of wanting to do the same to the parents she loved.

CHAPTER 9

1) Helmut Schoeck points out that one of the first persons to use the concept of 'institutionalized envy' was Eric Wolf, an expert on South American peasant cultures. He related the phenomenon to backbiting, the evil eye and the practice or fear of black magic. Helmut Schoeck, *Envy: A Theory of Social Behaviour*, op. cit., pp. 46-47.

2) Paul Johnson, "Farewell to the Labour Party", *New Statesman*, 9 September 1977, p. 330.

Johnson is especially critical of the closed shop and wildcat strikes which are, for him, ways in which the 'envious and incapable' retain power.

3) "The Wages of Sin", *London Standard*, 10 September 1985, p.7.

4) Helmut Schoeck, op. cit., pp. 218 & 222.

5) "Burma to Investigate Wealthy Citizens", *International Herald Tribune*, 17 March 1986, p. 2.

6) *New Larousse Encyclopedia of Mythology*, op. cit., p. 163.

7) The phrase was used by the philosopher, Søren Kierkegaard, in describing the envy-motive and the passion for social levelling.

Søren Kierkegaard, *En literair Anmeldelse to Tidsaldre (The Present Age)*, in, *Samlede Vaerker*, ed. H. O. Lange, Copenhagen, 1920-30, Vol. VIII, p. 76, quoted by Helmut Schoeck, op. cit., p. 173.

8) Lee Lorenz, *New Yorker*, 15 July 1985, p. 29.

9) There are many instances when the term *institutionalized grenvy* provides the most appropriate description of business or bureaucratic practices.

10) Lee Iacocca, *Iacocca: An Autobiography*, Bantam Books, London, 1986, p. 109.

11) "No study of the English landed family makes any sense unless the principle and practice of primogeniture is constantly born in mind. It was something that went far to determine the behaviour and character of both parents and children, and to govern the relationship between siblings" Lawrence Stone, *The Family, Sex and Marriage: In England 1500-1800*, op. cit., pp. 87-88.

12) The potential Sultans were locked in the Cage with only a handful of sterilized women and attendants to keep them company. "The Sultan Ibrahim was caged from the age of two until he succeeded at 24; Suleiman II for a total of 39 years; and Osman III, in the eighteenth century, for 50. The Cage was not only a living death, but a guarantee that any sultan who emerged from it would be a weak one...." Reay Tannahill, *Sex in History*, op. cit., p. 228.

13) Sigmund Freud, "Group Psychology and the Analysis of the Ego", *S.E.*, Vol. 18, op cit., pp.119-121.

14) Ibid., pp. 120-121.

15) J. M. Roberts, *The Hutchinson History of the World*, Hutchinson & Co, London, 1976.

Roberts discusses the impact of ideological and nationalistic movements at different points in world history. The group amplifies the underlying antagonisms which may surface at times of collective action. Alternatively, a murderous hatred may emerge when identification with the group breaks down and the individual is left unprotected against inner chaos caused by loss of pride, preexistent malice and vengeful resentment for feelings of helpless rootlessness.

16) It is worth noting that these hostilities are based on the continual interaction of imagined and actual grievances, each serving to bolster the other.

17) Freud concluded that far from being a "herd animal", man is really "a horde animal, an individual creature in a horde led by a chief." Sigmund Freud, "Group Psychology and the Analysis of the Ego", op cit., p. 121.

18) Helmut Schoeck, *Envy: A Theory of Social Behaviour*, op. cit., p. 66.

19) Paul Johnson, *A History of the Modern World: From 1917 to the 1980's*, Weidenfeld and Nicolson, London, 1983, pp.704 -708.

20) Peter Drucker, "The Monster and The Lamb", *Atlantic*, December 1978, pp.82-87.

Reinhold Hensch commanded the annihilation troops. The 'enemies' included mental and physical defectives and resistance fighters. He was so cruel, ferocious and bloodthirsty that he was known as "The Monster" (Das Ungeheuer) even to his own men. Hensch killed himself after being captured by the Americans.

21) Ibid., p. 84

22) After taking up the post of press advisor to the Nazi commissar for Frankfurt, he told Peter Drucker, a colleague on the *Frankfurter General Anzeiger*: "I get scared when I hear all that talk in the Nazi inner councils- and I do sit in now, you know. There are madmen there who talk about killing the Jews and about going to war and about jailing and killing anyone who holds a dissenting opinion and questions the Führer's word. It's all insane, but it frightens me. I know you said to me a year ago that the Nazis believed

these things and that I had better take them seriously. But I thought that it was the usual campaign rhetoric and didn't mean a thing......After all, this is the twentieth century." Ibid., p. 85.

23) Ibid., p. 85.

24) Paul Johnson, *A History of the Modern World: From 1917 to the 1980's*, op. cit., p. 376.

Johnson adds that neither man consulted their citizens, nor spoke for collegiate bodies. "Their lieutenants obeyed blindly or in apathetic terror, and the vast nations over which they ruled seem to have had no choice but to stumble in their wake towards mutual destruction. We have here the very opposite of historical determinism – the apotheosis of the single autocrat." Ibid., p. 376.

25) For servicemen with decorations there was to be polygamy and a free choice of women. Ibid., p. 381.

26) Ibid., pp 435-441.

27) Louise Branson, "Russia writes off poison pen", *The Sunday Times*, 30 March 1986, p. 16.

28) "Crackdown on libelous mail", *The Times*, 21 April 1986, p. 9.

29) *Private Eye* exemplifies the use of the media to extend personal prejudices and grudges, particularly by people in the media, against each other, and against major social, business and political figures. This has led to many law suits with substantial damages having to be paid, a confirmation of the fact that the magazine does publish malicious rumors and lies. Alan Hamilton, "Ingrams step down at Private Eye", *The Times*, 15 March 1986, p. 2.

30) Bryron Rogers, "Dempster and the Princess", *Sunday Telegraph Magazine*, No. 266, 1 November 1981, p. 59.

31) Ibid., p. 60.

32) Ibid., p. 60.

33) "All is not well in Fairyland," is a typical Dempster quip. Ibid., p. 56.

I could quote almost endless examples of journalists' pandering to public envy. Typically, an extended piece on the Marks and Sieff families chronicled the rich Jewish families who controlled Marks and Spencer, Britain's most successful retail chain. Concurrently it used the occasion to parade those family member who "were littered with bizarre tragedies, rattling skeletons and clandestine love affairs." Or, a report on Britain's highest earner, Mr. Christopher Heath, told how his privacy was destroyed by journalistic intrusions the moment his income became public knowledge. Mr. Heath pointed out: "In any other country one would have been congratulated for being successful in business. Instead we were made to feel guilty. In America I would have been a hero." See: Russell Miller, "The Family hides its skeletons", *The Sunday Times Magazine*, 14 October 1984, pp. 90-97; Stephen Markeson, "At home with Britain's highest earner", *The Times*, 23 November 1987, p. 3.

34) Agnew would advise businessmen who wished to make campaign contributions,"Tell them you gave at the office." He meant his office. John T. Noonan Jr., *Bribes*, MacMillan Publishing Co, New York, 1984, p. 581.

35) Morton Mintz, *At Any Cost: Corporate Greed, Women and the Dalkon Shield*, Pantheon Books Inc., New York, 1985.

36) Quoted by Robin M. Henig, in her review of several books on the Dalkon Shield disaster, *International Herald Tribune*, 21 November. 1985, p. 22.

37) R. Barry O'Brien, "Pay-Bed Militant Sacked", *The Daily Telegraph*, 26 May 1979, p. 1.

At a union conference Geddes was quoted, "Let us make sure that every single rich bastard in our hospitals will be treated on a Health Service basis and not because he has the money to pay for a consultant. Private medicine is the hand round the neck of the Health Service. It is our duty to cut that hand off." In fact, most of the patients treated at the Hammersmith Hospital are poor people in need of special treatment and are sponsored by their home governments or charities.

Geddes was eventually dismissed for painting slogans on hospital walls.

38) *Fortune*, July 1962, p. 60, quoted by Helmut Schoeck, *Envy: A Theory of Social Behaviour*, op. cit., pp. 112-113.

39) Bertrand Russell, *The Conquest of Happiness*, op. cit. pp. 70-71.

H. L. Mencken, *The Vintage Mencken*, edited by Alistair Cooke, New York, 1956, pp. 75-77, quoted by Helmut Schoeck, *Envy: A Theory of Social Behaviour*, op. cit., p. 194.

The Biblical King Solomon illustrated the relation between law, justice and equity by proposing to divide a baby in two, rather than leave one or two women feeling hard done by, that is, envious of the other.

40) Gay Talese, *Thy Neighbor's Wife*, Collins, London, 1980, pp. 53-64.

Comstock lived from 1844 to 1915. Prior to the passage of the Comstock Act in 1873 there were no federal laws against eroticism, or, what Comstock called, sexual obscenity.

In 1959, a federal judge, influenced by a new definition of obscenity a couple of years previously (Roth vs The Supreme Court) rescinded the ban against D.H. Lawrence's, *Lady Chatterley's Lover*, and effectively overturned the Comstock regulations.

41) As an adult Comstock came to believe that eroticism was the plague of the young leading to moral, physical and social degeneracy through masturbation, fornication, abortion and venereal disease. Quoted by Gay Talese. Ibid, p. 57.

42) J. P. Morgan was an prominent banker who himself had a large collection of pornography. He was a strong supporter of Comstock.

Comstock was also aided by rampant church groups and fanatical British anti-vice societies which were influential on the continent and in America. Ibid., p. 56.

43) The Comstock Act, as it was known, banned from the mails "every obscene, lewd, lascivious or filthy book, pamphlet, picture, paper, letter, writing, print or other publication of an independent character." Ibid., p. 57.

44) The Comstock Law was deliberately vague so that almost any item useful for sexual relations could and did qualify as obscene. The various charges against the women who killed themselves included prostitution, performing abortions, disseminating birth-control devices and writing a marriage manual. Other victims of the Comstock Law included a New York publisher who was jailed and fined for having in stock Ovid's, *Art of Love*, a bookseller who received a similar sentence for selling Dr. Ashton's, *Book of Nature and Marriage Guide*, and numerous pharmacists who were jailed for selling condoms or vaginal syringes. Ibid. p. 58.

45) Quoted by Heywood Broun and Margaret Leech, *Anthony Comstock: Roundsman of the Lord*, New York, 1927, p. 15 and quoted by Reay Tannahill, *Sex in History*, op. cit., p. 399.

46) Hoover was obsessed with sex and communism, Anslinger with biochemical bliss and McCarthy with class conflict. Paul Fussel points out that while McCarthy talked about communists, the people he was really getting at were the envied upper-middle and upper classes. Speaking in West Virginia in 1950 McCarthy claimed: "It has not been the less fortunate or members of minority groups who have been selling this nation out, but rather those who have had all the benefits...the finest homes, the finest college education..." Quoted by Paul Fussel, *Caste Marks: Style and Status in the U.S.A.*, William Heinemann Ltd., London, 1984, p. 20.

47) As the journalist George Will points out: "....the U.S. economy depends on the endless inculcation of envy (i.e. grenvy). If consumers succumbed to contentment, commerce would slow, dangerously." George Will, "The Rich: Maligned Minority?", *International Herald Tribune*, 21-22 February 1981, p. 4.

48) The slogan was coined in 1948 and has been in continual use since then. See: Edward Jay Epstein, *The Rise and Fall of Diamonds: The Shattering of a Brilliant Illusion*, Simon and Schuster, New York, 1982 and David Koskoff, *The Diamond World*, Harper & Row, New York, 1982.

49) Robert Sherill, review of Edward Jay Epstein, *The Rise and Fall of Diamonds: The Shattering of a Brilliant Illusion* and David Koskoff, *The Diamond World*, in *International Herald Tribune*, 27 May 1982.

50) "Albany at large - Goldman Sachs recruit", *Sunday Telegraph*, 20 April 1986, p.4.

51) Edward Jay Epstein, "The Billion Dollar Junk Business" *The Sunday Times*, 30 August 1987, p. 45.

52) Although the son of an immigrant Russian delicatessen owner in Detroit, Boesky did not start with nothing. He received a $700,000 inheritance which according to Douglas Frantz, he managed to turn into a $200,000,000 fortune. Douglas Frantz, "Diamond on the Rocks", *The Times*, 16 October 1987, p. 10.

53) Many people (his Wall Street enemies, perhaps) reported that Boesky was a nasty person "painfully short of charm." He used his wealth and position to build himself up, often it seemed, in order to put others down. Aside from buying himself into the Harvard Club and Republican political affairs, he lived on a lavish scale. At the same time that he was under investigation for fraud, he arranged for extensive improvements to his 200 acre Westchester County (New York) estate complete with bass ponds, flocks of sheep and a herd of white-tailed deer. Alexander Chancellor, "Stocks of which American heroes are made...", *The Independent*, 20 November 1986, p.8.

54) Ibid., p. 8

55) Fox Butterfield, "3,000 Pairs of Shoes: What the Marcoses Left Behind", *International Herald Tribune*, 10 March 1986, p. 2..

56) The $100 million represented both a fine and returned profits. Ibid., p. 8.

It is not clear that Boesky acted differently or necessarily on a larger scale than other investment bankers. He certainly was a visible personality and well hated. Other traders, Lew Glucksman, for example, have acted with equal ambition and contempt for conventions. Glucksman's grenvy led to the inglorious demise of a great banking house, Lehmann Brothers. Ken Auletta, *Greed and Glory on Wall Street*, Random House, New York, 1987.

Boesky himself and other corporate raiders have been caricatured (via a mogul called Gekko) in a 1987 film by Oliver Stone simply titled *Wall Street*.

57) Milken can be quite flamboyant in his business dealings, wining and dining clients in the most luxurious manner, but personally he is more retiring. He refuses to be photographed and he lives with his wife and three children in a four bedroomed house

near Los Angeles. He spends his spare time coaching his son's baseball team. Edward Jay Epstein, "The Billion Dollar Junk Business" *The Sunday Times*, op. cit., p. 45.

58) Nicholas Ashford, "Gorged on a surfeit of lawsuits", *The Times*, 18 May 1984, p. 28.

Ashford points out that there are now more than 620,000 lawyers in the United States, one third of whom started practicing since the beginning of the 80's.

59) Ian Brodie, "California -where litigation has become big business", *The Daily Telegraph*, 28 January 1986, p. 12.

California is the most litigious state. Civil cases have been increasing seven times faster than the rate of population growth.

60) Paul Johnson, "Long arms in search of a deep pocket", *The Daily Telegraph*, 16 August 1980, p. 8.

61) Quoted by Ian Brodie, "California -where litigation has become big business", op. cit., p. 12.

62) Paul Johnson, op. cit., p. 8.

63) "Malpractice Suits Set Records in the U.S.", *International Herald Tribune*, 18 January 1985, p. 3.

64) Nicholas Ashford, "Gorged on a surfeit of lawsuits", op. cit., p. 28.

65) Ibid., p. 28.

Equally ridiculous was a million dollar award to a woman who claimed that her psychic powers had been curtailed after a brain scan. Rhoderick Sharp, "California gives lead on lawsuits", *The Times*, 5 June 1986, p.6.

66) David Wastell in "The soaring cost of doctors' blunders", *The Sunday Telegraph*, 19 July 1987, p.9.

67) Disgruntled patients and their families have attacked psychiatrists for using psychotherapy, instead of psychotropic medication, on the basis that they didn't like the effects of psychotherapy and that medication was common practice. At other times psychiatrists have been attacked for using these drugs on the basis that they have deleterious side effects, even though the patients and their families had requested them.

68) Malpractice insurance premiums now cost some physicians upwards of $80,000 per year. Obstetricians, in particular, have been affected by these huge premiums and in many areas have decided to retire or change specialties to avoid the risk of expensive, disruptive litigation. Hence the public may find it difficult or impossible to obtain obstetrical care.

69) Tony Allen-Mills, "Doctors Hit Back at Lawyers", *The Daily Telegraph*, 19 May 1986, p. 8.

70) Ian Brodie, "California -where litigation has become big business", op. cit., p. 12.

71) Milton Shulman, "Londoner's Diary", *Evening Standard*, 17 April 1978, p. 16.

At this time the top rate of tax was 83% on earned income and 98% on investment income. In fact for self-employed people the tax rate on earned income was even higher because it included an extra assessment for national insurance without extra benefits (ie a tax on self-employment).

72) The extremely high rate of taxation was a major reason why the Swedish film maker, Ingmar Bergman, became a tax exile. He was later prosecuted by the Swedish authorities for tax evasion, a case which he fought and won.

73) Helmut Schoeck, *Envy: A Theory of Social Behaviour*, op. cit., p. 27.

Schoeck points out that in Sweden a private firm produces a much-consulted list of family incomes above a few thousand dollars.

74) Ibid., p. 28.

75) Ibid., p. 323.

76) The income tax was invented in Tuscany in the early fifteen century. In fact it echoed certain Roman practices. But use of this tax generally lapsed until the Napoleonic wars when the British government introduced it as a temporary measure to help pay for the war. Afterwards it lapsed again, but in 1840 Sir Robert Peel appealed for seven pence on the pound. Since then this originally modest tax has become the basis of public finance in England, and most other countries as well. Hugh Thomas, *An Unfinished History of the World*, Hamish Hamilton, London, 1982, pp. 547-548.

77) Helmut Schoeck, *Envy: A Theory of Social Behaviour*, op. cit., pp. 327-329.

78) Jonathan Lynn and Antony Jay, *Yes Prime Minister*, produced by Sydney Lotterby for BBC-TV, 1986.

79) In the United States Internal Revenue agents, no less than their F.B.I. counterparts, depend on paid and unpaid informants to gain information on allegedly delinquent tax payers. The treasury service receives an estimated 100,000 communications per year about others' assets and income, information often motivated by 'revenge, envy, anger, patriotism and spite.' Helmut Schoeck, *Envy: A Theory of Social Behaviour*, op. cit., p. 323.

Moreover, former agents have testified before congressional committees that enforcement agents are under great pressure to seize the money and property of taxpayers even before they have had a chance to appeal against an assessment. Gary Klott, "A Bully Approach to Tax Collecting", *International Herald Tribune*, 13 April 1987, p. 2.

See also, David Burnham, "The Abuse of Power: Misuse of the I.R.S.," *New York Times Magazine*, 3 September 1989, pp. 25-61. Burnham concludes, "The I.R.S., which intrudes on more Americans than any Federal agency, may be the most powerful instrument of social control in the United States."

80) "Sociological research has shown the extent to which this demand for levelling originates with certain groups of intellectuals, the average voter feeling hardly any definite envy towards those with really high incomes, for the objects of our envy are generally those who are almost our equals." Helmut Schoeck, *Envy: A Theory of Social Behaviour*, op. cit., pp. 194-195. See also pp. 325-327.

81) E. J. Mishan, "A Survey of Welfare Economics, 1939-1959", *The Economic Journal* (London), Vol. LXX, June 1960, p. 247, quoted by Helmut Schoeck, *Envy: A Theory of Social Behaviour*, op. cit., p. 306.

82) Schoeck points out that one poll asked members of the lowest classes in the United States how much tax higher income group should pay. The people queried consistently named a much lower figure as fair or right than that imposed by the government at the time. Ibid., p. 325.

83) This view is well conveyed by J. S. Duesenberry: "...any net increase of output–for instance, more of 'every' good without additional effort–will not advance the welfare of the community no matter how it is distributed. Indeed, any increase of output makes the community worse off, since no matter how the additional goods are distributed, the additional envy generated cannot be adequately compensated for out of these extra goods." J. S. Duesenberry, *Income, Saving, and the Theory of Consumer Behavior*,

Cambridge (Mass.), 1949, quoted by E. J. Mishan, "A Survey of Welfare Economics, 1939-1959", op. cit., p. 247.

84) In 1981 the top rate stood at 70% and was reduced to 50%. Far from reducing the tax take, studies show that the decrease resulted in more revenue being collected from top rate taxpayers (and about half of the lost revenue from lower bracket taxpayers). In other words, it has become less worthwhile for people to diminish their economic activity or remain within the black economy. Paul Craig Roberts, "Slash top tax rates - and all will benefit", *The Times*, 6 June 1986, p.12.

Paul Craig Roberts, who was President Reagan's Assistant Treasury Secretary for Economic Policy, comments: "Lower tax rates, moreover, signify that popular democracy in the US is now sufficiently mature to set aside envy and to focus on opportunity as the galvanizing force in politics. American legislators of all parties no longer believe that high rates are necessary." Ibid., p. 12

A drastic reduction in tax rates does not necessarily mean, however, that the politics of malice has been equally diminished. Many wealthy people and businesses had become extremely proficient in avoiding taxation. This aroused the envy of those who could not use tax shelters as well as guilt among some who did. Since the decrease in tax rates was accompanied by the elimination of a host of favoured exemptions, the new law can be seen as an expression of envy (against the wealthy for using tax shelters for they will become liable for substantial amounts of tax) and as a defense against envy (by taking several million citizens out of the tax net there may be less pressure to reduce the remaining shelters).

85) R. E. Money-Kyrle, *Man's Picture of His World: A psycho-analytic study*, Duckworth, London, 1978. See especially chapters 10, "On Avoidable Sources of Conflict" and 11, "On Political Philosophies."

86) At best wealthy individuals viewed the required redistributive measures with contempt, that is, as a form of charity which did more harm than good. Money-Kyrle adds: "Of course, taxation or inflation may injure an otherwise free economy if carried to excess. But the exaggerated fear of them, which had an unconscious source, was, I think, a major factor in delaying the discovery of an effective means to alleviate distress." Ibid., p. 165.

87) Marx often inherited or was given large sums of money. David Aberbach, "Marx and his Tormented Vision", *Jewish Chronicle*, 11 March 1983, p. 22.

His wife was Jenny von Westphalen, daughter of a prominent Prussian Government Councilor, Ludwig von Westphalen. The family was aristocratic, well-to-do and well connected. Fritz Raddatz, *Karl Marx: A Political Biography*, trans. Richard Barry, Weidenfeld and Nicolson, London, 1978, pp. 21-22.

88) Robert Hinshelwood, "Projective Identification and Marx's Concept of Man", *Int. Rev. Psycho-Anal.*, Vol. 10, 1983, pp. 221-226.

Typically Marx attributed inner pains to outer conditions through the use of the word 'we'. As a teenager Marx wrote:

> "We are chained, shattered, empty, frightened,
>
> Eternally chained to this marble block of Being,
>
> Chained, eternally chained, eternally -
>
> And the worlds drag us with them in their rounds,
>
> Howling their songs of death, and we -

We are the apes of a cold God."

David Aberbach, "Marx and his Tormented Vision", op. cit., p. 22.

89) The millennial belief in absolute egalitarianism provides another defense against as well as expression of envy. It is a long, often violent history which has been traced in great detail by Norman Cohn, *The Pursuit of the Millennium: Revolutionary Millennarians and Mystical Anarchists of the Middle Ages*, Paladin Books, London, 1978.

90) Leszek Kolakowski, "The Fantasy of Marxism", *Encounter*, December 1978, No. 303, pp. 83-84.

91) R. E. Money-Kyrle, *Man's Picture of His World: A psycho-analytic study*, op. cit., p. 181.

92) Ralph Waldo Emerson (1803-1882), American essayist, philosopher and poet, quoted by Robert Nisbet, *Prejudices: A Philosophical Dictionary*, Harvard University Press, Cambridge, Massachusetts, 1982, p. 108.

93) It is interesting to speculate that Marx's intense hatred of the bourgeoisie was, at least in parts, a displacement of an even more insatiable hatred initially directed to the non-transferable knowledge and skills of his father, a successful lawyer, and his heritage, the tradition of a long and distinguished line of rabbis. In fact, Marx totally rejected this heritage and remained a virulent anti-semite throughout his adult life. He himself was baptized, confirmed and married in church. His attacks on 'the huckerstering Jew' appears to be a veiled attack on his father for converting to Christianity as part of a general thrust for acceptance and 'upward mobility.' A fiercely denied sense of guilt about this lost patrimony may also have been involved.

Fritz Raddatz, *Karl Marx: A Political Biography*, op. cit., pp.3-6, 40-41.

94) Leslie Farber points out that the entire advertising industry is devoted to this proposition that man is what he owns and that, ironically, the Marxist sociology of class is devoted to the same view. In consequence: "So long as I believe that you are your possessions and that my motive is greed, I can avoid any acknowledgement of the essential inequality between us." Leslie Farber, *lying, despair, jealousy, envy, sex, suicide, drugs, and the good life*, op. cit. p. 40.

95) Helmut Schoeck, *Envy: A Theory of Social Behaviour*, op. cit., pp. 216-217.

96) Ibid., p. 217.

See also Norman Cohn's discussion of the English peasant revolt led by the priest, John Ball. His most enthusiastic followers were to be found among the lower clergy and Londoners "envious of the rich and the nobility". Norman Cohn, *The Pursuit of the Millennium*, op. cit., pp. 198-204.

97) Helmut Schoeck points out that there is no absolute criteria of luxury. Much depends on the degree of envy of those who stand in judgment. "Luxury *as such* has never existed, and never will exist, but only *envy* of consumer behaviour that is branded as luxury." Helmut Schoeck, *Envy: A Theory of Social Behaviour*, op. cit., p. 216.

98) Quoted by Paul Fussel, *Caste Marks: Style and Status in the U.S.A.*, op. cit., p. 19.

99) A British tommy trying to explain the difference between conscripts and officers during the North Africa campaign of World War Two neatly captured the bitterness that class and status distinctions evoke:

"I'll tell you what it means, it means Vickers-Armstrong booking a profit to look like a loss, and Churchill lighting a new cigar, and the *Times* explaining Liberty and Democracy, and me sitting on my arse in Libya splashing a fainting man with water out of my steel helmet. It's a very fine thing if only you're in the right class-that's highly important, sir, because one class gets the sugar and the other gets the shit." Ibid., p. 25.

100) $100 was the rental in 1979. Presumably it is now much higher. John Brooks, *Showing Off in America: From Conspicuous Consumption to Parody Display*, Little, Brown and Company, Boston, 1979, p. 271.

101) Paul Fussell has devised a 'living-room scale' for ascertaining social class. His scale would serve just as well for denoting status distinctions. Thus, someone with a threadbare rug or carpet would gain 8 points, while someone with a new oriental would lose 2. He reckons that 245 points are needed for membership in the upper class, or the highest status group. Paul Fussel, *Caste Marks: Style and Status in the U.S.A.*, op. cit., pp. 194-197.

102) G. Rudé, *The Crowd in the French Revolution*, Oxford and New York, 1959, pp. 201-202, discussed by Helmut Schoeck, *Envy: A Theory of Social Behaviour*, op. cit. p.342.

103) "The inescapable conclusion remains that the primary and most constant motive impelling revolutionary crowds during this period was the concern for the provision of cheap and plentiful food. This more than any other factor, was the raw material out of which the popular Revolution was forged...Even more it accounts for the occasional outbreaks of independent activity by the *menu peuple*, going beyond or running counter to, the interests of their *bourgeois* allies...Yet without the impact of political ideas, mainly derived from their *bourgeois* leaders, such movements would have remained strangely purposeless and barren of result." G. Rudé, *The Crowd in the French Revolution*, op. cit., p. 208,

104) Eric Hobsbawm, Professor of Economic and Social History at Birkbeck College, University of London, has written detailed studies of revolutions, revolutionary processes and revolutionaries. See: E. J. Hobsbawm, *Social Bandits and Primitive Rebels. Studies in Archaic Forms of Social Movement in the 19th and 20th Centuries*, Glencoe, Ill., 1959, pp. 116, 118, 122, discussed by Helmut Schoeck, *Envy: A Theory of Social Behaviour*, op. cit. p.343.

105) These conclusions concern urban insurrections and revolutions. Hobsbawm points out that the situation is markedly different in the case of rural areas and peasant revolutions which are usually egalitarian and often utopian in character. E. J. Hobsbawm, *Social Bandits and Primitive Rebels. Studies in Archaic Forms of Social Movement in the 19th and 20th Centuries*, op. cit., pp. 26, 187, 122.

106) Roger Money-Kyrle states: ".....the witch-hunts which will then break out will arise from motives of a paradoxical nature characteristic only of the unconscious. For those who perish as suspected, but not actual, traitors to the revolution are also the scapegoats for the unacknowledged sense of guilt at being revolutionaries which their executioners project onto them." R. E. Money-Kyrle, *Man's Picture of His World: A psycho-analytic study*, op. cit., p. 182.

107) B. L. Garrison, "Congo Rebels Kill "Intellectuals" as Enemies of Their Revolution", *New York Times*, 4 October 1964, p. 4, quoted by Helmut Schoeck, *Envy: A Theory of Social Behaviour*, op. cit. pp. 345-46.

In northern and eastern provinces of the Congo where the rebels held sway, even the clerks were wiped out. A Catholic missionary reported that in Moyen province, ".... there is hardly a Congolese alive with more than a primary education. This means, quite simply, that this part of the Congo has been set back thirty years." op.cit.., p. 346.

Fascist generals during the Spanish Civil War voiced similar sentiments. One of their slogans was: "Down with intelligence; long live death." Norman Stone, "When Spain tore itself to pieces", *The Sunday Telegraph*, 13 July 1986, p. 8.

108) Bernard Levin, "Punching holes in this earthly paradise", *The Times*, 16 December 1977, p. 16.

109) The 'red-eyed disease' is the tendency of envious eyes to become engorged with hostility at the sight of others prosperity or envied possessions. This is not an affliction limited to Chinese, but one widely recognized by them. Under Deng Xiaoping and the new policies of economic liberalization, the press has openly criticized the red-eyed envy of peasants left behind in the race for prosperity. A typical news item described how a woman in Jiangsu (one of the richest provinces) poisoned her neighbour's ducks because she resented his success. Christopher Wren, "Profits, Pop Music and Videodating in a New China: China Under Deng", *International Herald Tribune*, 28 December 1984, p. 2.

See also the account of Nien Cheng, a British educated Chinese woman, who observed and suffered the "Rampage of the Red Guards" in Shanghai in the 1960's. Nien Cheng, *Life and Death in Shanghai*, Grafton Books, London, 1986.

110) The 11+ exam was the principle means of sorting students according to academic ability and slotting them into grammar schools, or not. Although condemned for putting too much pressure on students too soon, the absence of state streaming has also proven unhelpful, while selection exams continue in the private sector.

Even into the late 1980's Labour leader Neil Kinnock affirmed the need to eliminate private education because it set unfair high standards which the state sector could not meet. Commenting on such attacks, educator John Rae quipped that Labour's answer to low standards was to make sure they applied to all. See: Anthony Bevins, "Kinnock calls for the end to private schools", *The Independent*, 1 June 87, p. 1; John Rae, "Shooting the piano player", *The Times*, 8 May 1987, p. 14.

111) Sue Reid, "Grammars are Best", *Evening Standard*, 2 August 1979, pp. 1-2. The article refers to a government survey of 384 grammar and comprehensive schools. Many were short of books and equipment and only a minority were performing with distinction. In many schools basic subjects like English, foreign languages, maths and science were neglected because teachers were underqualified and facilities were poor.

In subsequent years academic standards continued to deteriorate. In particular the ILEA (Inner London Education Authority) seemed to be obsessed with anti-sexism and anti-racism in place of academic excellence, which led Cabinet Minister Norman Tebbit to refer to the ILEA as an "education free zone". Simon Heffer, "Where the quality of learning is strained by socialist aims", *The Daily Telegraph*, 23 June 1986, p. 18.

112) John Izbicki, "Return of Grammar School Urged", *The Daily Telegraph*, 10 March 1986, p. 26.

113) I am not only describing a British problem. State educational standards have suffered in many countries for reasons which include inner city blight, cost constraints, changes in educational priorities, politicization of the curriculum, grade inflation and an excessive emphasis on self-expression and consciousness raising as opposed to basic skills. Some of these factors indicate envy or the fear of envy. Nonetheless, the process seems to have been taken to more destructive extremes in Britain.

Christopher Lasch, among many observers, has commented on the baleful effects of diluted standards in the American system, especially in the education of minority groups. Christopher Lasch, *The Culture of Narcissism*,, op. cit., pp. 140-145.

114) Women who wore the device had a much higher risk of developing pelvic inflammatory disease. Robin Henig, op. cit., p. 22.

115) Even as an IUD, the Dalkon Shield wasn't very effective. An initial study by Dr. Hugh Davis, inventor of the device, claimed it was superior to other IUD's. But the study was flawed and the Robins Company apparently knew this. Other studies demonstrated

its diminished capacity to prevent pregnancy in comparison to other IUD's or other methods. Ibid., p. 22.

116) L. P. Hartley, *Facial Justice*, Hamish Hamilton, London, 1960.

117) George Orwell, *Nineteen Eighty-four*, Penguin Books, London, 1984.

118) L. P. Hartley, *Facial Justice*, op. cit., p. 43.

119) Joab replied: "Brains are not a cause of Bad E, Jael, like money or beauty," an obvious denial of his sister's threat. But Jael continued the attack: "They might become so. It isn't fair that you should be cleverer than other people." Ibid., p.172.

120) Ibid., p. 43.

121) Journalist George Will has described the experience of living in Soviet Russia where the excessive control of overt sensuality, for reasons not unlike Hartley details, caused him acute discomfort, akin to severe sensory deprivation. "In the West, the social atmosphere may be overdosed with aphrodisiacs. However, a sojourn in an anti-sensualist society such as this underscores a theme of Orwell's "1984": Eroticism is feared by a regime that feels threatened by any realm of privacy or flicker of spontaneity." George Will, "Moscow's Stalinist Values Excite Longing for Neon", *International Herald Tribune*, 13 March 1986, p. 8.

122) Similarly, Valium addiction has been called, 'bottled happiness'. Alan Massam, "Happy end to my mother's long misery", *London Standard*, 3 April 1986, p. 14.

123) There exists a plethora of material which documents the misinformation about drug use and the history of repressive counter measures as well as attempts to redress the balance. See for example: *Drug Addiction: Crime or Disease? Interim and Final Reports of the Joint Committee of the American Bar Association and the American Medical Association on Narcotic Drugs*, Indiana University Press, Bloomington,1963; Joel Fort, *The Pleasure Seekers: The Drug Crisis, Youth and Society*, Grove Press, New York, 1969; Joseph Berke, "The Fickle Fix", *The Radical Therapist*, Vol. 1, No. 2, June-July 1970; Charles Tart (editor), *Altered States of Consciousness*, Anchor Books, New York, 1972.

124) L. P. Hartley, *Facial Justice*, op. cit., p. 43.

125) Paul Johnson, "Farewell to the Labour Party", op. cit. p. 329.

126) Paul Johnson, "Whatever happened to the Lucky Country?", *The Sunday Telegraph*, 2 January 1983, pp. 8-9.

127) Ibid., p. 8.

128) The voyagers on the First Fleet in 1788, as well as subsequent settlers, were under the orders of the British government. As Paul Johnson points out, "Australia has never wholly lost its sense of dependence on a paternalist power." According to Johnson, the biggest threat to Australia's prosperity comes from ingrained habits of looking to the State and Federal governments to provide basic necessities. Ibid., pp. 8 -9.

129) Johnson comments on the 'heavy hand of Canberra' as well as the big unions which seek to centralize and control individual rights and initiatives. Ibid. pp. 8 -9. Others have commented on the dominating position of big business. Collectively they share many features of 'Big Brother'.

130) Since the 1960's significant numbers of Australian women have adopted radical, leftwing feminist positions. Ibid., p.8.

This militancy is not simply a reaction to the overvaluation of maleness, or specific male oppression, but results from a general diminution of femaleness, and can be seen as an attempt to compensate for the loss of valued female roles. Years earlier Clara

Thompson discussed the cultural implications of this issue in, ""Penis Envy" in Women", Jean Baker Miller (ed.), *Psychoanalysis and Women*, op. cit., pp. 55-57.

131) Plutarch, *Alcibiades*, (13,4), quoted in Peter Walcot, *Envy and the Greeks*, op cit., p. 58.

132) Walcot points out that Greek audiences thoroughly enjoyed seeing prominent people being brought down to earth by public humiliation. They could not stand anyone excelling 'the democratic norm'. Then, as now, one of the best areas for a flank attack was personal morality. Ibid., p. 66.

133) "Anyone for Losing", *The Times*, 6 July 1985, p. 9.

The same editorial gloated over the demise of Jimmy Connors ("the great old grunter) and Ivan Lendl ("a money-making machine with little compensating grace").

134) Michael Wise, "'Big Bang' Ignites a Wage Explosion", *International Herald Tribune*, 10 April 1986, pp. 7 & 13.

135) Many staff were 'head-hunted' or poached from other firms. Approximately one thousand people received remuneration running to several hundred thousand dollars a year, while a few executives reported deals worth millions. These packages were not unusual on the world financial market, but extremely large by British standards. Ibid., p. 8.

136) Quoted by Michael Wise, Ibid., p. 8.

137) Quoted by Michael Wise, Ibid., p. 8.

Prominent business figures also parroted the resentment of 'new money'. Thus, Charles John Constable, director general of the British Institute of Management commented: "People here will become increasingly disturbed by one group gaining extraordinary wealth for creating nothing, for simply turning over money. British attitudes are quite different from those in America." Quoted by Steve Lohr, "City's New Traders" Young, Cheeky", *International Herald Tribune*, 27-28 September 1986, pp. 17-19.

The idea that newcomers were getting rich for doing nothing does not fit the facts. The new traders worked long hours, bore heavy responsibilities and generated significant wealth in and for 'the City'. The denial of their efforts represents a typical envious response to people who had successfully infiltrated previously cordoned off areas of financial enrichment. Many were sneeringly labeled 'Yuppies' by the press, representing a public which resented thrusting ambitions and accomplishments. 'Yuppies' were alleged to be spoiled brats (like 'hippies') who did little and took everything, while simultaneously flaunting the proceeds. Yet, as journalist Peter McKay points out, this is a good description of their predecessors, "greedy, stupid city types" many of whom had gotten their jobs through family connections and then sat on their ass for years. McKay concludes: "No one who is honest can really claim that the yuppification of rundown London has not been a great and lasting restorative movement." Peter McKay, "Some of our best friends were yuppies", *The London Evening Standard*, 22 October 1987, p. 7.

138) Roy Mason, "De Lorean is a winner, damn it!", *The Times*, 12 October 1981, p. 6.

"Share deal that gave De Lorean the bargain of a lifetime", Business News, *The Sunday Times*, 11 October 1981, pp. 53 & 72.

139) De Lorean had been charged with racketeering on the basis of a 1978 law designed to put the Mafiosi behind bars. He was acquitted of 15 counts of racketeering, fraud and tax evasion. His defense attorneys proved that $8.9 million which he had used for personal purposes, had, in fact, been legitimately provided by Group Lotus for design work. "De Lorean Innocent of Embezzlement", *International Herald Tribune*, 18 December 1986, p. 2.

By the spring of 1987 De Lorean managed to reach a financial settlement with his major creditors. "De Lorean bouncing back", *The London Evening Standard*, 28 May 1987, p. 53.

CHAPTER 10

1) Jean-Paul Sartre, "My Political Will", *Strike*, Vol. 2, No. 3, October 1978, p. 5, translated and reprinted from *Mon Testament politique* (Edition "Gare L'explosion", 1977) courtesy of Edizioni della Rivisto "Anarchismo".

2) The French existentialist philosopher, playwright and novelist, Jean-Paul Sartre (1905-1980) was also a noted political activist who espoused many radical causes on behalf of the working class, the third world and especially oppressed youth.

3) "Who would dare criticize the servants of the Middle Ages who burned down their lord's castles, dipping their hands into the intestines to pull out his guts and then dance among the smoking ruins of the castle? Who would dare criticize those servants for creating with iron and fire their own freedom. Which one of you would dare to criticize the slaves of ancient time who struck the patrician, catching him in the midst of an orgy, snatching from him the golden cup, and after having emptied it, escaping, taking along the pillage and murdering the robbed one?....Let's resurrect the tradition of Brutus, Spartacus, and the rebellious peasants of past history! Stand Up! Action! Insurrection! Revolution!" Ibid., p.4.

4) Errico Malatesta, *Anarchy*, trans. by Vernon Richards, Freedom Press, London, 1974, p. 13.

5) "Things fall apart; the centre cannot hold;

Mere anarchy is loose upon the world,

The blood-dimmed tide is loosed, and everywhere

The ceremony of innocence is drowned;"

Although written about the Irish uprising, this excerpt from "The Second Coming", by W.B. Yeats, describes the impact of the vandal and anarchist, and is often quoted by their friends and enemies. W. B. Yeats, *Selected Poetry*, Pan Books, London, 1974, pp. 99-100.

6) During the 17th century opponents of the radical Levellers called them "Switzerising anarchists". Later the Girondin leader, Jacques-Pierre Brissot, used the epithet to denounce his Enragé rivals: "Laws that are not carried into effect, authorities without force and despised, crime unpunished, property attacked, the safety of the individual violated, the morality of the people corrupted, no constitution, no government, no justice, these are the features of anarchy."

The New Encyclopedia Britannica, 15th ed., 1985, p. 458.

7) William Godwin (1756-1836). Ibid., p. 458. The famous phrase, "From each according to his means, to each according to his needs" was popularized by the nineteenth century anarchist leader, Peter Kropotkin. But it had been clearly anticipated by Godwin, who, in turn, had been influenced by Sir Thomas More's, *Utopia*.

Godwin also commented: "Normal man seeks the light just as the flowers do. Man, if not too much interfered with, will make for himself the best possible environment and create for his children right conditions, because the instinct for peace and liberty is deeply rooted in his nature." Quoted by George Woodcock in, *Anarchy or Chaos*, Freedom Press, London, 1944, p. 32.

8) Pierre-Joseph Proudhon (1809-1865). Quoted by George Woodcock, Ibid., p. 35.

9) Idealists frequently insist this violence is justified even if the volence and consequent destruction violate the very beliefs they are trying to sustain.

10) Mikhail Bakunin (1814-1876) was an idealist who saw violent revolution as a necessary prelude to a new millennium. Nonetheless he was a brilliant instigator who inspired hatred and discord throughout Europe and America. His violent actions became models for future generations of revolutionaries which belied his hopes for human harmony and perfection "Bloody revolutions are often necessary, thanks to human stupidity; yet they are always an evil, a monstrous evil and a great disaster, not only with regard to the victims, but also for the sake of the purity and the perfection of the purpose in whose name they take place." Quoted by George Woodcock, Ibid., p. 37.

11) Ibid., p. 68.

In Italy Malatesta concurred with Nechaïeff's doctrine and helped to popularize it throughout Europe. However, just at the time that anarchism was becoming popular in the West, the Russian revolutionaries were abandoning the term in favor of terrorism. But the work of writers like Kropotkin and Kravchinsky led terroristic tactics to be identified with anarchist ideals. James Billington points out: "Thus anarchism tinged with idealism and sanctified with martyrdom became a new verbal talisman for many otherwise dispirited revolutionaries." James Billington, *Fire in the Minds of Men: Origins of the Revolutionary Faith*, Temple Smith, London, 1980, p. 414. See also pp. 415 - 416.

12) Action Directe, for example, has been one of the more prominent extremist groups operating in Europe in the 1980's. It was founded in France by Jean Marc Rouillan, the leader, and Nathalie Menogon in 1979. After bombing the Interpol headquarters outside Paris in May 1985 it vowed to continue "to hit central installations which link their political, economic and military strategy, and at the heart of which are found the strongest antagonisms of the international proletariat/imperialist bourgeoisie: to concretize the qualitative leap of all antagonisms of the masses and develop them toward a global revolutionary strategy." Diana Geddes, "Seven-year history of terror," *The Times*, 19 November 1986, p. 9

See also: Stephen Segaller, *Invisible Armies: Terrorism into the 1990s*, Michael Joseph, London, 1986.

Aum is a Japanese neo-Buddhist Japanese sect led by Shouko Asahara. Aum was responsible for attacking a Tokyo subway train with nerve gas in March 1995, killing 12 and injuring 5,500. Hisako Watanabe, "Paranoia and persecution on modern Japanese life," in Joseph H. Berke, et.al, (eds) *Even Paranoids Have Enemies*, Routledge, London, 1998, p. 190.

13) As a slogan and state of mind, 'saving the world' equals the wish to overcome starvation, oppression, disease and inequality, indeed, all the ostensibly positive features of anarchist thought. This psychic situation, which Herbert Rosenfeld has termed *libidinal narcissism*, precedes and lays the foundation for the more intransigent *destructive narcissism.*

Herbert Rosenfeld, "A clinical approach to the psychoanalytic theory of the life and death instincts: an investigation into the aggressive aspects of narcissism.", op. cit., p. 173.

In common usage the term *narcissism* equals what Rosenfeld calls libidinal narcissism.

14) Ibid. 174

"This narcissistic organization is in my experience not primarily directed against guilt and anxiety, but seems to have the purpose of maintaining the idealization and superior power of the destructive narcissism." Ibid., p. 174.

An important implication of Rosenfeld's work is that the contradictory currents of at least some political theories (such as the anarchists' millennial expectations and terrorist plans) reflect the ebb and flow of libidinal and destructive narcissism. The purpose of both of these strategies is to allow the envier to attack envied objects, while at the same time diminish envious tension and concomitant feelings of worthlessness in himself.

15) Helaire Belloc, "About John", *Selected Cautionary Verses*, Puffin Books, London, 1983, pp. 70-71. See also pp. 72-78.

16) In February 1959 a new school opened in East Harlem. By November 589 windows had been broken. In 1958 the New York Department of Education had to replace 160,000 broken windows and repair damage caused by 75 cases of arson. Helmut Schoeck, *Envy: A Theory of Social Behaviour*, op. cit., p. 112.

17) In 1978 the Tory Spokesman on Home Affairs, William Whitelaw, pointed out that schools and railways suffered £20 million of wanton damage per year. The current figure is probably higher. Oliver Pritchett, "The World of the Vandal", *The Sunday Telegraph*, 29 October 1978, p. 21.

Train vandals are so pervasive that they can severely disrpt train services. "In the northeast of England, upwards of 50 people are arrested per week for 'cutting and stealing trackside signalling cable, damaging high-voltage overhead power lines and placing obstacles such as a motorcycle and supermarket trolley on the tracks." Michael Dynes, "Rail vandals bring fast train services to a halt," *The Times*, 21 December 1991.

18) This man abandoned his Middlesborough farm after his crops had been attacked fifty times during a single harvest.

According to the National Farmers' Union Mutual Insurance Society, the problem of vandalism is the greatest at the edge of large cities and new towns. The damage done includes: "setting fire to crops, hayricks and buildings, sabotage of farm machinery, the theft of sheep, cattle and vegetables, and the killing and maiming of livestock by dogs or guns." John Young, "Vandalism is costing farms £5m each year", *The Times*, 18 April 1987, p. 4.

19) Helmut Schoeck, *Envy: A Theory of Social Behaviour*, op. cit., p.111.

20) *The New Encyclopedia Britannica*, 15th ed., 1985, p. 459.

For hundreds of years property had indeed been the main source of generating wealth. Yet, by the time of Proudhon's declaration, this had long since begun to change, precipitated by the growth of financial markets and the industrial revolution. Although Proudhon was trying to make a point about man's exploitation of man, his conclusions were inaccurate. "Property is theft" reflects envy of wealth.

Sartre's preoccupations were also nonsensical. By the time of his statement he had long known that "information is wealth". Even in his "Political Will", he talks about killing the rich to get money to buy printing presses, that is, convey valuable information, if only "the propaganda of the word".

21) Sartre assailed the rich and privileged and asserted that the "sword of Damocles" should be constantly held over their heads, so that "snakes of terror, like those of Nemesis, hiss night and day into their ears frightening them out of their luxury and their lives; that their position would become unbearable and that tired of such anguish,

they would see themselves forced to fall on their knees to demand forgiveness, begging the proletariat to grant them life in exchange for their privilege and the common joy in exchange for the general disgrace." Jean-Paul Sartre, "My Political Will", op. cit., p. 5.

22) Ibid., p. 5.

23) Ibid., p. 5.

24) Ibid., p. 5.

Sartre's anarchy links millennialism with economic and political vandalism.

25) Annie Cohen-Solal, *Sartre: A Life*, Heinemann, London, 1987.

26) Ronald Hayman, *Writing Against: A Biography of Sartre*, Weidenfeld & Nicolson, London, 1986.

27) Jean-Paul Sartre, "My Political Will", op. cit., p. 5.

28) Paul Webster, "Anarchists loot top Paris shops", *The Guardian*, 9 June 1979, p.8.

The raid described in the article was one of several similar incidents blamed on Autonome in the previous six months.

29) Ian Henry, "Gang 'Robbed to Finance Anarchy'", *The Daily Telegraph*, 27 September 1979, p. 3.

Interestingly, in England the right wing counterparts of left wing anarchist and semi-anarchist groups ('the violent fringe') often share similar hatreds. These include Mrs. Thatcher, nuclear energy, the capitalist press and Zionism. Cal McCrystal, "Warlords of the Fringe", *The Sunday Times*, 12 October 1986, pp. 36-43.

30) The Angry Brigade, "Communique 8", *The Angry Brigade 1967-1984 Documents and Chronology*, Anarchist Pocketbooks 3, Elephant Editions, London, 1985, pp. 20-21, 31.

31) According to the Opinion-Poll Institute of Professor Noelle-Neumann, the number of people in West Germany who feel intense boredom (Langeweile) has been steadily increasing. Professor Noelle-Neumann says the data demonstrates a positive correlation between those confessing boredom and those professing hatred of technology and the market economy as well as sympathy for the Green Party and egalitarian politics. Discussed by Helmut Schoeck, personal communication, letter of 8 July 1987.

There is a certain paradox in the fear of boredom and the desire for egalitarianism. In practice an egalitarian society is much less stimulating than a non-egalitarian society. To demonstrate this, one only has to talk to people who have lived in places like the People's Republic of China.

32) Aside from other causes, war is certainly a major antidote for mass boredom. One has only to consider the reactions of the populations of the major powers before say, World War One, or the Falkland's crisis.

33) Throughout the eighties the responses of large numbers of young people to unemployment in Europe and the United States have included violent resentful vandalism and drug induced withdrawal. The latter may reflect an underlying condition of over-stimulation, through television and the 'consumer spectacle'. So a state of boredom can serve as a defense against degrees of stimulation which cannot be assimilated.

34) When ghetto people were asked why they participated in riots, many answered, "Because I was bored." Understimulation in their daily lives, and overstimulation by TV appeared to be essential issues.

35) Theodore Roszak, *The Making of a Counter Culture: Reflections on the technocratic society and its youthful opposition*, Anchor Books, New York, 1969.

Joseph Berke (editor), *Counter Culture: The Creation of an Alternative Society*, Peter Owen, London, 1969.

36) David Mairowitz, "The Diggers", Ibid., pp. 378

37) The 'Diggers', 30-40 in number, established themselves on St. George's Hill, near Walton-on-Thames, on 1 April 1649, and remained there until March of the following year. They were led by Gerrard Winstanley, a tradesman whose business had failed during the economic depression of the 1640's. He articulated the basic ideas that he and his followers tried to put into practice. Winstanley asserted, for example, that people could only remove social injustice by their own deeds and called upon the common folk "...to manure and work upon the Common lands". Quoted by George Woodcock, *Anarchy or Chaos*, op. cit., p 29. See also pp. 27-31.

According to Woodcock, Winstanley anticipated Peter Kropotkin's idea of Mutual Aid. Kropotkin (1842-1921) was the most significant anarchist leader after Bakunin and essentially crystallized anarchist theory.

38) "The Digger Papers", excerpts, see: Joseph Berke (editor), *Counter Culture: The Creation of an Alternative Society*, op. cit., pp. 380-382.

39) Among the many goods and services the Digger manifesto advocated, there were 'Free': Garages, Food Stores, Information, Bank, Housing, 'Medical Thing', Hospital, Design Gang, Schools, News, Communication, Events, Garbage Collection, Radio, TV, Computer Stations, 'Tinkers and Gunsmiths'. Ibid., pp 380-381.

40) The Diggers deployed the politics of the preposterous to emphasize the anomalies between wealth and poverty. At one point they sent a van from the 'Free City Distribution Company' into wealthy neighborhoods to ask whether the people needed anything, and offered goods from the van. I think this action was not a labor of love, nor irony, rather a further form of intimidation, designed to facilitate 'begging with menaces', as happened later on.

41) Ibid., p.380. The Diggers hoped that the tone and content of this statement would help them forge cooperative links with other groups including the Black Panthers, Provos and Mission Rebels.

42) The Diggers were successful models for other groups which blazed briefly on the international underground scene. This included the White Panther Party (white radicals who named themselves after Black Liberationists) with adherents in the U.S. and the U.K. Point 10 of their 10 point programme against state oppression stated: "WE WANT A FREE PLANET. WE WANT FREE LAND..FREE FOOD..FREE SHELTER..FREE CLOTHING.. FREE MUSIC..FREE CULTURE..FREE MEDIA....FREE BODIES..FREE TECHNOLOGY... FREE EDUCATION..FREE HEALTH CARE....FREE PEOPLE...FREE TIME AND SPACE.. EVERYTHING FREE..FOR EVERYBODY.." White Panther Party, Abbey Wood Chapter "Ten Point Programme", *Chapter?*, No. 1, London, 1971, p. 15. This programme appears like a 'manic feast'.

The San Francisco Diggers (and kindred groups like the White Panthers) suffered the same fate as their English namesake, they broke up and seemingly disappeared. Winstanley himself vanished into such obscurity that his date and place of death are unknown.

43) One investigation uncovered benefits frauds of £8,500 per week at Newquay. These involved 173 claims, out of 451 that had been made in the town that week. The claimants were mostly young people who claimed from false address, and who, in some cases, were also working. Sarah Thompson, "£8,500-a-week benefits fiddle in seaside town", *The Daily Telegraph*, 22 August 1986, p. 3.

44) *Computer Security*, Time-Life Books, Alexandria, Virginia, 1986, p.42.

45) Ibid., p. 44.

46) Ibid., pp. 17-18, 60-61.

47) Ibid., pp. 18-19.

An expert programmer can write a logic bomb that is practically impossible to detect, because it takes up only a few lines amidst a larger program of tens of thousands of lines. Yet it can wreak havoc when it goes off such as by suddenly deleting huge chunks of data.

48) The consultant, Ross Greenberg, goes on to say, "I guess the people who devise these things take pleasure in destroying other people's work." Quoted by Mark McCain, "U.S. Computer Vandals Learn to Program Havoc", *International Herald Tribune*, 20 May 1987, p. 1.

Greenberg himself has devised several "tools of defense" against electronic terrorists. These include a software program that alerts him to suspicious activity within his computer.

49) Headlines about ecological 'rape' remain all too familiar. Of course, this kind of damage can and is done by organizations as well as individuals. Godfrey Brown, "Photographs show rape of the countryside", *The Daily Telegraph*, 4 September 1986, p. 4.

50) Helmut Schoeck, *Envy: A Theory of Social Behaviour*, op. cit., p. 107.

51) "Teacher gets life sentence for double axe murders", *The Times*, 16 April 1987, p. 3.

52) "The Tingling Fingers that Meant Death for 26", *The Daily Telegraph*, 21 January 1981, p. 3. The killings were done in the the city of Hull, Britain, over a five year period. Lee used to prowl the streets with a bottle of paraffin under his coat.

53) While damage to the fatherland may focus judicial interest, violation of the mother country makes the public crave for revenge.

54) Quoted by George Woodcock, *Anarchy or Chaos*, op. cit., pp. 54-55.

55) The manifesto ends with the call "to overthrow governments by whatever name they may be called." A century later Sartre used similar language to urge the overthrow of tyrannies "called a provisional government, government of liberation, constituent, legislative assembly, presidency; today his name is Giscard, tomorrow he will be called Marchais or Mitterand." Jean-Paul Sartre, "My Political Will", op. cit., p. 4.

56) George Woodcock, *Anarchy or Chaos*, op. cit., pp. 107-108.

57) "...to the last fiber of his being Marx was a politician; he was like lava, a revolutionary natural element; for him politics were the essence of all things; nothing else motivated him." Ibid., p. 49.

58) Recollection by the Italian politician Mazzini, quoted by Fritz Raddatz, Ibid., p. 66.

Similarly James Guillaume, the historian of the International, said that Marx maintained the attitude of "a ruling sovereign." Ibid., p. 66.

59) Lieutenant Techow who fought with Marx during the 1848 revolution and later met him again during his exile in London observed that Marx was eaten away by ambition. He ridiculed comrades who parroted his words and reserved real respect only for aristocrats: "I came away with the impression that the aim of all his endeavors was personal domination, that all his associates were far beneath him, lagging behind him, and that, if they should dare to forget it for a moment, he would put them back into their

place with a shameless impudence worthy of Napoleon." Quoted by Fritz Raddatz, Ibid., p. 66.

60) *Computer Security*, Time-Life Books, op. cit., p. 10.

61) Ibid., p. 72.

62) Ibid., p. 65.

War Games: directed by John Badham, produced by Harold Schneider. Warner Communication Inc., 1983

63) Ibid., p. 59.

See also discussion by Andrew Emmerson, "Phantoms of the operating system", *New Scientist*, 28 January 1988, p. 69.

American companies are also beginning to implant 'bombs' and 'worms' into their software to prevent illicit copying. Any program that is copied will self-destruct.

64) Ibid., pp. 10 & 67.

Most 'viruses' are malicious in origin. Armed with them, terrorists, hackers or plain practical jokers can wreak havoc on a mainframe computer within an hour, or a computer network within several days. Vin McLellan, "Sabotaged Computers Are Passing on the Bug", *International Herald Tribune*, 1 February 1988, pp. 1&11.

65) According to *Computer Security* computer-related frauds in Britain cost between £500 million and £2.5 billion per year and $300 million to $5 billion in the United States. These figures mostly concern embezzlement and do not take into account extensive malicious damage. Ibid., p. 19.

66) Ibid., p. 10.

Similarly a saboteur damaged the internal computer network of the IBM corporation with a Christmas greeting in December 1987. Essentially a picture of a Christmas tree began to appear on all the computer terminals, which brought all the other computer traffic to a halt. Although IBM played down the incident, the 'virus' took the huge network, known as the "Big Blue", out of action for over two hours. Charles Bremner, "'Virus' plague wreaks havoc with computers", *The Times*, 13 January 1988, p. 6.

67) Quoted by Bremner, ibid., p. 6.

68) Irving Berlin, "Anything You Can Do", *Annie Get Your Gun*, Irving Berlin, Ltd., London, 1947, pp. 128-137.

69) *Computer Security*, Time-Life Books, op. cit., p. 40.

Similarly American right wing groups like 'The Aryan Nations" claim the right to bomb federal buildings on the basis of beliefs which include: "Caucasians are the chosen people". "Official Links Idaho Blasts, Rights Effort", *The International Herald Tribune*, 3 October 1986, p. 4.

70) Computer Security, op. cit., p. 40.

71) In Americas most guerrilla attacks have focussed on military or military related installations. In 1970 anti-war activists bombed the Army Mathematics Research Center at the University of Wisconsin. In addition to doing about $18 million worth of damage to the buildings, computer hardware and twenty year accumulation of research data, they killed a young graduate student. Ibid., pp. 35, 40.

72) Robin Smyth, "Swiss 'losers' fight rat race", *The Observer*, 3 August 1980, p. 3.

73) Previously the youths paraded with fireworks, trumpets and bongo drums down the main streets demanding an amnesty for comrades arrested in earlier demonstrations. The attack on the opera house, site of a £14 million renovation was related to the decision of the city fathers to close a youth center.

74) Wallace Turner, "18 Hell's Angels Arrested in Drug Probe", *The International Herald Tribune*, 20 June 1979, p. 3.

75) The distinction is between "libidinal narcissism" (equivalent to 'The Jesus complex') and "destructive narcissism" (equivalent to 'The Hitler complex'). See: Herbert Rosenfeld, "A clinical approach to the psychoanalytic theory of the life and death instincts: an investigation into the aggressive aspects of narcissism.", op. cit., pp. 172 -173.

76) In this context, I refer, in particular, to the 'destructive phallicist' whose primary targets are the signs and symbols of phallic potency.

77) "A Nameless, Ancient Crime", editorial from *The New York Times* reprinted in *The International Herald Tribune*, 6 June 1982, p. 6.

78) Laurence Marks, William Keegan, Michael Nally and Kirsty White, "Our short hot summer of discontent," *The Observer*, 12 July 1981, p. 13.

79) There seem to be too many acts to cover adequately, because they saturate the imagination. Thus, in early September 1986, at a time when terrorists had hijacked a Pan Am jumbo jet in Karachi and shot up a synagogue in Istanbul, there occurred a host of other activities which were generally ignored. These included a bomb blast at the Paris City Hall, another bomb blast at the Cologne headquarters of the West Germany counterespionage agency and a grenade attack in a Philippines church. "Terrorism: No letup after gory weekend," *USA Today (International Edition)*, 9 September 1986, p.1.

80) In fact, since the mid 1980's, there has been a slow improvement in the subway system. Billions of dollars have been spent on graffiti free trains. By 1986 the Transit Authority claimed that riders had a one-in-four chance of riding a new or rehabilitated car. As one conductor, Harry Nugent, put it, "After you hit bottom, there's no place to go but up." Michael Roddy, "N.Y. Glimpses Graffiti-Free Future", *The International Herald Tribune*, 15-16 November 1986, p. 1.

81) New York subway graffiti, circa 1987.

82) There is an alternative to bombs, logic bombs and spray cans. I refer to men who "fuck the world" with envious erections. Indeed, the German legal system recognizes people who are willing to incur great expense to hurt a neighbor. The old Augsburg building code defines a malicious building as one which has little or no purpose in itself, but which causes loss of light and air to a neighbor. And Zinck's *Ökonomisches Lexikon* comments on buildings which exist solely to annoy or disadvantage others. Although it is hard to prove, it is easy to imagine a developer who would site a building to destroy a view, pollute the environment or damage the structure of the society in which he lived. The payoff is omnipotence, unstoppable revenge and the unshaken belief that there is no-one or no-thing bigger than oneself. See: Helmut Schoeck, *Envy: A Theory of Social Behavior*, op. cit., p. 113.

83) Jules Henry, *Culture Against Man*, Knopf, New York, 1978. See also: *Pathways to Madness*, Random House, New York, 1971.

84) Bruno Bettelheim discusses this issue in some detail in his chapter on the rise of fascism in Nazi Germany, "Remarks on the Psychological Appeal of Totalitarianism," in *Surviving the Holocaust*, Fontana Paperbacks, London, 1986, pp. 104 -119.

85) The Angry Brigade, Communique 7, op. cit., p. 27.

86) Editorial, White Panther Party, Abbey Wood Chapter, *Chapter?*, op. cit., p. 2.

87) Francis Bacon pointed this out while discussing envy: "But this is a sure rule, that if the envy upon the minister be great when the cause of it is small; or if the envy be general in a manner upon all the ministers of an estate, then the envy (though hidden) is truly upon the state itself." Francis Bacon, "Of Envy", *The Essays or Counsels, Civil and Moral,* op. cit., p. 61.

88) Among various cartoons the White Panther journal showed ridiculous pot smoking pig police under the caption: "A pig is a person who exploits for his own benefit...A pig is a low natured beast that has no regard for law, justice or the rights of the people; a creature that bites the hand that feeds it; a foul depraved traducer......"White Panther Party, Abbey Wood Chapter, *Chapter?,* op. cit., p. 9.

The image of a tyrannical soldier with a gun forcing a naked man to lick his boots featured in: Richard Livermore, "Notes for the Anarchy & Order Brigade", *Anarchy,* No. 38, p. 25.

89) Pete Mastin, 1985 Faction 12, *Black Flag,* No. 131, 29 April 1985.

90) The emotional context was the threat generated by the Vietnam war and the cultural upheaval that was taking place in American society as a whole. Each side appealed to the worst fears of the other.

See: David Mairowitz, *The Radical Soap Opera,* Penguin Books, London, 1976, pp. 222-226. Mairowitz called the occasion, "The Politics of Gesture".

91) Peter Steinberger, "John Sinclair is Free", *Big Fat Magazine,* June 1970, reprinted in *Chapter?,* op. cit., p 35.

See also: David Mairowitz, *The Radical Soap Opera,* op. cit., pp. 226-228.

92) Ibid., p.5.

Sinclair emphasized that 'We' have to make use of "every tool, every energy, and every medium we can get our collective hands on."

93) This was Sinclair's third offense. He was released in 1972 after three years in jail.

94) Throughout the '50's and '60's many youngsters suffered comparable punishments for infringements of drug laws and sexual mores, really for transgressing a moral code based on the denial of sensual impulses and hatred of those who took pleasure in them. For example, in some states people could be jailed for cohabiting without being married and in West Virginia they could be jailed for using sexually explicit words in public.

95) Pete Mastin, 1985 Faction 12, *Black Flag,* No. 131, 29 April 1985.

96) Catherine Bennett, "Poison Post", *The Mail on Sunday,* 23 May 1982, p. 19.

News writers are not the only victims of hate mailers. All the media lies at risk. Bob Booth, Head of Correspondence at the BBC, says he handles 500,000 hate letters per year. When asked for reasons, psychologist Jane Firebank pointed out, "Behind the letters is often very bitter envy. The writers are frustrated - not necessarily sexually but in their lives and achievements - so they resent other people becoming famous." Ibid., p. 19.

97) Sinclair came to idealize the Black Panthers and modeled his revolutionary organization after them. Certainly he had links with underground groups like the Weathermen. After his drug busts, he was indicted for bombing the Ann Arbor office of the C.I.A. As for M.C.5., he turned it into a mouthpiece for violent insurrectionary activities. Roger Lewis, *Outlaws of America,* Pelican Books, London, 1972, pp. 100, 158-162. See also: David Mairowitz, *The Radical Soap Opera,* op. cit., pp. 226-228.

CHAPTER 11a

1) Eugène Raiga, *L'Envie*, Paris, 1932, discussed by H. Schoeck, *Envy: A Theory of Social Behaviour*, op. cit., p. 190.

2) "Over a period of sixty years, from roughly 1470-1530, the secular spirit of the age was exemplified in a succession of six popes - five Italians and a Spaniard who carried it to an excess of venality, amorality, avarice and spectacularly calamitous power politics.......Theirs was a folly of perversity, perhaps the most consequential in Western history, if measured by its result in centuries of ensuing hostility and fratricidal war." Barbara Tuchman, *The March of Folly: From Troy to Vietnam*, Abacus Books, London, 1984.

3) Niccolò Machiavelli (1469-1527), Florentine statesman and writer on government.

Jean Bodin (1530- 1596), French philosopher and jurist.

4) The concept of 'personalismo' comes from the British political sociologist, J. P. Nettl, "The State as a Conceptual Variable", and is quoted by Gabriel Ben-Dor, *State and Conflict in the Middle East: Emergence of the Postcolonial State*, Praeger Publishers, New York, 1983, p. 14.

5) Jean Jacques Rousseau (1712-1778), French political philosopher and writer.

6) The term nation or state are frequently used synonymously. Strictly speaking 'nation' refers to community of people characterized by a common language and culture and often, but not necessarily living with a specific territory. When this nation has agreed sovereign boundaries, then it is a state.

According to Elie Kedourie, Professor of Politics at the University of London, a nation is a body of people who collectively constitute a political unit, indeed, any "body of people associating together, and deciding on a scheme for their own government, form a nation." Elie Kedourie, *Nationalism*, Hutchinson University Library, Hutchinson & Co (Publishers) Ltd., London, 1966., p. 15.

The key word here is 'body', which implies that a nation, like a person has boundaries, feelings, wishes, a soul and so forth related to the skin, the mind, the heart, etc. Thus, if citizens direct elemental feelings towards their national body, then this body, 'the body politic', can and does reflect, expand and express the feelings of its citizens, irrational as well as rational, destructive as well as creative.

7) See Ernest Jones, "Psychopathology and International Tension" in *Psycho-Myth, Psycho-History*, Vol.1, Hillstone, New York, 1974, pp. 301-2.

8) Elias Canetti, *Crowds and Power*, op. cit., pp. 15-16.

9) Concurrently, nationalistic self-seeking disguises individual inferiority. This goal is consistent with Canetti's description of two other crowd features: growth and direction seeking (common goals).

10) See discussion by Nettl quoted by Gabriel Ben-Dor, *State and Conflict in the Middle East: Emergence of the Postcolonial State*, op. cit., pp.4-5.

11) Max Montgelas and Walter Schücking, eds. *Outbreak of the World War: German Documents Collected by Karl Kautsky*, Oxford University Press, Oxford, 1924, pp. 63, 161, 266 & 307, quoted by Lloyd deMause, ed., *The New Psychohistory*, op. cit., p. 14.

12) I am aware that my brief discussion hardly does justice to the complexity of stateness, and in particular, the intrasocietal (nationness, self-definition, institutional viability) dimensions as opposed to the extrasocietal ones. However, this one area of

stateness, supranational relations, is especially useful for the purpose of illustrating the ultimate expressions of (and detachments from) powerful emotional currents, often expressed in modern times via nationalism and charismatic leaders.

In all places, citizens can and do use the state to 'lose' their individual hopes and sorrows. Then, as frequently happens, a further degree of detachment takes place. The state 'loses' these feelings by attributing them to other states, and engaging in a variety of alliances or conflicts in order to justify the loss. Conversely, people may be given (or retrieve) self-esteem through their country's extrasocietal relations. For example, for many postcolonial states, the preferred way to gain status (which may or may not be passed down to the populace) is by establishing a presence at the United Nations or other international organizations. See: Gabriel Ben-Dor, *State and Conflict in the Middle East: Emergence of the Postcolonial State*, op. cit. pp. 1-34.

13) Daniel Moynihan, "The United States in Opposition", *Commentary*, Vol. 59, No.3, March 1975, p.37.

14) Barbara Tuchman's, for example, has given a detailed description of the Renaissance Church (Saint Peter's See transformed into "the supreme pork barrel") whose avaricious internal and external policies led to a devastating series of intra- and extra- European wars. Barbara Tuchman, *The March of Folly*, op. cit., pp. 144 -154.

15) The actions of Stalinist Russia and Maoist China were formal attacks by one part of state against another part of itself. Hence a state can act like humans to greedily or enviously attack internal as well as external targets. See: Robert Conquest, *The Harvest of Sorrow*, Hutchinson & Co., London, 1986.

16) Mel Brooks, *To Be Or Not To Be*, 1984. Directed by Alan Johnson. The film itself was a remake of an Ernst Lubitsch classic.

17) On 16 October 1973 OPEC (Organization of Petroleum Exporting Countries) cut production and raised the oil price by 70%. On 23 December they raised the price again and within one year it had been increased by four times. According to Henry Kissinger, this "was one of the pivotal events in the history of this century." Quoted by Paul Johnson, *A History of the Modern World: From 1917 to the 1980's*, Weidenfeld & Nicolson, London, 1983, p. 669.

Interestingly, an analysis by the *Economist* subsequently showed that greed is not an effective economic policy. In six years of massive price increases from 1973 the OPEC countries accumulated $1.3 trillion. But, if they had not acted so precipitously, and extortionately, they could have achieved the same profits, while maintaining a better price and a larger share of the market. Charles Krauthammer, "OPEC is Dead, But There's No Need for Mourning", *The International Herald Tribune*, 21-22 December 1985, p. 4.

Aside from oil, the greedy aggrandizement of gold and silver from Latin America by Spain, or minerals from the Congo by Belgium also did not confer unambiguous economic benefits. J. M. Roberts, *The Hutchinson History of the World*, Hutchinson & Co, London, 1976, pp. 668 & 847.

18) Much of the angry, guilt-ridden opprobrium was self-inflicted, both before and after the war. Thus, a student group at Cambridge (England) published a pamphlet which declaimed, "We took the rubber from Malaya, the tea from India, raw materials from all over the world and gave almost nothing in return." Quoted by Luis Burstin, "A Few Home Truths About Latin America", *Commentary*, Vol. 79, No. 2, February 1985, p. 49.

In fact the reverse was true. The British took rubber to Malaya from Brazil and tea to India from China, greatly invigorating the economies of both countries.

19) Paraphrased by Luis Burstin, Ibid., p. 47.

Among many critics of the United States, Burstin quotes the left-wing Mexican writer, Carlos Fuentes, who blames the United States government and corporations for Latin "turmoil, instability, terrorism, hunger and weakness".

20) United Nations World Population Conference, Stockholm, 1974. Quoted by Daniel Moynihan, "The United States in Opposition", op. cit., p. 37.

21) Professor Dumont contributed to the Population Tribune, an unofficial, parallel conference in Stockholm. His report, "Population and Cannibals" subsequently received front page coverage in *Development Forum*, an official UN publication. Dumont blamed the West for being "Plunders of the Third World". He stated: "Eating little children. I have already had occasion to show that the rich white man, with his overconsumption of meat and his lack of generosity towards poor populations, acts like a true cannibal, albeit indirectly. Ibid., pp. 37-38.

22) China, for example, has the strictest of all population-control programs. Yet the Chinese delegation furiously assailed the very idea of population control as "fundamentally subversive to the future of the Third World". The Chinese insisted that population control was the means by which "hegemonists" and "imperialists" sought to spoil the future of mankind. Consumerism, not population, was the true source of the world's problems. Ibid., p. 37.

23) I refer to the United Nations Conference on the Human Environment held in Stockholm in 1972. Ibid., p. 36.

24) Ibid., p. 39.

The Fabian Society is an organization of English socialists, established in 1884, which aims to bring about socialism by gradual reforms rather than revolutionary action. The complement, of course, of this language, is that of the Marxist-Leninists, whose words demonstrate a more extreme form of abuse, but are still continuous with the rhetoric of resentment.

25) It has often been noted that the London School of Economics is "the most important institution of higher education in Asia and Africa." Ibid., p. 33.

26) Beatrice Webb wrote in her autobiography: My husband and I felt "assured that with the School (LSE) as the teaching body, the Fabian Society as a propagandist organization, the LCC (London County Council) as object lesson in electoral success, our books as the only original work in economic fact and theory, no young man or woman who is anxious to study or work in public affairs can fail *to come under our influence.*" (my italics) Quoted by Daniel Moynihan, ibid., p. 33.

27) Anthony Lewis, "Embracing the Disaster, Entrenching the Follies", *International Herald Tribune*, 6 February 1987, p. 4.

28) DeMause quotes from Kaiser Wilhelm, for example, who prior to World War One referred to the monarchy as being "seized by throat" and "strangled". As regards Germany, the Kaiser asserted England had suddenly thrown a net "over our head, and.... we squirm isolated in the net." These comments were made at a time when England was friendly towards Germany. But the Kaiser, on behalf of many people including himself, felt that way (and acted accordingly). That was his reality, in the same way that other commentators prior to war have described their nations as "unable to draw a breath of relief," "unable to see the light at the end of the tunnel," moving with "naked force" into "the descent into the abyss." Lloyd deMause, ed., *The New Psychohistory*, op. cit., pp. 16-22.

29) Henry Steele Commager and Richard B. Morris, eds., *The Spirit of Seventy-Six*, Vol. 1, Bobbs-Merrill Co., New York, 1970, p. 294, quoted by Lloyd deMause, ibid., p. 20.

30) Kedourie points out that nationalism is essentially related to the idea of self determination. Self-determination (economic, military, political autonomy) then tends

to be seen as the highest moral and political goal. Elie Kedourie, *Nationalism*, op. cit., pp. 32, 62-91.

31) Tuchman has described the attitude of the British government towards its American colony prior to the revolution: "They were not interested in the Americans because they considered them rabble or at best children whom it was inconceivable to treat - or even fight - as equals. " Barbara Tuchman, *The March of Folly*, op. cit., p. 286.

32) In the late 20th century Egypt, Libya and Syria have all acted liked vandals, although the phenomenon is by no means limited to Arab states. Nasser was particularly successful in mobilizing the internal antagonisms of the Egyptian and Arab masses and redirecting it outwards towards their former colonial masters. As the British political scientist, P. J. Vatikiotis, points out Nasser was very skillful "in evoking hazy pictures of past oppression and bitterness." For example, after Suez, but essentially repeated in many other contexts, Nasser exclaimed: "We shall not submit to anyone's influence or authority." And, "It was only when we succeeded in giving Egypt back to all the Egyptians that we were able to achieve this victory and rout the great powers." P. J. Vatikiotis, *Nasser and His Generation*, Croom Helm, London, 1978, p. 276.

Nasser was also the hero and model for Colonel Gaddafi who, in the eyes of many Western powers, turned Libya into a 'rogue state'. See: David Blundy and Andrew Lycett, *Qaddafi and the Libyan Revolution*, Weidenfeld and Nicolson, London, 1987.

33) The speech was made at an A.F.L.-C.I.O. dinner in June 1975 to an audience of distinguished trade unionists and politicians. Given Solzhenitsyn's personality, it is unlikely he simply made these comments to ingratiate himself with his American hosts. Quoted by Daniel Moynihan, *A Dangerous Place*, Secker & Warburg, London, 1979, p. 76.

34) During the 1970's Tanzania received more aid from Western Europe, Canada and the United States than any other African country (about £1.5 billion), with little effect. Throughout this period the country was led by Julius Nyerere, a doctrinaire socialist and Pan African nationalist, who had a seminal influence on the economic policies which misused the resources received. At the same time Nyerere gained international respect by attacking the West for colonialism, imperialism, materialism and so forth.

35) Helmut Schoeck points out that the relationship between Western donors and hostile third world countries in the period 1955-1965 provides experimental proof of Kant's dictum that a display of ingratitude does not necessarily bring about a decrease in benefaction. On the contrary, the benefactor "may well be convinced that the very disdain of any such reward as gratitude only adds to the inner worth of his benefaction." Quoted by Helmut Schoeck, *Envy: A Theory of Social Behavior*, op. cit., pp. 168-169.

36) Tim Jones, "Stewed tea at Cliveden", *The Times*, 20 October 1986, p. 3.

Hilary Rubinstein, who is editor of *The Good Hotel Guide, 1987*, reports: "There is a growing fashion to denigrate Americans, behaviour as distasteful as anti-Semitism or mindless prejudice against women or blacks or gays. My correspondence files bear witness to all these forms of bias, but the habit of rubbishing Americans ....almost always (stems) from envy." Hilary Rubinstein, "Un-American activities keeping tourists away", *The Independent*, 16 October 1986, p. 17.

37) *The Scotsman* published a poem entitled, "The American Visitors," which began:

"They think the city's been put up for grabs:

The dollar's strength turns everything to trash.

they come, they see, they conquer with their cash."

Quoted by Rubinstein, ibid., p. 17.

38) Thomas Friedman, "American Power and an Envious, Angry World." *International Herald Tribune*, 2 March 1998, p. 7.

39) Eugène Raiga predicted that the setting up of socialist governments devoted to mutual aid would not inhibit these envious and jealous rivalries. As Helmut Schoeck points out this has been amply proven. Satellites of the Eastern bloc jealously guard their privileges, while other nations vigorously compete for development aid from the United States and Europe. Eugène Raiga, *L'Envie*, Paris, 1932, pp. 233, 236, discussed by Helmut Schoeck, *Envy: A Theory of Social Behavior*, op. cit., p. 190.

40) in 1987, United States Secretary of State, George Shultz, reflected on the strategic, economic, ideological and altruistic factors that determined American aid. The latter was much less important than the practical as well as narcissistic wish for developing countries to remake their economies in the American image. David Shipler, "Shultz's Goals in Africa: Building Markets, Cutting Soviet Influence Were Among Priorities", *International Herald Tribune*, 19 January 1987, p. 2.

41) Low's cartoon was published in J. M. Roberts, *The Hutchinson History of the World*, op. cit., p. 1077.

42) Jonathan Mirsky, "The western flower that may not bloom", *The Times*, 20 January 1987, p. 14.

43) Daniel Southerland, "Door Still Open, Deng Declares", *International Herald Tribune*, 21 January 1987, p. 1.

44) Jonathan Mirsky, "The western flower that may not bloom", op. cit., p. 14.

Since the 19th century the Chinese have tried to distinguish between western learning for "practical matters" (xixue wei yong) and "Chinese learning for the fundamentals" (zhongxue wei ti). The distinction is an attempt to avoid the severe loss of pride, threatened loss of national identity and consequent narcissistic rage that follows whenever their sense of superiority is called into question.

45) *L'Observateur*, 14 August 1952, quoted by Hugh Thomas, *An Unfinished History of the World*, op. cit., pp. 722-723.

46) Richard Bernstein, "Washington and the UN: What Went Wrong?" *International Herald Tribune*, 1 February 1984, p. 6.

47) Helen Caldicott, *Missile Envy*, op. cit., p. 297.

48) Ibid., p. 297.

49) The Olympic Games are at least 3,500 years old. The first games of the modern era began in Athens in 1896. Although ideally contests between individuals, not countries, the games have been increasingly marred by severe nationalistic disputes. This is not a new phenomenon. Past games often got out of hand with results not unlike the pitched battles that can erupt at present day international football matches. At Constantinople the rivalries between the 'blues' and 'greens' led to civil wars and the death of thousands, a situation Edward Gibbon called the 'blue livery of disorder'. Hugh Thomas, *An Unfinished History of the World*, op. cit., pp.614-617.

50) Distraught at signs of weakness, France saw herself as the fighting-cock of Europe, an evident illusion. She blamed the German people for her inability occupy a dominant role as from the times of Louis XIV to Napoleon I. Paul Johnson, *A History of the Modern World: From 1917 to the 1980's*, op. cit., p. 140.

51) In 1915 Bérillon's diagnoses were polychesia and bromidrosis (excessive defecation and body-smells). Ibid., p. 145.

52) Ibid., p. 142.

53) The British found it inconceivable to treat or fight the Americans colonials as equals. Thus, in all their military dispatches, they never once referred to the American Commander-in-Chief, George Washington, as General, but only as Mister. Barbara Tuchman, *The March of Folly*, op. cit., p. 286.

54) Quoted by Barbara Tuchman, ibid., p. 287.

55) Moreover, foreigners are frequently portrayed as goons, thugs and rapists, all victimizing innocent Japanese. Andrew Horvat, "The 'little Japan' mentality", *The Independent*, 29 December 1986, p. 10.

As if to demonstrate that 'there is nothing new under the sun', Nigerians hold similar views about their black neighbours as do Argentines towards other Latin Americans. See: Karan Thapar, "Nigeria: so much money and so many problems", *The Times*, 16 Match 1981, p. 12; also Miguel Acoca, "A Critical View of Argentina: Ethnic Pride Takes a Fall", *International Herald Tribune*, 16 June 1982, p. 4.

56) J. M. Roberts, *The Hutchinson History of the World*, op. cit., pp. 839-840.

57) The division of society into a multiplicity of classes or castes with equally large gradations of inferiority and superiority can be traced to ancient Egypt, Rome and many other societies. Hugh Thomas argues against the alleged existence of three fundamental classes as postulated by Karl Marx, Matthew Arnold and others. Hugh Thomas, *An Unfinished History of the World*, op. cit., pp. 696 -705.

Often classes or castes seem to be created by real or potential members for purposes of self-aggrandizement. According to Nietzsche Christianity is based on the resentment of the weak towards the strong, the haves versus the have-nots. Nietzsche argued that the idea, 'the meek shall inherit the earth', simply serves to elevate sickness and poverty into virtues, and to allow the downtrodden to trod on their masters. Thomas makes the same point in terms of the concept of 'the proletariat'. Ibid. pp. 700-701.

58) Conor Cruise O'Brien, *The Siege: The Saga of Israel and Zionism*, Simon and Schuster, New York, 1986, pp. 335-336.

59) 'Dhimmi' status for Jews and Christians in Muslim lands was generally preferable to the non-status (and consequent persecution) of Jews and Muslims in Christian lands. Ibid., p. 336.

The Arabs saw the end of 'dhimmi' status as the Ottoman reaction to growing European power and prestige. For them it marked the unwelcome encroachment of Jews and Christians on their way of life. The placid contempt which had previously marked the Muslim side of 'dhimmi' turned into sullen resentment. From the mid-nineteenth century onwards Muslim intellectuals began to speak out. For instance, the Egyptian historian, al-Jabarti, was appalled that: "......contrary to ancient custom, (non-Muslims) wear fine clothes and bear arms, wield authority over Muslims and generally behave in a way which inverts the order of things established by divine law." Bernard Lewis, "L'Islam et les Non-Musulmans", *Annales: Economies, Sociétés, Civilisations*, 3, 4 (Mai, Aout 1980), quoted by Conor Cruise O'Brien, ibid., p. 339.

60) According to an American intelligence agent operating in Iraq during the mid 1940's: "Most Jews, in the Arab mind, are miserable, cowardly and unclean. So the idea of a portion of the Arab world being governed by Jews is intolerable. Palestine, therefore, has become more than a remote political problem, it is now a question of personal religion and honour." O.S.S. Report of February 3, 1945; quoted in Luks, "Iraqi Jews during World War II", in *Weiner Library Bulletin*, No. XXX (43/44), 1977; quoted by Conor Cruise O'Brien, ibid., p. 340.

61) Ye'or, "Aspects of the Arab-Israel Conflict", in *Weiner Library Bulletin*, No. XXXII (49/50), 1979; quoted by Conor Cruise O'Brien, ibid., p. 340.

62) Gamal Abdel Nasser, 1918-1970. I refer to the situation during the 1950's and 1960's. Subsequently Nasser's role as the scourge of Western interests was taken over by the Iranian leader, Ayatollah Khomeini. However, as far as the Arabs were concerned, the Ayatollah was a mixed blessing for he was leader of the Shiite Muslims who, as underdogs, were themselves in conflict with the predominant Sunnite sect.

63) The prominent writer, Tawfiq al-Hakim described the relationship between Nasser and Egypt as that of a man who "had become the idol, the worshipped of the people... They became a collection of waving arms and applauding hands, and cheering mouths. And the Chief in his dominating presence, towering over them from his podium, spoke alone for long hours, interrupted only by the hysterical cries: "Nasser, Nasser, Nasser."

al-Hakim's descriptions of Nasser delineate the transformation of personal inflation to national narcissism: "....he overwhelmed us with his magic...and the hopes, dreams and promises which underlay the victories of the revolution which he repeatedly announced to us....with their pipes and drums, anthems, songs and films, which made us see ourselves as a great industrial state, leaders of the developing world....and the strongest military power in the Middle East." Tawfiq al-Hakim, *'Awdat al-wa'i*, Beirut, 1974, quoted by P. J. Vatikiotis, *Nasser and His Generation*, op. cit., pp. 291, 320.

64) Hussein Sabri observed: "He pushed Egypt ahead, but soon let his phantasy take over, leading to the disaster of 5 June 1967....Suez was the turning point. It led him to believe that revolutionary Egypt vanquished Imperialism and that had it not been for Nasser this would not have happened. Victory was his victory, protected by Providence. Everyone forgot Egypt was not victorious in 1956!" Hussein Dhu'l-Fiqar Sabri in *Rose el-Youssef*, 18 July 1975, quoted by P. J. Vatikiotis, ibid., p. 290.

65) Herbert Rosenfeld, *Impasse and Interpretation*, Tavistock, London, 1987, p. 109. The concept of 'destructive narcissism' was described in detail by Rosenfeld in, "A Clinical Approach to the Psychoanalytic Theory of the Lifre and Death Instincts: An Investigation into the Aggressive Aspects of Narcissism," Int. J. Psycho-Anal., 1971, Vol. 52. Part 1, pp. 169-178.

66) Chauvinism or Jingoism represents the merger and submergence of ordinary nationalism (equivalent to a positive or libidinal narcissism) with and by destructive nationalism. (equivalent to a negative or anti-libidinal narcissism). The former was named after the alleged Nicolas Chauvin, a soldier of Napoleon 1, famous for his bellicose attachment to lost imperial causes, and the latter follows the refrain of an aggressive Victorian music hall song:

G. W. Hunt, "We don't want to fight" 1878

67) P. J. Vatikiotis, *Nasser and His Generation*, op. cit., p. 270.

68) Immanuel Kant quoted by Hugh Thomas, *An Unfinished History of the World*, op. cit., p. 645.

69) *Das Deutsche Vaterland* was one of Germany's most popular patriotic songs. It was written by the poet Ernst Moritz Arndt (1769-1860) and appealed to the expansionist voice of German nationalism:

"What is the German Fatherland?
The Prussian, or the Swabian kind?
Where Rhenish grapes bloom ripe and full,
Where curves his flight the Baltic gull?
Ah, no! No! No!
His Fatherland must greater grow!"

Quoted by Robert Waite, *The Psychopathic God: Adolf Hitler*, Basic Books, New York, 1977, pp. 259-260.

70) Adam Müller quoted by Robert Waite, ibid., p. 287.

71) Johann Gottlieb Fichte (1762-1814), nationalist philosopher, wrote *Addresses to the German People* in the period 1807-08. Quoted by Robert Waite, ibid., p. 261.

72) Prince Otto von Bismarck (1815-1898) was the Prussian chancellor of the German Empire (1871-1890.)

73) Thus, in 1900 Kaiser Wilhelm wrote: "You should give the name of Germany such cause to be remembered in China for a thousand years, so that no Chinaman, no matter whether his eyes be slit or not, will dare to look a German in the face." Quoted by Hugh Thomas, *An Unfinished History of the World*, op. cit., p. 670.

74) ".......France is and will remain by far the most dangerous enemy, The French people, who are becoming more and more obsessed by negroid ideas, represent a threatening menace to the existence of the white race in Europe, because they are bound up with the Jewish campaign for world-domination." Adolf Hitler, *Mein Kampf*, translated by James Murphy, Hurst and Blackett Ltd., London, 1930, p. 508.

75) In the period prior to World War 1 Germany was still preoccupied with being liked. "In a series of crises, she showed that she wanted to frighten other nations with her displeasure and make herself esteemed." J. M. Roberts, *The Hutchinson History of the World*, op. cit., p. 910.

76) Victoria was queen of Great Britain and Ireland from 1837 to 1901. Her Prince Consort was Albert from Saxe-Coburg-Gotha. Their first and second generation descendents either ruled or married the rulers of Germany (as a whole as well as Hesse, Schleswig-Holstein, and Battenberg) and Russia, Norway, Denmark and Greece. See end plate family tree from Kenneth Rose, *King George V*, Weidenfeld and Nicolson, London, 1983.

These sibling rivalries may have exacerbated colonial rivalries, but the latter were not of primary significance in and of themselves. "....the issue was not really one of colonial rivalry, but of whether Germany could bully France without fear of her being supported by others. Quarrels over non-European affairs before 1914 seem in fact to have been a positive distraction from the more dangerous rivalries of Europe itself; they may even have helped to preserve the peace." J. M. Roberts, *The Hutchinson History of the World*, op. cit., p. 843.

77) James Murphy, in his introduction to *Mein Kampf*, points out that the concept of 'volk' had an almost mythical meaning for Germans. Much more than 'people' or 'citizens', it was a primary word which conveyed a sense of the basic national stock, without regard to caste or class. "Now, after the defeat of 1918, the downfall of the Monarchy and the destruction of the aristocracy and the upper classes, the concept of *Das Volk* came into prominence as the unifying coefficient which would embrace the whole German people." James Murphy, "Translator's Introduction", *Mein Kampf*, op. cit., p. 13.

78) Paul Johnson, *A History of the Modern World: From 1917 to the 1980's*, op. cit., p. 106.

In fact Germany did become the dominant force in Europe in the decades after World War 2. The war simply postponed this outcome.

79) The Germans were outraged because they were forced to hand over entire German communities to the 'barbarous slavs'. This overlooked the fact that only a short time before Ludendorff had occupied the Ukraine and laid the basis for the whole area to become a German satellite-colony. They thought they had been swindled, although the

Silesian plebiscite had been an important concession secured for Germany by the British Lloyd George. All this was never explained by their government. Paul Johnson, ibid., pp. 105-106.

The German hatred of Slav rule was surely related to a collective denial of their Slav origins. Hugh Thomas points out that far from being racially pure, the German people, most particularly the Prussians, who were half Slav, had registered themselves as a Slav monarchy at the Congress of Vienna. Hugh Thomas, *An Unfinished History of the World*, op. cit., p. 666.

80) Generations of Germans glorified war and death. The "Schoolmaster of Germany", the popular historian Heinrich von Trietschke, whose views complemented the pedagogy of father Daniel Schreber, instilled the idea that peace is "immoral" and that "human reason" can only triumph through battle. "The army, not parliament is the most valuable institution of the State". Quoted by Robert Waite, ibid., p. 289.

81) The work of Heinrich von Kleist (1777-1810), especially, *Michael Kohlhaas*, symbolizes Germany and illustrates the rage that follows a narcissistic injury. Heinz Kohut, "Thoughts of Narcissism and Narcissistic Rage", op. cit., pp. 360-362.

82) Children of the Volksschulen were required to memorize this poem during the period 1900-1914. Quoted by Robert Waite, *The Psychopathic God: Adolf Hitler*, op. cit., p. 260.

83) Joseph Paul Goebbels (1897-1845) was later to become the Nazi Propaganda Minister. An early diary entry recalls: "....he is like a child, kind, good, merciful. Like a cat: cunning, clever, agile. Like a lion: roaring, great and gigantic. A great guy, a man! (ein Kerl, ein Mann!)" Quoted by Robert Waite, ibid., p. 3.

84) David Lloyd George (1863-1945), Prime Minister from 1916 to 1922. His remarks were published in an article in the London *Daily Express* on 7 November 1930. Quoted by Robert Waite, ibid., p. 4.

85) Ian Kershaw, *The Hitler Myth: Image and Reality in the Third Reich*, Oxford University Press, London, 1989. p. 68

In a later book, Kershaw explores the hubris involved in identifying himself with Germany and Germany with himself ('The Party is Hitler. But Hitler is Germany, just as Germany is Hitler. Hitler! Sieg Heil'), which allowed him overstep all institutional and moral barriers. Ian Kershaw: *Hitler: 1889-1936: Hubris (Vol1)*, W. W. Norton & Co., New York, 1999.

86) Joseph Goebbels, *The Early Goebbels Diaries: 1925 -1926*, ed., Helmut Heiber, trans. Oliver Watson, New York, 1963.

87) Ibid. p. 91.

In *Mein Kampf* Hitler proclaimed that hate was much more powerful than love, and that "wrathful hatred" was the most valuable of all political qualities.

88) Conversation with Harold Nicolson, in *Diaries and Letters: The War Years, 1939-1945*, 3 Volumes, New York, 1967, Vol. 2, p. 39, quoted by Robert Waite, *The Psychopathic God: Adolf Hitler*, op. cit., p. 330.

89) It would be wrong to conclude that these thrusts were justified by past hurts. That view was part of the big lie that Hitler used in order to release guilt free aggression and amplify the scope of his policies. For most Germans the lie worked. It camouflaged their inherent as well as acquired cruelties. The full truth did not begin to emerge until after World War Two, and especially after 1961, when the historian Fritz Fisher published the seminal, *Griff nach der Weltmacht* (translated as *Germany's Aims in the First World War*). His study documents the continuous aggressive, expansionist intentions that have underpinned Germany's foreign relations since the time of Bismarck.

Fritz Fisher, *Griff nach der Weltmacht*, London, 1967. The intentions had to do with dominating Europe and diminishing internal social tensions by war. See discussion by Paul Johnson, *A History of the Modern World: From 1917 to the 1980's*, op. cit., pp. 106-107.

90) Hugh Thomas points out that the need for land was an illusion. The German population, like others in Europe had ceased to grow, especially because huge numbers of people had previously emigrated to the United States. Hugh Thomas, *An Unfinished History of the World*, op. cit., p. 671.

91) Quoted by Waite, ibid., p. 79.

92) In the 18th and 19th century the British policy of transportation anticipated future mass purification programs, related to the wish to create a national "mother/fatherland", devoid of bad foreign elements. Transportation involved shipping large numbers of 'the criminal class' to Australia, at that time, a primitive and inhospitable backwater. Either during the passage, or afterwards, many of the transportees died from disease, neglect or direct physical abuse. All this has been documented by Robert Hughes in *The Fatal Shore: A History of the Transportation of Convicts to Australia, 1787-1868*, Collins Harvill, London, 1987.

Jeremy Bentham quoted by Robert Hughes, ibid., p. 2.

93) My discussion is based on the extensive research of the American historian Rudolph Binion. In particular I refer to his paper, "Hitler's Concept of *Lebensraum* : The Psychological Basis". This was originally delivered at the American Historical Association meeting in New Orleans on 28 December 1972 and was published in the *History of Childhood Quarterly*, Vol. 1, No. 2, Fall 1973, pp. 187-215.

94) August Kubizek, *Adolf Hitler, mein Jugendfreund*, Graz, 1953, p. 50, quoted by Rudolph Binion, ibid., p. 192.

95) Rudolph Binion points out that Hitler was not an overt anti-semite until after World War One. Despite his own account in *Mein Kampf*, Hitler's deadly hatred of Jews can be dated quite precisely, to the period October-November 1918 when he was hospitalized for mustard gas poisoning and suffered a breakdown. See discussion, ibid., pp. 189-190.

Ian Kershaw also emphasizes that Hitler could be very careful about discussing 'the Jewish problem,' and could conceal his hostility against the Jews when politically expedient, particularly during the 1930's. Ian Kershaw, *The Hitler Myth: Image and Reality in the Third Reich*, op. cit. p. 250.

96) Robert Waite, *The Psychopathic God: Adolf Hitler*, op. cit., 248-251.

97) Daniel Goldhagen, *Hitler's Willing Executioners:Ordinary Germans and the Holocaust*, Little, Brown & Co, New York, 1996, pp. 39-40

98) Robert Waite, *The Psychopathic God: Adolf Hitler*, op. cit., pp.237-239.

99) Elaine Pagels, *The Origins of Satan*, Random House, New York, 1995.

Pagels is Professor of Religion at Princeton University.

100) Richard L. Rubenstein, "Religion and the Origins of the Death Camps," in *After Auschwitz*, Bobbs-Merrill, Indianapolis, 1976, pp. 1-44.

101) Goldhagen, op. cit., pp. 389-393.

102) The Nazis appropriated the passage about 'magnificent blond beasts' from the philosopher Friedrich Nietzsche (1844-1900). See discussion by Robert Waite, *The Psychopathic God: Adolf Hitler*, op. cit., pp. 275-282.

103) As I have previously described, envy is both an interpersonal transaction and a perceptual transformation. By forcing the Jews and others to live in sub-human conditions, the Nazis acted to make them become (sub-human) as they Nazis wanted to see them. Moreover, the Nazis acted to alter these peoples' view of themselves so that they not only accepted, but could not challenge how they were seen or treated.

104) Richard L. Rubenstein, op. cit., p. 34.

105) Hitler rode to power on the promise to rebuild the army after 'The Diktat of Versailles'. Elias Canetti asserts that without the prohibition on universal military service after Versailles, National Socialism would not have been born. He emphasizes that the army was an essential component of the German mystique, what he calls its 'crowd symbol', its 'marching forest'. Elias Canetti, *Crowds and Power*, op. cit., pp. 173-174, 179-183.

106) Throughout his life, Hitler was infatuated with death. Even at moments of triumph, such as at the conclusion of the Nuremberg Rally in 1934, Hitler would exclaim: "When my eyes are closed in death, I do not know, but the Party will live on." Quoted by Robert Waite, *The Psychopathic God: Adolf Hitler*, op. cit., p. 18, see pp. 18-22.

107) Peter Nichols, "Chancellor blames envy for dislike of Germans", *The Times*, October 1977, p. 4.

108) "The blessing of a late birth" refers to Germans who were born after the war and did not suffer terrible privations or take part in the Nazi dictatorship. The term has been popularized by politicians like Chancellor Helmut Kohl. However, "the blessing of a late birth" does attract the envy of older Germans, especially for the younger generation's relative freedom from guilt. Peter Sichrovsky, *Schuldig geboren (Born Guilty)*, Kiepenheurer & Witsch, Cologne, 1987, discussed by Tony Caterall, "Born Guilty", *The Observer*, 1 March 1987, p. 51.

109) Gerard Wright and Stuart Millar, "A clique within a clique, obsessed with guns, death and Hitler,' *The Guardian*, 22 April 1999, p. 3.

110) John Hiscock, "Bloody revenge of Internet nerds obsessed with Satan and Nazis," *The Daily Telegraph*, 22 April 1999. pp. 1-2.

CHAPTER 11b

1) Elie Kedourie, *Nationalism, op. cit.*, p. 87.

2) Alan Dershowitz, *Why Terrorism Works*, p. 79.

3) Reuben Levy, *The Social Structure of Islam*, p. 191. The 9th century Muslim philosopher, Ibn Qutayba referred to *jihad* as a 'holy war.' (*Uyun al-akhbar*, p.18).

4) Sunni, from the Arabic, *ahl al-sunnah wa-l-jamaa* (the people of the custom/tradition of the Prophet). Sunni Islam is the largest division of Islam that accepts the first four caliphs (known as *Rashidun* – the Rightly Guided Caliphs) as the rightful successors of Muhammad.

5) Shi'ites, from the Arabic *si'a* (partisans). Shi'ites regard Ali and his descendants as the legitimate successors to Muhammad and reject the first three caliphs. This branch of Islam account for 10-15% of all Muslims.

6) Bernard Lewis, "The Revolt of Islam," *The New Yorker*, 19 November 2001, p. 59.

7) Ibid, p.63. In the words of the Koran (1:7): "...let not Satan seduce you..."

8) In a review of several books on terrorism, Louise Richardson notes the motivating

power of the desire of revenge for real or imagined hurts, "Blasts from the Past," *Financial Times Magazine*, 2-3 July 2005, pp. 26-27.

9) Saul Friedländer, *Nazi Germany and the Jews*, p. 36.

10) The Harvard psychiatrist, Kenneth Levin, explains that there is a widespread belief in the Islamic-Arab world, that people blame Western colonialism for their having been 'stripped of their place in the sun.' Even more so, Israel is seen as a direct vestige of European colonialism. *The Oslo Syndrome: Delusions of a People Under Siege*, p. 339. Presumably this is a further reason why anti-Zionism is so popular in left-wing politics and among revisionist historians (p.vxi).

It is more likely that the situation is the result of centuries of brutal domination by Muslim, but non-Arab, Turks.

11) "...be ye changed into apes driven away from the society of men" (1:2, p.198); "He whom God hath cursed and with whom he hath been angry, having changed some of them into apes and swine..." (1:5, p.304).

12) The number 72 probably comes from various 'sayings' and 'teachings' (*hadith* in Arabic) where rewards to those who reach Heaven are measured in terms of thousands of servants and 72 wives (*The Jerusalem Post Internet Edition*, September 6, 2001.

13) *Memri* (Middle East Media Research Institute) Special report No 24, 26 December 2003, p.2.

14) "...all suicide missions are backed up by organizations." Richardson, *op. cit.*,p. 27.

15) "...reveals the existence of a malignant form of triangulation aligned towards incarceration and death rather than freedom and life, and which reflects the dynamics of terrorism, This is the domain of the psychotic 'super' superego...This form of pathological, intrapsychic triangulation, with its links to an internal fundamentalist morality, bears a striking resemblance to terrorist tactics and their rationale." Paul Williams, "Terror, terrorising, terrorism," unpublished paper, London, 2005.

16) B. Lewis, *op. cit.*, p. 56.

17) *Kamikaze* is a Japanese word which means 'a divine wind,' and is historically related to the name of a typhoon that saved Japan from a Mongol invasion in 1281. It has come to be known (since World War II) as suicide attacks by Japanese aircrews against Allied ships. In modern parlance, it refers to a person who is 'reckless' and is involved in self-destructive behavior. Of late, terrorists who are suicide bombers are performing kamikaze acts in the sense that they are willing to sacrifice their lives in the hope that they can extract a large toll of innocent victims.

18) Yassir Arafat's 'real' name was: Rahman Abdel-Raouf Arafat al-Qudwa al-Husseini. His father was a merchant of the Husseini family and, on his mother's side, he was related to the Grand Mufti of Jerusalem, Haj Amin El Husseini (Mideast Web: *http://mideastweb.org*).

19) Geoffrey Alderman, "Either a catastrophe or a conspiracy," *Jewish Chronicle*, 3 June 2005, p 25.

20) *Memri*, No. 24, *op. cit.*, p. 1.

21) Alderman, *op. cit.*, p. 25. Text of Ibrahim Mudaires's sermon, *Jerusalem Post*, Online Edition, 19 May 2005, p.1.

22) "...perceived humiliation could be an important factor in explaining terrorism...." Jessica Stern, "Holy Avengers," *Financial Times Magazine*, 12 June 2004.

23) Arno Gruen, *The Betrayal of the Self*, p.41.

24) Sigmund Freud, "Mourning and Melancholy." Cathexis is a psychoanalytic term that refers to the attachment of emotional feeling and significance to an idea, object or person. We are using it in the sense of intense erotic investment.

25) Robert Stoller, *Perversion: The Erotic Form of Hatred*, p.106. Stoller makes the important connection between a driven erotic desire and hatred (and other extreme forms of aggression).

26) Otto F. Kernberg, *Aggression in Personality Disorders and Perversions*, p. 23.

27) Freud, "Mourning and Melancholy," p.251.

28) Kernberg, *op.cit.* , p. 22.

29) Robert Robins & Jerrold Post, *Political Paranoia: The Psychopolitics of Hatred*, p. 178.

30) Ibid, p. 150.

31) Stanley Schneider, "Fundamentalism and Paranoia in Groups and Society."

32) *Memri*, No. 24, *op. cit.*, p. 5.

33) Wolfgang Sofsky, *The Order of Terror*, p.16.

34) *http:/www.answers.com/topic/osama-bin-ladin*, June 2005.

35) Herbert Rosenfeld, "A Clinical Approach to the Psychoanalytic Theory of the Life and Death Instincts: An Investigation into the Aggressive Aspects of Narcissism,", p. 173.

36) Ibid., p. 174.

37) Sigmund Freud elaborated over the years of his clinical work and publications, a increasingly more sophisticated theoretical formulation of instincts, drives and trauma. Some classical examples: "Three Essays on Sexuality," "Instincts and their Vicissitudes," "Beyond the Pleasure Principle," and "Inhibitions, Symptoms and Anxieties."

38) Melanie Klein, *The Psycho-Analysis of Children*, p.150.

39) Ibid

40) Abu Zaid seems to have been in a state of shock after a relative and Islamic militant had been killed in an exchange of gunfire with Israeli troops. Afterwards he became religious and '...started talking about being a martyr and going to heaven.' "Suicide Bomber Expressed Desire to be a Martyr,"*Haaretz*, 28 October 2005, p.A2.

41) "Private Jordan TV Station Airing Anti-Semitic Series," *Jerusalem Post*, 26 October 2005, p.4.

42) Rafael López-Corvo, *The Dictionary of the Work of W.R.Bion*, p.146.

43) W.R.Bion, *Cogitations*, p.122.

44) López-Corvo, *op. cit.* , p.272.

45) Ibid, pp. 71-72.

46) W.R.Bion, *Learning from Experience*, p.97.

47) Tim Butcher, "Moment a suicide bombing mission failed," *The Daily Telegraph*, 22 June 2005, p. 13.

48) Editorial, "Asking for death," *Jerusalem Post*, Online Edition,13 January 2005, p.2.

49) Ibid.,p. 4.

50) Martin Fletcher, "Bunker-buster bombs blast Bin Laden caves," *The Times*, 20 November 2001, p.8.

51) "The Shahids who are in heaven next to Allah...As the Shahids are indeed in the highest paradise. The superior qualities and miracles of the Shahids are too numerous to count..." Sermon, 2 May 2003, Sheikh Ibrahim Mudaires, Sheikh Ijlin Mosque, Gaza, *Memri, op. cit.* p 11.

52) *Al-Iqtisadiyya* (Saudi Arabia), 15 November 2005. English translation: *The Saudi Gazette* (Saudi Arabia) 17 November 2005. Republished by *MEMRI,* Special Dispatch Series No. 1032, 23 November 2005.

53) Tom Tugend, "Glee as 'Paradise' lost," Jewish Chronicle, 10 March 2006, p.16

54) Nonie Darwish, "What a Muslim Learned on Yom Kippur," *FrontPageMagazine.com,* 5 October 2004, pp.1-2.

55) To view the interview on Al-Jazeera see:

http://switch3.castup.net/cunet/gm.asp?ai=214&ar=105owm&ak=null

The Egyptian cleric with whom Wafa Sultan debated was Ibrahim Al-Khouli. He essentially called her a heretic and blasphemer. Joseph Millis, "Islam slammed by American Muslim," Jewish Chronicle, 10 March 2006, p. 14.

After the program was shown, Wafa Sultan was inundated with death threats. John M. Broder, "For Muslim Who Says Violence Destroys Islam, Violent Threats," The Saturday Profile, *The New York Times International*, 11 March 2006 pp. 1-5.

56) "If individuals can experience psychosis, so too can a group mind and so too can a culture...Examples of cultural self-destructiveness that run counter to any rationale explanation are not all that difficult to find – the destruction of their own heritage in Afghanistan ..." Paul Williams, *op. cit.*, p. 6.

57) Melanie Klein, "A Contribution to the Psychogenesis of Manic-Depressive States," (1935) *The Writings of Melanie Klein*,, Vol. 1, The Hogarth Oress, London, 1975, p. 264-266.

58) Melanie Klein, "Notes on Schizoid Mechanisms," (1946) *The Writings of Melanie Klein*,, Vol. 3, The Hogarth Oress, London, 1975, pp.7 -11.

59) Geoffrey Alderman, op. cit., p.25.

60) Text of Ibrahim Mudaires sermon, op. cit., p.1.

61) George W. Bush, "Remarks by the President at the 20th Anniversary of the National Endowment for Democracy."

CHAPTER 12

1) Arthur Koestler, Hungarian born journalist and writer (1905-1983)

2) Arthur Koestler in, *The God that Failed*, ed. R. Crossman, New York, 1949, p. 18, quoted by Helmut Schoeck, *Envy: A Theory of Social Behaviour*, op. cit., p. 279.

3) For these same reasons many people admire and identify with the underprivileged or oppressed peoples of the world. By doing so they try to overcome their own sense of guilt about matters closer at hand. Helmut Schoeck believes that large social, religious or political organizations can behave in the same way. He cites contemporary Christian churches (like the Church of England) which try to deal with a pervasive guilt about

spiritual poverty at home by attacking 'the rich' for material poverty abroad. Helmut Schoeck, "The Less Developed Countries as a Moral Issue: Risky Assignments of Guilt and Responsibility", *Humanitas: Journal of the Institute of Man*, Vol. IX, No. 2, May 1973, p. 211.

4) David Hughes and Jill Hartley, "Labour's moral crusade vs Tory consumer power", *The Sunday Times*, London, 10 May 1987, p. 1.

5) Roy Hattersly, *Choose Freedom: the Future of Democratic Socialism*, Michael Joseph, London, 1987. Roy Hattersly was Deputy Leader of the Labour Party during the 1987 campaign.

6) As Matthew Arnold, the nineteenth century English essayist and critic put it, "Choose equality and flee greed." Quoted by R. H. Tawney, *Equality*, George Allen and Unwin Ltd., London,1931, p. 24.

Tawney himself believed that equality was not "to pamper the gross bodily appetites of an envious multitude, but to free the spirit of all." Ibid., p. 290.

7) Helmut Schoeck, "Individuality vs Equality", *Essays in Individuality*, edited by Felix Morley, University of Pennsylvania Press, 1958, pp. 168-169.

8) See, for example, the work of the Israeli novelist, Amos Oz, as well as the discussion by Helmut Schoeck in, *Envy: A Theory of Social Behaviour*, op. cit., pp. 286-315.

9) In the late 1980's the Cuban leader Fidel Castro angrily halted the successful liberalization of the economy to prevent imaginative, hard working farmers from becoming too rich, as well as to conserve foreign exchange. He was reported to be stunned by the fact that many people were making big money on the private farmers' markets which he himself had introduced in 1980 to stimulate production and reduce shortages. Weeks later, after closing these markets, he halted the right to private home ownership. Castro complained that homeowners were "getting rich" buying, selling and trading houses. He told a Communist Party congress: "No one was born a revolutionary. We must cultivate man's sense of shame." Joseph Treaster, "To Cure 'Capitalist Vice', Cuba Applies Austerity", *The International Herald Tribune*, 9 February 1987, pp. 13+17.

10) Despite the egalitarian reforms since the War, John Rae, the former headmaster of London's Westminster School, concurs: "In some parts of the country, a working-class child has less chance of leaving school literate and numerate than he would have done in 1945." John Rae, "Shooting the piano tuner", *The Times*, 7 May 1987, p. 14.

11) Adamischin was quoted in the mass circulation daily, *Kurier*. He was attempting to explain ideological mistakes that had reduced socialist achievements, especially in view of the socialist principle of equality. The interview was related to the decision of the Soviet leader, Mikhail Gorbachev, to introduce a modern form of socialism to the Soviet Union. Quoted in "Russia ends 'equal pay' red tape", *The London Standard*, 24 July 1986, p. 12.

12) William Manchester, "Levelling American Society", *The International Herald Tribune*, 24 July 1978, p. 4. Manchester asserts levelling has become "a secular religion, a faith as powerful and intolerant as Puritanism in 17th-century New England.

13) Ibid. p. 4.

14) Frank Ching, "Upward Mobility for Chinese Comrades", *The International Herald Tribune*, 7 January 1985, p. 4.

"The result of trying to make everyone equal is a lost generation of graduates in China who can't read classical Chinese. When Mao died, and you could get a reasonable education again, what happened was that these younger people are being promoted above the heads of older ones–which leads to more tension, this time between generations."

Quoted from "Walking on the Chinese Wall", *The Hampstead and Highgate Express*, London, 9 August 1985, p. 13.

15) Peter Bauer, *Equality, the Third World, and Economic Delusion*, Methuen, London 1982.

16) I refer to the destruction of the kulaks, another example of economic tyranny and political genocide. Millions of Russian peasants were killed both for ideological and practical reasons.

17) Sir Keith Joseph, "The tyranny hidden in the pursuit of equality.", *The Times*, 9 June 1978, p. 14.

See also, Keith Joseph and Jonathan Sumption, *Equality*, John Murray Publishers Ltd., London, 1979, p. 54.

18) Procrustus was the celebrated Greek highwayman who used to tie travelers to a bed and stretch their spines or cut off their legs in order to make them fit in. Nowadays the term Procrustean refers to policies or actions designed to ensure conformity and 'fairness'. Ibid., p. 63.

19) Roy Hattersly clearly coveys this attitude in his book, *Choose Freedom: the Future of Democratic Socialism*. His central thesis is that socialists are the real lovers of freedom.

20) Cyprian, *On Jealousy and Envy*, [10], quoted by Peter Walcot, *Envy and the Greeks*, op. cit. p. 93.

21) Ibid., pp. 96-98.

22) The work of Iambulus is known from the writings of Diodorus Siculus (c. 60- c.20 B.C.E.)

23) Aristotle (384-322 B. C. E.), *Politics*, (1266a, 1266b, 1267a) discussed by Walcot, ibid., p. 99.

24) This was a state of affairs further characterized by the end of exploitation and oppression of men by men, universal good faith and brotherly love. Norman Cohn, *The Pursuit of the Millennium*, op. cit. p. 187, see also pp. 188-197.

25) Orthodox preachers reserved their most virulent criticism for the rich and powerful. "Their satiety was our famine; their merriment was our wretchedness; their jousts and tournaments were our torments......Their feasts, delectations, pomps, vanities, excesses and superfluities were our fastings, penalties, wants, calamities and spoilation. " In many cases sermons like these were all that was needed to ignite social revolt. Ibid. p. 201-202.

In general, see Norman Cohn's three chapters on "The Egalitarian Millennium", ibid., pp. 198-281.

26) Ibid., pp. 201-202.

27) Ibid., pp. 214-222.

28) Melvin Lasky, *Utopia and Revolution*, Macmillan London Ltd., London, 1977, p. 4.

29) Radicals from as far away as Japan, France and the United States have favoured one particular sentence of Bakunin: "There will be a qualitative transformation, a new living, life-giving revelation, a new heaven and a new earth, a young and mighty world in which all our present dissonances will be resolved into a harmonious whole." *The New Encyclopedia Britannica*, 15th edition, 1985, p. 462.

30) George Foster points out that feelings of inferiority due to influences outside one control may be bearable, but feelings of inferiority clearly relatable to personal faults

or others' superiority are very damaging to self-esteem and are much more difficult to accept. George Foster, "The Anatomy of Envy: A Study of Symbolic Behavior", op. cit., p. 184.

31) Margaret Norton Briggs, "The Rat Race for Glamour", *The Sunday Times*, 5 November 1978, p. 14.

32) Interestingly, the word 'luck' comes from the Middle High German 'gelücke' which denotes a chance combination of factors which may turn out favourably or unfavourably for a person or group. Subsequently the English term 'luck' became differentiated from 'happiness' which originally meant something like 'a condition due to haphazard happenings'. See discussion by Helmut Schoeck in *Envy: A Theory of Social Behaviour*, op. cit., pp. 238-239.

33) Ibid., pp. 30-31.

34) See discussion in Peter Walcot, *Envy and the Greeks*, op. cit. pp. 101-102.

35) Ibid., p. 101 Poverty's argument was the same as that of Hesiod in his poem, *Works and Days*. There Hesiod claimed that strife is an incentive. It inspires men to action, especially in the face of a wealthy neighbour. Essentially Hesiod argued that men need incentives like envy, whether to emulate others or to discharge tension in themselves. Ibid. 102.

36) Arguably the ancient Egyptians could have benefited from a bit more chaos and disorder. But then they suffered Pharaonic despotisms so pervasive that the opportunity for ordinary citizens to express envy might not have been obvious. Utopias can be equally oppressive. Then 'Big Brother' is an inner envier projected onto the group as a whole. See discussion in Melvin Lasky, *Utopia and Revolution*, op. cit., pp. 6-7, 10-11.

37) Helmut Schoeck, *Envy: A Theory of Social Behaviour*, op. cit., pp. 255.

Schoeck adds that: "We need envy for our social existence, though no society that hopes to endure can afford to raise it to a value principle or to an institution."

38) Geoffrey Chaucer, "The Parson's Tale", in *Canterbury Tales*, op. cit., p. 506.

39) Wilfred Bion, *Learning from Experience*, in *Seven Servants*, Jason Aronson, Inc., New York, 1977.

40) Pindar, *Nemean Odes*, quoted by Peter Walcot, *Envy and the Greeks*, op. cit., p. 80.

About the same time, the Chinese sage, Lao-tse (604 B C.E.?) was writing that "The value in relations is benevolence. The value in words is sincerity." from "No. 8 - Noncompetitive Values", *The Tao of Power*, trans. by R. L. Wing, The Aquarian Press, Wellingborough, Northamptonshire, England, 1986.

41) Norman Cohn, *Europe's Inner Demons*, op. cit., pp. 216-217.

42) Jacob and Wilhelm Grimm, "Briar-Rose" in *Selected Tales*, op. cit., pp. 70-73.

43) Ibid., p. 70.

44) The fact that a wise-woman could turn bad is also consistent with traditional folk-beliefs. The "beautiful ladies" were known to enter through the cracks in the door of a well ordered house. If they were treated well, given food, wine and entertainments, then they gave every kind of good blessing in return. But if they were mistreated, i.e. left out, then poverty, sickness and death would follow. Norman Cohn, *Europe's Inner Demons*, op. cit., p. 216.

45) Melanie Klein, "Love, Guilt and Reparation" in *Love, Guilt and Reparation and other Works 1921-1945*, The Hogarth Press, London, 1975, p. 330.

46) Helmut Schoeck adds: "Perhaps from the psychoanalytical and therapeutical perspectives one is inclined to underestimate self- and mutual compensating, alleviating processes and mechanisms in many families, despite the fact that one can prove the existence of classic antagonisms." Quoted from letter to Joseph Berke, 8 July 1986.

47) This example reflects the many famous accounts which foretell the transformation of bad bits into good. Thus, the culmination of Aeschylus's *Oresteia, The Eumenides*, tells how and why Athena's wisdom and understanding of Orestes was able to change the Erinyes, "the Furies" or destructive forces, into the Eumenides, "the kindly ones" or beneficent forces. See Melanie Klein, "Some Reflections on the Oresteia", *Envy and Gratitude and Other Works 1916-1963*, op. cit., p. 276.

48) "The ideal breast, introjected with love, gratification and gratitude, becomes part of the ego, the ego is more full of goodness itself. And thus, in a benevolent cycle, envy lessens as gratification increases, the diminution of envy allows more gratification which in turn furthers the lessening of envy." Hanna Segal, *Introduction to the Work of Melanie Klein*, op. cit. p. 52.

49) Specifically the three goddesses were Aglaia (Brilliance), Euphrosyne (Joy) and Thalia (Bloom).

50) Peter Walcot, *Envy and the Greeks*, op. cit., p. 74.

51) Ibid., p. 73.

52) Quoted by Cindy Blake, "Good deeds- bad thoughts", *The Sunday Times*, 24 March 1985, p. 37.

53) Ibid., p. 37.

54) "By contrast, with people in whom this feeling of inner wealth and strength is not sufficiently established, bouts of generosity are often followed by an exaggerated need for appreciation and gratitude, and consequently by persecutory anxieties of having been impoverished and robbed." Melanie Klein, "Envy and Gratitude", *Envy and Gratitude and Other Works 1946 -1963*, op. cit., p. 189.

55) Bertrand Russell, *The Conquest of Happiness*, op. cit., p. 67.

56) *Forms of Prayer for Jewish Worship: Prayers for the High Holydays*, edited by the Assembly of Rabbis of the Reform Synagogues of Great Britain, 8th edition, London, 1985, pp. 569-571.

57) Quoted by: Joseph H. Berke, "Psychoanalysis and Kabbalah," in *Psychoanalytic Review*, Vol. 83, No. 6, December 1996, p.857.

58) The original law of compensation was passed in March 1953. It was followed by a federal Law of Indemnification which indemnified individuals or their dependants for loss of life or limb, damage to health, loss of career, property, pensions, and insurance as well as compensation for loss of liberty, imprisonment, etc.Paul Johnson, *A History of the Jews*, Weidenfeld and Nicolson, London, 1987, pp. 514-516.

59) The Arbours Crisis Centre was founded in 1973 by myself and others to help people in emotional distress and as an alternative to traditional mental hospital treatment. The Crisis Centre itself provides personal and psychotherapeutic support and accommodation for individuals, couples or families in a quiet residential setting.

See The Centre's website: www.arbourscentre.org.uk. Also, Joseph Berke, *I Haven't Had To Go Mad Here*, Pelican Books, London, 1979; Joseph Berke, "The Arbours Centre," *International Journal of Therapeutic Communities*, Vol. 3, No. 4, 1982, pp. 248-261; Joseph Berke (et al), *Beyond Madness: PsychoSocial Interventions in Psychosis*, Jessica Kingsley, London, 2002.

60) Personal communication, 1985.

Bibliography

Abraham, Karl. *Selected Papers on Psycho-Analysis*. London: The Hogarth Press, 1973.

–. "Manifestations of the Female Castration Complex." In *Selected Papers on Psycho-Analysis*.

–. "A Short Study of the Development of the Libido, Viewed in the Light of Mental Disorders." In *Selected Papers on Psycho-Analysis*.

Aeschylus. *The Agamemnon*. Translated by Gilbert Murray. London: George Allen & Unwin Ltd., 1925.

–. *The Oresteia*. Translated by Robert Fagles. London: Penguin Books, 1983.

–. *The Eumenides*. Translated by Richmond Lattimore. In *Greek Tragedies: Volume 3*, edited by David Grene and Richmond Lattimore. Chicago: Phoenix Books, University of Chicago Press, 1963.

Alcalay, R. *Words of the Wise*. Israel: Masada Press.

Alderman, G. (3 June 2005) "Either a catastrophe or a conspiracy," London: *The Jewish Chronicle*.

al-Hakim, Tawfiq. *'Awdat al-wa'i*. Beirut: 1974.

Al-Sowayan, S. (15 November 2005) Saudi Arabia: *Al-Iqtisadiyya*. English translation: *The Saudi Gazette* (Saudi Arabia) 17 November 2005. Republished by *MEMRI*, Special Dispatch Series No. 1032, 23 November 2005.

Allen, Woody. *Annie Hall*. In *Four Films of Woody Allen*. London: Faber and Faber, 1983.

Angry Brigade, the. "Communique 8." In *The Angry Brigade 1967-1984 Documents and Chronology*. London: Anarchist Pocketbooks 3, Elephant Editions, 1985

Aristides, "A Few Kind Words for Envy," *American Scholar*, Autumn 1989.

Aristophanes. *The Birds*. Translated by Gilbert Murray. London: George Allen & Unwin, 1950.

Aristotle. *The Politics of Aristotle*. Translated by E. Barker. Oxford: The Clarendon Press, 1946.

Auletta, Ken. *Greed and Glory on Wall Street*. New York: Random House, 1987.

Bacon, Francis. *The Essays or Counsels, Civil and Moral*. Edited by S. H. Reynolds. Oxford: The Clarendon Press, 1890.

Banfield, Edward. *The Moral Basis of a Backward Society*. Glencoe, Ill.: Glencoe Free Press, 1958.

Bank, Stephen, and Michael Kahn. *The Sibling Bond*. New York: Basic Books, 1982.

Barnes, Mary, and Joseph Berke. *Mary Barnes: Two Accounts of a Journey Through Madness.* London: Penguin Books, 1982.

Bat Ye'or. (1985). "The Dhimmi: Jews and Christians Under Islam." Cranbury, NJ: *Farleigh Dickinson University Press,* 1996.

Bauer, Peter. *Equality, The Third World, and Economic Delusion.* London: Methuen, 1982.

Baumgarten, Edward. *"Versuch uber mögliche Fortschritte im theoretischen und praktischen Umgang mit Macht."* Studium Generale, 1951.

Belloc, Hilaire. "About John." In *Selected Cautionary Verses.* London: Puffin Books, 1983.

Ben-Dor, Gabriel. *State and Conflict in the Middle East: Emergence of the Postcolonial State.* New York: Praeger Publishers, 1983.

Berke, Joseph, ed. *Counter Culture: The Creation of an Alternative Society.* London: Peter Owen, 1969.

–. "The Fickle Fix." *The Radical Therapist 1,* no. 2. (June-July 1970).

–. *I Haven't Had to Go Mad Here.* London: Pelican Books, 1979.

–. "The Arbours Centre." *Int. J. Therapeutic Communities* 3, no. 4 (1982).

–. "Primitive Mental Mechanisms: A Study of Introjection, Projection and Identification." Unpublished paper (1982).

–. "Differentiation of the Pre-Genital Phase from the Genital Phase of the Early Oedipus Complex." Unpublished paper (1983).

–. "Envy Loveth Not: A Study of the Origin, Influence and Confluence of Envy and Narcissism." *Brit. J. Psychoth.* 1, no. 3 (1985).

–. "Shame and Envy." *Brit. J. Psychoth.* 2, no. 4 (1986).

–. "Psychoanalysis and Kabbalah," in *Psychoanalytic Review,* Vol.83, No.6, December 1996.

Berke, J. et. al. (eds.) *Beyond Madness: PsychoSocial Interventions in Psychosis,* London: Jessica Kingsley, 2002.

Berlin, Irving. "Anything You Can Do." *Annie Get Your Gun.* London: Irving Berlin Ltd., 1947.

Bethe, E. *Die Dorische Knabenliebe, ihre Ethik and ihre Idee.* Neue Folge: Rheinisches Museum für Philologie, 1907.

Bett, Henry, *Nursery Rhymes and Tales: Their Origin and History.* New York: 1924.

Bettelheim, Bruno. *Symbolic Wounds.* London: Thames & Hudson, 1955.

–. *The Empty Fortress: Infantile Autism and the Birth of the Self.* New York: The Free Press, Macmillan Publishing Co., 1967.

–. The Uses of Enchantment: The Meaning and Importance of Fairy Tales. London: Thames & Hudson, 1976.

–. *Freud and Man's Soul.* London: Chatto & Windus, 1983.

–. *Surviving the Holocaust.* London: Flamingo Books, Fontana Paperbacks, 1986.

Billington, James. *Fire in the Minds of Men: Origins of the Revolutionary Faith.* London: Temple Smith, 1980.

Binion, Rudolph. "Hitler's Concept of *Lebensraum:* The Psychological Basis." *History of Childhood Quarterly* 1, no. 2 (Fall 1973).

Bion, Wilfred R. "Attacks on Linking." *Int. J. Psycho-Anal.* 40 (1959).

–. *Learning from Experience.* Reprinted in *Seven Servants: Four Works by Wilfred R. Bion.* New York: Jason Aronson, 1977.

–. "Attention and Interpretation." London: *Tavistock.* (1970)

–. "Cogitations." London: *Karnac* (1992)

Blundy, David, and Andrew Lycett. *Qaddafi and the Libyan Revolution.* London:

Weidenfeld & Nicolson, 1987.

Blumenfeld, Laura. "Bill Clinton's Nemesis, Or Rancorous Remains Of an Old Friendship," *International Herald Tribune*, 31 December 1993.

Bodansky, Y. (1999). "Islamic Anti-Semitism as a Political Instrument." Israel: *Shaarei Tikva*, Ariel Centre for Policy Research.

Boehm, Felix. "The Femininity Complex in Men." In *Psychoanalysis and Male Sexuality*, edited by H. Ruitenbeek.

Brayfield, Celia. *Glitter: The Truth about Fame*. London: Chatto & Windus, 1985.

Bremner, R. H. *Children and Youth in America*. Cambridge, Mass.: Harvard University Press, 1970.

Brenner, Charles. "The Psychoanalytic Concept of Aggression." *Int. J. Psycho-Anal.* 52, no. 2 (1971).

Broder, John. "For Muslim Who Says Violence Destroys Islam, Violent Threats,"

The New York Times, Saturday Profile, 11 March 2006.

Brooks, John. *Showing Off in America: From Conspicuous Consumption to Parody Display.* Boston: Little, Brown & Company, 1979.

Broun, Heywood, and Margaret Leech. *Anthony Comstock: Roundsman of the Lord*. New York: 1927.

Bryk, F. *Die Beschneidung bei Mann and Weib*. Neubrandenburg: Gustav Feller, 1931.

Burnham, David. "The Abuse of Power: Misuse of the I.R.S.," *New York Times Magazine*, 3 September 1989

Burstin, Luis. "A Few Home Truths About Latin America." *Commentary* 79, no. 2 (February 1985).

Bush, G.W. (2005) "Remarks by the President at the 20th Anniversary of the National Endowment for Democracy." 12 October 2005.

Butcher, T. (22 June 2005) "Moment a suicide bombing mission failed," London: *The Daily Telegraph*.

Butler, Samuel. *Erewhon*. London: Longman's & Co., 1890.

–. *Erewhon Revisited*. London: Grant Richards, 1901.

Caldicott, Helen. *Missile Envy.* New York: William Morrow & Co., 1984.

Calhoun, A. W. *A Social History of the American Family from Colonial Times to the Present*. New York: 1945.

Canetti, Elias. *Crowds and Power*. London: Victor Gollancz, 1962.

Carle, Eric. *The Very Hungry Caterpillar*. London: Hamish Hamilton, 1970.

Carr, Francis. *Mozart and Constanze*. New York: Franklin Watts, 1986.

Carroll, John. *Guilt: The Grey Eminence Behind Character, History and Culture*. London: Routledge & Kegan Paul, 1985.

Carroll, Lewis. *Alice's Adventures in Wonderland*, Penguin Classics, 1998.

–. *Through the Looking Glass*, Penguin Classics, 1998.

Carstairs, G. Morris. *The Twice-Born. A Study of a Community of High-Caste Hindus*. London: Hogarth Press, 1957.

Cartland, Barbara. *The Outrageous Queen: A Biography of Christina of Sweden*. London: Frederick Muller, 1956.

Chase-Marshall, Janet. "Who's Afraid of Phyllis Chesler?" *Human Behavior* (September 1978).

Chasseguet-Smirgel, Janine. *Female Sexuality.* Ann Arbor, Mich.: University of Michigan Press, 1970.

Chaucer, Geoffrey. "The Parson's Tale." In *Canterbury Tales*. Translated by Nevill Coghill. London: Penguin Books, 1982.

Cheng, Nien. *Life and Death in Shanghai*. London: Grafton Books, 1986.

Chesler, Phyllis. *Women and Madness*. New York: Doubleday & Co., 1952.

Cirlot, J. E. *A Dictionary of Symbols*. Translated by J. Sage. London: Routledge & Kegan Paul, 1962.

Clanton, Gordon. "Frontiers of Jealousy Research." *Alternative Lifestyles* 4, no. 3 (August 1981).

Cohen-Solal, Annie. *Sartre: A Life*. London: Heinemann, 1987.

Cohn, Norman. *Europe's Inner Demons*. London: Paladin Books, 1976.

–. *The Pursuit of the Millennium: Revolutionary Millennarians and Mystical Anarchists of the Middle Ages*. London: Paladin Books, 1978.

Commager, Henry Steele, and Richard B. Morris, eds. *The Spirit of Seventy-Six*, vol. 1. New York: Bobbs-Merrill Co., 1970.

Computer Security. Alexandria, Va.: Time-Life Books, 1986.

Conquest, Robert. *The Harvest of Sorrow*. London: Hutchinson & Co., 1986.

Corless, F. and Mulchrone, P. "Moslem's jackpot angers Mosque leaders," *Daily Mirror*, 14 December 1994.

Court, Joan. "Battering Parents." *Social Work* 26, no. 1 (January 1969).

Crawford, Christina. *Mommie Dearest*. London: Hart-Davis, 1979.

Creighton, Susan. *Child Victims of Physical Abuse*, 1976. London: NSPCC.

–, *Trends in Child Abuse*. London: NSPCC, 1984.

–, "Child Abuse Deaths." *NSPCC Information Briefing No. 5*. London: NSPCC, 1985.

Cyprian. "On Jealousy and Envy." In *The Writings of Cyprian*. Translated by R. E. Wallis. Edinburgh: T. & T. Clark, 1868.

Dahl, Roald. *Danny: Champion of the World*. New York: Bantam Books, 1979.

Dante (Aligheri). *Inferno*. Translated by L. Lockert. Princeton, N.J.: Princeton University Press, 1931.

Davies, Paul. *The Cosmic Blueprint*. London: Heinemann, 1987.

DeMause, Lloyd, ed. *The History of Childhood*. New York: Psychohistory Press, 1974.

–. "The Evolution of Childhood." In *The History of Childhood*, edited by Lloyd DeMause.

–. ed. *The New Psychohistory*. New York: Psychohistory Press, 1975.

Dershowitz, A.M. (2002). "Why Terrorism Works". New Haven: *Yale University Press*.

Devereux, G. "Why Oedipus Killed Laius, A Note on the Complementary Oedipus Complex in Greek Drama." *Int. J. Psycho-Anal.* 34 (1953).

Dickenson, R. L. *Human Sexual Anatomy*. 2d ed. Baltimore, Md.: Williams & Wilkens, 1949.

Dickins, Aileen. "Uterine Ligaments and the Treatment of Prolapse." *Journal of the Royal Society of Medicine 77* (May 1984).

"The Digger Papers." In *Counter Culture: The Creation of an Alternative Society*, edited by Joseph Berke.

Dodds, John W. *The Age of Paradox: A Biography of England 1841-1851*. London: Victor Gollancz Ltd. 1953.

Donne, John. *The Complete Poetry and Prose of John Donne and The Complete Poetry of William Blake*. New York: The Modern Library, Random House, 1941.

Dooley, Dennis, and Gary Engle, eds. *Superman at Fifty: The Persistence of the Legend*. Cleveland, Oh.: Octavia Press, 1987.

Driver, G. R., and John C. Miles. "Middle Assyrian Laws." In *The Assyrian Laws.* Oxford: Oxford University Press 1935.

Drucker, Peter. "The Monster and the Lamb." *Atlantic* (December 1978).

Drug Addiction: Crime or Disease? Interim and Final Reports of the Joint Committee of the American Bar Association and the American Medical Association on Narcotic Drugs. Bloomington, Ind.: Indiana University Press, 1963.

Duesenberry, J. S. *Income, Saving, and the Theory of Consumer Behavior.* Cambridge, Mass.: 1949.

Dunn, Judy. "Sibling Relationships in Early Childhood." *Child Development* 54 (1983).

—. *Sisters and Brothers.* London: Fontana Paperbacks, 1984.

Dynes, Michael. "Rail vandals bring fast train services to a halt," *The Times,* 21 December 1991.

Eibl-Eibesfeldt, Irenaus. *Love and Hate.* Translated by G. Stachan. London: Methuen, 1971.

Emmerson, Andrew. "Phantoms of the Operating System." *New Scientist* (28 January 1988).

Encyclopaedia Britannica. 15th ed. Chicago: Encyclopaedia Britannica, Inc., 1974.

Encyclopedia Judaica. Jerusalem: Keter Books, 1972.

Engle, Bernice Schultz. "The Amazons in Ancient Greece." *Psychoanalytic Quarterly* 11 (1942).

Enoch, M. O., W. H. Trethowan, and J. C. Barker, eds. "The Othello Syndrome." *Some Uncommon Psychiatric Symptoms.* Bristol: Wright & Son, 1967.

Epstein, Edward Jay. *The Rise and Fall of Diamonds: The Shattering of a Brilliant Illusion.* New York: Simon & Schuster, 1982.

Euripides. *The Plays of Euripides.* Translated by Gilbert Murray. 2 vols. Newtown: Gregynog Press, 1931.

Faulkner, William. *Absalom, Absalom.* New York: Random House, 1966.

Farber, Leslie. "The Faces of Envy." In *lying, despair, jealousy, envy, sex, suicide, drugs, and the good life.* New York: Basic Books, Inc., 1976.

Fenichel, Otto. *The Psychoanalytic Theory of Neurosis.* New York: W. W. Norton & Co., 1945.

Ferenczi, Sandor. *Thalassa: A Theory of Genitality.* New York: The Norton Library, W. W. Norton & Co., 1968.

Fischer, Fritz. *Griff nach der Weltmacht* (Germany's Aims in the First World War). New York: W. W. Norton & Co., 1967.

Food and Drink Through the Ages: 2500 B.C. to 1937 A.D. London: Maggs Bros., 1937.

Forms of Prayer for Jewish Worship: Prayers for the High Holydays. Edited by the Assembly of Rabbis of the Reform Synagogues of Great Britain. 8th ed. London: Reform Synagogues of Great Britain, 1985.

Fletcher, M. (20 November 2001). "Bunker-buster bombs blast Bin Laden caves," London: *The Times.*

Fort, Joel. *The Pleasure Seekers: The Drug Crisis, Youth and Society.* New York: Grove Press, 1969.

Foster, George M., "The Anatomy of Envy: A Study in Symbolic Behavior." *Current Anthropology* 13, no. 2 (April 1972).

Freud, Sigmund. *Standard Edition of the Complete Psychological Works of Freud.* Edited by J. Strachey. London: The Hogarth Press, 1968. *(S.E.)*

–. "Three Essays on Sexuality." *S.E.* 7 (1905). London: *Hogarth*, 1981.

–. "Instincts and Their Vicissitudes." *S.E.* 14 (1915).

–. "Mourning and Melancholia." *S.E* 14 (1917). London: *Hogarth*, 1981.

–. "On the Sexual Theories of Children." *S.E.* 9 (1908).

–. "A Special Type of Choice of Object Made by Men." *S.E. 11* (1910).

–. "Psycho-Analytic Notes upon an Autobiographical Account of a Case of Paranoia (Dementia Paranoides)." *S.E.* 12 (1911).

–. "The Taboo of Virginity." *S.E. 11* (1918).

–. "Beyond the Pleasure Principle." *S.E.* 18 (1920).

–. "Group Psychology and the Analysis of the Ego." *S.E.* 18 (1921).

–. "Some Neurotic Mechanisms in Jealousy, Paranoia and Homosexuality." *S.E.* 18 (1922).

–. "The Economic Problem of Masochism." *S.E.* 19 (1924).

–. "The Dissolution of the Oedipus Complex." *S.E.* 19 (1924).

–. "Some Psychical Consequences of the Anatomical Distinction between the Sexes." *S.E.* 19 (1925).

–. "Inhibitions, Symptoms and Anxiety." *S.E* 20 (1926). London: *Hogarth*, 1981.

–. "New Introductory Lectures on Psycho-Analysis." *S.E.* 22 (1932).

–. "Anxiety and Instinctual Life," in "New Introductory Lectures on Psycho-Analysis," *S.E.* 22 (1932).

–. "Femininity." In "New Introductory Lectures on Psycho-Analysis," *S.E.* 22 (1932).

–. "Analysis Terminable and Interminable." *S.E.* 23 (1937).

–. *The Complete Letters of Sigmund Freud to Wilhelm Fliess.* Edited by Jeffrey Masson. Cambridge, Mass.: The Belknap Press of Harvard University Press, 1985.

Friday, Nancy. *Jealousy.* New York: William Morrow & Co., 1985.

Friedlander, S. (1997). "Nazi Germany and the Jews," vol. I. New York: *Harper Collins*

Friedman, Thomas. "American Power and an Envious, Angry World." *International Herald Tribune*, 2 March 1998.

Friedrich, Otto. "The New Origins of Life: How the Science of Conception Brings Hope to Childless Couples." *Time* (10 September 1984).

Fromm, Erich. *The Anatomy of Human Destructiveness.* New York: Holt, Rinehart & Winston, 1973.

Fussell, Paul. *Caste Marks: Style and Status in the U.S.A.* London: William Heinemann, 1984.

Garinet, Jules. *Histoire de la magic en France.* Paris: Foulon, 1818

Garner, Clare. "More than 100 children die of abuse and neglect every year," *The Independent*, 15 March 1999.

Gifford, Edward S. Jr. *The Evil Eye: Studies in the Folklore of Vision.* New York: The Macmillan Co., 1958.

Glenn, Jules. "Psychoanalysis of a Constipated Girl: Clinical Observations During the Fourth and Fifth Years." Paper presented at the Panel on the Psychology of Women: Infancy and Early Childhood, at the May 1974 meetings of the American Psychoanalytic Association.

Goebbels, Joseph. *The Early Goebbels Diaries: 1925-1926.* Translated by Oliver Watson. New York: Helmut Heiber, *1963.*

Goldhagen, Daniel. "Hitler's Willing Executioners; Ordinary Germans and the Holocaust," New York: *Little, Brown & Co.*, 1996

Greenacre, Phyllis. *Trauma, Growth, and Personality.* London: The Hogarth Press, 1953.

–. "Penis Awe and Its Relation to Penis Envy." In *Drives, Affects and Behavior.* Edited by R. M. Loewenstein.

Greenson, R. R. "Disidentifying from the Mother: Its Special Importance for the Boy." *Int. J. Psycho-Anal.* 49 (1968).

Greer, Germaine. *The Female Eunuch.* London: MacGibbon & Kee, 1970.

Greven, P. *Child-Rearing Concepts, 1628-1861.* Itasca: 1973.

Grimm, Jacob and Wilhelm. *Selected Tales.* Translated by David Luke. London: Penguin Classics, 1982.

Gruen, A. (1988). "The Betrayal of the Self: The Fear of Autonomy in Men and Women." New York: *Grove Press.*

Halberstam, David. *The Best and the Brightest.* London: Barrie & Jenkins, 1972.

Hall, Peter. *Peter Hall's Diaries.* Edited by John Goodwin. London: Hamish Hamilton, 1983.

Hamady, Sania. *Temperament and Character of the Arabs.* New York: Twayne, 1960.

Hartley, L. P. *Facial Justice.* London: Hamish Hamilton, 1960.

Hattersly, Roy. *Choose Freedom: The Future of Democratic Socialism.* London: Michael Joseph, 1987.

Hayley, Thomas T. S. "Khoba Khobee." Unpublished article.

Hayman, Ronald. *Writing Against: A Biography of Sartre.* London: Weidenfeld & Nicolson, 1986.

Hayman, Suzie. "10 Times Better." *Forum* 17, no. 10 (October 1984).

Henry, Jules. *Culture Against Man.* New York: Knopf, 1978.

–. Pathways to Madness. New York: Random House, 1971.

Herodotus. *History.* New York: Dutton, 1912.

Hesiod. *Works and Days.* Translated by R. Lattimore, Ann Arbor Michigan, University of Michigan Press, 1959.

Hinshelwood, Robert. "Projective Identification and Marx's Concept of Man." *Int. Rev. Psycho-Anal.* 10 (1983).

Hiscock, John. "Bloody revenge of Internet nerds obsessed with Satan and Nazis," *The Daily Telegraph,* 22 April 1999.

Hitler, Adolf. *Mein Kampf.* Translated by James Murphy. London: Hurst and Blackett, 1930.

Hobsbawm, E. J. *Social Bandits and Primitive Rebels: Studies in Archaic Forms of Social Movement in the 19th and 20th Centuries.* Glencoe, Ill.: Glencoe Free Press, 1959.

Hobson, Robert. "Psychological Aspects of Circumcision." *Journal of Analytical Psychology* 6, no. 1 (1961).

Hodder, Elizabeth. *The Step-Parents' Handbook.* London: Sphere Books, 1985.

Homber, A. R. *Nomads of the Long Bow, The Siriono of Eastern Bolivia.* Smithsonian Institution: Institute of Social Anthropology Publication, no. 10. Washington, D.C. (1950).

Horney, Karen. "On the Genesis of the Castration Complex in Women." *Int. J. Psycho-Anal.* 5 (1924).

–. "The Dread of Women." In *Psychoanalysis and Male Sexuality.* Edited by Henrik Ruitenbeek.

Horsnell, Michael. "Girl, 13, denies twin murders," *The Times,* 30 January 1991.

Hughes, Robert. *The Fatal Shore: A History of the Transportation of Convicts to Australia, 1787-1868.* London: Collins Harvill, *1987.*

Hunter, G. K. Introduction to *King Lear.* In *King Lear,* William Shakespeare. London: Penguin Books, *1972.*

Hunter, Richard, and Ida Macalpine, eds. *Three Hundred Years of Psychiatry 1535-1860.* London: Oxford University Press, 1963.

Iacocca, Lee. *Iacocca: An Autobiography.* London: Bantam Books, 1986.

Ibn Qutyba. (1900-1908). "Uyun al-akhbar." Edited by C. Brockelmann. Berlin: *Georg Olms.*

Isocrates. *Antidosis.* In *Greek Orations.* Edited by W. R. Connor. Ann Arbor, Michigan: University of Michigan Press, 1966.

Jackson, Brian. *Fatherhood.* London: George Allen and Unwin, 1984.

Jaffe, Daniel. "The Masculine Envy of Woman's Procreative Function." *J. Amer. Psychoanal. Assoc.* 16 (1968).

Jahoda, Marie. *Freud and the Dilemmas of Psychology.* London: The Hogarth Press, 1977.

Joffe, Walter G. "A Critical Review of the Status of the Envy Concept." *Int. J. Psycho-Anal.* 50, no. 4 (1969).

Johnson, Paul. "Farewell to the Labour Party." *New Statesman* (9 September 1977).

–. *A History of the Modern World: From 1917 to the 1980s.* London: Weidenfeld & Nicolson, 1983.

–. *A History of the Jews.* London: Weidenfeld & Nicolson, 1987.

Jones, Derek Llewelyn. *Fundamentals of Obstetrics and Gynaecology* 1. London: Faber & Co., 1982.

Jones, Ernest. *Papers on Psycho-Analysis.* Boston: Beacon Press, 1961.

–. "The Early Development of Female Sexuality." In *Papers on Psycho-Analysis* (1927).

–. "The Phallic Phase." In *Papers on Psycho-Analysis* (1933).

–. *Psycho-Myth, Psycho-History* 1. New York: Hillstone, 1974.

–. "Psychopathology and International Tension." In *Psycho-Myth, Psycho-History* (1949).

Jones, R. V. "The Rise and Fall of British Industry." *New Scientist* (10 July 1986).

Joseph, Betty. "Some Characteristics of the Psychopathic Personality." *Int. J. Psycho-Anal.* 41 (1960).

Joseph, Keith, and Jonathan Sumption. *Equality.* London: John Murray Publishers Ltd., 1979.

Jung, Carl. "Versuch einer Darstellung der psychoanalytischen Theorie." *Jahrbuch für psychoanalytische and psychopathologische Forschungen* V (1913): 370. (*The theory of psycho-analysis.* New York: 1915.)

Kant, Immanuel. *Metaphysik der Sitten.* In Sämtliche Werke, edited by K. Vorlander. Vol. 3, 4th ed. Leipzig: Felix Meiner, 1922.

Karme, Laila. "The Penis As Umbilical Cord." *Psychoanalytic Quarterly* 47 (1978).

Karon, Bertram, and Gary VandenBos. *Psychotherapy of Schizophrenia: Treatment of Choice.* New York: Jason Aronson, 1981.

Kedourie, Elie. *Nationalism.* London: Hutchinson University Library, Hutchinson & Co., 1966.

Kern, Stephen. "Explosive Intimacy: Psychodynamics of the Victorian Family." In *The New Psychohistory,* edited by Lloyd DeMause.

Kernberg, Otto (1992). "Aggression in Personality Disorders and Perversions." New Haven: *Yale University Press.*

–. *Borderline Conditions and Pathological Narcissism.* New York: Jason Aronson, 1975.

–. "Why Some People Can't Love." An interview by Linda Wolfe, in *Psychology Today* (June 1978).

Kershaw, Ian. "The Hitler Myth: Image and Reality in the Third Reich," London: *Oxford University Press,* 1989.

Kershaw, Ian. Hitler: 1889-1936: Hubris (Vol. 1), New York: *W.W. Norton & Co.,* 1999.

Kierkegaard, Soren. *En literair Anmeldelse to Tidsaldre* (The present age). In *Samlede Vaerker,* edited by H. O. Lange, vol. 8. Copenhagen: 1920-30.

Klein, M. (1935). "A Contribution to the Psychogenesis of Manic-Depressive States." In: "The Writings of Melanie Klein", vol. 1, London: *The Hogarth Press,* 1975.

–. "Notes on Some Schizoid Mechanisms." In: "The Writings of Melanie Klein," vol. 3, London: *The Hogarth Press,* 1975. (1946).

–. "On the Development of Mental Functioning." *International Journal of Psycho-Analysis,* 39:84-90. (1958).

Klein, Melanie. *Love, Guilt and Reparation and Other Works 1921-1945.* Collected Works (C. W.), vol. 1. London: The Hogarth Press, 1975.

–. *The Psycho-Analysis of Children. C. W.,* vol. 2. Translated by A. Strachey. London: The Hogarth Press, 1975.

–. *Envy and Gratitude and Other Works 1946-1963.* C. W., vol. 3. London: The Hogarth Press, 1975.

–. "An Obsessional Neurosis in a Six-Year-Old Girl." C. W., vol. 2 *(1924).*

–. "Early Stages of the Oedipus Conflict and Superego Formation." C. W., vol. 2 (1928).

–. "The Significance of Early Anxiety Situations in the Development of the Ego." C. W., vol. 2 (1932).

–. "The Effects of Early Anxiety-Situations on the Sexual Development of the Girl." C. W., vol. 2 (1932).

–."A Contribution to the Psychogenesis of Manic-Depressive States," C.W. vol. 1 (1935)

–. "Love, Guilt and Reparation." C. W., vol. 1 (1937).

–. "Notes on Some Schizoid Mechanism," C.W. Vol. 3, (1946)

–. "On Observing the Behaviour of Young Infants." C. W., vol. 3 (1952).

–. "Some Theoretical Conclusions Regarding the Emotional Life of the Infant." C. W., vol. 3 (1952).

–. "Envy and Gratitude." C. W., vol. 3 (1957). This work was originally published as a separate volume, *Envy and Gratitude: A Study of Unconscious Sources.* London: Tavistock Publications, *1957.*

–. "Some Reflections on 'The Oresteia.' " C. W., vol. 3 (1963).

von Kleist, Heinrich. *Michael Kohlhaas.* In *Twelve German Novellas.* Edited and translated by H. Steinhawer. Berkeley: University of California Press, 1977.

Koestler, Arthur, et. al. *The God That Failed.* Edited by R. Crossman. London: Hamish Hamilton, 1950.

Kohut, Heinz. "Thoughts of Narcissism and Narcissistic Rage." *Psychoanalytic Study of the Child.* Vol. 27. New York: Quadrangle, 1972.

Kolakowski, Leszek. "The Fantasy of Marxism." *Encounter* (December *1978).*

The Koran. Translated by N. J. Dawood. London: Penguin Books, 1956.

Koskoff, David. *The Diamond World.* New York: Harper & Row, *1982.*

Kramer, Heinrich, and James Sprenger. *Malleus Maleficarum.* Translated by Montague Summers. London: Pushkin Press, 1951.

Kubizek, August. *Adolf Hitler, mein Jugendfreund.* Graz: 1953.

Kundera, Milan. *The Book of Laughter and Forgetting.* Translated by H. Heim. London: King Penguin, Penguin Books, 1985.

Laing, R. D. "Violence and Love." *Journal of Existentialism 5,* no. 20 (1965).

–. *The Politics of Experience.* New York: Pantheon Books, 1967.

–. "The Mystification of Experience." In *The Politics of Experience.*

–. *The Facts of Life.* New York: Pantheon Books, 1976.

Lang, P. H. *Music in Western Civilization.* New York: W. W. Norton & Co., 1940.

Langer, Marie. "Sterility and Envy." *Int. J. Psycho-Anal. 39 (1958).*

Laplanche, J., and J.-B. Pontalis. *The Language of Psycho-Analysis.* London: The Hogarth Press, 1973.

Lasch, Christopher. *The Culture of Narcissism: American Life in an Age of Diminishing Expectations.* New York: W. W. Norton & Co., 1978.

Lasky, Melvin. *Utopia and Revolution.* London: Macmillan London Ltd., 1977.

Lawrence, D. H. *Lady Chatterley's Lover.* New York: Grove Press, 1969.

Leach, Edmund. "Envy and the English Sickness." *The Listener* (26 March 1970).

–. "The Big Fish in the Biblical Wilderness." *Int. Rev. Psycho-Anal.* 13, part 2 (1986).

Lee, Laurie. *Cider with Rosie.* London: Penguin Books, 1959.

Leo, John. "Battling the Green-Eyed Monster." *Time* (25 November 1985).

Levin, K. (2005). "The Oslo Syndrome: Delusions of a People Under Siege," New Hampshire: *Smith & Kraus, Inc.*

Levin, Shmarya. *Childhood in Exile.* New York: 1929.

Levy, G. R. *The Gate of Horn.* London: Faber & Faber, 1946.

Levy, R. (1969). "The Social Structure of Islam." Cambridge: *Cambridge University Press.*

Lewis, B. (19 November 2001). "The Revolt of Islam", New York: *The New Yorker.*

Lewis, Bernard. "L'Islam et les Non-Musulmans." *Annales: Economies, Sociétés, Civilisations* 3, 4 (Mai, Aoft 1980).

Lewis, Roger. *Outlaws of America.* London: Pelican Books, 1972.

Lidz, Ruth and Theodor. "Male Menstruation: A Ritual Alternative to the Oedipal Transition." *Int. J. Psycho-Anal.* 58 (1977).

Liebaut, Jean. *Thresor des remedes secretes pour les maladies des femmes.* Paris: 1597.

Lightfoot-Klein, Hanny. "Pharonic Circumcision of Females in the Sudan." *Medicine and Law* 2 (1983).

Littlewood, Roland. "The Imitation of Madness: The Influence of Psychopathology upon Culture." *Soc. Sci. Med.* 19, no. 7 (1984

–. *Pathology and Identity in Northeast Trinidad.* Unpublished D. Phil. thesis.

–. *Pathology and Identity*, Cambridge University Press, 1993.

Livermore, Richard. "Notes for the Anarchy and Order Brigade." *Anarchy,* no. 3.

Loewenstein, R. M., ed. *Drives, Affects and Behavior.* Vol. 1. *Contributions to the Theory and Practice of Psychoanalysis and Its Applications.* New York: International Universities Press, 1960.

Lomas, Peter. "Dread of Envy As an Aetiological Factor in Puerperal Breakdown." *Brit. J. Med. Psychol.* 33 (1960).

–. "Ritualistic Elements in the Management of Childbirth." *Brit. J. Med. Psychol.* 9 (1966).

López-Corvo, R.E. (2003). "The Dictionary of the Work of W.R. Bion." London: *Karnac*

Luke, David. "Introduction." In *Selected Tales.* Jacob and Wilhelm Grimm.

Luks, Harold. "Iraqi Jews During World War II." *Weiner Library Bulletin* 30 (1977).

Lynn, Jonathan, and Antony Jay. *Yes, Prime Minister.* 2 vols. London: BBC Books, 1986/7.

Lysias. *Epitaph.* Translated by W. R. M. Lamb. New York: Putnam, 1930.

Mackay, Charles. *Memoirs of Extraordinary Popular Delusions.* London: Richard Bentley, 1841.

Mailer, Norman. *The Prisoner of Sex.* New York: New American Library, 1971.

Mairowitz, David. *The Radical Soap Opera.* London: Penguin Books, 1976.

Maizel, Neil. "Self-Envy, the Womb and the Nature of Goodness." *Int. J. Psycho-Anal.* 66 (1985).

Malatesta, Enrico. *Anarchy.* Translated by Vernon Richards. London: Freedom Press, 1974.

Marc, Olivier. *Psychology of the House.* London: Thames & Hudson, 1977.

Marmor, Judd. "Changing Patterns of Femininity: Psychoanalytic Implications." In *Psychoanalysis and Women.* Edited by Jean Baker Miller.

Marvick, Elizabeth W. "Childhood History and Decisions of State: The Case of Louis XIII." In *The New Psychohistory.* Edited by Lloyd DeMause.

Masson, Georgina. *Queen Christina.* London: Secker & Warburg, 1968.

Masson, Jeffrey. *The Assault on Truth: Freud's Suppression of the Seduction Theory.* London: Penguin Books, 1985.

May, Rollo. "Guilt and Awareness." In *Man and Society.* Edited by Roger W. Smith. New York: Anchor Books, Doubleday & Co., 1971.

McConville, Brigid. *Sisters: Love and Conflict within the Lifelong Bond.* London: Pan Books, 1985.

Mead, Margaret. *Male and Female.* London: Victor Gollancz, 1950.

Melville, Herman. *The Portable Melville.* Edited by J. Leyda. London: Penguin Books, 1976.

Memri, (Middle East Media Research Institute) Special Report No.24, 26 December 2003.

Memri, Special Dispatch Series No.1032, 23 November 2005.

Mencken, H. L. *The Vintage Mencken.* Edited by Alistair Cooke. New York: 1956.

Middlemore, Merell. *The Nursing Couple.* London: Hamish Hamilton Medical Books, 1941.

Miller, Alice. *Thou Shalt Not Be Aware.* London: Pluto Press, 1985.

Miller, Jean Baker, ed. *Psychoanalysis and Women.* London: Penguin Books, 1974.

Miller, Jonathan. *States of Mind.* London: British Broadcasting Corporation, 1983.

Millis, Joseph. "Islam slammed by American Muslim," *Jewish Chronicle*, 10 March 2006.

Milton, John. *Paradise Lost.* New York: W. W. Norton & Co., 1975.

Miner, Horace. *The Primitive City of Timbuctoo.* Princeton: Princeton University Press, 1953.

Mintz, Morton. *At Any Cost: Corporate Greed, Women and the Dalkon Shield.* New York: Pantheon Books, 1985.

Mishan, E. J. "A Survey of Welfare Economics, 1939-1959." *The Economic Journal* 70 (London: June 1960).

Mitchell, Juliet. *Psychoanalysis and Feminism.* London: Allen Lane, 1974.

Mitford, Jessica. *Hons and Rebels.* London: Victor Gollancz, 1960.

Money-Kyrle, R. E. *Man's Picture of His World: A Psycho-Analytic Study.* London: Duckworth, 1978.

Montagu, Ashley. *The Nature of Human Aggression.* London: Oxford University Press, 1976.

Montgelas, Max, and Walter Schucking, eds. *Outbreak of the World War: German Documents Collected by Karl Kautsky.* Oxford: Oxford University Press, 1924.

Moore, Jean, and Beryl Day. "Family Interaction Associated with Abuse of Children Over 5 Years of Age." In *Child Abuse and Neglect*. London: Pergamon Press, 1979.

More, Thomas. *Utopia*. New York: W. W. Norton & Co., 1976.

Morrison, R. "Who Killed Mozart.?" *The Sunday Times Magazine*, 29 July 1990.

Moulton, Ruth. "A Survey and Reevaluation of the Concept of Penis Envy." In *Psychoanalysis and Women*. Edited by Jean Baker Miller.

Moynihan, Daniel. "The United States in Opposition." *Commentary* 59, no. 3 (March 1975).

—. *A Dangerous Place*. London: Secker & Warburg, 1979.

Mudaires, I. (2 May 2003). "Sermon Sheikh Ijlin Mosque," Gaza: *Memri Special Report* No.24, 26 December 2003.

Mullahy, Patrick. *Oedipus: Myth and Complex*. New York: Evergreen Books, Grove Press, 1955.

Murphy, James. "Introduction." In *Mein Kampf*, Adolf Hitler.

Neumann, Erich. *The Great Mother: An Analysis of the Archetype*. New York: Bollingen Series XLVII, Pantheon Books, 1963.

Newall, Venetia, ed. *The Witch Figure*. London: Routledge & Kegan Paul, 1973.

—. "The Jew As Witch Figure." In *The Witch Figure*.

New Encyclopaedia Britannica. 15th ed. Chicago: Encyclopaedia Britannica, Inc., 1985.

New Larousse Encyclopedia of Mythology. London: Paul Hamlyn, 1969.

Nicolson, Harold. *Diaries and Letters: The War Years, 1939-1945*. 3 vols. New York: 1967.

Niederland, William. *The Schreber Case: Psychoanalytic Profile of a Paranoid Personality*. Hillsdale, N.J.: Analytic Press, 1984.

Nin, Anais. *Cities of the Interior*. Distributed by The Phoenix Book Shop. New York: 1959.

Nisbet, Robert. *Prejudices: A Philosophical Dictionary*. Cambridge, Mass.: Harvard University Press, 1982.

Noonan, John T., Jr. *Bribes*. New York: Macmillan Publishing Co., 1984.

Not Private Eye 1 (10 December 1986). Published by Daily Mirror Newspapers, London.

Oakley, Ann. *The Captured Womb: A History of the Medical Care of Pregnant Women*. Oxford: Blackwell, 1984.

O'Brien, Conor Cruise. *The Siege: The Saga of Israel and Zionism*. New York: Simon & Schuster, 1986.

Olesha, Yuri. *Envy*. Garden City, N.Y.: Anchor Books, Doubleday & Co., 1967.

Opie, Iona and Peter. *The Classic Fairy Tales*. London: Paladin Books, 1980.

Orwell, George. *1984*. London: Penguin Books, 1984.

Ovid. *Metamorphoses*. London: Penguin Books, 1955.

Oxford Universal Dictionary. 3rd rev. ed. Edited by C. T. Onions. New York: Oxford University Press, 1955.

Pagels, Elaine. "The Origins of Satan," New York: *Random House* 1995.

Paul, B. D. "Symbolic Sibling Rivalry in a Guatemalan Indian Village." *American Anthropologist* 52 (1950).

Penn, Jean. "Everybody and His Brother." *Playboy* (January 1986).

Penny, Alexandra. *How to Make Love to a Man*. London: Papermac, 1981.

The Pentateuch. In *The Twenty-four Books of the Old Testament*. Vol. 1. Translated by

Alexander Harkavy. New York: Hebrew Publishing Co., 1926.

Pepitone, Leslie. Review of *The Sibling Bond*. In *Am. J. Orthopsych.* 54, no. 2 (April 1984).

Pepys, Samuel. *The Diary of Samuel Pepys*. Vol. 2. London: J. M. Dent & Sons, 1906.

–, *The Diary of Samuel Pepys*. Vol 1. London: J. M. Dent & Sons, 1927.

Piers, Gerhart, and Milton Singer. *Shame and Guilt: A Psychoanalytical and Cultural Study*. Springfield, Ill.: Thomas Publishers, 1953.

Pindar. *The Odes of Pindar*. Translated by R. Lattimore. Chicago: University of Chicago Press, *1976*.

Plath, Sylvia. *The Journals of Sylvia Plath*. New York: Ballantine Books, 1983.

Plato. *Symposium*. Translated by B. Jowett. New York: Bobbs Merrill & Co., 1956.

Plutarch. *Alcibiades*. In *The Rise and Fall of Athens: Nine Greek Lives*. Translated by Ian Scott-Kilvert. London: Penguin Books, 1987.

–. *Moralia*. Translated by P. Holland. London: Everyman's Library, 1906.

Potter, David. *People of Plenty: Economic Abundance and the American Character*. Chicago: 1954.

Prentice, Thomson. "Lennon: The Rebellious Voice of a Generation." *Now* (12 December 1980).

Pushkin, Alexander. *Mozart and Salieri: The Little Tragedies*. Translated by Anthony Wood. London: Angel Books, 1982.

Raddatz, Fritz. *Karl Marx: A Political Biography*. Translated by Richard Barry. London: Weidenfeld & Nicolson, 1978.

Radice, Betty. *Who's Who in the Ancient World*. London: Penguin Books, 1984.

Rae, John. "Success." *Punch* (11 March 1981).

Raiga, Eugene. *L'Envie*. Paris: Alcan, 1932.

Raphael-Leff, Joan. "Facilitators and Regulators: Participators and Renouncers: Mothers' and Fathers' Orientations Towards Pregnancy and Parenthood." *J. Psychosomatic Obstetrics & Gynecology* 4 (1985).

Restak, Richard M. "Newborn Knowledge." *Science/82 3*, no. 1 (1982).

Rheingold, Joseph. *The Fear of Being a Woman: A Theory of Maternal Destructiveness*. New York: Grune & Stratton, 1964.

–. *The Mother, Anxiety, and Death: The Catastrophic Death Complex*. Boston: 1967.

Richardson, L. (2-3 July 2005). "Blasts from the Past," London: *Financial Times Magazine*.

Riviere, Joan. "Jealousy As a Mechanism of Defense." *Int. J. Psycho-Anal.* 13 (1932).

–, and Melanie Klein. *Love, Hate and Reparation*. London: The Hogarth Press, 1967.

–. "Hate, Greed and Aggression." In *Love, Hate and Reparation*.

Roberts, J. M. *The Hutchinson History of the World*. London: Hutchinson & Co., 1976. *The Pelican History of the World*. Rev. ed. London: Pelican Books, 1987.

Robins, R.S. & Post, J. M. (1997). "Political Paranoia: The Psychopolitics of Hatred." New Haven: *Yale University Press*.

Róheim, Géza. *The Eternal Ones of the Dream*. New York: International Universities Press, 1945.

–. "Aphrodite or the Woman with a Penis." In *The Panic of the Gods and Other Essays*. New York: Harper Torchbooks, 1972.

–. *Psychoanalysis and Anthropology: Culture, Personality and the Unconscious*. New York: International Universities Press, 1973.

Rose, Kenneth. *King George V*. London: Weidenfeld & Nicolson, 1983.

Rosenfeld, H. (1987). "Destructive Narcissism and the Death Instinct." In: H. Rosenfeld, "Impasse and Interpretation." London: *Tavistock.*

Rosenfeld, Herbert. *Psychotic States: A Psycho-Analytical Approach.* London: The Hogarth Press, 1965.

–, "The Psychopathology of Hypochondriasis." In *Psychotic States.*

–, "A Clinical Approach to the Psychoanalytic Theory of the Life and Death Instincts: An Investigation into the Aggressive Aspects of Narcissism." *Int. J. Psycho-Anal. 52,* part 1 (1971).

–. "Negative Therapeutic Reaction." In *Tactics and Techniques in Psychoanalytic Therapy: Volume II, Countertrans ference.* Edited by Peter Giovacchini. New York: Jason Aronson, 1975.

Ross, Anne. "The Divine Hag of the Pagan Celts." In *The Witch Figure.* Edited by Venetia Newall.

Ross, John. "Oedipus Revisited: Laius and the 'Laius Complex.' " *Psychoanalytic Study of the Child* 37. New Haven, Conn.: Yale University Press, 1982.

Roszak, Theodore. *The Making of a Counter Culture: Reflections on the Technocratic Society and Its Youthful Opposition.* New York: Anchor Books, 1969.

Roth, Philip. *Goodbye Columbus.* London: Andre Deutsch, 1959.

–, *The Breast.* London: Jonathan Cape, 1973.

Roubin, Lucienne. *Chambrettes des Provencaux.* Paris: Plon, 1970.

Rubinstein, Hilary, ed. *The Good Hotel Guide,* 1987. London: Consumer's Association and Hodder & Stoughton, *1987.*

Rubinstein, Richard L. "Religion and the Origins of the Death Camps," in After Auschwitz, Indianapolis: *Bobbs-Merrill,* 1976.

Rudé, G. *The Crowd in the French Revolution.* London: Greenwood Press, 1986.

Ruitenbeek, Henrik, ed. *Psychoanalysis and Male Sexuality.* New Haven, Conn.: College and University Press, 1966.

Runciman, W. G. *Relative Deprivation and Social Justice: A Study of Attitudes to Social Inequality in Twentieth Century England.* London: Routledge & Kegan Paul, 1966.

Russell, Bertrand. *The Conquest of Happiness.* London: Unwin Paperbacks, 1978.

Ryan, Thomas. "The Roots of Masculinity." In *The Sexuality of Man.* Edited by A. Metcalf and M. Humphries. London: Pluto Press, 1985.

Rycroft, Charles. *A Critical Dictionary of Psychoanalysis.* London: Penguin Books, 1972.

Sabbadini, Andrea. "Possession Anxiety: The Other Side of the Castration Complex." *Brit. J. Psychoth.* 3, no. 1 (Fall 1986).

Sabri, Hussein Dhu'l-Figar. *Rose el-Youssef* (18 July 1975).

Sale, G. (1833). (translator & editor). "Koran." Philadelphia: *Thomas Wardle.*

Sapsted, David, "Dancer's 60 inch breasts 'gave me whiplash,'" *Daily Telegraph,*

3 July 1998.

Sartre, Jean Paul. "My Political *Will." Strike* 2, no. 3 (October 1978). Translated and reprinted from *Mon Testament politique* (Edition "Gare L'explosion," 1977*),* courtesy of Edizioni della Rivisto "Anarchismo."

Schaffer, Rudolph. "*Mothering.* London: Fontana/Open Books, 1977.

Schatzman, Morton. *Soul Murder: Persecution in the Family.* New York: Random House, 1973.

Schneider, S. (2002). "Fundamentalism and Paranoia in Groups and Society." *Group* 26:17-27.

Schoeck, Helmut. *Envy: A Theory of Social Behavior.* Translated by M. Glenny and B.

Ross. New York: Harcourt, Brace & World, 1970. (Reprinted Indianapolis, Ind: The Liberty Press, 1987.)

–. "Individuality vs. Equality." In *Essays in Individuality*. Edited by Felix Morley. Philadelphia, Pa.: University of Pennsylvania Press, 1958.

–. "The Less Developed Countries As a Moral Issue: Risky Assignments of Guilt and Responsibility." *Humanitas: Journal of the Institute of Man* 9, no. 2 (May 1973).

Schreber, Daniel Gottlieb. *Kallipädie oder Erziehung zur Schonheit durch naturgetreue and gleichmässige Förderung normaler Korperbildung* (Education toward beauty by natural and balanced furtherance of normal body growth). Leipzig: Fleischer, 1858.

Schreber, Daniel Paul. *Denkwürdigkeiten eines Nervenkranken*. Leipzig: Oswald Mutze, 1903. *Memoirs of My Nervous Illness*. Edited and translated by Ida Macalpine and Richard Hunter. London: Dawson & Son, 1955.

Schüking, L. L. *The Puritan Family*. New York: 1970.

Schwenger, Peter. *Phallic Critiques: Masculinity and Twentieth-Century Literature*. London: Routledge & Kegan Paul, 1984.

Scott, J. "Evil Eyes," *The Sun*, 10 July 1990.

Scott, W. Clifford M. "Self-Envy and Envy of Dreams and Dreaming." In *Remembering Sleep and Dreams, Int. Rev. Psycho-Anal.* 2, part 3 (1975).

Segal, Hanna. *Introduction to the Work of Melanie Klein*. London: The Hogarth Press, 1975.

–, *Klein*. London: Fontana Modern Masters, 1979.

–, "Notes on Symbol Formation." *Int. J. Psycho-Anal.* 38 (1957).

–, "Some Clinical Implications of Melanie Klein's Work: Emergence from Narcissism." *Int. J. Psycho-Anal.* 64, no. 3 (1983).

Segal, Julia. "Mother, Sex, and Envy in a Children's Story." *Int. Rev. Psycho-Anal.* 6 (1979).

Segaller, Stephen. *Invisible Armies: Terrorism into the 1990s*. London: Michael Joseph, 1986.

Shaffer, Peter. *Amadeus*. London: Andre Deutsch, 1980.

Shakespeare, William. *The Tragedy of Othello*. New York: Pocket Books, 1957.

–. *Merry Wives of Windsor*. In *The Complete Pelican Shakespeare: The Comedies and the Romances*. Edited by Alfred Harbage. London: Penguin Books,
1969.

–. *King Lear*. London: Penguin Books, 1972.

Shamash, Jack.. "Warding off an evil eye," *The Times*, 13 March 1999.

Shelley, Mary Wollstonecraft. *Frankenstein*. London: Gibbings & Co., 1897.

Shorter, Edward. *A History of Women's Bodies*. London: Penguin Books, 1982.

Showalter, Elaine. *Hystories, Hysterical Epidemics and Modern Culture*. New York: Columbia University Press, 1997.

Shuttle, Penelope, and Peter Redgrove. *The Wise Wound: Menstruation and Everywoman*. London: Victor Gollancz, 1978.

Sichrovsky, Peter. *Schuldig Geboren* (Born Guilty). Cologne: Kiepenheurer & Witsch, 1987.

Simon, Julian L. "Resources, Population, Environment: An Oversupply of False Bad News." *Science* 208 (27 June 1980).

Skinner, Angela, and Raymond Castle. *78 Battered Children: A Retrospective Study*. London: NSPCC, 1969.

Slater, Philip. *The Glory of Hera: Greek Mythology and the Greek Family*. Boston: Beacon Press, 1968.

Smakowska, Christine. "Marital Problems and Family Violence." *NSPCC Information Briefing No. 7*. London: NSPCC, 1985.

Sofsky, W. (1999). "The Order of Terror: The Concentration Camp." Princeton, New Jersey: *Princeton University Press.*

Sophocles. *Oedipus Rex*. Translated by Albert Cook. In *Ten Greek Plays*. Edited by L. R. Lind. Cambridge, Mass.: Riverside Editions, Houghton Mifflin Co., 1957.

–. *Oedipus at Colonus*. Translated by Robert Fitzgerald. In *Greek Tragedies*. Edited by David Grene and Richmond Lattimore. Chicago, Ill.: Phoenix Books, University of Chicago Press, 1960.

Spencer, B., and F. J. Gillen. *The Native Tribes of Central Australia*. London: Macmillan & Co., 1899.

Stärcke, August. "The Castration Complex." *Int. J. Psycho-Anal.* 2 (1921).

Starr, Kevin. *Americans and the California Dream 1850-1915*. Oxford: Oxford University Press, 1973.

Steinbeck, John. *East of Eden*. New York: Viking Press, 1952.

Steinberger, Peter. "John Sinclair Is Free." *Big Fat Magazine* (June 1970).

Steiner, John. "Turning a Blind Eye: The Cover Up for Oedipus." *Int. Rev. Psycho-Anal.* 12 (1985).

Stern, J. (12 June 2004). "Holy Avengers," London: *Financial Times Magazine.*

Stern, Karl. *The Flight from Women*. London: George Allen & Unwin, 1966.

Stoller, R.J. (1975). "Perversion: The Erotic Form of Hatred." London: *Maresfield*, 1986.

Stoller, Robert. *The Transsexual Experiment*. London: The Hogarth Press, 1975.

–. *Sex and Gender: Volume 1, The Development of Masculinity and Femininity*. London: Maresfield Reprints, 1984.

Stone, Lawrence. *The Family, Sex and Marriage in England 1500-1800*. London: Weidenfeld & Nicolson, 1977.

Sullivan, Harry Stack. *Clinical Studies in Psychiatry*. New York: W. W. Norton, 1956.

Suttie, J. D. *The Origins of Love and Hate*. London: Paul, French Trubner & Co., 1935.

Taillevent, Guillaume Tirel *dit. La Viandier*. 1375.

Talese, Gay. *Thy Neighbor's Wife*, London: Collins, 1980.

Tannahill, Reay. *Sex in History*. London: Abacus, 1981.

The Tao of Power. Translated by R. L. Wing. Wellingborough, Northamptonshire, England: Aquarian Press, 1986.

Tart, Charles, ed. *Altered States of Consciousness*. New York: Anchor Books, 1972.

Tavris, Carol. *Anger: The Misunderstood Emotion*. New York: Simon & Schuster, 1983.

Tawney, R. H. *Equality*. London: George Allen & Unwin, 1931.

Teresi, Dick, and Kathleen McAuliffe. "Male Pregnancy." *Omni* 8, no. 3 (December 1985).

Thomas, Hugh. *An Unfinished History of the World*. London: Hamish Hamilton, 1982.

Thompson, Clara. "'Penis Envy' in Women." In *Psychoanalysis and Women*. Edited by Jean Baker Miller.

Thomson, David. "Sam Shepard: An American Original." *Playgirl* 12, no. 7 (December 1984).

Todd, John and Kenneth Dewhurst. "The Othello Syndrome: A Study in the Psychopathology of Sexual Jealousy." *The Journal of Nervous and Mental Disease* 122, no. 4 (October 1955).

Todd, John, J. R. M. Mackie, and Kenneth Dewhurst. "Real or Imaginary Hypophallism." *Brit J. Psychiat.* 119, no. 550 (September 1971).

The Torah: A Modern Commentary. New York: Union of Hebrew Congregations, 1981.

Torok, Maria. "The Significance of Penis Envy in Women." In *Female Sexuality,* Janine Chasseguet-Smirgel.

Tournier, Paul. *Guilt and Grace.* London: Hodder & Stoughton, 1962.

Trachtenberg, Joshua. *Jewish Magic and Superstition: A Study in Folk Religion.* New York: Atheneum, 1970.

Tresemer, David Ward. *Fear of Success.* New York: Plenum Press, 1977.

Tuchman, Barbara. *The March of Folly: From Troy to Vietnam.* London: Abacus Books, 1984.

Tugend, Tom. "Glee as 'Paradise' lost," *Jewish Chronicle,* 10 March 2006.

The Twenty-four Books of the Old Testament. Vol. 1. Translated by Andrew Harkavy. New York: Hebrew Publishing Co., 1926.

Twemlow, S.W. (2000). "The Roots of Violence: Converging Psychoanalytic Explanatory Models for Power Struggles and Violence in Schools." *Psychoanalytic Quarterly,* 69:741-785.

Ulmer, Rivka, *The Evil Eye in the Bible and Rabbinic Literature,* New Jersey: Ktav Publishing, 1994.

Unamuno, Miguel de. *Abel Sanchez: The History of a Passion.* Translated by Anthony Kerrigan. Chicago: Gateway Editions, 1956.

Vanggaard, Thorkil. *Phallos: A Symbol and Its History in the Male World.* New York: International Universities Press, 1972.

van Leewen, Kato. "Pregnancy Envy in the Male." *Int. J. Psycho-Anal.* 47 (1966).

Vatikiotis, P. J. *Nasser and His Generation.* London: Croom Helm, 1978.

Veith, Ilza. *Hysteria: The History of a Disease.* Chicago: University of Chicago Press, 1965.

Vermaseren, Maarten. *Cybele and Attis: The Myth and the Cult.* London: Thames & Hudson, 1977.

Vickers, Hugo. *Cecil Beaton: The Authorized Biography.* London: Weidenfeld & Nicolson, 1985.

Vines, Gail. "Test-Tube Embryos." *New Scientist* (19 November 1987).

Waite, Robert. *The Psychopathic God: Adol f Hitler.* New York: Basic Books, 1977.

Walcot, Peter. *Envy and the Greeks.* Warminister, England: Aris & Phillips, 1978.

–. "Greek Attitudes Towards Women: The Mythological Evidence." *Greece and Rome* 31, no. 1 (April 1984).

Waley, Arthur. "Chinese Cinderella Story." *Folk-Lore* 58 (1947).

Watanabe, Hisako. "Paranoia and persecution in modern Japanese life," in Joseph H. Berke, et.al, (eds) "Even Paranoids Have Enemies", London: *Routledge,*1998.

Webster's New World Dictionary. New York: William Collins & World Publishing Co., Inc. 1974.

Weidegar, Paula. *Menstruation and Menopause: The Physiology and Psychology, the Myth and the Reality.* New York: Alfred Knopf, 1976.

Weigart, Edith. "The Cult and Mythology of the Magna Mater from the Standpoint of Psychoanalysis." *Psychiatry 1* (1938).

Wells, H. G. *H. G. Wells in Love.* London: Faber & Faber, 1984.

White, Rhoda. *From Infancy to Womanhood: A Book of Instructions for Young Mothers.* London: 1882.

White Panther Party, Abbey Wood Chapter. "Ten Point Programme." *Chapter? 1* (London, 1971).

Whitmont, Edward. *Return of the Goddess: Femininity, Aggression and the Modern Grail Quest.* London: Routledge & Kegan Paul, 1983.

Widdowson, John. "The Witch As a Frightening and Threatening Figure." In *The Witch Figure.* Edited by Venetia Newall. London: Routledge & Kegan Paul, 1973.

Wideman, John. *Brothers and Keepers.* London: Allison & Busby, 1985.

Williams, Tennessee. *A Streetcar Named Desire.* New York: New Directions, 1947.

Williams, P. (2005). "Terror, terrorising, terrorism," unpublished paper, London.

Willimott, Juliet. "Too Many Episiotomies." *Midwives Chronicle* (February 1970).

Wills, Garry. *The Kennedy Imprisonment: A Meditation on Power.* Boston: Little, Brown & Co., 1982.

Winnicott, D. W. *The Piggle: An Account of the Psychoanalytic Treatment of a Little Girl.* Edited by Ishak Ramzu. London: Penguin Books, 1980.

Woodcock, George. *Anarchy or Chaos.* London: Freedom Press, 1944.

Wright, Gerard and Stuart Millar. "A clique within a clique, obsessed with guns, death and Hitler," *The Guardian,* 22 April 1999.

Yeats, W. B. *Selected Poetry.* London: Pan Books, 1974.

Ye'or. "Aspects of the Arab-Israel Conflict." In *Weiner Library Bulletin* 32, 49/50 (1979).

Zilbergeld, Bernie. *Male Sexuality.* New York: Bantam Books, 1981.

Zilboorg, Gregory. "Masculine and Feminine: Some Biological and Cultural Aspects." *Psychiatry* 7 (1944).

This bibliography includes the books as well as journal and magazine articles that I have cited. It excludes newspaper and newspaper magazine articles. The following is a list of the newspapers to which I have referred in the text and notes:

BEIJING (P. REP. CHINA).
The People's Daily

CHICAGO (U.S.A.).
The *Chicago Tribune*

JEDDAH (Saudi Arabia)
The Saudi Gazette

JERUSALEM (Israel)
The Jerusalem Post

LONDON (G.B.).
The Daily Express
The Daily Telegraph
The Daily Telegraph magazine
ES (the Evening Standard magazine)
The Evening Standard
The Financial Times
The Guardian
The Hampstead and Highgate Express
The Independent
The Jewish Chronicle
The Jewish Chronicle magazine
The London Standard
The Mail on Sunday
The Observer
The Sun
The Sunday Times
The Sunday Times magazine
The Times
The Times Health Supplement

MOSCOW (U.S.S.R.)
Kurier

NEW YORK (U.S.A.)
The New York Times
The New York Times Book Review
The New York Post
USA Today (International Edition)

PARIS (FRANCE).
L'Observateur
The International Herald Tribune

TEL AVIV (Israel)
Haaretz

WASHINGTON (U.S.A.).
The Washington Post

Index

Further Approbations

It is a generally accepted fact that Freud, in particular, and psychoanalysts, in general, hesitate to focus on aggression as an important underlying element in the development and expression of the psyche. Most probably, the exploration of aggressiveness and anger is too difficult an emotional task for clinicians to investigate as it parallels their own discomfort with these emotions. Joseph Berke's book, *Malice Through the Looking Glass* analyzes to the core "our capacity for destruction" which Berke feels "lies in the origins of malice."

The important contribution of this book is that a gifted theoretician and clinician has written an in-depth study of malice, evil and envy which blends together the theoretical, clinical, anthropological, historical and literary, in a well-written, clearly elucidated manner with a unique blend of intellectual honesty interspersed with humor and freshness.

The section entitled: 'Elaborations,' is a massive array of endnotes which adds immeasurably to our understanding of the ideas and concepts presented in the body of the book, and shows us the wide range of the author's knowledge and expertise. This user-friendly tool can be read simultaneously with the main text or alone.

The book is a helpful entrance into understanding today's world of violence and fundamentalism. Berke has done a masterful job integrating a wide array of information and presenting it in a clear, understandable manner.

STANLEY SCHNEIDER: SUPERVISING & TRAINING PSYCHOANALYST; PROFESSOR & CHAIRMAN, INTEGRATIVE PSYCHOTHERAPY PROGRAM, HEBREW UNIVERSITY IN JERUSALEM.

Joseph Berke has made a distinctive place for himself in the history of psychoanalytic theory. He has produced a major output of books, articles and other writings (visit: www.jhberke.com) exploring psychotherapy, psychoanalytic concepts, psycho-social environments, the experiences of therapists and patients and the interface between Kabbalah and psychoanalysis.

This book is an updated, re-thought and expanded version of *The Tyranny of Malice,* which first appeared in 1988. The updating attends to events in the nearly two decades which have ensued, particularly related to terrorism.

In his introduction, Joe points out that there has been little serious work on envy, greed and jealousy – the dark side of character, the underpinning of malicious hatred, and the counterparts of the virtues of gratitude, generosity and compassion. He thinks that in our times, envy occupies a similar position to sex for the Victorians, an obsession best forgotten denied or avoided. To listen or read Joe Berke, speaking or writing about everyday human emotions, is an unforgettable experience, which will have a profound and salutary effect on the way we see ourselves. This is the intended effect of The Looking Glass.

Kate Loewenthal: Professor of Psychology, Royal Holloway, University of London

Prior Praise, The Tyranny of Malice

"A timely, important and penetrating book -- I know of no other work which illuminates aggression and human cruelty in as detailed and profound a manner as Dr. Berke does."

Malcolm Pines: Former President, International Association of Group Psychotherapy.

"Bold and stimulating. Berke's.......honesty, good sense and story telling ability, makes the book a good reading and good advice for everyone."

Kansas City Star

"Joseph Berke's anatomy of human cruelty and aggression is...... exhaustive, involved, and objective; and he thankfully does not hold himself up as the savior-shrink with the curative key to an elusive problem. By awakening these particular sleeping dogs into howling consciousness, however, Berke does much to render them less harmful and menacing."

The Bloomsbury Review

"Berke explores the implications of unacknowledged envy, greed, and jealousy. These malign influences range from invidious sibling rivalry to journalism's pandering to public envy of the successful and even to the group rancor of unbridled nationalism. But the dark imperative of aggressive envy is Berke's major focus; and the antidote is to acknowledge its narcissistic origins."

Library Journal

About the Author

Joseph Berke is a prolific author of many books and articles. His next work is: *Centres of Power: The Convergence of Psychoanalysis and Kabbalah*, written together with Prof. Stanley Schneider, the Hebrew University, Jerusalem.

Joseph Berke is a psychoanalytic psychotherapist working with individuals and families. He is a lecturer, writer, and founder and director of the Arbours Crisis Centre, London.

Joseph Berke attended Columbia College of Columbia University and graduated from the Albert Einstein College of Medicine in New York. In 1965 he moved to London to work with the late Dr. R. D. Laing and to establish the Kingsley Hall community. There he helped a middle aged nurse, Mary Barnes, pass through a profound regression and re-emerge into life as an artist, writer and mystic.

In 1970 he co-founded the Arbours Housing Association in order to provide housing and personal, psychotherapeutic care for individuals in emotional distress.

In 1973 he founded the Arbours Crisis Centre, a pioneering psychosocial facility for severely disturbed and disturbing individuals and families.

His principle psychological areas of interest include psychoanalysis, psychosis, therapeutic communities and transpersonal psychology. Other major areas of interest include the Jewish mystical tradition, Kabbalah and Chassidism.

Relevant websites:

www.jhberke.com

www.mary-barnes.net

www.arbourscentre.org.uk

www. tevapublications.com